HARRAP'S GERMAN AND ENGLISH

Glossary of Terms in International Law

Gerard Gilbertson BA Hons

Senior Lecturer in German
The Polytechnic, Wolverhampton

formerly Lecturer in English,
Institut für Übersetzen und Dolmetschen,
Universität des Saarlandes

HARRAP LONDON

First published in Great Britain 1980
by George G. Harrap & Co. Ltd
182–184 High Holborn, London WC1V 7AX

© *G. Gilbertson* 1980

ISBN 0 245 53524 1

Text set in 9/10 pt VIP Times, printed and bound
in Great Britain at The Pitman Press, Bath

TABLE OF CONTENTS

INTRODUCTION

Though in general those who compile dictionaries are supposedly aware of the basic correspondence (or lack of it), some dictionaries are formulated with apparent disregard for three fundamental presuppositions which must underlie all adequate semantic analysis: 1) no word (or semantic unit) ever has exactly the same meaning in two different utterances; 2) there are no complete synonyms within a language; 3) there are no exact correspondences between related words in different languages.

(EUGENE A. NIDA, *Analysis of Meaning and Dictionary Making*, 1958)

The purpose of this Glossary is to provide a basic reference work for all those involved professionally with the terminology of international law and international treaties in English and German. It is hoped that not only translators, interpreters, and legal experts will find it of use, but also those in the fields of politics, the media, education, and international business.

In offering the Glossary to the public, the author is not only aware of the shortcomings inherent in all bilingual or multilingual specialist dictionaries, but is also conscious of the specific limitations of his own work. Whilst most of the original principles on which the selection and presentation of the material are based have remained intact throughout the preparation, the vast range and depth of primary source material in the field, combined with the dictates of economy and sheer practicability, mean that the content of the Glossary is, of necessity, incomplete.

The evolution of the Glossary from a personal card index to its present format was determined by three principal realizations: firstly, that among the already extant reference works on legal terminology very few concentrated exclusively on *international* law; secondly, that to restrict the material included to a simple list of individual terms (however comprehensive this might be) would be to deny the user both an insight into the wide variation encountered even in this restricted register, and an appreciation of the overall style; thirdly, that wherever practicable the user should be assured of authenticity.

Within this basic framework, and subject to the constraints mentioned above, the author has attempted to produce a comprehensive selection of terms and authentic illustrative examples in a concise, single-volume format that permits of translation from and into both German and English. He has continually borne in mind the requirements of the trainee as well as of the practising expert.

All suggestions for improving or augmenting the content of the Glossary will be welcomed by the author.

Arrangement of the Glossary and pattern of entries

The Glossary consists of three main parts:

(i) Part I is the German-English section, in which the headword entries are arranged in strict alphabetical order. In most cases, *nouns*, rather than adjectives, verbs, etc., have been selected for the headwords introducing compound phrases, collocations, and the illustrative contextual examples. Hence a phrase such as *Rechtsmitteln unterliegen* is in principle to be

iv

found under *Rechtsmittel* and not under *unterliegen*. The associated verbs, adjectives, etc., are, of course, also listed separately, but normally without extensive exemplification, or a list of derived compound phrases. In the case of phrases consisting basically of two nouns (e.g. *Tragweite des Vorbehalts*), the entry is normally to be found under the second noun.

Where an extensive list of derived phrases and/or contextual examples is entered under a noun headword (e.g. *Vertrag*), the order of listing is in three groups: a) nominal collocations (e.g. *Auslegung eines Vertrags*); b) adjectival collocations (e.g. *mehrseitiger Vertrag*); c) verbal collocations (e.g. *einen Vertrag ratifizieren*). Within these three groups alphabetical order of the modifier is observed. All derived phrases, sub-entries and examples are indented.

There are some exceptions to this basic arrangement: certain key adjectives (e.g. *völkerrechtlich, territorial, diplomatisch*) function as headwords introducing a list of derived phrases.

(ii) Part II consists of the Annexes, i.e. a selection of extended extracts from a variety of international instruments. While the selection of these texts is limited and, in part, also arbitrary, it is hoped that all will fulfil one or more of the following functions: a) provide definitions for many terms; b) provide a wider linguistic and conceptual context than can be accommodated in the short contextual examples in Part I; c) provide an introduction to the typology of international instruments; d) provide an authentic illustration of the overall style of this technical register. The material presented in these Annexes (above all the first three, which are of an explanatory nature) should be of special interest to the trainee translator. Except where inappropriate, the English and German texts run in parallel. A list of the Annexes is to be found at the front of Part II.

(iii) Part III is the English register. Here all the English words and phrases appearing in Parts I and II are listed with a precise reference to where they can be found. The register, like Part I, is based primarily on noun entries, and the pattern of entries under an introductory headword follows that described above for Part I. Further details regarding the register and the format of the references are given separately at the beginning of Part III.

Cross references

Part I of the Glossary contains a cross reference system. The cross reference is indicated by the symbol *, is located at the end of a headword or sub-entry, and refers the user to other entries under which further information can be obtained, for example in the form of synonyms, further derived phrases, contextual examples, explanatory notes, or Annex material.

Source materials and source references

(i) A total of some two hundred international treaties, agreements, statutes and similar documents, together with a wide range of textbooks, have been used either as the sources or the verification of the words and phrases included in the Glossary. Of these, well over one hundred have been specifically quoted, either in the contextual examples, the individual entries, or the Annexes. In such cases, a reference to the source is given.

(ii) Each instrument quoted in this way has its own abbreviated 'symbol' (e.g. VCLOT for the Vienna Convention on the Law of Treaties), and this is placed in brackets after the appropriate entry. In most cases, a numerical reference is also given; this refers to the *article* of the pertinent instrument, with two exceptions: in the case of ILOC the numerical reference is to the Convention number, and in that of SF to the page number. A numerical reference is occasionally not provided where a) a term appears throughout the instrument, or b) the reference is to associated or subsidiary documents (e.g. Optional Protocols, Regulations for Execution).

(iii) A key to the abbreviations used to designate the sources quoted is provided at the front of Part I. The key is in strict alphabetical order, and lists not only the full titles of the instruments concerned, but also the date of their conclusion.

(iv) Only those instruments have been used for which both English and German versions are available. In the vast majority of cases, these versions are either the original *equally authentic texts* or *official and authorized translations*. In the case of only very few instruments, for which an official German translation is not available, was it necessary to take recourse to unofficial but *already published translations*.

Contextual examples

While every effort has been made to ensure the *authenticity* of these examples (see above under *Source materials and source references*), a word of caution must be offered regarding their application. It must not be forgotten that even in this highly restricted technical register, just as in any other linguistic register, one encounters variations that are sometimes quite considerable. These may result from paraphrasing and personal choice of style, from the ubiquitous problems of equivalence in translation, or even from inaccuracies. Hence, although the examples are, in the overwhelming majority of cases, authenticated by official usage, they may not always be the models of uniformity or perfection that one might justifiably expect. The user is therefore strongly urged to regard such material as *descriptive* of usage rather than *prescriptive*.

Additional reference works

Definitive versions of international instruments that may be of further assistance to the user of this Glossary may be found in the following sources:

(i)   *UN Treaty Series,* published by the Secretary General, New York;
(ii) *Verträge der Bundesrepublik, Serie A*, published by the Auswärtiges Amt, Bonn. This series now runs to well over 30 volumes, and contains for many instruments not only the German text but also English, French and other language versions;
(iii) *HMSO Treaty Series* and *Miscellaneous Series* with various Cmd and Cmnd numbers. In most cases only the English version is supplied;
(iv) the *Bundesgesetzblatt* (Federal Law Gazette);
(v)   documents of the Commission of the European Communities.

In addition, periodicals such as *Lebende Sprachen*, published by Langenscheidt, frequently contain contributions in the form of bilingual/multilingual extracts of instruments, with very useful small glossaries appended.

To present even a modest selection from the enormous bibliography of textbooks and similar publications in international law, international relations, and diplomatic practice is a task beyond the scope of this Introduction. However, the interested reader might like to consult works by the following authors: in German *Berber, Dahm, Frei, Krekeler, Menzel,*

Schlochauer, Seidl-hohenveldern, Verdross, and in English *Akehurst, Greig, Holsti, Nicholson, Oppenheim, Satow, Schwarzenberger, Starke.*

Acknowledgments

In the course of planning and preparing this Glossary I have been fortunate to receive the encouragement and assistance of a large number of individuals and institutions at home and abroad. I would like to express my gratitude and appreciation to all those colleagues, students and correspondents who have so kindly offered their expertise and critical comment at various stages. My particular thanks are due to

> Mr P. *Latham*, MA, LL.B, Solicitor (Lecturer in English Law at the Vrije Universiteit, Brussels, Principal Administrator in Directorate General III at the Commission of the European Communities), and *Mr G. E. MacGregor*, BA, FIL (former Head of Division at the Commission of the European Communities) who together examined the entire manuscript of Part I and suggested a large number of corrections and improvements;

> The *Sprachendienst des Auswärtigen Amts*, Bonn, for providing me with the German text of the Vienna Convention on the Law of Treaties prior to its publication in the *Bundesgesetzblatt*, and for permission to use it in preparing this Glossary;

> The staff of the Computer Centre, The Polytechnic, Wolverhampton, in particular *Mr S. Machin* and *Mr C. Farrell* (Senior Analyst Programmers), and *Mr S. Percival* (Applications Manager), for their assistance in the computerized compilation of the English register;

> *Mr C. Johnson*, my meticulous Editor.

Any shortcomings or errors that remain are, of course, the responsibility of the author.

The compilation of this glossary constitutes part of the research undertaken for my M.A. thesis, soon to be submitted to the University of Sheffield.

The Glossary is dedicated to Mark and Josette.

GERARD GILBERTSON
Wolverhampton, September 1980

ABBREVIATIONS

(*a*) *Abbreviations of treaties, conventions, statutes, etc., used as sources for contextual examples and/or authentication in Parts I and II*

Notes:
- (i) the number(s) appearing after the abbreviations refer(s) to the relevant article(s) of that instrument;
- (ii) in the case of SF the number refers to the relevant page;
- (iii) in the case of ILOC the number refers to the Convention number;
- (iv) where no number is given, the term appears frequently throughout the instrument;
- (v) Opt. Prot, Pr, Prot, SProt, RegEx after the abbreviation refer to *Optional Protocol, Preamble, Protocol, Supplementary Protocol, Regulations for the Execution of* respectively.

AACER	Articles of Agreement of the Council of Europe Resettlement Fund 6.3.59
ARS	Agreement relating to Refugee Seamen 23.11.57
CAC	Convention on International Civil Aviation 5.12.44
CCC	Convention establishing a Customs Co-operation Council 15.12.50
CCFTD	Convention on the Conflicts of Laws relating to the Form of Testamentary Dispositions 5.10.61
CE	Statute of the Council of Europe
CEFA	Convention on the Execution of Foreign Arbitral Awards 26.9.27
CERD	Convention on the Elimination of all Forms of Racial Discrimination 7.3.66
CFIMT	Convention on the Facilitation of International Maritime Traffic 9.4.65
CFW	Convention concerning Frontier Workers 17.4.50
CICES	Convention for the International Council for the Exploration of the Sea 12.9.64
CLPD	Convention abolishing the Requirement of Legalization for foreign public Documents 5.10.61
CNAF	International Convention for the Northwest Atlantic Fisheries 8.2.49
CREFA	Convention on the Recognition and Enforcement of Foreign Arbitral Awards 10.6.58
CRFF	Convention on the Rights and Obligations of Foreign Forces and their Members in the FRG 26.5.52
CRMN	European Convention on the Reduction of Multiple Nationality 6.5.63
CRPG	Convention on Relations between the Three Powers and the FRG 26.5.52
CSE	Convention on Student Employees 17.4.50
CSFT	Convention and Statute on Freedom of Transit 20.4.21
CSLS	International Convention for the Safety of Life at Sea 17.6.60
CSMW	Convention on the Settlement of Matters arising out of the War and the Occupation 23.10.54
CUN	Charter of the United Nations
EAEC	Treaty Establishing the European Atomic Energy Community
ECC	European Cultural Convention 19.12.54

ECE	Terms of Reference of the Economic Commission for Europe (as revised 15.12.55)
ECER	Rules of Procedure of the Economic Commission for Europe (as revised 9.4.56)
ECICA	European Convention on International Commercial Arbitration 21.4.61
ECICP	European Convention on the International Classification of Patents for Inventions 19.12.54
ECPSD	European Convention for the Peaceful Settlement of Disputes 29.4.57
ECSC	Treaty Establishing the European Coal and Steel Community
ECSM	European Convention on Social and Medical Assistance 11.12.53
EEC	Treaty Establishing the European Economic Community
EExt	European Convention on Extradition 13.12.57
EFTA	Convention Establishing the European Free Trade Association 4.1.60
ELDO	Convention for the Establishment of a European Organization for the Development and Construction of Space Vehicle Launchers 29.3.62
EMA	European Monetary Agreement 5.8.55
EONR	Convention for the Establishment of a European Organization for Nuclear Research 1.7.53
EPTV	European Agreement on the Protection of TV Broadcasts 22.6.60
EPU	Agreement for the Establishment of a European Payments Union 19.9.50
ES	European Social Charter 18.10.61
ESRO	Convention for the Establishment of a European Space Research Organization 14.6.62
ExFC	Agreement between the Government of the UK and the Government of the FRG on the Extradition of Fugitive Criminals 23.2.60
EXWC	Agreement on the Exchange of War Cripples between Member Countries of the Council of Europe with a view to Medical Treatment 13.12.55
FAO	Constitution of the Food and Agriculture Organization of the UN
FC	European Fisheries Convention 9.3.64
GATT	General Agreement on Tariffs and Trade 23.10.47
GC	= common to GC I — GC IV
GC I	First Geneva Convention for the Amelioration of the Condition of the Wounded and Sick in Armed Forces in the Field 12.8.49
GC II	Second Geneva Convention for the Amelioration of the Condition of the Wounded, Sick and Shipwrecked Members of Armed Forces at Sea 12.8.49
GC III	Third Geneva Convention relative to the Treatment of Prisoners of War 12.8.49
GC IV	Fourth Geneva Convention relative to the Protection of Civilian Persons in time of War 12.8.49
GCC	Geneva Convention on the Continental Shelf 29.4.58
GCF	Geneva Convention on the Fishing and Preservation of Living Resources 29.4.58
GCHS	Geneva Convention on the High Seas 29.4.58
GCTS	Geneva Convention on the Territorial Sea and Contiguous Zone 29.4.58
GG	Grundgesetz (Basic Law of the FRG)
GrV	Grundvertrag 21.12.72

HgI	Hague Convention on the Pacific Settlement of International Disputes 18.10.07
IAEA	Statute of the International Atomic Energy Agency
ICC	Agreement providing for the provisional application of the Draft International Customs Conventions on Touring, on Commercial Road Vehicles and on the International Transportation of Goods by Road 16.6.49
ICCA	Draft International Convention (Customs) on Touring 16.6.49
ICCB	Draft International Convention (Customs) on the Transport of Goods by Road 16.6.49
ICCC	International Convention for the Suppression of Counterfeiting Currency 20.4.29
ICCPR	International Covenant on Civil and Political Rights
ICPCP	Statutes of the International Centre for the Study of the Preservation and Restoration of Cultural Property, Nov. 56 + Amendments
IDA	Articles of Agreement of the International Development Association 20.1.60
ILO	Constitution of the International Labour Organization
ILOC	ILO Convention Number ....
IMCO	Convention on the Intergovernmental Maritime Consultative Organization 6.3.48
IMF	Articles of Agreement of the International Monetary Fund 27.12.45
IRU	Convention establishing the International Relief Union 12.7.27
MNTB	Moscow Nuclear Test Ban Treaty 5.8.63
NAT	North Atlantic Treaty 4.4.49
NATA	Agreement between the Parties to the North Atlantic Treaty for Co-operation regarding Atomic Information 22.6.55
NATOS	Agreement on the Status of the NATO National Representatives and International Staff 20.9.51
NATOSF	Agreement between the Parties to the North Atlantic Treaty regarding the Status of their Forces 1.7.63
OECD	Covenant on the Organization for Economic Co-operation and Development 14.12.60
OEEC	Convention for European Economic Co-operation 16.4.48
PCG	Convention on the Prevention and Punishment of the Crime of Genocide 9.12.48
PCP	Convention for the Protection of Cultural Property in the Event of Armed Conflict 14.5.54
PHR	Convention for the Protection of Human Rights and Fundamental Freedoms 4.11.50
PHR Prot	Protocol to PHR of 20.3.52
PPELDO	Protocol on Privileges and Immunities of ELDO 29.6.64
PPESRO	Protocol concerning the Privileges and Immunities of ESRO 31.10.63
PPSO	Convention on the Prevention of Pollution of the Sea by Oil 12.5.54
PrivExCE	Privileges and Exemptions of the Council of Europe (+ Protocols) 2.9.49
RMCE	European Agreement on Regulations governing the movement of Persons between Member States of the Council of Europe
SC	Slavery Convention 25.9.26
SCS	Supplementary Convention on the Abolition of Slavery, the Slave Trade and Institutions and Practices Similar to Slavery 7.9.56

SF	Standardformulierungen für deutsche Vertragstexte (Auswärtiges Amt, Bonn)
SICJ	Statute of the International Court of Justice
TDRef	Agreement relating to the Issue of a Travel Document to Refugees who are the Concern of the Intergovernmental Committee on Refugees 15.10.46
TNPNW	Treaty on the Non-proliferation of Nuclear Weapons 1.7.68
TORG	Protocol on the Termination of the Occupational Regime in the FRG 23.10.54
TRW	Treaty providing for the Renunciation of War as an Instrument of National Policy 27.8.28
UCC	Universal Copyright Convention 6.9.52
UDHR	Universal Declaration of Human Rights 10.12.48
UNCDD	UN Convention on the Declaration of Death of Missing Persons (+ Final Act of Conference) 6.4.50
UNESCO	Constitution of the UN Educational, Scientific and Cultural Organization
VCCR	Vienna Convention on Consular Relations 24.4.63
VCDR	Vienna Convention on Diplomatic Relations 18.4.61
VCLD	Vienna Convention on Civil Liability for Nuclear Damage 21.5.63
VCLOT	Vienna Convention on the Law of Treaties 23.5.69
WEU	Common to WEU I – WEU IV
WEU I	Protocol modifying and completing the Brussels Treaty (Western European Union) 23.10.54
WEU II	Protocol No. II on the Forces of Western European Union 23.10.54
WEU III	Protocol No. III on the Control of Armaments 23.10.54
WEU IV	Protocol No. IV on the Agency of Western European Union for the Control of Armaments 23.10.54
WEUS	Agreement on the Status of Western European Union, National Representatives and International Staff 11.5.55
WHO	Constitution of the World Health Organization
WMO	Constitution of the World Meteorological Organization

(b) Other abbreviations used in the text

adj. = adjective
adj.n. = adjectival noun, noun used as an adjective
dat. = dative
f. = feminine
gen. = genitive
m. = masculine
n. = neuter
pers. = person
pl. = plural
prep. = preposition
s.o. = someone
usu. = usually
usw. = und so weiter = etc.
/ = or
( ) = may be omitted
* = see under

A

1 **abändern**, to amend, to modify, to revise

2 **ganz oder teilweise abändern**, to revise in whole or in part (*note to* *Vertrag modifizieren)

3 **Abänderung**, *f.*, amendment, modification, revision

4 **die einvernehmliche Abänderung eines Vertrages**, the amendment of a treaty by agreement between the parties (*See* VCLOT 39–41 *in Annex* 16.)

5 **Abänderungsurkunde**, *f.*, instrument of amendment/revision/modification

6 **Abänderungsvorschlag**, *m.*, proposed amendment/revision/modification

7 **abberufen**, to recall

8 **eine Mission endgültig oder vorübergehend abberufen (VCDR 45)**, to permanently or temporarily recall a mission

9 **Abberufung**, *f.*, recall

10 **Abberufungsschreiben**, *n.*, letters of recall

11 **abbrechen**, to sever, to break off, to terminate (*Abbruch)

12 **Abbruch**, *m.*, severance, breaking off, termination

13 **Der Abbruch der diplomatischen Beziehungen hat nicht ohne weiteres den Abbruch der konsularischen Beziehungen zur Folge (VCCR 2)**, The severance of diplomatic relations shall not *ipso facto* involve the severance of consular relations

14 **Abdruck**, *m.*, copy

15 **beglaubigter Abdruck**, certified copy (*Abschrift)

16 **aberkennen**, to withdraw recognition of, to recognize no longer

17 **die Staatsangehörigkeit aberkennen**, to deprive of/to withdraw nationality/citizenship

18 **Aberkennung**, *f.*, withdrawal (of recognition)

19 **abfassen**, to draw up (*maßgebend)

20 **abfertigen**, to clear, to process

21 **Abfertigung**, *f.*, clearance, processing

22 **Maßnahmen zur Erleichterung der Abfertigung von Ladung, Fahrgästen und Gepäck (CFIMT An)**, measures to facilitate clearance of cargo, passengers and baggage

23 **Verfahren zur Abfertigung von Fahrgästen (CFIMT An)**, method of processing passengers

24 **Abgabe[1]**, *f.*, due, charge, duty

25 **das Verbot, zwischen Mitgliedstaaten Ein- und Ausfuhrzölle und Abgaben gleicher Wirkung zu erheben (EEC 9)**, the prohibition between member states of customs duties on imports and exports and of all charges of equivalent effect

26 **Steuern und Abgaben**, dues and taxes

27 **Die Räumlichkeiten der Mission sind von allen staatlichen, regionalen und kommunalen Steuern oder sonstigen Abgaben befreit (VCDR 23)**, The premises of the mission shall be exempt from all national, regional or municipal dues and taxes

28 **Personal- und Realsteuern oder -abgaben (VCDR 34)**, dues and taxes, personal or real

29 **Steuern, Gebühren und sonstige Abgaben**, taxes, fees and other charges

30 **alle Zölle, Steuern und ähnliche Abgaben (VCDR 36)**, all customs duties, taxes and related charges

31 **interne Abgaben (EFTA)**, internal charges

32 **kommunale Abgaben**, municipal dues (*see* Steuern und *Abgaben)

33 **regionale Abgaben**, regional dues

34 **staatliche Abgaben und Gebühren**, national duties and charges/fees

35 **Abgaben für**, dues on/for

1

36 **Brefreiung von Abgaben,** exemption from dues

37 **Eintreibung von Abgaben,** collection of dues

38 **Die Eintreibung von Abgaben würde die Mission der Zwangsgewalt des Empfangsstaates unterstellen,** The collection of dues would subject the mission to the jurisdiction of the receiving state

39 **Abgaben erheben,** to levy dues/charges

40 **Abgaben erlassen,** to remit dues/charges

41 **Abgaben erstatten,** to reimburse dues/charges

42 **Abgabe²,** *f.*, submission, lodging

43 **Abgabe eines Protestes,** submission/lodging of a protest

44 **Abgabenstrafsache,** *f.* (EExt 5), offence in connection with taxes and duties

45 **abgeändert,** *adj.*, amended, modified, revised

46 **abgeänderter Entwurf,** amended draft

47 **abgeänderter Vertragstext,** revised text of a/the treaty

48 **Abgeordneter,** *adj.n.*, representative

49 **die Abgeordneten der Beratenden Versammlung und ihre Stellvertreter** (PrivExCE 14), the representatives to the Consultative Assembly and their substitutes (*Vertreter)

50 **abgeschlossen,** *adj.*, concluded, entered into

51 **abgrenzen,** to delimit, to delimit/draw (up) the boundaries of

52 **Abgrenzung,** *f.*, delimiting, limit, demarcation

53 **bei der Abgrenzung des Festlandsockels** (GCC 6), in delimiting the boundaries of the continental shelf

54 **Grundsätze der geographischen Abgrenzung** (GCTS, GCF), principles of geographic demarcation

55 **abhängig,** *adj.*, dependent

56 **Abhängigkeit,** *f.*, dependence

57 **gegenseitige/wechselseitige Abhängigkeit,** interdependence

58 **die wechselseitige Abhängigkeit der Völker der Welt,** the interdependence of the peoples of the world

59 **Abkommen,** *n.*, agreement, convention (*see note to* *Vertrag *in Annex* 1)

60 **Abkommen zu/über,** agreement for/on

61 **Abkommen technischen/kulturellen Charakters,** agreement of a technical/cultural nature

62 **internationales Abkommen,** international agreement

63 **internationale Abkommen allgemeiner oder besonderer Natur,** international agreements, whether general or particular

64 **regionales Abkommen,** regional agreement

65 **universales Abkommen,** universal agreement

66 **völkerrechtliches Abkommen,** international agreement

67 **zwischenstaatliches Abkommen,** intergovernmental agreement (*See also extensively under* *Vertrag, *Vertrags-, *vertrags-, *and see note to* *Vertrag *in Annex* 1.)

68 **Ablauf,** *m.*, expiry, expiration, termination

69 **nach Ablauf von 2 Jahren nach Inkrafttreten dieser Verordnung,** after the expiry of the 2 year period following the entry into force of this regulation (*Frist, *Erlöschen)

70 **ablaufen,** to expire, to terminate (*erlöschen, *kündigen)

71 **ableiten,** to deduce, to infer (*Abweichen)

72 **ablösen,** to replace, to supersede

73 **Ablösung,** *f.*, replacement (*Amtsantritt)

74 **abmachen,** to agree, to come to/to reach an agreement

75 **Abmachung,** *f.*, agreement, arrangement (*see note to* *Vertrag *in Annex* 1)

76 **gemäß den von der Generalversammlung getroffenen Abmachungen,** in accordance with arrange-

ments made by the General Assembly

77 **wenn keine andere Abmachung besteht,** unless otherwise agreed (*gegenteilig)

78 **abordnen,** to delegate, to send as delegate

79 **Abordnung,** *f.*, delegation

80 **Abrechnung,** *f.*, account(ing)

81 **Abrechnungsperiode,** *f.*, period of account, accounting period

82 **Abreise,** *f.*, departure

83 **endgültige Abreise von Diplomaten** (VCDR 10), final departure of diplomatic agents

84 **abrüsten,** to disarm

85 **Abrüstung,** *f.*, disarmament

86 **allgemeine und vollständige Abrüstung,** general and complete disarmament

87 **Abrüstungsabkommen,** *n.*, disarmament agreement/convention (*see note to* *Vertrag *in Annex* 1)

88 **Abrüstungskonferenz,** *f.*, disarmament conference

89 **Abrüstungskontrolle,** *f.*, disarmament control

90 **Abrüstungsverhandlungen,** *f.pl.*, disarmament negotiations

91 **Abschiedsaudienz,** *f.*, farewell audience

92 **abschließen,** to conclude

93 **Dieses Übereinkommen wird auf unbegrenzte Zeit abgeschlossen,** The present convention is of unlimited duration (*schließen)

94 **Abschluß,** *m.*, conclusion

95 **Abschlub der Verhandlungen,** conclusion of the negotiations

96 **Abschluß eines Vertrags,** conclusion of a treaty

97 **Abschlußvollmacht,** *f.*, (full) power / powers / authority / authorization to conclude (a treaty) (*Vollmacht)

98 **Abschnitt,** *m.*, section

99 **Abschrift,** *f.*, copy

100 **beglaubigte Abschrift,** certified copy

101 **Amtlich beglaubigte Abschriften werden von dieser Regierung den Regierungen der anderen Signatarstaaten übermittelt,** Duly certified copies shall be transmitted by that government to the governments of the other signatory states (*Verwahrregierung, *Urschrift)

102 **Abschwemmung,** *f.*, decretion (erosion *only in geological sense*) (*Anschwemmung)

103 **Absicht,** *f.*, intent, intention

104 **in der Absicht,** intending (*in preamble*)

105 **in der Absicht, die Verbundenheit Europas mit den überseeischen Ländern zu bekräftigen** (EEC Pr), intending to confirm the solidarity which binds Europe and the overseas countries

106 **die gegenteilige Absicht eindeutig zum Ausdruck bringen** (VCLOT 20), to definitely express a contrary intention

107 **Absichtserklärung,** *f.*, declaration of intent

108 **Absprache,** *f.*, undertaking, agreement, understanding

109 **alle zwischen ihnen bestehenden Verpflichtungen und Absprachen** (CAC 82), all obligations and understandings between them

110 **Abstammungsprinzip,** *n.*, (the principle of) *jus sanguinis*

111 **abstellen,** to cease, to remove, to redress

112 **Abstellung,** *f.*, cessation, removal, redress

113 **das Recht der Selbsthilfe zur Abstellung eines Unrechts,** the right of self-help to redress a wrong

114 **abstimmen[1],** to harmonize, to concert

115 **abstimmen[2],** to vote, to cast (one's) vote

116 **Jeder Delegierte hat das Recht, unabhängig für sich selbst über alle der Konferenz unterbreiteten Fragen abzustimmen** (ILO 4), Every delegate shall be entitled to vote individually on all matters which are taken into consideration by the conference (*Beschluß)

117 **Abstimmung[1],** *f.*, harmonization

118 **Abstimmung**[2], *f.*, vote, voting, ballot

119 **die Abstimmung des Rates,** the Council vote (EEC 8)

120 **Fragen zur Abstimmung stellen,** to put questions to the vote

121 **geheime Abstimmung,** secret vote/ballot

122 **alle Wahlen erfolgen in geheimer Abstimmung** (ECER 38), all elections shall be decided by secret ballot

123 **namentliche Abstimmung,** roll call (ECER 37), voting by call

124 **offene Abstimmung,** open vote/ballot

125 **schriftliche Abstimmung,** written ballot, vote in writing, vote by correspondence (WMO 10)

126 **sich der Abstimmung enthalten,** to abstain from voting

127 **mit der Maßgabe, daß sich die Streitparteien der Abstimmung enthalten** (CUN 27), provided that a party to a dispute shall abstain from voting

128 **an der Abstimmung teilnehmen,** to vote, to participate in the ballot

129 **an den Abstimmungen nehmen (die Berater) nicht teil** (ILO 3), (the advisers) may not vote

130 **Abstimmungsergebnis,** *n.*, (result of the) voting

131 **Das Abstimmungsergebnis und abweichende oder getrennt abgegebene Meinungen werden nicht veröffentlicht** (FC An), The voting shall not be disclosed, nor any dissenting or separate opinions

132 **Abstimmungsverfahren,** *n.*, voting procedure

133 **Über Fragen, für die ein anderes Abstimmungsverfahren nicht vereinbart ist oder vereinbart wird, beschließt der Rat einstimmig** (WEU I), The Council shall decide by unanimous vote questions for which no other voting procedure has been or may be agreed

134 **Abstimmungsvorschrift,** *f.*, voting rule, voting regulation, regulation concerning the ballot

135 **Abstufung,** *f.*, level, grade

136 **Das Völkerrecht kennt Abstufungen in der Anerkennung,** In/At international law there are various levels of recognition

137 **abträglich,** *adj.*, destructive, hostile, prejudicial

138 **eine der Sicherheit des Staates abträgliche Tätigkeit betreiben** (GC IV), to engage in activities hostile/prejudicial to the security of the state

139 **abtreten**[1], to cede

140 **ein Gebiet abtreten,** to cede a territory

141 **abtreten**[2], to retire, to withdraw

142 **abtretend**[1], *adj.*, cedant, ceding

143 **abtretender Staat,** cedant state, state ceding (the territory)

144 **abtretend**[2], *adj.*, retiring, withdrawing

145 **abtretender Gouverneursrat** (IAEA), outgoing Board of Governors

146 **Abtretung,** *f.*, cession

147 **Abtretungsvertrag,** *m.*, treaty of cession

148 **abweichen (von),** to differ (from), to deviate (from), to be at variance (with), to depart (from), to derogate (from)

149 **In Kriegszeiten kann jede Vertragspartei Maßnahmen treffen, die von ihren Verpflichtungen aus dieser Charta abweichen** (ES 30), In time of war any contracting party may take measures derogating from its obligations under this charter

150 **Von den vorstehenden Bestimmungen kann nicht abgewichen werden** (GC I 10), No derogation from the preceding provisions shall be made (*Abweichung)

151 **Abweichen,** *n.*, deviation, derogation

152 **Aus den Absätzen 1 bis 4 kann eine Berechtigung zum Abweichen von ... nicht abgeleitet werden** (SF 64), Nothing in paragraphs 1 to 4 shall authorize any deviation from ... (*Abweichung)

153 **abweichend,** *adj.*, deviating, in derogation, derogating, dissenting

154   **abweichende Meinungen,** dissenting opinions (*see* *Abstimmungsergebnis)

155   **abweichend von,** notwithstanding, in derogation of

156   **abweichend von diesem Artikel,** notwithstanding the provisions of this article, in a manner that is at variance with this article

157   **Abweichung,** *f.*, derogation, deviation, variance

158   **jede Vertragspartei, die von diesem Recht der Abweichung Gebrauch gemacht hat** (ES 30), any contracting party which has availed itself of this right of derogation

159   **vorbehaltlich der in diesem Vertrag vorgesehenen Ausnahmen oder Abweichungen,** subject to the exceptions or deviations/derogations provided for in this treaty

160   **Abweichungen von internationalen Verfahren** (CAC 38), departures from international procedures

161   **... so sind die Einzelheiten dieser Abweichungen anzugeben** (ILOC 87.13), ... (it) shall give details of such modifications (*Abweichen, *Wortlaut, *maßgebend)

162   **Abwesenheitsverfahren,** *n.* (EExt 14), proceedings by default

163   **achten,** to respect

164   **das Recht der ... achten,** to respect the right of ...

165   **die Würde der Mission achten,** to respect the dignity of the mission

166   **ächten,** to outlaw (war, etc.)

167   **Achtung,** *f.*, respect

168   **Achtung der Ehre/Würde eines Staates,** respect for the honour/dignity of a state

169   **Achtung des Grundsatzes/Prinzips des ...,** respect for the principle of ...

170   **Achtung der Menschenrechte und Grundfreiheiten,** respect for human rights and fundamental freedoms

171   **Achtung der territorialen Integrität,** respect for (the) territorial integrity

172   **allgemeine Achtung,** universal respect (*but see note to* *allgemein)

173   **Ächtung,** *f.*, outlawry

174   **Adjudikation,** *f.*, adjudication

175   **Unter „Adjudikation" im engeren Sinne versteht man die Zuerkennung der Gebietshoheit an einen Staat durch ein internationales Gericht oder Schiedsgericht,** "Adjudication" in the narrower sense is understood as the granting of territorial sovereignty to a state by an international court or court of arbitration

176   **adoptieren,** to adopt

177   **Adoption,** *f.*, adoption

178   **spezifische Adoption,** specific adoption (*Übernahme, *Transformation, *Transformationstheorie)

179   **Adoptionstheorie,** *f.*, adoption theory, theory of adoption

180   **Agent,** *m.*, agent

181   **besonderer Agent,** special agent (*e.g. in commission of inquiry*)

182   **diplomatischer Agent,** diplomatic agent (*Diplomat, *Bevollmächtigter[2])

183   **Aggression,** *f.*, aggression (*Angriff)

184   **Aggressor,** *m.*, aggressor (*Angreifer)

185   **Agrément,** *n.*, *agrément*, permission, approval, authorization

186   **(das) Agrément einholen,** to receive/be granted (the) *agrément*

187   **(das) Agrément entziehen,** to withdraw (the) *agrément*

188   **(das) Agrément erhalten,** to receive/be granted (the) *agrément*

189   **(das) Agrément erteilen,** to grant/issue (the) *agrément*

190   **(das) Agrément verweigern,** to refuse to grant/issue (the) *agrément* (*Ernennung)

191   **ahnden,** to punish, to repress (*Verstoß)

192   **Ahndung,** *f.*, punishment, repression

193   **Aide-Mémoire,** *n.*, *aide-mémoire*

194   **akkreditieren,** to accredit

195   **Botschafter und Gesandte sind bei dem Staatsoberhaupt akkreditiert,** Ambassadors and envoys are accredited to the head of state (*beglaubigt)

196 **Akkreditierung,** *f.,* accrediting
197 **Akt,** *m.,* act, action
198 **die Vornahme eines Aktes,** the taking/adoption of an action
199 **ausländische Akte (UNCDD),** foreign acts
200 **einseitige Akte,** unilateral acts
201 **friedensstörende Akte,** acts/actions prejudicial to (the) peace
202 **unfreundliche Akte,** unfriendly acts (*Handlung, *Akte)
203 **Akte,** *f.,* act
204 **Akte über die Beitrittsbedingungen,** act concerning the conditions of accession (*beitreten)
205 **Allbeteiligungsklausel,** *f., si omnes* clause
206 **Alle-Staaten-Formel,** *f.,* all states formula/clause
207 **allgemein,** *adj.,* general (*often* universal, *but note e.g. the distinction sometimes made between* allgemeines *Völkerrecht *and* universales *Völkerrecht)
208 **allgemein anerkannt,** generally recognized
209 **von den zivilisierten Ländern allgemein anerkannt,** generally recognized by the civilized countries
210 **allgemeine Achtung der Menschenrechte,** universal respect for human rights
211 **allgemeine Konferenz der Mitgliedstaaten der UN,** general conference of the members of the UN
212 **allgemeiner Vertrag,** general treaty
213 **Altstaat,** *m.,* existing state, established state, parent state, mother state, tutelary state
214 **Wenn ein Neustaat sich von einem Altstaat abgetrennt hat ...,** If a new state has seceded from a parent state ...
215 **Amnestie,** *f.,* amnesty
216 **Amnestieklausel,** *f.,* amnesty clause
217 **Amt¹,** *n.,* office, duties
218 **Antritt eines Amtes,** assumption of office/duties
219 **vor Antritt seines Amtes,** prior to his assumption of office/assuming (his) duties

220 **Ausübung eines Amtes,** performance/exercise of duties
221 **die unabhängige und unparteiische Ausübung ihres Amtes,** the independent and impartial exercise of their duties
222 **Wahrnehmung eines Amtes,** exercise/performance of duties
223 **unvereinbar mit der normalen Wahrnehmung ihres Amtes (CRPG An),** incompatible with the proper exercise of their duties
224 **Weiterführung eines Amtes,** continuation of/in office
225 **Ist der Vorsitzende an der Weiterführung seines Amtes behindert ...,** If the Chairman is unable to continue/is prevented from continuing to hold office ...
226 **ein Amt antreten,** to assume/take up (one's) office/duties
227 **Der Präsident und die Vizepräsidenten treten ihr Amt an dem auf die Wahl folgenden 1. November für 3 Jahre an (CICES 10),** The President and Vice-Presidents shall assume office on the first day of November next following their election
228 **ein Amt ausüben,** to exercise office/duties
229 **sein Amt unparteiisch und gewissenhaft ausüben,** to exercise one's duties impartially and conscientiously
230 **im Amt bleiben,** to hold/remain in office, to continue to exercise/perform (one's) duties
231 **Diese bleiben für die Dauer der Tagung im Amt (IAEA V),** They shall hold office for the duration of the session (*see* *Amtsantritt)
232 **eines Amtes enthoben werden,** to be dismissed/removed from (an) office
233 **ein Amt versehen,** to occupy an office/a position
234 **Der Generaldirektor versieht das Amt des Generalsekretärs der Konferenz (ILO 15),** The director-general shall act as secretary-general of the conference

235   **ein Amt weiterführen,** to continue in office, to continue to discharge (one's) duties
236   **von Amts wegen,** *ex officio*
237   **Amt²**, *n.*, agency, office, board, bureau
238   **amtlich,** *adj.*, official, in an official capacity
239   **amtliche Eigenschaft,** official capacity
240   **amtliche Korrespondenz,** official correspondence
241   **Dritte Staaten gewähren in bezug auf die amtliche Korrespondenz und sonstige amtliche Mitteilungen im Durchgangsverkehr ... die gleiche Freiheit und den gleichen Schutz wie der Empfangsstaat** (VCDR 40), Third states shall accord to official correspondence and other official communications in transit . . . the same freedom and protection as is accorded by the receiving state
242   **amtliche Mitteilung,** official communication/notification
243   **amtlicher Schriftwechsel/Schriftverkehr,** official correspondence
244   **amtlich beglaubigt,** officially/duly certified
245   **Amtsakt,** *m.*, official act (*Amtshandlung)
246   **Amtsantritt,** *m.*, assumption of office/duties, entering into office, taking up of (official) duties/functions
247   **Als Zeitpunkt des Amtsantritts des Missionschefs gilt der Tag, an welchem ...** (VCDR 13), The head of the mission is considered as having taken up his functions when ...
248   **Die Mitglieder des Gerichtshofes bleiben im Amt bis zum Amtsantritt ihrer Nachfolger. Nach ihrer Ablösung ...** (PHR 40), The members of the court shall hold office until replaced. After having been replaced ...
249   **mit seinem/ihrem Amtsantritt,** on assuming office (*Rangfolge, *Eigenschaft)
250   **Amtsbezirk** *m.* **eines Konsuls** (= Konsularbezirk, *n.*), consular district

251   **Amtsblatt,** *n.*, official journal
252   **Amtsdauer,** *f.*, term (of office) (*Amtszeit)
253   **Amtsenthebung,** *f.*, dismissal/removal from office
254   **Amtsgebühr,** *f.*, official charge/fee
255   **die von der Mission erhobenen Amtsgebühren,** fees and charges levied by the mission in the course of its duties
256   **Amtsgeschäfte,** *n.pl.*, official business
257   **Amtsgeschäfte, mit deren Wahrnehmung der Entsendestaat die Mission beauftragt** (VCDR 41), official business entrusted to the mission by the sending state
258   **Amtsgewalt,** *f.*, authority
259   **Der Fonds ist dem Europarat angeschlossen und als solcher dessen Amtsgewalt unterstellt** (AACER I), The fund shall be attached to the Council of Europe and administered under its supreme authority
260   **Amtshandlung,** *f.*, official act
261   **in Ausübung seiner dienstlichen Tätigkeit vorgenommene Amtshandlungen** (VCDR 38), official acts performed in the exercise of his functions (*Handlung)
262   **Amtsperiode,** *f.*, term (of office) (*Amtszeit)
263   **der noch verbleibende Teil der Amtsperiode,** the unexpired portion of the term (of office)
264   **Amtssprache,** *f.*, official language
265   **Amtstätigkeit,** *f.*, official duty/duties/functions
266   **Amtsträger** *m.* **einer Organisation,** officer/official of an organization (*Bediensteter)
267   **Amtszeit,** *f.*, term (of office)
268   **nach Ablauf ihrer Amtszeit,** after the expiration of their terms of office, on leaving office
269   **die Mitglieder, deren Amtszeit nach der Anfangsperiode von 4 Jahren abläuft,** the members whose term of office is to expire at the end of the initial period of 4 years (*Amtsperiode)

270 **anberaumen,** to convene, to call
271 **anberaumt,** *adj.*, convened, called
272 **eine zu diesem Zweck anberaumte öffentliche Sitzung (SICJ 66),** a public sitting to be held for this purpose
273 **anberaumte Termine,** dates set/fixed/prescribed/appointed
274 **Anbetracht,** *f.*, **in,** in view of, considering, aware, noting, whereas, in consideration (*in preamble*)
275 **Anciennität,** *f.*, seniority of office
276 **Der Vorrang innerhalb der drei Rangklassen richtet sich nach der Anciennität, d.h. nach der Länge des Zeitraums, der seit der Überreichung des Beglaubigungsschreibens verflossen ist,** The order of precedence within the three classes is determined by the seniority of office, i.e. the time that has elapsed since the presentation of credentials
277 **örtliche Anciennität,** local seniority of office
278 **ändern,** to revise, to amend, to modify (*Änderung, *abändern, *note to* *Vertrag modifizieren, and* VCLOT 39–41 *in Annex* 16)
279 **ändernd,** *adj.*, modifying, revising, amending (*often in compounds such as* **vertragsändernd**)
280 **... so greift dieses Übereinkommen nur ändernd ein, wenn ...** (CLPD 8), ... the present Convention will only override such provisions if ...
281 **anderslautend,** *adj.*, contrary, to the contrary (*anderweitig)
282 **Änderung,** *f.*, revision, amendment, modification
283 **einschließlich aller Änderungen und Ergänzungen** (CUN 79), including any alteration or amendment
284 **dieses Abkommen, alle Änderungen und ...,** the present agreement, any amendment to/revision of it and ...
285 **Änderungen im Beglaubigungsschreiben,** alterations in the credentials
286 **Annahme der Änderung,** acceptance of the revision/amendment

287 **Vorschlag auf Änderung,** proposal for amendment
288 **Vorschläge auf Änderung dieser Satzung können dem Ministerkomitee unterbreitet werden (CE 41),** Proposals for the amendment of this statute may be made to the Committee of Ministers
289 **eine Änderung vornehmen,** to amend
290 **jede auf Grund dieses Absatzes vorgenommene Änderung der Anlage (CFIMT VII),** any amendment to the Annex under this paragraph
291 **eine Änderung vorschlagen,** to propose an amendment
292 **Jedes Mitglied des Europarates kann Änderungen dieser Charta vorschlagen,** Any member of the Council of Europe may/is entitled to propose amendments to this charter (*Abänderung, *Modifikation, *and* VCLOT 39 *in Annex* 16)
293 **Änderungsentwurf,** *m.*, draft revision/amendment/modification
294 **Der Wortlaut jedes Änderungsentwurfs ist dem Generalsekretär der UN zu übermitteln,** The text of any proposed amendment shall be transmitted to the Secretary-General of the UN
295 **Änderungsprotokoll,** *n.*, protocol of amendment, amending protocol
296 **Änderungsübereinkunft,** *f.* (VCLOT), amending agreement
297 **Änderungsvorschlag,** *m.*, proposed amendment, proposal for an amendment, proposal to amend
298 **anderweitig,** *adj.*, (to the) contrary, alternative
299 **wenn anderweitig feststeht** (VCLOT 13), when it is otherwise established
300 **anderweitige Maßnahmen,** alternative action
301 **anderweitige Vereinbarung,** agreement to the contrary, other agreement
302 **unbeschadet anderweitiger Vereinbarung,** unless otherwise agreed (*gegenteilig, *anderslautend)

303 **Androhung,** *f.*, threat
(* Anwendung)
304 **anerkannt,** *adj.*, recognized
305 **allgemein anerkannt,** generally recognized (*see note to* * allgemein)
306 **allgemein anerkannte Rechtsgrundsätze,** generally recognized principles of law
307 **anerkennen,** to recognize
308 **einen Staat/Erwerb/eine Regierung/Annexion (usw.) anerkennen,** to recognize a state/an acquisition/a government/an annexation (etc.)
309 **anerkennend,** *adj.*, recognizing
310 **der anerkennende Staat,** the recognizing state
311 **Anerkennender,** *adj.n.*, the recognizing party/state
312 **Anerkenntnis,** *f.*, **in,** recognizing (*in preamble*)
313 **Anerkennung,** *f.*, recognition
314 **Anerkennung eines Staates/einer Regierung (usw),** recognition of a state/government (etc.)
315 **in Anerkennung,** recognizing (*in preamble*)
316 **Anerkennung** *de facto*, recognition *de facto*
317 **Anerkennung** *de jure*, recognition *de jure*
318 **Kraft der Anerkennung,** effect of recognition
319 **konstitutive Kraft der Anerkennung,** constitutive effect of recognition
320 **rückwirkende Kraft der Anerkennung,** retroactive effect of recognition
321 **Rechtswirkung der Anerkennung,** legal effect of recognition
322 **Rücknahme der Anerkennung,** withdrawal of recognition
323 **Theorie der Anerkennung,** theory/doctrine of recognition
324 **deklaratorische Theorie der Anerkennung,** declaratory/evidentiary theory/doctrine of recognition
325 **konstitutive Theorie der Anerkennung,** constitutive theory/doctrine of recognition

326 **Verweigerung der Anerkennung,** refusal of recognition, refusal to grant recognition
327 **Ein Abbruch der diplomatischen Beziehungen kommt der Verweigerung der Anerkennung gleich,** The severance of diplomatic relations is tantamount to the refusal to recognize
328 **Widerruf der Anerkennung,** withdrawal of recognition
329 **allgemeine Anerkennung,** general recognition
330 **ausdrückliche Anerkennung,** express recognition
331 **eingekleidete Anerkennung,** implied/implicit recognition
332 **förmliche Anerkennung,** formal recognition
333 **frühere Anerkennung,** prior/earlier recognition
334 **kollektive Anerkennung,** collective recognition
335 **spätere Anerkennung,** subsequent recognition
336 **stillschweigende Anerkennung,** implied/implicit recognition
337 **Nimmt ein Staat diplomatische Beziehungen auf, dann liegt darin eine stillschweigende Anerkennung,** The establishing of diplomatic relations by a state implies recognition
338 **ursprüngliche Anerkennung,** original recognition
339 **völkerrechtliche Anerkennung,** international recognition, recognition at international law
340 **Die Bundesregierung erklärt, daß mit Unterzeichnung dieses Vertrags keine völkerrechtliche Anerkennung der DDR verbunden ist** (TNPNW, Statements on Signature), The Federal Government declares that signature of this treaty does not imply recognition of the GDR under international law
341 **vorzeitige Anerkennung,** premature recognition
342 **Die vorzeitige Anerkennung eines Neustaates ist eine unzulässige**

Einmischung in die inneren Angelegenheiten des Altstaates, The premature recognition of a nascent state is an inadmissible intervention in the internal affairs of the parent state

343 **Anerkennung aussprechen,** to declare/accord/grant recognition

344 **Anerkennung verweigern,** to refuse (to grant) recognition

345 **Anerkennung widerrufen,** to withdraw recognition

346 **Anerkennung zurücknehmen,** to withdraw recognition

347 **Anerkennungsakt,** *m.,* act of recognition

348 **Anerkennungsdoktrin,** *f.,* doctrine of recognition

349 **deklaratorische Anerkennungsdoktrin,** declaratory/evidentiary doctrine of recognition

350 **konstitutive Anerkennungsdoktrin,** constitutive doctrine of recognition

351 **Anerkennungserklärung,** *f.,* declaration of recognition (*see note to* *Erklärung)

352 **Anerkennungspraxis,** *f.,* practice of/as to recognition

353 **Anerkennungsurkunde,** *f.,* instrument of recognition

354 **Anerkennungsvertrag,** *m.,* treaty of recognition

355 **anfechtbar,** *adj.,* contestable, appealable, open to challenge

356 **nicht anfechtbar,** without appeal, not contestable

357 **anfechten,** to contest, to challenge, to dispute, to appeal against

358 **anführen,** to list, to set out, to set forth, to specify, to mention (*angeführt)

359 **Angabe** *f.,* **unter,** giving, giving details of, together with details of

360 **Angarie,** *f.,* angary

361 **Angarienrecht,** *n.,* right of angary

362 **angeblich,** *adj.,* alleged

363 **der angebliche Verstoß gegen die Ehre des Staates,** the alleged infringement/violation of the honour of the state

364 **angeführt,** *adj.,* listed, set out, set forth, specified

365 **die in Artikel 4 angeführten Bestimmungen,** the provisions set out/ referred to in Article 4

366 **die namentlich angeführten Mitglieder,** the members mentioned/ specified by name

367 **Angehöriger,** *adj.n.,* national, citizen

368 **Angehörige eines Mitgliedstaats der Organisation,** nationals of a member state of the organization

369 **Mitglieder des diplomatischen Personals der Mission sollten grundsätzlich Angehörige des Entsendestaats sein,** Members of the diplomatic staff of the mission should in principle be nationals of the sending state

370 **Angehörige anderer Staaten,** non-nationals, nationals of other states (*Staatsangehöriger)

371 **Angeklagter,** *adj.n.,* defendant, defending state/party (*Strafverfahren)

372 **Angelegenheit**[1], *f.,* matter, affair

373 **ein freundlicher Ausgleich der Angelegenheit** (PHR 28), an amicable settlement of the matter

374 **Angelegenheiten, die unter dieses Übereinkommen fallen** (WMO 8), matters within the provisions of the Convention

375 **Angelegenheiten, die zum Aufgabenbereich der Organisation gehören** (WMO 8), matters within the purposes of the organization

376 **außenpolitische/äußere Angelegenheiten eines Staates,** foreign/external affairs of a state

377 **innere Angelegenheiten eines Staates,** internal/domestic affairs of a state

378 **eine unzulässige Einmischung in die inneren Angelegenheiten,** an inadmissible/unlawful intervention in the internal/domestic affairs

379 **Angelegenheit**[2], *f.,* case

380 **alle dem Gerichtshof unterbreiteten Angelegenheiten,** all cases referred to the court

381 **die Arten von Angelegenheiten bestimmen** (CRPG An), to determine the categories of cases

382   die Erledigung einer Angelegenheit (CRPG An), the adjudication of a case (*anhängig, *Kammer, endgültige *Entscheidung, *Sache²)
383   **angemessen**, *adj.*, reasonable, just, fair, proper
384   **angesichts**, *prep.* (+ *gen.*), in view of, considering, aware of, noting, whereas (*in preamble*)
385   **angleichen**, to approximate
386   **Angleichung**, *f.*, approximation
387   **Angleichung ihrer innerstaatlichen Rechtsvorschriften**, approximation of their respective municipal law(s) (*Rechtssystem)
388   **angreifen**, to attack
389   **angreifender Staat**, aggressor state
390   **Angreifer**, *m.*, aggressor
391   **Bestimmung des Angreifers**, determination of the aggressor
392   **Angreiferstaat**, *m.*, aggressor state
393   **angrenzen**, to adjoin, to be adjacent (to), to be contiguous (with)
394   **Angrenzen**, *n.*, contiguity
395   **angrenzend**, *adj.*, adjoining, adjacent, contiguous
396   **angrenzender Staat**, contiguous state, adjacent state
397   **angrenzende Gewässer**, adjacent waters
398   **Angriff**, *m.*, attack, aggression, hostile action
399   **im Falle eines Angriffs oder unmittelbar drohenden Angriffs** (CRPG 5), in the event of attack or imminent threat of such attack
400   **Angriff auf die Person**, attack on the person
401   **Angriff auf das Leben und die Person** (GC I), violence to life and person
402   **Angriff mit Waffengewalt**, armed attack/aggression
403   **bewaffneter Angriff**, armed attack/aggression
404   **nichtprovozierter Angriff**, unprovoked attack/aggression
405   **Angriffsakt**, *m.*, aggression, aggressive act, act of aggression, hostile act/action

406   **nichtkriegerische Angriffsakte**, non-war aggressive acts (*Angriffshandlung)
407   **Angriffshandlung**, *f.*, aggression, aggressive act, act of aggression, hostile act/action
408   **Angriffshandlungen und andere Friedensbrüche unterdrücken**, to suppress acts of aggression and other breaches of the peace (*Angriffsakt)
409   **Angriffskrieg**, *m.*, war of aggression, aggressive war, offensive war
410   **Angriffspolitik**, *f.*, policy of aggression
411   **Wiederaufnahme der Angriffspolitik** (CUN 53), renewal of aggressive policy
412   **anhalten**, to stop, to stop and search, to arrest (*especially of ships*)
413   **Anhalten**, *n.*, stoppage
414   **Anhalterecht**, *n.*, right to stop, right to stop and search, right of stoppage
415   **Anhalte- und Durchsuchungsrecht**, right to stop and search
416   **Anhang**, *m.*, appendix, annex
417   **Der Anhang dieser Charta ist Bestandteil derselben** (ES 38), The appendix to this charter shall form an integral part of it
418   **... sind im Anhang, der Bestandteil dieses Übereinkommens ist, aufgeführt** (CFW 1), ... are specified in the annex to the convention which shall be an integral part thereof (*Anlage)
419   **anhängig**, *adj.*, pending, before the court
420   **seine Tätigkeit in anhängigen Angelegenheiten** (CRPG An), his duties respecting pending cases
421   **die bei dem Gerichtshof anhängig gemachte Angelegenheit**, the case before the court
422   **Die Rechtssachen werden beim Gerichtshof durch Notifizierung des Schiedsvertrags oder durch eine Klageschrift anhängig gemacht** (SICJ 40), Cases are brought before the court either by the notification

of the special agreement or by a written application

423 **Anhängigkeit,** *f.*, pendency

424 **anheischig,** *adj.*, bound, obliged

425 **die Vertragsmächte machen sich anheischig . . .,** the contracting states undertake to . . .

426 **anhören,** to hear, to consult

427 **Anhörung,** *f.*, hearing, consultation

428 **die Anhörung der Zeugen,** the hearing of the witnesses

429 **nach Anhörung der Versammlung** (EEC 7), after consulting the Assembly

430 **Anlage¹,** *f.*, annex, appendix

431 **in Anlage I aufgeführte Staaten** (WMO 3), any state listed in Annex I attached hereto (*Anhang)

432 **Anlage²,** *f.*, installation, plant (*Anlagenstaat, *Kernanlage)

433 **Anlagenstaat,** *m.* (VCLD), installation state (*i.e. a state in which a nuclear installation is situated*)

434 **Anliegerstaat,** *m.*, adjoining/adjacent state (*in context of rivers or lakes sometimes* littoral state, riparian state)

435 **Anmerkung,** *f.*, note

436 **erläuternde Anmerkungen,** interpretative notes (*Erläuterungen)

437 **Annahme,** *f.*, acceptance, adoption

438 **eine den Vertragsregierungen zur Annahme zugeleitete Änderung,** an amendment communicated to the contracting governments for their acceptance

439 **formgerechte Annahme,** formal acceptance

440 **zwei Monate nach deren/dessen formgerechter Annahme,** two months after it has been formally accepted

441 **nachträgliche Annahme,** subsequent/deferred acceptance (*ungültig, *Unterzeichnung, *and* VCLOT 2 *in Annex* 14)

442 **Annahmeerklärung,** *f.*, notification of acceptance (*see note to* *Erklärung)

443 **nach Eingang der Annahmeerklä-**

rung **bei der Interimskommission,** upon receipt by the Interim Commission of the notification of acceptance

444 **Annahmeklausel,** *f.*, acceptance clause

445 **Annahmeurkunde,** *f.*, instrument of acceptance

446 **annehmen,** to accept, to adopt

447 **Alle Mitglieder der UN nehmen das Statut des IGHs** *ipso facto* **an,** All members of the UN are *ipso facto* parties to the Statute of the ICJ

448 **annektieren,** to annex

449 **Annektierung,** *f.*, annexation

450 **Annexion,** *f.*, annexation

451 **die Annexion strittiger Gebiete,** the annexation of disputed territories

452 **Annexionserklärung,** *f.*, declaration of annexation (*see note to* *Erklärung)

453 **Annexionsrecht,** *n.*, right of annexation, right to annex

454 **Annexionsverbot,** *n.*, prohibition of annexation

455 **Anpassung,** *f.*, adjustment

456 **die Anpassungen der Verträge,** the adjustments to/of the treaties

457 **Anrainerstaat,** *m.*, adjacent state, adjoining state, littoral state

458 **da am Golf mehrere Anrainerstaaten vorhanden sind . . .,** as several states are adjacent to the gulf . . .

459 **anrufen,** to resort to, to have/take/seek recourse (to)

460 **Vereinbaren die Parteien, diese Kommission nicht anzurufen . . .** (ECPSD 5), If the parties agree not to have recourse to that Commission . . .

461 **Gewalt anrufen,** to resort to (armed) force (*Anrufung, *Streitgegenstand)

462 **Anrufender,** *adj.n.*, the party/state seeking recourse

463 **Anrufung,** *f.*, recourse, resort (to)

464 **Anrufung des Gerichts/des Gerichtshofes,** recourse to the court/court of justice

465 **vor Anrufung des IGHs,** before resorting to the ICJ, prior to recourse to the ICJ

466 **Anrufung der Gewalt,** resort/ recourse to (armed) force
467 **Anrufung regionaler Organe,** resort to regional agencies/organs
468 **Anrufung der Schiedssprechung,** recourse to arbitration
469 **unmittelbare Anrufung,** direct recourse (*Vergleichsverfahren)
470 **ansässig,** *adj.*, resident
471 **ständig ansässig,** permanently resident
472 **Anschluß,** *m.*, annexation, Anschluss (*in the particular case of Austria in* 1938)
473 **Anschlußzone,** *f.*, contiguous zone
474 **Die Anschlußzone darf sich nicht weiter als 12 Seemeilen über die Basislinie hinaus erstrecken, von der aus die Breite des Küstenmeeres gemessen wird** (GCTS 24), The contiguous zone may not extend beyond 12 miles from the baseline from which the breadth of the territorial sea is measured
475 **Anschwemmung,** *f.*, accretion (alluvium *used purely in geological sense*)
476 **Ansicht,** *f.*, opinion
477 **einstimmige/übereinstimmende Ansicht,** unanimous opinion
478 **Bringt das Urteil im ganzen oder in einzelnen Teilen nicht die übereinstimmende Ansicht der Richter zum Ausdruck, so hat jeder Richter das Recht, eine Darlegung seiner eigenen Ansicht beizufügen** (PHR 51), If the judgment does not represent in whole or in part the unanimous opinion of the judges, any judge shall be entitled to deliver a separate opinion (*Meinung)
479 **Anspruch¹,** *m.*, right
480 **Anspruch auf . . . haben,** to have a right of/to, to be entitled to (*The wide choice of equally valid terms should be noted, in German between* **Anspruch auf, Recht auf, Recht des/der,** *and in English between* right of, right to, (to be)

entitled to. *Even within* ES, PHR *and* UDHR *there exists wide variation. For expressions not listed here, see under* *Recht auf, *frei, *Freiheit, *and also* CERD 5 *in* Annex 9.)
Anspruch auf:
481 **Anerkennung als Rechtsperson** (UDHR 6), recognition as a person before the law
482 **Begrenzung der Arbeitszeit** (UDHR 24), limitation of working hours
483 **Erholung und Freizeit,** rest and leisure
484 **gleichen Schutz vor dem Gesetz** (UDHR 7), equal protection of the law
485 **Leistungen,** benefits
486 **periodischen, bezahlten Urlaub** (UDHR 24), periodic holidays with pay
487 **rechtliches Gehör** (UDHR 10), a hearing by a tribunal
488 **rechtlichen Schutz gegen Eingriffe in sein Privatleben** (UDHR 12), the protection of the law against interference with his privacy
489 **Staatsangehörigkeit,** nationality
490 **wirksamen Rechtsschutz,** effective protection at law/of the law
491 **Anspruch²,** *m.*, claim
492 **sich aus dem Krieg ergebende Ansprüche** (CSMW), claims arising out of the war
493 **Ansprüche gegen,** claims against
494 **Erledigung der Ansprüche,** disposal of claims (NATOSF VIII)
495 **Erlöschen eines Anspruchs,** extinction/lapse of a claim
496 **entgegengesetzte Ansprüche,** opposing claims
497 **entgegengesetzte Ansprüche ausgleichen,** to reconcile opposing claims
498 **Ansprüche geltend machen,** to make claims, to lodge claims
499 **Ansprüche auf den Kontinentalsockel geltend machen** (GCC 2), to make a claim to the continental shelf
500 **in Anspruch nehmen,** (i) to claim, to

claim the right of/entitlement to; (ii) to have recourse to

501 **..., kann kein Staat das Recht für sich in Anspruch nehmen, einen Teil davon seiner Souveränität zu unterstellen** (GCHS 2), ... no state may validly purport to subject any part of them to its sovereignty

502 **Ansprüche vorbringen,** to present/lodge claims

503 **anspruchsberechtigt,** *adj.*, entitled to claim

504 **anstellen,** to appoint, to engage

505 **Anstellung,** *f.*, appointment, engagement

506 **die Anstellung und die Entlassung von Personen als Mitglied der Mission** (VCDR 10), the engagement and dismissal of persons as members of the mission

507 **Anstellungsurkunde,** *f.*, letter/certificate of appointment

508 **Antrag,** *m.*, motion, request, claim, petition, application

509 **auf Antrag oder** *proprio motu*, on request or on its own initiative

510 **auf Antrag eines Drittels der Vertragsregierungen,** upon the request of one third of the contracting governments

511 **die bei Gericht eingehenden Anträge** (CRPG An), petitions submitted to the tribunal

512 **Antrag auf,** motion/request for

513 **einen Antrag stellen,** to file/submit/make a request, to file/submit a motion

514 **Ein Antrag auf Revision dieser Konvention kann jederzeit gestellt werden** (PCG 16), A request for the revision of the present convention may be made at any time (*Ersuchen, *einberufen, *Gegenpartei)

515 **antragstellend,** *adj.*, applying, making/submitting the request/application/claim, filing/tabling/submitting the motion (etc.)

516 **antragstellender Staat,** state which is the claimant (PPELDO 27)

517 **Antragsteller,** *m.*, applicant, claim-

ant, party making/submitting the request, filing/submitting the motion (etc.)

518 **antreten,** to assume, to enter on (*Amt antreten)

519 **Antritt,** *m.*, assumption (*e.g.* of office) (*Amtsantritt)

520 **Antwortnote,** *f.*, note in reply

521 **anwendbar,** *adj.*, applicable

522 **anwendbar werden,** to become applicable

523 **keine auf den Fall anwendbare Regel,** no rule applicable to the case

524 **selbständig anwendbare Regel des Völkerrechts,** self-executing rule of international law

525 **Anwendbarkeit,** *f.*, applicability

526 **... daß sie beabsichtigen, die Anwendbarkeit dieses Abkommens auf die Gesamtheit oder einen Teil ihrer Gebiete auszudehnen** (IRU 20), ... that he desires that the convention shall apply to all or any of his territories

527 **anwenden,** to apply

528 **ganz oder teilweise anwenden,** to apply in whole or in part

529 **vorläufig anwenden,** to apply provisionally/for the time being

530 **Gewalt anwenden,** to use (armed) force

531 **Anwendung,** *f.*, application, operation

532 **Anwendung bzw. Androhung militärischer Gewalt,** the use or threat of (armed/military) force

533 **Richter, die in Anwendung des Artikels 31 bestellt werden,** judges appointed under Article 31

534 **Die Anwendung der strittigen Maßnahmen hat zu unterbleiben** (GCF 10), The measures in dispute shall not be applied

535 **Die Anwendung des Übereinkommens findet mit ... sein Ende,** The application of the present convention shall cease on .../when ...

536 **Anwendung der Zwangsarbeit,** recourse to forced labour (SC 5)

537 **Aufhebung der Anwendung,** termination of (the) application

538   **Ausdehnung der Anwendung,** extension of (the) application (*normally territorial*)

539   **Verlängerung der Anwendung,** extension of (the) application (*normally temporal*)

540   **die Verlängerung der Anwendung von Artikel 11** (EPU 33), the extension of the operation of Article 11

541   **volle Anwendung,** full application

542   **bestimmte Gebiete von der vollen Anwendung der Artikel 3 und 4 ausschließen** (FC 11), to exclude particular areas from the full application of Articles 3 and 4

543   **vorläufige Anwendung,** provisional application

544   **die Anwendung aufheben,** to terminate the application

545   **die Anwendung aufschieben,** to postpone the application (*see* öffentliche *Ordnung)

546   **die Anwendung ausdehnen,** to extend the application

547   **die Anwendung aussetzen,** to suspend the application

548   **Die Anwendung der Maßnahmen wird ausgesetzt** (GCF 10), The measures shall be suspended

549   **Anwendung finden,** to apply, to be applicable

550   **ein Hoheitsgebiet, in dem die Charta Anwendung findet** (ES 37), a territory to which the said Charter is applicable

551   **(Personen), auf welche die Bestimmungen des Artikels 18 ganz oder teilweise Anwendung finden** (PrivExCE 17), (persons) to whom the provisions of Article 18 shall apply in whole or in part

552   **keine Anwendung mehr finden,** to cease to apply/be applicable

553   **die Anwendung sicherstellen,** to ensure (the) application

554   **die Anwendung der Bestimmungen dieser Konvention sicherstellen** (PCG 5), to give effect to the provisions of the present convention

555   **die Anwendung suspendieren,** to suspend (the) application

556   **die Anwendung verlängern,** to extend (the) application

557   **Anwendungsbereich,** *m.*, field/scope of application

558   **unbeschadet besonderer Bestimmungen dieses Vertrages ist in seinem Anwendungsbereich ...** (EEC 7), within the scope of application of this treaty and without prejudice to the special provisions contained therein ...

559   **ausgedehnter Anwendungsbereich,** wide field/scope of application

560   **Die Bestimmungen des zweiten Teils haben hingegen einen ausgedehnteren Anwendungsbereich** (GC IV 4), The provisions of Part II are, however, wider in application

561   **territorialer Anwendungsbereich,** territorial application

562   **anwesend,** *adj.*, present

563   **anwesende und abstimmende Mitglieder/Richter,** members/judges present and voting (*Beschluß)

564   **Arbeitsgruppe**[1], *f.*, working party/group

565   **Arbeitsgruppe**[2], *f.*, labour unit, labour detachment (GC I/IV)

566   **Arbeitskräfteausschuß,** *m.*, manpower committee

567   **Arbeitsrecht,** *n.*, law(s) relating to/governing labour/labour questions, labour law(s)

568   **Arbeitsschutz,** *m.*, protection of labour (GC III)

569   **Arbeitssprache,** *f.*, working language

570   **Die Arbeitssprachen der Organisation sind ...,** The working languages of the organization shall be ...

571   **Archiv,** *n.*, archive(s)

572   **Die Archive (der Mission usw.) sind unverletzlich, wo immer sie sich befinden,** The archives (of the mission, etc.) shall be inviolable wherever they may be

573   **Artikel,** *m.*, article

574   **Assoziation,** *f.*, association

575   **multilaterale Assoziation zur**

Beseitigung der Handelsschranken (EFTA Pr), multilateral association for the removal of trade barriers

576 **Assoziationsabkommen,** *n.*, association agreement, agreement of association

577 **Assoziationsrat,** *m.*, council of (the) association

578 **Assoziationsvertrag,** *m.*, treaty of association, association treaty

579 **assoziieren,** to associate

580 **Assoziierung,** *f.*, (act of) association

581 **die Assoziierung überseeischer Länder und Hoheitsgebiete** (EEC 3), the association of the overseas countries and territories

582 **Asyl,** *n.*, asylum, sanctuary

583 **um Asyl bitten/ersuchen,** to request/apply for asylum

584 **Asyl gewähren,** to grant/afford asylum

585 **Asylrecht,** *n.*, the right of asylum/sanctuary

586 **Atomenergie,** *f.*, atomic energy

587 **die friedliche Anwendung/Verwendung der Atomenergie,** the peaceful application/use of atomic energy

588 **die praktische Anwendung der Atomenergie zu friedlichen Zwecken** (IAEA III), the practical application of atomic energy for peaceful purposes

589 **der Beitrag der Atomenergie zum Frieden, zur Gesundheit und zum Wohlstand in der ganzen Welt** (IAEA II), the contribution of atomic energy to peace, health and prosperity throughout the world

590 **Atom-Information,** *f.* (NATA), atomic information

591 **Sicherung/Verteilung der Atom-Information,** safeguarding/dissemination of atomic information

592 **Atomkrieg,** *m.*, atomic/nuclear war

593 **Atomkriegführung,** *f.*, atomic/nuclear war(fare)

594 **Atomwettrüsten,** *n.*, atomic arms race

595 **Audienz,** *f.*, audience

596 **öffentliche/private Audienz,** public/private audience

597 **um eine Audienz bitten,** to request an audience

598 **eine Audienz gewähren,** to grant an audience

599 **um eine Audienz nachsuchen,** to request an audience

600 **aufbringen,** to seize

601 **aufbringender Staat,** state making the seizure

602 **Aufbringung,** *f.*, seizure

603 **die Aufbringung eines der Seeräuberei verdächtigten Schiffes** (GCHS 20), the seizure of a ship on suspicion of piracy

604 **Aufenthaltsland,** *n.*, country of (temporary) residence

605 **Aufenthaltsstaat,** *m.*, state of (temporary) residence (*Heimatstaat, *Wohnsitz *and note*)

606 **Aufenthaltsvorrecht,** *n.* (WEUS 2), privilege of residence

607 **auferlegen,** to impose (on) (*in a pejorative sense sometimes* to inflict on)

608 **Das Völkerrecht verleiht dem einzelnen Rechte und erlegt ihm Pflichten auf,** International law grants the individual rights and imposes duties on him

609 **Maßnahmen, die ihnen durch diese Entscheidungen auferlegt werden** (CRPG An), action required of them by such decisions

610 **auferlegt,** *adj.*, imposed (upon), incumbent (upon)

611 **die den Parteien auferlegte Pflicht,** the duty incumbent upon the parties

612 **Auferlegung,** *f.*, imposition, imposing, inflicting (*auferlegen)

613 **aufführen,** to list, to set forth/out, to enumerate (*aufgeführt)

614 **Aufgabe,** *f.*, task, duty, function

615 **Durchführung der Aufgaben,** performance/exercise of duties/functions

616 **Erfüllung der Aufgaben,** fulfilment of duties/functions

617 **Grenzen der Aufgaben,** limits of duties/functions (*Aufgaben überschreiten)

618 **Übertragung der Aufgaben,** delegation of duties/functions

619 **Wahrnehmung der Aufgaben,** performance/exercise of duties/functions

620 **beratende Aufgabe,** advisory/consultative function

621 **... unterstützt von einem Wirtschafts- und Sozialausschuß mit beratender Aufgabe (EEC 4),** ... assisted by an Economic and Social Committee acting in an advisory capacity

622 **dienstliche Aufgabe,** official duty/function

623 **humanitäre Aufgaben (GC),** humanitarian duties/functions

624 **Aufgaben durchführen,** to perform/exercise functions/duties

625 **Aufgaben erfüllen,** to fulfil/discharge duties/functions

626 **Aufgaben überschreiten,** to exceed duties/functions

627 **Die Vertreter ... dürfen keinesfalls die Grenzen ihrer Aufgabe überschreiten (GC I 8),** The representatives shall not in any case exceed their mission

628 **Aufgaben übertragen,** to delegate/entrust duties/functions

629 **die ihnen übertragenen Aufgaben,** the duties delegated/entrusted to them, the duties with which they are entrusted

630 **Aufgaben wahrnehmen,** to perform/exercise functions/duties (*Dienstobliegenheit, *Tätigkeit, *Funktion)

631 **Aufgabenbereich,** *m.,* scope/area/range of duties/functions

632 **mit unverändertem Aufgabenbereich (ECE III),** with unchanged terms of reference

633 **aufgeführt,** *adj.,* listed, set forth/out, enumerated

634 **die in Artikel ... aufgeführten Bestimmungen,** the provisions/terms set forth in Article ...

635 **die in Artikel III aufgeführten Handlungen (PCG 4),** the acts enumerated in Article III

636 **aufgehoben,** *adj.,* suspended, terminated, rescinded, repealed

aufgelegt: *see* *aufliegen

637 **aufgrund von,** by virtue of, pursuant to, on the basis of

638 **Verhandlungen aufgrund von Artikel 15,** negotiations pursuant to Article 15

639 **aufheben,** to suspend, to waive, to terminate, to set aside, to rescind, to repeal, to abrogate

640 **Gewohnheitsrecht kann durch einen Vertrag aufgehoben werden,** Custom(ary law) may be terminated by treaty

641 **Immunität aufheben,** to withdraw/to waive immunity (*kündigen, *erlöschen, *Immunität)

642 **Aufhebung,** *f.,* termination, suspension, waiver, repeal

643 **einvernehmliche Aufhebung eines Vertrags,** termination of a treaty by mutual consent/agreement (*Verzicht, *Immunität, *gelten, *Außerkraftsetzung)

644 **aufklären,** to clarify, to elucidate (*Tatfragen)

645 **Aufklärung,** *f.,* clarification, elucidation, inquiry

646 **Die Erlaubnis des Staates, auf dessen Gebiet zu der Aufklärung geschritten werden soll, ist einzuholen (HgI-20),** Permission must be obtained from the state on whose territory it is proposed to hold the inquiry

647 **Aufklärungsmittel,** *n.,* means of inquiry

648 **Auflage,** *f.,* condition, proviso

649 **(jedoch) mit der Auflage, daß ...,** subject to the condition that ...

650 **auflegen,** to open (*aufliegen, *Unterzeichnung)

651 **aufliegen (=aufgelegt werden),** to be open(ed)

652 **Der Vertrag liegt zum Beitritt auf,** The treaty shall be open for accession

653 **Der Vertrag liegt nach seinem Inkrafttreten noch 6 Monate zur Unterzeichnung auf,** The treaty shall remain open for signature for 6 months after it has entered into force (*Vertrag öffnen)

654 **auflösen**, to liquidate, to dissolve, to wind up (*e.g. an organization*)
655 **Auflösung,** *f.*, liquidation, dissolution, winding up (*e.g. of an organization*)
656 **Aufnahme¹,** *f.*, establishment (*e.g. of relations*)
657 **Aufnahme²,** *f.*, admission, acceptance (*e.g. of new members*)
658 **Aufnahme in die Mitgliedschaft,** admission to membership/as a member
659 **Aufnahme³,** *f.*, insertion (*e.g. of a clause*)
660 **Aufnahmeantrag,** *m.*, application for admission/membership
661 **Aufnahmebewerber,** *m.*, state/party applying for admission/membership
662 **Aufnahmegesuch,** *n.*, application for admission/membership
663 **Aufnahmestaat,** *m.* (NATOSF), receiving state (*Empfangsstaat)
664 **Aufnahmevoraussetzung,** *f.*, condition of admission/membership/acceptance/candidacy
665 **aufnehmen¹,** to establish (*e.g. relations*)
666 **aufnehmen²,** to admit/accept (*e.g. new members*)
667 **aufnehmen³,** to insert (*e.g. a clause*)
668 **aufrechterhalten,** to maintain
669 **den Weltfrieden aufrechterhalten,** to maintain world peace
670 **Aufrechterhaltung,** *f.*, maintenance
671 **Aufrechterhaltung der diplomatischen Beziehungen,** maintenance of diplomatic relations
672 **Aufrechterhaltung des Friedens/der internationalen Sicherheit,** maintenance of peace/international security
673 **aufreizen,** to incite (*Rassendiskriminierung *in* CERD 1 *in* Annex 12)
674 **Aufreizen,** *n.*, incitement (*Rassendiskriminierung *in* CERD 1 *in* Annex 12)
675 **Aufständischer,** *adj.n.*, rebel
676 **aufsuchen,** to explore

677 **Aufsuchung,** *f.*, exploration
678 **Auftrag,** *m.*, mission
679 **Vertreter mit vorübergehendem amtlichem Auftrag** (PPELDO 14), representatives on temporary official missions
680 **nach Beendigung ihres Auftrags,** after/on the termination of their mission
681 **heiliger Auftrag** (CUN 73), sacred mission
682 **einen Auftrag ausführen,** to carry out/execute/fulfil a mission (*Sachverständiger, *Mission)
683 **Augenschein,** *m.*, inspection of locality
684 **die Vorladung von Zeugen und Sachverständigen sowie die Vornahme des Augenscheins** (FC An), the summoning and hearing of witnesses and experts and to visit the localities in question
685 **die Vornahme des Augenscheins ermöglichen** (ECPSD 14), to allow (it) to visit the localities in question
686 **Augenscheinseinnahme,** *f.*, visit/inspection of locality
687 **Alle Augenscheinseinnahmen müssen in Gegenwart der Agenten und Rechtsbeistände der Parteien erfolgen** (HgI 21), Every examination of a locality must be made in the presence of the counsel of the parties
688 **Augenscheinsvornahme,** *f.*, visit/inspection of locality (*Augenschein)
689 **ausbeuten,** to exploit
690 **Ausbeutung,** *f.*, exploitation
691 **Ausbeutung der natürlichen Schätze/Naturschätze** (GCHS 26/GCC 1), exploitation of the natural resources
692 **ausbürgern,** to deprive of nationality/citizenship
693 **Ausbürgerung,** *f.*, deprivation of nationality/citizenship
694 **ausdehnen,** to extend
695 **Dieses Abkommen kann in der Folge auf ... ausgedehnt werden** (EXWC 1), The present agreement may in due course be extended to ...

696 **Ausdehnung,** *f.*, extension
697 **Ausdehnung von Vereinbarungen und Abmachungen,** extension of agreements and arrangements
698 **ausdrücklich,** *adj.*, express, explicit
699 **ausdrücklich oder stillschweigend,** express or implied
700 **ausdrückliche Anerkennung,** express recognition
701 **Auseinandersetzung,** *f.*, dispute, conflict, hostilities
702 **bewaffnete Auseinandersetzungen zwischen den Staaten,** armed conflicts between states
703 **kriegerische Auseinandersetzungen,** belligerent/armed conflicts
704 **militärische Auseinandersetzungen,** military/armed conflicts
705 **nichtkriegerische Auseinandersetzungen,** non-belligerent conflicts/non-war conflicts
       (*Konflikt, *Streit, *Streitigkeit)
706 **Ausfertigung,** *f.*, copy
707 **in einer einzelnen Ausfertigung,** in a single copy
       (*Abschrift)
708 **Ausfuhrbeschränkung,** *f.*, export restriction, restriction on export/exportation
709 **mengenmäßige Ausfuhrbeschränkung,** quantitative export restriction
710 **Ausfuhrbewilligung,** *f.*, export licence
711 **ausführen¹,** to export
712 **ausführen²,** to execute, to perform, to carry out
713 **ausführend¹,** *adj.*, exporting
714 **ausführender Mitgliedstaat,** exporting member state
715 **ausführend²,** *adj.*, executing, executive, performing
716 **ausführendes Organ,** executing/executive organ
       (*Exekutiv- *compounds*)
717 **Ausfuhrverbot,** *n.*, export prohibition
718 **Ausfuhrzoll,** *m.*, export duty
719 **Ausgangskontingent,** *n.* (EFTA), basic quota
720 **Ausgangsmaterial,** *n.* (IAEA), source material(s)

721 **der buchmäßige Nachweis über das Ausgangsmaterial** (IAEA XII), the accountability for source materials
722 **Ausgangsstoff,** *m.* (EAEC), source material(s)
723 **Ausgangszoll,** *m.* (EFTA), basic duty
724 **Ausgangszollamt,** *n.* (ICCB), customs office of departure
725 **Ausgebürgerter,** *adj.n.*, denaturalized person, person deprived of his nationality/citizenship
726 **Ausgelieferter,** *adj.n.*, extradited person, person who has been extradited
       (*ausliefern, *Auslieferung)
727 **Ausgleich,** *m.*, clearing, settlement, compensation
       (*Angelegenheit)
728 **Ausgleichsabgabe,** *f.*, countervailing charge
729 **Ausgleichsabgabe bei der Einfuhr** (EEC 46), countervailing charge on entry
730 **aushandeln,** to negotiate
731 **den Text eines Vertrags aushandeln,** to negotiate the text of a treaty
732 **Aushandlung,** *f.*, negotiating, negotiation
733 **Ausländer,** *m.*, alien, non-resident
734 **feindlicher Ausländer,** enemy alien
735 **Ausländermeldepflicht,** *f.*, duty/obligation of aliens to register
       (*Meldepflicht)
736 **Ausländerrecht,** *n.*, legislation/law(s) relating to aliens
       (*Fremdenrecht)
737 **Ausländerregistrierung,** *f.*, aliens' registration, registration of aliens
       (*Meldepflicht)
738 **Ausländerstatut¹,** *n.* = *Ausländerrecht, *n.*
739 **Ausländerstatut²,** *n.*, status of aliens
740 **ausländisch,** *adj.*, alien, foreign
741 **ausländische Schiedssprüche,** foreign awards/judgments
742 **ausländische Schiffe,** foreign vessels
743 **ausländische Seeleute,** alien seafarers (ARS)
744 **ausländische Urteile,** foreign awards/judgments

745 **Auslandsvertreter,** *m.*, diplomatic agent/envoy/representative

746 **auslegen,** to interpret, to construe

747 **Dieser Artikel ist nicht so auszulegen, als verpflichte er einen Vertragsstaat ...,** No provision of this article shall be construed to require any contracting state (to) ...

748 **Dieses Übereinkommen ist nicht so auszulegen, als schließe es ... aus** (VCDR 3), Nothing in the present convention shall be construed as preventing ...

749 **Dieses Übereinkommen und seine Anlage sind nicht so auszulegen, als verhinderten sie ...** (CFIMT V), Nothing in the present convention or its Annex shall be interpreted as preventing ... (*völkerrechtskonform)

750 **Auslegung,** *f.*, interpretation, construction

751 **die Auslegung des konstituierenden Aktes einer öffentlichen internationalen Organisation,** the construction of the constituent instrument of a public international organization

752 **Jede Streitigkeit zwischen Vertragsparteien über die Auslegung oder Anwendung dieses Übereinkommens wird ... einem Schiedsverfahren unterworfen** (FC 13), Any dispute which may arise between contracting parties concerning the interpretation or application of the present convention ... shall be submitted to arbitration

753 **authentische Auslegung,** authentic interpretation/construction

754 **einschränkende Auslegung,** restrictive interpretation

755 **enge Auslegung,** restrictive interpretation

756 **extensive Auslegung,** extensive interpretation (*Bedeutung^2)

757 **Auslegungsbestimmungen,** *f.pl.*, interpretations (ICCC), provisions relating to interpretation

758 **Auslegungsgrundsatz,** *m.*, principle of interpretation

759 **Oberster Auslegungsgrundsatz ist, daß ein Vertrag nach Treu und Glauben auszulegen ist,** The supreme principle of interpretation is that a treaty shall be interpreted/construed in good faith

760 **Auslegungsmittel,** *n.*, means of interpretation

761 **ergänzende Auslegungsmittel,** supplementary means of interpretation

762 **Ergänzende Auslegungsmittel, insbesondere die vorbereitenden Arbeiten, können herangezogen werden** (VCLOT 32), Recourse may be had to supplementary means of interpretation, including the preparatory work of the treaty

763 **Auslegungsprotokoll,** *n.*, protocol of interpretation

764 **Auslegungsregel,** *f.*, rule of interpretation

765 **die im Völkerrecht allgemein angewandten Auslegungsregeln** (CRPG An), the generally accepted rules of international law governing the interpretation of treaties

766 **souveränitätsfreundliche Auslegungsregeln,** rules of interpretation not prejudicial to/non-restrictive upon (the party's/parties') sovereignty

767 **ausliefern,** to extradite, to surrender

768 **die Personen ausliefern, die von den Justizbehörden des ersuchenden Staates wegen einer strafbaren Handlung ... verfolgt werden** (EExt 1), to surrender all persons against whom the competent authorities of the requesting state are proceeding for an offence

769 **einen Verbrecher ausliefern** (ExFC IV), to deliver up a criminal

770 **Auslieferung,** *f.*, extradition, surrender

771 **die Auslieferung flüchtiger Verbrecher** (ExFC), the extradition of fugitive criminals

772 **die Auslieferung eines Verfolgten** (EExt 8), the extradition of the person claimed

773 **eine Liste der strafbaren Handlungen, derentwegen die Aus-**

lieferung zulässig/ausgeschlossen ist (EExt 2), a list of offences for which extradition is allowed/excluded

774 **gegenseitige Auslieferung,** mutual extradition

775 **Auslieferung ablehnen,** to refuse extradition

776   **das Recht, die Auslieferung seiner Staatsangehörigen abzulehnen** (EExt 6), the right to refuse extradition of its nationals

777 **Auslieferung ausschließen,** to refuse extradition (EExt 2)

778 **Auslieferung begehren,** to request extradition (EExt 3)

779 **Auslieferung begründen,** to give reasons for the extradition

780 **Auslieferung bewilligen,** to grant extradition (EExt 2)

781 **Auslieferung gewähren,** to allow extradition (ExFC III)

782 **Auslieferung zulassen,** to allow extradition (EExt 2)

783   **Länder, die grundsätzlich die Auslieferung ihrer eigenen Staatsangehörigen nicht zulassen** (ICCC 8), countries where the principle of the extradition of nationals is not recognized (*Übergabe; *also* ExFC *Article* III *in Annex* 10)

784 **Auslieferungsabkommen,** *n.*, extradition agreement

785 **Auslieferungsersuchen,** *n.*, request for extradition (EExt/ExFC)

786 **die strafbare Handlung, die dem Auslieferungsersuchen zugrunde liegt** (EExt 7), the offence for which extradition is requested

787 **ein Auslieferungsersuchen stellen,** to make a request for extradition

788 **auslieferungsfähig,** *adj.*, extraditable

789 **auslieferungsfähige Straftaten** (ExFC VI), extradition crimes

790 **auslieferungsfähige strafbare Handlungen** (EExt 2), extraditable offences

791 **Auslieferungshaft,** *f.* (EExt 16), provisional arrest

792 **Auslieferungsübereinkommen,** *n.*, convention on extradition

793 **Auslieferungsverfahren,** *n.* (PHR 5), extradition action

794 **Auslieferungsverpflichtung,** *f.*, obligation to extradite

795 **Auslieferungsvertrag,** *m.*, extradition treaty, treaty of extradition

796 **Auslieferungszweck,** *m.*, purpose of extradition

797   **... und ... gelten für Auslieferungszwecke nicht als politische Straftaten** (PCG 7), ... and ... shall not be considered as political crimes for the purposes of extradition

798 **ausplündern,** to plunder, to despoil

799 **Ausplünderung,** *f.*, plundering, despoliation

800 **Ausreise,** *f.*, exit, departure

801 **endgültige Ausreise,** final departure

802 **Ausreisesichtvermerk,** *m.*, exit visa

803 **Ausreisevisum,** *n.*, exit visa

804 **Aussage,** *f.*, statement, evidence

805 **aussagen,** to give evidence, to make a statement

806   **als Zeuge/Sachverständiger aussagen,** to give evidence as a witness/expert

807 **ausscheiden,** to retire, to withdraw

808 **Ausscheidende Mitglieder können nicht unmittelbar wiedergewählt werden** (CUN 23), A retiring member shall not be eligible for immediate re-election

809 **Jedes Mitglied des Europarates kann aus diesem ausscheiden, indem es dem Generalsekretär gegenüber eine förmliche Erklärung hierüber abgibt** (CE 7), Any member of the Council of Europe may withdraw by formally notifying the Secretary-General of its intention to do so

810 **Ein Vertragsteil scheidet aus dieser Konvention, der aus dem Europarat ausscheidet,** Any contracting party which ceases to be a member of the Council of Europe shall cease to be a party to this convention

811 **Ausscheidung,** *f.*, withdrawal (*ausscheiden)

812 **Ausschiffung,** *f.*, disembarkation

813 **Ausschiffungshafen,** *m.* (CFIMT), port of disembarkation

814 **Ausschiffungskarte,** *f.* (CFIMT), disembarkation card
815 **Ausschlag** *m.* **geben,** to decide, to give the deciding vote
816 **bei Stimmengleichheit gibt die Stimme des ältesten Richters den Ausschlag,** in the event of an equality of votes the eldest judge has a casting vote
817 **ausschließen,** to expel, to exclude, to suspend, to deprive (*Kontrollrecht)
818 **Ausschluß,** *m.*, expulsion, exclusion, suspension
819 **Ausschluß eines Mitglieds,** expulsion of a member
820 **Ausschluß eines Staates,** exclusion/ expulsion of a state
821 **Der Ausschluß eines oder mehrerer Staaten von der Konvention engt nicht nur ihren Anwendungsbereich ein, sondern beeinträchtigt die Autorität der moralischen und humanitären Prinzipien, die ihre Basis darstellen,** The exclusion of one or more states from the convention not only restricts its area of application, but detracts from the moral and humanitarian principles on which it is based
822 **vorübergehender oder endgültiger Ausschluß** (ICPCP 13), suspension or exclusion
823 **Ausschuß,** *m.*, committee
824 **Ausschuß von Regierungsvertretern** (UCC), intergovernmental committee
825 **ad-hoc Ausschuß,** ad-hoc committee
826 **beratender Ausschuß,** consultative/advisory committee
827 **engerer Ausschuß,** select/restricted committee
828 **gemeinsamer Ausschuß,** joint committee
829 **gemischter Ausschuß,** mixed committee
830 **geschäftsführender Ausschuß,** executive committee, managing/management committee
831 **intersessionaler Ausschuß,** intersessional committee

832 **nachgeordneter Ausschuß,** subordinate committee
833 **regionaler Ausschuß,** regional committee
834 **ständiger Ausschuß,** standing/permanent committee
835 **technischer Ausschuß,** technical committee
836 **zuständiger Ausschuß,** competent/ appropriate committee
837 **zwischenstaatlicher Ausschuß,** intergovernmental committee
838 **außergerichtlich,** *adj.*, extrajudicial
839 **Außerkraftsetzung,** *f.*, repeal, suspension
840 **Außerkraftsetzung eines Gesetzes,** repeal of a law
841 **Eine solche Außerkraftsetzung kann auf einen weiteren Zeitraum von höchstens 240 Tagen ausgedehnt werden** (IMF XVI), Such suspension may be extended for an additional period of not more than 240 days
842 **Außerkraftsetzung von Rechtsvorschriften** (TORG 2), deprivation of effect of legislation
843 **zeitweilige Außerkraftsetzung,** temporary suspension (*Kraft, *Aufhebung)
844 **außerordentlich,** *adj.*, extraordinary, special (session, etc.)
845 **aussetzen,** to suspend, to cease to apply
846 **die Anwendung sämtlicher oder eines Teils der beigefügten Regeln aussetzen** (CSLS VI), to suspend the operation of the whole or any part of the regulations annexed hereto
847 **Aussetzung,** *f.*, suspension
848 **Aussetzung im Kriegsfall** (CSLS VI), suspension in case of war
849 **Aussprache,** *f.*, discussion, debate
850 **eine zur Aussprache stehende Frage,** a question under discussion/consideration
851 **die Vertagung der Aussprache beantragen,** to move the adjournment of the discussion
852 **eine Aussprache zwischen Regie-**

rungen (ECE VII), a discussion among governments

853 **aussprechen,** to deliver, to pronounce, to make (judgment, award, etc.)

854 **Ausspruch,** *m.*, decision, (delivery of) judgment

855 **ausstellen,** to issue

856 **ausstellende Behörde,** issuing authority

857 **Ausstellung,** *f.*, issue, issuing

858 **Ausstellungsland,** *n.*, country of issue

859 **Austausch,** *m.*, exchange

860 **Austausch der Urkunden,** exchange of instruments/documents

861 **der freie Austausch von Gedanken und Erkenntnissen** (UNESCO), the free exchange of ideas and knowledge

862 **austauschen,** to exchange

863 **Die Vertragsschließenden tauschen über den Generalsekretär des Europarates technische Informationen über ... aus** (EXWC 2), The contracting parties shall, through the Secretary-General of the Council of Europe, exchange technical information on ...

864 **austreten,** to withdraw

865 **Austritt,** *m.*, withdrawal

866 **Austritt aus einer Organisation,** withdrawal from an organization

867 **Austritt aus einem Vertrag,** withdrawal from a treaty

868 **Austrittsanzeige,** *f.*, notice of withdrawal

869 **Austrittserklärung,** *f.*, notification of withdrawal (*see note to* *Erklärung*)

870 **Austrittsrecht,** *n.*, right to withdraw/of withdrawal

871 **Austrittsrecht der Mitglieder,** right of members to withdraw

872 **Austrittsschreiben,** *n.*, notice/notice in writing/written notice of withdrawal

873 **ausüben,** to exercise, to perform

874 **Funktionen ausüben,** to exercise functions

875 **Hoheitsgewalt ausüben,** to exercise sovereignty

876 **Privilegien ausüben,** to exercise privileges

877 **Rechte ausüben,** to exercise rights

878 **Ausübung,** *f.*, exercise, performance

879 **Ausübung der Funktionen,** exercise/performance of functions

880 **Die Generalversammlung kann die zur Ausübung ihrer Funktionen für nötig erachteten Hilfsorgane schaffen,** The General Assembly may establish such subsidiary organs as it deems necessary for the performance of its functions

881 **wirksame Ausübung von Rechten,** effective exercise of rights (*Erfüllung, *Wahrnehmung)

882 **Ausweis,** *m.*, identity card, (identity) document, (identity) paper, *laissez-passer*

883 **Geltungsdauer des Ausweises** (TDRef), validity of the document

884 **Erneuerung/Verlängerung der Geltungsdauer des Ausweises,** renewal/extension of the validity of the (identity) document

885 **gelöschte/ungelöschte Ausweise** (ICCA), discharged/undischarged papers

886 **militärische Ausweise,** military identity papers/documents

887 **ausweisen**[1], to expel

888 **Niemand darf aus dem Hoheitsgebiet des Staates, dessen Staatsangehöriger er ist, durch eine Einzel- oder eine Kollektivmaßnahme ausgewiesen werden** (PHR Prot 4), No one shall be expelled, by means either of an individual or of a collective measure, from the territory of the state of which he is a national

889 **ausweisen**[2], to identify

890 **sich ausweisen,** to show/present one's papers

891 **Ausweiskarte,** *f.*, identity card

892 **Ausweisung,** *f.*, expulsion

893 **Ausweisungsverfahren,** *n.*, expulsion procedure

894 **Ausweisungsverfügung,** *f.*, expulsion order, order to leave the country

895 **Ausweisungsverfügung erlassen,** to issue an expulsion order
896 **authentisch,** *adj.*, authentic
897 **gleichermaßen authentisch,** equally authentic
898 **authentische Interpretation/Auslegung,** authentic interpretation/construction

899 **authentischer Vertragstext,** authentic text of the treaty
900 **als authentisch festlegen** (VCLOT 33), to authenticate (*maßgebend)
901 **autonom,** *adj.*, autonomous
902 **Autonomie,** *f.*, autonomy

B

1 **Bakterienkrieg,** *m.*, bacterial/bacteriological warfare
2 **Bannware,** *f.*, contraband, contraband good(s)
3 **die Bestimmung der Bannware,** destination of (the) contraband
4 **absolute Bannware,** absolute contraband
5 **relative Bannware,** relative contraband
6 **Bannwarenladung,** *f.*, contraband cargo
7 **Bannwarenrecht,** *n.*, law of contraband
8 **Basislinie,** *f.* (= Grundlinie, *f.*), baseline
9 **jede von einer Vertragspartei gezogene Basislinie und jede eine Bucht abschließende Linie** (FC 6), any straight baseline or bay-closing line which a contracting party may draw
10 **Trockenfallende Erhebungen dürfen nicht Ausgangs- oder Endpunkt von Basislinien sein** (GCTS 4), Baselines may not be drawn to and from low-tide elevations
11 **die normale Basislinie für die Messung der Breite des Küstenmeeres** (GCTS 3), the normal baseline for measuring the breadth of the territorial sea
12 **die Festlegung der Basislinie** (GCTS 4/5), the drawing/establishing of the baseline
13 **gerade Basislinien,** straight baselines
14 **das System/Verfahren der geraden Basislinien** (GCTS), the system/method of straight baselines (*Anschlußzone, *Küstenmeer, innere *Gewässer, *zerklüftet, Recht zu *fischen)
15 **Beamter,** *adj.n.*, official (*e.g.* UN, EEC), officer (*e.g.* ICJ)
16 **beantragen,** to apply for, to request, to submit a request for (*Antrag stellen)
17 **beaufsichtigen,** to supervise
18 **Beaufsichtigung,** *f.*, supervision

19 **ein internationales Treuhandsystem für die Verwaltung und Beaufsichtigung der Hoheitsgebiete, die ...** (CUN 75), an international trusteeship system for the administration and supervision of such territories as ...
20 **beauftragen,** to charge, to delegate
21 **beauftragt,** *adj.*, charged, delegated
22 **die Person, die beauftragt ist, in dieser Eigenschaft tätig zu sein** (VCDR 1), the person charged with the duty of acting in that capacity
23 **Beauftragter,** *adj.n.*, representative, delegate (*Delegierter)
24 **Bedeutung**[1]**,** *f.*, importance, significance
25 **die ständig wachsende Bedeutung der Verträge als Quelle des Völkerrechts** (VCLOT Pr), the ever-increasing importance of treaties as a source of international law
26 **Bedeutung**[2]**,** *f.*, meaning
27 **Diejenige Bedeutung, die die Texte am besten miteinander in Einklang bringt, wird zugrunde gelegt** (VCLOT 33), The meaning which best reconciles the texts shall be adopted
28 **die Bedeutung bestimmen, wenn die Auslegung (a) die Bedeutung mehrdeutig oder dunkel läßt oder (b) zu einem offensichtlich sinnwidrigen oder unvernünftigen Ergebnis führt** (VCLOT 32), to determine the meaning when the interpretation (a) leaves the meaning ambiguous or obscure, (b) leads to a result which is manifestly absurd or unreasonable (*Auslegung)
29 **Bediensteter,** *adj.n.*, employee, officer, staff member
30 **Bedienstete des Entsendestaates** (VCDR 1), employees of the sending state
31 **Bedienstete der Organisation,** staff/officers of the organization

32   **internationale Bedienstete,** international staff, international officers
33   **Bedingung,** *f.,* condition, term
34   **Verzicht auf Bedingungen,** waiver of conditions
35   **unter der Bedingung, daß ...,** on/subject to the condition that ...
36   **einheitliche Bedingungen,** uniform conditions
37   **Bedingungen annehmen,** to accept conditions
38   **Bedingungen auferlegen,** to impose conditions (*Vorbehalt)
39   **bedingungslos,** *adj.,* unconditional
40   **bedingungslose Kapitulation,** unconditional capitulation/surrender (*Gegenseitigkeit)
41   **bedrohen,** to threaten
42   **Bedrohung,** *f.,* threat
43   **Bedrohung des Friedens,** threat to (the) peace
44   **bedürfen** (+ *gen.*), to require
45   **Der Vertrag bedarf der Ratifikation/Annahme (usw.),** The treaty requires/is subject to ratification/acceptance (etc.)
46   **... bedarf der Zustimmung durch die Mehrheit der Vertragsstaaten** (SF 106), ... must be approved by the majority of all the contracting states (*verfassungsmäßiges Verfahren)
47   **Bedürfnis,** *f.,* necessity, requirement
48   **militärische Bedürfnisse** (CUN 47), military requirements
49   **beeinträchtigen,** to prejudice, to impair, to infringe, to (adversely) affect
50   **Dieser Artikel beeinträchtigt in keiner Weise die Anwendung der Artikel ... und ...,** This article in no way prejudices the application of articles ... and ... (*berühren²)
51   **Beeinträchtigung,** *f.,* prejudice, (adverse) effect, impairment
52   **ohne Beeinträchtigung (des),** without prejudice (to)
53   **beenden,** to terminate
54   **beendigen,** to terminate
55   **Beendigung,** *f.,* termination, expiry

56   **Dieses Protokoll bleibt bis zur Beendigung dieses Übereinkommens in Kraft** (PPELDO 36), This protocol shall remain in force until the expiry of the convention
57   **Beendigung der dienstlichen Tätigkeit** (VCDR 25), termination of functions
58   **Beendigung der Feindseligkeiten,** termination of hostilities
59   **Beendigung des Kriegszustandes,** termination of the state of war
60   **befassen,** to charge, to call upon, to refer to, to bring before
61   **Eine Partei kann die zuständigen Organe der UN damit befassen, ... zu machen,** Any party may call upon the competent organs of the UN to ...
62   **Ist eine Vergleichskommission mit der Streitigkeit befaßt, ...** (ECPSD 31), If the dispute is brought before a conciliation committee ...
63   **sich mit einem Fall/einer Sache befassen,** to deal with a case/matter
64   **Der Ausschuß befaßt sich mit einer an ihn verwiesenen Sache erst dann, wenn er sich Gewißheit verschafft hat, daß alle innerstaatlichen Rechtsbehelfe eingelegt und erschöpft worden sind** (CERD 11), The committee shall deal with a matter referred to it only after it has ascertained that all available domestic remedies have been invoked and exhausted (in the case)
65   **befindlich,** *adj.,* situated
66   **darüber befindlich,** superjacent (*Wasser, *Gewässer, *Luftraum)
67   **befreien¹ (von),** to liberate, to release (from)
68   **befreien² (von),** to exempt (from) (*Befreiung² von)
69   **Befreiung¹,** *f.,* liberation
70   **Befreiung²,** *f.,* exemption, immunity
71   **Befreiungen und Erleichterungen,** immunities and facilities
72   **Befreiungen und Vorrechte,** immunities and privileges
73   **die Befreiungen und Vorrechte, die diplomatischen Vertretern und**

ihrem amtlichen Personal vergleichbaren Ranges gewährt werden (WEUS 11), immunities and privileges accorded to diplomatic representatives and their official staff of comparable rank

74   Befreiung hinsichtlich ..., exemption/immunity in respect of ...
75   Befreiung von, exemption/immunity from
     Befreiung von:
76   Abgaben und Steuern, dues and taxes
77   Aufenthaltsgenehmigung (VCCR 46), residence permit(s)
78   Ausländerregistrierung (PrivExCE 9), aliens' registration
79   Besteuerung (VCCR 49), taxation
80   Einwanderungsbeschränkungen (PrivExCE 9), immigration restrictions
81   Festnahme oder Haft (WEUS 12), personal arrest or detention
82   gerichtlicher Verfolgung, prosecution, judicial process
83   Gerichtsbarkeit, legal/judicial process
84   jeder staatlichen Gerichtsbarkeit (CCC An), legal process of any kind
85   Gerichtsbarkeit auf ihre mündlichen und schriftlichen Äußerungen und Handlungen, die sie in Ausübung ihres Amtes vornehmen (PrivExCE 10), legal process in respect of words spoken or written and all acts done by them in discharging their duties
86   Haft und gerichtlicher Verfolgung (WEUS 18), detention and prosecution
87   persönlichen Dienstleistungen und Auflagen (VCCR 52), personal services and contributions
88   Sozialversicherung (VCCR 48), social security (provisions)
89   Zöllen und Zollkontrollen (VCCR 50), customs duties and inspection
90   die Befreiung aufheben, to waive immunity/exemption
91   die Befreiungen eines Abgeordne-

ten aufheben (PrivExCE 15), to waive the immunity of a representative
92   Befreiungen gewähren, to grant/to accord immunities/exemptions
93   auf Befreiungen verzichten, to waive immunities/exemptions
     (For further immunities, see under *Immunität von; see also *Beschlagnahme, *Rechtsfähigkeit, *Vorrecht, *Zwang, and Annex 7.)
94   Befreiungsarmee, f., liberation army, army of liberation
95   Befreiungsfront, f., liberation front
96   Befreiungskrieg, m., war of liberation
97   befugen, to authorize, to empower
98   Befugnis, f., authority, power
99   die auf dieser Charta beruhende Befugnis (CUN 51), the authority under the present charter
100 die Befugnis des Gerichtshofs, ex aequo et bono zu entscheiden (SICJ 38), the power of the court to decide a case ex aequo et bono
101 Die Befugnis hierzu ergibt sich aus den Artikeln ..., Authority to do this/to take such action derives from Articles ...
102 Befugnis zur Gesetzgebung, power to legislate, law-making power
103 Ausübung der Befugnisse, exercise of powers
104 Delegierung der Befugnisse, delegation of powers
105 Übertragung der Befugnisse, transfer/delegation of powers
106 aufgeführte Befugnisse, powers listed/specified/set forth
107 die in diesem Artikel aufgeführten Befugnisse (CUN 11), the powers set forth in this article
108 ausschließliche Befugnis, exclusive power
109 besondere Befugnis, special power
110 die (dem Sicherheitsrat) hierfür eingeräumten besonderen Befugnisse (CUN 24), the specific powers granted (to the Security Council) for the discharge of these duties

111 eingeräumte Befugnisse, powers granted/accorded/conferred

112 **Fälle, in denen ein Einschreiten auf einer vertraglich eingeräumten Befugnis beruht (GCHS 22),** where acts of interference derive from powers conferred by treaty

113 **eingeschränkte Befugnisse,** curtailed / reduced / restricted / limited powers

114 **implizierte Befugnisse** (= stillschweigend zuerkannte Befugnisse), implied powers

115 **Kraft implizierter Befugnisse versucht man, Lücken im Vertrag auszufüllen, falls der Vertragszweck sonst nicht zu erreichen ist,** In cases where the purpose of a treaty cannot otherwise be achieved, implied powers are used to eliminate shortcomings in the treaty

116 **notarielle Befugnisse,** powers notary

117 **notarielle, standesamtliche und ähnliche Befugnisse ausüben** · (VCCR 5), to act as notary and civil registrar
stillschweigend zuerkannte Befugnisse = implizierte *Befugnisse

118 **überschrittene Befugnisse,** abused powers

119 **vertraglich vereinbarte Befugnisse,** powers agreed on by treaty, powers conferred/as agreed by treaty (*Vertreter[2], *Obliegenheit, *Beisitzer)

120 **befugt,** *adj.*, authorized, empowered

121 **der Gerichtshof ist befugt ...,** the court shall have the power ...

122 **gehörig befugt,** duly authorized

123 **die hierzu gehörig befugten (Vertreter),** the (delegates), being duly authorized thereto/to that effect (*Unterschrift, *berechtigt)

124 **begehen,** to commit, to perpetrate

125 **ein völkerrechtliches Unrecht begehen,** to commit an international wrong

126 **begehren,** to request

127 **Begehren,** *n.*, request

128 **auf Begehren einer Partei,** at/on the request of a party/one of the parties

129 **Dem ersuchenden Staat ist mitzuteilen, inwieweit seinem Begehren Folge gegeben worden ist (EExt 6),** The requesting party shall be informed of the result of its request (*Ersuchen)

130 **Begehung,** *f.*, commission, committing, perpetration

131 **eine Darstellung der Handlungen, ... (und) Zeit und Ort ihrer Begehung (EExt 12),** a statement of the offences (together with) the time and place of their commission

132 **direkte Anreizung zur Begehung von ... (PCG 3),** direct incitement to commit ...

133 **Verschwörung zur Begehung von ... (PCG 3),** conspiracy to commit ...

134 **Begehungsland,** *n.*, country in which the crime/offence has been committed/perpetrated

135 **Begehungsort,** *m.* (EExt), place of commission (*Begehung)

136 **beglaubigen,** to accredit, to certify, to attest, to authenticate

137 **Der Wortlaut dieser Übereinkünfte in englischer und französischer Sprache ist dieser Schlußakte beigefügt und wird hiermit beglaubigt (SF 143),** The texts of these instruments in the English and French languages are annexed hereto and are hereby authenticated

138 **beglaubigt,** *adj.*, accredited, certified, attested, authenticated

139 **gehörig beglaubigt,** duly certified

140 **beim Staatsoberhaupt beglaubigt,** accredited to the head of state

141 **beglaubigte Abschrift,** certified copy

142 **beglaubigter Missionschef,** accredited head of mission

143 **beglaubigter Wortlaut,** authenticated text, certified text

144 **Beglaubigung,** *f.*, accreditation, attestation, certification, notarial authentication (CLPD 1)

145 **Beglaubigungsschreiben,** *n.*, credentials, letter(s) of credence, *lettre(s) de créance*

146 **Änderungen im Beglaubigungs-**

schreiben, alterations in the credentials

147 Überreichung des Beglaubigungsschreibens, presentation of credentials

148   die Reihenfolge der Überreichung der Beglaubigungsschreiben (VCDR 13), the order of the presentation of credentials

149   das Beglaubigungsschreiben überreichen, to present/deliver/hand over (one's) credentials

150   eine formgerechte Abschrift seines Beglaubigungsschreibens überreichen (VCDR 13), to present a true copy of his credentials

151 begnadigen, to pardon, to reprieve, to grant a pardon to

152 Begnadigung, *f.*, pardon, reprieve

153 Begriffsbestimmung, *f.*, definition, definition/use of terms

154   Begriffsbestimmungen und allgemeine Bestimmungen (CFIMT), definitions and general provisions (*See* VCLOT 2 *in Annex* 14.)

155 begründen, to justify, to give reasons for

156   Die Entscheidung ist zu begründen, The judgment shall state the reasons on which it is based

157   die Vereinbarungen, die die Zuständigkeit des Gerichts begründen, the agreements establishing the competence of the court

158   Der Gerichtshof muß sich vergewissern, daß die Anträge tatsächlich und rechtlich begründet sind (SICJ 53), The court must satisfy itself that the claims are well founded in fact and law

159   Diese Verordnung begründet keinen Anspruch auf ..., This regulation shall create no entitlement to ... (*Einspruch begründen)

160 Begründung, *f.*, justification, reason(s)

161   die Begründung des Urteils, the reasons for the award/judgment, the reasons on which the award/judgment is based (*begründen)

162 begutachten, to give an opinion/expert opinion on (*Gutachten)

163 Begutachtung, *f.*, (expert) opinion, advisory opinion (*Gutachten)

164 Behandlung, *f.*, treatment

165   diskriminierende Behandlung, discriminating/discriminatory treatment (*see* *diskriminierend)

166   entwürdigende Behandlung (GC I), degrading treatment

167   erniedrigende Behandlung (GC I), humiliating treatment

168   grausame Behandlung (GC I), cruel treatment

169   menschliche Behandlung (GC I), humane treatment

170   steuerliche Behandlung, tax treatment, fiscal treatment

171   unmenschliche Behandlung (GC I), inhuman treatment

172   zollrechtliche Behandlung, customs treatment

173 behauptet, *adj.*, alleged

174   behaupteter Verstoß, alleged infringement/violation

175 Behörde, *f.*, authority

176   amtliche Behörde, official authority

177   ausstellende Behörde, issuing authority

178   öffentliche Behörde, public authority

179   zuständige Behörde, competent/responsible authority (*Dienststelle)

180 beifügen, to append, to annex

181 beigefügt, *adj.*, appended, annexed

182   ... und ist der Schlußakte beigefügt, ... and is (hereby) annexed to the final act (*beglaubigter Wortlaut, *Vereinbarungsentwurf)

183 beigetreten, *adj.*, acceding, which have acceded

184   die Regierungen später beigetretener Staaten, the governments of states subsequently acceding

185   die so beigetretene Macht (TRW III), the power thus adhering (*beitretend)

186 Beihilfe, *f.*, aid, assistance

187   staatliche Beihilfe (EFTA), government aid

beilegbar 30

188 **beilegbar,** *adj.*, capable of settlement
189 **schiedsgerichtlich beilegbar,** arbitrable
190 **beilegen,** to settle, to let (a matter) drop
191 **einen Streit beilegen,** to settle a dispute
192 **auf gütlichem Wege beilegen,** to settle amicably
193 **durch unmittelbare Verhandlungen beilegen,** to settle by (means of) direct negotiations (*Streit, *Streit- *compounds*)
194 **Beilegung,** *f.*, settlement
195 **die Beilegung erfolgt durch ...,** the settlement shall be achieved by ...
196 **Die Beilegung der Streitigkeiten erfolgte durch die guten Dienste unparteiischer Stellen,** The settlement of the dispute(s) was achieved by the good offices of impartial bodies
197 **einvernehmliche Beilegung,** settlement by mutual consent, consensual settlement
198 **friedliche Beilegung,** pacific/peaceful settlement
199 **gerichtliche Beilegung,** judicial settlement
200 **gütliche Beilegung,** amicable settlement
201 **schiedsgerichtliche Beilegung,** arbitral settlement, settlement by arbitration, arbitration
202 **beiliegend,** *adj.*, annexed, appended
203 **gemäß beiliegendem Statut,** in accordance with the annexed statute (*beigefügt)
204 **Beirat,** *m.*, advisory council
205 **wissenschaftlicher Beirat,** scientific advisory council
206 **Beisitzer,** *m.*, assessor
207 **Erachten die Parteien die Ernennung von Beisitzern für nötig, so bestimmt das Untersuchungsabkommen die Art ihrer Bestellung und den Umfang ihrer Befugnisse** (HgI 10), If the parties consider it necessary to appoint assessors, the Convention of Inquiry shall determine the mode of their selection and the extent of their powers
208 **Beistand[1],** *m.*, assistance
209 **gegenseitiger Beistand** (EEC 108), mutual assistance
210 **Beistand[2],** *m.*, counsel
211 **der Bevollmächtigte oder Beistand einer Partei** (SICJ 17), the agent or counsel of a party
212 **Beistandspakt,** *m.* (= Beistandsvertrag, *m.*), treaty of (mutual) assistance (*see note to* *Vertrag *in Annex* 1)
213 **Beitrag,** *m.*, contribution
214 **alle nach Absatz (a) entrichteten Beiträge** (EONR VII), all contributions made in accordance with the provisions of sub-paragraph (a)
215 **freiwillige Beiträge,** voluntary contributions
216 **geschuldete Beiträge,** contributions due, unpaid contributions
217 **rückständige Beiträge,** contributions due, unpaid contributions
218 **Beitragsausschuß,** *m.*, committee on contributions
219 **Beitragsschlüssel,** *m.* (= Beitragstabelle, *f.*) scale of contributions
Beitragstabelle, *f.* = *Beitragsschlüssel, *m.*
220 **Beitragszahlung,** *f.*, contribution
221 **im Verhältnis zur Höhe ihrer Beitragszahlungen** (EMA 5), in proportion to the amounts of their contributions
222 **beitreten,** to accede to, to adhere to
223 **einem Vertrag/Abkommen beitreten,** to accede to a treaty/an agreement
224 **Nach dem 1.1.1950 kann jedes Mitglied der UN der Konvention beitreten,** After 1st January 1950 any member of the UN may accede to the present convention
225 **Die neuen Mitgliedstaaten treten durch diese Akte den Vereinbarungen der ... bei,** The new member states accede by this act to the agreements adopted by ...
226 **unter Vorbehalt beitreten,** to accede subject to reservation (*beigetreten)
227 **beitretend,** *adj.*, acceding, adhering

228   **die beitretenden Staaten/Regierungen,** the acceding states/governments

229   **jede später beitretende Regierung,** every government subsequently acceding (*beigetreten)

230   **Beitritt,** *m.*, accession (*more rarely:* adherence/adhesion)

231   **Der Beitritt erfolgt durch Hinterlegung einer Beitrittsurkunde beim Generaldirektor (PCP Prot),** Accession shall be effected by the deposit of an instrument of accession with the Director-General

232   **jede Urkunde über den Beitritt einer Macht (TRW III),** every instrument evidencing the adherence of a power

233   **zum Beitritt aufliegen,** to be open for accession

234   **Dieses Übereinkommen liegt für jede Regierung zum Beitritt auf (SF 96),** The present agreement shall be open for accession by any government

235   **Staaten zum Beitritt einladen,** to invite states to accede (*Vertrag öffnen, VCLOT 2 *in* Annex 14, VCLOT 83 *in Annex* 5)

236   **Beitrittsbedingung,** *f.*, condition of accession

237   **Beitrittserklärung,** *f.*, declaration/instrument of accession (*see note to* *Erklärung)

238   **Der Beitritt wird mit dem ersten Tag des Monats, der auf die Hinterlegung der Beitrittserklärung folgt, wirksam (EXWC 9),** Such accession shall take effect on the first day of the month following the deposit of the instrument of accession

239   **Beitrittsklausel,** *f.*, accession clause, clause of accession

240   **Beitrittsrecht,** *n.*, right of accession/to accede

241   **Beitrittsurkunde,** *f.*, instrument of accession (*Beitrittserklärung, *and* VCLOT 84 *in Annex* 5)

242   **beitrittswillig,** *adj.*, willing to accede, applying for accession/membership, candidate

243   **beiwohnen** (+ *dat.*), to be present at, to participate in, to attend (discussions, etc.)

244   **Beklagter,** *adj.n.*, defendant

245   **bekräftigen,** to affirm

246   **die BRD bekräftigt ihre Absicht ... (zu),** the FGR affirms its intention (to ...)

247   **Bekräftigung,** *f.*, affirmation

248   **in Bekräftigung,** affirming (*in preamble*)

249   **in Bekräftigung ihrer Absicht, ... herbeizuführen,** affirming their intention to achieve ...

250   **Bekundung,** *f.*, proclamation

251   **in Bekundung,** proclaiming (*in preamble*)

252   **in Bekundung ihres Hauptzieles, das aus ... besteht (MNTB Pr),** proclaiming as their principal aim the ...

253   **Bemühen,** *n.*, pains, endeavour, effort

254   **in dem Bemühen** (= bemüht), anxious (*in preamble*) **bemüht** = in dem *Bemühen

255   **benachrichtigen,** to inform, to give notice of, to notify

256   **Benachrichtigung,** *f.*, notice, informing

257   **nach ordnungsgemäßer Benachrichtigung der Bevollmächtigten (SICJ 58),** due notice having been given to the agents

258   **benennen,** to appoint (*ernennen)

259   **Benennung,** *f.*, appointment (*Ernennung)

260   **Beobachter,** *m.*, observer

261   **Die ... Organisation war ebenfalls durch einen Beobachter vertreten,** The ... organization was also represented by an observer

262   **Beobachter *ad hoc*,** observer *ad hoc*

263   **ständiger Beobachter,** permanent observer

264   **Beobachterstatus,** *m.*, observer status

265   **beraten,** to discuss, to consult, to deliberate

266   **Die Kommission vertagt sich, um ihren Bericht zu beraten und**

abzufassen, The commission adjourns to consider and draw up its report

267 über Änderungen der Anlage beraten (CFIMT VII), to consider amendments to the annex

268 beratend, *adj.*, consultative, advisory, deliberative

269 beratender Ausschuß, consultative committee

270 in beratender Eigenschaft, in an advisory capacity

271 beratende Versammlung, consultative assembly

272 Die beratende Versammlung ist das beratende Organ des Europarates (CE 22), The Consultative Assembly is the deliberative organ of the Council of Europe

273 Beratung, *f.*, consultation, deliberation, discussion

274 Der Gerichtshof zieht sich zur Beratung zurück (SICJ 54), The court shall withdraw to consider

275 Die Beratung der Kommission erfolgt nicht öffentlich und bleibt geheim (HgI 30), The commission considers its decisions in private and the proceedings are secret

276 Die Beratungen des Gerichtshofes sind und bleiben geheim (SICJ 54), The deliberations of the court shall take place in private and remain secret

277 Die Beratungen des Gerichts sind und bleiben geheim (CRPG An), The deliberations of the tribunal shall be and remain secret

278 Beratungen beiwohnen, to be present at discussions/deliberations

279 an Beratungen teilnehmen, to participate in discussions/deliberations

280 Beratungsamt, *n.*, advisory board

281 Beratungsausschuß, *m.*, advisory/consultative committee

282 Beratungsbefugnis, *f.*, power of deliberation

283 Beratungs- und Kontrollbefugnisse (EAEC), powers of deliberation and of control

284 Beratungsergebnisse, *n.pl.*, conclusions

285 Beratungskommission, *f.*, advisory/consultative commission

286 Beratungsorgan, *n.*, advisory/consultative organ
Beratungsstelle, *f.* = *Beratungsamt, *n.*

287 berauben, to pillage, to plunder

288 Beraubung, *f.*, pillage, plunder

289 berechtigen, to authorize, to entitle, to empower

290 berechtigt, *adj.*, authorized, entitled, empowered

291 Der Staat/die Mission (usw) ist berechtigt, ... zu machen, The state/the mission (etc.) shall have the right/power to ...

292 die zum Vertragsabschluß berechtigten Organe des Staates, the organs of the state authorized/empowered to conclude a treaty

293 die zum Vertragsaushandeln berechtigten Delegierten, the delegates authorized/empowered to negotiate a/the treaty
(*befugt)

294 Berechtigung, *f.*, right, entitlement, authorization

295 die Berechtigung aller Staaten, am internationalen Verkehr teilzunehmen, the right of all states to participate in international intercourse

296 Bereich, *m.*, field, sphere
(*Gebiet²)

297 Bereinigung, *f.*, adjustment

298 Maßnahmen zur friedlichen Bereinigung jeder Situation (CUN 14), measures for the peaceful adjustment of any situation

299 Bergungsort *m.* für Kulturgut (PCP), refuge for cultural property

300 Bericht, *m.*, report

301 einen Bericht abfassen, to draw up/prepare a report (*see* * beraten)

302 einen Bericht erstatten, to make/provide/submit a report

303 Der Rat erstattet jährlich einen Bericht über seine Tätigkeit (PMBT 5), The council shall make an annual report on its activities

304 einen Bericht verfassen, to draw up/prepare a report

305   ... verfaßt sie einen Bericht, den sie dem Vorsitzenden des Ausschusses vorlegt, und der ihre Feststellung über alle auf den Streit zwischen den Parteien bezüglichen Sachfragen enthält (CERD 13), ... it shall prepare and submit to the chairman of the committee a report embodying its findings on all questions of fact relevant to the issue between the parties

306   einen Bericht vorlegen, to submit a report

307   einen Bericht über die getroffenen Gesetzgebungs-, Gerichts-, Verwaltungs- und sonstigen Maßnahmen vorlegen (CERD 9), to submit a report on the legislative, judicial, administrative or other measures which they have adopted

308   berichten, to report, to submit a report

309   Berichterstatter, *m.*, *rapporteur,* reporter

310   Berichterstattung, *f.*, reporting, reports (submitted)

311   dem Ausschuß zur Untersuchung und Berichterstattung zugewiesen, referred to the committee for study and report

312   Berichtigung, *f.*, correction

313   die Berichtigung am Text vornehmen und paraphieren (VCLOT 79), to make and initial the correction in the text

314   berufen auf, sich, to invoke

315   sich auf seine Immunität berufen, to invoke one's immunity

316   sich auf einen Vertrag/ein Übereinkommen berufen, to invoke a treaty/convention

317   Ein Vertragsstaat darf sich gegenüber einem anderen Vertragsstaat nur insoweit auf dieses Übereinkommen berufen, als er selbst verpflichtet ist, es anzuwenden (CREFA XIV), A contracting state shall not be entitled to avail itself of the present convention against other contracting states except to the extent that it is itself bound to apply the convention

318   Berufskonsul, *m.* (VCCR), career consular officer

319   Berufskonsuln, die Leiter konsularischer Vertretungen sind (VCCR 16), career heads of consular posts

        Berufskonsulatsbeamter, *adj.n.* = *Berufskonsul, *m.*

320   Berufsverband, *m.*, industrial/professional organization

321   die maßgebenden Berufsverbände der Arbeitgeber oder Arbeitnehmer (ILO 3), the industrial organizations which are most representative of employers or work people

322   Berufung[1], *f.*, invocation, invoking

323   Eine Berufung auf Immunitäten vor der Gerichtsbarkeit ist ausgeschlossen (VCLD XIV), Jurisdictional immunities shall not be invoked

324   unter Berufung (+ *gen.*), by invoking

325   Berufung[2], *f.*, appeal, petition

326   Berufung einlegen (gegen), to appeal, to petition, to lodge/file an appeal (against) (*Rechtsmittel, *Nichtigkeitsbeschwerde)

327   Berufungsbeklagter, *adj.n.*, respondent, party/person appealed against/against whom the appeal is lodged/filed/entered

328   Berufungsgericht, *n.*, court/tribunal of appeal, appeal court/tribunal, appellate tribunal (CSMW 4)

329   Berufungsgrund, *m.*, ground(s) of/reason(s) for appeal

330   Berufungskläger, *m.*, appellant, the person/party appealing

331   Berufungsschrift, *f.*, notice of appeal

332   beruhen auf, to be based on, to derive from, to stem from

333   berühren[1], to concern, to affect

334   Fragen des Friedens, die die legitimen Interessen aller Staaten berühren, questions of peace affecting the legitimate interests of all states

335   berühren[2], to affect, to impair, to

prejudice, to have/exert a prejudicial effect on, to disturb

336 **Dieser Vertrag berührt nicht die von ihnen früher abgeschlossenen zweiseitigen und mehrseitigen Verträge und Vereinbarungen,** The present treaty shall be without prejudice to any bilateral and multilateral treaties and agreements that they have already concluded

337 **die Anwendung dieses Artikels berührt nicht ...,** the application of this article shall not prejudice/shall in no way prejudice ...

338 **... werden durch diese Vereinbarung nicht berührt (ARS 12),** nothing in this agreement shall be deemed to impair ...
(*beeinträchtigen, *unberührt)

339 **Besatzung[1],** *f.,* crew

340 **Besatzung[2],** *f.,* occupation (*see note to* *Besetzung)

341 **Besatzungsarmee,** *f.,* army of occupation

342 **Besatzungsbehörde,** *f.,* occupation/occupying authorities

343 **Besatzungsdokument,***n.* (CFIMT), crew document

344 **Besatzungsgewalt,** *f.,* occupational power/authority

345 **Besatzungskosten,** *pl.,* occupation costs

346 **Besatzungsliste,** *f.* (CFIMT), crew list

347 **Besatzungsmacht,** *f.,* occupying power

348 **Besatzungsmitglied,** *n.,* member of the crew

349 **zivile Besatzungsmitglieder von Militärflugzeugen (GC I),** civil members of military aircraft crews

350 **Besatzungsrecht,** *n.,* law of occupation

351 **Besatzungsregime,** *n.* (CRPG), occupation regime

352 **Besatzungsstatut,** *n.,* occupation statute

353 **Besatzungsstatut aufheben (CRPG),** to revoke the occupation statute

354 **Besatzungsstreitkräfte,** *f.pl.,* occupation forces, forces of occupation, occupying forces

355 **Besatzungsverwaltung,** *f.,* occupying administration, administration by the occupying power

356 **Besatzungszone,***f.,* zone of occupation

357 **Beschädigter[1],** *adj.n.,* injured person, person who has sustained damage, loss or injury

358 **Beschädigter[2],** *adj.n.,* cripple

359 **,,Beschädigte'' im Sinne dieses Abkommens sind alle Militär- und Zivilpersonen, die infolge des Krieges eine Amputation erlitten haben oder körperbehindert sind (EXWC 1),** The term "cripples", for the purpose of this agreement, shall include all persons, military or civilian, who, as a result of war, have suffered an amputation or who are suffering from an impairment of the power of movement

360 **Beschäftigungsbedingungen,** *f. pl.,* working conditions, conditions of employment

361 **stetige Verbesserung der Lebensbedingungen und Beschäftigungsbedingungen (EEC Pr),** constant improvement of the living and working conditions

362 **Beschlagnahme,***f.,* seizure, requisition

363 **Die Beschlagnahme erfolgt nach dem innerstaatlichen Recht jeder Vertragspartei (EPTV 4),** Seizure shall be effected in accordance with the domestic law of each party to this agreement

364 **... genießen Befreiung von jeder Form verwaltungsmäßiger Beschlagnahme, Einziehung, Enteignung und Zwangsverwaltung (PPELDO 5),** ... shall be immune from any form of requisition, confiscation, expropriation and sequestration

365 **Beschlagnahme ihres persönlichen Gepäcks (PPELDO 14),** seizure of their personal baggage

366 **das Recht zur Beschlagnahme (GC I 34),** the right of requisition

367 **Beschlagnahmen, Kontributionen und Einquartierungen (VCDR 35),**

requisitions, (military) contributions and billeting
(*Prisenrecht)

368 **beschlagnahmen,** to seize
369 **beschließen,** to decide, to approve, to carry
370 **einstimmig beschließen,** to decide by unanimous vote
(*Abstimmungsverfahren)
371 **Beschluß,** *m.,* decision, judicial decision, court order, order of the court, resolution
372 **in der Anlage zu diesem Beschluß,** in the annex to this decision
373 **durch einstimmigen Beschluß,** by unanimous decision, by unanimous vote (IMF XVI), by unanimous agreement (NAT 10)
374 **solange ein Beschluß des Rats nicht ergangen ist** (EEC 149), as long as the Council has not acted
375 **Beschlüsse der Generalversammlung bedürfen einer Zweidrittelmehrheit der anwesenden und abstimmenden Mitglieder** (CUN 18), Decisions of the General Assembly shall be made by a two-thirds majority of the members present and voting
376 **einen Beschluß ausführen,** to carry out/execute a decision
377 **einen Beschluß fassen,** to take/make a decision
378 **einem Beschluß Wirksamkeit verleihen,** to give effect to a decision
(*Urteil, *Entscheidung)
379 **beschlußfähig sein,** to be competent to make decisions, to be/constitute a quorum
380 **Die Kommission ist nur dann beschlußfähig, wenn alle Mitglieder anwesend sind** (ECPSD 13), Decisions of the commission shall be valid only if all its members are present
381 **Der Gerichtshof ist beschlußfähig, wenn 9 Richter anwesend sind** (SICJ 25), A quorum of 9 judges shall suffice to constitute the court
382 **Die Kommission ist bei Anwesenheit einer Mehrheit ihrer Mitglieder beschlußfähig** (ECER 23), A majority of the members of the commission shall constitute a quorum

383 **die Vertragsparteien sind nur dann beschlußfähig, wenn ...,** the contracting parties shall not take a decision unless ...
(*Beschlußfähigkeit)
384 **Beschußfähigkeit,** *f.,* competence to make decisions, (existence of a) quorum
385 **die zur Beschlußfähigkeit notwendige Mitgliederzahl** (CE 18), the quorum
386 **Zur Beschlußfähigkeit des Kongresses bei seinen Sitzungen ist die Anwesenheit von Delegierten der Mehrheit aller Mitglieder erforderlich** (WMO 12), The presence of delegates of a majority of the members shall be required to constitute a quorum for meetings of Congress
387 **die Beschlußfähigkeit feststellen,** to establish that a/the quorum is present/that (the number of) those present constitute(s) a quorum
388 **Beschlußfassung,** *f.,* decision(s), decision making
389 **bis zur Beschlußfassung durch den Rat** (IMF XVI), pending decision by the board
390 **beschränken,** to limit, to restrict
391 **Beschränkung,** *f.,* limitation, restriction
392 **die fortschreitende Beseitigung der Beschränkungen im zwischenstaatlichen Wirtschaftsverkehr** (EEC Pr), the progressive abolition of restrictions on international trade
393 **ohne Beschränkung durch Rasse, Staatsbürgerschaft oder Religion** (UDHR 16), without any limitation due to race, nationality or religion (*see* *Unterscheidung, *Unterschied)
394 **Beschränkungen unterworfen,** restricted
395 **mengenmäßige Beschränkungen,** quantitative restrictions
396 **beschuldigen,** to accuse of, to charge with
397 **Jeder Mensch, der einer strafbaren Handlung beschuldigt wird, ist so lange als unschuldig anzusehen, bis**

seine Schuld in einem öffentlichen Verfahren gemäß dem Gesetz nachgewiesen ist (UDHR 11), Everyone charged with a penal offence has the right to be presumed innocent until proved guilty according to law in a public trial
398 **Beschuldigung,** *f.*, charge, accusation
399 **eine strafrechtliche Beschuldigung erheben** (UDHR 10), to file/make a criminal charge
400 **Beschwerde¹,** *f.*, complaint
401 **das Recht, Beschwerde zu führen,** the right to enter/lay a complaint
402 **Beschwerde²,** *f.*, appeal, petition
403 **Beschwerdeführer¹,** *m.*, person/party entering/laying the complaint
404 **Beschwerdeführer²,** *m.*, appellant, party/person appealing, party/person filing/lodging the appeal
405 **Beschwerdegegner¹,** *m.*, person/party against whom the complaint is entered/laid
406 **Beschwerdegegner²,** *m.*, respondent in appeal proceedings
407 **Beschwerderecht,** *n.*, right of petition, right of complaint, right of/to appeal
408 **Mißbrauch des Beschwerderechts** (PHR), abuse of the right of petition (*For* *Beschwerde- *compounds see also under* *Berufungs-.)
409 **beschwichtigen,** to appease
410 **Beschwichtigung,** *f.*, appeasement
411 **Beschwichtigungspolitik,** *f.*, policy of appeasement
412 **besetzen,** to occupy
413 **ein Gebiet besetzen,** to occupy a territory
414 **eine Stelle/einen Sitz (neu) besetzen,** to fill a vacancy
415 **besetzend,** *adj.*, occupying
416 **der besetzende Staat,** the occupying state/occupant state (*See also under* *Besatzungs-.)
417 **Besetzender,** *adj.n.* (= *Okkupant, *m.*), occupant, occupying state/power, occupant state/power (*See also under* *Besatzungs-.)
418 **Besetzung,** *f.*, occupation (*i.e. the act*

of occupying, in contrast to *Besatzung, *i.e. the presence of* (foreign) occupying forces)
419 **friedliche Besetzung,** peaceful/pacific occupation
420 **kriegerische Besetzung,** belligerent occupation, occupation by force of arms
421 **Das Völkerrecht kennt typische Situationen einer Handlungsunfähigkeit, z.B. die der kriegerischen Besetzung** (*occupatio bellica*), In international law there are typical situations of an incapacity to act, e.g. that in the case of belligerent occupation (*occupatio bellica*)
422 **teilweise/vollständige Besetzung eines Gebiets** (GC IV), partial/total occupation of a territory (*Okkupation)
423 **Besitz,** *m.*, possession
424 **besitzen,** to possess
425 **Besitzung,** *f.*, possession
426 **Kolonien, Besitzungen und Protektorate,** colonies, possessions and protectorates
427 **überseeische Besitzungen,** overseas territories/possessions
428 **bestallen,** to appoint
429 **Bestallung,** *f.*, appointment
430 **die Bestallung eines Konsuls,** the commission of a consular agent/consul
431 **Bestallungsschreiben,** *n.*, commission
432 **eine Urkunde in Form eines Bestallungsschreibens oder eines entsprechenden Schriftstückes** (VCCR 11), a document in the form of a commission or similar document
433 **Der Entsendestaat übermittelt das Bestallungsschreiben auf diplomatischem oder einem anderen geeigneten Wege** (VCCR 11), The sending state shall transmit the commission through the diplomatic or other appropriate channel (*Ernennungsschreiben)
434 **Bestandteil,** *m.*, integral part
435 **... ist Bestandteil des Grundgesetzes,** ... is an integral part of the basic law

436   der Anhang, der Bestandteil des
       Übereinkommens ist ..., the annex/
       appendix which is/forms an integral
       part of the convention ...
437   bestätigen, to confirm
438   Bestätigung, f., confirmation
439   in Bestätigung ihrer (Absicht usw),
       confirming their (intention, etc.) (in
       preamble)
440   bestehend, adj., existing, present,
       extant
441   bestehendes Recht, existing law, pre-
       sent law
442   bestehende oder spätere Vorschrif-
       ten, present or future/subsequent
       rules (and regulations)
443   bestellen, to appoint, to designate
444   Vermittler bestellen (VCLOT An),
       to appoint conciliators
       (*ernennen)
445   Bestellung, f., appointment
       (*Ernennung, *Bestallung)
446   Bestellungsurkunde, f., letter/cer-
       tificate of appointment
447   besteuern, to tax, to impose a tax/
       taxation (on)
448   Besteuerung, f., taxation
449   Befreiung von der Besteuerung,
       immunity from taxation
450   bestimmen¹, to provide, to lay down
451   ... soweit nicht das Recht des zu-
       ständigen Gerichtes etwas anderes
       bestimmt, ... unless the law of the
       competent court otherwise pro-
       vides
452   bestimmen², to designate
453   als Vertreter bestimmen, to desig-
       nate as representative/delegate
       (*Verwahrregierung)
454   Bestimmung¹, f., provision, term
455   Annahme der Bestimmungen, adop-
       tion of the provisions
456   Anwendung der Bestimmungen,
       application of the provisions
457   Durchführung der Bestimmungen,
       execution / implementation / perfor-
       mance of the provisions
458   Erfüllung der Bestimmungen, com-
       pliance with/carrying out/fulfilment/
       discharge of the provisions
459   Nichterfüllung der Bestimmungen,
       failure to fulfil/discharge the provi-

sions, non-compliance with the provisions
460   Verstoß gegen die Bestimmungen,
       offence against/infringement of the
       provisions
461   allgemeine Bestimmung, general
       provision
462   anderslautende Bestimmung, provi-
       sion to the contrary, alternative pro-
       vision
463   anderweitige Bestimmung, provision
       to the contrary, alternative provision
464   angenommene Bestimmung, ac-
       cepted provision
465   einschränkende Bestimmung, res-
       trictive provision
466   erforderliche Bestimmungen, neces-
       sary provisions
467   Die für die Handhabung und
       wirksame Anwendung dieses
       Artikels erforderlichen Bestim-
       mungen sind in Anhang B enthal-
       ten (EFTA 4), Provisions neces-
       sary for the administration and
       effective application of this article
       are contained in Annex B
468   gegenteilige Bestimmung, contrary
       provision, contradictory provision
469   verschiedene Bestimmungen, miscel-
       laneous provisions
470   vorstehende Bestimmungen, preced-
       ing provisions, provisions set out/set
       forth/listed above
471   zuwiderlaufende Bestimmung, con-
       trary provision, provision to the con-
       trary
472   eine der innerstaatlichen Gesetz-
       gebung zuwiderlaufende Bestim-
       mung (ILOC 22.3), a provision
       contrary to the national law
       (nach *Maßgabe, *unbeschadet,
       *Begriffsbestimmung)
473   Bestimmung², f., destination (see
       under *Bestimmungs- compounds)
474   Bestimmung³, f., determination
475   Bestimmung des Angreifers, deter-
       mination of the aggressor
476   Bestimmungsgebiet, n., territory
       of destination (of both goods and
       persons, e.g. refugees)
477   endgültiges Bestimmungsgebiet, ter-
       ritory of final destination

478 **vorgesehenes Bestimmungsgebiet,** territory of intended destination

479 **Bestimmungshafen,** *m.*, port of destination

480 **Bestimmungszollamt,** *n.* (ICCB), customs office of destination

481 **bestrafen,** to punish, to penalize

482 **Personen, die ..., verfolgen und strafrechtlich oder disziplinarisch bestrafen** (PCP 28), to prosecute and impose penal or disciplinary sanctions upon those persons who ...

483 **Bestrafung,** *f.*, punishment

484 **Bestreben,** *n.*, endeavour, effort

485 **in dem Bestreben** (= in dem *Bemühen), anxious (*in preamble*)

486 **die Regierungen sind sich in dem Bestreben einig ...,** the governments agree to endeavour to ...

487 **bestrebt sein,** to endeavour to, to be anxious to

488 **bestrebt, ... herbeizuführen,** anxious to achieve (*in preamble*)

489 **die Vertragsschließenden werden bestrebt sein ...,** the contracting parties shall endeavour to ... (in dem *Bestreben, in dem *Bemühen)

490 **beteiligt,** *adj.*, concerned

491 **beteiligte Macht/Partei,** power/party concerned (*betroffen)

492 **Beteiligter,** *adj.n.*, the party concerned

493 **betrauen,** to charge

494 **Personen, die mit der Wahrnehmung von Aufgaben betraut sind,** persons charged with the execution of duties/functions (*beauftragt)

495 **betroffen,** *adj.*, concerned

496 **betroffener Staat,** state concerned (*beteiligt)

497 **Beutegut,** *n.*, booty

498 **Bevölkerung,** *f.*, population

499 **eingeborene Bevölkerung,** native population, indigenous population, native inhabitants

500 **einheimische Bevölkerung,** local population

501 **ständige Bevölkerung,** permanent population (*Staatsvolk)

502 **Bevölkerungsaustausch,** *m.*, exchange of populations (*e.g.* in the case of minorities)

503 **Bevölkerungsüberführung,** *f.*, transfer of population(s)

504 **bevollmächtigt,** *adj.*, authorized, empowered

505 **die von ihren Regierungen hierzu gehörig bevollmächtigten Unterzeichneten** (GCF 22), the undersigned plenipotentiaries, being duly authorized thereto by their respective governments (*Bevollmächtigter[1], *Vollmacht)

506 **Bevollmächtigtenkonferenz,** *f.*, conference of plenipotentiaries

507 **Bevollmächtigter[1],** *adj.n.*, plenipotentiary

508 **..., und haben zu ihren Bevollmächtigten ernannt: ...** (SF 44), ..., and have designated/appointed as their plenipotentiaries: ... (*bevollmächtigt, *Mittelsperson, *Benachrichtigung, *Unterschrift)

509 **Bevollmächtigter[2],** *adj.n.*, agent

510 **Ein Mitglied des Gerichtshofes darf nicht als Bevollmächtigter, Beistand oder Anwalt tätig sein** (SICJ 17), No member of the Court may act as agent, counsel or advocate

511 **Bevollmächtigung,** *f.*, authorization, granting of full powers (*Vollmacht)

512 **bewaffnen,** to arm

513 **bewaffnet,** *adj.*, armed, military

514 **bewaffneter Angriff,** armed/military attack/aggression

515 **bewaffnete Einmischung,** armed/military intervention

516 **bewaffneter Friede,** armed peace (*militärisch)

517 **Bewaffnung,** *f.*, armament, arming

518 **beweglich,** *adj.*, movable

519 **bewegliches Erbgut,** movable legacy, movable property of the deceased

520 **bewegliches Vermögen,** movable property (*see* *Vermögen)

521 **Bewegungsfreiheit,** *f.*, freedom of movement

522   Bewegungs- und Reisefreiheit (VCCR), freedom of movement and travel
523   Beweis, *m.*, evidence, proof
524   Beweis durch Vermutung, presumptive evidence (*see* *Vermutung)
525   Erheblichkeit des Beweises, relevance/relevancy of the evidence
526   Zulässigkeit des Beweises, admissibility of the evidence
527   schlüssiger Beweis, conclusive evidence
528   zulässiger Beweis, admissible evidence
529   Beweis antreten/erbringen/führen, to furnish/provide evidence
530   unter Beweis stellen, to prove, to establish, to substantiate
531   Beweis zulassen, to admit evidence
532   Beweisantritt, *m.*, presentation of the evidence
533   Beweisaufnahme, *f.* (= Beweiserhebung, *f.*), taking/hearing of the evidence, examination/hearing of witnesses
534   Beweisaufnahmen an Ort und Stelle herbeiführen (HgI 24), to procure evidence on the spot
535   Abschluß/Schluß der Beweisaufnahme, closing of the evidence
536   beweisen, to prove, to establish, to substantiate
537   Beweiserbringung, *f.*, presentation of the evidence
538   Beweiserhebung, *f.*, taking/hearing of the evidence, examination/hearing of witnesses (*Beweisaufnahme)
539   Beweisführung, *f.*, the giving/furnishing/presentation of evidence
540   Beweiskraft, *f.*, conclusive/probatory force
541   beweiskräftig, *adj.*, having conclusive force, having the force of evidence/proof, conclusive
542   Beweislast, *f.*, burden/onus of proof
543   die Beweislast auferlegen, to impose the burden/onus of proof (on s.o.)
544   die Beweislast verteilen, to apportion the burden/onus of proof
545   Beweismaterial, *n.*, evidence, proof
546   Beweismittel, *n.*, evidence, proof

547   nachdem der Gerichtshof die Beweismittel und Zeugenaussagen erhalten hat (SICJ 52), after the Court has received the proofs and evidence
548   mündliche oder schriftliche Beweismittel (SICJ 52), oral or written evidence
549   Beweismittel angeben, to state the evidence/proof
550   Beweismittel vorbringen, to tender/to submit evidence/proof
551   Beweisregel, *f.*, rule(s) of evidence
552   Beweiswürdigung, *f.*, consideration of the evidence
553   bewilligen, to grant, to (give) consent to, to authorize, to permit
554   Bewilligung, *f.*, consent, authority, authorization, permission, permit
555   Bewußtsein, *n.*, consciousness, awareness
556   in dem Bewußtsein, aware, conscious (*in preamble*)
557   Beziehung, *f.*, relation
558   Beziehungen zu anderen Organisationen, relations with other organizations
559   Beziehungen zwischen den Staaten, relations between states
560   Abbruch der Beziehungen, severance/breaking off of relations (*see* *Abbruch)
561   Aufnahme der Beziehungen, establishment of relations
562   Aufrechterhaltung der Beziehungen, maintenance of relations
563   Befestigung der Beziehungen, consolidation of relations
564   Normalisierung der Beziehungen, normalization of relations
565   bilaterale Beziehungen, bilateral relations
566   diplomatische Beziehungen, diplomatic relations (*see* *diplomatisch, *Abbruch)
567   feindliche Beziehungen, hostile relations
568   finanzielle Beziehungen, financial relations
569   friedliche Beziehungen, peaceful/pacific relations
570   friedliche und harmonische

Beziehungen zwischen den Völkern, peaceful and harmonious relations between (the) peoples

571 **Bruch der friedlichen Beziehungen** (HgI 8), rupture of pacific relations

572 **gegenseitige Beziehungen,** mutual/ reciprocal relations

573 **jede Veränderung in ihren gegenseitigen Beziehungen** (TRW Pr), all changes in their relations with one another

574 **in ihren gegenseitigen Beziehungen die Bestimmungen anwenden** (ICC I), to apply on a reciprocal basis the provisions

575 **gutnachbarliche Beziehungen,** good-neighbourly relations

576 **internationale Beziehungen,** international relations

577 **Gruppen von Ländern, die für die Gestaltung ihrer internationalen Beziehungen nicht verantwortlich sind** (WHO 8), groups of territories which are not responsible for the conduct of their international relations (*see* souveräne *Gleichheit)

578 **konsularische Beziehungen,** consular relations

579 **kulturelle Beziehungen,** cultural relations

580 **mehrseitige/multilaterale Beziehungen,** multilateral relations

581 **völkerrechtliche Beziehungen,** international relations

582 **wirtschaftliche Beziehungen,** economic relations

583 **wissenschaftliche Beziehungen,** scientific relations

584 **zweiseitige Beziehungen,** bilateral relations

585 **zwischenstaatliche Beziehungen,** relations between states, interstate relations, international relations

586 **Beziehungen abbrechen,** to sever/to break off relations

587 **Beziehungen aufnehmen,** to establish relations

588 **Beziehungen aufrechterhalten,** to maintain relations

589 **in Beziehungen treten (mit),** to enter into relations (with)

590 **Beziehungen unterhalten,** to maintain relations

591 **bilateral,** *adj.*, bilateral

592 **billig,** *adj.*, just, equitable, fair, reasonable

593 **billigen,** to approve
(*Billigung)

594 **billigerweise,** justly, equitably, fairly, reasonably

595 **Billigkeit,** *f.*, equity, *aequitas* (*the abstract concept of* justice/fair play)

596 **das der Billigkeit am meisten entsprechende Mittel, Streitigkeiten zu erledigen** (HgI 38), the most equitable means of settling disputes

597 **nach Billigkeit entscheiden,** to decide equitably/*ex aequo et bono*/in accordance with equitable principles

598 **Das Schiedsgericht entscheidet nach Billigkeit, wenn dies dem Willen der Parteien entspricht** (ECICA VII), The arbitrators shall act as *amiables compositeurs* if the parties so decide

599 **Billigkeitsentscheidung,** *f.*, decision *ex aequo et bono*

600 **Billigkeitsgedanke,** *m.*, concept/ idea of equity/fairness

601 **Billigkeitslösung,** *f.*, solution *ex aequo et bono*

602 **Billigkeitsrecht,** *n.*, equity, principles of equity

603 **Billigung,** *f.*, approval

604 **Billigung der Erweiterungen oder Änderungen** (ECICP 7), approval of any elaborations or modifications

605 **Billigungsurkunde,** *f.*, instrument of approval

606 **Bindekraft,** *f.*, binding force
(*Verbindlichkeit, *bindende Kraft)

607 **binden,** to bind, to be binding on

608 **es bindet nur diejenigen Mitglieder, deren ...** (ILOC 23.8), it shall be binding only upon those members whose ...

609 **bindend,** *adj.*, binding

610 **Die Entscheidung des Gerichtshofs ist nur für die Streitparteien bindend** (SICJ 59), The decision of the court has no binding force except between the parties

611   **für sich als bindend anerkennen** (PHR 22), to regard as binding on them

612   **bindende Kraft** (= Bindekraft, *f.*), binding force

613   **Solchen Empfehlungen der Generalversammlung kommt keine bindende Kraft zu,** No binding force is attached to such recommendations by the General Assembly/Such recommendations by the General Assembly possess no binding force (*Verbindlichkeit, *verbindlich)

614   **Bindung₁** *f.*, obligation, commitment

615   **juristische Bindung,** legal obligation

616   **vertragliche Bindung,** contractual obligation

617   **Bindung²,** *f.*, link, tie, bond

618   **Die Einbürgerung wurde nicht anerkannt, zumal keine echte Bindung bestand,** The naturalization was not recognized as there existed no genuine link/no qualifying connection

619   **Binnengewässer,** *n.* (*usu. in pl.*), internal waters (innere *Gewässer)

620   **Binnenmeer,** *n.* (= Binnensee, *m.*), land-locked sea

621   **Binnenstaat,** *m.*, non-coastal state, land-locked state

622   **Die Binnenstaaten sollen freien Zugang zum Meer haben, um die Freiheit des Meeres im gleichen Maße wie die Küstenstaaten zu genießen** (GCHS 3), In order to enjoy the freedom of the seas on equal terms with the coastal states, states having no sea-coast should have free access to the sea (*Küstenstaat)

623   **Binnenverkehr,** *m.*, inland transport

624   **Binnenwasserstraße,** *f.*, inland waterway

625   **bisherig,** *adj.*, previous

626   **bisheriges Recht,** previous law

627   **bisheriger Staat,** previous state, predecessor state, extinct state, mother/parent state (*see* *Altstaat)

628   **Blockade,** *f.*, blockade

629   **Regel der Wirksamkeit der Blockade,** rule of effectiveness of a blockade

630   **eine Blockade aufheben,** to raise/to lift a blockade

631   **eine Blockade bekanntgeben,** to notify a blockade, to give notice of a blockade

632   **eine Blockade brechen,** to violate/to break/to run a blockade

633   **eine Blockade errichten,** to establish a blockade

634   **eine Blockade notifizieren,** to notify/to give notice of a blockade

635   **eine Blockade verhängen,** to establish a blockade, to blockade

636   **Blockadebrecher,** *m.*, blockade runner

637   **Blockadebruch,** *m.*, breach of a blockade

638   **Blockaderecht¹,** *n.*, right of blockade

639   **Blockaderecht²,** *n.*, law governing/as to blockades

640   **Blockadestreitmacht,** *f.*, blockading force

641   **Blockadezustand,** *m.*, state of blockade

642   **Bodenschätze,** *m.pl.*, resources, natural resources (*Meeresgrund, *Schätze, *Naturschätze)

643   **bodenständig,** *adj.*, internal, inland

644   **bodenständige Verteidigung,** internal/inland defence (*see* *Verteidigung)

645   **Botschaft,** *f.*, embassy, mission (*Mission)

646   **Botschafter,** *m.*, ambassador (*Missionschef, *Gesandter)

647   **Botschafterkonferenz,** *f.*, conference of ambassadors

648   **Botschaftsrat,** *m.*, counsellor

649   **Botschaftssekretär,** *m.*, secretary (of the embassy)

650   **erster Botschaftssekretär,** first secretary

651   **Briefkopf** *m.* **der Botschaft,** letterhead of the embassy

652   **Briefschaften,** *f.pl.*, correspondence (*Schriftwechsel)

653 **Briefwechsel,** *m.,* exchange of letters, correspondence
654 **Bruch,** *m.,* breach, violation, rupture
655 **Bruch einer Regel,** breach of a rule
656 **Bruch eines Vertrags,** violation of a treaty
657 **Bruttoregistertonnen,** *f.pl.,* gross tonnage
658 **Schiffe von 20 000 und mehr Bruttoregistertonnen,** ships of 20,000 tons gross tonnage or more
659 **Buchstabe,** *m.,* letter, sub-paragraph (*if indicated by letter*)
660 **die Bestimmungen dieses Buchstabens** (MNTB 1), the provisions of this sub-paragraph
661 **Bucht,** *f.,* bay
662 **die natürlichen Öffnungspunkte einer Bucht** (GCTS 7), the natural entrance points of a bay
663 **jede eine Bucht abschließende Linie** (FC 6), any bay-closing line
664 **geschlossene Bucht,** land-locked bay
665 **historische Bucht,** historic bay (*Basislinie, *Einschnitt)
666 **Budget,** *n.,* budget
667 **die Budgets der Verwaltung der Spezialorganisationen der UN,** the administrative budgets of the specialized agencies of the UN
668 **Budgetabmachung,** *f.,* budgetary arrangement
669 **Budgetfrage,** *f.,* budgetary question
670 **Bund¹,** *m.,* federation
671 **Bund²,** *m.,* League (of Nations)
672 **Bundesgesetzblatt,** *n.* (BGBl), Federal Law Gazette
673 **Bundesmitglied¹,** *n.,* member of the League (of Nations)
674 **Bundesmitglied²,** *n.,* member of the federation, federal member
675 **Bundesstaat,** *m.,* federal state (*The essential distinctions between* **Bundesstaat**/federal state *and* **Staaten-**

bund/Confederation *are* (i) *that the former is a real state at international law, while the latter is not;* (ii) *the former has direct power over the member states and their citizens, while the latter does not normally. See also* *Realunion *and* *Staatenbund.*)
676 **bundesstaatlich,** *adj.,* federal
677 **Bündnis,** *n.,* alliance
678 **Bündnisabkommen,** *n.,* treaty/agreement of alliance (*see note to* *Vertrag *in Annex* 1)
679 **Bündnisfall,** *m., casus fœderis*
680 **Bündnispolitik,** *f.,* policy of alliances
681 **Bündnisvertrag,** *m.,* treaty of alliance
682 **Bureau,** *n.,* bureau, office (*Büro²)
683 **Bürge,** *m.,* surety, guarantor
684 **bürgen für,** to stand as surety, to guarantee, to act/stand as guarantor for
685 **Bürgerpflicht,** *f.,* civil duty, civil obligation
686 **Bürgerrechte,** *n.pl.,* civil rights (*for lists of some of the civil rights, see under* *Recht auf, *frei, *Freiheit, *Anspruch auf, -freiheit *compounds, and* CERD 5 *in Annex* 9)
687 **Bürgschaft,** *f.,* suretyship, guarantee, bond
688 **Bürgschaften und sonstige Arten der Sicherheitsleistung** (CFIMT), bonds and other forms of security
689 **Büro¹,** *n.,* officers, bureau
690 **Der Rat wählt sein Büro aus seinen Mitgliedern** (UNESCO V), The Board shall elect its officers from among its members
691 **Büro²,** *n.,* bureau, office
692 **ständiges Büro,** permanent office

C

1 **Charakter,** *m*., character, nature, status
2 **allgemeiner Charakter,** general character
3 **empfehlender Charakter von Resolutionen,** recommendatory character/nature of resolutions
4 **universaler Charakter,** universal character
5 **zwingender Charakter,** coercive character
6 **die Frage, ob dem universalen Recht zwingender Charakter zukommt oder nicht,** the question whether universal law is of a coercive nature
7 **ein Abkommen technischen/kulturellen (usw) Charakters,** an agreement of a technical/cultural (etc.) nature
8 **Konflikte nichtkriegerischen Charakters,** non-war conflicts, conflicts of a non-war character
9 **Charta,** *f*., (*e.g.* UN) charter (*Satzung)
10 **Chef,** *m*., head
11 **Chef der Delegation,** head of the delegation
12 **die Mission und ihr Chef** (VCDR 20), the mission and its head (*Leiter, *Missionschef)
13 **Chefdelegierter,** *adj.n*., head of the delegation
14 **Chiffreur,** *m*., code clerk
15 **Chiffrierabteilung,** *f*., ciphering section/service
    Chiffrierbeamter, *adj.n*. = *Chiffreur, *m*.
16 **Code,** *f*., code, cipher
17 **das Recht, Codes zu benutzen** (PrivExCE 9), the right to use codes (*verschlüsseln)

D

1 **Dachorganisation,** *f.*, overhead organization, central organization, national organization

2 **Dachverband,** *m.*, federation, confederation, central organization, national federation

3 **Dauer,** *f.*, term, period, duration

4 **für die Dauer von 2 Jahren, gerechnet vom Zeitpunkt des ...,** for a period/term of two years from the date of ...

5 **unbegrenzte Dauer,** unlimited duration (*Zeitraum)

6 **Dauervisum,** *n.*, permanent visa

7 **Debellatio(n),** *f.*, debellatio

8 **dechiffrieren,** to decode, to decipher

9 **Dechiffrierung,** *f.*, decoding, deciphering

10 **Defensivallianz,** *f.* (= Defensivbündnis, *n.*), defensive alliance

11 **Dekan,** *m.* (= *Doyen, *m.*), dean, doyen

12 **Dekartellisierung,** *f.*, decartellization

13 **Deklaration,** *f.*, declaration

14 **deklaratorisch,** *adj.*, declaratory

15 **deklaratorischer Ausdruck der bestehenden Rechtslage,** declaratory expression of existing law

16 **Delegat,** *m.*, delegate

17 **päpstlicher Delegat,** apostolic delegate (*Vertreter, *Delegierter, *Abgeordneter)

18 **Delegation,** *f.*, delegation

19 **Leiter der Delegation bei ...,** head of the delegation to ...

20 **Delegationschef,** *m.*, head of the delegation

21 **Delegationsleiter,** *m.*, head of the delegation

22 **Delegationstheorie,** *f.*, delegation theory

23 **delegieren,** to delegate (*übertragen)

24 **Delegierter,** *adj.n.*, delegate

25 **durch Delegierte vertreten,** represented by delegates

26 **Jede Vertragspartei ist im Rat durch höchstens 2 Delegierte vertreten** (CICES 6), Each contracting party shall be represented at the Council by not more than 2 delegates

27 **ständiger Delegierter,** permanent delegate

28 **stellvertretender Delegierter,** alternate/substitute delegate (*Vertreter, *Abgeordneter, *Delegat, *Eigenschaft)

29 **Delegierung,** *f.*, delegation, act of delegation

30 **Delegierung von Befugnissen,** delegation of powers

31 **Delikt,** *n.* (= Straftat, *f.*), delict, wrong, criminal act/offence, tortious act

32 **völkerrechtliches Delikt,** international wrong/offence/delict, an act illegal in/under/at international law (strafbare *Handlung)

33 **Demarkation,** *f.*, demarcation

34 **Demarkationslinie,** *f.*, demarcation line

35 **demobilisieren,** to demobilize

36 **Demobilisierung,** *f.*, demobilization

37 **Denkmalsort,** *m.* (PCP 8), centre containing monument(s)

38 **Denkschrift,** *f.*, (written) statement

39 **Die Gründe für den Einspruch sind in einer Denkschrift darzulegen,** The grounds for such objection shall be set forth in a (written) statement

40 **deponieren,** to deposit (*hinterlegen)

41 **Deponierung,** *f.*, deposit, deposition (*Hinterlegung)

42 **Deportation,** *f.*, deportation

43 **deportieren,** to deport

44 **Depositar,** *m.*, depositary

45 **die Hinterlegung der Urkunden beim Depositar,** the deposit of the instruments with the depositary

46 **Der Depositar handelt nicht in seiner Eigenschaft als eine der Vertragsparteien, sondern übt im Auftrag und im**

Namen der Staaten, die bereits Partner des Vertrags sind, oder es noch werden können, internationale Funktionen aus, The depositary (state) does not act in its capacity as one of the parties to the treaty, but exercises international functions on behalf of and in the name of those states already party to the treaty or which may (subsequently) become parties to it (*Verwahrer, and VCLOT 76-77 in Annex 15)

47 Depositaraufgaben, f.pl. (= Depositarfunktionen, f.pl.), duties/functions of a/the depositary

48 administrativer Charakter der Depositaraufgaben, administrative character/nature of the duties/functions of a depositary

49 Depositarregierung, f. (= *Verwahrregierung, f.), depositary government

50 Depositarstaat, m. (= Verwahrstaat, m.), depositary state

51 Dereliktion, f., dereliction

52 Derogation, f., derogation

53 Deutschlandvertrag, m., Convention on Relations between the Three Powers and the FGR (1952)

54 Dienst, m., service

55 nach ihrem Ausscheiden aus den Diensten der Organisation (PPELDO 16), after they have left the service of the organization

56 bei Beendigung ihrer Dienste, on the termination of their services/functions

57 diplomatischer Dienst, diplomatic service

58 gute Dienste, good offices

59 die guten Dienste unparteiischer Stellen, the good offices of impartial bodies/agents

60 Ausschuß für gute Dienste, good offices committee

61 Gute Dienste haben ausschließlich die Bedeutung eines Rates und niemals verbindliche Kraft (HgI 6), Good offices have exclusively the character of advice and never have binding force

62 gute Dienste leihen, to lend (one's) good offices

63 die Schutzmächte leihen ihre guten Dienste zur Beilegung des Streitfalles, the protecting powers shall lend their good offices with a view to settling the dispute

64 Dienste leisten, to render/perform services

65 Dienste leisten, um die die Sonderorganisationen ersuchen (CUN 66), to perform services at the request of specialized agencies

66 Dienstalter, n., length of service

67 der nach dem Dienstalter älteste Richter, the longest serving/the senior judge (*dienstältest)

68 dienstältest, adj., longest serving, longest accredited, senior

69 der dienstälteste anwesende Richter (SICJ 45), the senior judge present (*Dienstalter)

70 Dienstantritt, m., assumption of office, entry into office, assumption of duties/functions (*Amtsantritt)

71 Dienstbedingungen, f.pl., terms (of duty), conditions of service

72 Der Rat ernennt einen Generalsekretär. Er legt dessen Dienstobliegenheiten und -bedingungen fest (CICES 13), The Council shall appoint a General Secretary on such terms and to perform such duties as it may determine

73 Dienstbezeichnung, f., title

74 Dienstleistung, f., service

75 persönliche Dienstleistungen, personal services

76 Diplomaten von allen persönlichen Dienstleistungen, von allen öffentlichen Dienstleistungen jeder Art befreien (VCDR 35), to exempt diplomatic agents from all personal services and from all public service of any kind

77 Dienstleistungen im Hafen (CFIMT), services at ports/a port

78 Gegenwert für Dienstleistungen, charge for services (rendered), service charge

79 dienstlich, *adj.*, official
80 dienstliche Aufgaben/Funktionen/ Tätigkeit, official duties/functions
81 die Beendigung ihrer dienstlichen Tätigkeit bei der Mission (VCDR 10), the termination of their functions with the mission (*amtlich)
82 Dienstobliegenheit, *f.*, duty, official duty
83 bei der Wahrnehmung ihrer Dienstobliegenheiten (IAEA VII), in the performance of their duties (*Weisung, *Obliegenheit, *Dienstbedingung, *Aufgabe)
84 Dienstort, *m.*, location
85 Dienstpaß, *m.*, official pass
86 Dienstpersonal, *n.*, service staff (*Mission, *Personal)
87 Dienstsiegel, *n.*, (official) seal
88 Dienststelle, *f.*, agency, authority
89 Öffentliche Behörden: Die Dienststellen oder Bediensteten in einem Staat (CFIMT An), Public Authorities: The agencies or officials in a State
90 Die Mitteilungen dürfen niemandem außerhalb der Dienststellen der Assoziation oder der Regierungsstellen der Mitgliedstaaten bekanntgegeben werden (EFTA 5), The information shall not be disclosed to any person outside the service of the association or the government of any member state
91 zuständige Dienststelle, competent agency/authority
92 Dienstvergehen, *n.*, disciplinary offence
93 Dienstwohnung, *f.*, official residence
94 dinglich, *adj.*, real, *in rem*
95 dinglicher Erwerb, acquisition *in rem*, acquisition of real rights
96 dingliche Klage, real action, action *in rem* (*Klage)
97 Diplomat, *m.*, diplomatic agent, diplomat
98 Der Ausdruck „Diplomat" bezeichnet den Missionschef und die Mitglieder des diplomatischen Personals der Mission (VCDR 1), A "diploma-

tic agent" is the head of the mission or a member of the diplomatic staff of the mission
99 Abreise des Diplomaten, departure of the diplomatic agent
100 endgültige Abreise des Diplomaten (VCDR), final departure of the diplomatic agent
101 Befreiungen von Diplomaten, immunities of diplomatic agents (*see* *Befreiung[2] von)
102 Dienstwohnung des Diplomaten, official residence of the diplomatic agent
103 Eintreffen des Diplomaten, arrival of the diplomatic agent
104 Ernennung des Diplomaten, appointment of the diplomatic agent
105 Haushalt des Diplomaten, household of the diplomatic agent
106 die zum Haushalt eines Diplomaten gehörenden Familienmitglieder (VCDR), the members of the family of a diplomatic agent forming part of his household
107 Immunitäten von Diplomaten, immunities of diplomatic agents (*see* *Immunität von)
108 die Person des Diplomaten, the person of the diplomatic agent
109 Die Person des Diplomaten ist unverletzlich (VCDR 29), The person of the diplomatic agent shall be inviolable
110 Vorrechte von Diplomaten, privileges of diplomatic agents (*Klage, *Vollstreckungsmaßnahme, *Einrichtung, *and* VCDR 1 *in* Annex 8)
Diplomatenkonvention, *f.* = *Diplomatenübereinkommen, *n.*
111 Diplomatenpaß, *m.*, diplomatic passport
112 Diplomatenrecht, *n.*, law relating to diplomatic agents, law governing diplomatic rights and privileges
113 Diplomatenübereinkommen, *n.*, convention on diplomatic agents/relations (*normally refers to the Vienna Convention on Diplomatic Relations of* 18.4.1961)
114 Diplomatenvisum, *n.*, diplomatic visa

115 **Diplomatie,** *f.*, diplomacy
116 **ad-hoc Diplomatie,** ad-hoc diplomacy
117 **direkte Diplomatie,** direct diplomacy
118 **geheime Diplomatie,** secret diplomacy
119 **ständige Diplomatie,** permanent diplomacy
120 **diplomatisch,** *adj.*, diplomatic
121 **diplomatischer Agent** (= *Diplomat, m.*), diplomatic agent
122 **diplomatisches Asyl,** diplomatic asylum
123 **diplomatische Befreiungen,** diplomatic immunities (*Befreiung von)
124 **diplomatische Behälter** (WEUS 10), diplomatic bags (*see* *diplomatisches Kuriergepäck)
125 **diplomatische Beziehungen,** diplomatic relations
126 **Abbruch der diplomatischen Beziehungen,** severance/breaking off of diplomatic relations
127 **Aufnahme der diplomatischen Beziehungen,** establishment of diplomatic relations
128 **Aufrechterhaltung der diplomatischen Beziehungen,** maintenance of diplomatic relations
129 **Bereitschaft zu diplomatischen Beziehungen,** intention/desire to establish diplomatic relations
130 **Mit der Anerkennung wird auch die Bereitschaft zu diplomatischen Beziehungen ausdrücklich oder stillschweigend ausgedrückt,** The intention/desire to establish diplomatic relations is express or implicit in the declaration of recognition
131 **Unterbrechung der diplomatischen Beziehungen,** suspension of diplomatic relations
132 **Wiederaufnahme der diplomatischen Beziehungen,** resumption/re-establishment of diplomatic relations
133 **Wiederherstellung der diplomatischen Beziehungen,** resumption/re-establishment of diplomatic relations
134 **diplomatische Beziehungen abbrechen,** to break off/to sever diplomatic relations (*see* *Gesandtschaftspflicht)
135 **diplomatische Beziehungen aufnehmen,** to establish/to initiate diplomatic relations
136 **diplomatische Beziehungen aufrechterhalten,** to maintain diplomatic relations
137 **diplomatische Beziehungen unterbrechen,** to suspend diplomatic relations
138 **diplomatische Beziehungen wiederaufnehmen,** to resume/to re-establish diplomatic relations
139 **diplomatischer Brauch,** diplomatic custom
140 **Dieses Verfahren ist gegen jeden diplomatischen Brauch,** This procedure is contrary to all diplomatic custom
141 **diplomatischer Dienst,** diplomatic service
142 **diplomatische Immunitäten,** diplomatic immunities (*see* *Immunität von, *Befreiung² von)
143 **diplomatisches Korps,** diplomatic corps
144 **diplomatisches Kuriergepäck,** diplomatic bag (*see* *Kuriergepäck)
145 **diplomatische Liste,** diplomatic list
146 **diplomatische Note,** diplomatic note
147 **diplomatisches Personal,** diplomatic staff
148 **die Bestellung eines Mitgliedes des diplomatischen Personals für mehrere Staaten vornehmen** (VCDR 5), to assign any member of the diplomatic staff to more than one state (*see* Personal der *Mission)
149 **diplomatische Privilegien,** diplomatic privileges
150 **diplomatischer Rang,** diplomatic rank (*see* *Rang *and* *Rang- compounds*, diplomatisches *Personal)
151 **diplomatische Schriftstücke,** diplomatic documents
152 **diplomatischer Verkehr,** diplomatic intercourse
153 **diplomatischer Vertreter,** diplomatic envoy/representative/agent

154 **einen diplomatischen Vertreter bestellen/ernennen,** to appoint a diplomatic envoy

155 **diplomatische Vertretung,** (i) diplomatic representation; (ii) diplomatic post/mission

156 **diplomatische Vorrechte,** diplomatic privileges (*see* *Befreiungen und Vorrechte, *Befreiung² von, *Immunität von)

157 **diplomatischer Weg,** diplomatic channel

158 **auf diplomatischem Wege,** through (the) diplomatic channel(s), by diplomacy

159 **Direktionsausschuß,** *m.*, directing committee (SF 34), governing body (AACER), steering committee

160 **Direktionsausschuß für Kernenergie,** steering committee for nuclear energy

161 **Direktorenkonferenz,** *f.* (WMO), Conference of Directors

162 **Direktorium,** *n.*, managing board (*e.g.* EPU), board of management (*e.g.* EMA)

163 **diskriminieren,** to discriminate

164 **diskriminierend,** *adj.*, discriminatory

165 **diskriminierende Behandlung,** discriminatory treatment, discrimination

166 **Der Empfangsstaat unterläßt jede diskriminierende Behandlung von Staaten** (VCDR 47), The receiving state shall not discriminate as between states

167 **diskriminierende Handlung,** discriminatory act, act of discrimination (CERD 4)

168 **Diskriminierung,** *f.*, discrimination

169 **Diskriminierung von Staaten wegen deren politischer Ordnung,** discrimination against states because of their political system(s)

170 **Diskriminierung aus Gründen der (Staatsangehörigkeit usw),** discrimination on the grounds of (nationality, etc.)

171 **Diskriminierung im internationalen Handel** (GATT), discriminatory treatment in international commerce

172 **diskriminierungsfrei,** *adj.*, non-discriminatory

173 **diskriminierungsfreie Handels- und Zahlungspolitik** (EMA 2), non-discriminatory trade and payments policies

174 **Diskussionsgrundlage,** *f.*, basis of discussion

175 **der Konferenz lag ... als Diskussionsgrundlage vor,** the Conference had before it and used as a basis of discussion ... (+ *specific report/draft, etc.*)

176 **Disziplinarausschuß,** *m.*, disciplinary committee

177 **Disziplinargewalt,** *f.*, disciplinary power

178 **disziplinarisch,** *adj.*, disciplinary

179 **Disziplinarmaßnahme,** *f.*, disciplinary measure/action

180 **Disziplinarrat,** *m.*, disciplinary board

181 **Disziplinarstrafe,** *f.*, disciplinary punishment

182 **Disziplinarvergehen,** *n.*, disciplinary offence

183 **Dokument,** *n.*, document (*in pl. often* documentation)

184 **die Dokumente für Zoll-, Einwanderungs- und Gesundheitszwecke** (CFIMT An), documentation for customs, immigration and public health purposes

185 **ergänzende Dokumente,** related documents

186 **Dokumentenerfordernis,** *n.*, documentary requirement

187 **Domizil,** *n.*, (country of) domicile (*but see note to* *Wohnsitz)

188 **Donau-Kommission,** *f.*, Danube Commission

189 **Doppelbesteuerungsabkommen,** *n.*, double taxation agreement/convention

190 **Abkommen zur Vermeidung der Doppelbesteuerung und zur Verhinderung der Steuerverkürzung,** convention for the avoidance of double taxation and the prevention of fiscal evasion

191 **Doppelstaatler,** *m.*, person of dual nationality

192 **Doppelstaatsangehörigkeit,** *f.*,
dual nationality
(*Mehrstaatigkeit, *Staatsangehörigkeit)
193 **Doyen,***m.* (= Dekan,*m.*), dean, doyen
(*i.e. longest serving ambassador, etc.*)
194 **Die Aufgaben des Doyens sind vor-
wiegend zeremonieller Natur,** The
duties of the Dean are primarily of a
ceremonial character
195 **In einigen Staaten übernimmt der
Vertreter des Heiligen Stuhls —
ohne Rüchsicht auf die örtliche
Anciennität — die Rolle des Doyens,**
In some states the Representative of
the Holy See takes over the role of
Dean, irrespective of local seniority
(of office)
(*Anciennität)
196 **Drei-Elementen-Lehre,** *f.*, three-
elements theory (*for definition see
example under* *Staatsvolk)
Dreier- = *Dreimächte-
197 **Dreimächteabkommen,** *n.*, tripar-
tite/three-power agreement
198 **Dreimächteausschuß,** *m.*, tripar-
tite/three-power committee, committee of three
199 **Dreimächteerklärung,** *f.*, tripar-
tite/three-power declaration
200 **Dreimächtegruppe,** *f.*, tripartite/
three-power group, group of three
201 **Dreimächteübereinkommen,** *n.*,
tripartite/three-power agreement
202 **Dreimeilenzone,** *f.*, three-mile
zone/belt
Dreiparteien- = *Dreimächte-
203 **Dringlichkeitsverfahren,** *n.*,
emergency/expedited procedure
204 **in einem Dringlichkeitsverfahren,** by
an expedited procedure
205 **Dritter,***adj.n.*, third party, third state
206 **Drittstaat,** *m.*, third state
(*See* VCLOT 2 *in Annex* 14.)
207 **Dualismus,** *m.*, dualism
208 **Dualist,** *m.*, dualist
209 **dualistisch,** *adj.*, dualist
(*Transformationstheorie)
210 **Duplik,** *f.* (= Gegenerwiderung, *f.*),
rejoinder, defendant's rejoinder
(schriftliches *Verfahren)
211 **durchdringen,** to penetrate

212 **Durchdringung,** *f.*, penetration
213 **friedliche Durchdringung,** peaceful
penetration
214 **durchfahren,** to pass through
215 **ein das Küstenmeer durchfahrendes
fremdes Schiff** (GCTS 20), a foreign
ship passing through the territorial
sea
216 **Durchfahrt,** *f.*, transit, passage
(through), access
217 **Die Durchfahrt schließt das Recht
zum Stoppen und Ankern ein** (GCTS
14), Passage includes stopping and
anchoring
218 **freie Durchfahrt,** free/unhindered
passage/transit
219 **friedliche Durchfahrt,** innocent passage
220 **Die Schiffe aller Staaten, ob Küsten-
oder Binnenstaaten, genießen das
Recht der friedlichen Durchfahrt
durch das Küstenmeer** (GCTS 14),
Ships of all states, whether coastal
or not, shall enjoy the right of innocent passage through the territorial
sea
221 **die Durchfahrt fremder Fischerei-
schiffe gilt nicht als friedlich, wenn
sie die Gesetze und Vorschriften
nicht beachten, die ...** (GCTS
14), (the) passage of foreign fishing
vessels shall not be considered
innocent if they do not observe
such laws and regulations as ...
222 **die friedliche Durchfahrt behindern,** to hamper innocent passage
(GCTS 15)
223 **die friedliche Durchfahrt untersagen** (GCTS 16), to suspend innocent passage
224 **nichtfriedliche Durchfahrt** (GCTS
16), passage which is not innocent
unschädliche Durchfahrt = friedliche *Durchfahrt
(*Durchlaß, *Durchgang, *Durchreise)
225 **durchführbar,** *adj.*, enforceable,
capable of implementation
226 **Zwangsmittel, die ein Recht durchführbar machen,** means of coercion that make a law enforceable
(*Vollstreckungsmaßnahme)

227 **durchführen,** to execute, to implement, to discharge

228 **Durchführung,** *f.,* execution, implementation, discharge, performance

229 **in Durchführung des Beschlusses,** in (full) implementation/discharge of the decision

230 **bei der Durchführung des Vertrags arbeiten die Hohen Vertragsschließenden Parteien eng mit ... zusammen** (WEU I III), in the execution of the treaty the High Contracting Parties shall work in close cooperation with . . .

231 **bei der Durchführung ihrer besonderen Aufgaben** (CCC IX), in the achievement of their respective tasks

232 **Die Vertragsparteien kommen zusammen, um die Durchführung dieses Übereinkommens zu prüfen,** The contracting parties shall meet together to consider the operation of the present convention

233 **Durchführung von Inspektionen** (WEU IV), the conduct of inspections

234 **Durchfuhrverkehr,** *m.* (GATT 5), traffic in transit
(*Durchgangsverkehr, *Durchgangstransport)

235 **Durchgang,** *m.,* transit

236 **freier Durchgang,** free/unhindered transit

237 **alle den freien Durchgang und die Gleichbehandlung in den Häfen betreffenden Fragen** (GCHS 3), all matters relating to freedom of transit and equal treatment in ports
(*Durchlaß, *Durchfahrt, *Durchreise)

238 **Durchgangshafen,** *m.,* port of transit

239 **Durchgangslager,** *n.,* transit camp

240 **Durchgangsstaat,** *m.,* state of transit, transit state

241 **Durchgangstransport,** *m.* (CSFT), traffic in transit
(*Durchgangsverkehr)

242 **Durchgangsverkehr,** *m.,* traffic in transit, transit traffic

243 **Freiheit des Durchgangsverkehrs** (CSFT), freedom of transit

244 **freier Durchgangsverkehr** (CSFT), free transit

245 **internationaler Durchgangsverkehr,** international transit

246 **Durchgangszollamt,** *n.* (ICCB), customs office en route

247 **Durchlaß,** *m.,* passage

248 **freier Durchlaß,** free passage

249 **freien Durchlaß genehmigen,** to permit/to allow free passage

250 **freien Durchlaß gewähren,** to ensure free passage
(*Durchfahrt, *Durchgang, *Durchreise)

251 **durchlassen,** to allow passage, to allow to pass

252 **ungehindert durchlassen,** to allow/to permit free passage, to allow to pass unhindered

253 **Durchlieferung,** *f.* (EExt 21), transit (*i.e. during extradition*)

254 **Durchmarsch,** *m.,* passage/transit (of forces)

255 **Durchmarschrechte,** *n.pl.* (CUN 43), rights of passage

256 **Durchreise,** *f.,* transit

257 **alle für seine sichere Durchreise erforderlichen Immunitäten** (VCDR 40), any such immunities as may be required to ensure his transit
(*Durchfahrt, *Durchgang, *Durchlaß)

258 **Durchreisender,** *adj.n.,* passenger in transit

259 **Durchreisesichtvermerk,** *m.* (= Durchreisevisum, *n.*), transit visa

260 **Durchreisestaat,** *m.,* transit state, state of transit

261 **durchsetzbar,** *adj.,* enforceable, capable of enforcement/execution

262 **nicht (gerichtlich) durchsetzbar,** unenforceable, not capable of enforcement/execution (by means of court action/action in the courts)

263 **durchsetzen,** to enforce, to execute

264 **Durchsetzung,** *f.,* enforcement, execution

265 **zwangsweise Durchsetzung** (= Zwangsdurchsetzung, *f.*), coercive enforcement
(*Durchführung, *Vollstreckung)

266 **durchsuchen,** to (visit and) search
267 **Durchsuchung,** *f.*, (visit and) search
268   **Verweigerung der Durchsuchung,** resistance to (visit and) search
269 **Durchsuchungsrecht,** *n.*, the right of visit and search

270   **Durchsuchungs- und Wegnahmerecht,** the right of search and seizure
271   **das dem Kriegführenden zugestandene Durchsuchungsrecht,** the belligerent right of visit and search

E

1 **Effektivitätsgrundsatz,** *m.*, principle of effectiveness, the "effectiveness/efficacy" principle
2 **Ehre,** *f.*, honour
3 **Verletzung von Ehre,** act(s) injurious to honour
4 **Eigengewässer,** *n. (usu. in pl.)*, internal waters (*Binnengewässer, *Gewässer)
5 **Eigenschaft,** *f.*, capacity
6 **die Person, die beauftragt ist, in dieser Eigenschaft tätig zu sein** (VCDR 1), the person charged with the duty of acting in this capacity
7 **Mit seinem Amtsantritt verliert der Präsident die Eigenschaft als Delegierter** (CICES 10), On assuming office the President shall cease forthwith to be a delegate
8 **in ihrer Eigenschaft als Sachverständige** (PPELDO 17), in their capacity as experts
9 **amtliche Eigenschaft,** official capacity
10 **beratende Eigenschaft,** advisory capacity
11 **gutachterliche Eigenschaft,** capacity as an expert
12 **konsultative Eigenschaft,** consultative capacity
13 **persönliche Eigenschaft,** personal capacity
14 **Die Kommissionsmitglieder sind in persönlicher Eigenschaft tätig** (CERD 12), The members of the commission shall serve in their personal capacity
15 **Eigentum,** *n.*, property
16 **das Eigentum und die sonstigen Vermögenswerte der Organisation** (PPELDO 5), the organization's property and assets
17 **bewegliches Eigentum,** movable property
18 **feindliches Eigentum,** enemy property
19 **unbewegliches Eigentum,** immovable property
20 **Eigentum beschlagnahmen,** to seize/confiscate property
21 **Eigentum erwerben,** to acquire property
22 **Eigentum konfiszieren,** to confiscate property
23 **Eigentum einem Sequester unterstellen,** to sequestrate property (*Sache[1], *Vermögen)
24 **Eigentumsrecht,** *n.*, right to own property, right of ownership; property right (EAEC 91)
25 **einberufen,** to convene, to convoke, to call
26 **Auf Antrag eines Drittels der Vertragsregierungen beruft die Organisation jederzeit eine Konferenz der Regierungen zur Prüfung der ...ein** (PPSO An I), A conference of governments to consider ...shall at any time be called by the organization upon the request of one third of the contracting governments
27 **Einberufung,** *f.*, convocation, convening
28 **Einberufungsschreiben,** *n.*, letter of convocation
29 **Einbuchtung,** *f.*, indentation
30 **wo die Küste tiefe Einbuchtungen und Einschnitte aufweist** ... (GCTS 4), in localities where the coastline is deeply indented and cut into ... (*Einschnitt)
31 **einbürgern,** to naturalize
32 **Einbürgerung,** *f.*, naturalization
33 **Einbürgerungsanspruch,** *m.*, entitlement to naturalization
34 **Einbürgerungsanspruch haben,** to be entitled to naturalization/to be entitled to be registered as a citizen
35 **Einbürgerungsurkunde,** *f.*, certificate of naturalization, letters of naturalization, citizenship papers
36 **eindringen,** to invade
37 **eindringende Truppen bekämpfen** (GC I), to resist invading forces
38 **Einfuhr,** *f.*, import, importation
39 **Ausweis zur vorübergehenden Einfuhr** (ICCA), temporary importation papers

40   **Einfuhrabgabe,** *f.*, customs duty and any other duty/tax chargeable by reason of importation

41   **Unter ,,Einfuhrabgabe'' versteht man nicht nur Zölle, sondern alle bei der Einfuhr erhobenen Abgaben** (ICCA 1), The term "import duties and import taxes" shall mean not only customs duties but also all duties and taxes whatever chargeable by reason of importation

42   **Einfuhrbeschränkung,** *f.*, restrictions on imports/importation

43   **mengenmäßige Einfuhrbeschränkungen,** quantitative import restrictions, quantitative restrictions on importation

44   **Einfuhrbewilligung,** *f.*, import authorization/licence

45   **einführen**[1], to import

46   **einführen**[2], to introduce, to establish, to inaugurate

47   **Einfuhr-Förmlichkeiten,** *f.pl.*, import formalities

48   **Einfuhrgenehmigung,** *f.*, import authorization/licence

49   **Einfuhrkontingent,** *n.*, import quota

50   **Einfuhrland,** *n.*, country of importation

51   **Einfuhrlizenz,** *f.*, import licence

52   **Einfuhrmonopol,** *n.* (GATT), monopoly of importation

53   **Einfuhrquote,** *f.*, import quota

54   **Einfuhrrestriktion,** *f.*, import restriction

55   **Einführung,** *f.*, introduction, establishment, adoption

56   **die Einführung eines gemeinsamen Zolltarifs** (EEC 3), the establishment of a common customs tariff

57   **die Einführung einer gemeinsamen Politik auf dem Gebiet der Landwirtschaft/des Verkehrs** (EEC 3), the adoption of a common policy in the sphere of agriculture/transport

58   **Einfuhrverbot,** *n.*, import prohibition

59   **Einfuhrzoll,** *m.*, import duty (*Einfuhrabgabe)

60   **Eingang,** *m.*, receipt

61   **30 Tage nach Eingang der (Mitteilung usw),** 30 days after receipt of the (notification, etc.)

62   **1 Jahr nach Eingang der ...,** 1 year from the date on which the ... was received

63   **Eingebürgerter,** *adj.n.*, naturalized person

64   **eingedenk** (+ *gen.*), recalling, conscious of, having regard to (*in preamble*)

65   **eingedenk der Tatsache, daß die Völker der UN ...** (SCS Pr), mindful that the peoples of the UN ...

66   **eingegangen,** *adj.*, received

67   **jede eingegangene Notifizierung,** any/every notification received

68   **eingehen,** to be received (*Eingang, *eingegangen)

69   **eingreifen,** to intervene (*einmischen,*note to* *intervenieren)

70   **Eingreifen,** *n.*, intervention (*Einmischung, *Intervention)

71   **Eingriff,** *m.*, intervention (*Einmischung)

72   **einhalten,** to observe, to adhere to, to comply with, to perform, to fulfil, to respect, to abide by

73   **Die Hohen Vertragsparteien verpflichten sich, das vorliegende Abkommen unter allen Umständen einzuhalten** (GC IV 1), The High Contracting Parties undertake to respect the present convention in all circumstances

74   **Einhaltung,** *f.*, observance/observation (of), performance (of), respect (for), compliance (with), fulfilment (of)

75   **Einhaltungsversprechen,** *n.*, promise to observe/fulfil/perform/comply with/adhere to

76   **einheitlich,** *adj.*, standard, uniform

77   **Einheitsstaat,** *m.*, unitary state

78   **Für einen Bundesstaat oder einen Staat, der kein Einheitsstaat ist, gelten die folgenden Bestimmungen:** (CREFA XI), In the case of a Federal State or non-unitary state, the following provisions shall apply:

79   **einholen,** to obtain, to receive, to be granted

80 **das Exequatur einholen,** to obtain/ to receive the exequatur

81 **die Zustimmung des Parlaments einholen,** to obtain parliamentary approval

82 **Einholung,** *f.*, receipt, obtaining

83 **einigen, sich,** to agree, to come to an agreement

84 **Die unterzeichneten Regierungen haben sich auf gewisse Grundsätze und Übereinkommen geeinigt** (CAC Pr), The undersigned governments have agreed on certain principles and arrangements

85 **Einigung,** *f.*, agreement

86 **Einigung erzielen,** to reach an agreement

87 **Einkammer-,** unicameral, one-chamber, single-chamber

88 **Einkammersystem,** *n.*, unicameral system

89 **Einklang,** *m.*, accord, accordance

90 **im Einklang mit diesem Verfahren,** in accordance with this procedure (SF 141)
(*Schlußvermerk, *gemäß)

91 **einladen,** to invite

92 **zur Teilnahme/zum Beitritt (usw.) einladen,** to invite to participate/to accede (etc.)

93 **Einlaufhafen,** *m.* (CFIMT), port of arrival

94 **einmischen,** to intervene, to interfere

95 **sich in die inneren Angelegenheiten eines Staates einmischen,** to intervene in the internal/domestic affairs of a state
(*Angelegenheit, *note to* *intervenieren)

96 **Einmischung,** *f.*, intervention, interference

97 **bewaffnete Einmischung,** armed/ military intervention

98 **unzulässige Einmischung in,** inadmissible intervention in
(*Angelegenheit, *note to* *intervenieren)

99 **Einmischungsverbot,** *n.*, duty not to intervene, prohibition upon/ against intervention

100 **Einnahme,** *f.*, income, revenue

101 **Einnahmeentgang,** *m.*, loss of revenue

102 **der mit der Abgabenbefreiung verbundene Einnahmeentgang,** the loss of revenue arising from the exemption from dues

103 **einquartieren,** to billet

104 **Einquartierung,** *f.*, billeting

105 **einräumen,** to grant, to afford

106 **Befugnisse/Rechte einräumen,** to grant powers/rights

107 **Einräumung,** *f.*, grant, granting

108 **Einrede**[1]**,** *f.*, objection, traverse, contradiction

109 **Einrede**[2]**,** *f.*, plea

110 **Einrede erheben,** to raise a plea

111 **Einrede zulassen,** to admit a plea, to declare a plea admissible

112 **Einreise,** *f.*, entry, arrival, immigration

113 **Einreisegesetz,** *n.* (CFIMT An), immigration law

114 **einreisen,** to arrive, to enter

115 **... wenn ein Fahrgast aus diesem Grund nicht in den betreffenden Staat einreisen darf ...** (CFIMT An), ... if, for that reason, the passenger is found to be inadmissible to the state...

116 **Einreisevorschriften,** *f.pl.*, regulations on/concerning entry, regulations/laws relating to immigration

117 **einrichten,** to set up, to establish, to institute

118 **zur Mission gehörende Büros einrichten** (VCDR 12), to establish offices forming part of the mission

119 **Einrichtung**[1]**,** *f.*, establishment (*e.g. of diplomatic agents*), installation

120 **Gegenstände für den persönlichen Gebrauch des Diplomaten ... einschließlich die für seine Einrichtung vorgesehenen Gegenstände** (VCDR 36), articles for the personal use of a diplomatic agent including articles intended for his establishment

121 **Gegenstände, die anläßlich ihrer Ersteinrichtung eingeführt werden** (VCDR 37), articles imported at the time of first installation

122 **Einrichtung**[2]**,** *f.*, agency, organ, institution

123 **regionale Einrichtungen** (CUN), regional agencies

124   zwischenstaatliche Einrichtung (SF 28), intergovernmental agency
125   einschiffen, to embark (*Fahrgast)
126   Einschiffung, *f.*, embarkation
127   Einschiffungshafen, *m.*, port of embarkation
128   Einschiffungskarte, *f.*, embarkation card
129   Einschnitt, *m.*, indentation
130   Ein Einschnitt gilt jedoch nur dann als Bucht, wenn seine Fläche so groß oder größer ist, als die eines halben Kreises, dessen Durchmesser die quer über die Öffnung des Einschnittes gezogene Linie ist (GCTS 7), An indentation shall not, however, be regarded as a bay unless its area is as large as, or larger than, that of the semi-circle whose diameter is a line drawn across the mouth of that indentation (*Bucht, *Einbuchtung)
131   einschränken, to restrict, to limit
132   einschränkend, *adj. & adv.*, restrictive
133   einschränkend anwenden, to apply restrictively
134   Einschränkung, *f.*, restriction, limit
135   einschreiten, to intervene (*einmischen, *intervenieren *and note*)
136   Einschreiten, *n.*, intervention
137   einschüchtern, to intimidate
138   Einschüchterung, *f.*, intimidation
139   einseitig, *adj.*, unilateral
140   Einspruch, *m.*, objection
141   Einspruch begründen, to give reasons for the objection
142   der Einspruch muß begründet sein; er kann nur darauf gestützt werden, daß ... (PCP Reg Ex 14), such objection shall state the reasons giving rise to it, the only valid grounds being that ...
143   Einspruch einlegen, to file/submit/lodge an objection
144   Einspruch erheben, to raise/make an objection
145   es sei denn, daß einer der Empfangsstaaten ausdrücklich Einspruch erhebt (VCDR 5), unless

there is express objection by any of the receiving states
146   vorbehaltlich der Bestätigung, Zurückziehung oder Streichung noch zu erhebender oder bereits erhobener Einsprüche, pending the confirmation, withdrawal or cancellation of any objection that may be, or may have been, made (*Denkschrift)
147   Einspruchsbegründung, *f.*, the grounds/reasons for the objection, the grounds on which the objection is based
148   Einspruchsfrist, *f.*, period/time limit for filing/submitting the objection, period/time limit within which the objection must be filed/submitted
149   Einspruchsgrund, *m.*, the grounds/reasons for the objection, the grounds on which the objection is based
150   Einspruchsrecht, *n.*, right of objection/to object
151   Einspruchsschrift, *f.*, written grounds of objection
152   einstellen¹, to appoint
153   einstellen², to cease, to suspend
154   Einstellung¹, *f.*, appointment
155   Einstellung², *f.*, cessation, suspension
156   Einstellung der Feindseligkeiten, cessation of hostilities
157   Einstellung der Geschäftsfähigkeit (IDA VII), suspension of operations
158   Einstellung der Kampfhandlungen (GC IV), close of military operations
159   Einstellungsbefugnis, *f.*, power of appointment
160   einstimmig, *adj.*, unanimous
161   Einstimmigkeit, *f.*, unanimity, unanimous vote
162   kommt keine Einstimmigkeit zustande ... (EEC 8), failing unanimity (*Stimmengleichheit)
163   einstweilig, *adj.*, interim
164   einstweilige Maßnahmen (ECICA VI), interim measures
165   einstweilige Verfügung, interim injunction
166   eintragen, to register
167   Der Generalsekretär des Völker-

bundes hat dieses Abkommen ... einzutragen (ICCC 28), The present convention shall be registered by the Secretariat of the League of Nations (*registrieren)

168 **Eintragung**, *f.*, registration

169 **zwecks/zur Eintragung**, for (the purpose of) registration (*Registrierung, *Ratifikation)

170 **eintreiben**, to exact, to demand, to collect

171 **Eintreibung**, *f.*, collection, exacting

172 **einverleiben**, to annex

173 **Einverleibung**, *f.*, annexation

174 **Einverleibung des ganzen besetzten Gebietes oder eines Teils davon durch die Besatzungsmacht** (GC IV 47), annexation of the whole or part of the occupied territory by the occupying power

175 **gewaltsame Einverleibung**, annexation by armed force

176 **Einvernehmen**, *n.*, consent, agreement

177 **es besteht Einvernehmen, daß ...**, there is agreement that .../it is agreed that ...

178 **in den Verhandlungen ist Einvernehmen darüber erzielt worden, daß ...**, in the negotiations it has been agreed that ...

179 **in Einvernehmen**, in (common) agreement, by (mutual) consent

180 **durch Einvernehmen zwischen den Vertragsparteien** (VCLOT 57), by consent of the parties

181 **gegenseitiges Einvernehmen**, mutual/common agreement/consent

182 **in gegenseitigem Einvernehmen erfolgen** (VCDR 2), to take place by mutual consent

183 **Die Mitglieder werden im gegenseitigen Einvernehmen ausgewählt** (ECPSD 6), The Commissioners shall be chosen by agreement (*Einverständnis)

184 **Einvernehmenserklärung**, *f.*, declaration of agreement/understanding

185 **einvernehmlich**, *adj.*, by consent, by agreement, consensual

186 **die einvernehmliche Abänderung eines Vertrages**, the amendment of a treaty by mutual consent

187 **die Beseitigung der Hindernisse durch einvernehmliches Handeln der Parteien**, the removal of barriers by action agreed upon by the parties

188 **einvernehmliche Beilegung**, agreed/consensual settlement

189 **einverständlich**, *adj.*, by consent, by agreement, consensual

190 **einverständliches Vorgehen** (EEC Pr), concerted action

191 **Einverständnis**, *n.*, assent, consent, agreement

192 **es besteht Einverständnis, daß ...**, the parties agree that .../it is agreed that ...

193 **im Einverständnis zwischen den Parteien/Mitgliedern**, by consent/agreement between the parties/members (*Einvernehmen)

194 **Einwanderer**, *m.*, immigrant

195 **einwandern**, to immigrate

196 **Einwanderung**, *f.*, immigration

197 **Einwanderungsbehörde**, *f.*, immigration authority

198 **Einwanderungsbeschränkungen**, *f.pl.*, measures restricting immigration (PPELDO 16)

199 **Einwanderungsvorschrift**, *f.*, immigration regulation

200 **Einzelabkommen**, *n.*, individual treaty (*Treuhandschaftssystem *and note to* *Vertrag *in Annex* 1)

201 **Einzelaktion**, *f.*, individual action

202 **Einzelhilfssendung**, *f.* (GC), individual relief consignment/shipment

203 **Einzelmaßnahme**, *f.*, individual measure (*ausweisen)

204 **Einzelperson**, *f.*, individual

205 **regierende Personen, öffentliche Beamte oder private Einzelpersonen** (PCG 4), (constitutionally) responsible rulers, public officials or private individuals

206 **geschützte Einzelperson** (GC IV), individual protected person (*Person)

207 **Einzelschiedsrichter**, *m.* (ECICA

IV), sole arbitrator
(*Oberschiedsrichter)
208 **Einzelzwangsverschickung,** *f.*
(GC IV), individual forcible transfer
(*Zwangsverschickung)
209 **einziehen,** to withdraw (*pass, document, etc.*)
210 **Einziehung**[1], *f.*, withdrawal
211 **Einziehung**[2], *f.*, confiscation
(*Beschlagnahme)
212 **eklektisch,** *adj.*, eclectic
213 **eklektische Lehre,** eclectic theory/doctrine
214 **eklektische Schule,** eclectic school
215 **Eklektizismus,** *m.*, eclecticism
216 **Embargo,** *n.*, embargo
217 **Embargo auf Waffen,** arms embargo
218 **empfangen,** to receive
219 **der empfangende Staat,** the receiving state, the recipient state, host state
220 **Empfangsstaat,** *m.*, the receiving state, the recipient state, host state
221 **Angehörige des Empfangsstaates und Personen, die dort ständig ansässig sind** (VCCR 71), nationals or permanent residents of the receiving state
222 **empfehlen,** to recommend
223 **Empfehlung,** *f.*, recommendation
224 **auf Empfehlung des Sicherheitsrats,** upon the recommendation of the Security Council
225 **Empfehlungen bezüglich ...,** recommendations in respect of ...
226 **Empfehlungen ausarbeiten,** to draw up recommendations
227 **Empfehlungen aussprechen/erstatten/erteilen,** to make recommendations
228 **Empfehlungscharakter,** *m.*, recommendatory character/nature
229 **Endentscheidung,** *f.* (CSMW V), final decision
(*Entscheidung)
230 **endgültig,** *adj.*, final, definitive
(endgültige *Entscheidung, authentischer *Text)
231 **Endurteil,** *n.*, final judgment/award
232 **Enklave,** *f.*, enclave
233 **entbinden,** to relieve of, to release from
234 **Die Kündigung entbindet die Vertragsschließenden Parteien nicht von**

den Verpflichtungen (ECPSD 40), Denunciation shall not release the contracting parties from their obligations
235 **enteignen,** to expropriate, to confiscate
236 **der enteignende Staat,** the confiscating state
237 **Enteignung,** *f.*, expropriation, confiscation
(*Beschlagnahme)
238 **Entgegennahme,** *f.*, acceptance
239 **entgegennehmen,** to accept
240 **enthalten, sich** (+ *gen.*), to refrain from, to abstain from
241 **die Parteien enthalten sich jeder Maßnahme, die ...,** the parties shall abstain from any measure/all measures that ...
242 **Alle Mitglieder enthalten sich der Drohung mit Gewalt,** All members shall refrain from the threat of force
243 **sich der Stimme enthalten,** to abstain from voting
244 **entheben,** to relieve
245 **eines Amtes enthoben werden,** to be relieved of an office, to be dismissed from office
246 **entkolonisieren,** to decolonize
247 **Entkolonisierung,** *f.*, decolonization
248 **Entladehafen,** *m.*, port of discharge
249 **entlassen,** to dismiss, to discharge
250 **Entlassung,** *f.*, discharge, dismissal
251 **Entlassung eines Diplomaten,** discharge of a diplomatic agent
(*Anstellung)
252 **Entlassungsbefugnisse,** *f.pl.*, powers of dismissal
253 **entmilitarisieren,** to demilitarize
254 **Entmilitarisierung,** *f.*, demilitarization
255 **entmobilisieren,** to demobilize
256 **Entmobilisierung,** *f.*, demobilization
257 **entmündigen,** to deprive of (legal) capacity
258 **Entmündigter,** *adj.n.*, person lacking (full) (legal) capacity, person deprived of his (civic) rights/lacking full rights
(*Vormund)

259 **Entmündigung**, *f.*, deprivation of (legal) capacity

260 **entneutralisieren**, to deneutralize

261 **Entneutralisierung**, *f.*, deneutralization

262 **Entrattungsbescheinigung**, *f.*, deratting certificate

263 **entrechten**, to deprive of rights

264 **Entrechtung**, *f.*, deprivation of rights

265 **entschädigen**, to compensate, to make reparation

266 **Entschädigung**, *f.*, compensation, reparation

267 **Entschädigung für Arbeitsunfälle** (GC IV), compensation for occupational accidents

268 **Entschädigung für Opfer der nationalsozialistischen Verfolgung**, compensation for victims of Nazi persecution (*Schadenersatz)

269 **Entschädigungsanspruch**, *m.*, right/claim to compensation

270 **Entschädigungsantrag**, *m.*, application/claim for compensation

271 **entschädigungslos**, *adj.*, without compensation

272 **entscheiden**, to decide, to reach a decision

273 **Im Zweifelsfalle entscheidet der Gerichtshof** (SICJ 16), Any doubt on this point shall be settled by the decision of the court

274 **einen Fall *ex aequo et bono* entscheiden**, to decide a case *ex aequo et bono*

275 **... sofern der Gouverneursrat nicht anders entscheidet** (IAEA IX), ... in the absence of a contrary decision of the Board of Governors

276 **..., es sei denn, daß die Kommission anders entscheidet** (ECER 51), ... unless otherwise decided by the Commission (*Entscheidung, *Stimmenmehrheit)

277 **Entscheidung**, *f.*, decision (*compare with* *Beschluß), judgment

278 **Entscheidungen internationaler Gerichte**, decisions of/by international courts

279 **Entscheidungen von Organen inter-** nationaler Organisationen, decisions of/by organs of international organizations

280 **Entscheidungen in der Form von Urteilen oder Verfügungen** (CRPG An), decisions in the form of judgments or directives

281 **bei seinen/ihren Entscheidungen**, in reaching its decisions

282 **solange die Entscheidung noch nicht ergangen ist** (GCF 10), pending the/its award

283 **auf Grund einer Entscheidung der zuständigen Gerichtsbehörde** (VCCR 41), pursuant to a decision by the competent judicial authority

284 **Jede Entscheidung ergeht nach der Mehrheit der Mitglieder** (HgI 30), All questions are decided by a majority of members

285 **Sinn und Tragweite der Entscheidung** (SICJ 60), meaning and scope of the judgment

286 **Verkündung der Entscheidung**, pronouncement of the decision

287 **einstimmige Entscheidung**, unanimous decision

288 **endgültige Entscheidung**, final decision, decision with final effect

289 **bis eine endgültige Entscheidung in diesen Angelegenheiten ergangen ist** (CRPG An), until such cases have been finally decided

290 **Die Entscheidung des Gerichtshofs ist endgültig** (PHR 52), The judgment of the court shall be final

291 **Die Entscheidung ist endgültig und unterliegt keinem Rechtsmittel** (SICJ 60), The judgment is final and without appeal

292 **erstinstanzliche Entscheidung**, decision at first instance

293 **freie Entscheidung**, free decision

294 **Theoretisch steht den Staaten die Möglichkeit freier Entscheidungen zu**, In theory, states possess/enjoy liberty of action (*see* *Handlungsfähigkeit)

295 **gerichtliche Entscheidung**, judicial decision

296 **in Ausführung einer rechtskräftigen gerichtlichen Entscheidung**,

in execution of a judicial decision of/with final effect

297 **letzte Entscheidung,** final decision (*see* endgültige *Entscheidung)

298 **letztinstanzliche Entscheidung** (CSMW), decision of the last instance

299 **rechtskräftige Entscheidung,** decision in force/in effect; final decision, decision of/with final effect (*see* endgültige *Entscheidung, richterliche *Entscheidung, gerichtliche *Entscheidung)

300 **richterliche Entscheidung,** judicial decision

301 **eine rechtskräftige richterliche Entscheidung** (CRFF 6), a final judicial decision

302 **verbindliche Entscheidung,** binding decision

303 **... deren Entscheidung für alle Mitgliedstaaten und Organe verbindlich ist** (EEC 8), ... whose decision shall be binding upon all member states and upon the institutions

304 **vorläufige Entscheidung,** provisional decision

305 **eine Entscheidung erlassen,** to render/pronounce/give a decision

306 **Die Subkommission erläßt ihre Entscheidungen binnen 5 Monaten nach ihrer Ernennung** (GCF 9), The special commission shall render its decision within a period of 5 months from the time it is appointed

307 **eine Entscheidung, die von einer der vorgesehenen Kammern erlassen wird** (SICJ 27), a judgment given by any of the chambers provided for (*see* *Kammer)

308 **eine Entscheidung fällen,** to reach/pronounce/hand down a decision (*see* *Kammer)

309 **sich der Entscheidung fügen,** to comply with/abide by a decision

310 **einer Entscheidung nachkommen,** to comply with/abide by a decision

311 **sich nach den Entscheidungen des Gerichts richten** (PHR 53), to abide by the decision of the court

312 **eine Entscheidung verkünden,** to

pronounce/deliver a decision

313 **sich eine Entscheidung vorbehalten,** to reserve a decision

314 **... für die es sich die Entscheidung vorbehält** (ILOC 87 12), ... in respect of which it reserves its decision

315 **zur Entscheidung vorlegen,** to refer/submit for a decision

316 **Entscheidungsbefugnis,** *f.,* power of decision

317 **Entscheidungsbegründung,** *f.* (= Entscheidungsgründe, *m.pl.*), grounds of the decision/judgment, the grounds on which the decision/judgment is based (*begründen)

318 **Entscheidungsgewalt,** *f.,* power of decision

Entscheidungsgründe, *m.pl.* = *Entscheidungsbegründung, *f.*

319 **Entscheidungsinstanz,** *f.,* court, tribunal

320 **völkerrechtliche Entscheidungsinstanz,** international court/tribunal

321 **entschließen,** to resolve, to decide

322 **Entschließung,** *f.,* resolution, determination

323 **die Konferenz nahm die Entschließung zum Protokoll über ... zur Kenntnis** (PPESRO 7), the conference took note of the resolution concerning the protocol on ... (*Nichterfüllung, *Erklärung, *Unterausschuß)

324 **entschlossen,** *adj.* (= in dem Entschluß), decided, determined, having decided, resolved (*in preamble*)

325 **entschlossen, durch gemeinsames Handeln den wirtschaftlichen und sozialen Fortschritt zu sichern** (SF 49), decided to ensure the economic and social progress by common action

Entschluß *m.,* in dem = *entschlossen

326 **entschlüsseln,** to decipher/ to decode

327 **Entschlüsselung,** *f.,* deciphering/decoding

328 **entsenden,** to send

329 **Entsendestaat,** *m.,* sending state

330 **Entsendung,** f., sending
331 **Entspannung,** f., détente, relaxation of tension
332 **entstehen,** to emerge, to arise
333 **Entstehung,** f., emergence
334 **Entstehung eines Staates,** emergence of a state
335 **entwaffnen,** to disarm
336 **Entwaffnung,** f., disarmament
337 **entwerfen,** to draft, to draw up
338 **Entwurf,** m., draft, draft wording
339 **abgeänderter Entwurf,** amended draft
(See also under relevant compounds— e.g. * Vertragsentwurf.)
340 **entziehen,** to withdraw (*rights, agrément, etc.*)
entziffern = *entschlüsseln
Entzifferung, f. = *Entschlüsselung, f.
341 **Entzug,** m., withdrawal (*of rights, etc.*)
342 **Erbe,** n., heritage
(*kulturell)
343 **Erbschaft,** f., estate, succession, inheritance
344 **Erbschaftssteuer,** f., estate/succession/inheritance duty
345 **Erbschaftssteuern, die der Empfangsstaat erhebt** (VCDR 34), estate, succession or inheritance duties levied by the receiving state
346 **erfolgen,** to take place, to be effected (*Beitritt, *Kündigung, *Beschlagnahme)
347 **erforderlich,** *adj.,* necessary, required, requisite
348 **die . . ., die für . . . erforderlich ist/sind,** such . . . as may be necessary/required for . . .
349 **Erfordernis,** n., requirement, necessity
350 **grundlegende Erfordernisse** (ECSC 69), fundamental needs
351 **erforschen,** to explore
352 **Erforschung,** f., exploration (Erforschung des *Meeres, *Meeresgrund)
353 **erfüllen,** to fulfil, to implement, to perform, to discharge, to satisfy/to comply with
354 **nach Treu und Glauben erfüllen,** to fulfil in good faith

355 **einen Vertrag erfüllen,** to fulfil/implement (the terms/provisions of) a treaty
356 **Erfüllung,** f., fulfilment, implementation, performance, discharge
357 **bei der Erfüllung dieser Pflichten oder Funktionen,** in discharging these duties or functions
358 **nachträgliche Unmöglichkeit der Erfüllung** (VCLOT 61), supervening impossibility of performance
359 **ergänzen,** to supplement, to complement
360 **Ergänzung,** f., supplement, complement
361 **Ergänzungs-,** supplementary, complementary
362 **Ergänzungsabkommen,** n., supplementary agreement
363 **Ergänzungsprogramm** n. **einer Organisation,** supplementary programme of an organization
364 **ergehen,** to be entered/pronounced (*e.g. of judgment/decision*) (das *Urteil ergeht)
365 **erhalten,** to maintain, to preserve, to conserve
366 **Erhaltung,** f., maintenance, conservation, preservation
367 **Erhaltung des Friedens,** maintenance/preservation of peace (*Schätze, *Hilfsquellen)
368 **Erhaltungsmaßnahme,** f., measure of conservation (GCF 8), measure of preservation (PCP 5), conservation measure (GCF 6)
369 **international vereinbarte Erhaltungsmaßnahmen** (FC 5), internationally agreed measures of conservation
370 **erheben**[1]**,** to levy (taxes, etc.) (*Einfuhrabgabe)
371 **erheben**[2]**,** to make/to raise (an objection, etc.) (*Einspruch erheben)
372 **Erheblichkeit,** f., relevance (*e.g. of evidence*)
373 **Erhebung,** f., elevation
374 **Eine trockenfallende Erhebung ist natürlich entstandenes Land, das bei Ebbe von Wasser umgeben ist und über den Wasserspiegel hinausragt,**

jedoch bei Flut überspielt wird
(GCTS 11), A low-tide elevation is a
naturally formed area of land which is
surrounded by and above water at low
tide but submerged at high tide
(*Basislinie, *Insel)
375 erkennen, to recognize
376 Erkenntnis, f., realization, recognition
377 in der Erkenntnis, recognizing (in preamble)
378 erklären, to declare, to state
379 feierlich erklären, to solemnly declare
380 Erklärung, f., declaration, statement (sometimes used in the sense of Urkunde, instrument, as in Kündigungserklärung/Beitrittserklärung in e.g. PCP 33–37, or in durch schriftliche Erklärung, by an instrument in writing)
381 Erklärungen, Entschließungen und sonstige Stellungnahmen, declarations, resolutions or other positions
382 eine gemäß/nach diesem Artikel abgegebene Erklärung, a declaration made in accordance with/under this article
383 eine Erklärung über die persönliche Habe der Besatzung (CFIMT An), Crew's Effects Declaration
384 allgemeine Erklärung, general/universal declaration (see *Menschenrechte, and note to *allgemein)
385 anderslautende Erklärung, conflicting declaration, declaration to the contrary
386 gegenteilige Erklärung, declaration to the contrary
387 gemeinsame Erklärung, joint declaration
388 nachträgliche Erklärung, subsequent declaration
389 spätere Erklärung, subsequent declaration
390 ursprüngliche Erklärung, original declaration
391 vereinbarte Erklärung, agreed declaration, joint declaration
392 eine Erklärung abgeben, to make a declaration
393 eine Erklärung beim Generalsekretär

der UN hinterlegen, to deposit a declaration with the Secretary-General of the UN
394 Erlaubnis, f., authorization, authority, permit, permission
395 Erläuterungen, f.pl., notes, interpretative notes (e.g. in annex to a treaty)
396 erledigen, to settle (*beilegen)
397 Erledigung, f., settlement
398 freundschaftliche Erledigung eines Streitfalles, amicable settlement of a dispute
399 friedliche Erledigung eines Streitfalles, peaceful/pacific settlement of a dispute
400 gerichtliche/richterliche Erledigung, judicial settlement, settlement approved by a/the court
Erledigung des Geschäfts = *Geschäftsabwicklung, f.
(*Beilegung)
401 erleichtern, to facilitate
402 die Aufgabe der Vertreter erleichtern, to facilitate the task of the representatives
403 Erleichterung, f., facility, facilitation, easement, freer facility
404 Erleichterungen der Förmlichkeiten, facilitation of formalities
405 Erleichterung des internationalen Seeverkehrs (CFIMT Pr), facilitation of international maritime traffic
406 zur Erleichterung (+ gen.), in order to facilitate
407 Erleichterungsmaßnahme, f., measure of facilitation
408 erlöschen, to expire, to lapse, to become extinct, to terminate
409 die Rechte erlöschen, sobald ..., the rights shall lapse when ...
410 Ein Vertrag erlischt durch Erfüllung, Kündigung oder am Ende der vertraglich vereinbarten Geltungsdauer, A treaty terminates by fulfilment, by denunciation or at the end of the period of validity agreed on in the instrument/on the expiration date mutually agreed upon in the instrument
(*Gültigkeit, zwingende *Norm)

411 **Erlöschen**, *n.*, expiration, extinction, lapse, termination, cessation
412 **Das Recht des zuständigen Gerichts kann für das Erlöschen oder für die Verjährung eine Frist von nicht weniger als 3 Jahren festsetzen** (VCLD VI), The law of the competent court may establish a period of extinction or prescription of not less than 3 years
413 **zum Erlöschen bringen,** to terminate (*Schadenersatzanspruch)
Erlöschung, *f.* = *Erlöschen, *n.*
414 **Erlöschungsgrund**, *m.*, reason for termination/expiration/lapse/extinction
415 **ermächtigen,** to empower, to authorize
416 **ermächtigt,** *adj.*, authorized, empowered
417 **zur Vertretung ermächtigt,** authorized/empowered to represent
418 **zum Vertragsabschluß ermächtigt,** authorized/empowered to conclude a/the treaty
419 **Ermächtigung,** *f.*, authorization, power, authority
420 **mit Ermächtigung des Sicherheitsrates/durch den Sicherheitsrat,** with the authorization of the Security Council
421 **Ermangelung,** *f.*, **in,** in the absence of, failing, lacking
422 **in Ermangelung einer besonderen Übereinkunft** (SICJ 4), in the absence of a special agreement
423 **in Ermangelung eines solchen Verfahrens** (VCLOT 10), failing such procedure
424 **ernannt,** *adj.*, appointed, nominated
425 **ein ordnungsgemäß ernannter Delegierter,** a duly appointed delegate/a delegate duly appointed
426 **ernennen,** to appoint, to nominate
427 **im Einklang mit Regelungen ernennen, welche die Generalversammlung erläßt** (CUN 101), to appoint under regulations established by the General Assembly (*Wiederernennung)
428 **Ernennung,** *f.*, appointment, nomination

429 **Vor Ernennung eines Diplomaten ist das *Agrément* des Empfangsstaates einzuholen,** The *agrément* of the receiving state must be obtained prior to the appointment of a diplomatic agent
430 **Ordnungsmäßigkeit der Ernennung,** regularity of the appointment/nomination
431 **eine Ernennung vornehmen,** to make an appointment/a nomination
432 **Ernennungsausschuß,** *m.*, nomination(s) committee
433 **Ernennungsbefugnis,** *f.*, power of appointment/nomination
434 **Ernennungsschreiben,** *n.*, commission (*e.g. of a consul*), letter of appointment
435 **Ernennungsurkunde,** *f.*, letter/certificate of appointment
436 **erneuern,** to renew (*Vertragsdauer)
437 **Erneuerung,** *f.*, renewal
438 **errichten,** to establish, to set up
439 **Errichtung,** *f.*, establishment, setting up
440 **durch die Errichtung eines Gemeinsamen Marktes,** by establishing a Common Market
441 **Ersatzmann,** *m.* (*pl.* -leute) (CE 25), substitute
442 **erschöpfen,** to exhaust
443 **innerstaatliche Rechtsbehelfe erschöpfen,** to exhaust local remedies
444 **Erschöpfung,** *f.*, exhaustion
445 **nach Erschöpfung des innerstaatlichen Rechtsweges,** when (all) local remedies have been tried/exhausted
446 **Ersitzung,** *f.*, usucapion, acquisitive prescription
447 **erstrecken auf,** to extend to, to apply to
448 **die Geltung dieses Abkommens erstreckt sich nicht auf ...,** the present convention shall not apply to ...
449 **eine Regierung, deren Unterschrift oder Beitritt sich nicht auf alle 3 Entwürfe erstreckt ...** (ICC I), a government whose signature or accession does not apply to all 3 of the draft conventions ...

450   mit dem Ziel, dieses Übereinkommen
        auf das betreffende Hoheitsgebiet zu
        erstrecken (CFIMT XIII), in an
        endeavour to extend the present con-
        vention to that territory
        (*Verzicht auf, *Immunität, *Sou-
        veränität)
451   Erstreckung, f., extension
452   Die Erstreckung erfolgt durch eine an
        die ... Regierung gerichtete Notifi-
        zierung, Such extension shall be made
        by a notification to the ...Govern-
        ment
453   ersuchen, to request
        (*ersuchend)
454   Ersuchen, n., request
455   auf Ersuchen der Mitglieder, at the
        request of the members
456   die zu diesem Zweck erlassenen
        Ersuchen, (HgI 24), the requests for
        this purpose
457   Das Ersuchen wird schriftlich
        abgefaßt und auf dem diplomatischen
        Weg übermittelt (EExt 12), The
        request shall be in writing and shall be
        communicated through the diploma-
        tic channel
458   wird das Ersuchen an den Gouver-
        neur eines Gebietes gerichtet ...
        (EXFC V), is the requisition is made
        to the Governor of a territory ...
459   Ersuchen an die Kommission
        (ECPSD 9), invitation to the commis-
        sion
460   Ersuchen um Rechtshilfe (=*Rechts-
        hilfeersuchen, n.), letters rogatory
461   einem Ersuchen nachkommen, to
        grant a request
        (*Begehren)
462   ersuchend, adj., making the request
463   das ersuchende Land (ICCC 16), the
        country making the request
464   der ersuchende Staat (EExt 1-2), the
        requesting state
465   auf Begehren des ersuchenden
        Staates (EExt 6), at the request
        of the requesting state
466   ersucht, adj., requested, to which/
        whom the request is made/addressed
467   der ersuchte Staat, the requested
        state (EExt 1-2), the state to which
        the request is made/addressed, the

state receiving the request, the state
addressed
468   erteilen, to grant, to issue
469   Erteilung, f., issue, grant, granting
470   bis zur Erteilung der Exequatur
        (VCCR 13), pending delivery of the
        exequatur
471   erwachsen (aus), to arise (from)
472   Rechte, die aus diesem Vertrag
        erwachsen, rights arising from the
        present treaty
473   Erwägung, in der, considering, in
        consideration, whereas (in preamble)
474   erweitern, to extend, to elaborate
475   Erweiterung, f., extension, elabora-
        tion
        (*Billigung)
476   Erwerb, m., acquisition
        (*Erwerbung, Erwerb der *Staats-
        angehörigkeit)
477   erwerben, to acquire
478   (ein) Gebiet erwerben, to acquire (a)
        territory
479   Staatsangehörigkeit erwerben, to
        acquire nationality
480   Erwerberstaat, m., acquiring state,
        annexing state, successor state
481   Erwerbsgrund, m., reason for
        acquisition
        (Erwerb der *Staatsangehörigkeit)
482   Erwerbung, f., acquisition
483   territoriale Erwerbung, territorial
        acquisition
484   Anerkennung einer territorialen
        Erwerbung, recognition of a ter-
        ritorial acquisition
485   erworben, adj., acquired
486   Erzwingbarkeit, f., enforceability
487   die Erzwingbarkeit des Völkerrechts,
        the enforceability/possibility of
        enforcing international law
488   erzwingen, to enforce
489   die Beachtung einer Völker-
        rechtsregel erzwingen, to enforce the
        observance of a rule of international
        law
490   Etatismus, m., etatism
491   ethnisch, adj., ethnic(al)
492   ethnische Gruppe, ethnic group
        (See also under some *Volks- com-
        pounds — e.g. *Volkstum, *Volks-
        gruppe; and CERD 1 in Annex 12.)

493 **Etikette,** *f.*, etiquette

494 **Exekution,** *f.*, execution, enforcement

495 **die Exekution der Urteile internationaler Gerichte,** the execution of judgments/awards of/rendered by international courts (and tribunals) (*Vollstreckung)

496 **Exekutionsmaßnahme,** *f.*, execution measure, measure of execution (*Vollstreckungsmaßnahme)

497 **Exekutivausschuß,** *m.*, executive committee/board

498 **Der Exekutivausschuß ist das ausführende Organ der Organisation** (WMO 14), The executive committee is the executing body of the organization

499 **Exekutive,** *f.*, executive, executive power (*vollziehende Gewalt)

500 **Exekutivorgan,** *n.*, executive body/agency

501 **Exekutivrat,** *m.*, executive council, executive board

502 **Exekutivsekretär,** *m.*, executive secretary

503 **Exequatur,** *n.*, exequatur

504 **Der Leiter einer konsularischen Vertretung kann sein Amt nicht antreten, bevor ihm das Exequatur erteilt worden ist** (VCCR 12), The head of a consular post shall not enter upon his duties until he has received an exequatur

505 **das Exequatur einholen,** to receive/be granted the exequatur

506 **das Exequatur erteilen,** to issue/grant the exequatur

507 **das Exequatur verweigern,** to refuse (to grant) the exequatur

508 **Das Exequatur kann ohne Angabe von Gründen verweigert werden,** No reasons need be given for refusing (to grant) the exequatur

509 **das Exequatur zurückziehen,** to withdraw the exequatur

510 **Exil,** *n.*, exile

511 **Exilregierung,** *f.*, government in exile

512 **Exklave,** *f.*, exclave

513 **Experte,** *m.*, expert (*Sachverständiger *and* *Sachverständigen- *compounds*)

514 **exterritorial,** *adj.*, exterritorial

515 **Exterritorialität,** *f.*, exterritoriality

F

1 **Fachausschuß**, *m.*, technical committee, specialized committee

2 **Fachgruppe**, *f.*, specialized group (SF 39), technical group

3 **Fachkommission**, *f.*, technical commission (*e.g.* WMO), functional commission (SF 31), specialized commission

4 **fachlich**, *adj.*, technical

5 **fachliche Organisation**, technical organization

6 **Fachorganisation**, *f.*, technical organization

7 **Fachorganisation der UN** (IMCO 3), specialized agency of the UN

8 **Fachpersonal**, *n.*, technical staff

9 **Fachvorschriften**, *f.pl.*, technical regulations

10 **Fahnenflucht**, *f.*, desertion

11 **fahren**, to drive, to travel, to sail

12 **Unterseeboote haben ... über Wasser zu fahren** (GCTS 14), Submarines are required to navigate on the surface

13 **Schiffe unter seiner Flagge auf Hoher See fahren lassen** (GCHS 4), to sail ships under its flag on the high seas

14 **Fahrgast**, *m.*, passenger

15 **sich ein- oder ausschiffende Fahrgäste** (CFIMT An), embarking or disembarking passengers

16 **Fahrgastdokument**, *n.* (CFIMT), passenger document

17 **Fahrgastliste**, *f.* (CFIMT), passenger list

18 **fahrlässig**, *adj.*, careless, reckless, negligent (*vorsätzlich)

19 **Fahrlässigkeit**, *f.*, negligence

20 **wiederholte Fahrlässigkeit** (CFIMT), recurrent carelessness

21 **fakultativ**, *adj.*, optional

22 **Fakultativklausel**, *f.*, optional clause

23 **Fakultativprotokoll**, *n.*, optional protocol

24 **Fall**, *m.*, case (*Sache², *Angelegenheit²)

25 **fällen**, to pronounce/hand down (*a* judgment, *etc.*)

26 **fällig**, *adj.*, due, overdue

27 **eine fällige Zahlung**, a payment due

28 **Fallrecht**, *n.*, case law

29 **Fallsammlung**, *f.*, case-book

30 **Falschmünzerei**, *f.*, counterfeiting (currency)

31 **Familienrecht**, *n.*, family law

32 **Familienrechte**, *n.pl.*, family rights

33 **Familienzugehörigkeit**, *f.*, parentage

34 **Eintragung der Familienzugehörigkeit**, registration of parentage

35 **Fang**, *m.*, catch, fishing (*Fisch)

36 **Fanggebiet**, *n.* (GCF/FC), fishing grounds

37 **Fangmethode**, *f.* (GCF), method of fishing

38 **Fangperiode**, *f.* (GCF), (fishing) season

39 **fassen**, to word, to draft

40 **Fassung**, *f.*, wording, draft, form, version, text

41 **Geänderte Fassung vom 18.12.59. Der ursprüngliche Text lautete:** Revised wording of 18.12.59. The original text read: (*Wortlaut, *Text)

42 **feierlich**, *adj.*, solemn

43 **die Parteien erklären feierlich ...**, the parties solemnly declare ...

44 **sich feierlich verpflichten ...**, to undertake solemnly ...

45 **Feind**, *m.*, enemy

46 **Feindbestimmung**, *f.*, enemy/hostile destination

47 **die Beschlagnahme von Gütern mit Feindbestimmung**, the seizure of goods of hostile destination

48 **Feindeshand**, *f.*, enemy hands

49 **in Feindeshand geraten**, to fall into enemy hands

50 **feindlich**, *adj.*, enemy, hostile

51 **feindlicher Agent**, enemy agent

52 **feindlicher Ausländer**, enemy alien

53 **feindliche Bestimmung** (= *Feindbestimmung, *f.*), enemy/hostile destination

54   **feindliche Beziehungen,** hostile relations
55   **feindlicher Charakter,** hostile character/status/nature
56   **feindliches Eigentum,** enemy property
57   **feindliches Gebiet,** enemy territory
58   **feindliche Güter,** enemy goods
59   **feindliche Kombattanten,** hostile belligerents
60   **feindliche Kriegführende,** hostile belligerents
61   **feindliche Nationalität,** enemy nationality
62   **feindliche Person,** enemy person
63   **feindliches Privateigentum,** private enemy property
64   **feindliches Schiff,** enemy ship/vessel
65   **feindlicher Staat,** enemy/hostile state
66   **feindlicher Staatsangehöriger,** enemy national
67   **feindliches Staatseigentum,** public enemy property
68   **feindlicher Status,** enemy status/character
69   **feindliche Unterstützung,** unneutral service (*see* *neutralitätswidrig)
70   **feindliches Vermögen,** enemy property
71   **Feindseligkeit,** *f.,* hostility, hostile action
72   **Personen, die nicht unmittelbar an den Feindseligkeiten teilnehmen** (GCI 3), persons taking no active part in the hostilities
73   **Aussetzung der Feindseligkeiten,** suspension of hostilities
74   **Beendigung der Feindseligkeiten,** end of hostilities
75   **Beginn der Feindseligkeiten,** commencement of hostilities
76   **Einstellung der Feindseligkeiten,** cessation of hostilities
77   **Eröffnung der Feindseligkeiten,** opening of hostilities, outbreak of hostilities
78   **Feindstaat,** *m.,* enemy/hostile state
79   **Feindvermögen,** *n.,* enemy property
80   **Feldgeistlicher,** *adj.n.,* chaplain
81   **die den Streitkräften zugeteilten Feldgeistlichen** (GC I), chaplains attached to the armed forces

(*Seelsorgepersonal)
82   **Fernblockade,** *f.,* long-distance blockade
83   **Festlandsockel,** *m.* (= Kontinentalsockel, *m.*), continental shelf
84   **Im Sinne dieser Artikel bezeichnet der Ausdruck ,,Festlandsockel'' (a) den Meeresgrund und den Meeresuntergrund der an der Küste grenzenden Unterwasserzonen außerhalb des Küstenmeeres bis zu einer Tiefe von 200 m oder darüber hinaus, soweit die Tiefe des darüber befindlichen Wassers die Ausbeutung der Naturschätze gestattet; (b) den Meeresgrund und den Meeresuntergrund der entsprechenden an die Küste von Inseln grenzenden Unterwasserzonen** (GCC), For the purpose of these Articles the term "continental shelf" is used as referring (a) to the seabed and subsoil of the submarine areas adjacent to the coast but outside the area of the territorial sea, to a depth of 200 metres or, beyond that limit, to where the depth of the superjacent waters admits of the exploration of the natural resources of the said areas; (b) to the seabed and subsoil of similar submarine areas adjacent to the coasts of islands
85   **Festnahme,** *f.,* arrest
86   **ordnungsgemäße Festnahme** (PHR 2), lawful arrest
87   **Feuerpause,** *f.,* suspension of fire
88   **Fiktion,** *f.,* (legal) fiction
89   **Dies mag in der Praxis zu unrealistischen Resultaten führen, so z.B. als die USA bis 1933 die Fiktion aufrechterhielten, die Regierung Kerenski sei die Regierung Rußlands,** In practice this may lead to unrealistic consequences: for example, until 1933 the USA maintained the fiction that the Kerenski Government was the Government of Russia
(*fingieren)
90   **fingieren,** to maintain a fiction, to assume, to deem
91   **Es wird fingiert, daß in der Person des Geschädigten dessen Heimatstaat**

geschädigt wurde, The fiction is maintained that/It is deemed that in the person suffering injury, the state of which this person is a national has been injured
(* Fiktion)

92 **Fisch**, *m.*, fish

93 **den Fang eines oder mehrerer Bestände an Fischen betreiben** (GCF 3), to engage in fishing any stock or stocks of fish

94 **Fischbestand**, *m.*, stock of fish

95 **Erhaltung der Fischbestände des Nordwestatlantischen Ozeans** (CNAF Pr), Conservation of the fishery resources of the North West Atlantic Ocean

96 **fischen**, to fish

97 **gewohnheitsmäßig fischen**, to fish habitually

98 **die Fischer anderer Vertragsparteien, die gewohnheitsmäßig in der in Art. 2 bezeichneten Zone gefischt haben,** ... (FC 9), fishermen of other contracting parties who have habitually fished in the belt provided for in Art. 2 . . .

99 **das Recht zu fischen** (= Fischereirecht, *n.*), the right to fish

100 **Der Küstenstaat hat innerhalb der von der Basislinie seines Küstenmeeres aus gemessenen Sechsmeilenzone das ausschließliche Recht zu fischen** (FC 2), The coastal state has the exclusive right to fish ... within the belt of 6 miles measured from the baseline of its territorial sea

101 **Fischer**, *m.*, fisherman
(* fischen)

102 **Fischerei**, *f.*, fishery, fisheries, fishing

103 **die Erhaltung der Fischerei** (CNAF), conservation of fisheries

104 **eine dauerhafte Regelung über die Fischerei** (FC Pr), a régime of fisheries of a permanent character (*see* * Fischereiregelung)

105 **Vorschriften über die Fischerei erlassen** (FC), to regulate the fisheries

106 **Fischerei betreiben,** to be engaged in/to engage in/to carry on fishing

107 **Alle Staaten können für ihre Staatsangehörigen das Recht in Anspruch nehmen, Fischerei auf hoher See zu betreiben** (GCF 1), All states have the right for their nationals to engage in fishing on the high seas

108 **gewohnheitsmäßig betriebene Fischerei,** habitual fishing

109 **das Recht zu fischen auf Grund gewohnheitsmäßig betriebener Fischerei** (FC 8), the right to fish by virtue of habitual fishing

110 **Fischereiabkommen**, *n.*, fishing/fisheries agreement (*see note to* *Vertrag *in Annex* 1)

111 **Fischereiangelegenheiten**, *f.pl.*, fishery matters/cases

112 **die ausschließliche Hoheitsgewalt in Fischereiangelegenheiten** (FC 2), exclusive jurisdiction in matters of fisheries

113 **Fischereiboot**, *n.*, fishing boat/craft/vessel

114 **Fischereifahrzeug**, *n.* (GCF), fishing boat/craft/vessel

115 **Der Ausdruck ,,Fischereifahrzeug" bezeichnet ein Fahrzeug, das für den Fang von Fischen, Walen, Seehunden, Walrossen oder anderen Lebewesen des Meeres verwendet wird** (CSLS Reg 2), A fishing vessel is a vessel used for catching fish, whales, seals, walrus or other living resources of the sea

116 **Fischereikonvention**, *f.*, fisheries convention, fishing convention (*see note to* *Vertrag *in Annex* 1)

117 **Fischereirecht**, *n.* (= Recht *n.* zu *fischen), fishing/fishery right, the right to fish

118 **Ausdehnung der Fischereirechte auf 200 Seemeilen,** extension of (coastal) fishing rights to 200 nautical miles

119 **Fischereiregelung**, *f.*, fishery régime, regulation of fisheries

120 **Jede Vertragspartei erkennt das Recht jeder anderen Vertragspartei an, die in den Art. 2 bis 6 bezeichnete Fischereiregelung einzuführen** (FC 1), Each contracting party recognizes the right of any other contracting

party to establish the fishery régime described in Art. 2 to 6

121 **Fischfang**, *m*., fishing, fishery

122 **Fremde Schiffe haben kein Recht auf Fischfang**, Foreign vessels have no fishery rights

123 **Fischfang in den Küstengewässern**, fishing (with)in the maritime belt

124 **fiskalisch**, *adj*., fiscal

125 **fiskalische Abgaben** (EFTA), fiscal charges

126 **Fiskalzoll**, *m*., revenue duty

127 **Fiskalzölle und interne Steuern** (EFTA 6), revenue duties and internal taxation

128 **Flagge**, *f*., flag

129 **Ein Schiff darf seine Flagge während der Fahrt nicht wechseln**, A ship may not change its flag during a voyage

130 **auf dem Missionsgebäude Flagge und Wappen zeigen**, to use the flag and emblem on the premises of the mission

131 **ein unter deutscher Flagge fahrendes Schiff**, a ship sailing under German flag

132 **eine Flagge führen**, to fly a flag (* Hoheitszeichen, * Wappen)

133 **Flaggenführung**, *f*., flying the flag

134 **das Recht der Flaggenführung**, the right to use the flag

135 **die Verpflichtung der Schiffe zur Flaggenführung**, the obligation of ships to fly their flag

136 **Flaggenmißbrauch**, *m*., misuse of the flag

137 **Flaggenstaat**, *m*., flag state

138 **Flaggenwechsel**, *m*., change/transfer of flag

139 **Flottenabkommen**, *n*., naval agreement

140 **Flottenvertrag**, *m*., naval treaty

141 **Flüchtling**, *m*., refugee

142 **Hoher Kommissar der UN für Flüchtlinge**, UN High Commissioner for Refugees

143 **das Land, in welches der Flüchtling sich zu begeben wünscht** (TD Ref 10), the country to which the refugee desires to proceed

144 **Personal- und Reiseausweis für Flüchtlinge**, identity and travel document for refugees

145 **nationale Flüchtlinge** (AACER), national refugees

146 **politische Flüchtlinge**, political refugees

147 **Flüchtlingsfrage**, *f*., refugee problem

148 **Flüchtlingshilfe**, *f*., assistance to refugees, refugee aid

149 **Flüchtlingskategorie**, *f*., category of refugees

150 **Flüchtlingsproblem**, *n*., refugee problem

151 **Flüchtlingsseemann**, *m*. (*pl.* -leute), refugee seaman

152 **Flugfreiheit**, *f*., freedom to fly in/over/through, liberty of passage

153 **Fluß**, *m*., river

154 **internationaler Fluß**, international river

155 **internationalisierter Fluß**, internationalized river

156 **schiffbarer Fluß**, navigable river

157 **Flußgrenze**, *f*., river frontier/border/boundary

158 **Folge**, *f*., **in der**, subsequently, in due course, thereafter

159 **oder in der Folge** (PHR Prot 4), or at any time thereafter

160 **folgenden, im**, below, hereinafter

161 **im folgenden als ... bezeichnet**, hereinafter called ...

162 **Folgezeit**, *f*., **in der**, subsequently

163 **in der Folgezeit ratifizieren**, to ratify subsequently

164 **Folterung**, *f*., torture

165 **körperliche (oder) seelische Folterungen** (GC III), physical (or) mental torture

166 **Fonds**, *m*., fund

167 **fördern**, to promote, to facilitate, to encourage, to further

168 **eine engere Zusammenarbeit der Völker fördern**, to encourage a closer cooperation between peoples

169 **Form**, *f*., form

170 **in (guter und) gehöriger/ordnungsgemäßer Form befunden**, found in (good and) due/proper form

171 **formgerecht**, *adj*., formal, in due/proper form

172 **förmlich**, *adj*., formal

173 **Förmlichkeit**, *f.*, formality
     (*Vereinheitlichung)
174 **Forum**, *n.*, forum
175 **ein Forum für Erörterung und Infor-
     mationsaustausch** (ECE II), a forum
     for discussion and the exchange of
     information
176 **Fracht**, *f.*, cargo, freight
177 **Frachterklärung**, *f.*, cargo declara-
     tion
178 **Frachtschiff**, *n.*, cargo ship
179 **Frage**, *f.*, question, problem, matter
180 **jede vor den Sicherheitsrat gebrachte
     Frage** (CUN 31), any question
     brought before the Security Council
181 **frei¹**, *adj.*, free
     *(Many of the expressions below are
     from instruments dealing with human
     right and fundamental freedoms —
     e.g. CERD, PHR, UDHR, ES. For
     further examples, see under *Recht
     auf, *Freiheit, *Anspruch auf, and
     Art. 5 CERD in Annex 9.)*
182 **den Parteien steht es frei ...**, the
     parties shall be free to ...
183 **Alle Menschen sind frei und gleich an
     Würde und Rechten geboren** (UDHR
     1), All human beings are born free
     and equal in dignity and rights
184 **freier Austausch von Gedanken und
     Erkenntnissen** (UNESCO), free
     exchange of ideas and knowledge
185 **freie Berufswahl** (UDHR), free
     choice of employment
186 **freie Bewegung der Arbeitnehmer**
     (CFW), free movement of workers
187 **freie Fahrt im Luftraum**, freedom of
     passage through the air
188 **freier Gedankenaustausch durch
     Wort und Bild** (UNESCO), free flow
     of ideas by word and image
189 **freie Meinungsäußerung**, freedom of
     (opinion and) expression
190 **freier Personen-, Dienstleistungs- und
     Kapitalverkehr** (EEC 3), freedom
     of movement for persons, services
     and capital
191 **freie Religionsausübung**, freedom of
     worship, free practice of religion
192 **frei Schiff frei Gut**, the flag covers the
     goods
193 **freie Waren**, free goods/articles *(in

     contrast to* contraband goods)
194 **frei²**, *adj.*, vacant
195 **freier Sitz/freie Stelle**, vacancy
196 **Freibeuter**, *m.*, privateer
197 **Freigüter**, *n.pl.*, free goods/articles
     (in contrast to contraband goods)
198 **Freihafen**, *m.*, free port
199 **Freihandelszone**, *f.*, free trade area
200 **Freiheit**, *f.*, freedom, liberty
     *(Many of the freedoms listed below
     are part of the extensive list of Hu-
     man Rights and Fundamental Free-
     doms from e.g. CERD, PHR, ES,
     UDHR. For additional expressions
     and expressions formulated in other
     ways, see under *frei, *Recht auf,
     *Anspruch auf, and under the perti-
     nent compound, also Art. 5 CERD
     in Annex 9.)*
201 **die Grundlage von Freiheit, Gerech-
     tigkeit und Frieden in der Welt**
     (ICCPR Pr), the foundation of free-
     dom, justice and peace in the world
202 **in der Erwägung, daß die Freiheit das
     angeborene Recht jedes Menschen ist**
     (SCS Pr), considering that freedom is
     the birthright of every human being
203 **das Fünf-Freiheiten-Abkommen**, the
     Five Freedoms Document
204 **das Zwei-Freiheiten-Abkommen**, the
     Two Freedoms Document
205 **Freiheit des Durchgangsverkehrs**
     (CSFT), freedom of transit
206 **Freiheit zum Empfang und zur Mit-
     teilung von Nachrichten** (PMR 10),
     freedom to receive and impart in-
     formation
207 **Freiheit der Fischerei**, freedom of
     fishing
208 **Freiheit des Gedankens** (= Gedan-
     kenfreiheit, *f.*,*Meinungsfreiheit,
     f.), freedom of thought/opinion
209 **Freiheit der Hohen See**, freedom of
     the high seas/open sea
210 **Freiheit des Luftraumes**, freedom of
     the air
211 **Freiheit der Meere**, freedom of the
     (high) seas/open sea
212 **Freiheit der Meinung** (=
     Meinungsfreiheit, *f.*), freedom to
     hold opinions (PHR 10), freedom of
     thought/opinion

213 **Freiheit der Meinungsäußerung,** freedom of expression

214 **Freiheit der Schiffahrt,** freedom of navigation

215 **Freiheit im Schriftwechsel** (GC III), freedom to correspond

216 **Freiheit von Sklaverei und Dienstbarkeit,** freedom from slavery and servitude (*see* *Leibeigenschaft)

217 **Freiheit der Vereinigung** (= Vereinigungsfreiheit, *f.*), freedom of association

218 **Freiheit der Verkehrswege** (CSFT), freedom of communications

219 **Freiheit von willkürlicher Verhaftung und Haft,** freedom from arbitrary arrest and detention

220 **Freiheit des Wortes** (= Redefreiheit, *f.*), freedom of speech

221 **um den Vertretern im Ministerkomitee volle Freiheit des Wortes . . . zu gewährleisten** (PrivExCE 10), to secure for the representatives at the Committee of Ministers complete freedom of speech

222 **persönliche Freiheit,** individual liberty/freedom

223 **Wahrung der persönlichen Freiheit,** preservation of individual liberty

224 **Freiheit ausüben,** to exercise liberty/freedom

225 **Freiheit entziehen,** to withdraw/deprive of liberty/freedom

226 **Niemandem darf die Freiheit allein deshalb entzogen werden, weil er nicht in der Lage ist, eine vertragliche Verpflichtung zu erfüllen** (PHR Prot 4), No one shall be deprived of his liberty merely on the ground of inability to fulfil a contractual obligation

227 **Freiheit gewähren,** to grant/ensure freedom

228 **Freiheit gewährleisten,** to secure/ensure freedom

229 **freilassen,** to release

230 **auf Ehrenwort oder Versprechen freigelassen** (GC III), released on parole or promise

231 **Freilassung,** *f.*, release

232 **Freistaat,** *m.*, free state

233 **freistehen** (+ *dat. of pers.*), to be at liberty to, to be free to

234 **Jeder Vertragspartei steht es frei, das vorliegende Abkommen zu kündigen** (GC I 63), Each of the contracting parties shall be at liberty to denounce the present convention

235 **Freiwerden** *n.* **einer Stelle,** (occurrence of a) vacancy

236 **nach späterem Freiwerden der Stelle** (EONR VI), on the occurrence of a subsequent vacancy

237 **Freiwilligenkorps,** *n.*, volunteer corps

238 **Freizügigkeit,** *f.*, free movement, freedom of movement

239 **Freizügigkeit der Arbeitnehmer** (EEC), freedom of movement for workers

240 **freier Waren- und Kapitalverkehr und Freizügigkeit der Personen** (EEC 60), freedom of movement for goods, capital and persons

241 **Fremdenrecht,** *n.*, law(s) relating to/governing aliens

242 **Unter Fremden- oder Ausländerrecht ist die Gesamtheit der Rechtsvorschriften zu verstehen, die die Rechtsstellung dieser Personen in einem fremden Staat regeln,** The law relating to aliens signifies the sum of laws and regulations that regulate the legal position/status of these persons in a foreign state

243 **das völkerrechtliche Fremdenrecht,** international rules/laws relating to/governing aliens

244 **Fremder,** *adj.n.*, alien

245 **Fremder ist jede Person, die sich auf dem Gebiet eines Staates aufhält, dessen Staatsangehörigkeit sie nicht besitzt,** An alien is any person residing in the territory of a state the nationality of which that person does not possess

246 **Freundschaft,** *f.*, friendship

247 **Freundschaft und Verständnis zwischen den Staaten und Völkern der Welt wecken und erhalten** (CAC Pr), to help create and preserve friendship and understanding among the nations and peoples of the world

248 **Freundschaftsabkommen,** *n.*, agreement of friendship (*see note to* *Vertrag in Annex* 1)
249 **Freundschaftsvertrag,** *m.*, treaty of friendship (*see note to* *Vertrag in Annex* 1)
250 **Frieden,** *m.*, peace
251   **Aufrechterhaltung des Friedens,** maintenance of peace
252   **Aufrechterhaltung des Friedens und der internationalen Sicherheit,** maintenance of peace and of international security
253   **Bedrohung des Friedens** (CUN 39), threat to the peace
254   **Bruch des Friedens** (CUN 39), breach of the peace
255   **Maßnahmen bei Bedrohung oder Bruch des Friedens oder bei Angriffshandlungen** (CUN Ch. VII), action with respect to threats to the peace, breaches of the peace, or acts of aggression
256   **Festigung des Friedens,** strengthening/consolidation of peace
257   **Friede der Mission** (VCDR), peace of the mission
258   **ein auf Gerechtigkeit beruhender Frieden** (ECPSD Pr), a peace based upon justice
259   **bewaffneter Frieden,** armed peace
260   **dauerhafter Frieden,** enduring/lasting peace
261   **internationaler Frieden,** international peace
262   **Erhaltung des internationalen Friedens und der internationalen Sicherheit** (GATT), maintenance of international peace and security
263   **den Frieden aufrechterhalten,** to maintain peace
264   **den Frieden erhalten,** to maintain peace
265   **den Frieden festigen,** to consolidate peace
266   **den Frieden gefährden,** to endanger/be a threat to peace
267   **den Frieden schließen,** to conclude peace
268   **den Frieden wiederherstellen,** to restore peace

(*Weltfrieden)
269 **Friedensbedrohung,** *f.*, threat to the peace
270 **Friedensbemühungen,** *f.pl.*, efforts to achieve/maintain peace
271 **Friedensbeobachter,** *m.*, peace observer
272 **Friedensbeobachterkommission,** *f.*, peace observation/observer commission
273 **Friedensblockade,** *f.*, peacetime blockade
274 **Friedensbruch,** *m.*, breach of the peace
275 **friedenserhaltend,** *adj. & adv.*, in the maintenance of peace, maintaining peace
276   **friedenserhaltend eingreifen,** to intervene in the interests of the preservation/maintenance of peace
277 **friedensgefährdend,** *adj.*, endangering/likely to endanger peace
278 **Friedenskonferenz,** *f.*, peace conference
279 **Friedensoffensive,** *f.*, peace offensive
280 **Friedensregelung,** *f.*, peace settlement
281 **Friedensschluß,** *m.*, conclusion of peace
282   **beim Friedensschluß,** when peace is concluded
283 **friedensstörend,** *adj.*, disruptive of (the) peace, prejudicial to peace
284 **Friedensverhandlungen,** *f.pl.*, peace negotiations
285 **Friedensvertrag,** *m.*, peace treaty (*see note to* *Vertrag in Annex* 1)
286 **friedensvertraglich,** *adj.*, by peace treaty
287   **friedensvertragliche Regelung,** settlement by peace treaty
288 **Friedenswille,** *m.*, desire/will for peace
289 **Friedenszeit,** *f.*, peacetime
290   **in Friedenszeiten,** in time of peace, in peacetime
291 **Friedenszustand,** *m.*, state of peace
292 **friedlich,** *adj.*, pacific, peaceful, by pacific/peaceful means
293   **friedliche Beilegung,** pacific settlement

294 **friedliche Blockade,** pacific blockade
295 **friedliche Durchfahrt,** innocent passage
296 **Kriegs- und Handelsschiffen fremder Staaten muß der Küstenstaat das Recht der friedlichen Durchfahrt zugestehen,** The littoral state must grant foreign warships and merchant vessels the right of innocent passage
297 **friedliche Durchdringung,** peaceful penetration
298 **friedliche Koexistenz,** peaceful coexistence
299 **friedliche Mittel,** pacific means
300 **friedliche Mittel zur Beilegung eines Streits,** pacific means for the settlement of/for settling a dispute
301 **friedliche Ordnung,** (i) pacific adjustment/settlement; (ii) peaceful state/order of things
302 **friedliche Regelung,** pacific regulation/settlement
303 **friedliches und geordnetes Verfahren,** peaceful and orderly process/procedure
304 **auf friedlichem Wege,** by pacific means
305 **friedliche Zusammenarbeit,** peaceful cooperation
306 **friedliches Zusammenleben,** peaceful coexistence, peaceful relations
307 **friedliche Zwecke,** peaceful purposes (*Atomenergie, *Kernenergie)
308 **friedliebend,** *adj.*, peace-loving
309 **friedliebende Staaten/Völker,** peace-loving states/peoples
310 **Frist,** *f.*, period, notice, time limit
311 **innerhalb der oben hierfür vorgeschriebenen Frist** (VCLOT An), within the period described above
312 **Ablauf einer Frist,** expiry/expiration of a period/time limit
313 **vor Ablauf der genannten Frist von 10 Jahren,** prior to the expiry of the aforesaid period of 10 years

314 **einen Vertrag vor Ablauf der laufenden Frist kündigen,** to denounce a treaty before the expiry/expiration of the current period (*Kündigungsfrist, *wirksam)
315 **früher,** *adj.*, prior, previous, earlier (*law, treaty, rule, etc.*)
316 **Frühere Vereinbarungen werden dadurch nicht beeinträchtigt,** This shall not prejudice earlier agreements
317 **Führung** *f.* **des Verfahrens** (SICJ 48), conduct of the case (*Verfügung[1])
318 **Funkaufklärung,** *f.*, radio reconnaissance
319 **Funktion,** *f.*, function
320 **Ausübung/Wahrnehmung der Funktionen,** exercise/performance of functions
321 **die ihnen zugewiesenen Funktionen,** the functions assigned to them, such functions as may be assigned to them
322 **internationale Funktionen,** international functions (*see* *Depositar)
323 **Funktionen ausüben,** to exercise/perform functions
324 **Funktionen erfüllen,** to fulfil/discharge functions
325 **Funktionen wahrnehmen,** to exercise/perform functions (*Aufgabe, *Tätigkeit[1])
326 **Funkverbindung,** *f.*, wireless communication, radio contact
327 **missionseigene Funkverbindung,** wireless communication(s) under the control of the mission, wireless transmitter owned and operated by the mission
328 **Eine missionseigene Funkverbindung darf nur mit Zustimmung des Empfangsstaates errichtet werden,** The mission may install and use its own wireless transmitter only with the consent of the receiving state

G

1 **Gaskrieg,** *m.,* gas warfare
2 **Gebiet¹,** *n.,* region (*i.e. in a purely geographical sense, in contrast to* **Gebiet³** *below*)
3 **das Überfliegen bestimmter Gebiete in seinem Hoheitsgebiet** (CAC), the flying over certain regions of its territory
4 **... indem sie den Abstand zwischen einzelnen Gebieten und den Rückstand weniger begünstigter Gebiete verringern** (EEC Pr), ... by reducing the differences existing between the various regions and the backwardness of the less favoured regions
5 **Gebiet²,** *n.,* field (**internationale** *Zusammenarbeit)
6 **Gebiet³,** *n.,* territory, area of jurisdiction, area over which sovereignty is exercised (*see also* *Hoheitsgebiet)
7 **Als Gebiet eines Staates gelten die der Staatshoheit, der Oberhoheit, dem Schutz oder der Mandatsgewalt dieses Staates unterstehenden Landgebiete und angrenzenden Hoheitsgewässer** (CAC 2), The territory of a state shall be deemed to be the land areas and territorial waters adjacent thereto under the sovereignty, suzerainty, protection or mandate of such state
8 **die außerhalb des Mutterlandes gelegenen Gebiete, deren internationalen Beziehungen sie wahrnehmen, einschließlich aller Gebiete, deren Verwaltung ihnen als Treuhändern übertragen ist** (ILO 35), the non-metropolitan territories for whose international relations they are responsible, including any trust territories for which they are the administering authority
9 **Gebiete, die sich nicht selbst regieren,** non-self-governing territories
10 **nicht unter Selbstregierung stehende Gebiete** (SCS 12), non-self-governing territories
11 **Gebiete, deren Völker noch nicht die volle Selbstregierung erreicht haben,** territories whose peoples have not yet attained a full measure of self-government
12 **seinem Schutz unterstehende/unterstellte Gebiete,** territories placed under its protection
13 **unter Treuhandschaft gestellte Gebiete,** trusteeship territories
14 **die Unantastbarkeit/Unversehrtheit des Gebietes,** territorial integrity
15 **Aufenthalt in einem Gebiet,** residence in a territory
16 **Durchreise durch ein Gebiet,** transit through a territory
17 **Niederlassung in einem Gebiet,** establishment in a territory
18 **Zulassung zu einem Gebiet,** admission to a territory
19 **autonomes Gebiet,** autonomous/self-governing territory
20 **besetztes Gebiet,** occupied territory
21 **feindliches Gebiet,** enemy territory
22 **herrenloses Gebiet,** *terra nullius, territorium nullius*
23 **neutrales Gebiet,** neutral territory
24 **nichtautonomes Gebiet,** non-self-governing territory
25 **treuhänderisch verwaltetes Gebiet** (SCS 12), trust territory
26 **überseeisches Gebiet,** overseas territory
27 **Gebiet abtreten,** to cede territory
28 **Gebiet beanspruchen,** to claim territory
29 **Gebiet einverleiben,** to annex/to incorporate territory
30 **Gebiet erwerben,** to acquire territory
31 **Gebiet räumen,** to evacuate territory
32 **Gebietsabtretung,** *f.,* cession of territory
33 **Gebietsanspruch,** *m.,* territorial claim
34 **Sie erklären, daß sie keine Gebietsansprüche gegen irgend jemand haben und solche in Zukunft auch nicht erheben werden,** They declare that they have no territorial claims against anyone and shall not make any such claims in the future

35 **Gebietsaustausch**, *m.*, exchange of territory

36 **Gebietseinheit**, *f.* (CSMW), territorial entity

37 **Gebietseinverleibung**, *f.*, territorial annexation/incorporation

38 **Gebietserwerb**, *m.*, territorial acquisition

39 **Gebietserwerber**, *m.*, acquiring state/party, the state/party acquiring territory

40 **Gebietsherrschaft**, *f.*, territorial sovereignty

41 **Gebietshoheit**, *f.*, sovereignty, territorial sovereignty, sovereign rights exercisable by states

42 **ausschließliche Gebietshoheit,** exclusive (territorial) sovereignty

43 **Gebietskörperschaft**, *f.*, territorial (sub)division, territorial corporation

44 **die Vertragsparteien oder deren Gebietskörperschaften wie Staaten oder Republiken** (VCLD VII), the contracting parties or any of their constituent subdivisions such as states or republics

45 **Gebietsstand**, *m.* (ECPSD 35), territorial status

46 **Gebietsveränderung**, *f.*, territorial change, change in/of (the extent/size of) territory

47 **gewaltsame Gebietsveränderung,** change of territory brought about by (use of) (armed/military) force

48 **Gebietsverlust**, *m.*, loss of territory

49 **Gebrauch**, *m.*, custom

50 **die Gebräuche des Krieges,** the customs of war

51 **Gebühr**, *f.*, fee

52 **über Gebühr,** undue, excessive (*Rechtsbehelf²)

53 **gebunden,** *adj.*, bound

54 **Die Vertragsparteien bleiben in ihren gegenseitigen Beziehungen durch das Abkommen gebunden** (GC IV 2), The powers party to the convention shall remain bound by it in their mutual relations

55 **Gedankenfreiheit**, *f.* (CERD/UDHR), freedom of thought

56 **geeignet,** *adj.*, suitable, appropriate

57 **alle geeigneten Maßnahmen,** all appropriate action/measures

58 **Maßnahmen, die geeignet sind, ... zu machen,** action/measures appropriate for ... (-ing) (*in a pejorative sense:* measures calculated to ...)

59 **gefährden,** to endanger, to jeopardize, to prejudice, to be detrimental to

60 **die innere und äußere finanzielle Stabilität der Mitgliedstaaten gefährden** (EEC 6), to prejudice the internal and external financial stability of the member states

61 **den Frieden/Weltfrieden gefährden,** to endanger peace/international peace

62 **Gefährdung,** *f.*, endangering, jeopardizing

63 **Gefährdung der öffentlichen Ordnung,** endangering of public order

64 **Gefährdung der Staatssicherheit,** endangering of national security

65 **Gefallenenliste,** *f.*, list of the dead

66 **Gefallener,** *adj.n.*, dead/fallen (person), person killed in action/on active duty

67 **geborgene Gefallene** (GC I), dead persons found

68 **die Gefallenen ausplündern** (GC I), to despoil the dead

69 **die Gefallenen bergen** (GC I), to find/collect the dead

70 **gefangenhalten,** to detain, to imprison

71 **Gefangenhaltung,** *f.*, detention, imprisonment

72 **Gefangenhaltungsort,** *m.* (GC), place of detention/imprisonment

73 **Gefangennahme,** *f.*, capture, detention

74 **gefangennehmen,** to capture, to take prisoner

75 **die gefangennehmende Macht** (GC I), the capturing power

76 **Gefangenschaft,** *f.*, detention, captivity

77 **Gefangenschaftsbedingungen,** *f. pl.* (GC III), conditions of captivity

78 **Gefangenschaftskarte,** *f.*, capture card

79 **gegeben in (der Stadt ...),** done at (the city of ...) (*geschehen zu)

80 **Gegenpartei**, *f.*, the other party (to the dispute), the opposite/opposing party, the adverse party (GC I)
81 **Geht der Antrag nur von einer Partei aus, so hat diese ihn unverzüglich der Gegenpartei zu notifizieren** (ECPSD 9), If the application emanates from only one of the parties, the other party shall, without delay, be notified of it by that party
82 **Gegenrepressalie**, *f.*, counter-reprisal
83 **zu Gegenrepressalien greifen**, to resort to counter-reprisals
84 **Gegenschrift**, *f.*, counter-memorial (*Klagebeantwortung)
85 **Gegenschriftsatz**, *m.*, counter-case
86 **gegenseitig**, *adj.*, reciprocal, mutual
87 **in ihren gegenseitigen Beziehungen,** in their mutual relations/in their relations with each other
88 **gegenseitiger   Garantievertrag,** treaty of mutual guarantee
89 **Gegenseitigkeit**, *f.*, reciprocity
90 **auf der Grundlage der Gegenseitigkeit,** on the basis of reciprocity
91 **auf der Grundlage der Gegenseitigkeit behandeln** (CSMW XII), to extend reciprocal treatment to
92 **bedingungslos oder unter der Bedingung der Gegenseitigkeit** (PHR 46), unconditionally or on condition of reciprocity
93 **vorbehaltlich der Gegenseitigkeit,** subject to reciprocity
94 **Gegenseitigkeitserklärung,** *f.*, declaration of reciprocity
95 **Gegenseitigkeitsklausel**, *f.*, reciprocity clause
96 **Gegenseitigkeitsvertrag,** *m.*, treaty of reciprocity (*see note to* *Vertrag in Annex* 1)
97 **Gegenstand**[1], *m.*, subject (matter), object
98 **Gegenstand eines Ersuchens**, object of the request
99 **Gegenstand eines Gerichtsverfahrens** (ECPSD), subject of judicial proceedings
100 **Gegenstand einer strafbaren Handlung**, subject matter/substance of a punishable act
101 **Gegenstand eines Schiedsgerichtsverfahrens** (ECPSD), subject of arbitration/arbitral proceedings
102 **Gegenstand des Schiedsspruchs,** subject of the award
103 **Gegenstand der Streitigkeit**, subject (matter) of the dispute
104 **Gegenstand eines Vertrags**, subject (matter) of a treaty
105 **es wird Gegenstand späterer Verträge sein ...,** it will be a matter for subsequent agreement/treaties
106 **Gegenstand**[2], *m.*, article
107 **Gegenstände für den amtlichen Gebrauch der Mission,** articles for the official use of the mission
108 **zollfrei eingeführte Gegenstände,** articles imported free of import duty (*Einrichtung)
109 **gegenteilig**, *adj.*, contrary, opposite, to the contrary
110 **gegenüber der Regierung eine gegenteilige Erklärung abgeben** (SF 84), to make a contrary declaration to the government
111 **gegenteilige Vereinbarung,** agreement to the contrary
112 **außer im Falle gegenteiliger Vereinbarungen** (GC I 32), unless otherwise agreed
113 **mangels einer gegenteiligen Vereinbarung zwischen den Vertragsparteien** (FC 7), failing agreement between the contracting parties to the contrary
114 **sofern durch die Vertragsparteien nichts Gegenteiliges beschlossen wird** (ICC III), unless the contracting governments agree otherwise
115 **gegnerisch**, *adj.*, opposing, opposite
116 **gegnerische Partei** (= *Gegenpartei, f.*), opposing party
117 **gehalten**, *adj.*, bound, obliged
118 **... ist jede der Parteien gehalten, mindestens die folgenden Bestimmungen anzuwenden** (GC IV 3), ... each party shall be bound to apply, as a minimum, the following provisions
119 **geheim**, *adj.*, secret
120 **geheime Abstimmung**, secret ballot

121   **geheime Beratungen,** secret delibera-
      tions
122   **geheime Wahl,** secret ballot
123   **Geheimabkommen,**   *n.,*   secret
      agreement (*see note to* *Vertrag *in
      Annex* 1)
124   **Geheimdiplomatie,** *f.,* secret dip-
      lomacy
125   **Geheimklausel,** *f.,* secret clause
126   **Geheimprotokoll,** *n.,* secret pro-
      tocol
127   **Geheimsitzung,**   *f.,*   secret   ses-
      sion/meeting,   session/meeting   in
      camera
128   **Geheimvertrag,** *m.,* secret treaty
      (*see note to* *Vertrag *in Annex* 1)
129   **gehörig,***adj.*, due, in due form, proper
130   **gehörig   befugt/ermächtigt,**   duly
      authorized
      (*Unterschrift, *Unterzeichneter)
131   **Geisel,** *m. and f.,* hostage
132   **Geiselerschießung,** *f.,* shooting/
      execution of hostages
133   **Geist,** *m.,* spirit
134   **im Geiste dieses Abkommens,** in the
      spirit of this agreement
135   **gelten,** to be valid, to apply, to be
      deemed/considered, to operate, to be
      effective
136   **die Änderung gilt als angenommen,**
      wenn . . ., the amendment shall be
      deemed to have been accepted when
      . . .
137   **die Bestimmungen gelten für . . .,**
      the(se) provisions shall apply to . . .
138   **Dasselbe gilt von ihrer Aufhebung**
      (RMCE 7), The same procedure shall
      apply as soon as this measure ceases
      to be operative
139   **sinngemäß gelten,** to apply *mutatis
      mutandis*/by analogy
      (*Wirkung, in *Kraft treten)
140   **geltend,** *adj.,* valid, in force/
      operation/effect
141   **alle geltenden Verträge,** all treaties in
      force
142   **gemäß ihren geltenden Gesetzen und**
      Verträgen (PCG 7), in accordance
      with their laws and treaties in force
143   **vorbehaltlich der im Empfangsstaat**
      geltenden Gepflogenheiten und Ver-
      fahren (VCCR 5), subject to the

practices and procedures obtaining in
the receiving state
144   **geltend machen,** to put into effect/
      operation, to exercise, to assert, to
      claim, to validate, to invoke
145   **einen Anspruch geltend machen,** to
      assert/make a claim, to claim a right
      (in *Kraft treten)
146   **Geltendmachung,**   *f.,*   assertion,
      asserting, exercise
147   **bei   der   Geltendmachung   ihrer**
      Rechte, in asserting/exercising their
      rights
148   **Geltung,** *f.,* validity, application,
      applicability, operation
149   **die Geltung dieses Abkommens er-**
      streckt sich nicht auf . . . (CEFA
      10), the present convention does
      not apply to . . .
150   **die Bestimmungen in Geltung setzen**
      (ILOC 23.10), to bring the pro-
      visions into operation
151   **Der Küstenstaat kann dieser Vor-**
      schrift Geltung verschaffen (FC 4),
      The coastal state may enforce this
      rule
152   **innerstaatliche   Geltung,**   validity
      under/in municipal law
153   **völkerrechtliche   Geltung,**   validity
      under/in international law
      (*Gültigkeit)
154   **Geltungsbereich,** *m.,* area of appli-
      cation,   territory   in/to   which   the
      treaty (etc.) applies, scope, territorial
      application
155   **Ausdehnung des Geltungsbereichs**
      der Konvention (PCP 35), territorial
      extension of the convention
156   **nicht in den Geltungsbereich dieses**
      Übereinkommens   fallende   interna-
      tionale Übereinkünfte (VCLOT 3),
      international agreements not within
      the scope of the present convention
157   **räumlicher Geltungsbereich,** territor-
      ial application/scope
158   **Geltungsdauer,** *f.,* duration, (period
      of) validity, period of operation
159   **die Geltungsdauer dieses Überein-**
      kommens beträgt 5 Jahre (SF 104),
      the duration of the present conven-
      tion shall be 5 years
160   **Dieser Vertrag hat unbegrenzte Gel-**

tungsdauer (MNTB), This treaty shall be of unlimited duration

161   nach 10 Jahren Geltungsdauer des Vertrags (NAT 12), after the treaty has been in force for 10 years

162   die Geltungsdauer erneuern/verlängern, to renew/extend the period of validity/operation

163   Die Geltungsdauer des Übereinkommens verlängert sich, außer im Falle der Kündigung, stillschweigend um jeweils 5 Jahre (CCFTD 19), If there has been no denunciation, it (the convention) shall be renewed tacitly every 5 years (*erlöschen)

164   gemäß, prep. (+ dat.), in accordance with, pursuant to, in pursuance of, under

165   gemäß der vorliegenden Satzung, in accordance with the present charter

166   gemäß dem beiliegenden Statut, in accordance with the annexed statute

167   gemäß den Bestimmungen des Artikels. . ., in accordance with (the provisions of) Article . . ./the provisions set forth/contained in Article . . .

168   nachdem er gemäß dem vorhergehenden Absatz in Kraft getreten ist (TRW III), when it has come into effect as prescribed in the preceding paragraph

169   gemeinsam, adj., common, joint

170   gemeinsam und einzeln, jointly. and severally

171   Gemeinschaft, f., community

172   Gemeinschaft der freien Nationen (CRPG 3), community of free nations

173   Gemeinschaft der Staaten, community of states (*Staatengemeinschaft)

174   Gemeinwille, m., common will

175   Gemeinwohl, n., common wellbeing/welfare/benefit

176   im Interesse des Gemeinwohls, in the common interest

177   genannt, adj., said, above-mentioned, set forth above, aforesaid

178   Anspruch auf die genannten Leistungen, entitlement to the said benefits

179   genehm, adj., acceptable

180   nicht genehm, not acceptable

181   eine Person als nicht genehm erklären, to declare a person not acceptable (see *persona non grata)

182   genehmigen, to approve, to permit, to authorize

183   Genehmigung, f., approval, permission, authorization

184   mit vorheriger oder nachträglicher Genehmigung der Kommission (ECE III), with prior or subsequent authorization of the commission

185   verfassungsmäßige Genehmigung, approval as provided for in/as required by the constitution, approval in accordance with (the terms of) the constitution (See VCLOT 2.1 (b) in Annex 14.)

186   Genehmigungsklausel, f., approval clause

187   Genehmigungsurkunde, f., instrument of approval; approval certificate (ICCB)

188   Generalakte, f., general act

189   Generalamnestie, f., general amnesty

190   Generaldirektor, m., director-general

191   Generalklausel, f., general clause

192   Generalkommissar, m., commissioner-general

193   Generalkonferenz, f., general conference

194   Generalkonsul, m., consul-general

195   Generalkonsulat, n., consulate-general

196   Generalmobilmachung, f., general mobilization

     Generalpardon, n. = *Generalamnestie, f.

197   Generalsekretär, m., secretary-general (CUN, CE, etc.); general secretary (e.g. CICES)

198   Generalstabsausschuß, m., Military Staff Committee

199   Der Generalstabsausschuß der UN besteht aus den Generalstabchefs der ständigen Mitglieder, The Military Staff Committee of the UN consists of the Chiefs of Staff of the permanent members

200 **Generalversammlung,** *f.*, general assembly

201 **Generalvertrag,** *m.*, general treaty (*e.g. Franco-German treaty of 23.10.54*)

202 **Genfer Kreuz,** *n.*, Geneva Cross

203 **Genocid/Genozid,** *f.*, genocide (**Völkermord*)

204 **Genugtuung,** *f.*, satisfaction, redress

205 **Genugtuung für ein völkerrechtliches Unrecht,** satisfaction/redress for an international wrong

206 **angemessene Genugtuung für jeden erlittenen Schaden (CERD 6),** adequate satisfaction for any damage suffered

207 **der geschädigten Partei eine angemessene Genugtuung zuerkennen,** to grant the injured party proper satisfaction

208 **Genugtuung erlangen,** to obtain satisfaction

209 **gelingt es dem Einsender der Petition nicht, von der nach Absatz 2 errichteten oder bezeichneten Stelle Genugtuung zu erlangen ... (CERD 14),** in the event of failure to obtain satisfaction from the body established or indicated in accordance with Paragraph 2, the petitioner ...

210 **Gepäck,** *n.*, bag, baggage

211 **diplomatisches Gepäck,** diplomatic baggage (**Kuriergepäck*)

212 **Gerechtigkeit,** *f.*, justice

213 **fundamentale Grundsätze der Gerechtigkeit (VCLD XII),** fundamental principles of justice

214 **in allen Fällen, in denen sie verhindern würden, daß der Gerechtigkeit Genüge geschieht (WEUS 14),** in any case where it would impede the course of justice

215 **Gericht,** *n.*, court, tribunal

216 **Das Gericht hat seinen Sitz an einem Ort des Bundesgebietes (CRPG An),** The seat of the tribunal shall be located within the Federal territory

217 **Das Gericht tagt entweder in Plenarsitzung oder in Kammern von 3 Mitgliedern,** The court/tribunal shall sit either in plenary session or in chambers of 3 members

218 **Mitglieder des Gerichts,** members of the court/tribunal

219 **Räumlichkeiten des Gerichts,** premises of the court/tribunal

220 **innerstaatliches Gericht,** national court

221 **internationales Gericht,** international court

222 **ordentlich bestelltes Gericht,** regularly constituted court

223 **ständiges Gericht,** permanent court

224 **unparteiisches Gericht,** impartial court

225 **das Recht auf ein gerechtes Verfahren vor einem unabhängigen und unparteiischen Gericht,** the right to a fair trial by an independent and impartial court

226 **zuständiges Gericht,** competent court

227 **„Recht des zuständigen Gerichts" bedeutet das Recht desjenigen Gerichts, das nach diesem Übereinkommen Gerichtsbarkeit ausübt (VCLD 1),** "Law of the competent court" means the law of the court having jurisdiction under this convention

228 **...wenn das Recht des zuständigen Gerichts es vorsieht, ...** if the law of the competent court so provides

229 **das Gericht ist für alle Streitigkeiten zuständig, die ... (CRPG An),** the tribunal shall have jurisdiction over all disputes that ...

230 **gerichtlich,** *adj.*, judicial, of the court

231 **gerichtliche Behörden,** judicial authorities

232 **gerichtliche Beilegung,** judicial settlement

233 **gerichtliche und außergerichtliche Urkunden (VCCR 5),** judicial and extra-judicial documents

234 **gerichtliche Verfolgung,** prosecution, trial

235 **Gerichtsbarkeit,** *f.*, jurisdiction

236 **Gerichtsbarkeit der gerichtlichen Behörden (VCCR 43),** jurisdiction of the judicial authorities

237   seiner Gerichtsbarkeit unterstellte
       Gebiete (SC 2), territories placed
       under its jurisdiction
238   Befreiung/Immunität   von   der
       Gerichtsbarkeit,   immunity   from
       jurisdiction/legal process
239   Immunität von der Zivil- und Ver-
           waltungsgerichtsbarkeit des Emp-
           fangsstaats (VCDR 37), immunity
           from   civil   and   administrative
           jurisdiction of the receiving state
240   ausschließliche Gerichtsbarkeit, ex-
       clusive jurisdiction
241   freiwillige Gerichtsbarkeit, volun-
       tary/non-contentious jurisdiction
242   innerstaatliche Gerichtsbarkeit, na-
       tional/domestic jurisdiction
243   internationale Gerichtsbarkeit, in-
       ternational jurisdiction
244   obligatorische Gerichtsbarkeit, com-
       pulsory jurisdiction
245   der Vorwurf, es fehle im Völker-
           recht eine generell obligatorische
           Gerichtsbarkeit, the criticism that
           international law does not possess
           a generally compulsory jurisdic-
           tion (see *Gerichtsbarkeit aner-
           kennen)
246   ordentliche   Gerichtsbarkeit,   reg-
       ular/ordinary jurisdiction
247   örtliche Gerichtsbarkeit, local juris-
       diction
248   staatliche Gerichtsbarkeit, nation-
       al/domestic jurisdiction
249   sich der Gerichtsbarkeit völkerrecht-
       licher Instanzen unterwerfen, to
       submit to the jurisdiction of interna-
       tional courts and tribunals
250   die Gerichtsbarkeit des Gerichts/
       Gerichtshofs in Anspruch nehmen,
       to have recourse to the court/court
       of justice
251   Gerichtsbarkeit anerkennen, to rec-
       ognize jurisdiction
252   Die USA erkennt die Gerichtsbar-
           keit des IGHs nicht an, wenn die
           Angelegenheit nach Auffassung
           der USA in deren ausschließlichen
           Zuständigkeitsbereich gehört, The
           USA does not recognize the juris-
           diction of the ICJ if, in the opin-
           ion of the USA, the matter comes

       within the field of its own exclu-
       sive jurisdiction
253   die Gerichtsbarkeit als obliga-
       torisch anerkennen, to recognize
       the jurisdiction as compulsory
254   ... die Erklärung abgeben, daß
           er   die   Gerichtsbarkeit   des
           Gerichtshofs ohne weiteres und
           ohne besonderes Abkommen als
           obligatorisch anerkennt (PHR
           46),   ... declare that it recog-
           nizes as compulsory ipso facto
           and without special agreement
           the jurisdiction of the court
255   die   Gerichtsbarkeit   des
       Gerichtshofs für alle Rechts-
       streitigkeiten als obligatorisch
       anerkennen, to recognize as
       compulsory the jurisdiction of
       the court in all legal disputes
       (*Zuständigkeit, *unterstellen)
256 Gerichtsbehörde,   f.,   judicial
       authority
257   Gerichts- und Verwaltungsbehör-
       den,   judicial   and   administrative
       authorities
258 Gerichtsferien, pl., judicial vaca-
       tions (ICJ)
259 Gerichtshof, m., court of justice
260   der Gerichtshof der Europäischen
       Gemeinschaften, the Court of Justice
       of the European Communities
261   der Internationale Gerichtshof (der
       IGH), the International Court of
       Justice (the ICJ) (often abbreviated
       to der Gerichtshof: the Court)
262   Der IGH ist das Hauptrecht-
           sprechungsorgan der UN (CUN
           92), The ICJ shall be the principal
           judicial organ of the UN
       der Ständige Internationale Gerichts-
263   hof (der SIGH), the Permanent
       Court of International Justice (the
       PCIJ)
264   Der Gerichtshof setzt sich zusammen
       aus unabhängigen Richtern, The
       court is composed of a body of inde-
       pendent judges
265   Der Gerichtshof ist beschlußfähig,
       wenn neun Richter anwesend sind
       (SICJ 25), A quorum of nine judges
       shall suffice to constitute the court

266 **Mitglieder des Gerichtshofs,** members of the court

267 **Parteien vor dem Gerichtshof,** parties (to cases) before the court

268 **Nur Staaten sind berechtigt, als Parteien vor dem Gerichtshof aufzutreten** (SICJ 34), Only states may be parties in cases before the court

269 **Zuständigkeit des Gerichtshofs,** competence of the court (*See also* CUN 92–94 *and* SICJ 1–3 *in Annex* 19.)

270 **Gerichtskosten,** *pl.*, court costs, expenses of the court

271 **die Gerichtskosten mitbestreiten,** to bear a share of the court costs/the expenses of the court

272 **Gerichtsmaßnahme,** *f.*, judicial measure/action

273 **Gerichtssprache,** *f.*, official language of the court

274 **Gerichtsstaat,** *m.*, state of the forum

275 **Gesamtarbeitsvertrag,** *m.* (ES 33), collective agreement (*see note to* *Vertrag in Annex* 1)

276 **Gesamtliste,** *f.*, general list (*e.g. of members of a court of arbitration*)

277 **Gesamtstimmenzahl,** *f.*, total number of votes, total voting power (IMF XVI) (*Stimmenzahl)

278 **Gesandter,** *adj.n.*, envoy

279 **In manchen Botschaften führt der erste dem Missionschef zugeteilte Beamte den Titel eines Gesandten: ein Gesandter ist also nicht notwendigerweise Missionschef,** In some embassies the senior officer assigned to the head of mission bears the title of "envoy": hence an envoy is not necessarily the head of mission

280 **Außerordentlicher Gesandter und bevollmächtigter Minister,** Envoy Extraordinary and Minister Plenipotentiary

281 **Gesandtschaft,** *f.*, legation, mission

282 **die Gesandtschaft zur Botschaft erheben,** to raise the legation to the rank/status of an embassy

283 **Gesandtschaftspflicht,** *f.*, duty/obligation to establish/maintain a legation/mission/diplomatic relations

284 **Da keine Gesandtschaftspflicht besteht, kann jedes Völkerrechtssubjekt zu jeder Zeit die diplomatischen Beziehungen zu anderen Staaten abbrechen,** As there exists no obligation to maintain a legation, any subject of international law may at any time break off diplomatic relations with other states

285 **Geschädigter,** *adj.n.*, person who suffers/sustains damage or injury, injured person/party

286 **Geschäft,** *n.*, business, activities, operations, transaction, dealing

287 **neben den sonst in diesem Abkommen genannten Geschäften kann die Organisation . . .** (IDA V), in addition to the operations specified elsewhere in this agreement the Association may . . .

288 **internationale Geschäfte,** international transactions/operations (*Tätigkeit²)

289 **Geschäftsabwicklung,** *f.*, despatch of business

290 **geschäftsfähig,** *adj.*, legally capable of conducting/transacting business/of entering into transactions/of possessing full (contractual) capacity

291 **die Interessen minderjähriger und anderer nicht voll geschäftsfähiger Angehöriger des Entsendestaates wahren** (VCCR 5), to safeguard the interests of minors and other persons lacking full capacity who are nationals of the sending state

292 **beschränkt geschäftsfähig,** of/possessing limited (contractual/legal) capacity (*handlungsfähig, *Handlungsfähigkeit, *Rechtsfähigkeit)

293 **Geschäftsfähiger,** *adj.n.*, person/party legally capable of conducting/transacting business/of entering into transactions/of possessing full (contractual) capacity

294 **Geschäftsfähigkeit,** *f.*, legal capacity to conduct/transact business/to enter into transactions, full (contractual) capacity

295 **Beschränkung der Geschäftsfähig-**

keit, limitation of (legal/contractual) capacity (*Rechtsfähigkeit, *Handlungsfähigkeit)
296 **geschäftsführend,** *adj.*, executive
297 **Geschäftsführung,** *f.*, execution/conduct of affairs
298 **Über die Tätigkeit der Organisation und ihre Geschäftsführung beschließen die Mitglieder** (WMO 5), The activities of the organization and the conduct of its affairs shall be decided by the members
299 **Geschäftsführung ohne Auftrag,** agency of necessity
300 **Geschäftsordnung,** *f.*, rules of procedure; regulations
301 **Der Ausschuß gibt sich eine Geschäftsordnung** (CERD 10), The committee shall adopt its own rules of procedure
302 **Im Rahmen dieses Übereinkommens gibt sich der Rat eine Geschäftsordnung** (CICES 9), Subject to the provisions of this convention the council shall draw up its own rules of procedure
303 **nach Maßgabe der Geschäftsordnung** (WMO 7), in accordance with the provisions of the regulations
304 **die Geschäftsordnung des Gerichtshofs,** the rules of the court
305 **allgemeine Geschäftsordnung,** general rules of procedure; general regulations (WMO)
306 **die Geschäftsordnung einhalten,** to observe/adhere to the rules of procedure (*Verfahrensregel)
307 **Geschäftsstelle,** *f.*, registry (*e.g. of court of justice*)
308 **Geschäftstätigkeit,** *f.*, operations, activities (*Geschäft, *Tätigkeit[2])
309 **Geschäftsträger,** *m.*, chargé d'affaires
310 **Geschäftsträger ad interim,** chargé d'affaires *ad interim*
311 **Ist der Posten des Missionschefs unbesetzt oder ist der Missionschef außerstande, seine Aufgaben wahrzunehmen, so ist ein**

Geschäftsträger *ad interim* **vorübergehend als Missionschef tätig** (VCDR 19), If the post of head of the mission is vacant, or if the head of the mission is unable to perform his functions, a chargé d'affaires *ad interim* shall act provisionally as head of mission
312 **ständiger Geschäftsträger,** chargé d'affaires *en pied/en titre*
313 **vorläufiger Geschäftsträger,** chargé d'affaires *ad interim* (*Missionschef)
314 **geschäftsunfähig,** *adj.*, incapacitated, lacking (full) capacity (*geschäftsfähig)
315 **Geschäftsunfähiger,** *adj.n.*, person/party lacking (full) capacity, (legally) incapacitated person/party
316 **Geschäftsunfähigkeit,** *f.*, (legal) incapacity, incapacity/inability to conduct/transact legal business
317 **geschehen zu,** done at (*Urschrift)
318 **geschlossen[1],** *adj.*, closed
319 **geschlossen[2],** *adj.*, concluded
320 **geschützt,** *adj.*, protected
321 **geschützte Person** (GC), protected person
322 **Gesellschaft[1],** *f.*, society; company; association (*of legal or natural persons or both*); partnership (*which may or may not have legal personality, according to the legal system*)
323 **Gesellschaft[2],** *f.*, society
324 **die menschliche Gesellschaft** (ICCPR Pr), the human family
325 **Gesetz,** *n.*, law, enacted law, statute
326 **gemäß dem Gesetz,** according to/in accordance with the law/statute/statutory provisions
327 **Herrschaft/Vorherrschaft des Gesetzes,** rule of law, primacy of law
337 **notwendige gesetzgeberische Maßnahmen ergreifen** (PCG 5), to enact (the) necessary legislation
330 **Gesetze und Vorschriften,** laws and regulations
331 **alle Gesetze und sonstigen Vorschriften ändern, aufheben oder für nichtig erklären** (CERD 2), to

amend, rescind or nullify any laws and regulations

332 **Gesetzesbestimmung,** *f.*, provision of (enacted) law, statutory provision

333 **gesetzgebend,** *adj.*, legislative

334 **gesetzgebende Gewalt,** legislative power/authority

335 **gesetzgebende Körperschaften** (SF 78), legislative bodies

336 **gesetzgeberisch,** *adj.*, legislative

337 **notwendige gesetzgeberische Maßnahmen ergreifen** (PCG 5), to enact (the) necessary legislation

338 **Gesetzgebung,** *f.*, the act of legislating/passing laws, the process of making/adopting legislation; the legislation

339 **soweit die Länder für die Gesetzgebung zuständig sind** (GG 32), in so far as the Laender have power to legislate

340 **im Wege der Gesetzgebung,** by (means of) legislation/legislative action, by legislating

341 **Akte der Gesetzgebung,** legislative acts

342 **innere/innerstaatliche/staatliche Gesetzgebung,** domestic/municipal/national legislation

343 **nur nach Maßgabe ihrer inneren Gesetzgebung** (ICCC Prot), only within the limits provided for by their domestic law

344 **von der innerstaatlichen Gesetzgebung gezogene geographische Grenzen** (ILOC 22.2), geographical limits determined by the national law

345 **Gesetzgebungsbefugnis,** *f.*, legislative jurisdiction/power/authority, jurisdiction/power/authority to legislate

346 **Gesetzgebungskompetenz,** *f.*, legislative competence/authority, competence/authority to legislate

347 **Gesetzgebungsmaßnahme,** *f.*, legislative measure

348 **Gesetzgebungs- und Verwaltungsmaßnahmen** (SF 78), legislative and administrative action/provisions

349 **Gesetzgebungswege** *m.*, **auf dem,**

by (means of) legislative action/legislation

350 **gesetzlich,** *adj.*, statutory, prescribed by/provided for in law/a text of law

351 **gesetzmäßig,** *adj.*, in accordance/compatible/consistent with the law, legal, lawful

352 **gesetzwidrig,** *adj.*, not in accordance/incompatible/not consistent with the law, illegal, unlawful

353 **gestrichen,** *adj.*, deleted, omitted (*e.g. of article in amended/revised text*)

354 **Gesuch,** *n.*, petition, request

355 **sollte ein Gesuch dieser Art unmittelbar an die ... Regierung gerichtet werden ...,** should a request/petition of this nature be made direct to the government of ...

356 **unzulässiges Gesuch,** inadmissible petition

357 **zulässiges Gesuch,** admissible petition

358 **ein Gesuch annehmen,** to accept a petition

359 **Gesuche entgegennehmen und prüfen** (CUN 87), to accept petitions and examine them

360 **ein Gesuch zurückweisen,** to reject a petition

361 **Die Kommission weist jedes Gesuch zurück, das sie für unzulässig hält** (PHR 27), The commission shall reject any petition referred to it which it considers inadmissible

362 **gewähren,** to accord, to grant, to ensure, to provide for

363 **Rechte/Immunitäten gewähren,** to grant rights/immunities

364 **gewährleisten,** to ensure, to uphold, to safeguard, to protect, to guarantee

365 **die Sicherheit der Mission gewährleisten,** to safeguard the security of the mission

366 **Gewahrsam,** *m.*, custody, detention

367 **Kulturgut in Gewahrsam nehmen,** to take into custody cultural property

368 **Gewahrsamsmacht,** *f.* (GC I), detaining power

369 **Gewahrsamsort,** *m.* (GC IV), place of detention

370 **Gewahrsamsstaat**, *m.* (GC I),
     detaining state, detaining power
371 **Gewalt¹**, *f.*, power, authority
372 **Die Gewalt geht vom Volke aus,**
     (The) Power emanates from the
     people
373 **ausführende Gewalt** (= vollziehende
     Gewalt), executive power
374 **gesetzgebende Gewalt,** legislative
     power/authority
375 **höchste Gewalt,** supreme authority
376 **höhere Gewalt,** *force majeure*
377   ... **wenn diese sich infolge höherer
        Gewalt im Hoheitsgebiet des drit-
        ten Staates befinden** (VCDR 40),
        ... whose presence in the territ-
        ory of the third state is due to *force
        majeure*
378 **oberste Gewalt,** supreme authority
379 **richterliche Gewalt,** judicial author-
     ity
380 **verfassungsgebende Gewalt,** con-
     stituent power
381 **verfassungsmäßige Gewalt,** constitu-
     tional power
382 **vollziehende Gewalt,** executive pow-
     er/authority
383 **Gewalt ausüben,** to exercise pow-
     er/authority
384 **Gewalt²**, *f.*, force, armed force
385 **Androhung mit Gewalt,** threat of
     force
386 **Anrufung der Gewalt,** recourse to
     force
387   **die Anrufung der Gewalt soweit
        wie möglich verhüten** (HgI 1), to
        obviate as far as possible recourse
        to force
388 **Anwendung von/der Gewalt,** use of
     force
389 **Drohung mit Gewalt,** threat of force
390 **Einsatz der Gewalt,** use of force
391 **bewaffnete/militärische   Gewalt,**
     armed/military force
     (*Gewalt- *compounds and* *Wille
     des Volkes)
392 **Gewaltandrohung,** *f.*, threat of
     force
393 **Gewaltanrufung,** *f.*, recourse to
     force
394 **Gewaltanwendung,** *f.*, use of force
395 **militärische Gewaltanwendung,** use

     of military/armed force
396 **rechtswidrige   Gewaltanwendung,**
     unlawful/illegal use of force, unlaw-
     ful violence (PHR)
397 **Gewaltanwendungsverbot,** *n.*
     (= Gewaltverbot, *n.*), the duty not to
     use (armed) force, prohibition of the
     use of (armed) force, duty to abstain
     from the use of (armed) force
398 **Gewaltenteilung,** *f.*, separation of
     powers
399 **gewaltsam,** *adj.*, forceful, armed,
     by/using armed force
400 **gewaltsame Angriffe gegen einen
     Staat,** armed attacks on a state
401 **gewaltsame Beseitigung fremder
     Herrschaft,** removal of foreign
     domination by (armed) force
402 **gewaltsame Einmischung,** armed
     intervention, intervention by/using
     (armed) force
403 **Gewalttat,** *f.*, violence, act of viol-
     ence
     Gewaltverbot, *n.* = *Gewaltanwen-
     dungsverbot, *n.*
404 **Gewässer,** *n.* (*usu. in pl.*), waters
405 **darüber   befindliche   Gewässer,**
     superjacent waters
406   **die Rechtsstellung der darüber be-
        findlichen Gewässer als Hohe See
        und   die   Rechtsstellung   des
        Luftraumes über diesem Gewässer**
        (GCC 3), the legal status of the
        superjacent waters as high seas
        and that of the airspace above
        those waters
407 **historische Gewässer,** historic waters
408 **innere Gewässer** (= *Binnengewäs-
     ser, *n.pl.*), internal waters
409 **Die landwärts der Basislinie des Kü-
     stenmeeres gelegenen Gewässer ge-
     hören zu den inneren Gewässern des
     Staates** (GCTS 5), Waters on the
     landward side of the baseline of the
     territorial sea form part of the in-
     ternal waters of the state
410 **von Land umschlossene Gewässer**
     (GCTS 7), land-locked waters
411 **vorgelagerte Gewässer,** adjacent
     waters
412   **Gewässer, die den in Anlage I
        aufgeführten Küsten der Ver-**

tragsparteien vorgelagert sind (FC 12), waters adjacent to the coasts of the contracting parties listed in Annex I

413 gewillt, *adj.*, intending, resolved, determined (*in preamble*) (fester *Wille)

414 Gewissensfreiheit, *f.* (UDHR/ CERD, etc.), freedom of conscience

415 Gewohnheit, *f.*, custom

416 gewohnheitsmäßig, *adj.*, customary, by custom (*fischen, *Fischerei)

417 Gewohnheitsnorm, *f.*, customary rule, rule of customary law

418 Gewohnheitsrecht, *n.*, customary law, custom (*In international law this appears more correctly as* Völkergewohnheitsrecht, international customary law, customary international law, international custom.)

419 allgemeines Gewohnheitsrecht, general customary law

420 bestehendes Gewohnheitsrecht, existing customary law

421 früheres Gewohnheitsrecht, prior/ earlier/previous customary law

422 internationales Gewohnheitsrecht, international customary law, international custom, customary international law

423 das internationale Gewohnheitsrecht als Ausdruck einer allgemeinen als Recht anerkannten Übung (SICJ 38), international custom as evidence of a general practice accepted as law

424 regionales Gewohnheitsrecht, regional customary law

425 späteres Gewohnheitsrecht, subsequent customary law

426 universales Gewohnheitsrecht, universal customary law

427 völkerrechtliches Gewohnheitsrecht, international customary law, international custom, customary international law (*Recht, *Völkerrecht, *kodifiziert, *aufheben, *Übernahme)

428 gewohnheitsrechtlich, *adj.*, customary, of customary law

429 gewohnheitsrechtliche Regeln, rules of customary law

430 Glauben, *m.*, faith

431 bösen Glaubens, in bad faith

432 guten Glaubens, in good faith, bona fide

433 nach Treu und Glauben, in good faith, bona fide

434 Glaubensfreiheit, *f.*, freedom of belief

435 Gläubiger, *adj.n.*, creditor

436 Gläubigerstaat, *m.*, creditor state

437 Gleichbehandlung, *f.*, equal treatment, equality of treatment

438 Gleichbehandlung von Staatsangehörigen und Staatsfremden, equal treatment of aliens and nationals

439 soziale und ärztliche Gleichbehandlung der Angehörigen der Mitgliedsländer (EXWC Pr), equal social and medical treatment for nationals of member countries

440 gleichberechtigt, *adj.*, having/enjoying equal rights, on the basis of equal rights

441 Gleichberechtigung, *f.*, equality, equality of rights, equal rights, emancipation

442 Grundsatz der Gleichberechtigung und Selbstbestimmung der Völker (CUN 1), principle of equal rights and self-determination of peoples

443 Gleichberechtigung von Mann und Frau (ICCPR 3), equal right of men and women

444 in voller Gleichberechtigung (UDHR 10), in full equality

445 Gleichheit, *f.*, equality

446 Gleichheit vor dem Gesetz, equality before the law

447 Gleichheit der Staaten, equality of states

448 souveräne Gleichheit, sovereign equality

449 der Grundsatz der souveränen Gleichheit aller ihrer Mitglieder (CUN 2), the principle of the sovereign equality of all its members

450 Das Prinzip der souveränen Gleichheit besagt, daß alle Staaten gleiche Rechte und Pflichten als Subjekte des Völkerrechts haben,

The principle of sovereign equality holds that all states as subjects of international law have equal rights and duties

451 **auf der Achtung der souveränen Gleichheit der Staaten beruhende internationale Beziehungen,** international relations based on the respect of the sovereign equality of states

452 **Gleichheitsgrundsatz,** *m.* (= Gleichheitsprinzip, *n.*), principle of equality

453 **gleichrangig,** *adj.*, of equal rank/ status (*ranggleich)

454 **Gleichrangigkeit,** *f.*, equality, equal rank/status

455 **Gleichrangigkeit der Staaten,** equality of states (*Gleichheit)

456 **gleichwertig,** *adj.*, equal, of equal value, equally authentic, equivalent

457 **. . . wobei beide Texte gleichwertig sind** (TRW III), . . . both texts having equal force (*authentisch, *maßgebend)

458 **Gleichwertigkeit,** *f.*, equality, equal value, equally authentic character/nature

459 **Gliedstaat,** *m.*, constituent state, state within a federation, member state (*but not to be confused with* *Mitglied(s)staat)

460 **die Gliedstaaten, die Provinzen oder die Kantone** (ILO 19), the constituent states, provinces or cantons

461 **der Bund und seine Gliedstaaten** (CREFA XI), the federation and its constituent units

462 **Gnade,** *f.*, pardon, reprieve

463 **Gnadengesuch,** *n.*, petition for pardon/reprieve

464 **ein Gnadengesuch abweisen,** to deny/refuse a petition for pardon

465 **ein Gnadengesuch einreichen,** to petition for/to submit a petition for pardon/reprieve

466 **Gnadenmaßnahme,** *f.*, act of clemency

467 **Gnadenrecht,** *n.*, right of pardon, prerogative of pardon (ICCC Prot)

468 **Gouverneursrat,** *m.*, Board of Governors (*e.g.* IAEA)

469 **Gräberdienst,** *m.* (GC I), Graves Registration Service

470 **Grausamkeiten,** *f.pl.* (GC), acts of cruelty/barbarity

471 **Grenzarbeitnehmer,** *m.* (CFW), frontier worker

472 **Grenzarbeitnehmer sind die Staatsangehörigen der Vertragsparteien, die unter Beibehaltung ihres Wohnortes in der Grenzzone einer der Parteien, an den sie in der Regel jeden Tag zurückkehren, in der benachbarten Grenzzone einer anderen Partei gegen Entgelt beschäftigt sind** (CFW 1), By frontier workers shall be understood nationals of the contracting parties who, while continuing to be ordinarily resident in the frontier zone of one of the parties, to which they normally return each day, are engaged in paid employment in the adjoining frontier zone of another of the parties (*Grenzgänger)

473 **Grenzarbeitnehmerkarte,** *f.*, frontier worker's card

474 **Grenzbereinigung,** *f.* (= Grenzberichtigung, *f.*), rectification/ adjustment of (the) border(s)/frontier(s)
Grenzberichtigung, *f.* = *Grenzbereinigung, *f.*

475 **Grenze¹,** *f.*, border, boundary, frontier

476 **Die Grenze darf nur an den zugelassenen Grenzübergangsstellen überschritten werden** (RMCE 2), The frontier shall be crossed only at authorized points

477 **Grenzen in Binnenseen,** frontiers in lakes or land-locked seas

478 **Flußgrenze,** river frontier

479 **Landgrenze,** land frontier

480 **Staatsgrenze,** national frontier

481 **Wassergrenze,** water frontier

482 **Grenze²,** *f.*, limit

483 **innerhalb der völkerrechtlich zulässigen Grenzen** (VCDR 3), within the limits permitted by international law

484 **grenzen an,** to adjoin, to border, to be adjacent to
(*angrenzend)

485 **Grenzfestsetzung,** *f.,* delimitation, drawing of (the) border(s)

486 **Grenzfluß,** *m.,* boundary river, frontier river

487 **Grenzgänger,** *m.,* frontier worker

488 **Grenzgänger und deren Familienangehörige,** frontier workers and their families/members of their families
(*Grenzarbeitnehmer)

489 **Grenzlinie,** *f.,* frontier/boundary line, line of delimitation

490 **Grenzpassierscheinheft,** *n.* (ICCA), *carnet de passage en douane*

491 **Grenzregulierung,** *f.,* regulation/adjustment of (the) border(s)

492 **Grenzregulierungsvertrag,** *m.,* treaty regulating/adjusting (the) border(s)

493 **Grenzstreit,** *m.,* frontier/border dispute

494 **Grenzübergangsstelle,** *f.,* frontier crossing point
(*Grenze[1])

495 **Grenzüberschreitung,** *f.,* crossing of frontiers (*frequently in sense of illegal crossing*)
(*Grenze[1])

496 **Grenzübertritt,** *m.,* crossing of frontiers

497 **Grenzverkehr,** *m.,* frontier traffic (EFTA)

498 **Grenzverletzung,** *f.,* frontier violation

499 **Grenzvertrag,** *m.,* frontier/border treaty, treaty regulating/relating to frontier(s)/border(s) (*see note to* *Vertrag in Annex* 1)

500 **Grenzziehung,** *f.,* delimitation, drawing of frontier(s)/border(s)

501 **Grenzzone,** *f.,* frontier zone

502 **Grenzzonen sind die beiderseits einer Grenze liegenden Zonen ... In der Regel haben diese Zonen eine Tiefe von 10 km** (CFW 2), Frontier zones shall be understood to be zones situated on each side of a frontier ... In principle these zones are 10 km in depth

(*Grenzarbeitnehmer)

503 **Grund[1],** *m.,* bed, seabed
(*Meeresgrund)

504 **Grund[2],** *m.,* reason, ground(s)

505 **Das Urteil ist mit Gründen zu versehen** (SICJ 56), The judgment shall state the reasons on which it is based

506 **auf Grund** (+ *gen.*), pursuant to, on the basis of, under

507 **aus Gründen** (+ *gen.*), on (the) grounds of

508 **Grundfreiheiten,** *f.pl.,* fundamental freedoms
(*Freiheit, *frei, *Menschenrechte, *Recht auf, *Anspruch auf)

509 **Grundgesetz,** *n.,* Basic Law of the FGR

510 **Grundlage,** *f.,* foundation, basis

511 **auf der Grundlage der Ziele und Grundsätze der Charta der UN,** on the basis of the aims and principles of the Charter of the UN

512 **auf der Grundlage gegenseitiger Vorteile,** on the basis of mutual advantages

513 **auf der Grundlage gleicher Rechte/der Gleichberechtigung,** on the basis of equal rights/of equality of rights

514 **Grundlinie,** *f.,* base line
(*zerklüftet, *Basislinie)

515 **Grundnorm,** *f.,* basic rule, basic standard

516 **Grundprinzip,** *n.,* fundamental principle

517 **Grundrecht,** *n.,* fundamental right, basic right
(*Rechte, *Recht auf, *Freiheit)

518 **Grundsatz,** *m.,* principle

519 **im Einklang mit den Grundsätzen und im Geiste dieses Abkommens** (ECSM 20), in accordance with the principles and spirit of this convention

520 **im Rahmen der Grundsätze der UN handeln** (ECE I), to act within the framework of the policies of the UN

521 **Handlungen, die mit diesem Grundsatz nicht vereinbar sind,** acts not compatible with/inconsistent with this principle
Grundsatz der: the principle of:

522 **Effektivität,** effectiveness/effectivity
523 **Gegenseitigkeit,** reciprocity
524 **Gerechtigkeit,** justice
525 **Gleichbehandlung,** equal treatment
526 **Gleichberechtigung,** equal rights
527 **Gleichberechtigung und Selbstbestimmung der Völker** (VCLOT Pr), equal rights and self-determination of peoples
528 **Gleichheit vor dem Gesetz,** equality at law/before the law
529 **souveränen Gleichheit und Unabhängigkeit aller Staaten,** sovereign equality and independence of all states
530 **Kontinuität der Staaten,** continuity of states
531 **Legalität,** legality
532 **Legitimität,** legitimacy
533 **Meeresfreiheit,** freedom of the seas
534 **Nichteinmischung,** non-intervention
535 **Proportionalität,** proportionality
536 **Rechtmäßigkeit,** legality
537 **Staatengleichheit,** equality of states
538 **Verhältnismäßigkeit,** proportionality
539 **Vorherrschaft des Rechts,** the rule of law
540 **Wirksamkeit,** effectiveness
541 **Grundsatzausschuß,** *m.* (SF 35), policy committee
542 **Grundsatzentscheidung,** *f.*, judgment/decision creating (legal) precedent/establishing a principle of law
543 **Grundsatzerklärung,** *f.*, declaration of principle
544 **Grundsatzfrage,** *f.*, matter/question of principle
545 **sofern nicht der Fall nach Ansicht des Rates eine Grundsatzfrage aufwirft** (PPELDO 5), unless, in the opinion of the council, the case raises a question of principle
546 **Grundsatzurteil,** *n.*, judgment/award creating a (legal) precedent/establishing a principle of law
547 **Gründungsakte,** *f.*, constituent act, constitution

548 **Gründungsmitglied,** *n.*, founding member, original member, initial member (*Mitglied)
549 **Gründungsurkunde,** *f.*, constituent document/instrument, instrument of constitution/formation, constitution
550 **Gründungsvertrag,** *m.*, treaty establishing/constituting
551 **Grundvertrag,** *m.*, Basic Treaty (DDR-BRD 21.12.72)
552 **Gruppe,** *f.*, group, category
553 **der Generalsekretär bestimmt die Gruppe der Beamten, die ... (**PrivExCE 17), the Secretary-General will specify the categories of officials who ...
554 **ad-hoc Gruppe,** ad-hoc group
555 **ethnische Gruppe** (= *Volksgruppe, *f.*), ethnic group
556 **eine Handlung, die in der Absicht begangen wird, eine nationale, ethnische, rassische oder religiöse Gruppe als solche ganz oder teilweise zu zerstören** (PCG 2), an act committed with intent to destroy, in whole or in part, a national, ethnical, racial or religious group as such (*Lebensbedingungen, *verfolgen)
557 **nationale Gruppe,** national group
558 **rassische Gruppe,** racial group
559 **religiöse Gruppe,** religious group
560 **Gruppenrechte,** *n.pl.*, rights of (minority) groups
561 **gültig,** *adj.*, valid, in force, applicable, operative, effective
562 **Gültigkeit,** *f.*, validity, applicability
563 **die Gültigkeit der Vereinbarung/des Vertrags erlischt/endet,** the validity of the agreement/treaty terminates/expires, the agreement/treaty shall cease to apply
564 **die Bestimmungen dieses Übereinkommens lassen die Gültigkeit von ... unberührt,** the provisions of the present convention shall not affect/prejudice the validity of ...
565 **die rechtliche Gültigkeit solcher Übereinkünfte** (VCLOT 3), the legal force of such agreements (*Geltung)

566 **Gültigkeitsdauer,** *f.,* (period of) validity
(*Geltungsdauer)

567 **Gut¹,** *n.,* a good (*in the economic sense*)

568 **Gut²,** *n.,* property

569 **bewegliches Gut,** movable property

570 **kulturelles Gut,** cultural property

571 **unbewegliches Gut,** immovable property
(*Vermögen, *Kulturgut)

572 **Gutachten,** *n.,* expert/expert's opinion, advisory opinion

573 **ein Gutachten abgeben/erstatten,** to give/to deliver an expert/advisory opinion

574 **den IGH ersuchen, ein Gutachten über jede Rechtsfrage zu erstatten,** to request the ICJ to give an advisory opinion on any legal question

575 **Der Gerichtshof gibt seine Gutachten in öffentlicher Sitzung ab** (SICJ 67), The court shall deliver its advisory opinions in open court

576 **Gutachter,** *m.,* expert
(*Sachverständiger)

577 **gutachterlich,** *adj.,* advisory

578 **bei der Ausübung seiner gutachterlichen Tätigkeit** (SICJ 68), in the exercise of its advisory functions
(*gutachtlich)

579 **Gutachterverfahren,** *n.,* advisory procedure

580 **gutachtlich,** *adj.,* advisory

581 **gutachtliche Aufgaben,** advisory functions

582 **Die Aufgaben der Organisation sind beratender und gutachtlicher Art** (IMCO 2), The functions of the organization shall be consultative and advisory

583 **gutachtliche Tätigkeit,** advisory function(s)
(*gutachterlich)

584 **gutgläubig,** *adj.,* acting in good faith, bona fide

585 **gütlich,** *adj.,* amicable, by agreement
(*beilegen)

586 **gutnachbarlich,** *adj.,* good-neighbourly

H

1 **Habe,** *f.,* effects
  (*Erklärung)
2 **Hafen,** *m.,* port, harbour
3 **Entsprechend dem Bedarf der sie anlaufenden Schiffe sind die Häfen mit geeigneten Anlagen zu versehen, die ...** (PPSO), According to the needs of ships using them, ports shall be provided with facilities adequate for ...
4 **Liegezeit im Hafen,** port time
5 **Ruhe und Ordnung im Hafen,** peace of the port
6 **angelaufener Hafen,** port of call
7 **Hafenanlagen,** *f.pl.,* harbour works
8 **die äußersten ständigen Hafenanlagen** (PPSO), the outermost permanent harbour works
9 **Hafengesundheitsbehörde,** *f.* (CFIMT), port health authorities
10 **Hafenverwaltung,** *f.* (CFIMT), port administration
11 **haftbar,** *adj.,* liable, responsible
12 **Sind wegen eines nuklearen Schadens mehrere Inhaber von Kernanlagen haftbar, so haften die Inhaber gemeinsam und einzeln nebeneinander** (VCLD II), Where nuclear damage engages the liability of more than one operator, the operators shall be jointly and severally liable
13 **haftbar machen,** to hold liable/responsible
14 **Die öffentlichen Behörden machen den Reeder nicht für die Vorlage oder Richtigkeit von Dokumenten haftbar, die ...** (CFIMT), Public authorities shall not hold the shipowner responsible for the presentation or accuracy of documents which ...
  (*haften, *Haftung)
15 **haften (für),** to accept responsibility (for), to be liable/responsible (for), to be held liable/responsible (for)
16 **... haftet nicht für ...,** no liability shall attach to ... for ... (VCLD IV)

17 **Kein Mitglied haftet auf Grund seiner Mitgliedschaft für die Verbindlichkeiten der Organisation** (IDA II), No member shall be liable, by reason of its membership, for obligations of the Association
18 **Je höher das staatliche Organ ist, das das Unrecht begangen hat, desto schwerer haftet der betroffene Staat,** The higher the state organ that has committed the offence, the more serious is the liability of the state concerned
19 **Der Inhaber haftet ohne Rücksicht auf Verschulden** (VCLD IV), The liability of the operator shall be absolute
20 **die haftenden Verbände** (ICCA), the guaranteeing associations
  (*haftbar, *Haftung, innerstaatliches *Recht)
21 **Haftung,** *f.,* liability, responsibility
22 **Bei Untergang eines Staates erlischt seine Haftung,** The extinction of a state results in the termination of its liability
23 **Durch die Vorschriften dieses Übereinkommens wird die Haftung von Personen, die haftbar gemacht werden können, in Zusammenhang mit ... weder eingeschränkt noch in sonstiger Weise berührt,** Nothing in this convention shall limit or otherwise affect the liability of any person who may be held liable in connection with ...
24 **Beschränkung der Haftung,** limitation of liability/responsibility
25 **Haftung des Staates,** state liability/responsibility, liability/responsibility of the state
26 **vertragliche Haftung,** contractual liability/responsibility
27 **völkerrechtliche Haftung,** international liability/responsibility, liability/responsibility under international law
  (*haften, *haftbar)
28 **Handel,** *m.,* trade, commerce, traffic

29 **unerlaubter Handel mit,** illicit traffic in

30 **handeln,** to act

31 **Die Organisation handelt gemäß den Zielen und Grundsätzen der UN** (IAEA III), The agency shall conduct its activities in accordance with the purposes and principles of the UN

32 **Handeln,** *n.*, action, measure(s)

33 **um ein schnelles und wirksames Handeln der UN zu gewährleisten** (CUN 24), in order to ensure prompt and effective action by the UN

34 **gemeinsames Handeln,** common/ joint action (*Handlung, *entschlossen, *Maßnahme)

35 **Handelsabkommen,** *n.*, commercial/trade agreement (*see note to* *Vertrag *in Annex* 1)

36 **Handelsabordnung,** *f.*, commercial/trade delegation

37 **Handelsattaché,** *m.*, commercial attaché

38 **Handelsbeschränkung,** *f.*, trade restriction, restriction on trade

39 **Handelsbeziehungen,** *f.pl.*, trade relations

40 **Handelsdelegation,** *f.*, commercial/trade delegation

41 **Handelsdirektorium,** *n.*, steering board for trade

42 **Handelsfreiheit,** *f.*, freedom of commerce

43 **Handels- und Gewerbefreiheit,** freedom of commerce and industry

44 **Handels- und Schiffahrtsfreiheit,** freedom of commerce and navigation

45 **Handelskrieg,** *m.*, trade war

46 **Handelskriegführung,** *f.*, trade war(fare)

47 **Handelsmission,** *f.*, commercial/ trade mission

48 **Handelsmonopol,** *n.*, trade monopoly

49 **staatliche Handelsmonopole** (EEC 37), state monopolies of a commercial character

50 **Handelspolitik,** *f.*, commercial/ trade policy

51 **gemeinsame Handelspolitik gegenüber dritten Ländern** (EEC 3), common commercial policy towards third countries

52 **Handelsrecht,** *n.*, commercial/mercantile law

53 **Handelsschiedsgerichtsbarkeit,** *f.* (ECICA), commercial arbitration

54 **Handelsschiff,** *n.*, merchant vessel/ ship, merchantman

55 **die Besatzungen der Handelsschiffe** (GC I 13), (members of) crews of the merchant marine

56 **Handelsschranke,** *f.*, trade barrier (*Assoziation)

57 **Handelsverkehr,** *m.*, trade, commerce

58 **ausgewogener Handelsverkehr** (EEC Pr), balanced trade

59 **Handelsvertrag,** *m.*, commercial treaty, treaty of commerce, trade treaty (*see note to* *Vertrag *in Annex* 1)

60 **Handelsverzerrung,** *f.*, deflection/distortion of trade

61 **eine Handelsverzerrung liegt vor, wenn . . .** (EFTA 5), trade is said to be deflected when . . .

62 **Handelszwecke,** *m.pl.*, commercial purposes (*Staatsschiff)

63 **Handlung,** *f.*, act, action

64 **Handlung mit/ohne Rechtswirkung,** act with/without legal effect

65 **Handlung gegen den Staat,** act against the state

66 **Handlungen, die den Feind schädigen** (GC I 21), acts harmful to the enemy

67 **ihre nicht in Ausübung ihrer dienstlichen Tätigkeit vorgenommenen Handlungen** (VCDR 37), acts performed outside the course of their duties

68 **von ihm in amtlicher Eigenschaft vorgenommene Handlungen** (WEUS 12), acts done by him in his official capacity

69 **die folgenden Handlungen sind zu bestrafen,** the following acts shall be punishable

70 **dienstliche Handlung** (= *Amtshandlung, *f.*), official act, act in an

official capacity, act performed as part of (their) duties, act performed in the exercise of (their) duties

71 **diskriminierende Handlung (CERD 4),** act of discrimination

72 **rassisch diskriminierende Handlung (CERD 6),** act of racial discrimination

73 **einseitige Handlung,** unilateral act

74 **feindselige Handlung,** hostile act, act of hostility

75 **konkludente Handlung,** conclusive act (*see* *konkludent *and note*)

76 **kriegerische Handlung,** belligerent act

77 **private Handlung,** private act, act performed in a private capacity

78 **richterliche Handlung,** judicial act

79 **strafbare Handlung,** crime, penal/criminal/punishable offence

80 **die dem Rechtshilfeersuchen zugrundeliegende strafbare Handlung,** the offence giving grounds for the letters rogatory

81 **das Zusammentreffen mehrerer strafbarer Handlungen,** the concurrence of offences

82 **die Folgen der strafbaren Handlung erstrecken sich auf ...,** the consequences of the crime extend to ...

83 **eine während der Durchfahrt an Bord des Schiffes begangene strafbare Handlung (GCTS 19),** a crime committed on board the ship during its passage

84 **strafbare Handlung ğegen die Sicherheit eines Staates (NATOSF VII),** security offence against a state

85 **im Zeitpunkt der Begehung der strafbaren Handlung (UDHR 11),** at the time the penal offence was committed

86 **auslieferungsfähige strafbare Handlung,** extraditable offence

87 **fiskalische strafbare Handlung (EExt 5),** fiscal offence

88 **militärische strafbare Handlung (EExt 4),** military offence

89 **politische strafbare Handlung (EExt 3),** political offence

90 **vorsätzliche strafbare Handlung (GC IV 68),** intentional offence (*beschuldigen, strafbare *Zuwiderhandlung)

91 **unerlaubte Handlung,** wrongful act, unlawful act

92 **unterlassene Handlung,** omission

93 **völkerrechtliche Handlung,** international act

94 **eine Handlung begehen,** to perform/commit an act

95 **sich einer Handlung enthalten,** to refrain from an act

96 **Sie haben sich aller Handlungen zu enthalten, die mit ihrer Stellung unvereinbar sind (ILO 9),** They shall refrain from any action that might reflect on their position

97 **eine Handlung unterlassen,** to omit to/to fail to perform an act

98 **eine Handlung vornehmen,** to perform an act

99 **die nachträgliche Bestätigung einer ohne Ermächtigung vorgenommenen Handlung (VCLOT 8),** the subsequent confirmation of an act performed without authorization (*Akt, *Unterlassung, *Auslieferung, *Last)

100 **handlungsfähig,** *adj.*, enjoying/of (legal) capacity, capable of action, enjoying capacity to act

101 **Das neue Mitglied der Völkerrechtsgemeinschaft muß handlungsfähig sein,** The new member of the international community must possess a capacity to act

102 **beschränkt handlungsfähig,** of limited (legal) capacity, capable of only limited action

103 **Handlungsfähiger ,** *adj.n.*, person/party enjoying/possessing capacity to act/legal capacity

104 **Handlungsfähigkeit,** *f.*, capacity to act, liberty of action

105 **Im Zweifelsfall sind Verträge so auszulegen, daß die weniger die Handlungsfähigkeit einschränkende Alternative zu wählen ist,** In cases of doubt, treaties must be interpreted in such a manner that the alternative

least restrictive upon liberty of action is selected

106 **beschränkte Handlungsfähigkeit,** limited capacity/liberty of action

107 **Die Souveränität der neutralen Staaten bleibt trotz der in ihrer Neutralität liegenden beschränkten Handlungsfähigkeit bestehen,** Despite the limitation on their capacity to act inherent in their neutrality, neutral states remain sovereign
(*Völkerrechtssubjektivität, *Rechtsfähigkeit)

108 **handlungsunfähig,** *adj.*, incapable of action, lacking (full) capacity to act, lacking legal capacity

109 **Handlungsunfähiger,** *adj.n.*, person/party lacking/not possessing capacity to act/legal capacity

110 **Handlungsunfähigkeit,** *f.*, incapacity to act
(kriegerische *Besetzung)

111 **Handzeichen,** *n.*, show of hands

112 **Abgestimmt wird normalerweise durch Handzeichen** (ECER 37), (The commission) shall normally vote by show of hands

113 **harmonisieren,** to harmonize

114 **Harmonisierung,** *f.*, harmonization

115 **Hauptausschuß,** *m.*, main committee

116 **Hauptberichterstatter,** *m., rapporteur-général*

117 **Hauptdelegierter,** *adj.n.*, principal delegate

118 **Hauptklage,** *f.*, principal claim
(*Widerklage)

119 **Hauptorgan,** *n.*, principal organ

120 **Hauptpflicht,** *f.*, principal/primary duty

121 **Hauptrechtsprechungsorgan,** *n.*, principal judicial organ (*see* CUN 92 *and* SICJ 1 *in Annex* 19)

122 **hauptrichterlich,** of/pertaining to the Chief Judge

123 **Hauptsache,** *f.*, primary case, primary matter/subject matter of the case

124 **Den Parteien steht es frei, das Recht zu vereinbaren, welches in der Hauptsache anzuwenden ist** (ECICA VII), The parties shall be free to determine, by agreement, the law to be applied to the substance of the dispute

125 **Hauptübereinkommen,** *n.*, principal agreement (*see note to* *Vertrag *in Annex* 1)

126 **Hauptverantwortung,** *f.*, primary responsibility

127 **Hauptverantwortung für die Wahrung des Friedens** (CUN 24), primary responsibility for the maintenance of peace

128 **Hauptverfahren,** *n.*, main proceedings

129 **Hauptversammlung,** *f.*, main/general assembly

130 **Hauptvertreter,** *m.*, principal representative

131 **ständiger Hauptvertreter** (WEUS), principal permanent representative
(*Vertreter[1])

132 **Hauptziel,** *n.*, principal/primary objective/aim
(*Hauptzweck)

133 **Hauptzweck,** *m.*, principal/primary objective/purpose

134 **die in Artikel 76 dargelegten Hauptzwecke** (CUN 83), the basic objectives set forth in Article 76

135 **Hausangestellter,** *adj.n.*, servant

136 **private Hausangestellte von Diplomaten,** private servants of diplomatic agents

137 **Haushalt[1],** *m.*, household

138 **die zum Haushalt eines Diplomaten gehörenden Familienmitglieder** (VCDR 37), the members of the family of a diplomatic agent forming part of his household

139 **Haushalt[2],** *m.*, budget

140 **außerordentlicher Haushalt,** extraordinary budget

141 **ordentlicher Haushalt,** ordinary budget

142 **Haushaltsausschuß,** *m.*, budget(ary) committee, committee of ways and means (SF 34)

143 **Haushaltsentwurf,** *m.*, proposed/draft budget

144 **Haushaltsjahr,** *n.*, financial year

145 **Haushaltsvoranschlag,** *m.*, draft budget, budget estimate

146 **Haushaltsvorlage,** *f.,* proposed budget
147 **Heer,** *n.,* army, armed forces
148 **Heere im Felde** (GC/HgI), armies/ armed forces in the field
149 **Heeresgefolge,** *n.,* army followers
150 **Heereslieferant,** *m.* (GC I), supply contractors (to the forces)
151 **Hegemonie,** *f.,* hegemony
152 **heilig,** *adj.,* holy, sacred
153 **heiliger Auftrag/heilige Mission,** sacred mission
154 **Heiliger Stuhl,** Holy See
155 **Heiligkeit,** *f.,* sanctity
156 **Heiligkeit der Verträge,** sanctity of treaties
157 **Heimat,** *f.,* home country/state (*Heimatstaat, *Heimatland)
158 **Heimatgebiet,** *n.* (OEEC), metropolitan territory (*Mutterland)
159 **Heimathafen,** *m.,* port of registry
160 **Heimatland,** *n.,* home country, native country, own country, country of domicile
161 **... hat Anspruch auf Rückbeförderung nach seinem Heimatland** (ILOC 23), ... shall be entitled to be taken back to his own country (*Heimatstaat *and note to* *Wohnsitz)
162 **Heimatort,** *m.* **der einzelnen Richter,** home of each judge (SICJ 23)
163 **Heimatrecht,** *n.,* national law, law of the state of which ... is a national
164 **Heimatstaat,** *m.,* native state/country, home state, state of which (one) is a national, country/state of origin
165 **Als ,,Heimatstaat'' wird der Staat bezeichnet, dessen Staatsangehörigkeit eine Person, auf die sich die Bestimmungen dieses Abkommens beziehen, besitzt** (ECSM 2), "Country of origin" means the country of which a person covered by the provisions of the present convention is a national
166 **in ihren Heimatstaat zurückkehren** (VCDR 40), to return to their country
167 **im Hoheitsgebiet ihres Heimatstaates**

(WEUS 18), on their national territory (*Heimatland)
168 **heimbefördern,** to repatriate
169 **Heimbeförderung,** *f.,* repatriation
170 **heimschaffen,** to repatriate
171 **Heimschaffung,** *f.,* repatriation
172 **Heimschaffungsbescheinigung,** *f.,* repatriation certificate
173 **heimsenden,** to repatriate
174 **Heimsendung,** *f.,* repatriation
175 **Herkunftsland,** *n.,* country of origin, home country (*Heimatland, *Heimatstaat)
176 **Herrschaft,** *f.,* rule, domination
177 **Herrschaft des Rechtes,** rule of law
178 **fremde Herrschaft,** foreign rule/ domination
179 **Herrschaftsgebiet,** *n.,* territory under (their) rule/jurisdiction (*Hoheitsgebiet)
180 **Herrschaftsgewalt,** *f.,* jurisdiction
181 **die ihrer Herrschaftsgewalt unterliegenden Personen,** persons subject to their jurisdiction (*Hoheit, *Hoheitsgewalt)
182 **herrühren,** to arise from (*erwachsen)
183 **Heuervertrag,** *m.* **der Schiffsleute** (ILOC 22), Seamen's Articles of Agreement
184 **Hilfeleistung,** *f.* **auf hoher See,** assistance to vessels in distress
185 **Hilfsausschuß,** *m.,* auxiliary committee
186 **Hilfsgesellschaft,** *f.* (GC), relief society, aid society
187 **freiwillige Hilfsgesellschaften** (GC I), Voluntary Aid Societies
188 **Hilfskrankenpfleger,** *m.* (GC I), hospital orderly/nurse
189 **Hilfskrankenträger,** *m.* (GC I), auxiliary stretcher bearer
190 **Hilfslieferungen,** *f.pl.* (GC), relief supplies
191 **ärztliche Hilfslieferungen** (GC), medical relief supplies
192 **Hilfsmittel,** *n.pl.,* (supplementary/ subsidiary) means
193 **Aufgaben, Hilfsmittel und Verpflichtungen** (WMO 26), functions, resources and obligations

194   **Hilfsmittel zur Feststellung von Völkerrechtsnormen,** supplementary
means for the determination of rules
of international law
(*Hilfsquelle[1])

195 **Hilfsorgan,** *n.*, auxiliary/subsidiary
organ/body

196   **die von ihr für erforderlich erachteten Hilfsorgane** (CFIMT An), any
subsidiary bodies it may consider
necessary

197   **Unterkommissionen, andere Hilfsorgane und Ausschüsse** (ECER 49),
sub-commissions, subsidiary bodies
and committees
(*Hilfsorganisation, *Ausübung der
Funktionen)

198 **Hilfsorganisation,** *f.* (GC), relief
organization, humanitarian organization

199 **Hilfspaket,** *n.* (GC), relief parcel

200 **Hilfsquelle[1],** *f.*, supplementary/sub-
sidiary/secondary source (of law)
(*Hilfsmittel)

201 **Hilfsquelle[2],** *f.*, resources

202   **durch Erschließung neuer Hilfsquellen** (EEC 3), by opening up fresh
resources

203   **die Erhaltung von natürlichen Hilfsquellen** (FAO), the conservation of
natural resources

204 **Hilfssendung,** *f.* (GC), relief con-
signment/shipment

205 **Hilfsspenden,** *f.pl.* (GC), relief

206 **Hilfswerk,** *n.*, relief agency

207 **Hinblick,** *m.*: **im Hinblick auf,** having regard to (*in preamble*)

208 **hinderlich,** *adj.*, inhibitive, restrictive
(hinderlicher *Vorbehalt)

209 **hinfällig,** *adj.*, void, null and void,
devoid of content

210   **Jede Vertragspartei kann ihre Verpflichtungen als hinfällig betrachten**
(ARS 13), A contracting party may
consider itself released from the
obligations incumbent on it

211 **hinsichtlich,** *prep.* (+ *gen.*), in
respect of

212   **Immunität hinsichtlich,** immunity in
respect of

213 **hinterlegen,** to deposit

214   **Die Ratifikations- oder Genehmi-
gungsurkunden sind im Archiv der
Regierung des Vereinigten Königreichs zu hinterlegen** (PPELDO 32),
The instruments of ratification or
approval shall be deposited with the
Government of the United Kingdom

215 **Hinterleger,** *m.*, depositor
(*Depositar, *Verwahrer, *and*
VCLOT 76–77 *in Annex* 15)

216 **Hinterlegung,** *f.*, deposit

217   **die Hinterlegung von (Ratifika-
tions-)Urkunden,** the deposit of instruments (of ratification)
(*Beitritt)

218 **Hinterlegungsakt,** *m.*, act of depositing, deposit

219 **Hinterlegungsmacht,** *f.*, depositary power/state
(*Mitglied(s)staat)

220 **Hinterlegungsstelle,** *f.*, depositary

221 **Hinweis,** *m.*: **unter Hinweis auf,**
recalling (*in preamble*)

222 **historisch,** *adj.*, historic

223   **historische Bucht,** historic bay

224   **historische Gewässer,** historic waters

225   **historischer Titel,** historic title

226 **Hochkommissar,** *m.*, high commissioner

227 **Hochkommissariat,** *n.*, office of
the high commissioner

228 **Hochverrat,** *m.*, high treason

229 **Hoheit,** *f.*, sovereignty, sovereign
rights, jurisdiction, supremacy,
authority

230   **ausschließliche Hoheit,** exclusive
sovereignty (etc.)

231   **gemeinsame Hoheit,** joint sovereignty (etc.)

232   **Untersteht ein Gebiet der gemeinsamen Hoheit von 2 oder mehr
Mitgliedern** ... (ILO 3), In the
case of a territory under the joint
authority of 2 or more members ...

233   **volle Hoheit** full/complete sovereignty (etc.)
(*Hoheitsgewalt)

234 **hoheitlich,** *adj.*, sovereign

235   **hoheitlicher Akt,** sovereign act

236   **hoheitlich handelnde Staatsorgane,**

organs of a state acting in a sovereign capacity

237 **Hoheitsakt,** *m.*, sovereign act

238 **Hoheitsausübung,** *f.*, exercise of sovereignty

239 **Hoheitsbereich,** *m.*, sovereign territory, jurisdiction (*Hoheitsgebiet)

240 **Hoheitsgebiet,** *n.*, territory, sovereign territory

241 **Hoheitsgebiete, deren Völker noch nicht die volle Selbstregierung erreicht haben** (CUN 73), territories whose peoples have not yet attained a full measure of self-government

242 **Als ,,Hoheitsgebiete'' eines Staates gelten die der Staatshoheit, der Oberhoheit, dem Schutz oder der Mandatsverwaltung dieses Staates unterstehenden Landgebiete und angrenzenden Hoheitsgewässer** (SF 71), The territories of a state shall be deemed to be the land areas and territorial waters adjacent thereto under the sovereignty, suzerainty, protection or mandate of such state

243 **Hoheitsgebiete ohne Selbstverwaltung,** non-self-governing territories

244 **die Vereinten Nationen, soweit sie Verwaltungsmacht eines Hoheitsgebietes sind** (CSLS XIII), the United Nations, in cases where they are the administering authority for a territory

245 **das Hoheitsgebiet, das in diesem Sinne als Mutterland gilt,** the territory which shall be considered to be its metropolitan territory for this purpose

246 **Flüge über dem Hoheitsgebiet von Vertragsstaaten** (CAC 5), flights over territory of contracting states

247 **Hoheitsgebiet zu Lande** (GCTS 1), land territory

248 **das Betreten oder Verlassen des Hoheitsgebietes** (NATOSF III), entering or leaving the territory

249 **ihre Hoheits- oder Herrschafts-**

gebiete (CSFT 2), territory under their sovereignty or authority (*Staatshoheit, *wahrnehmen, *Heimatstaat, *Gebiet, *Verwaltungsmacht, *Lufthoheit)

250 **Hoheitsgewalt,** *f.*, sovereignty, jurisdiction, sovereign acts

251 **Beschränkungen in der Ausübung der staatlichen Hoheitsgewalt, z.B. bei neutralisierten Staaten,** limitations on the exercise of national sovereignty, e.g. in the case of neutralized states

252 **Hoheitsgewässer,** *n.* (*usu. in pl.*), territorial waters (*Hoheitsgebiet, *Gebiet, *Gewässer)

253 **Hoheitsgrenze,** *f.*, territorial limit/boundary

254 **außerhalb der Hoheitsgrenzen des Staates** (MNTB 1), outside the territorial limits of the state

255 **Hoheitsrechte,** *n.pl.*, sovereign rights

256 **Der Ausschuß darf keine Empfehlungen unterbreiten, die zu einer Verletzung der Hoheitsrechte einer Regierung führen** (ECE XI), The committee shall not make recommendations leading to an infringement of the sovereign rights of any government

257 **in Ausübung seiner Hoheitsrechte** (EAEC 29), in exercising its sovereignty

258 **Hoheitszeichen,** *n.*, emblem

259 **Die Mission ist berechtigt, die Flagge und das Hoheitszeichen des Entsendestaates zu führen** (VCDR 20), The mission shall have the right to use the flag and emblem of the sending state

260 **Hohe See,** the high seas

261 **Honorarkonsul,** *m.*, honorary consul, honorary consular agent

262 **Humanitätsrecht,** *n.*, humanitarian law (*Menschenrechte)

I

1 **Ideal,** *n*., ideal

2 **Ideale und Grundsätze,** ideals and principles

3 **Ideale und Grundsätze, die ihr gemeinsames Erbe bilden** (EEC Pr), ideals and principles which are their common heritage

4 **Identitätsdokument,** *n*., identity document, document of identity

5 **die Anerkennung von amtlichen Identitätsdokumenten an Stelle von Reisepässen** (CFIMT An), the acceptance of official documents of identity in lieu of passports

6 **Einzel–Identitätsdokumente** (CFIMT), individual identity documents (*Ausweis)

7 **Identitätskarte,** *f*., identity card

8 **illegal,** *adj*., illegal, unlawful

9 **Illegalität,** *f*., illegality, unlawful nature

10 **Illegalitätsgrundsatz,** *m*. (= Illegalitätsprinzip, *n*.), principle of illegality

11 **Immobiliareigentum,** *n*., real property, immovable property (unbewegliches *Vermögen)

12 **Immunität,** *f*., immunity

13 **Immunität für,** immunity for/in respect of/with regard to

14 **Immunität für Amtshandlungen,** immunity for official acts/acts performed in an official capacity

15 **Immunität für private Handlungen,** immunity for private acts/acts performed in a private capacity

16 **Immunität gegen/gegenüber,** immunity from/in respect of (*see* *Immunität von, Verzicht auf *Immunität)

17 **Immunität hinsichtlich** (= *Immunität für), immunity, for/in respect of/with regard to

18 **Immunität von,** immunity from/in respect of

Immunität von:

19 **Beschlagnahme,** requisition

20 **Durchsuchung,** search

21 **Exekution(smaßnahmen),** execution (action/measures)

22 **gerichtlichem Verfahren,** judicial/legal prosecution/suit/process

23 **gerichtlicher Verfolgung,** judicial/legal prosecution/suit/process

24 **Gerichtsbarkeit,** jurisdiction

25 **Die Immunität des Diplomaten von der Gerichtsbarkeit des Empfangsstaates befreit ihn nicht von der Gerichtsbarkeit des Entsendestaates** (VCDR 31), The immunity of a diplomatic agent from the jurisdiction of the receiving state does not exempt him from the jurisdiction of the sending state

26 **Strafgerichtsbarkeit,** criminal jurisdiction

27 **Strafverfolgung,** criminal prosecution/process

28 **Verwaltungsgerichtsbarkeit,** administrative jurisdiction

29 **Vollstreckung(smaßnahmen),** execution (action/measures)

30 **Zivilgerichtsbarkeit,** civil jurisdiction

31 **Aufhebung der Immunität,** waiver of immunity (*see* *Immunität aufheben)

32 **Verzicht auf Immunität,** waiver of immunity

33 **Ein Verzicht auf Immunität erstreckt sich nicht auf die Immunität gegenüber Exekutionsmaßnahmen,** Waiver of immunity does not extend to immunity in respect of execution (of the judgment)

34 **Der Verzicht auf Immunität muß stets ausdrücklich sein,** Waiver of immunity must always be express

35 **absolute Immunität,** absolute immunity

36 **diplomatische Immunität,** diplomatic immunity

37   **konsularische Immunität,** consular
     immunity
38   **persönliche Immunität,** personal
     immunity, immunity of the person
39   **der Kurier genießt persönliche**
        Immunität, the courier shall enjoy
        personal immunity
40   **relative Immunität,** relative immun-
     ity
41   **steuerliche Immunität,** fiscal immun-
     ity
42   **strafrechtliche Immunität,** immunity
     from penal/criminal jurisdiction
43   **zivilrechtliche Immunität,** immunity
     from civil jurisdiction
     (*Many other immunities are listed*
     under *Befreiung[2]; *see also* *Vor-
     rechte, *Schutz[2], *and* PPELDO 14
     and VCDR 31–34 *in Annex 7.*)
44   **die Immunität erstreckt sich auf ...,**
     the immunity extends to ...
45   **Die Immunität der Diplomaten er-**
        streckt sich auch auf Angele-
        genheiten und Handlungen ihres
        privaten Lebensbereiches, The
        immunity of diplomatic agents
        also extends to matters and acts in
        their private capacity
46   **die Immunität gilt für ...,** the
     immunity applies to ...
47   **Immunität aufheben,** to waive im-
     munity
48   **Der Entsendestaat kann durch**
        eine ausdrückliche Erklärung die
        Immunität eines Diplomaten
        aufheben, The sending state can
        waive the immunity of a diploma-
        tic agent by an express declaration
49   **die Immunität in allen Fällen**
        aufheben, in denen sie ohne Beein-
        trächtigung der Zwecke, für die
        sie gewährt wird, aufgehoben
        werden kann (WEUS 14), to
        waive immunity in any case where
        it can be waived without prejudice
        to the purposes for which it is
        accorded
50   **sich auf die Immunität berufen,** to
     invoke immunity
51   **Immunität einräumen,** to grant/
     accord immunity
52   **Immunität geltend machen,** to in-

voke immunity, to invoke one's
right to immunity
53   **Diese Immunität kann nicht gel-**
        tend gemacht werden, wenn
        ... (WEUS 18), This immunity
        does not apply when ...
54   **Immunität genießen,** to enjoy im-
     munity
55   **Immunität gewähren,** to grant/
     accord immunity
56   **Immunität gewährleisten,** to se-
     cure/ensure immunity, to ensure
     that immunity is observed/respected
57   **auf Immunität verzichten,** to waive
     immunity
58   **Immunität zuerkennen,** to grant/
     accord immunity
59   **Immunitätsrecht,** *n.*, right of im-
     munity, immunity
60   **alle zur Wahrnehmung ihrer Auf-**
     gaben erforderlichen Vorrechte und
     Immunitätsrechte (CICES 15), such
     privileges and immunities necessary
     for the fulfilment of their functions
61   **Immunitätsverzicht,** *m.*, waiver of
     immunity
62   **Impfbescheinigungsformular,** *n.*
     (CFIMT An), vaccination certificate
     form
63   **Impfung,** *f.*, vaccination
64   **internationale Bescheinigung über**
     Impfung oder Wiederimpfung
     (CFIMT An), international certifi-
     cate of vaccination or revaccination
65   **implizieren,** to imply
66   **impliziert,** *adj.*, implied
67   **implizierte Befugnisse,** implied pow-
     ers
68   **Inanspruchnahme,** *f.*, claim(ing),
     resort, recourse
69   **die Inanspruchnahme regionaler**
     Einrichtungen (CUN 33), resort to
     regional agencies
70   **das Recht der Inanspruchnahme,**
     the right to claim, the right to have
     recourse to
71   **Individualbeschwerde,** *f.*, indi-
     vidual complaint (*e.g. to Human*
     Rights Committee)
72   **das Recht, eine Individualbe-**
     schwerde zu erheben (PHR Prot 4),
     the right of individual recourse

73 **Individualrechte,** *n.pl.,* individual rights, rights of the individual

74 **Informationsstelle,** *f.,* information centre/agency

75 **Inkorporation,** *f.,* incorporation

76 **Die Inkorporation oder die generelle Transformation beruht auf der grundsätzlichen Bereitschaft des Staates, den Inhalt der Völkerrechtsnorm auch als innerstaatliches Recht zur Anwendung zu bringen,** Incorporation or general transformation is based on the fundamental willingness of the state to apply as a rule of its municipal law the substance of a rule of international law (*Transformation)

77 **Inkorporationstheorie,** *f.,* incorporation theory

78 **inkorporieren,** to incorporate

79 **das Völkerrecht in das staatliche Recht inkorporieren,** to incorporate international law in municipal law

80 **Inkorporierung,** f. (= *Inkorporation, *f.),* incorporation

81 **automatische Inkorporierung der Völkerrechtsregeln,** automatic incorporation of rules of international law

82 **inkraftsetzen,** to put into force/effect (in *Kraft setzen)

83 **Inkraftsetzung,** *f.,* putting into force/effect, application (in *Kraft setzen)

84 **Inkrafttreten,** *n.,* entry into force/effect, taking force/effect

85 **vor/bis zum Inkrafttreten des Vertrags,** pending/prior to the entry into force of the treaty

86 **nach Inkrafttreten des Vertrags,** subsequent to the entry into force of the treaty

87 **Inkrafttreten durch** (+ *acc.*)/**aufgrund** (+ *gen.*), entry into force by/by virtue of

88 **Inkrafttreten durch Annahme/Unterzeichnung usw.,** entry into force by acceptance/signature, etc.

89 **Tag/Zeitpunkt des Inkrafttretens,** effective date, date of coming into force/effect

90 **Diese Konvention bleibt für die Dauer von 10 Jahren vom Zeitpunkt ihres Inkrafttretens an in Kraft** (CPG 14), The present convention shall remain in effect for a period of 10 years from the date of its coming into force (in *Kraft treten)

91 **Inlandszollamt,** *n.,* inland customs office

92 **innerstaatlich,** *adj.,* domestic, internal, state, national, municipal

93 **innerstaatliche Gesetzgebung,** national law (ILOC 23.3), national/domestic legislation

94 **innerstaatliches Recht,** municipal/state/national/internal/domestic law

95 **innerstaatliche Vorschriften,** municipal (etc.) rules/regulations/rules and regulations

96 **innerstaatliche Zuständigkeit,** municipal (etc.) jurisdiction/competence

97 **Inpflichtnahme,** *f.,* obligation, imposition of (an) obligation(s)

98 **Als Beispiel für die Inpflichtnahme von Einzelnen durch das Völkerrecht sei an das Problem des Völkerstrafrechts erinnert, das im Eichmannprozeß eine besondere Rolle spielte,** As an example of the imposition of rights and duties on individuals by international law, let us mention the problem of international criminal law which played a particular part in the Eichmann trial

99 **Insel,** *f.,* island

100 **Eine Insel ist natürlich entstandenes Land, das von Wasser umgeben ist und bei Flut über den Wasserspiegel hinausragt** (GCTS 10), An island is a naturally formed area of land, surrounded by water, which is above water at high tide (*Erhebung)

101 **Inselkette,** *f.,* fringe of islands (GCTS 4), chain of islands

102 **Instanz,** *f.,* court, tribunal, instance

103 **erste Instanz,** first instance

104 **höhere Instanz,** higher instance

105   untere Instanz, lower instance
      (* Vergleichsverfahren)
106   Institution, f., institution
107   Die Institutionen der Assoziation
      sind der Rat und jene anderen
      Organe, die der Rat schaffen kann
      (EFTA 1), The institutions of the
      association shall be a council and
      such other organs as the council may
      set up
108   bilaterale Institution, bilateral in-
      stitution
109   internationale Institution, interna-
      tional institution
110   multilaterale Institution, multilat-
      eral institution
111   regionale Institution, regional in-
      stitution
112   zwischenstaatliche Institution, inter-
      governmental institution
113   Insurgent, m., insurgent
114   Integrität, f., integrity
115   territoriale Integrität, territorial in-
      tegrity
116   die Bewahrung/Erhaltung der ter-
      ritorialen Integrität eines Staates,
      the maintenance/preservation of
      the territorial integrity of a state
117   Interesse, n., interest
118   die Interessen der Staatengemein-
      schaft als ganzes, the interests of the
      community of states as a whole
119   Schutz der Interessen, protection of
      interests
120   legitimes Interesse, legitimate inter-
      est (see * berühren[1])
121   öffentliches Interesse, public interest
122   verletztes Interesse, injured interest
123   Interimsausschuß, m., interim
      committee
124   Interimskommission, f., interim
      commission
125   Interimsrat, m., interim council
126   international, adj., international
127   internationaler Bahnhof, interna-
      tional station
128   internationaler Bediensteter, inter-
      national officer/official
129   internationale Behörde, interna-
      tional authority
130   internationale Binnengewässer,
      international internal waters

131   internationale Binnenschiffahrts-
      vorschriften, international inland
      waterway regulations
132   internationaler Charakter, interna-
      tional character/nature
133   der ausschließlich internationale
      Charakter der Verantwortung des
      Generalsekretärs (CUN 100), the
      exclusively international charac-
      ter of the responsibilities of the
      Secretary-General
134   internationaler Flughafen, interna-
      tional airport
135   internationaler Fluß, international
      river
136   Rechtsordnung der internationa-
      len Flüsse, law(s) of international
      rivers
137   internationaler Frieden, interna-
      tional peace
138   internationale Funktionen, interna-
      tional functions (see * Depositar)
139   internationales Gericht, interna-
      tional court
140   internationale Gerichtsbarkeit, in-
      ternational jurisdiction
141   internationaler Gerichtshof, interna-
      tional court of justice
142   internationale Gesundheitsvorschrif-
      ten (WHO), international sanitary
      regulations
143   internationale Gewohnheit, interna-
      tional custom
144   internationales Gewohnheitsrecht,
      international customary law, cus-
      tomary international law
145   internationales Gewohnheitsrecht
      als Ausdruck einer allgemeinen,
      als Recht anerkannten Übung, in-
      ternational custom as evidence of
      a general practice accepted as law
146   internationale Handelsschiffahrt
      (IMCO), shipping engaged in inter-
      national trade
147   internationaler Kanal, international
      canal
148   internationales Kartell, interna-
      tional cartel
149   internationale Konferenz, interna-
      tional conference
150   internationaler Konflikt, interna-
      tional conflict

151 **internationale Kontrolle,** international control/supervision

152 **internationaler Militärgerichtshof,** international military tribunal

153 **internationale Moral,** international morality

154 **internationale Ordnung,** international order

155 **internationale Organisation,** international organization

156 **internationale Person,** international person

157 **internationales Personal,** international staff

158 **internationale Persönlichkeit,** international personality

159 **internationale Praxis,** international practice

160 **internationales Prisengericht,** international prize court

161 **internationales Privatrecht,** private international law

162 **internationales Recht,** international law

(*Note:* **internationales Recht** *is a more comprehensive term than* international law, *as it applies also to areas that in English would normally require an additional adjectival component, e.g.* international criminal law *or* private international law. *The more precise equivalent for* international law *is* **Völkerrecht,** *which strictly speaking is only a subdivision of* **internationales Recht.** *For all examples and expressions see under* *Völkerrecht, *Völkerrechts-, *völkerrechtlich, and * Völker-)

163 **internationales Regime,** international régime

164 **internationale Reibungen,** international friction(s)

165 **internationaler Schutz,** international protection

166 **internationale Sicherheit,** international security (*see* *Weltfrieden)

167 **internationale Staatenordnung,** international order of states

168 **internationale Strafgerichtsbarkeit,** international criminal jurisdiction

169 **internationales Strafrecht,** international criminal law

170 **internationale Streitfälle,** international disputes

171 **internationale Streitigkeiten,** international disputes

172 **internationaler Strom,** international river

173 **internationales Treuhandsystem,** international trusteeship system

174 **internationale Übung,** international practice/usage

175 **internationale Verpflichtungen,** international obligations

176 **internationales Vertragsrecht,** international treaty law/law of treaties

177 **internationales Verwaltungsrecht,** international administrative law

178 **internationale Vorschriften,** international regulations

179 **internationale Wasserstraßen,** international waterways

180 **internationale Zivilluftfahrt,** international civil aviation

181 **internationale Zusammenarbeit,** international cooperation

182 **internationalisieren,** to internationalize

183 **internationalisiert,** *adj.,* internationalized

184 **Internationalisierung,** *f.,* internationalization

185 **Internationalisierung von Flüssen, Kanälen und Meerengen,** internationalization of rivers, canals and straits

186 **internieren,** to intern

187 **Interniertenausschuß,** *m.,* Internee Committee

188 **Internierter,** *adj.n.,* internee

189 **die Verlegung von Internierten** (GC IV), the transfer of internees

190 **Internierung,** *f.,* internment

191 **Internierungskarte,** *f.,* internment card

192 **Internierungslager,** *n.,* internment camp

193 **Die Internierungslager werden so mit den Buchstaben ,,IC" gekennzeichnet, daß sie tagsüber aus der Luft deutlich erkennbar sind** (GC IV 83), The internment camps shall be indicated by the letters "IC"

placed so as to be clearly visible in the daytime from the air

194 **Internierungsort,** *m*., place of internment

195 **Internuntius,** *m*. (*pl.* **-ien**), internuncio

196 **Interpretation,** *f*., interpretation

197 **authentische Interpretation,** authentic interpretation (**Auslegung*)

198 **interpretieren,** to interpret (**auslegen*)

199 **intervenieren,** to intervene (*both in the diplomatic sense of* **sich um eine Angelegenheit kümmern** *and the sense of* **sich einmischen,** *the pejorative sense of which may sometimes best be rendered by* to interfere) (**einmischen*)

200 **Intervention,** *f*., intervention (*note to* *intervenieren)

201 **Interventionismus,** *m*., interventionism

202 **interventionistisch,** *adj*., interventionist

203 **interventionistische Maßnahmen,** interventionist measures/action

204 **Interventionsabsicht,** *f*., intention to intervene

205 **Interventionsakt,** *m*., act of intervention

206 **Interventionsmaßnahme,** *f*., intervention measure/action

207 **Interventionsrecht,** *n*., right of intervention, right to intervene

208 **Interventionsverbot,** *n*., duty not to intervene, prohibition of intervention

J

1 **Jahrbuch,** *n.*, yearbook
2 **statistisches Jahrbuch,** statistical yearbook
3 **Jahresabrechnung,** *f.*, annual account(s)
   (*Jahresberechnung)
4 **Jahresbeitrag,** *m.*, annual contribution
5 **Jahresberechnung,** *f.*, annual account(s)
6 **durch Rechnungsprüfer kontrollierte Jahresberechnungen** (EONR V), audited annual accounts
7 **Jahresbericht,** *m.*, annual report
8 **Jahreshaushalt,** *m.*, annual budget
9 **Jahreshaushaltsplan,** *m.*, annual budget
10 **Jahrestagung,** *f.*, annual session, annual conference
11 **ordentliche Jahrestagung,** regular/ ordinary annual session
12 **Jahresversammlung,** *f.*, annual assembly
13 **Ja-Stimme,** *f.*, vote cast "for", affirmative vote
14 **Judikative,** *f.*, judiciary
15 **Jurisdiktion,** *f.*, jurisdiction
   (*Gerichtsbarkeit)
16 **juristisch,** *adj.*, judicial, juridical, juristic, legal
   (*gerichtlich, *richterlich)
17 **Justizbehörde,** *f.*, judicial authority/authorities
18 **Justizhoheit,** *f.*, judicial sovereignty
19 **justiziabel,** *adj.*, justiciable
20 **Justizverweigerung,** *f.*, denial of justice
   (*For further* **Justiz-** *compounds see under* *Rechts-.)

102

K

1 **Kabotage,** *f.*, cabotage
2 **Kabotagenprivilegien,** *n.pl.*, cabotage privileges
3 **Kammer,** *f.*, chamber
4 **Jedes Urteil, das von einer der Kammern erlassen wird, gilt als Urteil des Gerichtshofes (SICJ 27),** A judgment given by any of the chambers shall be considered as rendered by the court
5 **Jede Entscheidung, die eine Kammer in einer ihr zugewiesenen Angelegenheit gefällt hat, gilt als Entscheidung des Gerichts (CRPG An),** Any decision of a chamber, on a case assigned to it, shall be deemed to be a decision of the tribunal
6 **eine Kammer berufen/bestellen/bilden,** to form a chamber
7 **Kampf,** *m.*, combat
8 **außer Kampf,** *hors de combat*
9 **Personen, die durch Verwundung oder Gefangennahme außer Kampf gesetzt sind (GC IV 3),** persons placed *hors de combat* by wounds or detention
10 **Kampfgebiet,** *n.*, zone of military operations, region where fighting is taking place (GC IV)
11 **Kampfhandlung,** *f.*, (military) operation
12 **die allgemeine Einstellung der Kampfhandlungen (GC IV),** the general close of military operations
13 **Kampfzone,** *f.*, combat zone (GC III)
14 **Kandidat,** *m.*, candidate
15 **kandidieren,** to stand as candidate
16 **Kanonenschußweite,** *f.*, gunshot range
17 **Regel der Kanonenschußweite,** rule of the range of cannon
18 **Kanzler,** *m.*, Chancellor (*e.g. in consulate*)
19 **Kanzler des Gerichtshofes,** Registrar of the Court (ICJ, EAEC, etc.)
20 **Kapellenrecht,** *n.*, right of chapel

21 **Kaperbrief,** *m.*, letter(s) of marque (and reprisal)
22 **Kaperei,** *f.*, privateering
23 **Kaperer,** *m.*, captor, privateer
24 **kapern,** to capture
25 **Kaperschiff,** *n.*, privateer
26 **Kapitän,** *m.*, master
27 **die strafrechtliche oder disziplinarische Verantwortlichkeit des Kapitäns (GCHS 11),** the penal or disciplinary responsibility of the master
28 **Kapitänspatent,** *n.*, master's certificate
29 **Kapitel,** *m.*, chapter
30 **in Kapiteln gliedern,** to set out in chapters
31 **die in Kapitel II dieses Vertrags aufgeführten Bedingungen,** the provisions set forth in Chapter II of the present treaty
32 **Kapitulation,** *f.*, capitulation
33 **bedingungslose Kapitulation,** unconditional capitulation
34 **Kapitulationsvertrag,** *m.*, treaty of capitulation
35 **kapitulieren,** to capitulate
36 **Kategorie,** *f.*, category (*Klasse)
37 **Kenntnis, in,** aware (*in preamble*)
38 **in Kenntnis setzen,** to inform, to advise
39 **Der Generalsekretär setzt die anderen Parteien davon in Kenntnis,** The Secretary-General shall inform the other parties
40 **Kenntnis (davon) geben,** to inform/give notice of/advise
41 **Kenntnis (davon) nehmen,** to note, to be informed of
42 **Kernanlage,** *f.*, nuclear installation
43 **Eine Kernanlage bedeutet Kernreaktoren, Fabriken, die Kernbrennstoffe verwenden, Einrichtungen für die Lagerung von Kernmaterialien (VCLD 1),** "Nuclear installation" means any nuclear reactor, any factory using nuclear fuel, any facility where nuclear material is stored

44 **Inhaber einer Kernanlage** (VCLD), operator of a nuclear installation (*haftbar)

45 **Kernbrennstoff,** *m.*, nuclear fuel

46 **bestrahlte Kernbrennstoffe,** irradiated fuels

47 **Aufbereitung bestrahlter Kernbrennstoffe,** processing of irradiated nuclear fuels

48 **Kernenergie,** *f.*, nuclear energy

49 **die friedliche Anwendung/Verwendung/Nutzung von Kernenergie,** the peaceful use/uses of nuclear energy

50 **die friedliche Entwicklung der Kernenergie** (EAEC), the peaceful development of atomic energy

51 **Kernforschung,** *f.*, nuclear research

52 **gemeinsame Kernforschung** (EAEC), joint nuclear research

53 **Kernmaterial,** *n.* (*pl.* **-ien**), nuclear material

54 **besonderes Kernmaterial,** special nuclear material

55 **Kernsprengkörper,** *m.*, nuclear explosive device (TNPNW)

56 **Kernsprengmittel,** *n.pl.*, nuclear explosives

57 **Kernwaffen,** *f.pl.*, nuclear weapons

58 **Versuchsexplosionen von Kernwaffen,** test explosions of nuclear weapons (MNTB Pr), nuclear weapon test explosions (MNTB 1) (*nukleare Versuchsexplosionen)

59 **Kernwaffenstaat,** *m.*, nuclear weapon state (TNPNW)

60 **Kernwaffenversuch,** *m.*, nuclear weapon test
(*For terms not listed under* **Kern-** *see under* *nuklear.)

61 **Klage,** *f.*, action, proceeding, suit; statement of claim, writ, plaint; complaint

62 **Klagen in Nachlaßsachen** (VCDR 31), actions relating to succession

63 **Klagen in Zusammenhang mit einem freien Beruf oder einer gewerblichen Tätigkeit, die der Diplomat im Empfangsstaat ausübt** (VCDR 31), an action relating to a professional or commercial activity exercised by the diplomatic agent in the receiving state

64 **unmittelbar an der Klage beteiligt sein/ein unmittelbares Interesse an der Klage haben,** to be directly concerned in the action/complaint (etc.)

65 **dingliche Klagen,** real actions

66 **Ein Diplomat unterliegt der Zivilgerichtsbarkeit des Empfangsstaates hinsichtlich dinglicher Klagen,** A diplomatic agent is liable to the civil jurisdiction of the receiving state in respect of real actions

67 **(un)zulässige Klagen,** (in)admissible actions (etc.)

68 **einer Klage abhelfen,** to meet a complaint

69 **Vorschläge, wie der Klage abzuhelfen ist** (ILO 28), recommendations as to the steps which should be taken to meet the complaint

70 **eine Klage einbringen,** to bring/start/initiate/institute an action (etc.), to sue

71 **eine Klage einreichen,** to lodge/file/submit an action (etc.)

72 **Jedes Mitglied kann beim Internationalen Arbeitsamt Klage gegen ein anderes Mitglied einreichen** (ILO 26), Any of the members shall have the right to file a complaint with the International Labour Office against another member

73 **eine Klage erheben,** to bring/start/initiate/institute an action (etc.), to sue (*see* *Schadenersatzanspruch)

74 **eine Klage auf . . . stützen,** to base an action (etc.) on . . .

75 **eine Klage verweisen (an),** to refer/pass an action (etc.) (to)

76 **eine Klage an einen Untersuchungsausschuß verweisen** (ILO 27), to refer a complaint to a committee of inquiry

77 **Klagebeantwortung,** *f.*, countermemorials (CUN), answer to the complaint (CSMW An), defendant's answer (schriftliches *Verfahren)

78 **Klagebegründung,** *f.*, statement of

claim/action, (written) action/complaint

79 **Klageerhebung,** *f.*, submission of a case, commencement/initiation of an action/claim, commencement of the suit

80 **Klagegrund,** *m.*, grounds for/cause of the action/claim/complaint

81 **klagen,** to bring an action/-claim/complaint, to start/initiate proceedings, to sue

82 **klagend,** *adj.*, plaintiff

83 **die klagende Regierung,** the plaintiff government, the government making/filing/lodging the action/claim/complaint

84 **Kläger,** *m.*, plaintiff, plaintiff state/party, complainant

85 **als Kläger auftreten,** to appear as plaintiff, to sue

86 **Klagerücknahme,** *f.*, withdrawal of (the) action/claim/complaint

87 **Klageschrift,** *f.*, (written) complaint, statement of claim, (written) application (*anhängig, schriftliches *Verfahren, *Streitigkeit)

88 **Klagewege** *m.*, **im,** by (means of) action/claim/complaint

89 **die Streitigkeit im Klagewege dem Gerichtshof unterbreiten** (VCDR Opt Prot), to bring the dispute before the court by an application

90 **klären,** to clarify, to elucidate

91 **Klärung,** *f.*, clarification, elucidation

92 **alle Urkunden, die zur Klärung der Frage dienen können** (SICJ 65), all documents likely to throw light upon the question

93 **Klasse,** *f.*, class

94 **Die Staaten vereinbaren die Klasse, in welche ihre Missionschefs einzuordnen sind** (VCDR 15), The class to which the heads of their missions are to be assigned shall be agreed between states

95 **Kategorie und Klasse eines Leiters einer konsularischen Vertretung** (VCCR 9/11, VCDR 14), category and class of a head of a consular post (*see also under* *Rang, *Missionschef, *konsularische Vertretung)

96 **Klassifikation,** *f.*, classification

97 **vollständige Symbole der Internationalen Klassifikation,** complete symbols of the International Classification

98 **Klassifikationssystem,** *n.*, system of classification

99 **Klassifikationssystem für Erfindungspatente** (ECICP 1), system of classification of patents for inventions

100 **Klausel,** *f.*, clause

101 **Klausel** *rebus sic stantibus, rebus sic stantibus* clause

102 **Koalitionsfreiheit,** *f.*, freedom of (professional) association/coalition

103 **Kodifikation,** *f.*, codification

104 **völkerrechtliche Kodifikation,** codification of international law

105 **Kodifikationskonferenz,** *f.*, codification conference

106 **Kodifikationsvertrag,** *m.*, codification treaty

107 **kodifizieren,** to codify

108 **kodifiziert,** *adj.*, codified

109 **Weite Teile des Völkerrechts sind bisher nicht kodifiziert: sie beruhen auf Gewohnheitsrecht oder werden aus allgemeinen Rechtsgrundsätzen abgeleitet,** Large sections of international law have not yet been codified: they are based on customary law or are derived from general principles of law

110 **kodifiziertes Recht,** codified law

111 **vertraglich kodifizierte Regel,** rule codified in a treaty

112 **kodifiziertes Völkergewohnheitsrecht,** codified international custom(ary law)

113 **Kodifizierung,** *f.*, codification

114 **Koexistenz,** *f.*, coexistence

115 **friedliche Koexistenz,** peaceful coexistence

116 **koimperial,** *adj.*, coimperial

117 **koimperiale Herrschaftsform,** coimperial form of government

118 **Koimperium,** *n.*, coimperium (*Kondominium)

119 **kollektiv,** *adj.*, collective

120 **Kollektivaktion,** *f.*, collective action(s)

121 **Kollektivausweisung,** *f.*, collective expulsion

122 **Kollektivausweisungen von Ausländern** (PHR Prot 4), collective expulsion of aliens

123 **Kollektiveinbürgerung,** *f.*, collective naturalization

124 **Kollektivgarantie,** *f.*, collective guarantee

125 **Kollektivintervention,** *f.*, collective intervention

126 **Kollektivmaßnahme,** *f.*, collective measure/action

127 **wirksame Kollektivmaßnahmen treffen** (CUN 1), to take effective collective measures (*ausweisen)

128 **Kollektivnote,** *f.*, collective note

129 **Kollektivstrafe,** *f.*, collective punishment, collective penalty/penalties

130 **Kollektivverhandlungen,** *f.pl.*, collective bargaining

131 **Kollektivvertrag,** *m.*, collective treaty

132 **Kollision,** *f.*, conflict (*e.g. of laws*)

133 **Kollisionsnorm,** *f.*, rule of conflict

134 **die Kollisionsnormen, von denen auszugehen das Schiedsgericht jeweils für richtig erachtet** (ECICA VII), the rules of conflict that the arbitrators deem applicable

135 **Kollisionsrecht,** *n.*, rules governing the conflict of laws (zuständiges *Gericht)

136 **Kolonialgebiet,** *n.*, colonial territory

137 **Kolonialismus,** *m.*, colonialism

138 **kolonialistisch,** *adj.*, colonialist

139 **Kolonialmacht,** *f.*, colonial power

140 **Kolonialreich,** *n.*, colonial empire

141 **Kombattant,** *m.*, combatant

142 **illegaler Kombattant,** illegal combatant

143 **legaler Kombattant,** legal combatant

144 **Komitee,** *n.*, committee

145 **Komitees oder Ausschüsse beratenden Charakters** (CE 17), advisory and technical committees or commissions (*Ausschuß)

146 **Kommissar,** *m.*, commissioner (*e.g. of commission of inquiry*)

147 **Kommission,** *f.*, commission

148 **beratende Kommission,** advisory commission

149 **beratende gemischte Kommission,** mixed advisory commission

150 **ständige Kommission,** permanent commission

151 **vorbereitende Kommission,** preparatory commission

152 **Kommissionsmitglied,** *n.*, commissioner, member of a commission

153 **Kommuniqué,** *n.*, communiqué

154 **gemeinsames Kommuniqué,** joint communiqué

155 **kompetent,** *adj.*, competent, authorized (*zuständig)

156 **Kompetenz,** *f.*, competence, authority, power

157 **internationale Kompetenz,** international competence

158 **nationale/staatliche Kompetenz,** national/domestic/state competence (*Zuständigkeit)

159 **Kompetenzkompetenz,** *f.*, power to delegate authority/competence

160 **Kompetenz-Theorie,** *f.*, competence theory

161 **Kompetenzverteilung,** *f.*, division of competence

162 **Kompetenzverteilung zwischen Bund und Ländern** (GG 70), division of competence between the Federation and the Länder

163 **Kompromiß,** *m.*, compromise, *compromis* (*Schiedskompromiß, *Schiedsvergleich)

164 **Kompromißbereitschaft,** *f.*, readiness to (reach a) compromise

165 **Kompromißfrieden,** *m.*, compromise peace

166 **Kompromißlösung,** *f.*, compromise solution

167 **Kondominium,** *n.*, condominium

168 **Beim Kondominium wird die Staatsgewalt im eigenen Staatsgebiet ausgeübt, während beim Koimperium diese Befugnis über fremdes (drittstaatliches) Gebiet ausgeübt wird,** In a condominium sovereignty/state jurisdiction is exercised

within the territory of the state, whereas in a coimperium this authority is exercised over foreign territory (i.e. the territory of a third state)

169 **Konferenz,** *f.,* conference

170 **die Konferenz der UN über . . . tagte vom . . . bis . . .,** the UN conference on . . . met during the period from . . . to . . .

171 **die Regierungen der folgenden Staaten waren auf der Konferenz durch Delegationen/Beobachter vertreten:** the governments of the following states were represented at the conference by delegations/observers:

172 **Konferenz für/über,** conference on

173 **Allgemeine Konferenz,** General Conference (*e.g.* ILO)

174 **eine Konferenz einberufen,** to convene/convoke a conference

175 **eine Konferenz vertagen,** to adjourn/postpone a conference

176 **Konferenzdiplomatie,** *f.,* diplomacy by conference

177 **Konferenzteilnehmer,** *m.,* participants (at the conference), conference members

178 **konfiszieren,** to confiscate

179 **Konfiszierung,** *f.,* confiscation (*Beschlagnahme)

180 **Konflikt,** *m.,* conflict

181 **Konflikte nichtinternationalen Charakters** (PCP 19), conflicts not of an international character

182 **Konflikte nichtkriegerischen Charakters,** conflicts of a non-war character/status, non-war conflicts

183 **die am Konflikt beteiligten Mächte/Parteien** (GC I), the powers in conflict/the parties to the conflict

184 **bewaffneter Konflikt,** armed/military conflict

185 **bewaffneter Konflikt, der keinen internationalen Charakter hat** (GC I), armed conflict not of an international character

186 **internationaler Konflikt,** international conflict

187 **militärischer Konflikt,** armed/military conflict

188 **zwischenstaatlicher Konflikt,** international conflict (*Streit *and* *Streit- *compounds*)

189 **Konfliktspartei,** *f.,* party to the/a conflict

190 **konkludent,** *adj.,* implied, conclusive

191 **konkludente Anerkennung,** implied recognition

192 **konkludente Handlung,** conclusive act, act implying intent (*e.g. a major military attack by state* A *against state* B *may imply the intent of state* A *to wage war on state* B, *even without express notification in a declaration of war*)

193 **Konkordat,** *n.,* concordat

194 **konstituieren,** to constitute

195 **konstituierend,** *adj.,* constitutive, constituent (*Auslegung)

196 **Konstituierung,** *f.,* constitution

197 **konstitutiv,** *adj.,* constitutive

198 **Konsul,** *m.,* consular officer, consul (Leiter einer *konsularischen Vertretung)

199 **Konsularabkommen,** *n.,* consular agreement

200 **Konsularabteilung,** *f.,* consular section

201 **Konsularagent,** *m.,* consular agent

202 **Konsularagentur,** *f.,* consular agency

203 **Konsularbediensteter,** *adj.n.,* consular employee

204 **Konsularbehörde,** *f.,* consular authority

205 **Konsularbehörde des Flaggenstaates** (GCTS 19), consular authority of the flag state

206 **Konsularbezirk,** *m.,* consular district

207 **Konsulargericht,** *n.,* consular court

208 **Konsulargerichtsbarkeit,** *f.,* consular jurisdiction

209 **konsularisch,** *adj.,* consular

210 **konsularische Amtshandlungen,** consular acts, official consular acts

211 **für konsularische Amtshandlungen Gebühren und Kosten erheben** (VCCR 39), to levy fees and charges for consular acts

212 **konsularisches Archiv,** consular archive(s)

213 **konsularische Aufgaben,** consular duties/functions

214 **die Wahrnehmung der konsularischen Aufgaben für einen dritten Staat** (VCCR 8), the exercise of consular functions on behalf of a third state (*see* *Verantwortung)

215 **konsularische Außenstelle,** consular section

216 **konsularische Beziehungen,** consular relations

217 **konsularischer Dienst,** consular service

218 **konsularische Funktionen,** consular functions

219 **konsularische Immunitäten,** consular immunities (*see* *Immunität, *Befreiung)

220 **konsularisches Korps,** consular corps

221 **konsularisches Kuriergepäck,** consular bag (*see* *Kuriergepäck)

222 **konsularisches Personal,** consular staff

223 **konsularische Räumlichkeiten,** consular premises

224 **Unverletzlichkeit der konsularischen Räumlichkeiten** (VCCR 31), inviolability of the consular premises

225 **der Friede und die Würde der konsularischen Räumlichkeiten** (VCCR 31), the peace and dignity of the consular premises (*See also under* Räumlichkeiten der *Mission.)

226 **konsularische Vertretung,** (i) consular representation; (ii) consular post

227 **die Einstufung der konsularischen Vertretung** (VCCR), the classification of the consular post

228 **Leiter einer konsularischen Vertretung** (VCCR), head of a consular post

229 **Die Leiter konsularischer Vertretungen sind in folgende 4 Klassen eingeteilt: (1) Generalkonsuln; (2) Konsuln; (3) Vizekonsuln; (4) Konsularagenten** (VCCR 9), The heads of consular posts are divided into 4 classes, namely: (1) Consuls-General; (2) Consuls; (3) Vice-Consuls; (4) Consular Agents

230 **amtierender Leiter einer konsularischen Vertretung** (VCCR), acting head of a consular post

231 **konsularische Vorrechte,** consular privileges

232 **Konsularkonvention,** *f.*, consular convention (*normally refers to the Vienna Convention on Consular Relations* 24.4.63)

233 **Konsularposten,** *m.* (= *konsularische Vertretung), consular post

234 **Leiter eines Konsularpostens,** head of a consular post

235 **Konsularposten, deren Leiter ein Wahlkonsul ist** (VCCR 58), consular posts headed by an honorary consular officer

236 **Konsularrecht,** *n.*, consular law, law(s) relating to/governing consuls

237 **Konsularvertrag,** *m.*, consular treaty

Konsularvertretung, *f.* = *konsularische Vertretung

238 **Konsulat,** *n.*, consulate

239 **Generalkonsulat,** consulate-general

240 **Konsulatsdienst,** *m.*, consular service

241 **Konsulatsfaktura,** *f.*, consular invoice

242 **Konsultation,** *f.*, consultation

243 **Jede Vertragspartei leitet Konsultationen mit der Organisation ein/nimmt Konsultationen mit der Organisation auf** (SF 75), Any contracting party shall enter into consultations with the organization

244 **Konsultationen werden geführt/finden statt,** Consultations shall be held (SF 76)

245 **konsultativ,** *adj.*, consultative

246 **Konsultativabmachung,** *f.*, consultative arrangement

247 **Konsultativorgan,** *n.*, advisory/consultative organ/body

248 **Konsultativrat,** *m.*, advisory/consultative council

249   **konsultieren,** to consult

250   **die Parteien konsultieren einander,** the parties shall consult (with) each other (SF 76)

251   **Konsultierung,** *f.,* consultation

252   **nach Konsultierung des Ausschusses,** after consulting (with) the committee

253   **nach Konsultierung des betreffenden Staates** (IAEA XII), after consultation with the state concerned (*Konsultation)

254   **Konterbande,** *f.,* contraband

255   **absolute Konterbande,** absolute contraband

256   **bedingte/relative Konterbande,** conditional contraband

257   **unbedingte Konterbande,** absolute contraband

258   **Kontiguität,** *f.,* contiguity

259   **Kontiguitätszone,** *f.,* contiguous zone

260   **Kontinentalschelf,** *m.,* continental shelf (*Festlandsockel)

261   **Kontinentalsockel,** *m.,* continental shelf (*Festlandsockel)

262   **Kontingent[1],** *n.,* quota

263   **Erweiterung von Kontingenten** (EEC), enlargement of quotas

264   **Kontingent[2],** *n.,* contingent

265   **Mitglieder halten Kontingente ihrer Luftstreitkräfte zum sofortigen Einsatz bei gemeinsamen internationalen Zwangsmaßnahmen bereit** (CUN 45), Members shall hold immediately available national airforce contingents for combined international enforcement action

266   **Kontinuität,** *f.,* continuity

267   **Kontinuität von Staaten,** continuity of states

268   **kontradiktorisch,** *adj.,* contentious, by means of/involving counterarguments, by means of/involving statements/arguments by both parties

269   **Die Untersuchung erfolgt kontradiktorisch** (HgI 19), On the inquiry both sides must be heard

270   **Zum Zweck der Tatsachenfeststellung hat die Kommission mit den Vertretern der Parteien eine kontradiktorische Prüfung ... vorzunehmen** (PHR 28), With a view to ascertaining the facts the Commission shall undertake together with the representatives of both parties an examination

271   **Kontrollamt,** *n.,* board of control, supervisory board

272   **Kontrollausschuß,** *m.,* committee of control, supervisory committee

273   **Kontrollbefugnis,** *f.,* supervisory authority/power, authority/power of supervision/control

274   **Kontrolldokument,** *n.,* control document (CFIMT)

275   **Kontrolle,** *f.,* supervision, control; inspection; monitoring

276   **Kontrolle des persönlichen Gepäcks des Diplomaten** (VCDR 36), inspection of the personal baggage of the diplomatic agent

277   **Rechte zur Kontrolle und Aufsicht über Schiffe** (VCCR 5), rights of supervision and inspection in respect of vessels

278   **kontrollieren,** to inspect, to control, to examine, to monitor

279   **Kontrollmaßnahme,** *f.,* measure of control, control action

280   **Kontrollratsgesetz,** *n.,* Control Council Law

281   **Kontrollrecht,** *n.,* right of supervision/control, right to supervise/control

282   **Eine solche Erlaubnis schließt nicht ein Kontrollrecht der anderen Vertragsregierungen aus** (CSLS V), Such permission shall not deprive other contracting governments of any right of control

283   **Kontrollstelle,** *f.,* board of control, supervisory board

284   **Konvention,** *f.,* convention, covenant

285   **Konvention zu/über,** convention for/on (*Übereinkommen *and* *note* *to* *Vertrag *in Annex* 1)

286   **Konventionsabschluß,** *m.,* conclusion of a/the convention

287 **Konventionsentwurf,** *m.,* draft convention

288 **Konventionstext,** *m.,* text of the convention

289 **Konzession,** *f.,* concession

290 **Konzessionsvertrag,** *m.,* concession(ary) contract/treaty

291 **Konzessionsverträge zwischen Staaten und Privatpersonen,** concessionary treaties between states and individuals

292 **kooptieren,** to co-opt

293 **Kooptierung,** *f.,* co-option

294 **koordinieren,** to coordinate

295 **Koordinierung,** *f.,* coordination

296 **Koordinierungsausschuß,** *m.,* coordination/coordinating committee

297 **Körperschaft,** *f.,* corporate body, body

298 **beratende Körperschaft,** advisory/deliberative body

299 **gesetzgebende Körperschaft,** legislative body

300 **die Wahl der gesetzgebenden Körperschaften** (PHR Prot 3), the choice of the legislature

301 **nationale Körperschaften,** national bodies

302 **öffentlich-rechtliche Körperschaft,** public body, body corporate governed by public law

303 **Korps,** *n.,* corps

304 **diplomatisches Korps,** diplomatic corps

305 **konsularisches Korps,** consular corps

306 **Korrespondenz,** *f.,* correspondence

307 **amtliche Korrespondenz und sonstige amtliche Mitteilungen im Durchgangsverkehr** (VCDR 40), official correspondence and other official communications in transit (*Schriftstück, *Schriftverkehr)

308 **kraft,** *prep.* (+ *gen.*), by virtue of, by operation of

309 **kraft ihres Amtes,** in virtue of their functions (VCLOT 7), by virtue of their office, *ex officio*

310 **kraft internationaler Gewohnheit verbindlich** (VCLOT 38), binding through international custom

311 **kraft dieses Rechts** (ICCPR 1), by virtue of this right

312 **kraft der Rechtsvorschriften des Empfangsstaates** (VCDR Opt Prot), by the operation of the law of the receiving state

313 **Kraft,** *f.,* force, effect

314 **bindende Kraft,** binding force (*see* *Verbindlichkeit[1])

315 **konstituierende/konstitutive Kraft,** constitutive force

316 **normative/normsetzende Kraft,** normative force

317 **die normative Kraft völkerrechtlicher Verträge,** the normative effect/power of international treaties

318 **rückwirkende Kraft,** retroactive force, retroactivity

319 **verbindliche/verpflichtende Kraft,** binding force (*see* *Verbindlichkeit[1])

320 **außer Kraft,** not in force, not in effect

321 **außer Kraft setzen,** to repeal, to abolish, to terminate, to suspend (*see* *kündigen, *Außerkraftsetzung)

322 **außer Kraft treten,** to cease to be in force/effect, to terminate (*see* *erlöschen)

323 **in Kraft,** in force, in effect

324 **in Kraft befindlich,** in force, in effect

325 **bisher in Kraft befindliche Ordnungen** (UCC Pr), systems already in force

326 **auf Grund in Kraft befindlicher und für die Vertragsparteien verbindlicher Bestimmungen** (VCLOT 65), under any provisions in force binding the parties

327 **in Kraft bleiben,** to remain in force/effect

328 **Dieses Abkommen bleibt auf unbegrenzte Zeit in Kraft,** This agreement shall continue in effect/remain in effect for an unlimited period

329 **Diese Übereinkunft bleibt zeitlich unbegrenzt in Kraft**

(ECICP 8), This convention shall remain in force indefinitely

330 **ohne zeitliche Begrenzung in Kraft bleiben** (EXWC 11), to remain in force indefinitely

331 **in Kraft setzen,** to put/bring into force/effect

332 **die Bestimmungen dieses Abkommens ganz oder teilweise in Kraft setzen** (GC IV 3), to bring into force all or part of the provisions of the present convention

333 **in Kraft treten,** to enter into force/effect

334 **geltende oder künftig in Kraft tretende Bestimmungen** (ES 32), provisions which are already in force, or may come into force

335 **... tritt für die Staaten in Kraft, die ...,** ... shall enter into force in respect of those states which ... (*Inkrafttreten)

336 **Krankenpfleger,** *m.*, orderly, nurse

337 **bewaffneter Krankenpfleger** (GC I), armed orderly/nurse

338 **Kreuz, Rotes,** Red Cross

339 **Internationales Komitee des Roten Kreuzes,** International Committee of the Red Cross

340 **Krieg,** *m.*, war, warfare

341 **sich aus dem Krieg ergebende Ansprüche** (CSMW), claims arising out of the war

342 **durch den Krieg verursachte Leiden** (GC IV 13), sufferings caused by war

343 **infolge des Krieges verwaiste Kinder** (GC), children orphaned as a result of the war

344 **vom Krieg zerstreute Familien** (GC), families dispersed owing to the war

345 **Folgen des Krieges** (GC), consequences of war, results of war

346 **Gefahren des Krieges** (GC), hazards/dangers of war

347 **Gesetze und Gebräuche des Krieges,** laws and customs of war

348 **Verstoß gegen die Gesetze und Gebräuche des Krieges,** act in violation of the laws and customs of war

349 **Illegalität des Krieges,** illegality of war

350 **Illegitimität des Krieges,** illegitimacy/unjust cause of war

351 **Legalität des Krieges,** legality of war

352 **Legitimität des Krieges,** legitimacy/just cause of war

353 **Rechtmäßigkeit des Krieges,** legality of war

354 **Verhütung des Krieges,** prevention of war

355 **Verzicht auf Krieg,** renunciation of war

356 **Verzicht auf Krieg als Werkzeug ihrer nationalen Politik** (TRW Pr), renunciation of war as an instrument of their national policy

357 **beschränkter Krieg,** limited warfare

358 **biologischer Krieg,** biological warfare

359 **chemischer Krieg,** chemical warfare

360 **gerechter Krieg,** just war

361 **illegaler Krieg,** illegal/unlawful war

362 **illegitimer Krieg,** illegitimate/unjust war

363 **kalter Krieg,** cold war

364 **legaler Krieg,** legal/lawful war

365 **legitimer Krieg,** legitimate/just war

366 **psychologischer Krieg,** psychological warfare

367 **rechtmäßiger Krieg,** legal/lawful war

368 **rechtswidriger Krieg,** illegal/unlawful war

369 **totaler/unbeschränkter Krieg,** total/unlimited/unrestricted war(fare)

370 **ungerechter Krieg,** unjust war

371 **Krieg ächten,** to outlaw war

372 **Krieg erklären,** to declare war

373 **Krieg führen,** to wage war

374 **Krieg verhüten,** to prevent war

375 **Krieg verurteilen,** to condemn war

376 **den Krieg als Mittel für die Lösung internationaler Streitfälle verurteilen** (TRW I), to condemn recourse to war for the solution of international controversies

377 **zum Krieg schreiten** (TRW Pr), to resort to war

378 **kriegerisch**, *adj.*, belligerent
379 **kriegführend**, *adj.*, belligerent
380 **Kriegführender**, *adj.n.*, belligerent
381 **Kriegführende zur See,** maritime belligerents
382 **feindliche Kriegführende,** hostile belligerents
383 **Kriegführung,** *f.*, war(fare)
384 **maritime Kriegführung,** naval warfare, maritime warfare, war(fare) at sea (*Krieg)
385 **Kriegführungsrecht,** *n.*, the right to wage/resort to war
386 **Kriegsächtung,** *f.*, outlawry of war
387 **Kriegsausbruch,** *m.*, outbreak of war
388 **Kriegsberichterstatter,** *m.*, war correspondent
389 **kriegsbeschädigt,** *adj.*, (war) crippled
390 **kriegsbeschädigter Angehöriger von einem Mitgliedsland** (EXWC Pr), a war cripple being a national of a member country
391 **Kriegsbeschädigter,** *adj.n.*, person injured in war, war cripple
392 **Austausch von Kriegsbeschädigten** (EXWC), exchange of war cripples (*Beschädigter²)
393 **Kriegsbeteiligung,** *f.*, cobelligerency
394 **Kriegsbeute,** *f.*, booty, war booty
395 **Kriegsbrauch,** *m.*, usage of war
396 **Kriegsdrohung,** *f.*, threat of war
397 **Kriegseintritt,** *m.*, entry into (the) war
398 **Kriegsentschädigung,** *f.*, (war) reparation(s)
399 **Kriegsereignisse,** *n.pl.*, events of war
400 **infolge von Kriegsereignissen** (UNCDD 1), in consequence of events of war
401 **Kriegserklärung,** *f.*, declaration of war
402 **Kriegsfall,** *m.*, *casus belli*
403 **Kriegsfolgen,** *f.pl.* (GC IV), consequences/effects of war
404 **Kriegsfreiheit,** *f.*, freedom/right to wage war
405 **Kriegsgefahren,** *f.pl.* (GC), dangers/hazards of war
406 **eine den Kriegsgefahren besonders ausgesetzte Gegend,** an area particularly exposed to the dangers of war
407 **Kriegsgefangenenlager,** *n.*, prisoner of war camp
408 **Kriegsgefangenenpost,** *f.*, Prisoner of War Mail
409 **Kriegsgefangenenschriftwechsel,** *m.*, Prisoner of War Mail
410 **Kriegsgefangener,** *adj.n.*, prisoner of war
411 **Die Kriegsgefangenen unterstehen der Gewalt der feindlichen Macht, nicht jedoch der Gewalt der Personen oder Truppenteile, die sie gefangen haben** (GC III), Prisoners of war are in the hands of the enemy power, but not the individuals or military units who have captured them
412 **gesundheitliche/seelische Bedürfnisse der Kriegsgefangenen** (GC III), medical/spiritual needs of prisoners of war
413 **menschliche Behandlung der Kriegsgefangenen,** humane treatment of prisoners of war
414 **Arbeitslager für Kriegsgefangene** (GC III), labour camp for prisoners of war
415 **Heimschaffung der Kriegsgefangenen** (GC III), repatriation of prisoners of war
416 **Hospitalisierung von Kriegsgefangenen in neutralen Ländern** (GC III), accommodation of prisoners of war in neutral countries
417 **Internierung von Kriegsgefangenen** (GC III), internment of prisoners of war
418 **Verlegung der Kriegsgefangenen in ein anderes Lager** (GC III), transfer of prisoners of war to another camp
419 **Zentralauskunftsstelle für Kriegsgefangene** (GC III), Central Prisoners of War Information Agency
420 **Zentralstelle für Kriegsgefangene** (GC I), Central Prisoners of War Agency
421 **Kriegsgefangenschaft,** *f.*, captivity

422 **Kriegsgefangenschaftskarte,** *f.*, Capture Card for Prisoners of War

423 **Kriegsgerät,** *n.*, military equipment, implements of war

424 **für Kriegsgerät bestimmte Werkzeuge und Maschinen,** plant intended for the manufacture of military material

425 **Kriegsgesetze,** *n.pl.*, laws of war

426 **Fallen solche Transporte der Gegenpartei in die Hände, so unterliegen sie den Kriegsgesetzen (GC I 35),** Should such transports fall into the hands of the adverse party, they shall be subject to the laws of war

427 **Kriegsgesetzgebung,** *f.*, war legislation

428 **Kriegsgreuel,** *m.pl.*, war atrocities

429 **Kriegshandlung,** *f.*, act of war

430 **rechtmäßige Kriegshandlungen (PHR 15),** lawful acts of war

431 **Kriegshetze,** *f.*, warmongering, warmongery

432 **Kriegshetzer,** *m.*, warmonger

433 **Kriegskonterbande,** *f.*, contraband of war

434 **Kriegslist,** *f.*, war stratagem

435 **Kriegsmaterial,** *n.*, war material

436 **Kriegsopfer,** *n.*, war victim

437 **zivile Kriegsopfer,** civilian war victims

438 **Exhumierung und Überführung der Leichen von Kriegsopfern,** exhumation and removal of bodies of war victims

439 **Kriegspotential,** *n.*, war potential

440 **Kriegsraison,** *f.*, military necessity

441 **Kriegsrecht,** *n.*, law(s) of war, *jus in bello* (**Kriegsgesetze*)

442 **kriegsrechtlich,** *adj.*, of the rules of war(fare)

443 **kriegsrechtliche Vorschriften,** rules of the law of war

444 **Kriegsschäden,** *m.pl.*, war damage(s)

445 **Kriegsschauplatz,** *m.*, theatre of war

446 **Kriegsschiff,** *n.*, warship

447 **Kriegsschiffe Kriegführender,** belligerent warships, warships of belligerent states

448 **Kriegsschiffe und Schiffe, die als Hilfsschiffe im Dienst der Seestreitkräfte (sind)** (PPSO An), naval ships and ships used as naval auxiliaries

449 **Kriegsschiffe und Truppentransportschiffe** (CSLS Reg 3), ships of war and troopships

450 **Kriegstreiber,** *m.*, warmonger

451 **Kriegsverbot,** *n.*, outlawry/prohibition of war

452 **Kriegsverbrechen,** *n.*, war crime

453 **Kriegsverbrecher,** *m.*, war criminal

454 **Kriegsverhütung,** *f.*, prevention of war

455 **Kriegsvölkerrecht,** *n.*, international law of war

456 **Kriegsvorschrift,** *f.*, rule of war, rule relating to war(fare)

457 **Kriegszustand,** *m.*, state/status of war

458 **... auch wenn der Kriegszustand von einer dieser Parteien nicht anerkannt wird (GC IV 2),** ... even if the state of war is not recognized by one of the parties

459 **Kriegszustand beenden,** to terminate a state of war

460 **Kriegszustand erklären,** to declare a state of war

461 **Kultur,** *f.*, culture, civilization

462 **ihre gemeinsame Kultur (ECC Pr),** the civilization which is common to them all

463 **Kulturabkommen,** *n.*, cultural agreement, cultural convention (*e.g.* ECC)

464 **Kulturattaché,** *m.*, cultural attaché

465 **Kulturaustausch,** *m.*, cultural exchange

466 **kulturell,** *adj.*, cultural

467 **kulturelles Erbe der ganzen Menschheit/aller Völker** (PCP Pr/1), cultural heritage of all mankind/of every people

468 **im europäischen Interesse liegende kulturelle Maßnahmen** (ECC 3), cultural activities of European interest

469 **Kulturgut,** *n.*, cultural property (CSMW), object of cultural value (ECC)

470 Der Ausdruck „Kulturgüter" umfaßt bewegliche Sachen von religiösem, künstlerischem, urkundlichem, wissenschaftlichem oder historischem Wert (CSMW V 1), The term "cultural property" shall comprise movable goods of religious, artistic, documentary, scholarly or historic value

471 **Kulturgut unter Sonderschutz** (PCP), cultural property under special protection

472 **internationales Register für Kulturgut unter Sonderschutz,** international register for cultural property under special protection

473 **bewegliches Kulturgut,** movable cultural property

474 **Bergungsorte zur Sicherung beweglichen Kulturguts bei bewaffneten Konflikten** (PCP 8), refuges intended to shelter movable cultural property in the event of armed conflicts

475 **europäische Kulturgüter** (ECC 5), objects of European cultural value

476 **nationales Kulturgut,** national cultural property

477 **nationales Kulturgut von künstlerischem, geschichtlichem oder archäologischem Wert** (EEC 36), national treasures possessing artistic, historic or archaeological value

478 **unbewegliches Kulturgut,** immovable cultural property

479 **Eintragung von Kulturgut,** registration of cultural property

480 **Generalkommissar für Kulturgut,** Commissioner-General for cultural property

481 **Restaurierung von Kulturgut,** restoration of cultural property

482 **Rückführung von Kulturgut,** repatriation of cultural property

483 **Unverletzlichkeit des Kulturguts,** immunity of cultural property

484 **Verwahrer des Kulturguts,** depositary of cultural property

485 **Kultursachverständiger,** *adj.n.,* cultural expert

486 **Ausschuß der Kultursachverstän-**

digen des Europarats, committee of cultural experts of the Council of Europe

487 **kündbar,** *adj.*, subject to denunciation

488 **kündigen,** to denounce, to rescind, to repudiate, to terminate, to give notice of termination

489 **Eine Vertragspartei kann diese Charta erst nach Ablauf von 5 Jahren, nachdem die Charta für sie in Kraft getreten ist, kündigen** (ES 37), Any contracting party may denounce this charter only at the end of a period of 5 years from the date on which the charter entered into force for it

490 **die Vertragspartei, die das Übereinkommen kündigt** (SF 112), the denouncing party

491 **Jede Vertragspartei kann dieses Übereinkommen durch eine an den Generalsekretär der UN gerichtete Notifikation kündigen** (ECICA X), Any contracting party may denounce this convention by so notifying the Secretary-General of the UN
(*erlöschen, *aufheben, Ablauf einer *Frist)

492 **Kündigung,** *f.*, denunciation, termination, repudiation, rescission

493 **Die Kündigung wirkt nur für den Staat, der sie notifiziert** (CCFTD 19), The denunciation will only have effect as regards the state which has notified it

494 **Die Kündigung berührt nicht die Gültigkeit der Charta für die anderen Vertragsparteien** (ES 37), Such denunciation shall not affect the validity of the charter in respect of the other contracting parties

495 **Die Kündigung wird ein Jahr nach ihrer Notifizierung an die Regierung wirksam,** The denunciation shall take effect/become effective one year after notification thereof has been made to the government

496 **eine derartige Kündigung bewirkt nicht, daß . . .,** such (a) denunciation shall not have the effect of . . .

497   **Die Kündigung hat durch schriftliche Erklärung zu erfolgen** (PCP
Prot), The denunciation shall be
notified by an instrument in writing

498   **Jede Kündigung des Übereinkommens . . . hat die Kündigung dieses
Protokolls durch den betreffenden
Staat zur Folge** (PPELDO 36),
Denunciation of the convention . . .
shall imply denunciation by that
state of this protocol .

499   **außer im Falle der Kündigung** (SF
105), except in the event of denunciation

500   **Kündigungsanzeige,** *f.,* notice of
denunciation

501   **Kündigungserklärung,** *f.,* instrument of denunciation
(*note to* *Erklärung)

502   **Kündigungsfrist,** *f.,* period of
notice

503   **mit einer Kündigungsfrist von 12
Monaten,** on 12 months' notice

504   **unter Einhaltung einer Kündigungsfrist von einem Jahr,** by giving
one year's notice

505   **Kündigungsklausel,** *f.,* denunciation clause

506   **Kündigungsrecht,** *n.,* right of denunciation

507   **Kündigungsschreiben,** *n.,* notice
of denunciation

508   **Kündigungsurkunde,** *f.,* instrument of denunciation

509   **Kurier,** *m.,* courier

510   **diplomatischer Kurier,** diplomatic
courier

511   **konsularischer Kurier,** consular
courier

512   **Kurier** *ad hoc,* courier *ad hoc*

513   **Schriftstücke durch Kurier erhalten,**
to receive papers/documents by
courier

514   **Kuriergepäck,** *n.,* bag, pouch, diplomatic bag

515   **das Kuriergepäck dem Empfänger
aushändigen/zustellen** (VCCR), to
deliver the diplomatic bag to the
consignee

516   **das Kuriergepäck zurückhalten,** to
detain the diplomatic bag

517   **das Kuriergepäck entgegenneh-**
men/in Empfang nehmen (VCDR),
to take possession of the diplomatic
bag

518   **diplomatisches Kuriergepäck,** diplomatic bag

519   **Gepäckstücke, die das diplomatische Gepäck bilden, dürfen
nur diplomatische Schriftstücke
oder für den amtlichen Gebrauch
bestimmte Gegenstände enthalten**
(VCDR 27), The packages constituting the diplomatic bag may
contain only diplomatic documents or articles intended for official use

520   **konsularisches Kuriergepäck,** consular bag

521   **Kurzbericht,** *m.,* summary record/
report

522   **Kurzprotokoll,** *n.,* summary re-
cord/report

523   **Küste,** *f.,* coast

524   **Liegen die Küsten zweier Staaten
einander gegenüber, oder grenzen
sie aneinander . . .** (FC 7), Where
the coasts of two states are opposite
or adjacent to each other . . .

525   **von der allgemeinen Richtung der
Küste erheblich abweichen** (GCTS
4), to depart to an appreciable
extent from the general direction of
the coast

526   **eine Krümmung der Küste** (GCTS
7), a curvature of the coast
(*Festlandsockel, *Zerklüftung)

527   **Küsteneinrichtung,** *f.,* coastal
installation

528   **ortsfeste Küsteneinrichtungen,** fixed
coastal installations

529   **Küstenfischerei,** *f.,* coastal fish-
ery/fisheries/fishing
(*Fischerei)

530   **Küstenfrachtverkehr,** *m.,* cabotage

531   **Küstengewässer,** *n.* (*usu. in pl.*),
territorial sea, maritime belt (*Only
in a very general geographic or nautical sense to be translated by* coastal
waters.)
(*Küstenmeer)

532   **Küstenmeer,** *n.,* territorial sea

533   **Die Souveränität eines Staates er-**

streckt sich über sein Hoheitsgebiet zu Lande und seine inneren Gewässer hinaus auf einen an seine Küste grenzenden Meeresstreifen, der als Küstenmeer bezeichnet wird (GCTS 1), The sovereignty of a state extends beyond its land territory and its internal waters to a belt of sea adjacent to its coast, described as the territorial sea

534 **Die äußere Grenze des Küstenmeeres wird durch eine Linie gebildet, auf der jeder Punkt vom nächstgelegenen Punkt der Basislinie um die Breite des Küstenmeeres entfernt ist** (GCTS 6), The outer limit of the territorial sea is the line every point of which is at a distance from the nearest point of the baseline equal to the breadth of the territorial sea

535 **eine an das Küstenmeer eines Küstenstaates grenzende Zone der Hohen See** (GCF 6), an area of the high seas adjacent to the territorial sea of a coastal state

536 **für die Abgrenzung des Küstenmeeres** (GCTS 8), for the purposes of delimiting the territorial sea

537 **die Ordnung im Küstenmeer** (GCTS 19), the good order of the territorial sea

(friedliche *Durchfahrt, *Anschlußzone, *Basislinie)

538 **Küstenstaat**, *m*., coastal state, maritime state, littoral state

539 **alle Staaten, ob Küsten- oder Binnenstaaten** (GCTS 14), all states, whether coastal or not

L

1 **laden,** to summon
2 **die vor die Kommission geladenen Zeugen** (HgI), witnesses who have been summoned before the commission
3 **Ladung¹,** *f.*, summons, summoning
4 **nach gehöriger Ladung der Agenten der Parteien** (HgI 21), after the agents of the parties have been duly summoned
5 **erneute Ladung,** renewed summons
6 **mündliche Ladung,** verbal summons (*Vorladung)
7 **Ladung²,** *f.*, cargo, load
8 **Fluggäste, Ladung und Post aufnehmen/absetzen,** to take on/to put down passengers, cargo and mail
9 **Lagerung und Weiterversand der Ladung** (CFIMT An), warehousing and re-forwarding of the cargo
10 **gefährliche, verbotene oder Beschränkungen unterworfene Ladung** (CFIMT An), dangerous, prohibited or restricted cargo
11 **Lage,** *f.*, situation
12 **Die Regierung nimmt von dieser tatsächlichen Lage Kenntnis,** The Government shall take note of this situation of fact
13 **unter Berücksichtigung der derzeitigen Lage,** in consideration of the current/present situation
14 **Lagerstätte,** *f.*, deposit, mineral deposit (*of oil; sometimes* reservoir)
15 **Land,** *n.*, country (*In the context of a Federal state,* **Land** *may of course be a territorial subdivision, hence not an equivalent of* country *or a near-synonym for* **Staat.** *This is also true in many of the* **Landes-** *compounds, e.g.* **Landesgrenze** *which, in such a context, is an internal border/boundary quite distinct from* *Staatsgrenze.*)
16 **blockfreie/bündnisfreie Länder,** non-aligned countries (*For further adjectival phrases, see extensively under* *Staat.*)

17 **Landesfarben,** *f.pl.*, national colours (*e.g. on aircraft*)
18 **Landesflagge,** *f.*, national flag (*Flagge, *Wappen)
19 **Landesfriedensbruch,** *m.*, civil riot/disturbance
20 **Landesgrenze,** *f.*, national frontier, national border (*but see note to* *Land) (*Landgrenze) **Landesrecht,** *n.* = innerstaatliches *Recht
21 **Landesverrat,** *m.*, high treason
22 **Landesverteidigung,** *f.*, national defence
23 **Landeswährung,** *f.*, national currency, local currency
24 **Landgebiet,** *n.*, land area, land territory, land domain (GCTS 4), territory
25 **die Landgebiete und die angrenzenden Hoheitsgewässer** (SF 71), the land areas and the territorial waters adjacent thereto (*Gebiet³, *note to* *Gebiet¹, *Hoheitsgebiet, *Staatshoheit)
26 **Landgrenze,** *f.*, land frontier, land boundary (*Landesgrenze)
27 **Landkrieg,** *m.*, land warfare, war on land
28 **Gesetze und Gebräuche des Landkriegs,** laws and customs of land warfare
29 **Landkriegsführung,** *f.*, land warfare
30 **Landkriegsrecht,** *n.*, law of land warfare, law(s) governing/relating to land warfare
31 **Landmacht,** *f.*, land power
32 **Landstreitkräfte,** *f.pl.*, land forces, ground forces
33 **Landung,** *f.*, landing
34 **das Recht zum Überflug ohne Landung,** the right to fly across a territory without landing
35 **Landung für nichtgewerbliche Zwecke** (CAC), stop for non-traffic purposes

36 **Landungsfreiheit**, *f.*, freedom/liberty of landing/to land
37 **Landungsrecht,** *n.*, right of landing/to land
38 **Landungsstreitkräfte,** *f.pl.*, landing forces
39 **Landwirtschaft,** *f.*, agriculture (Erzeugnisse des *Meeres)
40 **Landwirtschaftsabkommen,** *n.*, agricultural agreement (*see note to* *Vertrag *in Annex* 1)
41 **Last,** *f.*, burden, charge
42 **Personen, denen eine Handlung zur Last gelegt wird,** persons charged with an act
43 **Laufzeit,** *f.*, duration
44 **unter Angabe ihrer Laufzeit (EMA 16),** together with details of their duration
45 **Lazarett**, *n.* (GC), hospital
46 **Lazarettschiff,** *n.* (GC), hospital ship
47 **militärische Lazarettschiffe** (GC), military hospital ships
48 **Die militärischen Lazarettschiffe (sind) die Schiffe, die von den Mächten einzig und allein dazu erbaut und eingerichtet worden sind, um Verwundeten, Kranken und Schiffbrüchigen Hilfe zu bringen (GC II 22),** Military hospital ships (are) ships built or equipped by the Powers specially and solely with a view to assisting the wounded, sick and shipwrecked
49 **in Lazarettschiffe umgewandelte Handelsschiffe** (GC II), merchant ships transformed into hospital ships
50 **Lazarettzug,** *m.* (GC), hospital train
51 **Lebensbedingungen,** *f.pl.*, living conditions
52 **die vorsätzliche Auferlegung von Lebensbedingungen für die Gruppe, die geeignet sind, ihre körperliche Zerstörung ganz oder teilweise herbeizuführen (CERD),** deliberately inflicting on the group conditions of life calculated to bring about its physical destruction in whole or in part

53 **Lebenshaltung,** *f.*, standard of living
54 **eine beschleunigte Hebung der Lebenshaltung (EEC 2),** an accelerated raising of the standard of living
55 **Lebensraum,** *m.*, *lebensraum*, living space
56 **Lebewesen,** *n.*, organism
57 **am Meeresgrund lebende Lebewesen** (FC, etc.), sedentary organisms
58 **der Fang von am Meeresgrund lebenden Lebewesen,** sedentary fishery/fisheries
59 **legal,** *adj.*, legal, lawful
60 **Legalisation,** *f.*, legalization
61 **diplomatische Legalisation,** diplomatic legalization
62 **konsularische Legalisation,** consular legalization (öffentliche *Urkunde)
63 **legalisieren,** to legalize
64 **Legalisierung,** *f.*, legalization
65 **Legalität,** *f.*, legality
66 **Legalitätsgrundsatz,** *m.*, principle of legality
67 **Legat,** *m.*, legate
68 **apostolischer Legat,** apostolic legate
69 **Legation,** *f.*, legation
70 **legitim,** *adj.*, legitimate
71 **Legitimation,** *f.*, authorization, identification
72 **Legitimationskarte,** *f.* (=* Teilnehmerkarte, *f.*), congress card, legitimation card
73 **legitimieren,** to legitimate, to authorize
74 **Legitimierung,** *f.*, authorization, legitimation
75 **Legitimist,** *m.*, legitimist
76 **Legitimität,** *f.*, legitimacy
77 **Legitimität der Staaten,** legitimacy of states
78 **verfassungsmäßige Legitimität,** constitutional legitimacy
79 **Legitimitätsgrundsatz,** *m.*, principle of legitimacy
80 **Lehre,** *f.*, doctrine, teaching, theory
81 **herrschende Lehre,** ruling doctrine
82 **heutige Lehre des Völkerrechts,** current doctrine of international law, current thought in international law (*Lehrmeinung)

83 **Lehrmeinung,** *f.*, teaching(s), doctrine, view
84 **die Lehrmeinung der fähigsten Völkerrechtler** (SICJ 38), the teachings of the most highly qualified publicists
(*Lehre)
85 **Leibeigenschaft,** *f.*, servitude
86 **Niemand darf in Sklaverei oder Leibeigenschaft gehalten werden** (PHR 4), No-one shall be held in slavery or servitude
87 **Leistung,** *f.*, benefit, payment
(*Sachleistung)
88 **Leistungsanspruch,** *m.*, entitlement to/right of benefit/payment, claim for benefit/payment
89 **leiten,** to head (*e.g. consular post*)
90 **Leiter,** *m.*, head of post (VCCR 15)
91 **amtierender Leiter,** acting head of post
92 **Zulassung als Leiter,** admission as head of post
(*konsularische Vertretung)
93 **Leitfälle,** *m.pl.*, leading cases
94 **Leitung,** *f.*, conduct, management
95 **Leitung eines Prozesses,** conduct of a case
96 **unter der Leitung des Gerichtshofes,** subject to/under the control of the court
(*Führung)
97 **Lenkungsausschuß,** *m.*, steering committee
98 **Lenkungsgruppe,** *f.*, steering group
99 *lettre(s) f.pl. de récréance, lettre(s) de récréance*
100 *levée f. en masse,* levée en masse
101 **Liberalisierungsliste,** *f.* (EEC), list of liberalization
102 **Liegenschaften,** *f.pl.*, immovable property
103 **dingliche Klagen betreffend einem Diplomaten gehörender Liegenschaften,** real actions relating to the private immovable property of a diplomat(ic agent)
104 **Liegenschaften der Streitkräfte** (CRFF 38), accommodation of the Forces (*includes such immovable installations as target ramps, airfields, etc.*)

(unbewegliches *Vermögen)
105 **Linie,** *f.*, line
106 **Zurücknahme der Truppen hinter bestimmte Linien,** withdrawal of troops behind certain lines
107 **mittlere Linie,** median line
(*Mittellinie)
108 **Liquidation,** *f.* (= Liquidierung, *f.*), liquidation
109 **Liquidation des Fonds** (EMA 17), liquidation of the Fund
(*Auflösung)
110 **liquidieren,** to liquidate
Liquidierung, *f.* = *Liquidation, f.*
111 **Liste**[1]**,** *f.*, list, panel (*e.g. of experts*)
(geheime *Wahl)
112 **Liste**[2]**,** *f.*, schedule
113 **Los**[1]**,** *n.*, lot
114 **das Los bestimmt . . .,** drawing lots determines . . .
115 **Los**[2]**,** *n.*, condition, fate
(*Verwundeter)
116 **lösen,** to solve, to resolve, to settle
(*beilegen, *regeln)
117 **Lösung,** *f.*, solution, settlement
(*Beilegung)
118 **Luftfahrtkonvention,** *f.*, aviation convention, aerial navigation convention
119 **Luftfahrzeug,** *n.*, aircraft
120 **inländische Luftfahrzeuge** (CAC 15), national aircraft
(*Staatszugehörigkeit)
121 **Luftfreiheit,** *f.*, freedom of the air
122 **Luftgebiet,** *n.*, airspace, air domain
123 **Luftherrschaft,** *f.*, air supremacy
124 **Lufthoheit,** *f.*, sovereignty over airspace
125 **. . . daß jeder Staat über seinem Hoheitsgebiet volle und ausschließliche Lufthoheit besitzt** (CAC 1), . . . that every state has complete and exclusive sovereignty over the airspace above its territory
126 **Luftinspektion,** *f.*, aerial inspection
127 **Luftkorridor,** *m.*, air corridor
128 **Luftkrieg,** *m.*, air warfare, aerial warfare
129 **Luftkriegsrecht,** *n.*, law of air warfare, law(s) governing/relating to aerial warfare
130 **Luftraum,** *m.*, airspace

131 **Luftraum über dem Küstenmeer** (GCTS 2), airspace over the territorial sea

132 **darüber befindlicher Luftraum,** airspace above (GCHS 25), superincumbent airspace

133 **Freiheit des Luftraumes,** freedom of the air

134 **Luftrecht,** *n.*, law(s) relating to/governing airspace

135 **Luftsperrgebiet,** *n.*, prohibited airspace

136 **Luftstreitkräfte,** *f.pl.*, air force(s)

137 **Lufttüchtigkeit,** *f.*, airworthiness

138 **Bescheinigung der Lufttüchtigkeit,** certificate of airworthiness

139 **Luftüberwachung,** *f.*, aerial inspection

140 **Luftverkehr,** *m.*, air traffic/transport

141 **Luftverkehrsabkommen,** *n.*, air transport agreement

142 **Luftverkehrsausschuß,** *m.*, air transport committee

143 **Luftverkehrsregeln,** *f.pl.* (CAC), rules of the air

144 **Luftverkehrsübereinkommen,** *n.*, air transport agreement/convention

145 **Luftverkehrsvorschriften,** *f.pl.* (CAC), air regulations

146 **Luftwaffenattaché,** *m.*, air attaché

147 **Luftzwischenfall,** *m.*, air/aerial incident

M

1 **Macht¹**, *f.*, power
2 **alliierte Macht,** allied power
3 **assoziierte Macht,** associated power
4 **beteiligte Macht,** power concerned
5 **feindliche Macht,** enemy/hostile power
6 **gefangennehmende Macht** (GC I), capturing power
7 **gegnerische Macht,** opposing power
8 **kriegführende Macht,** belligerent power
9 **neutrale Macht,** neutral power
   (*For adj. phrases not listed here, see under* *Staat.)
10 **Macht²**, *f.*, authority
11 **die volle Macht eines souveränen Staates** (CRPG 1), the full authority of a sovereign state
12 **Machtbereich**, *m., less often n.*, power, sphere of influence
13 **Personen, die sich im Machtbereich einer am Konflikt beteiligten Partei befinden** (GC IV 4), persons who find themselves in the hands of a party to the conflict
14 **Machtergreifung**, *f.*, seizure of power
15 **Machtpolitik**, *f.*, power politics
16 **Mandat**, *n.*, mandate, term of office
17 **Kein Vertreter kann im Laufe einer Sitzungsperiode . . . seines Mandats enthoben werden** (CE 25), No representative shall be deprived of his position as such during a session
18 **Dauer des Mandats,** term of office, duration of mandate/term of office
19 **Die gewöhnliche Dauer des Mandats der Vertreter beträgt 6 Jahre** (UCC Res XI), The normal duration of the term of office of the representative shall be 6 years
20 **Erlöschen des Mandats,** expiration of the term of office/mandate
   Mandatar, *m.* = *Mandatsmacht, *f.*
21 **Mandatsgebiet**, *n.*, mandate(d) territory (*established after WWI by the League of Nations; those remaining after WWII became trust territories*

under the auspices of the United Nations; see *Treuhandgebiet *and other* *Treuhand- *compounds*)
22 **Mandatsgewalt**, *f.*, mandate (*Gebiet³)
23 **Mandatsmacht**, *f.*, mandatory power
24 **Mandatssystem**, *n.*, mandate(s) system
25 **Mandatsverwaltung**, *f.*, mandate
26 **die Gebiete, die der Mandatsverwaltung eines Staates unterstehen,** the territories under the mandate of a state (*Gebiet³, *Hoheitsgebiet)
   mare clausum = geschlossenes *Meer
27 **Marineattaché**, *m.*, naval attaché
28 **Marinestreitkräfte**, *f.pl.*, naval forces
29 **Marionettenstaat**, *m.*, puppet state
30 **maritim**, *adj.*, maritime
31 **maritimer Staat,** maritime state
32 **Massenvernichtung**, *f.*, mass destruction
33 **Massenvernichtungswaffen**, *f.pl.*, weapons/arms of mass destruction
34 **Massenverschickung**, *f.*, mass transfer
35 **Massenzwangsverschickung**, *f.*, (GC IV), mass forcible transfer
36 **Maßgabe**, *f.*, measure, provision, proviso
37 **nach Maßgabe,** in accordance with, pursuant to, as prescribed in, under the conditions of
38 **nach Maßgabe der folgenden Bestimmungen** (EEC 8), in accordance with the provisions set out below
39 **nach Maßgabe dieses Vertrags** (SF 17), under the conditions provided for in this treaty
40 **nach Maßgabe der folgenden Bestimmungen und Bedingungen** (IAEA I), upon the terms and conditions hereinafter set forth
41 **nach Maßgabe seiner Zuständigkeit** (ICCC Prot), to the extent of its authority

42 **(jedoch) mit der Maßgabe, daß . . .,** except that/provided that/subject to the condition that

43 **mit der gleichen Maßgabe** (ECPSD 40), subject to the same conditions (*tätig, innere *Gesetzgebung)

44 **maßgebend,** *adj.*, authentic, authoritative, decisive, determining

45 **beide Texte sind maßgebend,** both texts are authentic

46 **maßgebender Wortlaut,** authentic text/wording

47 **Bei Abweichungen ist der Wortlaut in englischer Sprache, in der das Übereinkommen abgefaßt wurde, maßgebend** (SF 119), In the event of any inconsistency, the text in the English language, in which language the convention was drawn up, shall prevail (maßgebende *Urkunde, *Wortlaut)

48 **Maßnahme,** *f.*, measure, action, step

49 **Maßnahmen, die . . . gewährleisten,** measures to provide/providing/to ensure/ensuring

50 **die vom Sicherheitsrat beschlossenen Maßnahmen** (CUN 49), measures decided upon by the Security Council

51 **Maßnahmen bei Bedrohung oder Bruch des Friedens,** action with respect to threats to the peace/breaches of the peace (CUN Ch. VII)

52 **eine Gesamtheit von Maßnahmen** (EEC 8), a set of actions

53 **Maßnahmen, die auf die Verhinderung von . . . gerichtet sind,** measures intended to prevent . . .

54 **Maßnahme zur Behebung,** measure to remove/overcome

55 **Maßnahme zur Einschüchterung** (GC IV), measure of intimidation

56 **Maßnahme zur Erleichterung,** measure to facilitate

57 **Maßnahme zur Erzwingung,** measure to enforce

58 **anderweitige Maßnahmen,** alternative measures/action

59 **diskriminierende Maßnahmen,** discriminatory measures

60 **einschränkende Maßnahmen,** restrictive measures

61 **geeignete Maßnahmen,** appropriate/suitable measures

62 **gesetzgeberische Maßnahmen,** legislative measures/action, legislation

63 **Jeder Staat hat die erforderlichen gesetzgeberischen Maßnahmen zu treffen, die . . .** (GCHS 28), Every state shall take the necessary legislative measures to provide that . . .

64 **innere Maßnahmen,** domestic measures

65 **militärische Maßnahmen,** military measures

66 **dringende militärische Maßnahmen** (CUN 45), urgent military measures

67 **unmittelbare und wirksame Maßnahmen** (CERD 7), immediate and effective measures

68 **vorbeugende Maßnahmen,** preventive measures

69 **vorläufige Maßnahmen** (CUN 40), provisional measures

70 **vorübergehende Maßnahmen,** interim measures (EFTA), temporary/provisional measures

71 **wirksame Maßnahmen,** effective measures

72 **die Vertragsstaaten treffen alle wirksamen Maßnahmen, um sicherzustellen, daß . . .** (SCS 3), the states parties shall take all effective measures to ensure that . . .

73 **um sofortige und wirksame Maßnahmen durch die UN zu gewähren,** in order to ensure prompt and effective action by the UN

74 **Maßnahmen durchführen,** to execute/to carry out measures

75 **Maßnahmen einleiten,** to adopt/to initiate/to introduce measures

76 **Maßnahmen einstellen,** to cease measures

77 **Maßnahmen ergreifen,** to resort to/to adopt measures

78 **zu Maßnahmen Zuflucht nehmen,** to resort to measures

79   zu Maßnahmen Zuflucht nehmen
      zu müssen, die dem nationalen
      und internationalen Wohlstand
      abträglich sind (IMF 1), to resort
      to measures destructive of
      national or international prosper-
      ity
80   Maßnahmen treffen, to take/to
      adopt measures
81   Maßnahmen unterlassen, to refrain
      from/to abstain from measures
82   Maßnahmen untersagen, to pro-
      scribe/to forbid measures
83   Matrikelnummer, f., registration
      number, army number
84   Maximaltarif, m., maximum tariff
85   Mediatisierung, f., mediatization
86   Mediatisierung des Einzelnen,
      mediatization of the individual
87   Die Mediatisierung macht es dem
      Einzelnen in der Regel unmöglich,
      Träger völkerrechtlicher Rechte
      und Pflichten zu sein, As a rule,
      mediatization makes it impossible
      for the individual to be an incum-
      bent of international rights and
      duties
88   Meer, n., sea
89   Erforschung des Meeres, explora-
      tion of the sea, investigation of the
      sea, marine research
90   Studien und Untersuchungen zur
      Erforschung des Meeres (CICES
      1), research and investigations for
      the study of the sea
91   Erzeugnisse des Meeres, marine
      products/produce
92   In dieser Satzung umfaßt der Aus-
      druck „Landwirtschaft" auch die
      Fischerei und die Erzeugnisse des
      Meeres (FAO 1), In this constitu-
      tion the term "agriculture" in-
      cludes fisheries and marine pro-
      ducts (see *Fischerei)
93   Freiheit des Meeres, freedom of the
      seas (see *Binnenstaat)
94   Reichtum des Meeres, resources of
      the sea, marine resources
95   der lebende Reichtum des Meeres
      (GCC 5), the living resources of
      the sea (see *Schätze, *Meeres-
      schätze, *Naturschätze)

96   Verschmutzung/Verseuchung des
      Meeres (GCHS), pollution of the
      sea
97   angrenzendes Meer, adjacent/ad-
      joining sea
98   der Atlantische Ozean und die
      angrenzenden Meere (CICES 2),
      the Atlantic Ocean and its adja-
      cent seas
99   geschlossenes Meer, closed sea
100   offenes Meer, high sea(s), open sea
      (see die Hohe *See)
      (See further under *Meeres- com-
      pounds.)
101   Meerengen, f.pl., straits
102   für Kriegsschiffe gesperrte Meer-
      engen, straits closed to warships
103   Meerengen, die der internationalen
      Schiffahrt dienen (GCTS 17), straits
      which are used for international
      navigation
104   Kontrolle der Meerengen, control of
      the straits
105   Meerengenabkommen, n., straits
      agreement (in particular the 1936
      Montreux agreement)
106   Meerengenkontrolle, f., control of
      the straits
107   Meeresboden, m. (= *Meeres-
      grund, m.), seabed, bed of the
      sea
108   Meereserzeugnisse, n.pl. (GCF),
      marine products/produce
      (Erzeugnisse des *Meeres)
109   Meeresforschung, f., marine re-
      search, exploration of the sea
      (Erforschung des *Meeres)
110   Meeresfreiheit, f., freedom of the
      (high) seas
111   Meeresgrund, m., seabed, bed of
      the sea
112   seßhafte/unbewegliche Lebewesen
      am Meeresgrund (GCC 2), seden-
      tary/immobile organisms on the
      seabed
113   anorganische Bodenschätze des
      Meeresgrundes und des Meeresun-
      tergrundes (GCC 2), non-living
      resources of the seabed and subsoil
114   die Fischerei mit im Meeresgrund
      befestigten Geräten (GCF 13),
      fishery/fishing conducted by means

of equipment embedded on the floor of the sea

115 **die Ausbeutung und Erforschung des Meeresgrundes und Meeresuntergrundes** (GCHS 24), the exploitation and exploration of the seabed and its subsoil

116 **Naturschätze am Meeresgrund und im Meeresuntergrund,** natural resources on the surface and in the subsoil of the seabed (*Festlandsockel)

117 **Meeresprodukte,** *n.pl.*, marine products/produce

118 **Meeresschätze,** *m.pl.*, marine resources, resources of the sea (GCF)

119 **lebende Meeresschätze** (GCF), living marine resources

120 **die Ergiebigkeit der lebenden Meeresschätze** (GCF 7), the productivity of the living resources of the sea (*Schätze, *Naturschätze)

121 **Meeresstreifen,** *m.*, maritime belt, belt of sea (*Küstenmeer)

122 **Meeresuntergrund,** *m.*, subsoil of the seabed (*all examples under* *Meeresgrund)

123 **Mehrheit,** *f.*, majority

124 **absolute Mehrheit,** absolute majority

125 **mit der absoluten Mehrheit der abgegebenen Stimmen** (EAEC 111), by means of an absolute majority of the votes cast

126 **einfache Mehrheit,** simple majority

127 **qualifizierte Mehrheit,** qualified majority

128 **relative Mehrheit,** relative majority (*beschlußfähig, *Beschlußfähigkeit)

129 **Mehrheitsbericht,** *m.*, majority report

130 **Mehrheitsbeschluß,** *m.*, majority decision

131 **Mehrrassengesellschaft,** *f.*, multiracial society

132 **mehrseitig,** *adj.*, multilateral

133 **Mehrstaatigkeit,** *f.*, multiple nationality

134 **Verringerung der Mehrstaatigkeit**

(CRMN), reduction of cases of multiple nationality

135 **Mehrstaatler,** *m.*, person of/with multiple nationality

136 **Meinung,** *f.*, opinion

137 **abweichende Meinung,** dissenting opinion

138 **getrennt abgegebene Meinung,** separate opinion (*Ansicht, *Abstimmungsergebnis)

139 **Meinungsaustausch,** *m.*, exchange of views

140 **Meinungsfreiheit,** *f.*, freedom of thought/opinion

141 **Meinungsverschiedenheit,** *f.*, difference of opinion, dispute

142 **bei Meinungsverschiedenheiten,** in the event of any dispute

143 **Bei Meinungsverschiedenheiten über den Sinn oder die Tragweite der Entscheidung hat der Gerichtshof auf Ersuchen einer Partei sie auszulegen,** In the event of a dispute as to the meaning or scope of the judgment, the court shall construe it upon the request of any of the parties

144 **Jede Meinungsverschiedenheit zwischen den Vertragsparteien wird, soweit möglich, durch Verhandlungen beigelegt,** Any dispute between the contracting parties shall so far as is possible be settled by negotiation

145 **Meistbegünstigung,** *f.*, most-favoured-nation treatment

146 **Meistbegünstigungsklausel,** *f.*, most-favoured-nation clause

147 **Meistbegünstigungsprinzip,** *n.*, most-favoured-nation principle

148 **Meldepflicht** *f.* **für Ausländer,** duty of aliens to register

149 **Befreiung von der Meldepflicht für Ausländer** (PPELDO 14), exemption from aliens' registration formalities

150 **Memorandum,** *n.*, memorandum

151 **mengenmäßig,** *adj.*, quantitative

152 **mengenmäßige Beschränkungen,** quantitative restrictions

153 **Mensch,** *m.*, human being

154 **das Ideal vom freien Menschen**

(ICCPR Pr), the ideal of free human beings

155 **die Rechte und Freiheiten des Menschen** (ICCPR Pr), human rights and freedoms (*Menschenrechte)

156 **Menschenleben** *n. pl.* **auf See,** life at sea

157 **zur Rettung von Menschenleben auf See** (PPSO An), for the purpose of saving life at sea

158 **Menschenquarantänemaßnahmen,** *f.pl.* (CFIMT), public health quarantine measures

159 **Menschenrechte,** *n.pl.,* human rights

160 **die Menschenrechte durch die Herrschaft des Rechtes schützen** (UDHR Pr), to protect human rights by the rule of law

161 **Menschenrechte und Grundfreiheiten,** human rights and fundamental freedoms

162 **allgemeine Achtung und Verwirklichung der Menschenrechte und Grundfreiheiten ohne Unterschied der Rasse, des Geschlechts, der Sprache oder der Religion** (CUN 55), universal respect for, and observance of, human rights and fundamental freedoms without distinction as to race, sex, language or religion

163 **Achtung der Menschenrechte,** observance of human rights (PHR Pr), respect for human rights (CUN 76)

164 **Allgemeine Erklärung der Menschenrechte,** Universal Declaration of Human Rights

165 **Förderung der Menschenrechte,** promotion of human rights (CUN 68)

166 **Fortentwicklung der Menschenrechte** (CE 1), further realization of human rights

167 **Genuß der Menschenrechte,** enjoyment of human rights

168 **damit gewährleistet wird, daß sie in vollem Umfang und gleichberechtigt in den Genuß der Menschenrechte gelangen** (CERD 2), for the purpose of guaranteeing them the full and equal enjoyment of human rights

169 **Mißachtung der Menschenrechte** (UDHR), contempt for human rights

170 **Schutz der Menschenrechte,** maintenance of human rights (CE 1), protection of human rights

171 **Verkennung der Menschenrechte** (UDHR), disregard for human rights

172 **grundlegende Menschenrechte,** fundamental human rights

173 **politische Menschenrechte,** political rights

174 **soziale Menschenrechte,** social rights (*For a comprehensive list of human rights, see under* *Recht² auf, *Anspruch auf, *frei, *Freiheit.*)

175 **Menschenrechtsdeklaration,** *f.,* declaration of human rights

176 **Menschenrechtserklärung,** *f.,* declaration of human rights (*normally the UN declaration of 1948*)

177 **Menschenrechtskomitee,** *n.,* Human Rights Committee (*as provided for by the UN Covenant of 1966*)

178 **Menschenrechtskommission,** *f.,* Human Rights Commission (*as provided for by the European Convention of 1950*)

179 **Menschenrechtskonvention,** *f.,* Human Rights Convention (*i.e. European Convention of* 4.11.50), Human Rights Covenant *(UN Covenant of* 16.12.66)

180 **Menschenrechtsschutz,** *m.,* protection of human rights

181 **völkerrechtlicher Menschenrechtsschutz,** international protection of human rights, protection of human rights by international law

182 **menschlich¹,** *adj.,* human

183 **die menschliche Gesellschaft** (ICCPR), the human family

184 **menschliche Würde,** human dignity

185 **menschlich²,** *adj.,* humane

186 **menschliche Behandlung der Kriegsgefangenen,** humane treatment of prisoners of war

187 **Menschlichkeit,** *f.,* humanity

188   mit den Grundsätzen der Menschlichkeit vereinbar (GC IV), consistent with humanitarian principles

189   die Gesetze der Menschlichkeit (GC I), the laws of humanity

190   mit Menschlichkeit behandelt, humanely treated

191   Merkmal, n., characteristic, criterion

192   Merkmale, die der Rat festlegt, criteria established by the council

193   grundlegende technische Merkmale, fundamental technical criteria

194   Meuterei, f., mutiny

195   Meuterer, m., mutineer

196   meutern, to mutiny

197   Militärattaché, m., military attaché

198   Militärausschuß, m., military committee

199   Militärbehörde, f., military authority/authorities

200   Militärdienst, m., military service

201   Militärflugzeug, n., military aircraft

202   Militärfriedhof, m., war cemetery, military cemetery

203   Militärgericht, n., military court/tribunal, court martial

204   nichtpolitische und ordentlich bestellte Militärgerichte (GC IV), properly constituted, non-political courts

205   Militärgerichtshof, m., military court/tribunal, court martial

206   internationaler Militärgerichtshof, international military court/tribunal

207   Militärinternierter, adj.n., military internee

208   Militärinternierung, f., military internment

209   militärisch, adj., military, armed, using armed force

210   militärischer Angriff, military/armed attack/aggression

211   militärische Befehlsstelle, military command

212   militärische Besatzung, military occupation, armed occupation, occupying force(s)

213   militärische Besetzung, military occupation, armed occupation (see note to *Besetzung)

214   militärische Dienststelle, military agency

215   militärische Einheit, military unit

216   militärische Erfordernisse, military necessity/necessities

217   im Falle dringender militärischer Erfordernisse (GC I 33), in case of urgent military necessity

218   militärische Gesetze und Verordnungen, military laws and regulations

219   militärische Gewalt, military/armed force

220   militärische Intervention, military/armed intervention

221   militärische Repressalie, military/armed reprisal

222   militärische Schutzmaßnahme, military measure of protection, protective military action

223   militärische Sicherheit, military security

224   Militärisches Sicherheitsamt (TORG),Military Security Board (*bewaffnet)

225   Militärmission, f., military mission

226   Militärpakt, m., military pact/treaty (see note to *Vertrag in Annex 1)

227   Militärpersonen, f.pl. (GC I), armed forces, members of the armed forces

228   durch zivile Bedienstete oder Militärpersonen begangene Grausamkeiten (GC IV 32), measures of brutality applied by civilian or military agents

229   Miliz, f., militia

230   Minderheit, f., minority, minority group

231   ethnische Minderheit, ethnic minority

232   fremdvölkische Minderheit, alien/foreign minority

233   nationale Minderheit, national minority

234   rassische Minderheit, racial minority

235   religiöse Minderheit, religious minority

236   sprachliche Minderheit, linguistic minority (*Gruppe)

237 **Minderheitenrecht**, *n.*, law(s) relating to/governing minorities/ minority groups
238 **Minderheitenrechte**, *n.pl.*, rights of minorities/minority groups, minority rights
239 **Minderheitenschutz**, *m.*, protection of minorities/minority groups
240 **Minderheitenvertrag**, *m.*, minority treaty
241 **Minderheitsangehöriger**, *adj.n.*, member of a minority (group)
242 **Minderheitsbericht**, *m.*, minority report
243 **minderjährig**, *adj.*, minor, infant
244 **Minderjähriger**, *adj.n.*, minor, infant
245 **Minderjährigkeit**, *f.*, minority, infancy, age of minority
246 **die Volljährigkeit, die Minderjährigkeit, und die Voraussetzungen für die Ermächtigung und Vertretung** (CRMN 2), the age of majority and minority and the conditions for being empowered or represented
247 **Mindestnorm**, *f.*, minimum standard
248 **Mindestnormen zum Schutz der Staatsfremden**, minimum standards for the protection of aliens
249 **Mindesttarif**, *m.*, minimum tariff
250 **Ministerausschuß**, *m.*, ministerial committee, committee of ministers
251 **Ministerialrat**, *m.*, Committee of Ministers (PHR 54), council of ministers, ministerial council (* Urteil)
252 **Ministerkomitee**, *n.*, committee of ministers
253 **Ministerrat**, *m.*, council of ministers *(Often used (erroneously) when referring to the EC Council, which is normally but not necessarily composed of ministers representing each country.)*
254 **Ministerresident**, *m.*, Minister Resident
255 **Ministersitzung**, *f.*, ministerial meeting
256 **Mißbrauch**, *m.*, abuse, improper use, misuse

257 **Mißbrauch der Privilegien**, abuse of privileges
258 **mißbrauchen**, to abuse, to make improper use of, to misuse
259 **mißbräuchlich**, *adj.*, in abuse, in violation, improper, abusive
260 **die mißbräuchliche Anwendung einer Bestimmung**, the improper application of a provision
261 **Mission**, *f.*, mission
262 **zur Mission gehörende Büros an anderen Orten als denjenigen errichten, in denen die Mission selbst ihren Sitz hat** (VCDR 12), to establish offices forming part of the mission in localities other than those in which the mission itself is situated
263 **Angehöriger der Mission**, member of the mission
264 **Archive der Mission**, archives of the mission
265 **Mitglied der Mission**, member of the mission
266 **Der Ausdruck ,,Mitglieder der Mission'' bezeichnet den Missionschef und die Mitglieder des Personals der Mission** (VCDR 1), The "members of the mission" are the head of the mission and the members of the staff of the mission
267 **Familienangehörige eines Mitglieds der Mission** (VCDR 10), members of the family of a member of the mission
268 **die Ernennung von Mitgliedern der Mission, ihre Ankunft und ihre endgültige Abreise oder die Beendigung ihrer dienstlichen Tätigkeit bei der Mission** (VCDR 10), the appointment of members of the mission, their arrival and their final departure, or the termination of their functions with the mission
269 **die Anstellung und die Entlassung von im Empfangsstaat ansässigen Personen als Mitglied der Mission** (VCDR 10), the engagement or discharge of persons resident in the receiving state as members of the mission

270 **Personal der Mission,** staff of the mission

271 **Mitglied des Personals der Mission,** member of the staff of the mission

272 **Der Ausdruck „Mitglieder des Personals der Mission" bezeichnet die Mitglieder des diplomatischen Personals, des Verwaltungs- und technischen Personals und des dienstlichen Hauspersonals der Mission** (VCDR 1), The "members of the staff of the mission" are the members of the diplomatic staff, of the administrative and technical staff and of the service staff of the mission

273 **in diplomatischem Rang stehende Mitglieder des Personals der Mission** (VCDR 1), members of the staff of the mission having diplomatic rank

274 **diplomatisches Personal der Mission,** diplomatic staff of the mission

275 **dienstliches Hauspersonal/Dienstpersonal der Mission,** service staff of the mission

276 **Verwaltungspersonal der Mission,** administrative staff of the mission

277 **Räumlichkeiten der Mission,** premises of the mission

278 **Der Ausdruck „Räumlichkeiten der Mission" bezeichnet ungeachtet der Eigentumsverhältnisse die Gebäude oder Gebäudeteile und das dazugehörige Gelände, die für die Zwecke der Mission verwendet werden, einschließlich der Residenz des Missionschefs** (VCDR 1), The "premises of the mission" are the buildings or parts of buildings and the land ancillary thereto, irrespective of ownership, used for the purposes of the mission including the residence of the head of the mission

279 **Der Empfangsstaat erleichtert dem Entsendestaat den Erwerb der für dessen Mission benötigten Räumlichkeiten oder hilft ihm, sich auf andere Weise Räumlichkeiten zu beschaffen** (VCDR 21), The receiving state shall facilitate the acquisition by the sending state of premises necessary for its mission or assist the latter in obtaining accommodation in some other way

280 **die Obhut der Räumlichkeiten einem dritten Staat übertragen** (VCDR 45), to entrust the custody of the premises of the mission to a third state
(*konsularische Räumlichkeiten)

281 **Verkehr der Mission** (VCDR 27), communication on the part of the mission

282 **Vermögen der Mission,** property of the mission

283 **diplomatische Mission,** diplomatic mission

284 **ständige diplomatische Mission,** permanent diplomatic mission

285 **heilige Mission,** sacred mission

286 **. . . und übernehmen als heilige Mission die Verpflichtung . . . ,** . . . and accept as a sacred trust the obligation . . .

287 **eine Mission abberufen,** to recall a mission

288 **eine Mission endgültig oder vorübergehend abberufen** (VCDR 45), to permanently or temporarily recall a mission
(*See also* *Auftrag, *and* VCDR 1 *in* Annex 8.)

289 **Missionschef,** *m.*, head of (the) mission

290 **Die Missionschefs sind in folgende drei Klassen eingeteilt: (a) die Klasse der Botschafter oder Nuntien, die bei Staatsoberhäuptern beglaubigt sind, und sonstiger in gleichem Rang stehender Missionschefs; (b) die Klasse der Gesandten, Minister und Internuntien, die bei Staatsoberhäuptern beglaubigt sind; (c) die Klasse der Geschäftsträger, die bei Außenministern beglaubigt sind** (VCDR 14), Heads of mission are divided into three classes, namely: (a) that of Ambassadors or Nuncios

accredited to Heads of State, and
other Heads of mission of equivalent rank; (b) that of envoys, ministers and internuncios accredited to
Heads of State; (c) that of chargés
d'affaires accredited to Ministers for
Foreign Affairs
(*Rang, *Rangfolge, *Klasse, *Diplomat, *Geschäftsträger *ad interim*, *Gesandter)

291 **Missionsgebäude**, *n.*, premises of
the mission
(Räumlichkeiten der *Mission, *and*
VCDR *Art.* 1 (i) *in Annex* 8)

292 **Missionsmitglied**, *n.*, member of
the mission
(Mitglied der *Mission)

293 **Missionspersonal**, *n.*, staff of the
mission
(Personal der *Mission)

294 **Mißtrauensantrag**, *m.*, motion of
censure/no confidence

295 **Mißtrauensantrag annehmen**, to
adopt a motion of censure

296 **Mißtrauensantrag einbringen**, to
present/to introduce/to table a
motion of censure

297 **Mitglied**, *n.*, member; party

298 **Die Kommission besteht aus fünf
Mitgliedern. Jede Partei ernennt ein
Mitglied** (ECPSD 6), The Commission shall be composed of five members. The parties shall each nominate one Commissioner

299 **aus dem Kreis ihrer Mitglieder einen
Vorsitzenden wählen** (CNAF II), to
elect from its members a Chairman

300 **Mitglied eines Gerichts**, member of
a court/tribunal

301 **Mitglied der menschlichen Gesellschaft** (ICCPR Pr), member of the
human family

302 **Mitglied der Mission**, member of the
mission (*see* *Mission)

303 **Mitglied einer Organisation**,
member of an organization

304 **die Pflichten eines Mitglieds der
Organisation erfüllen** (IAEA IV),
to carry out the duties of membership

305 **Mitglied des Statuts des IGHs**, party
to the statute of the ICJ

306 **Mitglied eines Vertrags**, party to a
treaty

307 **assoziiertes Mitglied**, associate(d)
member

308 **Folgende Einrichtungen können
der Zentrale als assoziierte Mitglieder beitreten** (ICPCP 2), The
following shall be eligible for
associate membership of the centre

309 **ausscheidendes Mitglied**, retiring/
outgoing/withdrawing member

310 **Ein ausscheidendes Mitglied kann/
kann nicht unmittelbar wiedergewählt werden**, A retiring member shall/shall not be eligible for
immediate re-election

311 **nichtständiges Mitglied**, non-
permanent member

312 **nichtständige Mitglieder des
Sicherheitsrates**, non-permanent
members of the Security Council

313 **ordentliches Mitglied**, regular
member, full member, ordinary
member, member other than associate member (IMCO 15)

314 **ständiges Mitglied**, permanent
member

315 **ursprüngliches Mitglied**, founding/
initial/original member

316 **Mitgliedschaft**, *f.*, membership

317 **Die Mitgliedschaft steht den
Regierungen anderer Länder offen**
(IMF II), Membership shall be open
to the governments of other countries

318 **eine möglichst weltweite Mitgliedschaft**, a membership including/
covering/embracing as many (of the
world's) states as possible

319 **die aus der Mitgliedschaft erwachsenden Rechte und Vorteile**, the
rights and benefits arising/resulting
from membership

320 **bei der Empfehlung und Genehmigung der Mitgliedschaft eines
Staates** (IAEA IV), in recommen-
ding and approving a state for membership

321 **Antrag auf Mitgliedschaft**, appli-
cation/request for membership

322 **Erlöschen der Mitgliedschaft**, ter-

mination/expiry/expiration of membership

323 **Prinzip der Universalität der Mitgliedschaft,** principle of the universality of membership

324 **Mitgliedsland,** *n.*, member country

325 **Mitgliedsregierung,** *f.*, member government

326 **Mitglied(s)staat,** *m.*, member state (*i.e. of an organization*); contracting state (*i.e. to a treaty*)

327 **Die Hinterlegungsmacht teilt dann den Mitgliedsstaaten den Eingang der Ratifikationsurkunden mit,** The depositary state then notifies the (other) contracting states of the receipt of the instruments of ratification
(*beitreten)

328 **mitkriegführend,** *adj.*, co-belligerent

329 **mitteilen,** to notify, to communicate, to inform
(*Mitglied(s)staat)

330 **Mitteilung,** *f.*, notification, communication

331 **Er macht davon den Regierungen aller Mitgliedsstaaten Mitteilung** (PrivExCE 17), He shall communicate them to the governments of all members

332 **Mitteilung einer Handlung,** notification of an act

333 **nach Mitteilung der Vollmachten,** having communicated their full powers

334 **Eingang der Mitteilung,** receipt of notification
(*Notifikation, *unterliegen, *Dienststelle, *and* VCLOT 77 *in Annex* 15)

335 **Mittel¹,** *n.*, means, method(s)

336 **mit allen geeigneten Mitteln,** by all appropriate means

337 **Mittel²,** *n.*, means, funds, resources

338 **Mittellinie,** *f.*, median line

339 **Die Mittellinie in einem Fluß folgt dem jeweiligen mittleren Abstand zwischen den beiden Ufern,** The median line in a river follows the line at any point half-way between the two banks

340 **die Mittellinie, auf der jeder Punkt gleich weit von den nächstgelegenen Punkten der Niedrigwasserlinie der Küsten der betroffenen Vertragsparteien entfernt ist** (FC 7), the median line, every point of which is equidistant from the nearest points on the low water lines of the coasts of the contracting parties concerned
(*Talweg *and note*)

341 **Mittelsperson,** *f.*, intermediary

342 **Bevollmächtigte, deren Aufgabe es ist, als Mittelsperson zwischen ihnen und der Kommission zu handeln** (ECPSD 12), agents whose duty it shall be to act as intermediaries between them and the commission

343 **Mitunterzeichner,** *m.*, co-signatory

344 **Mitunterzeichnerregierung,** *f.*, co-signatory government

345 **Mitunterzeichnerstaat,** *m.*, co-signatory state

346 **Mobiliareigentum,** *n.*, personal property, movable property, movables
(bewegliches *Vermögen)

347 **mobilisieren,** to mobilize

348 **Mobilisierung,** *f.*, mobilization

349 **Mobilmachung,** *f.*, mobilization

350 **allgemeine Mobilmachung,** general mobilization

351 **Mobilmachung und andere den Krieg vorbereitende Maßnahmen** (HgI 7), mobilization or other measures of preparation for war

352 **Modalität,** *f.*, method, procedure, arrangement(s)

353 **geeignete Modalitäten für die Anwendung des Vertrags,** appropriate methods for the application of the treaty

354 **Modifikation,** *f.*, modification

355 **die Modifikation mehrseitiger Verträge** (VCLOT 41), the modification of multilateral treaties
(*Änderung, *Abänderung, *Vertrag modifizieren *and note, and* VCLOT 39–41 *in Annex* 16)

356 **modifizieren,** to modify
(*abändern, *Vertrag modifizieren *and note*)

357 **Modus,** *m.*, method, procedure
358 **Modus für die Bestellung des Vorsitzenden** (CE 18), method of appointment of its president
359 **Monismus,** *m.*, monism
360 **Monist,** *m.*, monist
361 **monistisch,** *adj.*, monist
362 **Moral,** *f.*, morality (öffentliche *Ordnung)
363 **multilateral,** *adj.*, multilateral
364 **Multilateralität,** *f.*, multilaterality, multilateral nature
365 **mündig,** *adj.*, of full age
366 **Mündigkeit,** *f.*, age of majority (*Minderjährigkeit)
367 **mündlich,** *adj.*, oral, not in writing
368 **mündliche Mitteilung,** oral notification/communication
369 **Munition,** *f.*, munition
370 **Munitions- oder Kriegsgerät,** munitions and implements of war
371 **Munitionshandel,** *m.*, trade in munitions
372 **Musterverfahren,** *n.*, standard practices, standard procedure
373 **Mustervorschriften,** *f.pl.*, standard procedures
374 **Mutterland,** *n.*, metropolitan territory, mother country

375 **Loslösung der Kolonien vom Mutterland,** separation of colonies from the mother country
376 **Dieses Abkommen findet auf das Mutterland der Parteien Anwendung** (EPTV 12), This agreement shall apply to the metropolitan territories of the parties
377 **Diese Charta gilt für das Mutterland jeder Vertragspartei** (ES 34), This charter shall apply to the metropolitan territory of each contracting party
378 **zum Mutterland gehörendes Hoheitsgebiet,** metropolitan territory
379 **außerhalb des Mutterlandes gelegene Gebiete,** non-metropolitan areas
380 **innerhalb des Mutterlandes gelegene Gebiete,** metropolitan areas
381 **das Mutterland der beteiligten Regierung** (ICC II), the metropolitan territory of the government concerned
382 **Zollgebiet des Mutterlandes** (GATT), metropolitan customs territory (*Gebiet[3])

N

1 **Nachbarland,** *n.*, neighbouring country
2 **nachbarlich,** *adj.*, neighbourly, voisinage
3 **nachbarliche Beziehungen,** neighbourly relations
4 **auf Grund nachbarlicher Vereinbarungen,** by virtue of voisinage arrangements
5 **nachbarlicher Verkehr zwischen den Staaten,** neighbourly intercourse among states
6 **Nachbarschaft,** *f.*, **gute** (CUN 74), good-neighbourliness
7 **Nachbarstaat,** *m.*, neighbouring state
8 **Nacheile,** *f.*, pursuit, hot pursuit
9 **die Nacheile nach einem fremden Schiff** (GCHS 23), the hot pursuit of a foreign ship
10 **im Falle einer Nacheile durch ein Flugzeug** (GCHS 23), where hot pursuit is effected by an aircraft
11 **Das Recht der Nacheile endet, sobald das verfolgte Schiff das Küstenmeer seines eigenen oder eines dritten Staates erreicht hat** (GCHS 23), The right of hot pursuit ceases as soon as the ship pursued enters the territorial sea of its own country or of a third state
12 **nacheilen,** to pursue
13 **nacheilend,** *adj.*, pursuing, in pursuit
14 **nacheilendes Schiff,** pursuing ship/vessel
15 **nacheilender Staat,** pursuing state
16 **Nachfolge,** *f.*, succession
17 **Nachfolge von Staaten,** succession of states
18 **nachfolgen,** to succeed to
19 **nachfolgend,** *adj.*, succeeding; subsequent, later
20 **nachfolgendes Recht,** subsequent law
21 **Nachfolgeorganisation,** *f.*, successor organization
22 **Nachfolger,** *m.*, successor, successor in title

23 **Nachfolgerstaat,** *m.*, successor state
24 **nachgeordnet,** *adj.*, subordinate, subsidiary
25 **nachgeordneter Ausschuß,** subordinate committee
26 **nachgeordnetes Organ,** subordinate organ
(nachgeordnete *Stelle, *Rangfolge)
27 **nachkommen,** to comply with, to fulfil, to discharge
28 **einer Verpflichtung nachkommen,** to comply with/fulfil/discharge an obligation
29 **Nachlaß,** *m.*, estate
30 **Klagen in Nachlaßsachen** (VCDR 31), actions relating to succession
31 **nachprüfen,** to review, to revise, to check
32 **Nachprüfung,** *f.*, review, revision, check
33 **Eine sachliche Nachprüfung des Anspruchs, auf dem das Urteil beruht, ist nicht zulässig,** The merits of the claim on which the judgment has been given shall not be reviewed/be open to review
34 **Die für . . . erhobenen Gebühren unterliegen einer Nachprüfung** (CAC 15), The charges imposed for . . . shall be subject to review (*Revision)
35 **Nachrichten,** *f.pl.*, communications, information, news
36 **Nachrichtenmittel,** *n.pl.*, (means of) communication (*Nachrichtenverkehr)
37 **Nachrichtensperre,** *f.*, communications/news blackout/ban
38 **Nachrichtenübermittlung,** *f.*, communication(s), act of communicating
39 **amtliche Nachrichtenübermittlung der Organisation** (WEUS 10), official communications of the organization (*Nachrichtenverkehr)
40 **Nachrichtenverbindungen,** *f.pl.*, communications

41   freie Nachrichtenverbindungen, free communication(s)
42   Nachrichtenverkehr, *m.*, communications
43   amtlicher Nachrichtenverkehr, official communications
44   **Der amtliche Nachrichtenverkehr der Organisation, gleichviel mit welchen Nachrichtenmitteln, unterliegt nicht der Zensur** (PPELDO 12), No censorship shall be applied to official communications of the organization by whatever means of communication
     (*Nachrichtenübermittlung)
45   nachstehend, *adj.*, following, below, set forth/out below
46   **nachstehend als ,,die Regierung'' bezeichnet,** hereinafter called "the Government"
47   **die nachstehenden Vorbehaltserklärungen** (ICCC Prot), the reservations set forth hereunder
48   nachteilig, *adj.*, of disadvantage, prejudicial
49   **eine Maßnahme, die eine nachteilige Rückwirkung auf . . . haben könnte,** a measure likely to react prejudicially upon . . .
50   nachträglich, *adj.*, subsequent, deferred, *a posteriori*
51   **wenn alle Vertragsparteien nachträglich vereinbart haben, daß . . .** (VCLOT 15), when all the parties have subsequently agreed that . . .
52   **nachträgliche Genehmigung,** subsequent approval, approval *a posteriori*
     (*später)
53   Nachtragshaushalt, *m.*, supplementary budget
54   Namen, im, in the name of, on behalf of
55   **im Namen meiner Regierung,** on behalf of my Government
     (*namens)
56   namens, on behalf of, in the name of
57   **die von oder namens der Organisation ein- oder ausgeführten Waren** (PPELDO 7), goods imported or

     exported by or on behalf of the organization
     (im *Namen)
58   namhaft machen, to nominate
59   **einen Vertreter namhaft machen** (ES 26), to nominate a representative
60   Nansen-Paß, *m.*, Nansen passport
61   Nationalfarben, *f.pl.*, national colours (*e.g. of an aircraft*)
62   Nationalflagge, *f.*, national flag (*Flagge, *Wappen)
63   Nationalität, *f.*, nationality
64   **Schiffe besitzen die Nationalität des Staates, dessen Flagge zu führen sie berechtigt sind** (GCHS 5), Ships have the nationality of the state whose flag they are entitled to fly
65   **Jeder Staat legt die Bedingungen fest, unter denen er Schiffen seine Nationalität gewährt** (GCHS 5), Each state shall fix the conditions for the grant of its nationality to ships
     (*Staatsangehörigkeit, *Staatszugehörigkeit, *and note to* *Staatszugehöriger)
     Nationalitätenstaat, *m.* = *Vielvölkerstaat, *m.*
66   Nationalstaat, *m.*, national state
67   NATO-Jahreserhebung, *f.*, NATO Annual Review
68   NATO-Kommandobehörden, *f. pl.*, NATO Commands
69   NATO-Militärausschuß, *m.*, NATO Military Committee
70   NATO-Stäbe, *m.pl.*, militärische, Military Staffs of NATO, NATO Military Staffs
71   NATO-Stellen, *f.pl.*, militärische, Military Authorities of NATO, NATO Military Authorities
72   naturalisieren, to naturalize
73   **Naturalisierung,** *f.*, naturalization
74   Naturalisierungsurkunde, *f.*, citizenship papers, letters/certificate of naturalization
75   Naturalrestitution, *f.*, restitution in kind
76   natürlich, *adj.*, natural

77 **natürliche und juristische Personen,**
    natural and legal persons
    (*Person)
78 **natürliche und künstliche Grenzen,**
    natural and artificial frontiers/borders
79 **Naturrecht¹**, *n.*, inherent/inalienable/natural right
    (naturgegebenes *Recht)
80 **Naturrecht²**, *n.*, law of nature, natural law
81 **naturrechtlich**, *adj.*, of the law of nature
82 **naturrechtliche Grundsätze,** principles of the law of nature
83 **Naturschätze,** *m.pl.*, natural resources
84 **die Ausbeutung der Naturschätze im Meeresuntergrund,** the exploitation of natural resources in the subsoil of the seabed
    (*Schätze, *Meeresgrund)
85 **Navicert,** *n.*, navicert (= navigation certificate)
86 **Navicertsystem,** *n.*, navicert system
87 **Nebenausschuß,** *m.*, subsidiary committee
88 **Nebenorgan,** *n.* (UN), subsidiary organ
    (*Wahrnehmung)
89 **Nehmestaat,** *m.*, captor state
90 **Nein-Stimme,** *f.*, vote (cast) "against", negative vote
91 **neufassen,** to redraft, to reword, to revise
92 **Neufassung,** *f.*, redrafting, rewording, revision
93 **neugefaßt,** *adj.*, new, redrafted, reworded, revised
94 **Neugier,** *f.*, **öffentliche,** public curiosity
95 **neutral,** *adj.*, neutral
96 **Neutraler,** *adj.n.*, neutral person/party/state
97 **neutralisieren,** to neutralize
98 **neutralisiert,** *adj.*, neutralized
99 **Neutralisierung,** *f.*, neutralization
100 **Neutralismus,** *m.*, neutralism
101 **Neutralist,** *m.*, neutralist
102 **neutralistisch,** *adj.*, neutralist
103 **Neutralität,** *f.*, neutrality
104 **„Neutralität" bedeutet die Nicht-**
    teilnahme eines Staates an den bewaffneten Auseinandersetzungen anderer Staaten, "Neutrality" signifies the non-participation of a state in the armed conflicts of other states
105 **Zustand der Neutralität,** state/status of neutrality
106 **Übereinstimmung   herrscht darüber, daß der Zustand der Neutralität ebenso wie der Kriegszustand bestimmte Rechte und Pflichten auferlegt,** It is generally agreed that the status of neutrality, like the status of war, imposes certain rights and duties
107 **absolute Neutralität,** absolute neutrality
108 **bewaffnete Neutralität,** armed neutrality
109 **ewige Neutralität,** perpetual/permanent neutrality
110 **freiwillige Neutralität,** voluntary neutrality
111 **immerwährende/ständige Neutralität,** perpetual/permanent neutrality
112 **unbedingte Neutralität,** unconditional neutrality
113 **wohlwollende Neutralität,** benevolent neutrality
114 **Neutralitätsbruch,** *m.*, breach of neutrality
115 **Neutralitätserklärung,** *f.*, declaration of neutrality
116 **Neutralitätsrecht¹,** *n.*, right of/to neutrality
117 **Neutralitätsrecht²,** *n.*, law(s) governing/relating to neutrality
118 **Neutralitätsverletzung,** *f.*, breach/violation of neutrality
119 **Neutralitätsvertrag,** *m.*, treaty of neutrality
120 **neutralitätswidrig,** *adj.*, unneutral, hostile, in breach of/in violation of (the) neutrality
121 **neutralitätswidrige Dienste,** unneutral service
122 **neutralitätswidrige Unterstützung,** unneutral service
123 **Nichtabgabe,** *f.*, non-submission, failure to submit (*e.g. of a protest*)

124 **Nichtaggression,** f., non-aggression
125 **Nichtangriff,** m., non-aggression
126 **Nichtangriffsvertrag,**   m.
   (= Nichtangriffspakt, m.), treaty of
   non-aggression, pact of non-
   aggression (see note to *Vertrag in
   Annex 1)
127 **Nichtauslieferung,**   f.,   non-
   extradition, failure to extradite
128 **nichtautonom,**   adj.,   non-self-
   governing, non-autonomous
129 **Nichtbeachtung,**   f.,   non-observance, failure to observe
   (*Nichteinhaltung)
130 **Nichtbefolgung,**   f.,   non-observance, failure to observe, non-compliance (with), failure to comply
   (with), failure to follow
   (*Nichteinhaltung)
131 **Nichtdiskriminierung,**   f.,   non-
   discrimination
132 **auf der Grundlage der Mehrseitig-
   keit   und   der   Nichtdiskriminierung** (OECD 1), on a multilateral, non-discriminatory basis
133 **Nichtdiskriminierungsklausel,**
   f., non-discrimination clause
134 **Nichteinhaltung,**   f.,   non-observance, failure to observe, non-
   compliance (with), failure to comply
   (with)
135 **Nichteinhaltung der Verpflichtungen
   des Staates A gegenüber dem Staat
   B,** failure of state A to comply with
   its obligations towards state B
136 **Nichteinhaltung   eines   Vertrages/
   Abkommens   usw.,**   non-observance / non-performance / non-
   fulfilment of a treaty/agreement,
   etc., failure to fulfil/observe/perform/
   comply with (the terms of) a
   treaty/agreement, etc.
137 **Nichteinheitsstaat,** m., non-unitary state
138 **Nichteinmischung,**   f.,   non-intervention
139 **Nichteinmischungspflicht,**   f.,
   duty not to intervene, duty of non-
   intervention
140 **Nichterfüllung,** f., non-fulfilment,
   failure to fulfil
141 **Nichterfüllung   völkerrechtlicher**

   Verpflichtungen/Pflichten, failure to
   fulfil international obligations/duties
142 **die   Nichterfüllung   von   Empfehlungen und Entschließungen des
   Rates** (CAC 54), failure to carry out
   recommendations or determinations
   of the Council
143 **Nichterfüllung eines Urteils,** failure
   to perform (the obligations incumbent under) a judgment
144 **Nichterreichen,**   n.,   non-attainment, failure to attain
145 **Nichterreichen der in der Präambel
   genannten Ziele,** failure to achieve
   the aims set forth in the preamble
146 **nichtfriedensgefährdend,**   adj.,
   non-prejudicial to peace, not likely
   to endanger peace and security
147 **Nichtgeltung,** f., non-validity
148 **Geltung   oder   Nichtgeltung   einer
   Völkerrechtsnorm,** validity or non-
   validity of an international norm
149 **Nichthandeln,** n., omission, failure
   to act
   (*Unterlassen, *Unterlassung)
150 **nichthoheitlich,** adj., non-sovereign
151 **nichthoheitliche   Akte,**   non-
   sovereign acts, acts done/performed
   in a non-sovereign capacity
152 **nichtig,** adj., void
153 **für nichtig erklären,** to declare void,
   to annul, to nullify, to denounce, to
   cancel
154 **null und nichtig,** null and void
   (zwingende *Norm)
155 **Nichtigkeit,** f., nullity
156 **völkerrechtliche   Nichtigkeit   eines
   Vertrages,** nullity of a treaty at/un-
   der international law
157 **Nichtigkeitsbeschwerde,**   f.,
   appeal based on the ground of nullity, pourvoi en cassation
   (endgültiger *Schiedsspruch)
158 **Nichtigkeitserklärung,** f., declaration of nullity, annulment
159 **Nichtigkeitsurteil,** n., judgment of
   nullity/annulment
160 **Nichtintervention,**   f.,   non-intervention
   (note to *intervenieren)
161 **nichtjustiziabel,**   adj.,   non-
   justiciable

162 **Nichtkämpfer,** *m.*, non-combatant

163 **Nichtkernwaffenmacht,** *f.* (TNPNW), non-nuclear-weapon power

164 **Nichtkernwaffenstaat,** *m.* (TNPNW), non-nuclear-weapon state

165 **Nichtkombattant,** *m.*, non-combatant

166 **nichtkriegerisch,** *adj.*, non-belligerent, pacific, non-war, of a non-war character

167 **nichtkriegerische Beilegung,** pacific settlement

168 **nichtkriegerischer Konflikt,** non-war conflict, conflict of a non-war nature/character/status

169 **nichtkriegerische Streitigkeiten,** non-war hostilities, hostilities of a non-war nature/character/status

170 **nichtkriegführend,** *adj.*, non-belligerent

171 **Nichtkriegführung,** *f.*, non-belligerency, non-belligerence

172 **Nichtmitglied,** *n.*, non-member

173 **Nichtmitgliedsregierung,** *f.*, non-member government

174 **Nichtmitgliedsstaat,** *m.*, non-member state

175 **die Mitglieder der UN and die in Artikel XI in Betracht gezogenen Nichtmitgliedsstaaten** (PCG 17), the members of the UN and the non-member states contemplated in Article XI

176 **nichtneutral,** *adj.*, non-neutral

177 **Nichtneutralität,** *f.*, non-neutrality

178 **Nichtparteinahme,** *f.*, impartiality

179 **Nichtregierungsvertreter,** *m.* (ILO), non-government delegate

180 **nichtrichterlich,** *adj.*, non-judicial

181 **nichtrückwirkend,** *adj.*, non-retroactive

182 **Nichtrückwirkung,** *f.*, non-retroactivity

183 **nichtselbständig,** *adj.*, dependent, non-autonomous

184 **nichtselbständig anwendbare Regeln,** non-self-executing rules

185 **nichtstaatlich,** *adj.*, non-governmental, non-state

186 **eine Konferenz nichtstaatlichen Charakters** (UNESCO IV), a non-governmental conference

187 **nichtstaatliches Gebilde,** non-state entity

188 **nichtstaatliche Organisationen,** non-governmental organizations

189 **nichtständig,** *adj.*, non-permanent

190 **nichtständige Mitglieder des Sicherheitsrates,** non-permanent members of the Security Council

191 **nichtstrafrechtlich,** *adj.*, non-criminal

192 **Nichtteilnahme,** *f.*, non-participation (*Neutralität)

193 **Nichtteilnehmer,** *m.*, non-participant

194 **Nichtteilnehmerregierung,** *f.*, non-participating government

195 **Nichtteilnehmerstaat,** *m.*, non-participating state

196 **Nichtunterzeichner,** *m.*, non-signatory

197 **Nichtunterzeichnerregierung,** *f.*, non-signatory government

198 **Nichtunterzeichnerstaat,** *m.*, non-signatory state

199 **Nichtverbreitung,** *f.*, non-proliferation

200 **Nichtverbreitungsvertrag,** *m.*, non-proliferation treaty

201 **nichtvertraglich,** *adj.*, non-contractual

202 **Nichtvertragsregierung,** *f.*, non-contracting government

203 **Nichtvertragsstaat,** *m.*, non-contracting state

204 **niederlassen, sich,** to establish oneself, to take up residence

205 **läßt sich ein Flüchtling rechtmäßig innerhalb eines anderen Gebietes nieder . . .** (TDRef 13), when a refugee has lawfully taken up residence in another territory . . .

206 **Niederlassung,** *f.*, establishment, settlement

207 **Niederlassungsfreiheit,** *f.*, freedom of establishment

208 **Niederlassungsrecht,** *n.*, right of establishment

209 **Niederlassungsvertrag,** *m.*, treaty of establishment

210 **niederlegen,** to establish, to set
forth/out, to lay down
211   **Grundsätze/Ziele, die in . . .
niedergelegt sind,** principles/aims set
forth in . . .
212 **Niederschrift,** *f.*, minute(s), record
213   **gemeinsame Niederschrift,** joint
minutes
214   **vereinbarte Niederschrift,** agreed
minutes
(*Protokoll²)
215 **Niedrigwasserlinie,** *f.*, low-tide
line, low-water line
216   **die nächstgelegenen Punkte der
Niedrigwasserlinie,** the nearest
points on the low-water line
(*Mittellinie)
217 **Niedrigwassermarke,** *f.*, low-tide
mark, low-water mark
218 **Niemandsland,** *n.*, no-man's land
219 **Nominierung,** *f.*, nomination
220 **Nominierungsausschuß,** *m.*,
nomination(s) committee
221 *non grata, non grata*
222   **zur Person** *non grata* **erklären,** to
declare *non grata*
223   **Eine Person kann als** *non grata* **erklärt werden, bevor sie im Hoheitsgebiet des Empfangsstaates eintrifft**
(VCDR 9), A person may be de-
clared *non grata* before arriving in
the territory of the receiving state
224 **Norm,** *f.*, rule, norm, standard
225   **Normen des innerstaatlichen Rechts,**
rules of municipal law
226   **Normen des Völkerrechts,** rules of
international law
227   **Summe der Normen,** total body/sum
of rules
228   **Verbindlichkeit der Normen,** binding nature of rules
229   **allgemeine Norm,** general rule
230   **anerkannte Norm,** recognized rule
231   **sich nach den allgemein anerkannten internationalen Normen rich-
ten** (GCHS 10), to conform to
generally accepted international
standards
232   **ausländische Norm,** foreign rule
233   **gewohnheitsrechtliche Norm,** customary rule
234   **gewohnheitsrechtlich geschaffene**

      Norm, rule established by cus-
tom(ary law)
235   **internationale Norm,** international
rule
236   **vertraglich geschaffene Norm,** contractual rule, rule created by treaty
237   **völkerrechtliche Norm,** international rule, rule of international law
238   **zwingende Norm,** cogent/manda-
tory/peremptory norm
239   **Entsteht eine neue zwingende
Norm des allgemeinen Völkerrechts, so wird jeder zu dieser
Norm im Widerspruch stehende
Vertrag nichtig und erlischt**
(VCLOT 64), If a new peremptory norm of general international
law emerges, any existing treaty
which is in conflict with that norm
becomes void and terminates
240   **zwischenstaatliche Norm,** international rule
241   **eine Norm niederlegen,** to establish a
rule
242 **normalisieren¹,** to normalize
243 **normalisieren²,** to standardize
244 **Normalisierung¹,** *f.*, normalization
245   **Normalisierung der Beziehungen,**
normalization of relations
246   **im Zuge der Normalisierung ihrer
Beziehungen** (GrV 7), in the
course of the normalization of
their relations
247 **Normalisierung²,** *f.*, standardization
248 **normativ,** *adj.*, normative
249 **normativistisch,** *adj.*, normative
250   **normativistische Lehre,** normative
theory/doctrine
251 **normsetzend,** *adj.*, normative
252 **Normsetzung,** *f.*, standardization
253 **Normung,** *f.*, standardization
254 **Note,** *f.*, note
255   **diplomatische Note,** diplomatic note
256   **gleichlautende Noten,** identical notes
257 **Notenaustausch,** *m.*, exchange of
notes
(*Notenwechsel)
258 **Notenwechsel,** *m.*, exchange of
notes
259   **durch Notenwechsel zwischen 2 oder
mehreren   Vertragsschließenden**

(EXWC 1), by an exchange of notes between 2 or more of the contracting parties

260   **diplomatischer Notenwechsel,** exchange of diplomatic notes
(*For an example see Annex* 6.)

261   **Notifikation,** *f.,* notification

262   **Durch eine Notifikation bringt der notifizierende Staat einem anderen Staat eine Tatsache zur Kenntnis,** By notification the notifying state informs another state of a fact

263   **30 Tage nach Eingang der Notifikation,** 30 days after receipt of the notification
(*Notifizierung, *zurücknehmen, *and* VCLOT 76–77 *in Annex* 15)

264   **Notifikationsurkunde,** *f.,* instrument of notification

265   **notifizieren,** to notify

266   **Jedes Mitglied notifiziert dem Amt die Anzahl . . .,** Each member shall notify the agency of the number(s) . . .

267   **Die Ankunft und die endgültige Abreise sind nach Möglichkeit im voraus zu notifizieren** (VCDR 10), Where possible, prior notification of arrival and departure shall be given

268   **Notifizierender,** *adj. n.,* the notifying party/state

269   **Notifizierung,** *f.,* notification

270   **jede gemäß Artikel 13 eingegangene Notifizierung** (RMCE 12), any notification received in accordance with Article 13

271   **durch eine an die . . . Regierung gerichtete Notifizierung,** by a notification addressed to the . . . Government
(*Notifikation)

272   **Notstand,** *m.,* emergency, state of (national) emergency

273   **öffentlicher Notstand,** public emergency

274   **öffentlicher Notstand, der das Leben der Nation bedroht** (ES 30), public emergency threatening the life of the nation

275   **Notstandsgesetz,** *n.,* emergency law

276   **Notwehr,** *f.,* self-defence

277   **Notwehrakt,** *m.,* act of self-defence

278   **Notwehrrecht,** *n.,* right of self-defence

279   **Notwendigkeit,** *f.,* necessity, requirement

280   **unter Berücksichtigung der örtlichen Notwendigkeiten** (PHR 63), with due regard to local requirements

281   **zwingende militärische Notwendigkeit** (GCI 8), imperative military necessity

282   **nuklear,** *adj.,* nuclear

283   **nukleare Anlagen,** nuclear facilities/plants

284   **friedliche nukleare Anlagen,** peaceful nuclear facilities

285   **nukleares Ereignis,** nuclear incident

286   **,,Nukleares Ereignis'' bedeutet ein nuklearen Schaden verursachendes Ereignis** (VCLD 1), "Nuclear incident" means any occurrence which causes nuclear damage

287   **nuklearer Schaden,** nuclear damage
(*nukleares Ereignis)

288   **nukleare Versuchsexplosionen,** nuclear test explosions (MNTB)
(*See also under* *Kern-*and* *Atom-.)

289   **null,** *adj.,* null
(*nichtig)

290   **Nuntiatur,** *f.,* nunciature

291   **Nuntio/Nuntius,** *m.* (*pl.* **-tien**), nuncio
(*Missionschef)

292   **NV-Vertrag,** *m.* (= Nichtverbreitungsvertrag, *m.*), non-proliferation treaty

O

1 **Oberausschuß**, *m.*, senior committee

2 **Obergutachten**, *n.*, chief expert's opinion

3 **Obergutachter**, *m.*, chief expert

4 **Oberherrlichkeit**, *f.*, suzerainty

5 **Oberhoheit**, *f.*, suzerainty, sovereignty
(*Staatshoheit)

6 **Oberschiedsrichter**, *m.*, umpire, chief arbitrator

7 **Der Präsident kann den Einzelschiedsrichter, den Obmann des Schiedsgerichts und den Oberschiedsrichter bestellen** (ECICA IV), The President shall be entitled to appoint the sole arbitrator, presiding arbitrator and umpire

8 **Die beiden Schiedsrichter wählen einen Oberschiedsrichter aus dem in Artikel 1 erwähnten internationalen Verzeichnis** (PCP RegEx 14), These two arbitrators shall select a chief arbitrator from the international list mentioned in Article 1
(*Obmann *and note*)

9 **Obhut**, *f.*, charge, custody, protection

10 **die Obhut der Räumlichkeiten der Mission einem dritten Staat übertragen** (VCDR 15), to entrust the custody of the mission to a third state

11 **Das Bureau hat das Archiv unter seiner Obhut** (HgI 43), The Bureau has charge of the archives

12 **Objekt**, *n.*, object

13 **Objekt der Repressalie**, object of (the) reprisal

14 **Objekt des Völkerrechts**, object of international law

15 **objektivistisch**, *adj.*, objectivist

16 **objektivistische Theorie**, objectivist theory

17 **obliegen** (+ *dat.*), to be the duty of, to be incumbent on/upon, to devolve on

18 **Es obliegt den Staaten, die Regeln des Völkerrechts zu beachten,** It is incumbent upon states to observe the rules of international law

19 **... dessen Ernennung der Organisation obliegt** (PPELDO 27), ... whose appointment devolves on the organization

20 **der Kommission obliegt es ...** (ECPSD 15), the task of the Commission shall be ...

21 **obliegend**, *adj.*, incumbent

22 **die ihnen obliegenden Verpflichtungen**, the duties/obligations incumbent upon them

23 **Obliegenheit**, *f.*, duty

24 **Erfüllung der Obliegenheiten**, performance of (their) duties

25 **in Wahrnehmung ihrer dienstlichen Obliegenheiten** (PrivExCE 14), in the exercise of their functions

26 **(dem Amt) stehen alle sonstigen Befugnisse und Obliegenheiten zu, die ihm übertragen werden** (ILO 10), (the office) shall have such other powers and duties as may be assigned to it
(*Dienstobliegenheit)

27 **Obliegerstaat**, *m.*, adjoining state

28 **obligatorisch**, *adj.*, compulsory

29 **obligatorische Gerichtsbarkeit**, compulsory jurisdiction

30 **die Anerkennung der obligatorischen Gerichtsbarkeit des IGHs,** the recognition of the compulsory jurisdiction of the ICJ

31 **Obmann**, *m.*, chairman, presiding arbitrator
(*There exists considerable inconsistency in the various instruments regarding the use of* **Obmann** *and* **Oberschiedsrichter**, *and the use of* umpire, chairman, presiding arbitrator, chief arbitrator, presiding member of the arbitral tribunal, chairman of the arbitral tribunal, *etc. See PCP, HgI, ECICA under* *Oberschiedsrichter *and* *Stimmengleichheit, *in addition to the examples given here.*)

32 **Der Obmann ist innerhalb von 3 Monaten zu bestellen** (SF 86), The

chairman shall be appointed within 3 months

33 **Die demgemäß bestellten Mitglieder einigen sich auf die Wahl eines Obmanns für das Schiedsgericht,** The members so appointed shall agree on the choice of a chairman of the arbitral tribunal

34 *occupatio bellica* (= kriegerische *Besetzung), belligerent occupation

35 **offenstehen,** to be open

36 **für den/zum Beitritt offenstehen,** to be open for accession (*aufliegen)

37 **öffentlich,** *adj.,* public

38 **öffentliche Dienstleistungen,** public (utility) services

39 **öffentliches Gewissen,** public conscience

40 **öffentliches Interesse,** public interest

41 **öffentlicher Notstand,** public emergency

42 **öffentliche Ordnung,** public policy, *ordre public,* public order (*see* öffentliche *Ordnung)

43 **öffentliches Recht,** public law

44 **öffentliche Sittlichkeit,** public morality

45 **öffentliche Sitzung,** public meeting/ session (*see* *Sitzung *and note,* öffentliche *Sitzung)

46 **Öffentlichkeit,** *f.,* public

47 **unter Ausschluß der Öffentlichkeit,** in camera, in closed session

48 **Die Sitzungen der Kommission finden unter Ausschluß der Öffentlichkeit statt** (PHR 33), The Commission shall sit in camera

49 **offiziös,** *adj.,* semi-official, pseudo-official

50 **offiziöse Handelsdelegation,** semi-official trade delegation

51 **öffnen,** to open (*for accession, etc.*) (*Vertrag öffnen, *aufliegen)

52 **Öffnung¹,** *f.,* mouth (*of indentation in coast*) (*Einschnitt)

53 **Öffnung²,** *f.,* opening (*for accession, etc.*)

54 **Öffnungspunkt,** *m.,* entrance point (*Bucht)

55 **Okkupant,** *m.,* occupant (power), occupying power

56 **Okkupation,** *f.,* occupation

57 **Unter ,,Okkupation'' versteht man die Inbesitznahme eines keiner Staatsgewalt unterworfenen Gebiets,** The term "occupation" signifies the taking possession of a territory not subject to the sovereignty of any (other) state

58 **Okkupationserklärung,** *f.,* declaration of occupation

59 **okkupieren,** to occupy

60 **Optant,** *m.,* the person/party opting (for)

61 **optieren für,** to opt for (*e.g. nationality*)

62 **Option,** *f.,* option

63 **Optionsklausel,** *f.,* option clause

64 **Optionsrecht,** *n.,* the right of option/to opt

65 **ordentlich,** *adj.,* regular, correct, as prescribed

66 **Ordnung¹,** *f.,* order, good order, system

67 **Erhaltung der Ordnung,** maintenance of order

68 **Ruhe und Ordnung im Hafen,** peace of the port

69 **öffentliche Ordnung,** public policy, *ordre public,* public order

70 **Anforderungen der Moral, der öffentlichen Ordnung und der allgemeinen Wohlfahrt** (UDHR 29), requirements of morality, public order and the general welfare

71 **Aufrechterhaltung der öffentlichen Ordnung und der guten Sitten,** maintenance of public order and morals

72 **grundlegende Erfordernisse der Gesundheit und der öffentlichen Ordnung** (ECSC 69), basic requirements of health and public policy

73 **aus Gründen der öffentlichen Ordnung** (RMCE 7), on grounds relating to *ordre public*

74 **verfassungsmäßige Ordnung,** constitutional order

75 **völkerrechtliche Ordnung,** international order

76 zwischenstaatliche Ordnung, international order, international system
77 bisher in Kraft befindliche zwischenstaatliche Ordnungen (UCC
Pr)., international systems
already in force
78 Ordnung², *f.*, adjustment, settlement, regulation
79 Ordnung internationaler Streitfälle,
adjustment of international disputes
(*Bereinigung)
80 ordnungsgemäß, *adj.*, due, in due
form, correct, as required/prescribed
81 Vollmachten, die in ordnungsgemäßer Form befunden worden
sind (ICCA Pr), full powers, found
in good and due form
(Austausch der *Vollmachten)
82 ordnungsmäßig, *adj.*, regular, due,
in due form, correct
83 Organ, *n.*, body, agency, organ
84 alle im Rahmen des Vertrags ge-
schaffenen Organe (WEU I III),
any organ established under the
treaty
85 ad-hoc-Organ, ad hoc body
86 beratendes Organ, advisory body
(*see* beratende *Versammlung)
87 leitendes Organ, governing body
88 nachgeordnetes Organ, subordinate
body
89 ständiges Organ, permanent body
(*Einrichtung²)
90 Organisation, *f.*, organization,
agency
91 Sonderorganisationen der UN,
specialized agencies of the UN
92 im folgenden „Organisation"
genannt (IAEA 1), hereinafter
referred to as "the Agency"
93 Organisationen der Arbeitnehmer
und Arbeitgeber (ILOC 87.3),
workers' and employers' organizations
94 amtliche Organisation, official/gov-
ernmental organization
95 angeschlossene Organisation, affiliated organization
96 fachliche Organisation, technical
organization
97 halbamtliche Organisation, semi-
official organization

98 humanitäre Organisation, humanitarian organization
99 internationale Organisation, international organization
100 nichtamtliche internationale Organisation, non-official international organization
101 nichtregierungsvertretende internationale Organisation, non-
governmental international organization
102 öffentliche internationale Organisation, public international organization
103 regierungsvertretende/staatliche Organisation, governmental organization
104 supranationale/übernationale Organisation, supranational organization
105 überstaatliche Organisation, supra-
national/suprastate organization
106 unparteiische Organisation, impartial organization
107 unparteiische humanitäre Organisation (GC I 3–8), impartial humanitarian organization/body
108 zwischenstaatliche Organisation,
intergovernmental organization
109 Aufnahme in eine Organisation,
admission to (membership of) an
organization
110 die Aufnahme in die Organisation
beantragen, to apply for admission to (membership of) the
organization
111 Ausschluß aus einer Organisation,
expulsion from an organization
112 Austritt aus einer Organisation,
withdrawal from an organization
113 Beitritt zu einer Organisation, accession to an organization
114 Zugehörigkeit zu einer Organisation, membership of an organization
115 Zulassung zu einer Organisation,
admission to (membership of) an
organization
116 aus einer Organisation austreten, to
withdraw from an organization
117 einer Organisation beitreten, to
join/accede to an organization
118 neue Mitglieder in eine Organisation
aufnehmen/zu einer Organisation

zulassen, to admit new members to an organization

119 **Organisationsausschuß,** *m.*, organizing committee

120 **örtlich,** *adj.*, local

121 **örtliche Anciennität,** local seniority (of office)

122 **örtliche Gerichtsbarkeit,** local jurisdiction

P

1 **Pachtabkommen,** *n.,* lease agreement

2 **Pachtvertrag,** *m.,* lease treaty (*see note to* *Vertrag *in Annex* 1)

3 **Pakt,** *m.,* pact (*see note to* *Vertrag *in Annex* 1)

4 **Papierblockade,** *f.,* paper blockade

5 **päpstlich,** *adj.,* apostolic

6 **paraphieren,** to initial (*Paraphierung)

7 **Paraphierung,** *f.,* initialling

8 **Die Richtigkeit des Vertragstextes wird dann von Seiten der Delegierten mit den Anfangsbuchstaben ihres Namens bestätigt: diesen Akt nennt man ,,die Paraphierung'',** The correctness of the text of the treaty is then verified by the delegates by the appendage of their initials, an act termed "the initialling"

9 **Parität,** *f.,* parity

10 **Paritätsklausel,** *f.,* parity clause

11 **Partei,** *f.,* party

12 **Partei an einem Rechtsgeschäft,** party to a legal transaction

13 **beklagte Partei,** defendant party

14 **klagende Partei,** party bringing the action, plaintiff (party)

15 **säumige Partei,** defaulting party

16 **vertragsschließende Partei,** contracting party

17 **Hohe Vertragsschließende Parteien,** High Contracting Parties (*See also under relevant compound, e.g.* *Streitpartei, *and Art.* 2 VCLOT *in Annex* 14.)

18 **Parteifähigkeit,** *f.,* ability/capability/authority to appear as party

19 **partikular,** *adj.,* particular/regional

20 **partikulares Gesetz,** particular law

21 **partikulares Gewohnheitsrecht,** particular customary law

22 **partikulare Konvention,** particular convention

23 **partikulares Völkerrecht,** particular international law

24 **Partisan,** *m.,* partisan

25 **Partisanenbewegung,** *f.,* partisan movement

26 **Partisanenkrieg,** *m.,* partisan warfare

27 **Passierschein,** *m.,* pass, permit, safe conduct (pass)

28 **Paßinhaber,** *m.,* passport holder

29 **Patent,** *n.,* patent

30 **Patentanmeldung,** *f.* (ECICP), patent application

31 **Patentklassifikation,** *f.* (ECICP), classification of patents (*Klassifikationssystem)

32 **pazifisch,** *adj.,* pacific, peaceful (*friedlich)

33 **Pazifismus,** *m.,* pacifism

34 **Pazifist,** *m.,* pacifist

35 **pazifistisch,** *adj.,* pacifist

36 **Person,** *f.,* person

37 **Achtung ihrer Person und ihrer Ehre** (GC III), respect for their persons and their honour

38 **jeder Angriff auf seine Person** (VCDR 29), any attack on his person

39 **Schutz der menschlichen Person in Verträgen humanitärer Art** (VCLOT 60), protection of the human person contained in treaties of a humanitarian character

40 **Unverletzlichkeit der Person** (VCDR 31), inviolability of the person

41 **aus der Sache oder aus der Person,** *ratione materiae* or *ratione personae*

42 **eine vor Gericht auftretende Person** (UCC III), a person seeking judicial relief

43 **seiner Hoheitsgewalt unterstehende Personen** (CERD 14), individuals within its jurisdiction

44 **geschützte Person,** protected person

45 **Die Anwesenheit einer geschützten Person darf nicht dazu benutzt werden, Kampfhandlungen von gewissen Punkten oder Gebieten fernzuhalten** (GC IV 28), The presence of a protected person may not be used to render certain points or areas immune from military operations

46 **Zentralauskunftstelle für geschützte Personen** (GC IV), Central Information Agency for Protected Persons

47 **internationale Person,** international person

48 **juristische Person,** legal person, juridical person, artificial legal person (*see note to* *Rechtsperson)

49 **natürliche oder juristische Person,** natural or legal person, person whether physical or legal (CREFA 1), person or entity (CSMW V)

50 **jede natürliche oder juristische Person** (ELDO Prot 2), any person, whether an individual, company or organization

51 **den Angehörigen des Entsendestaates, sowohl natürlichen als auch juristischen Personen, Hilfe und Beistand leisten** (VCCR 5), to help and assist nationals, both individuals and bodies corporate, of the sending state

52 **Der Rat ist eine juristische Person** (CCC An), The Council shall possess juridical personality

53 **Der Fonds besitzt die vollen Rechte einer juristischen Person** (IMF IX), The Fund shall possess full juridical personality (*Rechtsperson *and note*, *Rechtspersönlichkeit)

54 **die menschliche Person,** the human person

55 **die Würde und der Wert der menschlichen Person** (SCS Pr), the dignity and worth of the human person

56 **natürliche Person,** natural person (*See examples under* juristische *Person.)

57 **restitutionsberechtigte Person** (CSMW), person entitled to restitution, person whose claims for restitution have been approved

58 **rückgeschaffte Person,** repatriated person

59 **verfolgte Person,** persecuted person

60 **vermißte Person,** missing person (*see* *Verschollener)

61 **völkerrechtliche Person,** international person, person in/at international law

62 *persona non grata, persona non grata*

63 **. . . daß der Missionschef oder ein Mitglied des diplomatischen Personals *persona non grata,* oder daß ein anderes Mitglied des Personals der Mission . . . nicht genehm ist** (VCDR 9), . . . that the head of the mission or any member of the diplomatic staff of the mission is *persona non grata* or that any other member of the staff of the mission is not acceptable

64 **Personal,** *n.,* staff

65 **amtliches Personal,** official staff

66 **diplomatisches Personal,** diplomatic staff

67 **Der Ausdruck ,,Mitglieder des diplomatischen Personals" bezeichnet die in diplomatischem Rang stehenden Mitglieder des Personals der Mission** (VCDR 1), The "members of the diplomatic staff" are the members of the staff of the mission having diplomatic rank

68 **internationales Personal,** international staff

69 **technisches Personal,** technical staff (*See also under relevant compound, e.g.* **Dienstpersonal;** *Mission, and VCLOT 1 in Annex 8.)

70 **Personalabgaben,** *f.pl.,* personal dues

71 **Personalabteilung,** *f.,* staff department, personnel office

72 **Personalausschuß,** *m.,* staff committee

73 **Personalausweis,** *m.,* identity card, identity document

74 **Personalhoheit,** *f.,* personal sovereignty, personal jurisdiction

75 **Personalimmunität,** *f.,* personal immunity (*Immunität)

76 **Personalordnung,** *f.,* staff regulations (*e.g.* WMO)

77 **Personalstatut,** *n.,* staff regulations (*e.g.* WHO)

78 **Personalsteuern,** *f.pl.,* personal taxes (Steuern und *Abgaben)
79 **Personalunion,** *f.,* personal union (*Realunion)
80 **Personengruppe,** *f.* (PHR), group of individuals (*Gruppe)
81 **Personenrecht,** *n.,* the law relating to persons
82 **Personenverkehr,** *m.,* movement of persons
83 **die Beseitigung der Hindernisse für den freien Personen-, Dienstleistungs- und Kapitalverkehr** (EEC 3), the abolition of obstacles to freedom of movement for persons, services and capital
84 **Personen- und Güterverkehr zur See,** maritime travel and transport
85 **Persönlichkeit,** *f.,* personality
86 **internationale Persönlichkeit,** international personality
87 **juristische Persönlichkeit,** legal/judicial/juridical personality
88 **völkerrechtliche Persönlichkeit,** international (legal) personality (*Person, juristische *Person, *Rechtsperson, *Rechtspersönlichkeit)
89 **Petition,** *f.* (= *Gesuch, *n.*), petition
90 **Einsender einer Petition** (CERD 14), petitioner
91 **eine Petition entgegennehmen,** to accept a petition
92 **Petitionsrecht,** *n.,* right of petition
93 **das diesen Völkern in anderen internationalen Übereinkünften gewährte Petitionsrecht** (CERD 15), the right of petition granted to these peoples by other international instruments
94 **Petitionsregister,** *n.* (CERD 14), register of petitions
95 **pfänden,** to seize, to attach
96 **Pfändung,** *f.,* attachment, seizure
97 **Pflanzenquarantänemaßnahme,** *f.,* agricultural quarantine measure (CFIMT)
98 **Pflicht,** *f.,* duty, obligation
99 **Ausübung der Pflichten,** exercise of duties

100 **unabhängige Ausübung ihrer Pflichten,** independent exercise of their duties
101 **bürgerliche Pflichten,** civil duties
102 **völkerrechtliche Pflichten,** international duties, duties at/under international law (*Verpflichtung, *auferlegen, *auferlegt, *Rechte und Pflichten)
103 **Pflichtarbeit,** *f.,* compulsory labour
104 **Als ,,Zwangs- oder Pflichtarbeit'' gilt jede Art von Arbeit, die von einer Person unter Androhung irgendeiner Strafe verlangt wird** (ILOC 29.2), The term "forced or compulsory labour" shall mean all work which is exacted from any person under the menace of any penalty (*Zwangsarbeit)
105 **Pirat,** *m.,* pirate
106 **Piraterie,** *f.,* piracy
107 **Plädoyer,** *n.,* pleadings, plea
108 **Planungsausschuß,** *m.,* planning committee
109 **Planungsgruppe,** *f.,* planning group
110 **Plebiszit,** *n.,* plebiscite
111 **Plenarberatung,** *f.,* debate in plenary session, plenary debate
112 **Plenarsitzung,** *f.,* plenary session, full session, meeting in plenary session, plenum
113 **Das Gericht tagt/entscheidet (usw) in Plenarsitzung(en),** The court/tribunal shall sit/reach its decisions (etc.) in plenary session (*Vollsitzung, *Plenum *and note to* *Sitzung)
114 **Plenum,** *n.,* plenum, plenary session, full session
115 **Ein Quorum von 5 Mitgliedern genügt zur Bildung des Plenums** (CRPG An), A quorum of 5 members shall suffice to constitute a plenary session (*Vollsitzung, *Plenarsitzung)
116 **Polizeiaktion,** *f.,* police action, policing action
117 **Positivismus,** *m.,* positivism (*Wille)
118 **Positivist,** *m.,* positivist
119 **positivistisch,** *adj.,* positivist

120	**positivistische Lehre/Theorie,** positivist theory
(*Wille)

121	**Präambel,** *n.,* preamble
(*For samples see Annex* 4.)

122	**präjudizieren,** to prejudice

123	**Diese Bestimmungen präjudizieren nicht den Abschluß eines Vertrags, der zu . . . führt** (MNTB 1), These provisions are without prejudice to the conclusion of a treaty resulting in . . .
(*berühren², *beeinträchtigen)

124	**Präjudizwirkung,** *f.,* prejudicial effect

125	**Praktik,** *f.* (*usu. in pl.*), practice(s)
(*often in a pejorative sense, in contrast to* *Praxis)

126	**diskriminierende Praktiken** (ECSC 60), discriminatory practices

127	**Präsidialausschuß,** *m.,* Bureau (PPESRO 4), general committee (SF 34)

128	**Präventivkrieg,** *m.,* preventive war(fare)

129	**Präventivmaßnahme,** *f.,* preventive measure/action

130	**Präventiv- und Zwangsmaßnahmen,** preventive and enforcement action

131	**Praxis,** *f.,* practice

132	**diplomatische Praxis,** diplomatic practice

133	**herrschende Praxis,** prevailing/current practice

134	**völkerrechtliche Praxis,** international practice, practice under/in international law

135	**Präzedenz,** *f.,* precedent

136	**Präzedenzfall,** *m.,* precedent

137	**Presseattaché,** *m.,* press attaché

138	**Pressefreiheit,** *f.,* freedom of the press

139	**Primat,** *m.,* primacy, supremacy

140	**die Lehre des Primats des Völkerrechts,** the doctrine/theory of the primacy of international law
(*Vorrang², *vorgehen²)

141	**Prinzip,** *n.,* principle
(*See list under* *Grundsatz; *also under* **-prinzip** *and* **-grundsatz** *compounds.*)

142	**Prise,** *f.,* prize

143	**Schiffe, die von ihr als Prise beschlagnahmt werden** (NATOSF VIII), vessels seized by it in prize

144	**Prisengericht,** *n.,* prize court

145	**internationales Prisengericht,** international prize court

146	**nationales Prisengericht,** national prize court

147	**völkerrechtliches Prisengericht,** international prize court

148	**Prisenkommando,** *n.,* prize crew

149	**Prisenrecht,** *n.,* prize law

150	**Unverletzlichkeit in Bezug auf Beschlagnahme, Wegnahme und Ausübung des Prisenrechts** (PCP 14), immunity from seizure, capture and prize

151	**Prisenurteil,** *n.,* prize award, prize judgment

152	**Privateigentum,** *n.,* private property

153	**Privateigentum des Gegners/des Feindes,** private enemy property

154	**feindliches Privateigentum,** private enemy property

155	**Privatinteresse,** *n.,* private interest(s)

156	**die einem Privatinteresse zugefügte Schädigung** (FC An), the injury to private interests

157	**Privatkrieg,** *m.,* private war, war waged by private persons/individuals

158	**Privatpersonal,** *n.,* private staff

159	**Privatrecht,** *n.,* private law

160	**Verfahren, für die das Privatrecht maßgebend ist** (CSMW 3), proceedings based on private law

161	**internationales Privatrecht,** private international law

162	**privatrechtlich,** *adj.,* private, of/relating to private law

163	**Streitigkeiten, die sich aus privatrechtlichen Verträgen ergeben, sowie alle privatrechtlichen Streitigkeiten, bei denen die Organisation Streitpartei ist** (WEUS 26), disputes arising out of contracts or other disputes of a private character to which the organization is a party

164	**Privileg(ium),** *n.* (*pl.* **-ien**), privilege

165	**Privilegien und Immunitäten, die**

zur unabhängigen Ausübung ihrer
Pflichten nötig sind, privileges and
immunities necessary to the independent exercise of their duties
(*Vorrecht, *Befreiungen und Vorrechte)
166 Programmierungsausschuß, *m.*,
programme committee
167 Pronuntius, *m.* (*pl.* -tien), pronuncio
168 Protektor, *m.*, protector, protectory
power
(*Schutzmacht)
169 Protektorat, *n.*, protectorate
170 Protektoratsvertrag, *m.*, treaty of
protectorate, protectorate treaty
171 Protest, *m.*, protest
172 Protest einlegen, to submit a protest
173 Protestierender, *adj.n.*, protesting
party/state, party/state submitting
the protest
174 Protestnote, *f.*, protest note
175 Protokoll[1], *n.*, protocol (*see note to*
*Vertrag *in Annex* 1)
176 Protokoll zur Änderung des Teils
I und der Artikel . . . (SF 143),
protocol amending Part I and Articles . . .
177 Protokoll[2], *n.*, record, minutes,
procès-verbal
178 Protokoll aufsetzen, to draw up the
minutes/record
179 Zum Abschluß ihrer Arbeiten
setzt die Kommission ein Protokoll
auf (ECPSD 15), At the close of
its proceedings the commission
shall draw up a *procès-verbal* ˋ
180 Protokoll berichtigen, to correct/to
rectify the minutes
181 Protokoll verfassen, to draw up the
minutes/record
182 Protokoll[3], *n.*, ceremony, etiquette,
protocol
183 protokollarisch[1], *adj.*, on record,
in the minutes

184 Die Konferenz hat beschlossen,
folgendes protokollarisch festzuhal-
ten: (UNCDD), The conference
decided to place on record the following:
185 protokollarisch[2], *adj.*, ceremonial
186 Fragen der protokollarischen Rangordnung, questions of ceremonial
precedence
187 Protokollchef, *m.*, chief of protocol
188 provisorisch, *adj.*, provisional
(*Übergangs-)
189 Prozeß, *m.*, trial, proceedings
190 Prozeßbevollmächtigter, *adj.n.*
(= *Bevollmächtigter[2]), agent, representative authorized for the purpose of legal proceedings
191 Prozeßpartei, *f.*, party to the proceedings
192 als Prozeßpartei auftreten (ILO 39),
to institute legal proceedings
193 Prozeßrecht, *n.*, procedural law
194 prüfen, to examine, to consider
195 wohlwollend prüfen, to consider
favourably
196 Die Regierung wird wohlwollend
prüfen, ob . . ., The Government will favourably consider
whether . . .
197 . . . wird jede Vertragspartei
wohlwollend die Möglichkeit
prüfen . . . (ARS 5), . . . a contracting party shall give sympa-
thetic consideration to . . .
198 Prüfung, *f.*, consideration, examination, review
199 durch eine unparteiische und gewissenhafte Prüfung (HgI 9), by means
of an impartial and conscientious
investigation
200 Prüfungsgruppe, *f.* (SF 39), review
group
201 Prüfungskommission, *f.*, review/
examining commission
202 Pufferstaat, *m.*, buffer state

Q

1 **Qualifikation**, *f.*, qualification (*e.g. for membership*)

2 **Qualifikationsmerkmal**, *n.*, criterion of qualification

3 **Quarantäne**, *f.*, quarantine

4 **Quarantänegesetz**, *n.*, quarantine law

5 **Quarantänemaßnahme**, *f.*, quarantine measure

6 **quarantänepflichtig**, *adj.*, quarantinable

7 **quarantänepflichtige Krankheiten,** quarantinable diseases

8 **quarantänepflichtige pflanzliche/ tierische Erzeugnisse,** quarantinable plant/animal products

9 **Quarantäneschein**, *m.*, quarantine certificate

10 **Quarantänevorschrift**, *f.*, quarantine regulation

11 **Quarantänezwecke**, *m.pl.*, quarantine purposes

12 **der Besuch und die Überprüfung eines Schiffes zu Quarantäne- zwecken,** the visit to and inspection of a ship for quarantine purposes (**Quarantäne–** *entries all from* CFIMT)

13 **Quelle**, *f.*, source

14 **die Quellen des Völkerrechts,** the sources of international law (*Rechtsquelle, and* SICJ 38 *in Annex 20*)

15 **Quorum**, *n.*, quorum

16 **Ein Quorum von 9 Richtern genügt zur Bildung des Gerichtshofes,** A quorum of 9 judges shall suffice to constitute the court (*Beschlußfähigkeit, *Plenum)

17 **quotal**, *adj.*, proportionate, on a quota basis

18 **Quote**, *f.*, quota

19 **Überschreitung der Quoten** (EPU 13), exceeding the quotas

20 **quotenfrei**, *adj.*, non-quota, quota-free

21 **quotenfreie Bestimmungsländer,** non-quota countries of destination

R

1 **radioaktiv,** *adj.*, radioactive
2 **radioaktive Erzeugnisse oder Abfälle** (VCLD 1), radioactive products or waste
3 **radioaktiver Schutt,** radioactive debris
4 **radioaktive Stoffe,** radioactive substances
5   **Verseuchen der Umwelt des Menschen durch radioaktive Stoffe** (MNTB Pr), contamination of man's environment by radioactive substances
6 **radioaktive Verseuchung,** radioactive contamination
7   **radioaktive Verseuchung des Wassers, des Bodens oder des Luftraumes,** radioactive contamination of the water, soil or airspace
8 **Randstaat,** *m.*, peripheral state
9 **Rang,** *m.*, class, rank, status
10   **Die Staaten können frei den Rang der Missionschefs vereinbaren** (VCDR 15), The class to which heads of their missions are to be assigned is to be agreed between the states
11   **das im Rang nächstfolgende Mitglied des Gerichtshofes** (SF 87), the member of the court next in seniority
12   **die im Rang vergleichbaren Mitglieder diplomatischer Missionen** (PrivExCE 9), members of comparable rank of diplomatic missions (*see* *ranggleich)
13 **Rang der Völkerrechtsquellen,** ranking/order of precedence of the sources of international law
14 **diplomatischer Rang,** diplomatic rank
15   **die im diplomatischen Rang stehenden Mitglieder des Personals der Mission** (VCDR 1), the members of the staff of the mission having diplomatic rank
16 **vergleichbarer Rang,** comparable rank
17   **Vertreter vergleichbaren Ranges** (IMF IX), representatives of comparable rank

(*ranggleich)
18 **vorgehender Rang,** priority of rank, precedence
(*Klasse)
19 **rangältest,** *adj.*, highest ranking, of/having highest rank, the senior ranking
(*dienstältest)
20 **Rangänderung,** *f.*, change/alteration of rank/order of rank
21 **Rangfolge,** *f.*, precedence, order of precedence
22   **Innerhalb jeder Klasse richtet sich die Rangfolge der Missionschefs nach Tag und Zeit ihres Amtsantritts** (VCDR 16), Heads of mission shall take precedence in their respective classes in the order of the date and time of taking up their functions
23   **Rangfolge der Leiter konsularischer Vertretungen** (VCCR), precedence as between heads of consular posts
24   **in der Rangfolge nachgeordnet sein** (VCDR 16), to rank after
(*Klasse, *Rang, *Rangordnung)
25 **ranggleich,** *adj.*, of equal/comparable rank
26 **ranggleiche Mitglieder diplomatischer Vertretung** (CCC An), members of comparable rank of diplomatic missions
27 **ranghöchst,** *adj.*, the senior ranking, highest ranking, having/of highest rank
(*dienstältest)
28 **Rangklasse,** *f.*, class, rank, status
(*Rang, *Anciennität)
29 **Rangliste,** *f.* **der Kriegsmarine** (GCHS 8), Navy List
30 **Rangordnung,** *f.*, precedence, order of precedence
31 **Rangordnung und Protokoll,** precedence and etiquette
32 **Rangordnung der Quellen des Völkerrechts,** order of precedence of the sources of international law
33   **protokollarische Rangordnung,** ceremonial precedence
(*Rangfolge)

34 **Rangunterschied**, *m.*, difference/distinction of/as to class/rank
35 **Das Völkerrecht kennt keine Rangunterschiede zwischen den verschiedenen Völkerrechtsquellen,** International law makes no distinction between the importance of the various sources of international law/in international law there is no hierarchy of sources of international law
36 **Rasse,** *f.*, race
37 **Überlegenheit einer Rasse** (CERD 4), racial superiority
38 **Lehre von der Gleichheit/Ungleichheit der Rassen und Menschen** (UNESCO), doctrine of the equality/inequality of men and races
39 **Rassendiskriminierung,** *f.*, racial discrimination
40 **Aufreizen zur Rassendiskriminierung** (CERD 4), incitement to racial discrimination
41 **Rassendiskriminierung beseitigen** (CERD 5), to eliminate racial discrimination
42 **Rassendiskriminierung fördern oder dazu aufreizen** (CERD 4), to promote or incite racial discrimination
43 **Rassendiskriminierung rechtfertigen** (CERD 4), to justify racial discrimination
44 **Rassendiskriminierung mit allen geeigneten Mitteln verbieten** (CERD 2), to prohibit racial discrimination by all appropriate means (*see also* CERD 1 *in Annex* 12)
45 **Rassengruppe,** *f.* (CERD 1), racial group
46 **Rassen- oder Volksgruppe** (CERD 7), racial or ethnical group
47 **Rassenhaß,** *m.*, racial hatred
48 **Rassenintegrierung,** *f.*, racial integration
49 **alle eine Rassenintegrierung anstrebenden vielrassischen Organisationen** (CERD 2), all integrationist multiracial organizations
50 **rassenkämpferische Betätigung** (CERD 4), racist activity
51 **Rassenschranke,** *f.* (CERD 2), barrier between races, racial barrier

52 **Rassentrennung,** *f.*, racial division RD 2), racial segregation (*Segregationspolitik)
53 **Rassenverfolgung,** *f.*, racial persecution
54 **rassisch,** *adj.*, racial
55 **rassische Gruppe** (UDHR, CERD, etc.), racial group
56 **Rat,** *m.*, council (*e.g.* ELDO, ESRO), board (*e.g.* UNESCO)
57 **Vorstand des Rates,** Bureau of the Council (CICES)
58 **Zusammensetzung des Rats,** council composition (ESRO 10), composition of the council
59 **parlamentarischer Rat,** parliamentary council
60 **ständiger Rat,** permanent/standing council
61 **Ratgeber,** *m.*, adviser
62 **Jedem Delegierten können Ratgeber beigegeben werden** (ILO 3), Each delegate may be accompanied by advisers
63 **Ratifikation,** *f.*, ratification
64 **Dieser Vertrag bedarf der Ratifikation,** The present treaty is subject to ratification
65 **Eintragung der Ratifikationen, die später mitgeteilt werden** (ILOC 274), registration of ratifications which may be communicated subsequently
66 **förmliche Ratifikation,** formal ratification
67 **spätere Ratifikation,** subsequent ratification (*Ratifizierung, ohne *Vorbehalt, VCLOT 2 *in Annex* 14, *and* VCLOT 82 *in Annex* 5)
68 **ratifikationsbedürftig,** *adj.*, requiring ratification
69 **Ratifikationserklärung,** *f.*, declaration/instrument of ratification (*note to* *Erklärung)
70 **Ratifikationsklausel,** *f.*, ratification clause
71 **Ratifikationsurkunde,** *f.*, instrument of ratification
72 **Austausch der Ratifikationsurkunden,** exchange of instruments of ratification

73 **Hinterlegung der Ratifikationsur-kunden,** deposit of instruments of ratification (*hinterlegen, *Mitgliedstaat, *Ratifizierung, *and* VCLOT 84 *in Annex* 5)
74 **Ratifikationsvorbehalt,** *m.*, reservation in respect of ratification
75 **ratifizieren,** to ratify
76 **ein Unterzeichner, der diese Charta in der Folge ratifiziert** (ES 35), a signatory government ratifying this charter subsequently
77 **jede Regierung, die (sie) später ratifiziert** (ECICP 4), any government which subsequently ratifies it (ohne *Vorbehalt)
78 **Ratifizierender,** *adj.n.*, the ratifying party/state
79 **Ratifizierung,** *f.*, ratification
80 **Dieses Übereinkommen bedarf der Ratifizierung. Die Ratifizierungsur-kunden sind beim Generalsekretär der UN zu hinterlegen** (VCDR 49), The present convention is subject to ratification. The instruments of ratification shall be deposited with the Secretary-General of the UN
81 **unvollständige Ratifizierung,** imperfect/incomplete ratification (*Ratifikation, ohne *Vorbehalt, VCLOT 2 *in Annex* 14, *and* VCLOT 82 *in Annex* 5) **Räume,** *m.pl.* = *Räumlichkeiten, f.pl.*
82 **räumen,** to evacuate
83 **räumlich,** *adj.*, territorial, geographical
84 **räumlicher Geltungsbereich,** territorial application
85 **Räumlichkeiten,** *f.pl.*, premises, accommodation
86 **Die Räumlichkeiten und Gebäude des Rates sind unverletzlich** (PrivExCE 4), The buildings and premises of the Council shall be inviolable
87 **die Räumlichkeiten der Mission,** the premises of the mission
88 **die Räumlichkeiten, das Vermögen und die Archive der Mission achten und schützen** (VCDR 45), to respect and protect the premises of the mission, together with its property and archives
89 **Der Empfangsstaat erleichtert dem Entsendestaat den Erwerb der für dessen Mission benötigten Räum-lichkeiten, oder hilft ihm, sich auf andere Weise Räumlichkeiten zu beschaffen** (VCDR 21), The receiving state shall facilitate the acquisition by the sending state of premises necessary for its mission or assist the latter in obtaining accommodation in some other way
90 **Räumung,** *f.*, evacuation (*Verschickung)
91 **Realabgaben,** *f.pl.*, real dues (*Abgaben)
92 **Realsteuern,** *f.pl.*, real taxes (*Abgaben)
93 **Realunion,** *f.*, real union
94 **Die Realunion ist eine Staatenverbin-dung zweier oder mehrerer Staaten unter dem gleichen Staatsoberhaupt und mit gemeinsamen Staatsor-ganen,** Real union is a composite state of two or more states under the same head of state and with joint state organs (*note to* *Bundesstaat)
95 **Rechenschaft,** *f.*, account
96 **Die Abgeordneten . . . können nicht . . . amtlich zur Rechenschaft gezogen werden** (PrivExCE 14), The representatives . . . shall be immune from all official interrogation
97 **Rechenschaftsbericht,** *m.*, account
98 **ein Rechenschaftsbericht über die vom Sicherheitsrat beschlossenen oder ergriffenen Maßnahmen,** an account of the measures decided upon or taken by the Security Council
99 **Rechnungsdefizit,** *n.*, accounting deficit
100 **kumulative Rechnungsdefizite** (EPU), cumulative accounting deficits
101 **Rechnungseinheit,** *f.*, unit of account
102 **Betrag an Rechnungseinheiten im Gegenwert von . . .,** amount of units of account equivalent to . . .

103 **eine Rechnungseinheit von 0,888 . . . Gramm Feingold,** a unit of account of 0.888 . . . grammes of fine gold

104 **Rechnungsjahr,** *n.,* financial year

105 **laufendes Rechnungsjahr,** current financial year

106 **das unmittelbar voraufgegangene Rechnungsjahr,** the immediately preceding financial year

107 **Rechnungsprüfer,** *m.,* auditor (*Jahresabrechnung)

108 **Rechnungsprüferausschuß,** *m.,* auditing committee, committee of auditors

109 **Rechnungsprüfung,** *f.,* auditing

110 **Rechnungsüberschuß,** *m.,* accounting surplus

111 **kumulative Rechnungsüberschüsse (EPU),** cumulative accounting surpluses

112 **Rechnungszeitraum,** *m.,* period of account, financial period

113 **Recht¹,** *n.,* law

114 **Herrschaft/Vorherrschaft des Rechtes,** the rule of law

115 **von Rechts wegen,** by operation/virtue of law, by law

116 **allegemeines Recht,** the general law, the ordinary law, the law obtaining in the absence of specific (statutory) provisions

117 **anwendbares Recht,** applicable law, law applicable, law to be applied

118 **Diese Vereinbarung hat das anwendbare Recht anzugeben (PPELDO 25),** This agreement shall specify the law applicable

119 **anzuwendendes Recht,** applicable law, law applicable, law to be applied

120 **gemeinsame Regeln zur Lösung der Frage des anzuwendenden Rechts aufstellen (CCFTD Pr),** to establish common provisions on the conflict of laws

121 **ausländisches Recht,** foreign law

122 **bestehendes Recht,** existing law

123 **bürgerliches Recht,** civil law

124 **dispositives Recht,** permissive law (*i.e. non-mandatory*), dispositive law

125 **früheres Recht,** prior/earlier/previous law

126 **innerstaatliches Recht** (= staatliches Recht, nationales Recht, internes Recht), municipal law, state law, internal law, domestic law, national law

127 **Verhältnis zwischen der Charta und dem innerstaatlichen Recht sowie internationalen Übereinkünften (ES 32),** relations between the Charter and domestic law or international agreements

128 **Im Konfliktsfall zwischen Völkerrecht und innerstaatlichem Recht haftet der Staat Dritten gegenüber für die Einhaltung der zwischenstaatlichen Normen,** In the event of conflict between international law and municipal/domestic law, a state is responsible to third states for ensuring that the international rules are observed

129 **internationales Recht,** international law (*note to* *internationales Recht; *for examples see under* *Völkerrecht, *Völkerrechts-, *and* *völkerrechtlich*) **internes Recht** = innerstaatliches *Recht

130 **kodifiziertes Recht,** codified law

131 **materiales Recht (CSMW 4),** substantive law

132 **nachfolgendes Recht,** subsequent law

133 **nachgiebiges Recht,** permissive law, dispositive law

134 **nationales Recht,** national law (innerstaatliches *Recht)

135 **öffentliches Recht,** public law

136 **partikulares Recht,** particular law (*i.e. law of particular application*)

137 **positives Recht,** positive law

138 **privates Recht,** private law

139 **regionales Recht,** regional law

140 **späteres Recht,** subsequent law

141 **staatliches Recht,** state law (innerstaatliches *Recht)

142 **supranationales Recht,** supranational law

143 **universales Recht,** universal law (*i.e. law of universal application*)

144 **vergleichendes Recht,** comparative law

145 **zwingendes Recht,** mandatory law, peremptory law, *jus cogens*
146 **Recht²,** *n.,* right
147 **jeder, der in seinen Rechten verletzt worden ist** (ICCPR 2), any person whose rights are violated
148 **die Rechte Einzelner,** individual rights, rights of individuals
149 **Rechte, die aus einem Vertrag (usw.) erwachsen/herrühren,** rights arising from/resulting from a treaty (etc.)
150 **die aus der Mitgliedschaft erwachsenden Rechte** (CUN 2), the rights resulting from membership
151 **alle Rechte, die aus den Verträgen herrühren** (CSMW 2), all rights arising under the treaties
152 **internationalen Organisationen steht das Recht zu, . . .,** international organizations are entitled to . . .
153 **bestehende oder zukünftig erwachsende Rechte,** rights now existing or hereafter arising
154 **Rechte und Pflichten,** rights and duties/obligations
155 **Rechte und Pflichten auferlegen,** to impose rights and duties
156 **ein allgemeines Übereinkommen, das ihnen Rechte verleiht und Pflichten auferlegt** (SC 3), a general convention which will give them rights and impose upon them duties
157 **Art und Umfang seiner Rechte und Pflichten** (ILOC 22.8), the nature and extent of his rights and obligations
158 **Rechte und Vergünstigungen,** rights and benefits
159 **Rechte und Vorteile,** rights and benefits/privileges
160 **die aus der Mitgliedschaft erwachsenden Rechte und Vorteile** (IAEA IV), the rights and benefits resulting from membership
161 **Abschaffung der Rechte,** abolition of rights
162 **Abschaffung der in diesem Pakt anerkannten Rechte** (ICCPR 5), destruction of any of the rights recognized herein (in this covenant)

163 **Abtretung der Rechte,** assignment of rights
164 **Achtung der Rechte,** respect for/observance of rights
165 **Ausübung der Rechte,** exercise of rights
166 **Delegierung der Rechte,** delegation of rights
167 **Entzug der Rechte,** suspension of rights, withdrawal of rights
168 **zeitweiliger Entzug der Rechte,** (temporary) suspension of rights
169 **Erlöschen der Rechte,** extinction/lapse of rights
170 **Genuß der Rechte,** enjoyment of rights
171 **Schutz der Rechte,** protection of rights
172 **Sicherstellung der Rechte,** maintenance/securing/protection of rights
173 **Übergang der Rechte,** transfer of rights, subrogation of rights (VCLD IX)
174 **Übertragung der Rechte,** transfer of rights
175 **Untergang der Rechte,** extinction/lapse of rights
176 **Wahrung der Rechte,** preservation/upholding of rights
177 **alleiniges Recht,** exclusive right
178 **angeborenes Recht,** inherent right, birthright
179 **bürgerliche Rechte** (= Bürgerrechte), civil rights, civil law rights, rights in civil law, rights accorded by/available under civil law
180 **erworbene Rechte,** acquired rights
181 **geschützte Rechte,** protected rights
182 **gleiche Rechte,** equal rights, equivalent rights
183 **auf der Grundlage der gleichen Rechte,** on the basis of equal rights (* Gleichberechtigung)
184 **kulturelle Rechte,** cultural rights
185 **naturgegebene Rechte,** inherent rights
186 **das naturgegebene Recht zur Selbstverteidigung** (CUN 51), the inherent right of self-defence
187 **politische Rechte,** political rights
188 **souveräne Rechte,** sovereign rights
189 **soziale Rechte,** social rights

190 **territoriale Rechte,** territorial rights
191 **unveräußerliche Rechte,** inalienable rights
192 **wirtschaftliche Rechte,** economic rights
193 **die Rechte erlöschen,** the rights lapse/become extinct
194 **Diese Rechte erlöschen, wenn die Vertragspartner den Vertrag aufheben,** These rights become extinct if the contracting parties terminate the treaty
195 **die Rechte erwachsen aus . . .,** the rights arise from . . .
196 **Rechte ausüben,** to exercise rights
197 **sich seiner Rechte begeben,** to forgo one's rights
198 **Rechte (bei)behalten,** to retain rights
199 **die drei Mächte behalten weiterhin ihre bisher ausgeübten Rechte** (CRPG 4), The three Powers retain the rights heretofore exercised by them
200 **sich auf seine Rechte berufen,** to invoke/to claim one's rights
201 **Rechte delegieren,** to delegate rights
202 **Rechte einräumen,** to accord/to grant rights
203 **Rechte geltend machen,** to invoke/claim/exercise rights, to put rights into effect
204 **Rechte innehaben,** to hold/to possess rights
205 **Rechte übertragen,** to transfer rights
206 **Rechte verleihen,** to confer/to grant rights (see *Rechte und Pflichten)
207 **der Rechte verlustig werden,** to forfeit rights (see *verlustig)
208 **sich das Recht vorbehalten,** to reserve the right
209 **das Recht auf,** the right to/of
     (*The extensive rights both of individuals (e.g. in PHR, ES, UDHR) and of states and other international persons appear in various constructions, using das Recht auf, das Recht zu, das Recht + gen., das Recht + zu + infinitive, der Anspruch auf, or in expressions using Freiheit or frei, or even combinations of these. To reduce unnecessary entries, the*

*first three of the above are all listed here under das Recht auf. For rights and freedoms not listed here, see also under *Anspruch auf, *Freiheit, *frei, and under the relevant compound noun, e.g. *Landungsrecht, *Vereinigungsfreiheit. See also CERD 5 in Annex 9. The list below is arranged alphabetically according to the word immediately following das Recht auf (ein).*)
     das Recht auf:
210 **Achtung (seines) Eigentums** (PHR), the peaceful enjoyment of (his) possessions
211 **Achtung der Würde der Person,** respect for the dignity of the person
212 **angemessene und befriedigende Arbeitsbedingungen** (UDHR), just and favourable conditions of work
213 **angemessene und befriedigende Entlohnung** (UDHR), just and favourable remuneration
214 **angemessenen Lebensstandard,** adequate standard of living
215 **angemessenen sozialen, gesetzlichen und wirtschaftlichen Schutz** (ES), appropriate social, legal and economic protection
216 **Ausübung einer Erwerbstätigkeit** (ES), to engage in a gainful occupation
217 **besonderen Schutz bei der Arbeit** (ES), special protection in (their) work
218 **besonderen Schutz gegen körperliche und sittliche Gefahren** (ES), special protection against physical and moral hazards
219 **Eheschließung,** to marry
220 **Eigentum,** property
221 **allein oder in der Gemeinschaft mit anderen das Recht auf Eigentum haben** (UDHR), the right to own property alone as well as in association with others
222 **Erziehung,** education
223 **Flaggenführung,** to use the flag
224 **freie Berufs(aus)wahl** (CERD/

UDHR), free choice of profession
225   **freie Entscheidung,** free decision/freedom of decision
226   **freie Meinungsäußerung,** freedom of expression
227   **freie Wahl des Wohnsitzes** (UDHR), freedom of residence
228   **freie Zufahrt,** free access
229   **Freiheit,** liberty
230   **Freiheit zur Vereinigung** (ES), freedom of association
231   **Freizügigkeit,** freedom of movement
232   **Fürsorge** (ES), social and medical assistance
233   **geeignete Möglichkeiten der Berufsberatung/Berufsausbildung** (ES), appropriate facilities for vocational guidance/training
234   **gerechtes Arbeitsentgelt** (ES), fair remuneration
235   **gerechtes Verfahren,** fair trial
236   **Gleichbehandlung,** equal treatment
237   **Gleichberechtigung,** equality, equal rights
238   **gleichen Lohn für gleiche Arbeit** (CERD/UDHR), equal pay for equal work
239   **Gründung einer Familie,** to found a family
240   **Handel,** trade
241   **individuelle und kollektive Selbstverteidigung** (CUN 51), individual or collective self-defence
242   **Kollektivverhandlungen,** collective bargaining (EAEC), to bargain collectively (ES)
243   **Kriegführung,** to wage/make/resort to war
244   **Leben,** life
245   **Nacheile,** (hot) pursuit
246   **Niederlassung,** establishment/settlement
247   **ordentliches und unparteiisches Gerichtsverfahren** (GC III), fair and impartial trial
248   **persönliche Sicherheit,** security of the person
249   **Schutz gegen Arbeitslosigkeit** (CERD, UDHR), protection against unemployment

250   **Schutz und Beistand** (ES), protection and assistance
251   **Selbstbestimmung,** self-determination
252   **Selbsthilfe,** self-help, self-defence
253   **Selbstverteidigung,** self-defence
254   **sichere und gesunde Arbeitsbedingungen** (ES), safe and healthy working conditions
255   **Sicherheit,** security
256   **Sicherheit der Person,** security of the person
257   **soziale Sicherheit** (ES), social security
258   **Staatsangehörigkeit,** nationality
259   **Überflug,** to fly across (a territory)
260   **Überflug ohne Landung,** to fly across (a territory) without landing
261   **Unabhängigkeit,** independence
262   **Versammlungs- und Vereinigungsfreiheit zu friedlichen Zwecken** (UDHR), freedom of peaceful assembly and association
263   **Zulassung zu öffentlichen Ämtern in seinem Lande** (UDHR), access to public service in his country
264   **Zusammenschluß,** association
265   **das Recht, . . . zu (machen),** the right to (do) . . ./the right of (doing)
266   **Berufsvereinigungen zu bilden und solchen beizutreten,** to form and to join trade unions/professional associations
267   **Beschwerde zu führen** (GC III), of complaint/appeal, to complain
268   **eine Ehe einzugehen,** to marry
269   **eine Familie zu gründen,** to found a family
270   **ein Gnadengesuch einzureichen** (GC IV), petition for pardon or reprieve
271   **seinen Wohnsitz frei zu wählen** (PHR Prot 4), to choose one's residence
272   **Verbände zu bilden,** to form associations
273   **rechtlich,** *adj.*, legal, consistent with the law, within the law
274   **rechtliche Stellung,** legal status
275   **rechtmäßig**, *adj.*, lawful, legal, rightful, legitimate, licit

276 **Rechtmäßigkeit,** *f.,* lawfulness, legality, legitimacy

277 **Rechtsanspruch,** *m.,* legal claim, legal right

278 **Personen, die einen Rechtsanspruch auf . . . haben,** persons who are/may be legally entitled to . . .

279 **Rechtsauffassung,** *f.,* legal view/interpretation, attitude to/interpretation of law

280 **Rechtsausschuß,** *m.,* legal affairs committee

281 **Rechtsbehelf¹,** *m.,* plea, argument, point of argument

282 **Die Verhandlung besteht in dem mündlichen Vortrage der Rechtsbehelfe der Parteien vor dem Schiedsgericht** (HgI 63), The discussions consist in the oral development before the tribunal of the arguments of the parties

283 **Rechtsbehelf²,** *m.,* (legal) remedy

284 **wenn das Verfahren der Rechtsbehelfe über Gebühr in die Länge gezogen wird** (CERD 11), when the application of the remedies is unreasonably prolonged

285 **innerstaatliche Rechtsbehelfe,** domestic/internal/national (legal) remedies

286 **örtliche Rechtsbehelfe,** local (legal) remedies

287 **sonstige verfügbare örtliche Rechtsbehelfe** (CERD 14), other available local remedies

288 **die Erschöpfung der örtlichen Rechtsbehelfe,** the exhaustion of local (legal) remedies (*see* *Sache²)

289 **wirksame Rechtsbehelfe** (CERD 6), effective remedies (*Rechtsmittel)

290 **Rechtsbeistand,** *m.,* counsel, legal counsel

291 **. . . sind berechtigt, Rechtsbeistände oder Anwälte zu ernennen** (HgI 14), . . . shall be authorized to engage counsel or advocates

292 **einheimischer Rechtsbeistand** (UCC III), domestic counsel

293 **unentgeltlicher Rechtsbeistand,** free legal counsel (*Beistand²)

294 **Rechtsberater,** *m.,* counsel

295 **Sie können Rechtsberater hinzuziehen** (CRPG An), They may be assisted by counsel

296 **Rechtsbeziehung,** *f.,* legal relation(ship)

297 **Die Rechtsbeziehungen zwischen den Staaten werden allgemein durch das Völkerrecht geregelt,** Legal relations between states are in general regulated by international law

298 **Rechtsetzungsbefugnis,** *f.,* (= Rechtsetzungskompetenz, *f.*), law-making power/authority

299 **rechtsfähig,** *adj.,* having/possessing legal status/capacity (*Rechtsfähigkeit)

300 **Rechtsfähigkeit,** *f.,* legal capacity

301 **Ferner zeigt die Staatenpraxis, daß Rechtsfähigkeit nicht mit Handlungsfähigkeit verwechselt werden darf,** Moreover, practice as between states shows that legal capacity must not be confused with capacity to act

302 **die Rechtsfähigkeit, die für die Wahrnehmung ihrer Aufgaben notwendig ist** (WMO 27), such legal capacity as may be necessary for the exercise of its functions

303 **Die IAEA besitzt im Hoheitsgebiet jedes Mitgliedes die Rechtsfähigkeit, Vorrechte und Befreiungen, die zur Durchführung ihrer Aufgaben erforderlich sind** (IAEA XV), The Agency shall enjoy in the territory of each member such legal capacity and such privileges and immunities as are necessary for the exercise of its functions

304 **Die Organisation besitzt die Rechtsfähigkeit einer juristischen Person** (FAO XV), The organization shall have the capacity of a legal person (*Handlungsfähigkeit, juristische *Person)

305 **bürgerliche Rechtsfähigkeit,** civil capacity

306 **Die Kriegsgefangenen behalten ihre volle bürgerliche Rechtsfähigkeit** (GC III 14), Prisoners of war shall retain their full civil capacity

307 **Rechtsfrage,** *f.*, legal question, legal matter
(*Gutachten)

308 **Rechtsgarantie,** *f.*, legal/judicial guarantee

309 **die von den zivilisierten Völkern als unerläßlich anerkannten Rechtsgarantien** (GC I 3), the judicial guarantees which are recognized as indispensable by civilized peoples

310 **Rechtsgelehrsamkeit,** *f.*, jurisprudence

311 **Rechtsgelehrter,** *adj.n.*, jurisconsult, legal scholar, lawyer, jurist, one learned in the law

312 **Rechtsgelehrte von anerkanntem Ruf** (PHR 39), jurisconsults of recognized competence

313 **Rechtsgelehrte von anerkannter Sachkenntnis auf dem Gebiet des internationalen Rechts** (CRPG An), lawyers of recognized competence in international law

314 **Rechtsgeschäft,** *n.*, (legal) transaction/act, act in the law

315 **einseitiges Rechtsgeschäft,** unilateral (legal) transaction

316 **völkerrechtliche Rechtsgeschäfte,** acts at international law

317 **zweiseitiges Rechtsgeschäft,** bilateral (legal) transaction

318 **Rechtsgeschichte,** *f.*, history of law/ jurisprudence

319 **Rechtsgrundsatz,** *m.*, legal principle, principle of law

320 **allgemeine Rechtsgrundsätze,** general principles of law (*see* *kodifiziert)

321 **allgemein anerkannte Rechtsgrundsätze,** generally recognized principles of law
(zivilisierter *Staat)

322 **rechtsgültig,** *adj.*, valid in/at law, legally valid

323 **Die Beschlüsse sind nur dann rechtsgültig, wenn alle Mitglieder anwesend sind** (FC An), Decisions shall be valid only if all members are present

324 **Rechtsgültigkeit,** *f.*, validity in/at law, legal validity

325 **die Rechtsgültigkeit gesetzlicher Maßnahmen** (FC An), the validity of legal measures

326 **Rechtsgutachten,** *n.*, advisory (legal) opinion, counsel's opinion

327 **Die Rechtsgutachten haben keine bindende Wirkung** (CRPG An), Advisory opinions shall not be binding

328 **Rechtsgutachten erstatten,** to give an advisory opinion
(*Gutachten)

329 **Rechtshandlung,** *f.*, legal act

330 **rechtshängig,** *adj.*, pending
(*anhängig)

331 **Rechtshängigkeit,** *f.*, pendency (of proceedings)

332 **nach Rechtshängigkeit,** subsequent to/after action brought

333 **vor Rechtshängigkeit,** prior to/before action brought

334 **von der Rechtshängigkeit an** (CRPG An), at any time after the institution of proceedings

335 **Eintritt der Rechtshängigkeit,** commencement of proceedings

336 **Rechtshilfe,** *f.*, legal assistance, advice on legal matters, legal aid

337 **Konsuln leisten für die Staatsangehörigen des Entsendestaates Rechtshilfe,** Consular officers provide legal assistance/guidance to the nationals of the sending state

338 **Rechtshilfeersuchen,** *n.*, letters of request (ICCC 16), letters rogatory

339 **dem Rechtshilfeersuchen zugrunde liegende strafbare Handlung,** the offence motivating the letters rogatory

340 **Ausführung/Erledigung des Rechtshilfeersuchens,** execution of the letters rogatory

341 **Rechtshilfeersuchen ausführen/erledigen,** to execute the letters rogatory

342 **Rechtsinhaber,** *m.*, possessor/ holder/owner of a right, person entitled to a right

343 **Rechtskollision,** *f.*, conflict of laws

344 **Rechtskonflikt,** *m.*, conflict of laws

345 **Rechtskraft,** *f.*, legal force, legal efficacy

346 **Rechtskraft erhalten,** to come/enter into force

347   die durch die Besatzungsmacht
       erlassenen Bestimmungen erhalten
       erst dann Rechtskraft, wenn . . .
       (GC IV 65), the provisions
       enacted by the occupying power
       shall   not   come   into   force
       before . . .
       (in *Kraft treten)

348   rechtskräftig, *adj.*, binding (as be-
       tween parties), in force, having legal
       force

349   Alle Urteile . . . bleiben in jeder
       Hinsicht rechtskräftig und rechts-
       wirksam (CSMW 7), All judgments
       . . . shall remain final and valid for
       all purposes
       (endgültige   *Entscheidung,   in
       *Kraft   treten/bleiben,   rechtskräf-
       tiges/endgültiges *Urteil)

350   Rechtskreis¹, *m.*, school of (legal)
       thought, school of law
       (*Völkerrechtskreis)

351   Rechtskreis², *m.*, law district, area
       of jurisdiction

352   Rechtslage, *f.*, legal position, legal
       status

353   die Rechtslage von Ausländern, the
       legal status of aliens

354   die Rechtslage einer veränderten
       Sachlage anpassen, to adapt the legal
       position to a changed situation

355   Rechtslehre, *f.*, legal doctrine, legal
       theory, books of authority

356   Rechtsmißbrauch,   *m.*,   abuse/
       misuse/misapplication of the law

357   rechtsmißbräuchlich,   *adj.*,   in
       abuse of law

358   Rechtsmittel, *n.*, appeal, (means of)
       redress, remedy, appeal at law

359   Die Entscheidung ist endgültig und
       ohne Rechtsmittel, The decision is
       final and without appeal

360   innerstaatliche Rechtsmittel, domes-
       tic/local/internal/national remedies

361   erst nach Erschöpfung der inner-
       staatlichen Rechtsmittel, only
       when local remedies have been
       exhausted

362   Rechtsmittel ergreifen/einlegen, to
       appeal, to lodge/to file an appeal

363   wenn das Rechtsmittel nicht in-
       nerhalb von 30 Tagen nach

       Gewährung der Zulassung ein-
       gelegt wird (CSMW An), if no
       appeal is lodged within 30 days
       from the date on which it is
       granted

364   Gegen die Entscheidungen des
       Schiedsgerichts kann kein Rechts-
       mittel eingelegt werden (PCP Re-
       gEx 14), There shall be no appeal
       from the decisions of the arbitral
       tribunal

365   Gegen den Spruch des Schieds-
       gerichts kann ein Rechtsmittel
       nicht eingelegt werden (PPELDO
       26), No appeal shall lie against the
       award of the arbitration tribunal

366   Jeder Verurteilte hat das Recht,
       diejenigen   Rechtsmittel   zu
       ergreifen, die in dem vom Gericht
       angewendeten Recht vorgesehen
       sind (GC IV 72), A convicted per-
       son shall have the right of appeal
       provided for by the law applied by
       the court

367   Rechtsmitteln unterliegen, to be sub-
       ject to/susceptible of appeal
       (*Rechtsbehelf²,   *Rechtsweg,
       rechtskräftiges *Urteil)

368   Rechtsmittelfrist,   *f.*,   period
       allowed for appeal

369   Rechtsmittelverfahren,   *n.*,
       appeal, remedy, proceedings by way
       of (legal) remedy/appeal

370   erst nach Erschöpfung der inner-
       staatlichen   Rechtsmittelverfahren
       (PHR 26), only after all domestic
       remedies have been exhausted
       (*Rechtsmittel, *Rechtsweg)

371   Rechtsnachfolger, *m.*, successor in
       title, legal successor

372   Rechtsnorm, *f.*, (a) rule of law (con-
       trast with Herrschaft des *Rechts)

373   Hilfsmittel   zur   Feststellung   von
       Rechtsnormen (SICJ 38), subsidiary
       means for the determination of rules
       of law

374   Rechtsordnung, *f.*, legal system,
       legal order, law(s)

375   eine Stelle innerhalb seiner nationa-
       len Rechtsordnung (CERD 14), a
       body within its national legal order

376   Ist die Rechtsordnung nicht ver-

einheitlicht . . . (CCFTD 1), If the
law consists of a non-unified system
. . .

377 **Rechtsordnung verletzen,** to in-
fringe/to violate laws (and regulations)

378 **Rechtsperson**, *f.*, person before the
law, legal person (*i.e. person whom
the law recognizes as having rights
and duties, whether natural or artificial. Contrast this sense with that of*
legal person *under* juristische **Person. See also under* *Rechtspersönlichkeit.)

379 **Jeder Mensch hat überall Anspruch
auf Anerkennung als Rechtsperson**
(UDHR 6), Everyone has the right
to recognition everywhere as a person before the law

380 **Rechtspersönlichkeit,** *f.*, juridical
personality, legal personality, personality in law

381 **Die Organisation besitzt Rechtspersönlichkeit. Sie kann insbesondere
Vertrage Schließen, bewegliches und
unbewegliches Vermögen erwerben
und veräußern** (PPELDO 1), The
organization shall have legal personality. It shall in particular have
the capacity to contract, to acquire
and dispose of movable and immovable property

382 **Der Rat besitzt im Hoheitsgebiet der
Vertragsparteien Rechtspersönlichkeit, wenn zwischen ihm und der
Regierung der betreffenden Vertragspartei eine entsprechende Vereinbarung getroffen worden ist**
(CICES 15), The Council shall
enjoy, in the territories of the contracting parties, such legal capacity
as may be agreed between the Council and the Government of the contracting party concerned

383 **Die Internierten behalten ihre volle
zivile Rechtspersönlichkeit** (GC IV
80), Internees shall retain their full
civil capacity
(*Rechtsstellung, juristische *Person, *and note to* *Rechtsperson)

384 **Rechtspflege,** *f.*, administration of
justice

385 **Gleichbehandlung der Staatsangehörigen in der Rechtspflege** (CUN
76), equal treatment of nationals in
the administration of justice

386 **Behinderung der Rechtspflege,** obstruction of justice

387 **die Rechtspflege fördern** (PPELDO
22), to facilitate the proper administration of justice

388 **Rechtsprechung,** *f.*, the decided
cases, the decisions/judgments of the
courts

389 **die Gesetzgebung und Rechtsprechung** (CRFF 3), legislation and
judicial action

390 **Unparteilichkeit der Rechtsprechung**
(PHR 10), impartiality of the judiciary

391 **die Rechtsprechung der Schieds-
gerichte,** arbitral decisions/adjudica-
tions

392 **die Rechtsprechung des IGHs,** decisions delivered/handed down by the
ICJ

393 **Rechtsprechungsaufgaben,** *f.pl.*,
judicial duties

394 **Rechtsquelle,** *f.*, source of law

395 **Die Rechtsquellen des Völkerrechts
sind Gewohnheitsrecht, Vertragsrecht und allgemeine Rechtsgrundsätze,** The sources of international
law are customary law, law of treaties
and general principles of law

396 **Rechtsquellenkatalog,** *m.*, list of
sources of law

397 **der Rechtsquellenkatalog des Statuts
des IGHs,** the list of sources of law
contained/set forth in the Statute of
the ICJ

398 **Rechtsregel,** *f.*, a rule of law (*contrast with* Herrschaft des *Rechtes)
(*Rechtsnorm)

399 **Rechtssache,** *f.*, case
(*anhängig, *Sache²)

400 **Rechtssatz,** *m.*, legal principle/dic-
tum

401 **Rechtsschutz,** *m.*, legal protection,
protection at/by the law

402 **Rechtsschutz ohne Erfüllung von
Förmlichkeiten** (UCC III), legal
means of protecting without formalities

403 **gerichtlicher Rechtsschutz** (ICCPR 2), judicial remedy

404 **Rechtsspruch**, *m*., award, judgment (*Urteil, *Schiedsspruch)

405 **Rechtsstaat**, *m*., constitutional state, state governed according to a (free) constitution, state in which the rule of law prevails

406 **Rechtsstellung**, *f*., legal status, legal position

407 **Die Anwendung der vorstehenden Bestimmungen hat auf die Rechtsstellung der Parteien keinen Einfluß** (GC IV 4), The application of the preceding provisions shall not affect the legal status of the parties

408 **der Rat hat die Rechtsstellung inne, die . . .** (CCC XIII), the Council shall enjoy such legal capacity as . . .

409 **Die Organisation hat die Rechtsstellung einer juristischen Person,** The organization shall possess juridical personality

410 **Diese Anlagen haben jedoch nicht die Rechtsstellung von Inseln** (GCC 5), Such installations do not possess the status of islands

411 **Rechtsstellung, Vorrechte und Immunitäten** (OEEC 22), legal capacity, privileges and immunities

412 **Rechtsstellung sowie die Vorrechte und Befreiungen der Organisation** (PPESRO 1), legal status, the privileges and the immunities of the organization

413 **die allgemeine Rechtsstellung dieser Zonen als Hohe See** (GCF 13), the general status of the areas as high seas

414 **Rechtsstreitigkeit**, *f*., legal dispute (*Gerichtsbarkeit anerkennen)

415 **Rechtssubjekt**, *n*., subject of law

416 **Rechtssubjekt sein, heißt Träger von Rechten und Pflichten sein,** To be a subject of law means to be the incumbent of rights and duties (*Völkerrechtssubjektivität)

417 **Rechtssystem**, *n*., legal system, system/body of law

418 **Angleichung der nationalen Rechtssysteme,** approximation of national laws

419 **Rechtsvergleichung**, *f*., comparative law

420 **Rechtsverhältnis**, *n*., legal relationship

421 **Rechtsverhältnisse, sei es vertraglicher oder nichtvertraglicher Art** (CREFA 1), legal relationships whether contractual or not

422 **Rechtsverordnung**, *f*., statutory order/regulation/enactment

423 **Rechtsverweigerung**, *f*., denial of justice

424 **Rechtsvorgänger**, *m*., predecessor in title

425 **Rechtsvorschrift**, *f*., provision of law, legal provision (*In pl. often* legislation, *i.e.* the body of laws *in contrast to* *Gesetzgebung.)

426 **Gesetze und Rechtsvorschriften,** statutory and other legal provisions

427 **Der in diesem Vertrag verwendete Ausdruck ,,Rechtsvorschriften'' umfaßt Proklamationen, Gesetze, Verordnungen, Entscheidungen, Direktiven, Durchführungsbestimmungen, Genehmigungen oder sonstige Vorschriften ähnlicher Art** (CSMW 1), The term "legislation" as used in the present convention includes proclamations, laws, ordinances, decisions, directives, regulations, orders, licences or any other similar enactments

428 **Der Ausdruck ,,Rechtsvorschriften'' bezeichnet die bestehenden und künftigen Gesetze, Verordnungen und Satzungen jedes Mitgliedstaates** (SF 77), The term "legislation" designates any present or future laws, regulations and statutes of every member state

429 **Alle Angelegenheiten . . . unterliegen weiterhin den Rechtsvorschriften der Vertragsregierungen** (CFIMT V), All matters . . . remain subject to the legislation of the contracting governments

430 **die Rechtsvorschriften über die inneren Gewässer** (GCTS 4), the régime of internal waters

431 **Die Vollstreckung des gefällten Spruchs richtet sich nach den**

Rechtsvorschriften des Staates, in dem ... (PPELDO 25), The enforcement of the award shall be governed by the rules in force in the state in which ...

432 **Wenn genügend Beweise vorliegen, um auf Grund ihrer Rechtsvorschriften eine Strafverfolgung des ... einzuleiten (PPSO An),** If sufficient evidence is available in the form required by its law to enable proceedings against ...

433 **nach den Rechtsvorschriften des Empfangsstaates** (VCDR 23), under the law of the receiving state

434 **nach den Rechtsvorschriften eines anderen Mitgliedstaates,** under/in accordance with the legislation/laws of any other/another member state

435 **ein Mitgliedstaat, nach dessen Rechtsvorschriften ... von ... abhängig ist,** a member state whose legislation makes ... dependent/ conditional on ...

436 **kraft der Rechtsvorschriften des Empfangsstaates** (VCDR Opt. Prot), by the operation of the law of the receiving state

437 **vorbehaltlich seiner Gesetze und anderen Rechtsvorschriften über ...** (VCDR 26), subject to its laws and regulations concerning ...

438 **nach Maßgabe seiner Rechtsvorschriften** (VCDR 21), in accordance with its laws

439 **Angleichung der Rechtsvorschriften** (EEC 100), approximation of provisions laid down by law

440 **Aufhebung der Rechtsvorschriften** (TORG 2), repeal of legislation

441 **Außerkraftsetzung von Rechtsvorschriften** (TORG 2), deprivation of effect of legislation

442 **durch den Erlaß von Rechtsvorschriften,** by (means of) legislative measures, by adopting provisions of law

443 **Harmonisierung der Rechts- und Verwaltungsvorschriften,** harmonization of provisions laid down by legislation or administrative action

444 **Rechtsweg,** *m.*, course of law, process of law, legal remedies, remedies in/at law

445 **auf dem Rechtsweg,** by recourse to law, by (taking) legal proceedings/ measures, by legal process

446 **den Rechtsweg beschreiten,** to institute/to take legal proceedings/ measures

447 **Nach Erschöpfung des innerstaatlichen Rechtswegs kann sich der Einzelne an das Menschenrechtskomitee wenden,** After exhausting local remedies the individual may apply to the Human Rights Committee (*Rechtsmittel, *Rechtsmittelverfahren)

448 **rechtswidrig,** *adj.*, unlawful, illegal, contrary to/inconsistent/incompatible with the law

449 **handelt ein Organ eines Staates im Ausland rechtswidrig ...,** where an organ of a state acts illegally abroad

450 **rechtswirksam,** *adj.*, operative/ effective in law, in legal operation, operating in law, having legal effect

451 **Das Übereinkommen wird mit dem Tag der Hinterlegung seiner Ratifikation rechtswirksám** (SC 12), The convention will come into operation on the date of the deposit of its ratification

452 **vor dem Datum seines rechtswirksamen Ausscheidens** (PHR 65), before the date at which the denunciation became effective (*rechtskräftig, in *Kraft)

453 **Rechtszug,** *m.*, (legal) recourse

454 **Rechtszug an höhere Instanzen,** recourse to higher courts (*Anrufung)

455 **Redaktionsausschuß,** *m.*, drafting committee

456 **Redefreiheit,** *f.*, freedom of speech

457 **Reede,** *f.*, anchorage, roadstead

458 **Reeden, die Schiffen üblicherweise zum Laden, Löschen und Ankern dienen** (GCTS 9), roadsteads which are normally used for the loading, unloading and anchorage of ships

459 **Der Küstenstaat hat diese Reeden deutlich zu kennzeichnen, mit ihren Grenzen in Seekarten einzutragen,**

und diese gebührend bekanntzumachen (GCTS 9), The coastal state must clearly demarcate such roadsteads and indicate them on charts together with their boundaries, to which due publicity must be given

460 **Regel,** *f.*, rule
461 **Regeln für alle Schiffe** (GCTS), rules applicable to all ships
462 **Befolgung einer Regel,** adherence to a rule, observation of a rule
463 **Bruch einer Regel,** breach of a rule
464 **Gesamtheit von Regeln,** body/sum of rules
465 **Verletzung einer Regel,** breach/ violation/infringement of a rule
466 **restriktive Regel,** restrictive rule
467 **die Beseitigung/Eliminierung einer restriktiven Regel,** the elimination of a restrictive rule
468 **selbstanwendbare Regel,** self-executing rule
469 **völkerrechtliche Regel,** rule of international law, international rule
470 **eine Regel befolgen,** to observe a rule, to adhere to a rule
471 **eine Regel brechen,** to break a rule
472 **eine Regel verletzen,** to violate/to infringe a rule (*Norm, *Regelung, *Vorschrift)
473 **regeln,** to regulate, to settle, to resolve, to govern
474 **... werden zusätzlich/in einem Zusatzprotokoll geregelt,** ... shall be regulated separately/in a supplementary protocol
475 **Fragen, die in diesem Übereinkommen nicht geregelt sind** (VCLOT Pr.), questions not regulated by the provisions of the present convention
476 **Regelung,** *f.*, regulation, rule, settlement, régime
477 **eine von der Generalversammlung beschlossene Regelung** (SICJ 32), a regulation made by the General Assembly
478 **Regelung eines Streitfalles,** regulation/settlement/adjustment of a dispute (*see* *Beilegung)
479 **Regelung für Wahlkonsuln und von ihnen geleiteten konsularischen Ver-**

tretungen (VCCR Ch. III), régime relating to honorary consular officers and consular posts headed by them

480 **angemessene Regelung,** suitable/appropriate regulation
481 **die ihr angemessen erscheinende Regelung** (ECPSD 15), the terms of settlement which seem suitable to it
482 **friedensvertragliche Regelung** (CRPG 2), peaceful settlement
483 **frei vereinbarte friedensvertragliche Regelung** (CRPG 7), freely negotiated peace settlement
484 **Regelungen treffen für,** to lay down rules in respect of/with regard to (*Sondervereinbarung)
485 **regieren,** to govern, to regulate
486 **Regierung,** *f.*, government
487 **betroffene Regierung,** government affected/concerned
488 *de facto/de jure* **Regierung,** *de facto/de jure* government
489 **legitime Regierung,** legitimate government
490 **vertragschließende Regierung,** contracting government (*For further adjectival expressions see mainly under* *Staat, *and under relevant compound, e.g.* *Unterzeichnerregierung.)
491 **Regierungsabkommen,** *n.*, intergovernmental agreement (*see note to* *Vertrag)
492 **Regierungsanspruch,** *m.* (CSMW), governmental claim
493 **Regierungsdelegierter,** *adj.n.*, government delegate (*e.g.* ILO)
494 **Regierungsgewalt,** *f.*, authority
495 **oberste Regierungsgewalt,** supreme authority
496 **Regierungssozialausschuß,** *m.* (CE), Governmental Social Committee
497 **Regierungsstelle,** *f.* (= staatliche Stelle, *Dienststelle, *f.*), governmental/government agency
498 **Regierungsübereinkommen,** *n.*, intergovernmental convention
499 **Regierungsvertreter,** *m.*, government representative/delegate
500 **ausländische Regierungsvertreter**

(WEUS 16), representatives of foreign governments
(*Stimmrecht)

501 **regional**, *adj*., regional
502 **regionales Abkommen,** regional agreement (*see note to* *Vertrag *in* Annex* 1)
503 **regionale Ebene,** regional level
504 **Beziehungen zwischen Staaten auf regionaler Ebene,** relations between states at a regional level
505 **regionales Organ,** regional agency
506 **regionale Organisation,** regional organization
507 **Jede regionale Organisation besteht aus einem regionalen Ausschuß und einem regionalen Büro** (WHO 46), Each regional organization shall consist of a regional committee and a regional office
508 **Regionalabkommen,** *n*., regional agreement (*see note to* *Vertrag *in* Annex* 1)
509 **Regionalausschuß,** *m*., Regional Association (*e.g.* WMO), Regional Committee (*e.g.* WHO)
510 **Regionaldirektor,** *m*., Regional Director (*e.g.* WHO)
511 **Registerhafen,** *m*., port of registry
512 **registrieren,** to register
513 **Jeder Vertrag muß beim Sekretariat der UN registriert und von diesem veröffentlicht werden,** Every treaty must be registered with the Secretariat of the UN and published by it
514 **Registrierung,** *f*., registration
515 **Registrierung eines Schiffes,** registration/registry of a ship
516 **Registrierung eines Vertrags,** registration of a treaty
517 **Registrierungspflicht,** *f*., duty/obligation to register
518 **Registrierungspflicht für Ausländer** (IMF IX), alien registration requirements
(*Meldepflicht)
519 **Regnicole,** *m*., regnicole
520 **Reichtum,** *m*., resources
521 **lebender Reichtum,** living resources
522 **natürlicher Reichtum,** natural resources
(*Schätze)

523 **Reise,** *f*., journey
524 **fortgesetzte Reise,** continuous voyage
525 **Doktrin der fortgesetzten Reise,** doctrine of continuous voyage
526 **freie Reise** (WEUS 16), free movement
527 **ununterbrochene Reise,** continuous voyage
528 **Doktrin der ununterbrochenen Reise,** doctrine of continuous voyage
529 **Reiseausweis,** *m*., travel document (*Flüchtling)
530 **Reiseerleichterungen** *f.pl.* **für Flüchtlinge,** facilities for/measures facilitating the movement of refugees
531 **Rekreditiv,** *n*., *lettre(s) de récréance*
532 **Religionsfreiheit,** *f*. (CERD/UDHR), freedom of religion
533 **Religionshoheit,** *f*., spiritual sovereignty
534 **religiöse Gruppe,** *f*. (CERD/UDHR), religious group
535 **Reparation,** *f*., reparation
536 **Reparationsanspruch,** *m*., claim for reparation(s), right to reparation(s)
537 **Reparationszweck,** *m*., reparation (purposes)
538 **In keinem Fall darf solches Gut für Reparationszwecke zurückgehalten werden** (PCP Prot), Such property shall never be retained as war reparations
539 **repatriieren,** to repatriate
540 **Repatriierung,** *f*., repatriation
541 **Replik,** *f*., reply (schriftliches *Verfahren)
542 **Repressalie,** *f*., reprisal
543 **Sie enthalten sich jeder Repressalie gegenüber Kulturgut** (PCP 4), They shall refrain from any act directed by way of reprisals against cultural property
544 **militärische Repressalie,** military/armed reprisal, reprisal with armed force
545 **wirtschaftliche Repressalie,** economic reprisal (Vergeltung eines *Unrechts, *Verhältnismäßigkeit)

546 **Repressalienakt,** *m.,* act of reprisal
547 **Repressalienhandlung,** *f.,* act of reprisal
548 **Repressalienmaßnahme,** *f.,* measure/act of reprisal
549 **Repressalienobjekt,** *n.,* object of (the) reprisal
550 **Repressalienrecht,** *n.,* right of reprisal
551 **requirieren,** to requisition, to obtain by requisition
552 **alle requirierten Beförderungsmittel** (GC I 35), all means of transportation obtained by requisition
553 **Requirierung,** *f.,* requisition (*Beschlagnahme)
554 **Requisition,** *f.,* requisition (*Beschlagnahme)
555 **Requisitionsrecht,** *n.,* right of requisition
556 **das den Kriegführenden nach den Gesetzen und Gebräuchen des Krieges zuerkannte Requisitionsrecht** (GC I 34), the right of requisition recognized for belligerents by the laws and customs of war
557 **Resolution,** *f.,* resolution
558 **Resolutionsentwurf,** *m.,* draft resolution
559 **respektieren,** to respect
560 **Sie respektieren die Unabhängigkeit jedes der beiden Staaten** (GrV 6), They shall respect the independence of each of the two states
561 **restituieren,** to restitute
562 **eine zu restituierende Sache** (CSMW), property to be restituted (*rückerstatten)
563 **Restitution,** *f.,* restitution
564 **äußere Restitution** (CSMW), external restitution
565 **die Sache, deren Restitution begehrt wird** (CSMW), the property restitution of which is demanded
566 **Restitutionsanspruch,** *m.,* claim for restitution, right of restitution
567 **der Sachverhalt, der den Restitutionsanspruch begründet,** the facts on which the restitution claim is based
568 **Restitutionsantrag,** *m.* (CSMW), restitution request, claim/application for restitution

569 **restitutionsberechtigt,** *adj.,* entitled to restitution
570 **restitutionsberechtigte Personen** (CSMW), persons entitled to restitution, persons whose claims for restitution have been approved
571 **Restitutionsberechtigter,** *adj.n.,* person entitled to restitution
572 **Restitutionsklage,** *f.* (CSMW), restitution action, action for restitution
573 **Retorsion,** *f.,* retorsion
574 **Rettungsstelle,** *f.* (GC I), aid station
575 **revidieren,** to revise, to review
576 **Revision,** *f.,* revision, review
577 **Revision der Charta** (CUN 109), review of the Charter
578 **Revision der Entscheidung,** revision of the judgment
579 **Revision oder Änderung eines Übereinkommens,** revision or amendment of a Convention
580 **allgemeine Revision einer Satzung** (IAEA XVIII), general review of a statute
581 **einen Antrag auf Revision des Übereinkommens stellen** (GCE 13), to make a request for the revision of the Convention
582 **eine Revision beantragen** (SF 107), to request a revision (*Nachprüfung)
583 **Revisionsantrag,** *m.,* application/request for revision
584 **einen Revisionsantrag stellen,** to make an application/a request for revision
   Revisionsbegehren, *n.* = *Revisionsantrag, *m.*
585 **Revisionsklausel,** *f.,* revision clause
586 **Revisionskonferenz,** *f.,* revision conference, conference for revision
587 **Revisionsverfahren,** *n.,* revision procedure, proceedings for revision
588 **richten,** to address (*a request, etc.*) (*Notifizierung)
589 **Richter,** *m.,* judge
590 **ältester Richter,** eldest judge, senior judge
591 **anwesende Richter,** judges present (and attending)

592 **der dienstälteste Richter,** the senior judge
593 **unabhängiger Richter,** independent judge
594 **Der Gerichtshof besteht aus unabhängigen Richtern,** The court shall be composed of a body of independent judges
595 **die Richter,** the judges, the judiciary (*see also* SICJ 2 *in Annex* 19)
596 **Richterbank,** *f.*, Bench
597 **richterlich,** *adj.*, judicial, juridical
598 **richterliches Amt,** judicial office
599 **richterliche Beilegung,** judicial settlement
600 **richterliche Entscheidung,** judicial decision
601 **Richterrecht,** *n.*, judge-made law
602 **Richterspruch,** *m.*, judicial pronouncement/award
603 **Richtlinie,** *f.*, directive, guide line, guidance
604 **Richtlinien der Generalversammlung** (ICPCP 8), directives of the General Assembly
605 **Der Kongreß legt allgemeine Richtlinien fest** (WMO 8), Congress shall determine general policies
606 **Internationale Richtlinien und Empfehlungen** (CAC 37), International Standards and Recommended Practices
607 **Roter Halbmond,** Red Crescent
608 **Roter Löwe mit roter Sonne,** Red Lion and Sun
609 **Rotes Kreuz,** Red Cross
610 **Rote Sonne,** Red Sun
611 **Rotkreuzabkommen,** *n.*, Red Cross Convention
612 **Rotkreuzflagge,** *f.*, Red Cross flag
613 **Rotkreuzliga,** *f.*, League of Red Cross Societies
614 **Rückäußerung,** *f.*, reply
615 **rückerstatten,** to restitute, to refund
616 **Rückerstattung,** *f.*, restitution, refund (*Restitution)
617 **Rückerstattungsanspruch,** *m.*, restitution claim, right of restitution (*Restitutionsanspruch)
618 **Rückerstattungsbehörde,** *f.*

(CSMW), Restitution Agency
619 **Rückerstattungsberechtigter,** *adj.n.*, restitute, person entitled to restitution
620 **Rückerstattungsberufungsgericht,** *n.* (CSMW), Court of Restitution Appeals
621 **Rückerstattungsgericht,** *n.*, Restitution Court
622 **oberstes Rückerstattungsgericht** (CSMW), Supreme Restitution Court
623 **Rückerstattungsklage,** *f.*, action for restitution
624 **Rückerstattungsrecht¹,** *n.*, right to restitution
625 **Rückerstattungsrecht²,** *n.*, restitution law/legislation
626 **rückführen,** to repatriate, to return
627 **Rückführung,** *f.*, repatriation, return
628 **Erleichterungen bei der Rückführung in das Heimatland** (CCC An), repatriation facilities
629 **Rückführung in ihren Heimatstaat** (PPELDO), repatriation
630 **rückgängig,** *adj.*, retrograde, retrogressive, null and void
631 **rückgängig machen,** to redress (*e.g.* a *wrong*), to cancel, to annul, to revoke
632 **Rückgängigmachung,** *f.*, annulment, revoking, cancellation
633 **Maßnahmen zur Rückgängigmachung eines völkerrechtlichen Unrechts,** measures to secure redress for an international wrong
634 **Rückgriff,** *m.*, recourse
635 **Rückgriffsrecht,** *n.*, right of recourse
636 **Rücknahme,** *f.*, revocation, withdrawal
637 **Rücknahme von Notifikationen** (VCLOT 68), revocation of notifications (*zurücknehmen, *Widerruf)
638 **rückschaffen** (ECSM), to repatriate
639 **Rückschaffung,** *f.*, repatriation
640 **Rücktritt,** *m.*, withdrawal
641 **Rücktritt von einem Vertrag,** withdrawal from a treaty
642 **Rücktrittsanzeige,** *f.*, notice of withdrawal

643 **Rücktrittsrecht**, *n*., right of withdrawal

644 **sofern ein Kündigungs- oder Rücktrittsrecht sich nicht aus der Natur
des Vertrags herleiten läßt** (VCLOT
56), unless a right of denunciation or
withdrawal may be implied by the
nature of the treaty

645 **Rücktrittsschreiben**, *n*., notice (in
writing) of withdrawal

646 **rückwirkend**, *adj*., retroactive,
retrospective

647 **rückwirkendes Gesetz**, retroactive
law, law with retroactive effect

648 **Rückwirkung**, *f*., retroaction,
retroactive/retrospective effect

649 **Ruhe** *f*. **und Ordnung** *f*. **im
Hafen**, peace of the port

650 **Rüstung**, *f*., armament(s), arms

651 **Regelung von Rüstungen** (CUN 11),
regulation of armaments

652 **kontrollierte Rüstung** (WEU),
armaments to be controlled

653 **Rüstungsausschuß**, *m*., armaments
committee

654 **Rüstungsbegrenzung**, *f*., arms
limitation, limitation of arms/arma-
ments

655 **Rüstungsbeschränkung**, *f*., arms
limitation, limitation of arms/arma-
ments

Rüstungskontrollamt, *n*. = Amt
für *Rüstungskontrolle

656 **Rüstungskontrolle**, *f*., control of
armaments

657 **Amt für Rüstungskontrolle** (WEU),
Agency for the Control of Armaments

658 **Rüstungsproduktion**, *f*., armaments production

659 **unzulässige Rüstungsproduktion**
(WEU), armaments not to be manufactured

660 **Rüstungswettlauf**, *m*., arms/arm-
aments race

S

1 **Sabotage,** *f.*, sabotage
2 **Sabotageakt,** *m.*, act of sabotage
3 **schwere Sabotageakte** (GC IV), serious acts of sabotage
4 **Saboteur,** *m.*, saboteur
5 **sabotieren,** to sabotage
6 **sachdienlich,** *adj.*, relevant, pertaining, pertinent
7 **sachdienliche Urkunden und Auskünfte,** relevant documents and information (*e.g.* in arbitration)
8 **Sache¹,** *f.*, property
9 **bewegliche/unbewegliche Sachen,** movable/immovable property
10 **bewegliche Sachen und Grundstücke** (CCC An), movable and immovable property
11 **herausverlangte Sachen** (CSMW V), claimed property (*Eigentum, *Vermögen, *restituieren)
12 **Sache²,** *f.*, matter, case, item
13 **Der Ausschuß befaßt sich mit einer an ihn verwiesenen Sache erst dann, wenn er sich Gewißheit verschafft hat, daß alle innerstaatlichen Rechtsbehelfe eingelegt und erschöpft worden sind** (CERD 11), The committee shall deal with a matter referred to it only after it has ascertained that all available domestic remedies have been invoked and exhausted in the case
14 **für eine bestimmte Sache bestellte Richter/Schiedsrichter,** judges/arbitrators appointed for a specific case
15 **eine Sache beilegen,** to settle a case/matter
16 **Wird die Sache nicht zur Zufriedenheit beider Parteien beigelegt . . .** (CERD 11), If the matter is not adjusted to the satisfaction of both parties . . .
17 **Sachleistung,** *f.*, benefit in kind
18 **Sachverhalt,** *m.*, situation, facts (*e.g. of dispute*)
19 **der Sachverhalt, der . . . begründet,** the facts on which . . . is based
20 **kurze Angabe des Sachverhalts** (PHR 30), brief statement of the facts
21 **kurze Darstellung des Sachverhalts,** summary of the facts
22 **Klärung des Sachverhalts,** clarification/elucidation of the facts
23 **Sachverständigenausschuß,** *m.*, committee of experts, expert committee
24 **Sachverständigenausschuß für die Durchführung von Übereinkommen und Empfehlungen,** committee of experts on the application of conventions and recommendations
25 **Sachverständigenbegutachtung,** *f.*, (the giving of an) expert/expert's opinion
26 **Sachverständigenbericht,** *m.*, experts'/expert's report
27 **Sachverständigengruppe,** *f.*, group of experts
28 **Sachverständigengutachten,** *n.*, experts'/expert's opinion
29 **Sachverständiger,** *adj.n.*, expert (*e.g. as called upon to give evidence/ an opinion on a dispute*)
30 **18 Sachverständige von hohem sittlichen Rang und anerkannter Unparteilichkeit** (CERD 8), 18 experts of high moral standing and acknowledged impartiality
31 **Sachverständige im Dienste der Organisation** (OEEC SProt), experts on missions for the organization
32 **Sachverständige, die im Auftrag der Organisation tätig sind/für die Organisation tätige Sachverständige** (WEUS 19–23), experts employed on missions on behalf of the organization/experts on missions for the organization
33 **hochqualifizierte/höchstqualifizierte Sachverständige** (ICPCP 5), highly/ the best qualified technical experts
34 **korrespondierende Sachverständige** (ICPCP 9), corresponding experts/ correspondents
35 **unabhängige Sachverständige von**

167

höchster Integrität und anerkannter Sachkenntnis (EC 25), independent experts of the highest integrity and of recognized competence

36 **ad-hoc Arbeitsgruppe von Sachverständigen** (CFIMT An), ad-hoc working group of experts

37 **Liste von Sachverständigen,** list/panel of experts

38 **Sammelhilfssendung,** *f.* (GC III), collective relief shipment/consignment

39 **Sammelhilfsspenden,** *f.pl.* (GC), collective relief

40 **Sammelvisum,** *n.*, collective visa

41 **Sanitätsdienst,** *m.*, medical service

42 **bewegliche Einheiten des Sanitätsdienstes** (GC I), mobile medical units

43 **ständiger Sanitätsdienst der Streitkräfte** (GC I), regular medical service of the armed forces

44 **sanitätsdienstlich,** *adj.*, medical, of the medical service

45 **bei der Ausübung sanitätsdienstlicher Verrichtungen** (GC I 41), while carrying out medical duties

46 **Sanitätseinheit,** *f.*, medical unit

47 **bewegliche Sanitätseinheit,** mobile medical unit (*Sanitätsdienst)

48 **Sanitätseinrichtung,** *f.* (GC I), medical establishment

49 **ortsfeste Sanitätseinrichtung** (GC I), fixed medical establishment

50 **Sanitätsluftfahrzeug,** *n.* (GC I), medical aircraft

51 **Sanitätsmaterial,** *n.* (GC), medical material/equipment

52 **Sendungen von Arzneimitteln und Sanitätsmaterial** (GC IV 23), consignments of medical and hospital stores

53 **Sanitätsort,** *m.*, hospital locality

54 **Sanitätspersonal,** *n.*, medical personnel

55 **Sanitätstransport,** *m.* (GC I), medical transport

56 **Sanitätszone,** *f.* (GC I), hospital zone

57 **Sicherheits- und Sanitätszonen und -orte** (GC IV), hospital and safety zones and localities

58 **Sanktion,** *f.*, sanction

59 **militärische Sanktion,** military sanction

60 **wirtschaftliche Sanktion,** economic sanction

61 **Satzung,** *f.*, statute (*e.g.* ICJ, CE), charter (*e.g.* UN), constitution (*e.g.* UNESCO, ILO), covenant (*e.g.* League of Nations)

62 **Angelegenheiten im Bereich der Satzung** (IAEA V), matters within the scope of this statute

63 **Satzungsänderung,** *f.*, amendment of the statute/charter, etc.

64 **satzungsmäßig,** *adj.*, constitutional, in accordance with the statute/charter

65 **säumig,** *adj.*, at fault, defaulting

66 **säumige Partei/säumiger Staat,** party/state at fault, defaulting party/state

67 **schaden,** to damage, to injure

68 **Schaden,** *m.*, damage, injury

69 **Schadenersatz,** *m.*, compensation

70 **Schadenersatz beanspruchen,** to claim compensation

71 **Schadenersatz erhalten,** to recover/receive compensation

72 **Eine Person ist nicht berechtigt, Schadenersatz zu erhalten** (VCLD XVI), No person shall be entitled to recover compensation

73 **Schadenersatz leisten,** to pay compensation

74 **Schadenersatzanspruch,** *m.*, right to compensation; claim for compensation

75 **Schadenersatzansprüche erlöschen, wenn eine Klage nicht binnen 10 Jahren nach dem nuklearen Ereignis erhoben wird** (VCLD VI), Rights of compensation shall be extinguished if an action is not brought within 10 years from the date of the (nuclear) incident

76 **Eine Verlängerung der Frist für das Erlöschen darf in keinem Fall die Schadenersatzansprüche berühren** (VCLD VI), An extension of the extinction period shall in no case affect rights of compensation

77 **Schadenersatzleistung,** *f.*, compensation, payment(s) made in compensation

78 **Schadenersatzleistungsempfänger,** *m.*, beneficiary of compensation

79 **Schadenersatzpflicht,** *f.*, obligation to pay compensation/make payment(s) in compensation

80 **Schädigung,** *f.*, damage, injury

81 **Schallsignal,** *n.*, auditory signal (*Sichtsignal)

82 **Schätze,** *m.pl.*, resources

83 **Maßnahmen zur Erhaltung der in Frage kommenden Schätze** (GCF 3), measures necessary for the purpose of the conservation of the resources affected

84 **lebende Schätze,** living resources

85 **die Erhaltung der lebenden Schätze der Hohen See** (GCF), the conservation of the living resources of the high seas

86 **natürliche Schätze** (GCHS), natural resources (*Meeresschätze, *Meeresgrund)

87 **Schiedsabkommen,** *n.*, arbitration agreement (*Schiedsvereinbarung, *Schiedsvertrag)

88 **Schiedsabrede,** *f.*, arbitration arrangement/agreement

89 **eine Abschrift einer zwischen ihnen getroffenen Schiedsabrede** (Hgl 4), a copy of any conditions of arbitration arrived at between them (*Schiedsvereinbarung)

90 **Schiedsausschuß,** *m.*, arbitral committee, committee of arbitration

91 **Schiedsfähigkeit,** *f.*, capacity/right to submit to/to resort to arbitration

92 **Schiedsfähigkeit der juristischen Personen des öffentlichen Rechts** (ECICA II), right of legal persons of public law to resort to arbitration

93 **Schiedsgericht,** *n.*, court of arbitration, arbitral tribunal (*sometimes rendered by* the arbitrators; *see under* *Billigkeit)

94 **Das Schiedsgericht wird von Fall zu Fall gebildet** (SF 85), The arbitral tribunal shall be constituted for each individual case

95 **Kann eine Streitigkeit auf diese Weise nicht beigelegt werden, so ist sie auf Verlangen einer der beiden Vertragsparteien einem Schiedsgericht zu unterbreiten,** If the dispute cannot thus be settled, it shall upon the request of either contracting party be submitted to an arbitral tribunal

96 **Wird eine Streitigkeit zwischen zwei oder mehr Mitgliedstaaten . . . nicht durch die guten Dienste des Rates beigelegt, so ist auf Antrag einer der Parteien ein Schiedsgericht einzusetzen** (ELDO 22), In the event of any dispute between two or more states, members of the organization, . . . not being settled by the good offices of the Council, an arbitral tribunal shall be set up at the request of one of the parties

97 **die Anrufung eines Schiedsgerichts,** the recourse/appeal to a court of arbitration, the reference to arbitration (ILOC 22.4)

98 **gemischtes Schiedsgericht,** mixed arbitral tribunal/court of arbitration (*Rechtsmittel ergreifen)

99 **schiedsgerichtlich,** *adj.*, arbitral, by arbitration, by an arbitral tribunal

100 **schiedsgerichtliche Beilegung völkerrechtlicher Streitfälle,** settlement of international disputes by arbitration, arbitral settlement of international disputes

101 **schiedsgerichtlich beilegbar,** arbitrable

102 **schiedsgerichtliches Urteil,** award (*see* *Schiedsspruch)

103 **Schiedsgerichtsbarkeit,** *f.*, arbitration

104 **obligatorische/verbindliche Schiedsgerichtsbarkeit,** compulsory arbitration

105 **Schiedsgerichtshof,** *m.*, court of arbitration, arbitral tribunal

106 **Ständiger Schiedsgerichtshof,** Permanent Court of Arbitration

107 **Schiedsgerichtsmitglied,** *n.*, member of the/an arbitral tribunal/court of arbitration

108 **Schiedsgerichtsordnung,** *f.*, statutes/rules of the arbitral tribunal/court of arbitration

109 **Schiedsgerichtsverfahren,** *n.*, arbitration, arbitral procedure

110 **Einem Schiedsgerichtsverfahren kann ein Vergleichsverfahren vorausgehen,** Conciliation may precede arbitration

111 **Schiedsgerichtswesen,** *n.*, (the system of) arbitration

Schiedshof, *m.* = *Schiedsgericht, *n.*, *Schiedsgerichtshof, *m.*

112 **Schiedsinstanz,** *f.*, court of arbitration, arbitral tribunal (*in pl. often best translated by* courts and tribunals of arbitration *as in the following example*)

113 **Schiedsinstanzen und deren Anrufung,** courts and tribunals of arbitration and recourse to them

114 **Schiedsklausel,** *f.*, arbitration/arbitral clause

115 **auf Grund einer Schiedsklausel** (EAEC 153), pursuant to any arbitration clause

116 **Schiedskollegium,** *n.*, panel of arbiters/arbitrators, the arbitrators

117 **Schiedskommission,** *f.*, arbitral commission, commission of arbitration

118 **Schiedskommission für Güter, Rechte und Interessen in Deutschland,** Arbitral Commission on Property, Rights and Interests in Germany

119 **Anrufung der Schiedskommission/Berufung an die Schiedskommission,** appeal/recourse to the arbitral commission

120 **Schiedskompromiß,** *m.*, (arbitration/arbitral) compromise

121 **Schiedsrichter,** *m.*, arbiter, arbitrator

122 **Mehrere Regierungen können ein und dieselbe Person als Schiedsrichter benennen** (FC An), The same person may be nominated arbiter by more than one government

123 **die Aufgaben eines Schiedsrichters wahrnehmen,** to undertake/exercise the duties of an arbiter/arbitrator (*Oberschiedsrichter)

124 **Schiedsrichteramt,** *n.*, office/duties of (an) arbiter/arbitrator

125 **schiedsrichterlich,** *adj.*, arbitral, by arbitration

126 **schiedsrichterliche Beilegung,** arbitral settlement

127 **Schiedsrichterliste,** *f.*, list/panel of arbitrators/arbiters

128 **Schiedsrichterverzeichnis,** *n.*, list/panel of arbitrators/arbiters

129 **Schiedssprechung,** *f.*, arbitration

130 **Mächte/Staaten, welche die Schiedssprechung anrufen,** powers/states having/seeking recourse to arbitration

131 **Schiedsspruch,** *m.*, arbitral award, award of an arbitral tribunal/court of arbitration

132 **Unter „Schiedssprüchen" sind nicht nur Schiedssprüche von Schiedsrichtern, die für eine bestimmte Sache bestellt worden sind, sondern auch solche eines ständigen Schiedsgerichts, dem sich die Parteien unterworfen haben, zu verstehen** (CREFA 1), The term "arbitral awards" shall include not only awards made by arbitrators appointed for each case but also those made by permanent arbitral bodies to which the parties have submitted

133 **Anerkennung eines Schiedsspruchs,** recognition of an arbitral award

134 **Anerkennung und Vollstreckung ausländischer Schiedssprüche** (CREFA), recognition and enforcement of foreign arbitral awards

135 **Antrag auf (einen) Schiedsspruch,** request for arbitration/an arbitral award

136 **Aufhebung eines Schiedsspruchs** (ECICA IX), setting aside of an arbitral award

137 **Gegenstand eines Schiedsspruchs,** subject matter of an arbitral award

138 **Gültigkeit eines Schiedsspruchs,** validity of an arbitral award

139 **Sinn und Tragweite des Schiedsspruchs** (PPELDO 27), import or scope of the award

140 **Urschrift des Schiedsspruchs,** the original of the award

141 **endgültiger Schiedsspruch,** final (arbitral) award

142 **(der Schiedsspruch) gilt nicht als endgültig, wenn er dem Einspruch, der Berufung oder der Nichtigkeitsbeschwerde unterworfen ist** (CEFA 1), (the award) shall not be considered as final if it is open to *opposition, appel* or *pourvoi en cassation*

143 **der Schiedsspruch ergeht . . .,** the award is made . . .

144 **die Partei, zu deren Ungunsten der Schiedsspruch ergangen ist** (CEFA 3), the party against whom the award has been made

145 **einen Schiedsspruch anerkennen,** to recognize an award

146 **einen Schiedsspruch aufheben,** to set aside an award

147 **einen Schiedsspruch für nichtig erklären** (CEFA 2), to annul an award

148 **einen Schiedsspruch erlassen,** to make an award

149 **ein von einem Schiedsgericht erlassener Schiedsspruch,** an award of/by an arbitral tribunal

150 **einen Schiedsspruch geltend machen,** to assert/enforce an award

151 **die Partei, die den Schiedsspruch geltend macht** (CEFA 4), the party relying upon the award/who seeks to rely upon the award

152 **einem Schiedsspruch nachkommen,** to comply with an arbitral award

153 **einen Schiedsspruch vollstrecken,** to execute an award

154 **Schiedsstelle,** *f.,* arbitral body, arbitration body/board

155 **Wird eine Streitfrage nicht innerhalb von 3 Monaten geregelt, so ist sie einer Schiedsstelle zu unterbreiten** (ECSM 20), If any such dispute has not been resolved within a period of 3 months, the dispute shall be submitted to arbitration by an arbitral body

156 **beim Rat die Bestellung einer Schiedsstelle beantragen** (EEC 8), to call upon the Council to appoint an arbitration board
(*See also* CSE 15 *in Annex* 17.)

157 **Schiedsvereinbarung,** *f.,* arbitration agreement

158 **Im Sinne dieses Übereinkommens bedeutet „Schiedsvereinbarung" eine Schiedsklausel in einem Vertrag, oder eine Schiedsabrede** (ECICA I), For the purposes of this Convention the term "arbitration agreement" shall mean either an arbitral clause in a contract or an arbitration agreement (*Schiedsvertrag)

159 **Schiedsverfahren,** *n.,* arbitration, arbitral procedure

160 **Gegenstand eines Schiedsverfahrens,** subject (matter) of arbitration

161 **die Partei, die ein Schiedsverfahren beantragt,** the party requesting arbitration

162 **privates Schiedsverfahren,** private arbitration

163 **. . . einem Schiedsverfahren unterwerfen,** to submit . . . to arbitration (*Schiedsgerichtsverfahren)

164 **Schiedsvergleich,** *m.,* (arbitration/arbitral) compromise

165 **Schiedsvertrag,** *m.,* arbitration agreement, special agreement, *compromis*

166 **Die Parteien schließen einen Schiedsvertrag, in dem sie den Streitgegenstand und das Verfahren festlegen** (ECPSD 23), The parties shall draw up a special agreement determining the subject of the dispute and the details of procedure

167 **Notifizierung des Schiedsvertrags** (SICJ 40), notification of the special agreement

168 **Schiedsweg,** *m.,* arbitration, arbitral procedure

169 **auf dem Schiedsweg,** by (means of) arbitration, by arbitral process, by recourse to arbitration

170 **Schiff,** *n.,* ship, vessel

171 **Schiffe, die der Fischerei/dem Walfang dienen,** ships engaged in fishing/whaling

172 **der Betrieb von Schiffen mit wissenschaftlichem Auftrag** (CFIMT

An), the operation of ships in scientific services

173 **Einlaufen, Aufenthalt und Auslaufen von Schiffen auf Auslandsfahrt** (CFIMT), arrival, stay and departure of ships engaged in international voyages

174 **Schiffe von Küstenstaaten und Nichtküstenstaaten,** ships of coastal and non-coastal states

175 **registriertes/nichtregistriertes Schiff,** registered/non-registered ship

176 **verfolgtes Schiff,** pursued ship (see *Nacheile)

177 Schiffahrt, *f.*, shipping, navigation

178 **internationale Handelsschiffahrt** (CFIMT), shipping engaged in international trade

179 **die Schiffahrt unbillig behindern** (GCC 5), to interfere unjustifiably with navigation

180 Schiffahrtsabkommen, *n.*, shipping/navigation agreement

181 Schiffahrtsdienste, *m.pl.*, shipping services (CFIMT)

182 Schiffahrtsfreiheit, *f.*, freedom of navigation

183 Schiffahrtsvertrag, *m.*, shipping/navigation treaty (see note to *Vertrag in Annex 1)

184 schiffbar, *adj.*, navigable

185 **Die Grenze in einem Fluß folgt der Mittellinie, wenn der Fluß nicht schiffbar ist,** In a non-navigable river the boundary follows the median line

186 Schiffbrüchige *m.pl.* **der Streitkräfte zur See,** shipwrecked members of armed forces at sea

187 Schiffsbesatzung, *f.*, crew

188 Schiffsdokument, *n.*, ship's document

189 Schiffsführer, *m.*, master

190 **Der Ausdruck ,,Schiffsführer'' umfaßt jede Person, die Führer des Schiffes ist, mit Ausnahme der Lotsen** (ILOC 23.2), The term ''master'' includes every person having command of a vessel except pilots

191 Schiffsmann, *m.* (*pl.* Schiffsleute), seaman (ILOC 23)

192 **Schiffspapiere,** *n.pl.*, the ship's papers

193 **die Schiffspapiere prüfen und stempeln** (VCCR 5), to examine and stamp the ship's papers

194 **Schiffssicherheit,** *f.*, safety of the ship

195 **aus Gründen der Schiffssicherheit** (PPSO), for the purpose of securing the safety of the ship

196 schlichten, to settle, to regulate (*beilegen)

197 Schlichtung, *f.*, settlement, regulation (*Beilegung)

198 schließen, to conclude

199 **einen Vertrag/ein Abkommen schließen,** to conclude a treaty/an agreement

200 Schlußakte, *f.*, final act (zu *Urkund dessen)

201 Schlußantrag, *m.*, final argument, conclusion (of argument)

202 **die Einbringung der Schlußanträge durch jede Partei** (SICJ 48), the conclusion of its arguments by each party

203 Schlußartikel, *m.*, final article

204 Schlußbericht, *m.*, final report

205 Schlußbestimmung, *f.*, final provision, final clause (See VCLOT 81–85 in Annex 5.)

206 Schlüssel[1], *m.*, code

207 Schlüssel[2], *m.*, scale

208 **Die Kosten . . . werden nach einem vom Rat festgesetzten Schlüssel umgelegt** (CCC XII), The expenses . . . shall be levied in accordance with a scale to be determined by the Council

209 Schlußklausel, *f.*, final clause

210 Schlußprotokoll, *n.*, final protocol

211 Schlußvermerk, *m.*, final remark, testimonium

212 **Im Einklang mit Artikel 31 und mit dem Schlußvermerk des Protokolls wird es bei der Regierung der französischen Republik hinterlegt** (PPESRO 9), In accordance with the provisions of Article 31 and with the testimonium of the protocol it shall be deposited with the government of the French Republic

213 **Schmuggelware,** *f.*, contraband, contraband goods (*Bannware)
214 **Schnellverfahren,** *n.*, summary procedure
215 **Schranke,** *f.*, barrier
216 **die Europa trennenden Schranken** (EEC Pr), the barriers which divide Europe
217 **Schriftform,** *f.*, written form
218 **Die Notifikation nach Artikel 65 bedarf der Schriftform** (VCLOT 67), The notification provided for under Article 65 must be made in writing
219 **schriftlich,** *adj.*, written, in writing, in written form
220 **auf schriftlichem Wege,** in writing, by correspondence
221 **Schriftsatz,** *m.*, petition, paper, document, written pleadings
222 **nach Eingang des ersten Schriftsatzes gemäß Art. 14** (CRPG An), upon receipt of the first petition filed pursuant to Art. 14
223 **durch Einreichung weiterer Schriftsätze** (CSMW 10), by filing additional papers
224 **Schriftsätze eines Beteiligten,** documents filed by a party concerned
225 **Schriftsätze und Gegenschriftsätze,** cases and counter cases
226 **Schriftstück,** *n.*, document, paper
227 **amtliche Schriftstücke der Mission,** official documents of the mission
228 **das Recht, . . . Schriftstücke oder Schriftwechsel durch Kuriere oder in versiegelten Behältern zu erhalten** (PrivExCE 9), the right to receive papers or correspondence by courier or in sealed bags
229 **Schriftverkehr,** *m.*, correspondence
230 **durch unmittelbaren Schriftverkehr der Justizminister der beiden Länder** (ICCC 16), by direct correspondence between the Ministers of Justice of the two countries
231 **Schriftwechsel,** *m.*, correspondence (*Schriftstück)
232 **schuldhaft,** *adj.*, culpable, liable, negligent
233 **Schuldhaftung,** *f.*, liability
234 **schuldig,** *adj.*, guilty, at fault, delinquent
235 **schuldiger Staat,** guilty state, delinquent state, state at fault
236 **die für schuldig befundene Regierung** (ILO 34), the defaulting government
237 **sich einer Handlung/eines Unrechts schuldig machen,** to be guilty of an act/a wrong
238 **Schuldnerstaat,** *m.*, debtor state
239 **Schule,** *f.*, school, school of thought
240 **eklektische Schule,** eclectic school
241 **naturalistische Schule,** naturalist school
242 **positivistische Schule,** positivist school
243 **Schutz**[1]**,** *m.*, protection
244 **Schutz der Ehre,** protection of honour
245 **Schutz der Staatsangehörigen im Ausland,** protection of nationals/citizens abroad
246 **Schutz der Zivilbevölkerung,** protection of the civilian population
247 **der den Zivilkrankenhäusern gebührende Schutz** (GC), the protection to which civilian hospitals are entitled
248 **Schutz gegen Mißbräuche,** protection against abuses (CUN 73)
249 **diplomatischer Schutz,** diplomatic protection
250 **Schutz**[2]**,** *m.*, exemption, immunity
251 **Schutz gegen Festnahme oder Haft** (CCC An), immunity from personal arrest or detention
252 **Schutz gegen Verhaftung und gerichtlicher Verfolgung** (PrivExCE 15), exemption from arrest and prosecution (*Befreiung, *Immunität)
253 **Schutzgebiet,** *n.*, protected territory
254 **Schutzmacht,** *f.*, protecting power
255 **Ein Staat kann eine Schutzmacht mit der Wahrung seiner Interessen betreuen,** A state may entrust the protection of its interests to a protecting power
256 **unter Aufsicht der Schutzmächte**

(GC I 8), under the scrutiny of the protecting powers

257 **Schutzzeichen,** *n.* (GC I), distinctive emblem
   Schutzzone, *f.* = *Anschlußzone, *f.*

258 **Sechsmeilenzone,** *f.*, six mile belt, belt of six miles (*Zone)

259 **See,** *f.*, sea

260 **die Hohe See,** the high seas

261 **Unter ,,Hohe See" sind alle Teile des Meeres zu verstehen, die nicht zum Küstenmeer oder zu den inneren Gewässern eines Staates gehören** (GCHS 1), The term "high seas" means all parts of the sea that are not included in the territorial sea or in the internal waters of a state

262 **da die Hohe See allen Nationen offen steht** . . . (GCHS 2), the high seas being open to all nations . . .

263 **das Anhalten eines Schiffes auf Hoher See** (GCHS 23), the arrest of a ship on the high seas (*Meer, *Küstenmeer, *Gewässer)

264 **Seebeuterecht,** *n.*, prize law (*Prise, *Prisenrecht)

265 **Seeblockade,** *f.*, maritime blockade, naval blockade

266 **Seegebiet,** *n.*, maritime territory

267 **Seegesundheitserklärung,** *f.*, Maritime Declaration of Health

268 **Seegrenze,** *f.*, sea frontier/boundary

269 **Seekarte,** *f.*, maritime chart

270 **amtlich anerkannte Seekarten großen Maßstabes** (GCTS 2), officially recognized large-scale charts

271 **Seekrieg,** *m.*, naval war, naval warfare, maritime war, maritime warfare, war at sea

272 **Seekriegführung,** *f.*, maritime warfare, naval warfare, warfare at sea

273 **Seekriegsrecht,** *n.*, the law(s) of/governing/relating to maritime/naval war/warfare

274 **Seelsorgepersonal,** *n.* (GC I), chaplains

275 **Seelsorgepersonal der Streitkräfte** (GC I), chaplains of the armed forces/religious personnel of the armed forces (*Feldgeistlicher)

276 **Seemacht,** *f.*, sea/maritime/naval power

277 **Seemann,** *m.* (CFIMT), seafarer

278 **Seemannsausweis,** *m.*, seafarer's identity card

279 **Seeräuber,** *m.*, pirate

280 **Seeräuberei,** *f.*, piracy

281 **die Seeräuberei auf Hoher See unterdrücken** (GCHS 14), to repress piracy on the high seas

282 **seeräuberisch,** *adj.*, of piracy, pirate

283 **seeräuberische Handlungen,** acts of piracy (GCHS 19)

284 **Seeräuberluftfahrzeug,** *n.*, pirate aircraft (GCHS 17)

285 **Seeräuberschiff,** *n.*, pirate ship

286 **Seerecht,** *n.*, law of the sea, maritime law

287 **Seerechtskonferenz,** *f.*, conference on the law of the sea

288 **Seeschiff,** *n.*, sea-going vessel/ship

289 **Seeschiffahrt,** *f.*, maritime shipping/navigation

290 **Seeschiffahrtskonferenz,** *f.*, maritime conference, conference on maritime shipping/navigation

291 **Seestreitkräfte,** *f.pl.*, naval forces, maritime forces, sea forces

292 **Beschießung durch Seestreitkräfte,** naval bombardment

293 **seetüchtig,** *adj.*, seaworthy

294 **Seetüchtigkeit,** *f.*, seaworthiness

295 **seeuntüchtig,** *adj.*, unseaworthy

296 **Seeuntüchtigkeit,** *f.*, unseaworthiness

297 **Seeverkehr,** *m.*, maritime traffic

298 **Seevölkerrecht,** *n.*, international law of the sea

299 **Seeweg,** *m.*, sea lane

300 **anerkannte und für die internationale Schiffahrt wesentliche Seewege** (GCC 5), recognized sea lanes essential to international navigation

301 **Segregation,** *f.* (CERD 3), segregation

302 **Segregationspolitik,** *f.*, policy of segregation

303   Apartheids-, Segregations- oder son-
      stige Rassentrennungspolitik (CERD
      Pr), other policies of apartheid, seg-
      regation or separation
304   Seite, f., party
305   Hohe   Vertragschließende   Seite,
      High Contracting Party
      (*Partei)
306   Sekretariat, n., secretariat
307   Sekretariatsgeschäfte, n.pl., bus-
      iness of the secretariat
308   Die Sekretariatsgeschäfte der Kom-
      mission   werden   von   dem
      Generalsekretär des Europarats
      wahrgenommen (PHR 37), The Sec-
      retariat of the Commission shall be
      provided by the Secretary-General
      of the Council of Europe
309   selbständig, adj., independent,
      autonomous
310   selbständig anwendbare Regel, self-
      executing rule
311   Selbständigkeit, f., independence,
      autonomy
312   Selbstbeschränkung, f., auto-
      limitation
313   Selbstbeschränkungslehre, f.,
      theory/doctrine of auto-limitation
314   Selbstbestimmung, f., self-
      determination
      (*Staatengemeinschaft)
315   Selbstbestimmungsrecht, n.,
      right of self-determination
      (*Gleichberechtigung)
316   Selbsterhaltung, f., self-
      preservation
317   Selbsterhaltungsrecht, n., right of
      self-preservation
318   Selbsthilfe, f., self-help
319   Selbstregierung, f., self-
      government, autonomy
320   Gebiete ohne Selbstregierung, non-
      self-governing territories
321   Völker, die noch nicht die volle
      Selbstregierung   erreicht   haben
      (CUN 73), peoples who have not yet
      attained a full measure of self-
      government
322   Selbstregierungsbefugnisse, f.
      pl., power(s) of self-government
323   Selbstschutz, m., self-protection
324   Selbstverteidigung, f., self-defence

325   Naturrecht individueller und kollek-
      tiver Selbstverteidigung, natural/
      inherent right of individual and
      collective self-defence
326   selbstverwaltend, adj., self-
      governing, autonomous
327   Selbstverwaltung, f., self-
      government, autonomy
      (*Selbstregierung)
328   Servitut, f., servitude
329   Sezession, f., secession
330   Sezessionskrieg, m., war of seces-
      sion
331   Sicherheit, f., security
332   Sicherheit auf See, maritime safety,
      safety at sea
333   Sicherheit der Person, security of
      the person
334   Sicherheit des Staates, security of
      the state
335   Bedrohung   der   allgemeinen
      Sicherheit (CAC Pr), threat to gen-
      eral security
336   kollektive Sicherheit, collective sec-
      urity
      (*abträglich, *Weltfrieden)
337   Sicherheitsbedürfnis, n., neces-
      sity/need of security
338   die zwingenden Sicherheitsbedürf-
      nisse des Staates (GC I 8), the
      imperative necessities of security of
      the state
339   Sicherheitsdienst, m., security ser-
      vice
340   Sicherheitsmaßnahme, f., security
      measure, safety measure, safeguard
341   Sicherheitsnorm, f., standard of
      safety (IAEA), safety standard
      (EAEC)
342   Sicherheitsort, m. (GC IV), safety
      locality
343   Sicherheitspakt, m., security pact
344   Sicherheitsrat, m., Security Coun-
      cil
345   Sicherheitsregelung, f., security
      arrangement
346   die   kollektiven   Sicherheits-
      regelungen der NATO, the collective
      security arrangements of NATO
347   Sicherheitszone, f., safety zone
348   Die Sicherheitszonen können sich bis
      zu einem Abstand von 500m um die

erstellten Anlagen oder sonstigen
Vorrichtungen erstrecken (GCC 5),
The safety zones may extend to a
distance of 500m around the installations and other devices

349 **sicherstellen,** to ensure

350 **Maßnahmen, die die Durchführung
des Abkommens sicherstellen,**
actions/measures ensuring the
execution of the (provisions of) the
agreement

351 **Sicherung,** *f.,* ensuring, safeguarding, safeguard

352 **Sicherungsabkommen,** *n.,* safeguards agreement (TNPNW)

353 **Sicherungsmaßnahme,** *f.,* safeguard (TNPNW), measure of safeguard (PCP 4)

354 **Sicherungssystem,** *n.,* safeguards
system (IAEA)

355 **Sichtsignal,** *n.,* visual signal

356 **Sicht- oder Schallsignal zum Anhalten** (GCHS 23), a visual or auditory
signal to stop

357 **Sichtvermerk,** *m.,* visa

358 **Sichtvermerkzwang,** *m.,* obligation to obtain a visa

359 **Aufhebung des Sichtvermerkzwangs
für Flüchtlinge,** abolition of visas for
refugees

360 **Siegel,** *n.,* seal

361 **mit einem Siegel/Dienstsiegel versehen,** to affix a seal/an official seal to

362 **Siegermacht,** *f.,* victorious power

363 **Signatar,** *m.,* signatory

364 **Signatarstaat,** *m.,* signatory state
(beglaubigte *Abschrift)

365 **Sinn,** *m.,* spirit, meaning

366 **Sinn und Tragweite des Vertrags,**
meaning and scope of the treaty

367 **im Sinne dieses Artikels umfaßt
der Ausdruck . . .,** in this Article
(the term) . . . shall be deemed to
include . . .

368 **sinngemäß,** *adv., mutatis mutandis,*
by analogy

369 **si** *omnes* **Klausel,** *f., si omnes*
clause

370 **Sitte**[1]**,** *f.,* custom

371 **Sitte**[2]**,** *f.* (*usu. in pl*), morals, morality

372 **Sittengesetz,** *n.,* law of/relating to
morality

373 **wegen schwerster Verletzung des
internationalen Sittengesetzes und
der Heiligkeit der Verträge,** for a
supreme offence against international morality and the sanctity of
treaties

374 **Sitz**[1]**,** *m.,* seat, location

375 **Der IGH hat seinen Sitz im Haag,**
The seat of the ICJ is in the Hague

376 **Sitz des Sekretariats,** location of the
Secretariat

377 **am Sitz der UN** (CERD 10), at UN
Headquarters

378 **der Ort, in dem die Mission ihren
Sitz hat** (VCDR 12), the locality in
which the mission is situated

379 **das Land, in dem die Kommission
ihren Sitz hat** (CNAF XI), the country in which the seat of the Commission is located

380 **Sitz**[2]**,** *m.,* seat, place

381 **erledigte Sitze,** vacancies, empty/
vacant seats

382 **das Verfahren zur Besetzung
erledigter Sitze** (ILO 7), the
method of filling vacancies

383 **freie/freiwerdende/freigewordene
Sitze,** vacancies, empty/vacant seats

384 **Bleiben nach dem ersten Wahlgang noch Sitze frei, so findet in
derselben Weise ein zweiter und
erforderlichenfalls ein dritter
Wahlgang statt** (SICJ 11), If, after
the first meeting held for the purpose of the election, one or more
seats remain to be filled, a second
and if necessary a third meeting
shall take place

385 **verwaiste Sitze,** vacancies, seats that
have fallen empty/vacant

386 **zur Besetzung eines unerwartet
verwaisten Sitzes** (CERD 8), for
the filling of casual vacancies

387 **Sitzung,** *f.,* session, sitting, meeting,
hearing (Session *and* sitting *may be
interchangeable; on the other hand a*
session *may equal* **Sitzungsperiode,**
*i.e. a whole series of individual sit-
tings, as in the first example.*)

388 **Heute nachmittag findet die letzte
Sitzung von dieser Sitzungsperiode
statt,** The last sitting of this/the cur-

rent session will take place this
afternoon
389 **Öffentlichkeit der Sitzungen**, publicity of meetings
390 **außerordentliche Sitzung**, extraordinary session
391 **formelle Sitzung**, formal session
392 **formlose Sitzung**, informal session
393 **geschlossene Sitzung**, closed/private
session
394 **informelle Sitzung**, informal session
395 **nichtöffentliche Sitzung**, closed/pri-
vate session
396 **öffentliche Sitzung**, open/public session
397 **Die Sitzungen der Kommission
sind normalerweise öffentlich**
(ECER 46), The meetings of the
Commission shall ordinarily be
held in public
398 **in öffentlicher Sitzung**, in open
court (ICJ)
399 **ordentliche Sitzung**, ordinary session
400 **periodische Sitzung**, periodic session
401 **zwanglose Sitzung**, informal session
402 **Sitzungsperiode**, *f.*, session
(*note to* *Sitzung, *Tagung)
403 **Sklave**, *m.*, slave
404 **Jeder Sklave, der auf ein Schiff
gleich welcher Flagge flüchtet, ist
ipso facto frei** (GCHS 13), Any slave
taking refuge on board any ship,
whatever its flag, shall *ipso facto* be
free
405 **Sklavenhandel**, *m.*, slave trade
406 **die Bekämpfung des Sklavenhan-
dels**, the repression of the slave
trade
407 **den Sklavenhandel verhindern und
unterdrücken** (SC 2), to prevent and
suppress the slave trade
408 **Sklaverei**, *f.*, slavery
409 **Sklaverei ist der Zustand oder die
Stellung einer Person, an der die mit
dem Eigentumsrechte verbundenen
Befugnisse oder einzelne davon
ausgeübt werden** (SC 1), Slavery is
the status or condition of a person
over whom any or all of the powers
attaching to the right of ownership
are exercised

410 **Niemand darf in Sklaverei oder
Leibeigenschaft gehalten werden.
Sklaverei und Sklavenhandel sind in
allen Formen verboten** (UDHR 4),
No-one shall be held in slavery or
servitude; slavery and the slave
trade shall be prohibited in all their
forms
411 **sklavereiähnlich**, *adj.*, similar to
slavery
412 **sklavereiähnliche Einrichtungen und
Praktiken** (SCS), institutions and
practices similar to slavery
413 **Sockel**, *m.*, (continental) shelf
(*Festlandsockel)
414 **Sockelteil**, *m.*, section/area of the
(continental) shelf
(*Festlandsockel)
415 **Solidarität**, *f.*, solidarity
416 **geistige und moralische Solidarität
der Menschheit** (UNESCO), intel-
lectual and moral solidarity of mankind
417 **Sonderabkommen**, *n.*, special
agreement (*see note to* *Vertrag *in*
Annex 1)
418 **Sonderarbeitsgruppe**, *f.*, special
working group
419 **Sonderausschuß**, *m.*, special committee
420 **Sonderbeauftragter**, *adj.n.*, spe-
cial/ad-hoc envoy/representative
421 **Sonderbefugnis**, *f.*, special power/
authorization
422 **Sonderbotschafter**, *m.*, special/
ad-hoc envoy, roving ambassador
423 **Sonderfonds**, *m.*, special fund
Sondergesandter, *adj.n.* = *Sonderbeauftragter, *adj.n.*, *Sonderbotschafter, *m.*
424 **Sonderinstitution**, *f.*, special
agency
425 **Sonderkommission**, *f.*, special
commission
426 **Sondermitglied**, *n.*, special member
427 **Sonderorgan**, *n.*, special organ/
agency
428 **Sonderorganisation**, *f.*, specialized agency (UN)
429 **zwischenstaatliche Sonderorganisation**, specialized intergovernmental
organization

430 **Sonderprotokoll**, *n.*, special protocol

431 **Sonderregelung**, *f.*, special regulation/settlement/arrangement/provision

432 **Sonderungslager**, *n.* (GC III), screening camp

433 **Sondervereinbarung**, *f.*, special arrangement/agreement (*see note to* *Vertrag *in Annex* 1)

434 **Die Hohen Vertragsparteien können Sondervereinbarungen über alle Fragen treffen, deren besondere Regelung ihnen zweckmäßig erscheint** (PCP 24), The High Contracting Parties may conclude special agreements for all matters concerning which they deem it suitable to make special provision

435 **Sondervollmachten**, *f.pl.*, special power(s) (*Vollmacht)

436 **souverän**, *adj.*, sovereign

437 **souveräne Gleichheit aller Staaten,** sovereign equality of all states

438 **souveräne Rechte,** sovereign rights

439 **Souveräne Rechte stehen den Küstenstaaten zum Zweck der Ausbeutung von Naturschätzen im Festlandsockel zu,** Littoral states enjoy sovereign rights for the purpose of exploiting the natural resources of the continental shelf

440 **Souveränität**, *f.*, sovereignty

441 **die Souveränität eines Staates erstreckt sich auf . . .,** the sovereignty of a state extends to . . .

442 **absolute Souveränität,** absolute sovereignty

443 **äußere Souveränität,** external sovereignty

444 **innere Souveränität,** domestic/internal sovereignty

445 **relative Souveränität,** relative sovereignty

446 **staatliche Souveränität,** state sovereignty, national sovereignty, sovereignty of states

447 **territoriale Souveränität,** territorial sovereignty

448 **eine Ausdehnung der territorialen Souveränität am Meeresgrund über die Grenze der Küstengewässer hinaus,** an extension of the territorial sovereignty over the seabed beyond (the limit of) the territorial waters

449 **Souveränität besitzen,** to possess sovereignty

450 **Normalerweise besitzt ein Staat Souveränität innerhalb seines Staatsgebietes,** A state normally possesses sovereignty within its national territory/territorial limits

451 **Souveränitätsdenken**, *n.*, concept of sovereignty

452 **souveränitätsfreundlich**, *adj.*, non-prejudicial to sovereignty

453 **souveränitätsfreundliche Auslegungsregeln,** rules of interpretation non-restrictive upon sovereignty/non-prejudicial to sovereignty

454 **Souveränitätsgrundsatz**, *m.*, principle of sovereignty
Souveränitätsidee, *f.* = *Souveränitätsdenken, *n.*

455 **souveränitätskonform**, *adj.*, in conformity with sovereignty, non-detrimental/non-prejudicial to sovereignty (*souveränitätsfreundlich)
Souveränitätsprinzip, *n.* = *Souveränitätsgrundsatz, *m.*

456 **Sozialcharta**, *f.*, Social Charter

457 **Sozialfonds**, *m.*, social fund

458 **Sozialversicherungsträger**, *m.*, social security institution/fund

459 **von Pflichtbeiträgen an staatliche Sozialversicherungsträger befreit, sofern die Organisation ein eigenes Sozialversicherungssystem einrichtet** (PPELDO 20), exempt from all compulsory contributions to national social security schemes should the organization establish its own social security system

460 **spaltbar**, *adj.*, fissionable (*Stoff)

461 **später**, *adj.*, subsequent

462 **späteres Recht,** subsequent law/legislation

463 **spätere Verträge,** subsequent treaties

464 **später beitretend,** subsequently acceding
465 **jeder Staat, der (ihn) später ratifiziert,** every state subsequently ratifying it
466 **Sperrbereich,** *m.*, security band (*radio*)
467 **Sperrklausel,** *f.*, restrictive clause, blocking clause
468 **bestimmte Staaten durch Sperrklauseln von der Teilnahme an multilateralen Verträgen und internationalen Organisationen ausschließen,** to exclude certain states from participation in multilateral treaties and international organizations by (the inclusion of) restrictive clauses
469 **Sperrzone,** *f.*, prohibited/restricted area/zone, area/zone into which entry is prohibited/restricted
     Spezialorganisation, *f.* = *Sonderorganisation, f.*
470 **Spruch,** *m.*, award
471 **der von den Schiedsrichtern gefällte Spruch** (PPELDO 25), the award of the arbitrators (*Schiedsspruch)
472 **Staat,** *m.*, state
473 **Anerkennung eines Staates,** recognition of a state
474 **Entstehung eines Staates,** emergence of a state
475 **Kontinuität der Staaten,** continuity of states
476 **Nachfolge von Staaten,** succession of states
477 **Untergang eines Staates,** extinction of a state
478 **abhängiger Staat,** dependent state
479 **anerkannter Staat,** recognized state
480 **anerkennender Staat,** recognizing state
481 **ausländischer Staat,** foreign state
482 **beitretender Staat,** acceding state
483 **beitrittswilliger Staat,** state applying for membership/admission, state requesting/requiring/desiring admission/membership/accession, candidate state
484 **beschützter Staat,** protected state
485 **dritter Staat,** third state, other state

(*see* VCLOT 2.1(h) *in Annex* 14)
486 **embryonaler Staat,** embryonic state
487 **ersuchender Staat,** requesting state, state submitting the request
488 **ersuchter Staat,** requested state, state to which the request is/has been addressed, state to which the application is/has been made
489 **erwerbender Staat,** acquiring state
490 **föderativer Staat,** federal state
491 **fremder Staat,** foreign state
492 **friedliebender Staat,** peace-loving state (*now frequently with ideological overtones*)
493 **geschädigter Staat,** injured state
494 **halbsouveräner Staat,** semi-sovereign state (*a somewhat nonsensical term: a state is either sovereign or it is not; nevertheless frequently encountered*)
495 **kriegführender Staat,** belligerent state
496 **maritimer Staat,** maritime state
497 **mitkriegführender Staat,** co-belligerent state
498 **multinationaler Staat,** multinational state
499 **neuentstandener Staat,** new state, newly emerged state
500 **neuer Staat,** new state (*see* *Neustaat)
501 **neutraler Staat,** neutral state
502 **neutralisierter Staat,** neutralized state
503 **nichtselbständiger Staat,** dependent state
504 **okkupierender Staat** (= besetzender Staat), occupying state
505 **okkupierter Staat** (= besetzter Staat), occupied state
506 **schuldiger Staat,** delinquent state, state at fault
507 **selbständiger Staat,** independent state
508 **souveräner Staat,** sovereign state
509 **unabhängiger Staat,** independent state
510 **vertragsbrüchiger Staat,** state acting in violation of the treaty, treaty-breaking state
511 **zivilisierter Staat,** civilized state
512 **die von den zivilisierten Staaten**

anerkannten allgemeinen Rechtsgrundsätzen, the general principles of law recognized by civilized
states

513 staatenähnlich, adj., state-like

514 ein staatenähnliches Gebilde, z.B.
der Heilige Stuhl, a state-like entity,
e.g. the Holy See

515 Staatenbund, m., confederation

516 Ein Staatenbund ist eine lockere
Vereinigung von selbständigen
Staaten, A confederation is a loose
association of independent states
(*Realunion, and note to *Bundes-
staat)

517 Staatengemeinschaft, f., community of states/nations

518 Das Ziel der Selbstbestimmung eines
Volkes besteht u.a. darin, die gleiche
Stellung in der Staatengemeinschaft
einzunehmen, die andere Völker
bereits innehaben, The purpose of
the self-determination of a people is
inter alia to enable this people to
take up the same position in the
community of states as other peoples already hold

519 Staatengleichheit, f., equality of
states, state equality

520 Staatenhaftung, f., responsibility of
states, state responsibility

521 völkerrechtliche Staatenhaftung,
responsibility of states in international law

522 Staatenkonferenz, f., state conference

523 staatenlos, adj., stateless

524 Staatenloser, adj.n., stateless person

525 Staatenlosigkeit, f., statelessness

526 Staatennachfolge, f., state succession, succession of states

527 Staatennachfolger, m., successor
state

528 Staatenpraxis, f., state practice,
practice as between states

529 Staatenstreitigkeit, f., dispute
between states
Staatensukzession, f. = *Staatennachfolge, f.

530 Staatensystem, n., state system

531 Staatenverbindung, f., union of

states, composite states
(*Realunion, and note to *Bundesstaat)

532 staatlich, adj., domestic, state, of a
state, national

533 staatliche Abgaben und Gebühren
(CAC), national duties and charges

534 staatliche Monopole, state monopolies

535 staatliche Organe, state organs,
organs of the state

536 staatliche Organisationen, governmental organizations (WMO)

537 staatliches Recht, state law, domestic law, municipal law, internal law

538 Staatlichkeit, f., statehood, status
of/as a state

539 neu entstehende und schon bestehende Staatlichkeiten, newly
arising and already existing states/
state entities

540 Staatsangehöriger, adj.n., national, citizen

541 Staatsangehörige der UN, UN
nationals (CSMW)

542 Staatsangehörige der Vertragsparteien, nationals of the contracting
parties

543 einheimische Staatsangehörige (IMF
IX), local nationals

544 minderjähriger/volljähriger Staatsangehöriger (CRMN 2), a national
who is a minor/who is of full age

545 unerwünschter Staatsangehöriger,
undesirable national

546 die ihr unerwünschten Staatsangehörigen einer anderen Partei
(RMCE 6), the nationals of
another party whom it considers
undesirable

547 Staatsangehörigkeit, f., nationality

548 Diskriminierung aus Gründen der
Staatsangehörigkeit (EEC 7), discrimination on grounds of nationality

549 ohne Unterschied/Unterscheidung
der Staatsangehörigkeit, without
distinction as to nationality

550 ohne Rücksicht auf Staatsangehörigkeit und Rasse (IRU 3),
whatever their nationality or race

551   **Beibehaltung der vorherigen Staats-
      angehörigkeit** (CRMN 1), retention
      of (the) former nationality
552   **Erwerb der (neuen) Staats-
      angehörigkeit durch . . .**, acquisi-
      tion of (new) nationality by (virtue
      of) . . .
553   **durch Adoption,** by adoption
554   **durch Besitz früherer Staats-
      angehörigkeit,** by previous/earlier
      nationality
555   **durch Eheschließung,** by marriage
556   **durch Einbürgerung,** by natural-
      ization
557   **durch Eintritt in den Staatsdienst,**
      by entry into the (civil) service of
      the state
558   **durch Geburt,** by birth
559   **durch Heirat,** by marriage
560   **durch Legitimation,** by legitima-
      tion
561   **Verlust der Staatsangehörigkeit
      durch . . .**, loss of nationality by
      (virtue of) . . .
562   **durch Ausbürgerung,** by
      denaturalization
563   **durch Eheschließung/Heirat mit
      einem Ausländer,** by marriage to a
      foreign national
564   **durch Eintritt in einen fremden
      Staatsdienst,** by entry into the
      (civil) service of a foreign state
565   **durch Erwerb einer fremden
      Staatsangehörigkeit,** by acquisi-
      of another/a foreign nationality
566   **durch Gebietsveränderungen,** by
      territorial changes
567   **Verzicht auf (eine) Staatsangehörig-
      keit,** renunciation of (one) national-
      ity
568   **Wiedererwerb der Staatsangehörig-
      keit** (CRMN 1), recovery of nation-
      ality
569   **doppelte Staatsangehörigkeit,** dual
      nationality
570   **mehrfache Staatsangehörigkeit,**
      multiple nationality
571   **Staatsangehörigkeit aberkennen,** to
      deprive of nationality
572   **Staatsangehörigkeit aufgeben,** to
      give up nationality
573   **. . . wenn sein Heimatrecht ihm**

      **gestattet, seine Staatsangehörig-
      keit durch einfache Erklärung
      aufzugeben** (CRMN 2), . . . pro-
      vided that his national law permits
      him to give up his nationality by a
      simple declaration
574   **Staatsangehörigkeit beibehalten,** to
      retain the (former) nationality
575   **Staatsangehörigkeit besitzen,** to pos-
      sess nationality
576   **Staatsangehörigkeit entziehen,** to
      deprive of nationality
577   **Staatsangehörigkeit erwerben,** to
      acquire nationality
578   **die Staatsangehörigkeit durch
      Einbürgerung, Option oder
      Wiedereinbürgerung erwerben**
      (CRMN 1), to acquire nationality
      by means of naturalization, option
      or recovery
579   **für eine Staatsangehörigkeit
      optieren,** to opt for a/one nationality
580   **Staatsangehörigkeit verleihen,** to
      grant nationality
581   **Staatsangehörigkeit verlieren,** to
      lose (one's) nationality
582   **auf eine Staatsangehörigkeit verzich-
      ten,** to renounce a/one nationality
583   **Staatsangehörigkeit wiedererwer-
      ben,** to recover nationality
      (*Staatszugehörigkeit, *Nationali-
      tät, *Staatsbürgerschaft)
584   **Staatsangehörigkeitsdekrete,** *n.
      pl.*, nationality decrees
585   **Staatsangehörigkeitserwerb,**
      m., acquisition of nationality
      (Erwerb der *Staatsangehörigkeit)
586   **Staatsangehörigkeitsverlust,**
      m., loss of nationality
      (Verlust der *Staatsangehörigkeit)
587   **Staatsattribute,** *m.pl.*, attributes of
      a state
      (*Staatsvolk)
588   **Staatsbürger,** *m.*, citizen, national
      (*Staatsangehöriger)
589   **staatsbürgerlich,** *adj.*, civic, civil,
      of the citizens
590   **staatsbürgerliche Rechte und Pflich-
      ten** (GG 33), political rights and
      duties
591   **Staatsbürgerschaft,** *f.*, citizenship,
      nationality

592 **Staatsangehörigkeit, Staatsbürgerschaft oder Einbürgerung** (CERD
1), nationality, citizenship or
naturalization
(*Staatsangehörigkeit)

593 **Staatselement,** *n.*, element of a
state
(*Staatsvolk)

594 **Staatsfremder,** *adj.n.*, alien, non-
national, non-citizen
(*Mindestnorm)

595 **Staatsgebiet,** *n.*, state/national territory

596 **Unversehrtheit des Staatsgebiets,**
territorial integrity

597 **Erwerb/Verlust von Staatsgebiet,**
acquisition/loss of state territory
(*Gebiet³, *Hoheitsgebiet, *Staatsvolk)

598 **Staatsgebilde,** *n.*, state entity

599 **das sich formende Staatsgebilde,** the
nascent state, the emerging state,
the nascent state entity

600 **Staatsgewalt,** *f.*, sovereignty, state
jurisdiction, government, the state,
state authority

601 **eine Staatsgewalt, die nur dem Völkerrecht untersteht,** a state that is
subordinate only to international
law

602 **Die Staatsgewalt übt über das Staatsvolk Personalhoheit aus,** The state
exercises personal jurisdiction over
the population

603 **selbstregierende Staatsgewalt,**
sovereign government

604 **souveräne Staatsgewalt,** sovereign
government

605 **unmittelbare Staatsgewalt,** direct
state authority
(*Staatshoheit)

606 **Staatsgrenze,** *f.*, state frontier,
national frontier

607 **Staatshoheit,** *f.*, sovereignty, state
sovereignty

608 **Als Hoheitsgebiete eines Staates gelten die der Staatshoheit, der
Oberhoheit, dem Schutz oder der
Mandatsverwaltung dieses Staates
unterstehenden Landgebiete und
angrenzende Hoheitsgewässer** (SF
71), The territories of a state shall

be deemed to be the land areas and
territorial waters adjacent thereto
under the sovereignty, suzerainty,
protection or mandate of such a
state

609 **Staatshoheitsakt,** *m.*, sovereign act
of a state

610 **Staatskontinuität,** *f.*, continuity of
the state

611 **Staatslehre,** *f.*, theory of constitutional law

612 **Staatsluftfahrzeug,** *n.* (CAC),
state aircraft

613 **Staatsnotstand,** *m.*, national/state
emergency

614 **Staatsoberhaupt,** *n.*, head of state

615 **Staatsorgan,** *n.*, state organ, organ
of (the) state

616 **Staatsrecht,** *n.*, constitutional law

617 **Staatsschiff,** *n.*, government ship,
state ship

618 **Staatsschiffe, die nicht Kriegsschiffe
sind** (GCTS 21), government ships
other than warships

619 **Staatsschiffe, die Handelszwek-
ken/anderen als Handelszwecken
dienen** (GCTS 20), government
ships operated for commercial/non-
commercial reasons

620 **Staatsschiffe, die nicht der Handelsschiffahrt dienen** (ILOC 22.1),
government vessels not engaged in
trade

621 **Staatssicherheit,** *f.*, state security,
national security

622 **eine Verletzung der Staatssicherheit,**
a breach of state security, an act
endangering/jeopardizing state security

623 **Staatsvertrag,** *m.*, treaty, international treaty, treaty between states
(*within the FRG this term is also used
for a treaty between the individual*
Länder)

624 **Staatsvolk,** *n.*, population, national
population

625 **Ein Staatsvolk, ein Staatsgebiet und
eine selbstregierende Staatsgewalt
sind die drei Attribute eines souveränen Staates,** A permanent population, a defined national territory and
a sovereign government are the

three attributes/elements of a
sovereign state
626 **Staatszugehöriger,** *adj.n.*, national
627 **In den Artikeln . . . bezeichnet der
Ausdruck ,,Staatszugehöriger'' Fi-
scherboote und sonstige Fischer-
fahrzeuge jeder Größe, die die
Nationalität des betroffenen Staates
besitzen** (GCF 14), In Articles . . .
the term "nationals" means fishing
boats or craft of any size having the
nationality of the state concerned
(**Staatszugehöriger**/**Staatszugehörigkeit** *are more likely to be used in the
context of inanimates, in contrast to*
Staatsangehöriger / **Staatsangehörigkeit.** *See under* *Staatszugehörigkeit, *Staatsangehörigkeit, *Staatsangehöriger, *Nationalität *and*
*Staatsbürgerschaft.)
628 **Staatszugehörigkeit,** *f.,* nationality
629 **Luftfahrzeuge haben die Staatszugehörigkeit des Staates, in dem sie
eingetragen sind** (CAC 17), Aircraft
have the nationality of the state in
which they are registered
630 **Schiffe, welche die Staatszugehörigkeit des Entsendestaates besitzen**
(VCCR 5), vessels having the
nationality of the sending state
(*note to* *Staatszugehöriger)
631 **ständig,** *adj.,* standing, permanent
632 **ständiges Gericht,** permanent/stand-
ing court/tribunal
633 **der Ständige Internationale
Gerichtshof** (SIGH), the Permanent Court of International Justice
(PCIJ)
634 **ständiges Mitglied,** permanent
member
635 **der Ständige Schiedshof,** the Permanent Court of Arbitration
636 **Status,** *m.,* status
637 **den Status eines Beobachters haben,**
to have the status of an observer
638 **völkerrechtlicher Status eines neuen
Staates,** international status of a new
state
639 **Statut¹,** *n.,* statute
640 **Statut²,** *n.,* status
(*Truppenstatut, *Personalstatut)
641 **Stelle,** *f.,* agency, authority, organ,

body, board
642 **ad-hoc Stelle,** ad-hoc agency (etc.)
643 **nachgeordnete Stelle,** subordinate
agency (etc.)
644 **,,Nachgeordnete Stellen'' bedeutet
jegliche Organe, Ausschüsse oder
Dienste, die vom Rat eingesetzt oder
ihm unterstellt sind** (WEUS 1),
"Subsidiary bodies" means any
organ, committee or service established by the Council or placed
under its authority
645 **nichtstaatliche Stelle,** non-
governmental agency (etc.)
646 **staatliche Stelle,** government(al)
agency (etc.)
647 **unparteiische Stelle,** impartial agency
(etc.)
648 **Beilegung durch die guten Dienste
unparteiischer Stellen,** settlement
by the good offices of impartial
bodies
649 **Der Oberschiedsrichter kann von
einer im Schiedsvertrag benannten
unparteiischen dritten Stelle (z.B.
Staatsoberhaupt eines dritten
Staates) ernannt werden,** The
chief arbitrator may be appointed
by an impartial third party (e.g.
the head of state of a third state)
nominated in the arbitration
agreement
650 **zuständige Stelle,** competent authority
651 **die als zuständig angesehene/
erachtete Stelle,** the authority
regarded as competent
652 **Stellungnahme,** *f.,* position, statement, opinion
(*Erklärung)
653 **stellvertretend,** *adj.,* alternate,
substitute, deputy
(*Stellvertreter)
654 **Stellvertreter,** *m.,* alternate, substitute, deputy
655 **ein Delegierter, der von Stellvertretern und Beratern begleitet werden
kann** (IAEA V), a delegate who may
be accompanied by alternates and by
advisers
656 **Jeder Vertreter kann zu den Tagungen Stellvertreter und Berater**

hinzuziehen und sich in seiner Abwesenheit durch einen Stellvertreter vertreten lassen (ECER 10), A representative may be accompanied to the sessions by alternate representatives and advisers, and, when absent, he may be replaced by an alternate representative

657 das Verfahren zur Bestimmung von Stellvertretern (ILO 7), the method of appointing substitutes

658 **Steuer**, *f.*, tax

659 **Steuern und Abgaben, die nach den Rechtsvorschriften des Empfangsstaates zu entrichten sind** (VCDR 23), dues and taxes payable under the law of the receiving state

660 **kommunale Steuern,** municipal taxes

661 **regionale Steuern,** regional taxes

662 **staatliche Steuern,** national taxes (Steuern und *Abgaben)

663 **Steuerbefreiung,** *f.*, exemption from taxes/taxation, fiscal immunity **Steuerfreiheit,** *f.* = *Steuerbefreiung, *f.*

664 **Steuerstrafsache,** *f.*, fiscal offence

665 **Stillhalteanordnungen,** *f.pl.*, moratoria (WEUS 7)

666 **Stillhaltemaßnahmen,** *f.pl.*, standstill measures (SF 136)

667 **stillschweigend,** *adj.*, tacit, implied (*Geltungsdauer erneuern)·

668 **Stimmabgabe,** *f.*, voting, ballot

669 **geheime Stimmabgabe,** secret ballot

670 **stimmberechtigt,** *adj.*, entitled to vote

671 **ein Mitgliedstaat ist im Rat nicht stimmberechtigt, wenn . . .,** a member state shall have no vote in the council if . . .

672 **Stimme,** *f.*, vote

673 **eine Stimme abgeben,** to vote, to cast a vote

674 **die von den anwesenden Delegierten abgegebenen Stimmen** (ILO 3), the votes cast by the delegates present

675 **sich der Stimme enthalten,** to abstain from voting (*Abstimmung²)

676 **Stimmengleichheit,** *f.*, equality of votes, equal division of votes

677 **Bei Stimmengleichheit gibt die**

Stimme des ältesten Richters den Ausschlag (SICJ 12), In the event of an equality of votes the eldest judge has the deciding vote

678 **Bei Stimmengleichheit wird die Wahl des Obmanns einer dritten Macht anvertraut** (HgI 45), If the votes are equally divided the choice of the umpire is entrusted to a third power

679 **ergibt auch diese Abstimmung Stimmengleichheit . . .** (ECER 39), if this vote also results in equality . . .

680 **Stimmenmehrheit,** *f.*, majority of votes, majority vote

681 **Das Gericht entscheidet mit Stimmenmehrheit,** The court shall decide/reach its decisions by a majority vote

682 **Stimmenthaltung,** *f.*, abstention

683 **Stimmenzahl,** *f.*, number of votes (cast)

684 **eine 4/5 Mehrheit der gesamten Stimmenzahl** (IMF III), a 4/5 majority of the total voting power

685 **Stimmrecht,** *n.*, right to vote, voting right(s)/power

686 **die anwesenden und ihr Stimmrecht ausübenden Regierungsvertreter** (ILO 1), the government delegates present and voting

687 **zeitweilige Aufhebung des Stimmrechts** (CAC 62), suspension of voting power

688 **Stoff,** *m.*, material

689 **spaltbare Stoffe,** fissionable materials

690 **überschüssige besondere spaltbare Stoffe** (EAEC 80), excess of any special fissionable materials

691 **strafbar,** *adj.*, punishable

692 **strafbare Handlung,** punishable offence/act (strafbare *Handlung, strafbare *Zuwiderhandlung)

693 **Strafbestimmung,** *f.*, penal provision, penal sanction

694 **Strafe,** *f.*, sentence, punishment, penalty

695 **die Strafen, welche das Recht einer Vertragspartei vorsieht** (PPSO An), the penalties which may be imposed under the law of a contracting party

696 **Aussetzung der Strafe,** interruption of sentence

697 **Beendigung der Strafe,** termination of sentence

698 **Herabsetzung der Strafe,** reduction of sentence

699 **erniedrigende Strafe,** degrading punishment (PHR)

700 **unmenschliche Strafe,** inhuman punishment (PHR)

701 **die Strafe aussetzen** (CSMW), to interrupt the sentence

702 **die Strafe beendigen,** to terminate the sentence

703 **eine Strafe verhängen,** to impose a sentence

704 **Strafexpedition,** *f.,* punitive expedition

705 **Strafgericht,** *n.,* criminal court, penal court, penal tribunal

706 **. . . werden vor das zuständige internationale Strafgericht gestellt** (PCG 6), . . . shall be tried by such international penal tribunal as may have jurisdiction

707 **Strafgerichtsbarkeit,** *f.,* criminal jurisdiction

708 **Die Strafgerichtsbarkeit des Küstenstaates soll an Bord eines das Küstenmeer durchfahrenden Schiffes nicht ausgeübt werden,** The criminal jurisdiction of the coastal state should not be exercised on board a foreign vessel passing through the territorial sea

709 **internationale/völkerrechtliche Strafgerichtsbarkeit,** international criminal jurisdiction

710 **Strafmaßnahme,** *f.,* punitive measure, sanction

711 **die Anwendung der in Art. 13 vorgesehenen Strafmaßnahmen** (ICPCP 6), the application of sanctions as laid down in Art. 13

712 **Strafprozeß,** *m.,* criminal trial

713 **Strafprozeßordnung,** *f.,* code of criminal procedure

714 **Strafprozeßrecht,** *n.,* law relating to/governing criminal procedure

715 **Strafrecht,** *n.,* criminal law/code, penal law/code

716 **internationales/völkerrechtliches**

Strafrecht, international criminal law

717 **strafrechtlich,** *adj.,* penal, criminal, of penal/criminal law (*bestrafen, *Beschuldigung)

718 **Strafsache,** *f.,* criminal matter/case

719 **Straftat,** *f.,* offence, punishable act, criminal act/deed, penal act/deed (strafbare *Handlung)

720 **Strafverfahren,** *n.,* criminal proceedings

721 **wenn ein Angeklagter in einem Strafverfahren . . . freigesprochen worden ist oder . . . verurteilt worden ist** (NATOSF VII), where an accused has been tried . . . and has been acquitted, or has been convicted

Strafverfahrensrecht, *n.* = *Strafprozeßrecht, *n.*

722 **Strafverfolgung,** *f.,* prosecution, criminal proceedings

723 **die Pflicht zur Strafverfolgung** (ICCC 9), the obligation to take proceedings

724 **vorläufiger Schutz vor Strafverfolgung,** temporary protection from prosecution

725 **Strafverfolgung einleiten,** to initiate/take (criminal) proceedings

726 **Strafvollstreckung,** *f.,* punishment, execution/enforcement of punishment/sentence

727 **Strafvollzug,** *m.,* punishment, execution/enforcement of punishment/sentence

728 **nach den Grundsätzen eines humanen Strafvollzuges** (CSMW 7), in accordance with humane penological principles

729 **Streifen,** *m.,* belt (*Küstengewässer)

730 **Streikrecht,** *n.,* right to strike

731 **Streit,** *m.,* dispute

732 **die in Streit/im Streite befindlichen Staaten,** the states at variance, the contesting states, the states involved in a dispute

733 **die am Streite nicht beteiligten Mächte** (HgI 3), powers strangers to the dispute

734 **die auf den Streit bezüglichen Sachfragen,** the questions of fact relevant to the issue (*see* *Bericht verfassen)

735 **Gegenstand des Streites,** subject (matter) of the dispute (*see* *Streitgegenstand)

736 **einen Streit beilegen/erledigen,** to settle/regulate a dispute

737 **einen Streit lösen,** to resolve a dispute

738 **einen Streit regeln/schlichten,** to settle/regulate a dispute (*Streitfall, *Streitigkeit)

739 **Streitbeilegung,** *f.*, settlement of a dispute

740 **richterliche Streitbeilegung,** judicial settlement of a dispute

741 **schiedsrichterliche Streitbeilegung,** arbitral settlement of a dispute, settlement of a dispute by arbitration

742 **streiten,** to dispute, to be engaged in a dispute

743 **Streiterledigung,** *f.*, settlement of a dispute (*Streitbeilegung)

744 **Streitfall,** *m.*, dispute

745 **die Aufmerksamkeit der Generalversammlung auf einen Streitfall lenken,** to draw a dispute to the attention of the General Assembly

746 **der Streitfall zwischen den Parteien** (ILO 28), the issue between the parties

747 **internationale Streitfälle,** international disputes, disputes between states

748 **örtliche Streitfälle,** local disputes

749 **zwischenstaatliche Streitfälle,** disputes between states, international disputes (*Streit, *Streitigkeit)

750 **Streitfrage,** *f.*, dispute, matter in dispute

751 **Die Parteien werden ihre Streitfragen ausschließlich mit friedlichen Mitteln lösen,** The parties shall resolve their disputes exclusively by peaceful means (*Streit, *Streitfall, *Streitigkeit, *Schiedsstelle)

752 **Streitgegenstand,** *m.*, subject (matter) of the dispute

753 **kurze Darstellung des Streitgegenstandes** (ECPSD 9), summary account of the dispute

754 **wird ein Gericht eines Vertragsstaates wegen eines Streitgegenstandes angerufen . . .** (CEFA II), the court of a contracting state, when seized of an action . . . (*Schiedsvertrag)

755 **Streitgenossen,** *m.pl.* (CRPG An), parties to the dispute

756 **Streitgenossenschaft,** *f.*, parties in/having the same interest

757 **bilden mehrere Parteien eine Streitgenossenschaft . . .,** should there be several parties in the same interest . . . (SICJ 31)

758 **Streithängigkeit,** *f.*, pendency (*Rechtshängigkeit)

759 **streitig,** *adj.*, at issue, at/in/under dispute, disputed

760 **die streitigen Fragen klären** (ECPSD 15), to elucidate the questions in dispute (*strittig)

761 **Streitigkeit,** *f.*, dispute

762 **Jede Partei kann die Streitigkeit durch eine Klageschrift dem IGH unterbreiten** (VCLOT 66), Any one of the parties may, by a written application, submit the dispute to the ICJ

763 **eine Streitigkeit einem Schiedsverfahren unterwerfen** (VCLOT 66), to submit a dispute to arbitration

764 **ist eine Vergleichskommission mit der Streitigkeit befaßt** (ECPSD 31), if the dispute is brought before a conciliation commission

765 **ein berechtigtes Interesse an der Streitigkeit haben** (ECPSD 33), to have a legitimate interest in the dispute (*Streit, *Streitfall, *Schiedsgericht)

766 **Streitkräfte,** *f.pl.*, forces, armed forces, military forces

767 **ausländische Streitkräfte,** foreign forces

768 **Rechte und Pflichten ausländischer Streitkräfte** (CRPG), rights and obligations of foreign forces

769 **bewaffnete Streitkräfte** (GC I), armed (fighting) forces

770 **freiwillige Streitkräfte,** volunteer

forces (CUN 84)
771 reguläre   Streitkräfte,   regular
     (armed) forces
772   Bildung regulärer Streitkräfte
         (GC I 13), formation of regular
         armed units
773   an Land gesetzte Streitkräfte (GC I),
         forces put ashore
774   an Bord befindliche Streitkräfte (GC
         I), forces on board ship
775   Streitkräfte im Felde (GC), (armed)
         forces in the field
776   Herabsetzung der Streitkräfte, re-
         duction of (armed/military) forces
777   Manneszucht der Streitkräfte, discip-
         line of the forces
778   Rechtsstellung   der   Streitkräfte,
         (legal) status of the forces (CRFF)
779   Verminderung   der   Streitkräfte,
         reduction of (armed/military) forces
780 Streitpartei, f., party to the dispute,
     litigant
781   . . . sofern nicht die Streitparteien
         einer anderen Art der Beilegung zu-
         stimmen (CERD 22), . . . unless
         the disputants agree to another
         mode of settlement
     Streitteil, m. = *Streitpartei, f.
782 Streitwert, m., value in litigation,
     value/amount which is in contention
783   jede Streitigkeit, deren Streitwert
         50 000 französische Franken nicht
         überschreitet (PPESRO 7), any case
         of a dispute of which the value in

litigation does not exceed 50,000
French francs
784 strittig, adj., at issue, at/in/under dis-
     pute, disputed
785   die Punkte, die zwischen den Streit-
         parteien strittig sind, the points at
         issue between the two parties
786   strittiges Gebiet, disputed territory
         (*streitig)
787 Studiengruppe, f., study group
788 Subjekt, n., subject
789   Subjekt des Völkerrechts, subject of
         international law
790   handelndes Subjekt, subject capable
         of (legal) transactions, subject with
         (legal) capacity (see *handlungs-
         fähig)
791 Suchtstoffkommission, f., Com-
     mission on Narcotic Drugs
792 Sukzessionsstaat, m., successor
     state
793 suspendieren, to suspend
794 Suspendierung, f., suspension
795   die gänzliche oder teilweise Suspen-
         dierung eines Vertrags (VCLOT 60),
         suspending the treaty in whole or in
         part
796   Während der Suspendierung ist das
         Mitglied nicht berechtigt . . . (IDA
         VII), While under suspension, a
         member shall not be entitled . . .
         (*Ausschluß, *Aufhebung)
797 suzerän, adj., suzerain
798 Suzeränität, f., suzerainty

T

1 Tadelsantrag, *m*., motion of censure (*Mißtrauensantrag)

2 tagen , to sit, to meet, to be in session

3 **Der Gerichtshof tagt ständig,** The Court remains permanently in session

4 **Der Gerichtshof tagt in Plenarsitzungen,** The full Court shall sit/the Court of Justice shall sit in plenary session (*note to* *Sitzung)

5 Tagesordnung, *f*., agenda, orders of the day

6 **eine Frage auf die Tagesordnung setzen,** to place an item on the agenda

7 **eine Frage von der Tagesordnung absetzen,** to withdraw an item from the agenda

8 **endgültige Tagesordnung,** final/approved agenda

9 **vorläufige Tagesordnung,** provisional agenda

10 **die Tagesordnung annehmen,** to approve the agenda

11 **die Tagesordnung aufstellen,** to draw up/fix the agenda

12 **die Tagesordnung erschöpfen,** to exhaust/cover all the points/items of/on the agenda

13 **die Tagesordnung überladen,** to overload the agenda

14 Tagesordnungsausschuß, *m*., agenda committee

15 Tagesordnungsentwurf, *m*., draft agenda

16 Tagesordnungspunkt, *m*., item/point on the agenda

17 Tagung, *f*., session, meeting

18 **der zu einer Tagung zusammengetretene Kongreß** (WMO 5), the Congress in session

19 **außerordentliche Tagung,** extraordinary session/meeting

20 **ordentliche Tagung,** ordinary session/meeting

21 **Der Rat tritt einmal jährlich zu einer ordentlichen Tagung zusammen** (CICES 7), The Council shall meet in ordinary session once a year (*note to* *Sitzung)

22 Talweg , *m*., talweg/thalweg (*the median line of the principal channel in a navigable river; some texts reserve the term* median line *for non-navigable rivers.* *Mittellinie)

23 Tat, *f*., deed, act, action

24 **auf frischer Tat,** (in the) committing (of) an act, *in flagrante delicto*

25 **... wenn der Betreffende auf frischer Tat getroffen wird** (WEUS 18), ... when the representatives ... are found committing, attempting to commit, or just having committed an offence (*Handlung, *Tun)

26 Tatbestand, *m*., facts (of the case), situation

27 **Jede Partei hat ihre Darstellung des Tatbestandes einzureichen** (HgI 10), Each party must deposit its statement of facts (*Tatsache, *Tatfragen)

28 Täter, *m*., offender, person/party committing the act/offence

29 Tatfragen , *f.pl*., facts (*e.g. of a dispute*)

30 **... indem sie durch eine unparteiische und gewissenhafte Prüfung der Tatfragen aufklären** (HgI 9), ... by elucidating the facts by means of an impartial and conscientious investigation

31 **sämtliche für den Streitfall bedeutsame Tatfragen** (ILO 28), all questions of fact relevant to determining the issue

32 tätig, *adj*., active, employed

33 **in dieser Eigenschaft tätig sein** (VCDR 1), to act in this capacity

34 **Der Rat bleibt nach Maßgabe dieses Übereinkommens weiterhin tätig** (CICES 2), The Council shall be maintained in accordance with the provisions of this treaty (*Tätigkeit[1], *Eigenschaft)

35 Tätigkeit[1], *f*., activity, function,

capacity (*particularly of individuals: compare* *Tätigkeit² *below*)

36 Der Rat erstattet jährlich einen Bericht über seine Tätigkeit (PMBT V), The Council shall make an annual report of its activities

37 die Tätigkeit des (Rates usw) erstreckt sich auf. . . (CICES 2), the (Council, etc.) shall be concerned with . . .

38 Aufnahme der Tätigkeit, assumption of (one's) function(s)/activities/office

39   vor Aufnahme (seiner) Tätigkeit, before taking office, prior to (his) assuming office

40 Ausübung der Tätigkeit, exercise of (one's) function(s)/activities

41 Beendigung der Tätigkeit, termination of (one's) function(s)/activities

42 Einstellung der Tätigkeit, suspension of (one's) function(s)/activities

43 Fortsetzung der Tätigkeit, continuation of (one's) function(s)/activities

44 dienstliche Tätigkeit, (official) function(s)/duties

45   nach Beendigung ihrer dienstlichen Tätigkeiten (VCDR 10), on the termination of their functions

46 gutachtliche Tätigkeit, advisory function/capacity (*see* *Gutachten)

47 humanitäre Tätigkeit (GC I/II), humanitarian activities/missions

48 rechtsberatende Tätigkeit (CRFF 13), legal consultancy

49 seelsorgerische Tätigkeit (GC I 28), religious duties

50   ärztliche und seelsorgerische Tätigkeit (GC III 33), medical and spiritual functions

51 vermittelnde Tätigkeit, mediatory function/capacity

52 Tätigkeit aufnehmen, to commence (one's) activities, to take up (one's) functions

53 Tätigkeit ausüben, to exercise (one's) functions

54   Die Mitglieder des Gerichts dürfen keine Tätigkeit ausüben, die mit der normalen Wahrnehmung ihres Amtes unvereinbar ist (CRPG An), The members of the tribunal shall not engage in any activity incompatible with the proper exercise of their duties

55 Tätigkeit beendigen, to terminate (one's) functions

56 Tätigkeit einstellen, to suspend (one's) functions

57 Tätigkeit fortsetzen, to continue (to discharge) (one's) functions (*Amtshandlung, *Aufgabe, *Vorrechte und Befreiungen)

58 Tätigkeit², *f.*, operations (*particularly of agencies/bodies*)

59   Die Tätigkeit des Amts beschränkt sich auf das europäische Festland (WEU IV), The operations of the Agency shall be confined to the mainland of Europe

60   bei Beendigung der Tätigkeit der EZU (EMA Pr), when the operations of the EPU are terminated

61 Tätigkeitsbereich, *m.*, scope/field of activities/functions

62 Tätigkeitsbeschreibung, *f.*, description of activities/functions, duties

63 Tatsache, *f.*, fact

64   das Bestehen jeder Tatsache, die, wäre sie bewiesen, die Verletzung einer internationalen Verpflichtung darstellt (SICJ 36), the existence of a fact which, if established, would constitute a breach of an international obligation

65   . . . ob sich aus den festgestellten Tatsachen ergibt, daß. . . (PHR 31), . . . whether the facts found disclose that . . . (*Tatbestand, *Tatfragen)

66 Tatsachenfeststellung, *f.*, ascertaining of the facts (*kontradiktorisch)

67 Täuschung, *f.*, deceit, deception, fraud

68   arglistige Täuschung, fraud (*Urteil erlangen)

69 Teil¹, *m.*, portion, part

70   der noch verbleibende Teil der Periode/Amtszeit, the unexpired portion of the term/period/period of office

71   die im zweiten Teil dieses Abkommens aufgeführten Sondervereinbarungen, the special arrangements

set forth in Part II of this Agreement
72 **Teil²**, *m.*, party
73 **der betreffende Hohe Vertragsschließende Teil** (PHR), the High Contracting Party concerned (*Partei, *Vertragspartei)
74 **Teilabkommen,** *n.*, partial agreement (*see note to* * Vertrag *in Annex* 1)
75 **Teilabrüstung,** *f.*, partial disarmament, reduction of armaments
76 **Teilnahme,** *f.*, participation, accession
77 **Teilnahme ohne Stimmrecht** (CAC 53), participation without a vote
78 **ihre Teilnahme unter diesen Vorbehalten** (ICCC Prot), their participation, subject to the said reservations
79 **die zur Teilnahme an den Sitzungen des Ausschusses berechtigten Mitglieder** (PHR 32), the members entitled to sit on the committee
80 **die Teilnahme an einem Vertrag/einer Organisation,** participation in/accession to a treaty/an organization
81 **das Recht aller Staaten auf Teilnahme an universalen multilateralen Verträgen,** the right of all states to participate in/accede to universal multilateral treaties
82 **Teilnahme durch/aufgrund,** participation by/by virtue of
83 **Teilnahme durch Unterzeichnung/ Annahme / Ratifikation / Genehmigung,** participation/accession by signature/acceptance, ratification/approval
84 **gleichberechtigte Teilnahme,** participation on the basis of equal rights
85 **Teilnahmeklausel,** *f.*, clause relating to/regulating participation
86 **Teilnahmerecht,** *n.*, right of participation/to participate
87 **Teilnehmer,** *m.*, participant, delegate
88 **Teilnehmerabzeichen,** *n.*, (conference/congress) badge
89 **Teilnehmerkarte,** *f.*, congress/conference card, delegate's card, legitimation card

90 **Teilnehmerland,** *n.*, participating country
91 **Teilnehmerregierung,** *f.*, participating government
92 **Teilnehmerstaat,** *m.*, participating state
93 **Teilrechtsnachfolge,** *f.*, partial succession
94 **Teilstaat,** *m.*, state member (*e.g. of a federation*) (*Gliedstaat)
95 **teilweise,** *adv.*, in part
96 **ganz oder teilweise abändern,** to modify in whole or in part
97 **territorial,** *adj.*, territorial
98 **territoriale Abgrenzung,** territorial delimitation
99 **territorialer Anspruch,** territorial claim
100 **territorialer Erwerb,** territorial acquisition
101 **territoriale Erwerbung,** territorial acquisition
102 **territoriale Gerichtsbarkeit,** territorial jurisdiction
103 **territoriale Gewässer,** territorial waters (*see* *Küstengewässer, *Küstenmeer)
104 **territoriale Hoheit,** territorial sovereignty
105 **territoriale Integrität,** territorial integrity
106 **territoriale Souveränität,** territorial sovereignty
107 **territoriale Streitigkeit,** territorial dispute
108 **territoriale Unversehrtheit,** territorial integrity
109 **Territorialgewässer,** *n.* (*usu. in pl.*), territorial waters (*Küstenmeer)
110 **Territorialhoheit,** *f.*, territorial sovereignty
111 **Territorialität,** *f.*, territoriality
112 **Territorialitätsprinzip,** *n.*, *jus soli*
113 **Territorialmeer,** *n.*, territorial sea (*Küstenmeer, *Küstengewässer)
114 **Territorium,** *n.*, territory (*Gebiet³, *Hoheitsgebiet)
115 **Text,** *m.*, text, wording
116 **authentischer Text,** authentic text
117 **Festlegung des authentischen Tex-**

tes (VCLOT 10), authentication of the text

118   Der Text eines Vertrages wird als authentisch und endgültig festgelegt (VCLOT 10), The text of a treaty is established as authentic and definitive
119   berichtigter Text, corrected text (see mangelhafter *Text)
120   geänderter Text, modified text
121   mangelhafter Text, defective text
122   Der berichtigte Text tritt *ab initio* an die Stelle des mangelhaften Textes (VCLOT 79), The corrected text replaces the defective text *ab initio*
123   modifizierter Text, modified text
124   ursprünglicher Text, original text (*Wortlaut, *Vertragstext, *Fassung, *Urschrift, *and* VCLOT 85 *in Annex* 5)
125   Theorie, *f.,* theory
126   dualistische Theorie, dualist theory
127   monistische Theorie, monist theory
128   normativistische Theorie, normativist theory
129   objektivistische Theorie, objectivist theory
130   Todeserklärung, *f.,* declaration of death
131   die Todeserklärung Verschollener (UNCDD), the declaration of death of missing persons
132   Tötung, *f.,* killing, murder (GC I), deprivation of life (PHR 2)
133   vorsätzliche Tötung, killing/causing the death of another with malice aforethought
134   Träger¹, *m.,* incumbent
135   Träger von Rechten und Pflichten, incumbent of rights and duties
136   diejenigen, die Träger völkerrechtlicher Rechte und Pflichten sind und somit Völkerrechtssubjekte sein können, those who are incumbents of international rights and duties and hence can be subjects of international law
137   Träger², *m.: sometimes found as an abbreviation of such compounds as* Versicherungsträger, *hence* = institution
138   der zuständige Träger eines Mit-

gliedstaats, the responsible institution of a member state
139   Tragweite, *f.,* scope
140   Tragweite des Schiedsspruchs, the scope of the award
141   Tragweite des Vertrags, the scope of the treaty
142   Tragweite der Vorbehalte, the scope of (the) reservations
143   Transformation, *f.,* transformation
144   Transformation oder Adoption des Völkerrechts im innerstaatlichen Recht, transformation or adoption of international law in/into municipal law
145   automatische Transformation einer Völkerrechtsnorm, automatic transformation of a rule of international law
146   generelle Transformation, general transformation
147   spezifische Transformation, specific transformation (*Inkorporation)
148   Transformationstheorie, *f.,* transformation theory, theory of transformation
149   Die Transformationstheorie geht von der dualistischen Grundposition aus und läßt deshalb eine automatische *en bloc* Übernahme des Völkerrechts in das nationale Recht nicht zu, The theory of transformation proceeds from the fundamental position of the dualists and hence does not permit the *en bloc* adoption of international law into state law
150   transformieren, to transform
151   ein in innerstaatliches Recht transformierter Vertrag, a treaty transformed into municipal law
152   Transitabkommen, *n.,* transit agreement
153   Transitreisender, *adj.n.,* through traveller, person in transit
154   Transitverkehr, *m.,* transit traffic
155   Transitweg, *m.,* transit route
156   Mißbrauch der Transitwege, misuse/abuse of transit routes
157   Trennbarkeit *f.* von Vertragsbestimmungen (VCLOT 44), separability of treaty provisions

158 **Treu** *f.* **und Glauben,** good faith
159   nach **Treu und Glauben,** in good faith, *bona fide*
160   **Alle Mitglieder erfüllen nach Treu und Glauben die Verpflichtungen, die sie übernehmen** (CUN 2), All members shall fulfil in good faith the obligations assumed by them
161 **Treueid,** *n.,* oath of allegiance
162 **Treuepflicht,** *f.,* duty of allegiance
163 **Treueverpflichtung,** *f.,* duty of allegiance
164   **einem Staat gegenüber durch eine Treueverpflichtung gebunden sein,** to be bound to a state by a duty of allegiance
165 **Treuhandabkommen,** *n.,* trusteeship agreement
166 **Treuhänder,** *m.,* trustee
         (*Gebiet³)
167 **treuhänderisch,** *adj.,* trust, under trust
168   **alle treuhänderisch verwalteten Gebiete** (SCS 12), all trust territories
169 **Treuhänderrat,** *m.,* trusteeship council
170 **Treuhandgebiet,** *n.,* trust territory
171   **ein Treuhandgebiet verwalten,** to administer a trust territory
172   **regelmäßige Bereisungen der Treuhandgebiete veranlassen** (CUN 87), to provide for periodic visits to trust territories
         (*Mandatsgebiet *and note*)
173 **Treuhandrat,** *m.,* trusteeship council
174 **Treuhandschaft,** *f.,* trusteeship
175 **Treuhandschaftsgebiet,** *n.,* trusteeship territory

176 **Treuhandschaftsrat,** *m.,* trusteeship council
177 **Treuhandschaftssystem,** *n.,* trusteeship system
178   **ein internationales Treuhandschaftssystem für die Verwaltung und Beaufsichtigung der Hoheitsgebiete, die auf Grund späterer Einzelabkommen in dieses System einbezogen werden** (CUN 75), an international trusteeship system for the administration and supervision of such territories as may be placed thereunder by subsequent individual treaties
179 **Treuhandschaftsvertrag,** *m.,* trusteeship treaty/agreement (*see note to* *Vertrag *in Annex* 1)
180 **Treuhandstaat,** *m.,* trustee state, administering state
181 **trockenfallend,** *adj.,* low-tide, above water at low-tide
         (*Erhebung)
182 **Truppen,** *f.pl.,* troops
183   **eindringende Truppen** (GC I), invading troops
         (*Streitkräfte)
184 **Truppenstatut,** *n.,* status of forces agreement (NAT)
185 **Truppenvertrag,** *m.,* forces convention (*normally refers to* Convention on the Rights and Obligations of Foreign Forces and their Members in the FRG, 26.5.52)
186 **Tun,** *n.,* act
187   **ein Tun oder ein Unterlassen,** an act or omission
         (*zurechnen, *Handlung)

U

1 **übereinkommen**, to agree, to reach/come to an agreement

2 **die Regierungen sind wie folgt übereingekommen** (SF 46), the Governments have agreed as follows/ have agreed on the following provisions (*vereinbaren)

3 **Übereinkommen**, *n.*, agreement, convention (*see note to* *Vertrag *in Annex* 1)

4 **gewisse Grundsätze und Übereinkommen** (CAC Pr), certain principles and arrangements

5 **ein neues Ubereinkommen, welches das vorliegende Übereinkommen ganz oder teilweise abändert** (ILOC 27.7), a new Convention revising this Convention in whole or in part

6 **in dem Wunsch, zu diesem Zweck ein Übereinkommen zu schließen,** desiring for these purposes to conclude a Convention (*For further expressions and collocations see under* *Vertrag.)

7 **Übereinkunft,** *f.*, agreement (*sometimes translated by* instrument, *especially in pl. See also note to* *Vertrag *in Annex* 1)

8 **Der Wortlaut dieser Übereinkünfte in englischer und französischer Sprache ist dieser Schlußakte beigefügt und wird hiermit beglaubigt** (SF 143), The texts of these instruments in the English and French languages are annexed hereto, and are hereby authenticated

9 **örtlich begrenzte Übereinkünfte,** local agreements

10 **übereinstimmen,** to agree

11 **Übereinstimmung,** *f.*, agreement

12 **in Übereinstimmung mit,** in agreement/conformity with

13 **in Übereinstimmung mit allen abgeschlossenen internationalen Vereinbarungen** (IAEA III), in conformity with any international agreements entered into

14 **überfliegen,** to fly over

15 **Überfliegung,** *f.*, flight(s)/flying over

16 **die Überfliegung feindlichen Gebiets,** flights over enemy territory

17 **Übergabe,** *f.*, handing over, delivery (up), surrender (*e.g. in extradition*)

18 **aufgeschobene oder bedingte Übergabe** (EExt 19), postponed or conditional surrender (*Auslieferung)

19 **Übergangsbestimmung,** *f.*, transitional/interim provision, provision for a transitional period

20 **Übergangsmaßnahme,** *f.*, transitional/interim measure

21 **Übergangsregelung,** *f.*, transitional/interim regulation/rule/arrangement

22 **Übergangszeit,** *f.*, transitional/interim period

23 **Die Übergangszeit besteht aus drei Stufen** (EEC 8), This transitional period shall be divided into three stages

24 **übergeben,** to surrender, to extradite (*ausliefern, *Auslieferung)

25 **übermitteln,** to transmit, to communicate (*documents, etc.*) (beglaubigte *Abschrift, *Verwahrregierung)

26 **Übermittlung,** *f.*, transmission, communication

27 **Übernahme,** *f.*, adoption

28 **die uneingeschränkte Übernahme des völkerrechtlichen Gewohnheitsrechts in das staatliche Recht,** the unrestricted adoption of customary international law in municipal law (*Transformation(stheorie))

29 **übernational,** *adj.*, supranational

30 **übernehmen,** to adopt

31 **überprüfen,** to review

32 **Überprüfung,** *f.*, review

33 **eine umfassende Überprüfung der Wirkungsweise dieses Teils des Abkommens** (EMA 14), a comprehensive review of the operation

of the provisions of the present part
of the Agreement
(*Revision)

34 **überreichen,** to present, to hand
over (*e.g. credentials*)

35 **Überreichung,** *f.,* presentation,
handing over

36 **die Reihenfolge der Überreichung
von   Beglaubigungsschreiben**
(VCDR 13), the order of presentation of credentials

37 **überschreiten,** to overstep, to exceed, to cross (*illegally, e.g. frontier*), to abuse (powers, etc.)

38 **Überschreitung,** *f.,* (illegal) crossing (*e.g. of frontier*), abuse (*e.g. of
rights*)

39 **Überschreitung der ihnen übertragenen Befugnisse,** misuse/abuse
of the powers delegated to them

40 **Überseegebiet,** *n.,* overseas territory

41 **Übersiedlungsgut,** *n.,* goods/arti-
cles of establishment

42 **das von einem Diplomaten mitge-
brachte Übersiedlungsgut,** articles
brought by a diplomat and intended
for his establishment

43 **überstimmen,** to overrule, to outvote

44 **übertragen¹,** to delegate (to), to
confer (on), to invest (in)

45 **Funktionen, die dem . . . übertragen
sind,** functions entrusted to the . . .

46 **übertragen²,** *adj.,* delegated, conferred, invested

47 **die ihr übertragenen Aufgaben**
(IAEA III), its authorized functions

48 **die durch das vorliegende Abkommen den Schutzmächten übertragenen Aufgaben** (GC I 10), the duties
incumbent on the protecting powers
by virtue of the present convention

49 **Übertragung,** *f.,* delegation

50 **übertreten,** to transgress, to violate,
to infringe

51 **Übertretung,** *f.,* transgression,
minor/petty offence (*see note to
*Verbrechen)

52 **überwachen,** to supervise

53 **Überwachung,** *f.,* supervision

54 **Überwachungsausschuß,**   *m.,*
supervisory committee

55 **Überwachungsstelle,** *f.,* supervisory body/organ

56 **Überwasserkriegsschiff,** *n.,* surface warship

57 **Überwasserschiff,** *n.,* surface vessel

überzeugt = in der *Überzeugung

58 **Überzeugung,** *f.,* conviction

59 **in der Überzeugung,** convinced, in
the   conviction,   persuaded   (*in
preamble*)

60 **U-Boot-Krieg,** *m.* (= Unterseebootkrieg, *m.*), submarine warfare

61 **Übung,** *f.,* usage, practice

62 **wenn aus der Übung der beteiligten
Staaten oder aus anderen Umständen hervorgeht, daß . . .** (VCLOT
6), if it appears from the practice of
the states concerned or from other
circumstances that . . .

63 **durch   lange   Übung   eindeutig
erwiesen   sein** (GCTS 4), to be
clearly evidenced by a long usage

64 **dieser Artikel läßt die Übung unberührt . . .** (VCDR 16), this Article
is without prejudice to any practice. . .
(internationales   *Gewohnheitsrecht)

65 **Uferstaat,** *m.,* riparian state

66 **Umlagen,** *f.pl.,* levies

67 **Veranlagung der Umlagen,** assessment of levies

68 **umlegen,** to apportion, to divide, to
levy

69 **Die Kommission bestimmt . . . wie
die   Kosten   . . .   umzulegen   sind**
(GCF 9), The Commission shall
determine . . . how the costs . . .
shall be divided
(*Schlüssel²)

70 **umwandeln,** to transform

71 **Umwandlung,** *f.* (= *Transformation, f.*), transformation

72 **unabdingbar,** *adj.,* irrevocable,
inalienable, indispensable

73 **unabdingbare Voraussetzungen des
Vertrags,** indispensable prerequis-
ites to the treaty

74 **Unabdingbarkeit,** *f.,* inalienability,
irrevocability

75 **unabhängig,** adj., independent
76 **unabhängige Ausübung der Pflichten,** independent exercise of their duties
77 **unabhängige Richter,** independent judges
78 **unabhängige Sachverständige,** independent experts (*Privileg)
79 **Unabhängigkeit,** f., independence
80 **die Unabhängigkeit erlangen,** to gain/attain independence (*Unparteilichkeit)
81 **Unabhängigkeitserklärung,** f., declaration of independence
82 **einseitige Unabhängigkeitserklärung,** unilateral declaration of independence
83 **Unabhängigkeitskrieg,** m., war of independence
84 **Unabhängigkeitsvertrag,** m., treaty of independence
85 **unabsetzbar,** adj., not subject to dismissal/removal
86 **unanfechtbar,** adj., incontestable, without appeal
87 **Unanfechtbarkeit,** f., incontestability
88 **unbegründet,** adj., unfounded
89 **unbenommen,** adj., permitted, open
90 **es bleibt jedoch jedem Staat unbenommen . . . ,** it shall, nevertheless, be open to any state to . . ./each state shall, nevertheless, be free to . . .
91 **unberücksichtigt,** adj., not considered, not taken into account
92 **bleiben diese Empfehlungen unberücksichtigt . . .** (EMA 16), if effect is not given to such recommendations . . .
93 **unberührt,** adj., unaffected
94 **unberührt lassen,** to be without prejudice to, not to affect
95 **das vorliegende Abkommen läßt . . . unberührt** (UCC XVIII), this Convention shall not abrogate . . .
96 **lassen die Gültigkeit von . . . unberührt,** shall not affect the validity of . . .
97 **dieser Artikel läßt . . . unberührt** (VCDR 16), this article is without

prejudice to . . .
98 **Artikel 1 läßt die Verpflichtungen unberührt, durch welche . . .** (ECPSD 2), the provisions of Article 1 shall not affect undertakings by which . . . (*berühren², *beeinträchtigen)
99 **unbeschadet,** prep. (+ gen.), without prejudice to, subject to, notwithstanding
100 **unbeschadet der Bestimmungen des Absatzes 5,** subject to the provisions of paragraph 5
101 **unbeschadet der vorstehenden oder jeglicher sonstigen Bestimmungen** (WEUS 2), notwithstanding the foregoing or any other provisions
102 **unbesetzt,** adj., vacant
103 **ist der Posten des Missionschefs unbesetzt . . .** (VCDR 19), if the post of head of the mission is vacant . . .
104 **unbillig,** adj., unfair, unjust
105 **in einer Weise, die den Nichtkernwaffenstaaten keine unbilligen Lasten aufbürdet,** in a way that does not place unfair burdens on non-nuclear-weapon states
106 **undurchführbar,** adj., unenforceable, impossible to execute
107 **Undurchführbarkeit,** f., unenforceability, impossibility of enforcement/execution/implementation
108 **unerwünscht,** adj., undesirable, not acceptable
109 **unerwünschter Ausländer,** undesirable alien
110 **unerwünschter Staatsangehöriger einer anderen Partei,** undesirable national of another party (*non grata)
111 **ungerecht,** adj., unjust, unfair
112 **ungerechtfertigt,** adj., unjustified, non-justifiable
113 **ungerechtfertigte Einmischung in die inneren Angelegenheiten eines Staates,** non-justifiable intervention in the internal affairs of a state
114 **Ungerechtigkeit,** f., injustice, unfairness
115 **ungültig,** adj., invalid, not in force, non-applicable, inoperative

116 keine Bestimmung der Satzung macht . . . ungültig, nothing in the Charter invalidates . . .

117 Der Staat kann geltend machen, daß seine Zustimmung wegen der Bestechung ungültig sei (VCLOT 50), The state may invoke such corruption as invalidating its consent to be bound by a treaty

118 Die Annahme ist ungültig, falls nicht vorher oder nachher die Unterzeichnung erfolgt (UNESCO XV), No acceptance shall be valid unless preceded or followed by signature

119 Ungültigkeit, f., invalidity

120 unhaltbar, adj., untenable

121 die Abänderung unhaltbar gewordener Bestimmungen, the amendment of provisions that have become untenable

122 universal, adj., universal

123 universal akzeptiert, universally accepted

124 universal anerkannt, universally recognized

125 universal verbindlich, universally binding

126 universale Verbindlichkeit der Ziele und Grundsätze der Satzung der UN, universal binding nature/force of the aims and principles of the Charter of the UN

127 universaler Vertrag, universal treaty, treaty with universal application

128 Universalismus, m., universalism

129 Universalist, m., universalist

130 Universalität, f., universality, universal nature

131 die Universalität völkerrechtlicher Verträge, the universality of international treaties

132 Universalitätsgrundsatz, m., principle of universality

133 unkündbar, adj., not subject to denunciation

134 Dieses Übereinkommen ist unkündbar (SF 113), This Agreement shall not be subject to denunciation

135 unmittelbar, adj., direct

136 durch unmittelbare Verhandlungen, by direct negotiation(s)

137 unparteiisch, adj., impartial

138 die Beilegung durch gute Dienste unparteiischer Stellen, the settlement through the good offices of impartial bodies

139 . . . seine Aufgaben und Befugnisse unparteiisch und gewissenhaft ausüben, . . . to exercise his functions and powers impartially and conscientiously (see VCLOT 76 (2) in Annex 15)

140 Unparteilichkeit, f., impartiality

141 Aufgaben mit Unparteilichkeit erfüllen (GC I 10), to discharge duties impartially

142 in völliger Unparteilichkeit und Unabhängigkeit (EAEC 138), with complete impartiality and independence

143 Unrecht, n., wrong, tort, delinquency

144 Abstellung eines Unrechts, cessation of a wrong

145 Vergeltung eines Unrechts, retaliation against a wrong

146 bei der Repressalie handelt es sich um die Vergeltung eines völkerrechtlichen Unrechts durch ein anderes, (a) reprisal is the retaliation against one international wrong by another

147 (ein) Unrecht begehen, to commit (a) wrong

148 unrechtmäßig, adj., unlawful, wrongful, illicit, illegal

149 Unrechtmäßigkeit, f., illegality, character of something which is illegal/unlawful

150 unschuldig, adj., innocent (*beschuldigen)

151 Untätigkeit, f., omission, failure to act

152 Der Staat haftet auch für die Untätigkeit seiner Organe, The state is also (held) responsible for the failure of its organs/agents to act (*Unterlassen)

153 Unterabsatz, m., sub-paragraph (*Buchstabe)

154 Unterausschuß, m., sub-committee

155 der Unterausschuß wurde kraft der Entschließung der Kommission Nummer . . . zur Rechtsstellung

eines Ausschusses erhoben (ECE V),
the sub-committee was raised to
committee status by virtue of Commission Resolution . . .

156 unterbinden, to suppress
157 Unterbindung, f., suppression
158 unterbrechen, to break off, to suspend
159 Unterbrechung, f., breaking off,
suspension
160 unterbreiten, to submit, to refer
161 einem Gericht einen Streitfall unterbreiten, to submit a dispute to a court/
tribunal
162 unterdrücken, to suppress
163 verhindern und unterdrücken, to
prevent and suppress
164 Angriffshandlungen unterdrücken
(CUN 1), to suppress acts of aggression
165 Unterdrückung, f., suppression
166 Unterdrückung des unerlaubten
Handels mit . . ., the suppression of
illicit traffic in . . .
167 unterfertigt, adj., undersigned
168 die unterfertigten Bevollmächtigten
(ICCA), the undersigned plenipotentiaries
(*unterzeichnet)
169 Untergang, m., extinction, lapse,
disappearance
170 bei Untergang eines Staates, where/
when a state has become extinct/ex-
tinguished
171 Untergang eines Vertragspartners,
extinction of a party to a/the treaty
172 Untergang eines Rechtes/Anspruchs,
extinction/lapse of a right
173 untergehen, to be extinguished, to
lapse, to disappear
174 untergeordnet, adj., subordinate
175 Untergliederung, f., sub-division
176 politische Untergliederungen der
Vertragspartei (NATOSF I), political sub-divisions of the contracting
party
(*Gebietskörperschaft)
177 Untergruppe, f., sub-group
178 Unterhändler, m., representative,
delegate, delegate to conduct
negotiations
(*Vertreter)

179 Unterhändlervollmachten, f.pl.,
full powers (to negotiate), pleins
pouvoirs
(*Vollmachten)
180 Unterkommission, f., sub-commission
181 unterlassen, to omit, to fail (to do),
to refrain (from doing) (often best
translated by . . . shall not . . .)
182 der Empfangsstaat unterläßt alle
Maßnahmen, die . . ., the receiving
state shall not take any action
which . . .
183 Alle Mitglieder unterlassen jede
Androhung oder Anwendung von
Gewalt (CUN 2), All members shall
refrain from the threat or use of
force
184 unterläßt es ein Vertragsstaat . . .,
in the event of a contracting state
failing to . . .
185 Unterlassen, n., omission, failure to
act
186 ein Tun oder ein Unterlassen, an act
or omission
187 Unterlassung, f., omission, failure
to act
188 eine vor Inkrafttreten dieses Vertrags begangene Handlung oder
Unterlassung (CSMW 3), an act or
omission which occurred before the
date of entry into force of the present Convention
189 unterliegen, to be subject/liable to
190 Der diplomatische Kurier unterliegt
keiner Festnahme oder Haft irgendwelcher Art (VCDR 27), The diplomatic courier shall not be liable to
any form of arrest or detention
191 Der amtliche Schriftverkehr und die
übrigen amtlichen Mitteilungen des
Ministerkomitees unterliegen nicht
der Zensur (PrivExCE 8), No censorship shall be applied to the official correspondence and other
communications of the Committee
of Ministers
192 die freie Reise . . . unterliegt keiner
Beschränkung (WEUS 16), no restriction shall be imposed on the
free movement . . .
193 Unterordnungsverhältnis,   n.

(= *Vasallenverhältnis, *n.*), vassalage

194 **unterscheiden,** to distinguish

195 **Unterscheidung,** *f.*, distinction

196   **ohne Unterscheidung zwischen ständigen und nichtständigen Mitgliedern des Sicherheitsrats,** without any distinction between permanent and non-permanent members of the Security Council

197   **(ohne) Unterscheidung nach Rasse, Farbe, Geschlecht, Sprache, Religion, politischer und sonstiger Überzeugung, nationaler oder sozialer Herkunft, nach Eigentum, Geburt oder sonstigen Umständen (UDHR 2),** (without) distinction of race, colour, sex, language, religion, political or other opinion, national or social origin, property, birth or other status (*Unterschied, *Beschränkung)

198 **Unterschied,** *m.*, distinction

199   **ohne Unterschied der Rasse,** without distinction of/as to race

200   **zu einer größeren Harmonie unter den Völkern beitragen, unabhängig von den Unterschieden in ihren politischen Systemen,** to contribute to a greater harmony between peoples, regardless of differences in their political systems (*Unterscheidung, *Beschränkung, *and* Art. 5 CERD *in Annex* 9)

201 **unterschreiben,** to sign

202 **Unterschrift,** *f.*, signature

203   **mit seiner Unterschrift versehen,** to append one's signature

204   **Zu Urkund dessen haben die unterzeichneten, hierzu gehörig befugten Bevollmächtigten dieses Abkommen mit ihren Unterschriften versehen,** In witness whereof the undersigned Plenipotentiaries, duly empowered, have appended their signatures to the present Agreement

205 **Unterseebootkrieg,** *m.*, submarine warfare

206   **uneingeschränkter Unterseebootkrieg,** unrestricted submarine warfare

207 **unterstehen,** to be under/subject to (the authority of) (gemeinsame *Hoheit)

208 **unterstellen,** to place under, to subject to

209   **der örtlichen Gerichtsbarkeit unterstellt,** subject to local jurisdiction

210 **untersuchen,** to examine, to inquire into, to conduct an inquiry into

211 **Untersuchung,** *f.*, inquiry, examination

212   **Eine Untersuchung stellt den Sachverhalt eines Streitfalles fest,** An inquiry elicits the facts of a dispute

213   **Die Untersuchung erfolgt kontradiktorisch** (HgI 19), At the inquiry both sides must be heard

214   **eine Untersuchung vornehmen,** to carry out/conduct an inquiry

215 **Untersuchungsabkommen,** *n.*, Inquiry Convention, Convention of Inquiry (*both* HgI) (*Beisitzer)

216 **Untersuchungsausschuß,** *m.*, committee of inquiry

217 **Untersuchungsausschußverfahren,** *n.*, procedure of/for/(to be) used by committees of inquiry

218 **Untersuchungskommission,** *f.*, commission of inquiry

219 **Untersuchungsverfahren,** *n.*, inquiry procedure, procedure of inquiry

220 **unterwerfen** (+ *dat.*), to subject (to)

221   **sich unterwerfen** (+ *dat.*), to submit (to)

222   **sich der obligatorischen Gerichtsbarkeit des IGHs unterwerfen,** to submit to the compulsory jurisdiction of the ICJ (*unterworfen)

223 **Unterwerfung,** *f.*, subjugation, submission

224   **Unterwerfung von Völkern unter ein fremdes Joch,** subjugation of peoples to (a) foreign jurisdiction/power

225   **kriegerische Unterwerfung,** subjugation by armed force

226 **unterworfen,** *adj.*, subjected; subjugated

227 **alle dem Staat unterworfenen Personen,** all persons subject to the state/to the state's jurisdiction (*unterwerfen)

228 **unterzeichnen,** to sign

229 **einen Vertrag/ein Abkommen unterzeichnen,** to sign a treaty/agreement

230 **Unterzeichner,** *m.,* signatory, signatory state/government, state/government signatory to (a treaty)

231 **Unterzeichnerpartei,** *f.,* signatory party

232 **Unterzeichnerregierung,** *f.,* signatory government

233 **Unterzeichner- und beitretende Regierungen,** signatory and acceding governments

234 **die in Anlage . . . aufgeführten Unterzeichnerregierungen,** the Governments signatory hereto and listed in Annex . . .

235 **Unterzeichnerstaat,** *m.,* signatory state/country

236 **unterzeichnet,** *adj.,* undersigned, signatory

237 **die unterzeichneten Regierungen, Mitglieder des Europarats (ECSM Pr),** the Governments signatory hereto, being members of the Council of Europe

238 **Unterzeichneter,** *adj.n.,* undersigned

239 **die hierzu gehörig befugten Unterzeichneten (SF 117),** the undersigned, being duly authorized thereto/to that effect

240 **die hierzu gehörig beglaubigten Unterzeichneten (ECC 11),** the undersigned, duly authorized thereto

241 **Unterzeichnung,** *f.,* signing, signature

242 **Die Unterzeichnung verpflichtet die Staaten, den Vertrag zur Annahme oder Ablehnung den dazu ermächtigten Stellen vorzulegen,** The signing of a treaty obliges the States to present the treaty for acceptance or rejection to those organs which are empowered to accept or reject it

243 **Dieses Abkommen tritt einen Monat nach seiner Unterzeichnung in Kraft,** The present agreement shall enter into force one month from the date of signature thereof

244 **Nicht-Mitgliedstaaten, an die die Generalversammlung eine Aufforderung zur Unterzeichnung gerichtet hat (PCG 11),** non-member states to which an invitation to sign has been addressed by the General Assembly

245 **Die Satzung wird zur Unterzeichnung aufgelegt (SF 96),** The statute shall be opened for signature

246 **Unterzeichnung ohne Vorbehalt/ unter Vorbehalt der Ratifizierung,** signature without/with reservation in respect of ratification

247 **im Zeitpunkt der Unterzeichnung (PHR Prot 4),** at the time of signature

248 **nachträgliche Unterzeichnung,** deferred/subsequent signature

249 **Unterzeichnung** *ad referendum,* signature *ad referendum* (*Unterschrift, *and* VCLOT 77 *and* 81 *in Annexes* 15 *and* 5)

250 **Unterzeichnungsprotokoll,** *n.,* protocol of signature

251 **Unterzeichnungsurkunde,** *f.,* instrument of signature

252 **unveräußerlich,** *adj.,* inherent, inalienable

253 **unveräußerliche Rechte,** inalienable rights

254 **unveräußerliches Vermögen,** inalienable property

255 **unverbindlich,** *adj.,* non-binding, non-obligatory, non-compulsory, non-mandatory

256 **Unverbindlichkeit,***f.,*non-binding/ non-obligatory/ non-compulsory/ non-mandatory nature/ character

257 **unvereinbar,** *adj.,* incompatible, inconsistent

258 **mit den Zielen der UN unvereinbare Androhung von Gewalt (CUN 2),** use of force inconsistent with the purposes of the UN

259 **unvereinbar mit Ziel und Zweck des Vertrags (VCLOT 19),** incompatible with the object and purpose of the treaty

260 **Unvereinbarkeit,** *f.*, incompatibility, inconsistency

261 **Es besteht keine Unvereinbarkeit zwischen den Zielen des NV-Vertrags und des EURATOM-Vertrags,** There is no incompatibility between the aims of the Non-Proliferation Treaty and those of the Treaty establishing EURATOM

262 **unverletzbar,** *adj.*, inviolable

263 **Unverletzbarkeit,** *f.*, inviolability (*Unverletzlichkeit)

264 **unverletzlich,** *adj.*, inviolable

265 **Unverletzlichkeit,** *f.*, inviolability

266 **Unverletzlichkeit der Person,** inviolability of the person

267 **die Unverletzlichkeit seiner Person oder seiner Wohnung beeinträchtigen** (VCDR 31), to infringe the inviolability of his person or of his residence

268 **die Unverletzlichkeit der Grenzen und die Achtung der territorialen Integrität** (GrV), the inviolability of frontiers and the respect for territorial integrity

269 **Unverletzlichkeit der Mission,** inviolability of the mission

270 **Unverletzlichkeit aller Schriftstücke und Dokumente/Urkunden,** inviolability of all papers and documents

271 **Verfahren zur Erlangung der Unverletzlichkeit** (PCP), procedure to obtain immunity

272 **Aufhebung der Unverletzlichkeit** (PCP 11), withdrawal of immunity

273 **persönliche Unverletzlichkeit,** personal inviolability

274 **unverteidigt,** *adj.*, undefended

275 **unverteidigte Städte,** undefended towns (HgI), open cities

276 **unvollstreckbar,** *adj.*, unenforceable, incapable of execution

277 **Unvollstreckbarkeit,** *f.*, impossibility of execution, unenforceability

278 **unwirksam,** *adj.*, inoperative, not in effect, not having efficacy

279 **unzulässig,** *adj.*, inadmissible, illegal, unlawful, illicit

280 **Unzulässigkeit,** *f.*, inadmissibility, illegality, unlawfulness

281 **unzuständig** *adj.* **(für),** not responsible, not competent, lacking/not possessing responsibility/competence (for) (*zuständig)

282 **Unzuständigkeit,** *f.*, lack of responsibility/competence, incompetence (*Zuständigkeit)

283 **Urheberrecht,** *n.* (UCC), copyright

284 **Ausübung des Urheberrechts,** enjoyment of copyright

285 **Erwerb des Urheberrechts,** acquisition of copyright

286 **Inhaber des Urheberrechts,** copyright proprietor

287 **Schutz des Urheberrechts,** protection of copyright

288 **Urkund: zu Urkund dessen,** in witness whereof, in faith whereof

289 **Zu Urkund dessen haben die hierzu gehörig befugten Vertreter der Regierungen, die an dieser Tagung teilgenommen haben, diese Schlußakte unterzeichnet** (SF 144), In witness whereof the duly authorized representatives of the Governments which have taken part in that session have signed the present Final Act (*Unterschrift *and* VCLOT 85 *in Annex* 5)

290 **Urkunde,** *f.*, document, instrument

291 **Urkunden, die einen Vertrag bilden** (VCLOT 18), instruments constituting a treaty

292 **eine Übereinkunft in einer oder in mehreren zusammengehörigen Urkunden** (VCLOT 2), an agreement in a single instrument or in two or more related instruments

293 **Urkunden der Verwaltungsbehörden** (CLPD 1), administrative documents

294 **Urkunden, die von diplomatischen Vertretern errichtet sind** (CLPD 1), documents executed by diplomatic agents

295 **außergerichtliche Urkunden** (VCCR 5), extra-judicial documents

296 **gerichtliche Urkunden,** judicial documents

297 **maßgebende Urkunden,** authoritative documents
298 **die für die Organisationen maßgebenden Urkunden** (SF 77), the basic instruments/documents of the organizations
299 **notarielle Urkunden** (CLPD 1), notarial acts
300 **öffentliche Urkunden,** public documents
301 **ausländische öffentliche Urkunden von der diplomatischen oder konsularischen Legalisation befreien** (CLPD Pr), to abolish the requirement of diplomatic or consular legalization for foreign public documents
302 **sachdienliche Urkunden,** relevant documents
303 **zwischenstaatliche Urkunden** (ECE VII), intergovernmental documents (*Beitritt, *also relevant compounds, e.g.* *Beitrittsurkunde)
304 **Urschrift,** *f.,* original, original text
305 **beglaubigte Abschriften der Urschrift sowie weitere Texte des Vertrags in zusätzlichen Sprachen** (VCLOT 77), certified copies of the original text and any further text of the treaty in additional languages
306 **in doppelter Urschrift,** in duplicate
307 **in einer Urschrift,** in a single copy
308 **geschehen zu Genf am 10.3.55 in einer Urschrift in englischer und französischer Sprache, wobei jeder Wortlaut gleichermaßen verbindlich ist** (SF 144), done at Geneva in a single copy in the English and French languages, both texts authentic, this 10th day of March 1955
309 **in zwei Urschriften,** in duplicate
310 **Ursprung,** *m.,* origin
311 **ethnischer Ursprung,** ethnic origin
312 **nationaler Ursprung,** national origin
313 **ursprünglich,** *adj.,* original
314 **ursprüngliche Anerkennung,** original recognition
315 **ursprüngliches Mitglied,** original member
316 **ursprüngliche Mitgliedschaft,** original membership
317 **ursprünglicher Mitgliedstaat,** original member state
318 **ursprünglicher Vertrag,** original treaty
319 **ursprüngliche Vertragspartei,** original party to a/the treaty
320 **Ursprungsgebiet,** *n.,* area/territory of origin
321 **Ursprungsland,** *n.,* country of origin
322 **Ursprungsregeln,** *f.pl.* (EFTA), rules of origin
323 **Ursprungszeugnis,** *n.,* certificate of origin
324 **Urstück,** *n.,* original (text) (*Urschrift)
325 **Urteil,** *n.,* judgment, award (sentence *normally in criminal cases only, rare in international law*)
326 **Entscheidungen in der Form von Urteilen,** decisions in the form of written judgments
327 **Die Urteile sind mit Gründen zu versehen/sind zu begründen,** Judgments shall state the reasons on which they are based
328 **Das Urteil des Gerichtshofes ist dem Ministerialrat zuzuleiten: dieser überwacht seine Durchführung** (PHR 54), The judgment of the court shall be transmitted to the Committee of Ministers which shall supervise its execution
329 **jede einem Urteil vorausgehende Maßnahme** (PPELDO 5), any provisional judicial constraint
330 **Urteile und Verfügungen** (CSMW An), judgments and orders
331 **Durchführung des Urteils,** execution of the judgment
332 **Erlaß des Urteils,** pronouncement of the judgment
333 **vor Erlaß des Urteils,** prior to the pronouncement of the judgment
334 **bis zum Erlaß des Urteils des Gerichts** (CRPG An), pending the judgment of the tribunal
335 **Erläuterung des Urteils,** reasoning of the judgment
336 **Revision des Urteils,** revision of the judgment
337 **Vollstreckung des Urteils,**

execution/enforcement of the judgment

338 abweisendes Urteil, adverse judgment, judgment against

339 berufungsfähiges Urteil, appealable judgment

340 bestätigendes Urteil, confirmatory judgment

341 bindendes Urteil, binding judgment

342 endgültiges Urteil, final judgment

343 endgültige Urteile, die von einem Gericht erlassen werden, dem die Gerichtsbarkeit gemäß Art. XI zusteht (VCLD XII), final judgments entered by a court having jurisdiction under Art. XI

344 rechtskräftiges Urteil, final judgment/judgment binding between the parties

345 Die Urteile sind rechtskräftig und unterliegen keinem Rechtsmittel (CRPG An), Judgments shall be final and not subject to appeal
schiedsgerichtliches Urteil = * Schiedsspruch, *m.*

346 vollstreckbares Urteil, enforceable judgment

347 vorbereitendes Urteil, interlocutory judgment

348 vorhergehendes Urteil, previous judgment (*see* * Verurteilung)

349 das Urteil ergeht, the judgment is pronounced/entered

350 solange noch kein endgültiges Urteil ergangen ist (VCLD VI), provided that final judgment has not been entered

351 die Partei, gegen die das Urteil ergangen ist (VCLD XII), the party against whom judgment was pronounced

352 ein Urteil anfechten, to contest/challenge a judgment, to appeal/lodge an appeal against a judgment

353 ein Urteil ausfertigen, to engross a judgment

354 ein Urteil aussprechen, to give/pass/pronounce/hand down/enter/deliver a judgment

355 ein Urteil erlangen, to obtain a judgment

356 in Fällen, in denen das Urteil durch eine Täuschung erlangt wurde (VCLD XII), where judgment was obtained by fraud

357 ein Urteil erlassen/fällen/verkünden, to give/pass/pronounce/hand down/enter/deliver a judgment

358 ein Urteil vollstrecken, to enforce/execute a judgment

359 ein Urteil zustellen, to serve notice of judgment
(* Entscheidung,   * Nachprüfung, * Kammer)

360 Urteilsspruch, *m.,* judgment, award, verdict

361 Usurpation, *f.,* usurpation

362 Usurpator, *m.,* usurpator

363 usurpieren, to usurp

364 Usurpierung, *f.,* usurpation

V

1 **Vasallenstaat**, *m.*, vassal state
2 **Vasallenverhältnis,** *n.* (= Vassalität, *f.*), vassalage
3 **verantworten,** to be responsible/liable (for), to accept/undertake/bear the responsibility/liability (for) (*haften)
4 **verantwortlich,** *adj.*, responsible, liable (*haftbar, *Verantwortlichkeit)
5 **Verantwortlichkeit,** *f.*, responsibility, liability
6 **Eine Hohe Vertragspartei kann weder sich noch eine andere Vertragspartei von den Verantwortlichkeiten befreien, die ihr selbst oder einer anderen Vertragspartei auf Grund von Verletzungen im Sinne des vorstehenden Artikels zufallen** (GC I 51), No High Contracting Party shall be allowed to absolve itself or any other High Contracting Party of any liability incurred by itself or by another High Contracting Party in respect of breaches referred to in the preceding Article
7 **strafrechtliche oder disziplinarische Verantwortlichkeit** (GCHS 11), penal or disciplinary responsibility (* Haftung, *Verantwortung)
8 **Verantwortung,** *f.*, responsibility, liability
9 **einen Staat für Handlungen seiner Organe zur Verantwortung ziehen,** to hold a state responsible for the acts of its organs
10 **Konsuln können wegen Handlungen, die sie in Wahrnehmung konsularischer Aufgaben vorgenommen haben, nicht von den Gerichts- oder Verwaltungsbehörden des Empfangsstaates zur Verantwortung gezogen werden** (VCCR 43), Consular officers shall not be amenable to the jurisdiction of the judicial or administrative authorities of the receiving state in respect of acts performed in the exercise of consular functions

(*Verantwortlichkeit, *Haftung)
11 **Verbalnote,** *f.*, verbal note, *note verbale*
12 **Verband,** *m.*, association, federation, organization, institution (*Berufsverband)
13 **verbieten,** to prohibit, to ban
14 **verbindlich,** *adj.*, binding, obligatory, compulsory
15 **Die Entscheidung ist verbindlich für alle,** The decision shall be binding on all (parties)
16 **gleichermaßen verbindlich,** (*of texts, etc.*) equally authentic
17 **völkerrechtlich verbindlich,** binding under/at international law (*bindend, * Urschrift)
18 **Verbindlichkeit¹,** *f.*, binding nature, binding force
19 **Sie verlieren ihre Verbindlichkeit für eine Vertragspartei** (EMA 19), They shall cease to be binding on a contracting party (*bindende Kraft)
20 **Verbindlichkeit der Normen/Regeln,** binding nature of rules
21 **Verbindlichkeit des Vertragsrechts,** binding force of the law of treaties
22 **Verbindlichkeit²,** *f.*, obligation, liability
23 **alle bestehenden oder zukünftig erwachsenden Verbindlichkeiten** (CSMW IX), all liabilities, either now existing or hereafter arising
24 **eine Verbindlichkeit eingehen,** to contract/to assume a liability/obligation (*haften)
25 **Verbindung,** *f.*, link, connection, liaison
26 **echte Verbindung,** genuine link (*Bindung²)
27 **eine engere Verbindung zwischen den Mitgliedern,** a closer link between the members
28 **Verbindungsausschuß,** *m.*, liaison committee
29 **Verbindungsgruppe,** *f.*, liaison group

30 **Verbindungsstelle,** *f.,* liaison office

31 **Verbindungsstelle der ILO,** ILO liaison office

32 **Verbot,** *n.,* prohibition, interdiction, ban, proscription, duty not to

33 **Verbot chartawidriger Gewaltanwendung,** prohibition/proscription of the use of (armed) force in violation of the charter

34 **das Verbot der Einmischung,** ban/prohibition on/against intervention, duty not to intervene

35 **Verbote und Beschränkungen,** prohibitions and restrictions

36 **ein Verbot erlassen,** to order a prohibition/ban

37 **einem Verbot unterliegen,** to be prohibited/banned

38 **verboten,** *adj.,* prohibited, proscribed, banned, unlawful, illegal

39 **Verbotsnorm,** *f.,* rule prohibiting

40 **Verbotszone,** *f.,* prohibited zone, zone into which entry is prohibited

41 **Verbrechen,** *n.,* offence, crime (*normally a major offence, more serious than* *Vergehen, *which is in turn more serious than* *Übertretung)

42 **Verbrechen gegen den Frieden,** crime against peace

43 **Verbrechen gegen die Menschheit,** crime against humanity

44 **Verbrechen gegen das Völkerrecht,** offence against international law

45 **verbreiten,** to spread, to proliferate

46 **Verbreitung,** *f.,* spread, proliferation

47 **Verbreitung von Kernwaffen,** proliferation of nuclear weapons

48 **Verbundenheit,** *f.,* solidarity

49 **die Verbundenheit Europas mit den überseeischen Ländern zu bekräftigen** (EEC Pr), to confirm the solidarity which binds Europe and the overseas countries

50 **vereinbar** *adj.* **mit,** compatible/consistent with

51 **vereinbaren,** to arrange, to agree, to agree upon

52 **die Regierungen haben folgendes vereinbart:** the Governments have agreed as follows/have agreed on the following provisions:

53 **die Hohen Vertragsschließenden Parteien vereinbaren, daß ...** (TRW II), the High Contracting Parties agree that ...

54 **sofern die Parteien nichts anderes vereinbaren,** in the absence of agreement to the contrary between the parties (*übereinkommen)

55 **Vereinbarkeit** *f.* **mit,** compatibility/consistency with

56 **vereinbart,** *adj.,* agreed, agreed upon

57 **vereinbarte Erklärung,** agreed declaration

58 **vereinbarte Niederschrift,** agreed minutes

59 **hierbei gilt als vereinbart, daß ...,** it is understood/agreed in this connection that ...

60 **Vereinbarung,** *f.,* agreement, arrangement, memorandum of agreement/understanding, consent

61 **... daß Ihre Note und diese Antwortnote eine Vereinbarung zwischen unseren beiden Regierungen bilden sollen, ...** that your note and this note in reply shall constitute an agreement between our two Governments

62 **anderweitige Vereinbarung,** agreement to the contrary

63 **besondere Vereinbarung,** special agreement

64 **gegenteilige Vereinbarung,** agreement to the contrary

65 **mündliche Vereinbarung,** oral agreement

66 **nachbarliche Vereinbarung,** voisinage arrangement (FC 6)

67 **schriftliche Vereinbarung,** agreement in writing

68 **zweiseitige Vereinbarung,** bilateral agreement

69 **Die Vertragschließenden können durch zweiseitige Vereinbarungen Übergangsregelungen treffen** (ECSM 17), The contracting parties may, by bilateral arrangement, take interim measures

(*See particularly note to* *Vertrag *in*
Annex 1.)

70 **Vereinbarungsentwurf, m.**, draft
agreement

71 **der dem vorliegenden Abkommen
beigefügte Vereinbarungsentwurf,**
the draft agreement annexed to the
present convention

72 **Vereinbarungslehre,** *f.*, theory of
consent/common consent

73 **Vereinheitlichung,** *f.*, creation/
achievement of uniformity

74 **eine möglichst weitgehende
Vereinheitlichung der Förmlichkeiten, Dokumentenerfordernisse
und Verfahren** (CFIMT II), the
highest practicable degree of uniformity in formalities, documentary
requirements and procedures

75 **Vereinigung,** *f.*, association

76 **Vereinigungsfreiheit,** *f.*, (= *Vereins
freiheit, *f:*), freedom of association

77 **Vereinigungsrecht, n.**, right of
association, right to organize (ES 5)
Vereinsfreiheit, *f.* = *Vereinigungsfreiheit, *f.*

78 **vereiteln,** to frustrate, to impair, to
thwart

79 **Verpflichtung, Ziel und Zweck eines
Vertrags vor seinem Inkrafttreten
nicht zu vereiteln** (VCLOT 18),
obligation not to defeat the object
and purpose of a treaty prior to its
entry into force
(*See* CERD 1 *in Annex* 12.)

80 **Verfahren, n.**, procedure, proceed-
ing(s), process, method

81 **Die Kommission legt selbst ihr Verfahren fest** (GCF 9), The Commission shall determine its own procedure

82 **das gleiche Verfahren wird ange-
wendet, wenn . . .,** the same procedure shall apply if . . .

83 **Das Verfahren gliedert sich in ein
schriftliches und ein mündliches
Verfahren** (SICJ 43), The procedure
shall consist of two parts: written
and oral

84 **das Verfahren der Generalversammlung** (CUN 35), the proceedings of the General Assembly

85 **das Verfahren für die Wahl des
Präsidenten des Wirtschafts- und
Sozialrats** (CUN 72), the method of
selecting the President of the
Economic and Social Council

86 **die Führung des Verfahrens** (SICJ
48), the conduct of the case

87 **abgekürztes Verfahren,** summary
procedure

88 **festgelegtes Verfahren,** established
procedure

89 **geltendes Verfahren,** current/estab-
lished procedure

90 **gerichtliches/gesetzliches Verfahren,**
legal proceedings/process, judicial
proceedings/process

91 **Immunität gegen gerichtliche Verfahren** (IMF IX), immunity from
judicial process/legal process

92 **nach ordnungsgemäßem gesetz-
lichem Verfahren** (GCHS 11),
after due legal process

93 **mehrseitiges Verfahren,** multilateral
procedure(s)

94 **mündliches Verfahren,** oral proceedings

95 **das mündliche Verfahren besteht
in . . .** (SICJ 43), the oral proceedings shall consist of . . .

96 **nichtstrafrechtliches Verfahren,**
non-criminal proceedings

97 **öffentliches Verfahren,** public trial,
public proceedings (*see* *beschuldigen)

98 **ordentliches Verfahren,** regular trial
(GC IV), regular proceedings

99 **schriftliches Verfahren,** written proceedings

100 **Abschriften des gesamten schriftlichen Verfahrens übermitteln**
(SICJ 34), to communicate copies
of the written proceedings

101 **Das schriftliche Verfahren besteht
aus Klageschrift, Klagebeantwortung, und aus einer Replik und
einer Duplik** (CRPG An), written
proceedings shall consist of a
statement of the complainant's
case, the defendant's answer, and
a reply and a rejoinder

102 **strafrechtliches Verfahren,** criminal
proceedings

103   summarisches Verfahren, summary
       procedure
104   verfassungsmäßiges Verfahren, con-
       stitutional procedure
105   im Einklang mit seinem verfas-
          sungsmäßigen Verfahren (ICCPR
          2), in accordance with its constitu-
          tional processes
106   Verfahrensantrag, m., procedural
       motion
107   Verfahrensausschuß, m., pro-
       cedural committee
108   Verfahrensfrage, f., procedural
       matter, question of procedure
109   Verfahrensordnung f. des Gerichts-
       hofs (SICJ 25), rules of the court
110   Verfahrensrecht, n., procedural
       law
111   Verfahrensregel, f., rule of proce-
       dure
112   Verfassung, f., constitution
       (*Satzung)
113   Verfassungsakt, m., constitutional
       act
114   Verfassungsbruch, m., breach/vio-
       lation of the constitution
115   Verfassungsgericht, n., constitu-
       tional court
116   verfassungsmäßig, adj., constitu-
       tional
117   verfassungsmäßige Ordnung, con-
          stitutional order/system
118   verfassungsmäßiges Verfahren, con-
          stitutional procedure
119   dieses Protokoll bedarf der Rati-
          fikation   durch   die   Unter-
          zeichnerstaaten nach Maßgabe ih-
          rer eigenen verfassungsmäßigen
          Verfahren (PCP Prot), the pre-
          sent protocol shall be subject to
          ratification by signatory states in
          accordance with their respective
          constitutional procedures
120   Verfassungsmäßigkeit, f., con-
       stitutionality
121   Verfassungsordnung, f., constitu-
       tional order/system
122   nach der Verfassungsordnung des
          Bundes, under the constitutional
          system of the federation
123   Verfassungsrecht, n., constitu-
       tional law

124   Ratifizierung durch die Unterzeich-
          nerstaaten nach Maßgabe ihres Ver-
          fassungsrechts (CUN 110), ratifica-
          tion by the signatory states in accor-
          dance with their constitutional pro-
          cesses
          (verfassungsmäßiges *Verfahren)
125   verfassungsrechtlich, adj., con-
       stitutional
126   verfassungsrechtliche   Bestim-
          mungen, constitutional provisions
127   verfassungsrechtliche Erfordernisse,
          constitutional requirements
128   verfassungsrechtliche   Gepflogen-
          heiten,   constitutional   customs/
          usage, customary constitutional pro-
          cedures
129   verfassungsrechtliches   Verfahren,
          constitutional procedure/process
130   verfassungsrechtliche   Vorschriften,
          constitutional   rules   (and regula-
          tions)
131   Verfassungsvorschrift, f., con-
       stitutional rule
132   nach den Verfassungsvorschriften
          eines jeden von ihnen (SC 8), in
          accordance with the constitutional
          procedure of each (state)
133   Verfassungswidrigkeit, f., uncon-
       stitutionality
134   verfolgen¹, to persecute
135   ... die begründete Befürchtung
          hegt, wegen seiner Rasse, Religion,
          Staatsangehörigkeit, Zugehörigkeit
          zu einer bestimmten sozialen Gruppe
          oder wegen seiner politischen Über-
          zeugung verfolgt zu werden (ARS
          3), ... has well-founded fear of
          being persecuted for reasons of
          race, religion, nationality, mem-
          bership of a particular social group
          or political opinion
136   verfolgen², to pursue
       (*nacheilen)
137   verfolgen³, to prosecute
       (*Verfolgung³)
138   Verfolgung¹, f., persecution
139   nationale/politische/rassische   Ver-
          folgung,   national/political/racial
          persecution
140   Verfolgung², f., pursuit
       (*Nacheile)

141 **Verfolgung**[3], *f.*, prosecution
142   **gerichtliche Verfolgung,** prosecution, suit
143   **Schutz gegen Verhaftung und gerichtliche Verfolgung** (PrivEx-CE 15), exemption from arrest and prosecution
144   **im Falle einer gerichtlichen Verfolgung** (GC IV 5), in the case of trial
145 **Verfügung**[1], *f.*, order, directive, direction, injunction
146   **der Gerichtshof erläßt Verfügungen für die Führung des Verfahrens** (SICJ 48), the court shall make orders for the conduct of the case
147   **einstweilige Verfügung,** interim injunction (*Entscheidung)
148 **Verfügung**[2], *f.*, disposal, disposition
149   **endgültige Verfügung** (CSMW), final disposal
150   **letztwillige Verfügung** (CSMW X), testamentary disposition, last will and testament
151 **Vergehen,** *n.*, offence (*note to* *Verbrechen)
152 **vergelten,** to retaliate against
153 **Vergeltung,** *f.*, retaliation, reprisal
154 **Vergeltungsakt,** *m.*, retaliatory act
155 **Vergeltungsmaßnahme,** *f.*, retaliatory measure
156   **Vergeltungsmaßnahmen gegen Kriegsgefangene sind untersagt** (GC III 13), Measures of reprisal against prisoners of war are prohibited
157 **Vergleich,** *m.*, conciliation, composition, arrangement
158   **einen Vergleich zwischen den Parteien herbeiführen** (ECPSD 15), to bring the parties to an agreement
159 **Vergleichsausschuß,** *m.*, conciliation committee
160 **Vergleichskommission,** *f.*, conciliation commission
161   **Besondere Vergleichskommission** (ECPSD), Special Conciliation Commission
162 **Vergleichsverfahren,** *n.*, (procedure of) conciliation, composition proceedings, proceedings leading to

an arrangement
163   **vor Anrufung des IGHs ein Vergleichsverfahren einleiten** (VCDR Opt. Prot), to adopt a conciliation procedure before resorting to the ICJ
164   **Bei einem Vergleichsverfahren versucht die internationale Instanz nicht, den Parteien eine bestimmte Lösung aufzuzwingen,** In conciliation the international tribunal does not attempt to impose a specific solution on the parties
165 **Vergütung,** *f.*, emoluments (*e.g. of members of an arbitral tribunal*)
166 **Verhältnismäßigkeit,** *f.*, proportionality
167   **Grundsatz der Verhältnismäßigkeit bei Repressalien,** principle of proportionality in the case of reprisals
168 **verhandeln**[1], to negotiate
169 **verhandeln**[2], to hear (a case)
170 **Verhandlung**[1], *f.*, negotiation
171   **durch Verhandlungen beilegen,** to resolve/settle by negotiation(s)
172   **Abbruch der Verhandlungen,** breaking off of negotiations
173   **Aufnahme der Verhandlungen,** start/commencement of negotiations
174   **Führung der Verhandlungen,** conduct of negotiations
175   **Vertagung der Verhandlungen,** adjournment of negotiations
176 **Verhandlung**[2], *f.*, proceedings, hearing(s)
177   **Die Verhandlungen werden vom Präsidenten geleitet** (SICJ 45), The hearing shall be under the control of the President
178   **Die Verhandlungen sind öffentlich** (CRPG An), The tribunal shall sit in public
179   **Die mündliche Verhandlung ist öffentlich** (SICJ 46), The hearing in court shall be public (*Rechtsbehelf[1])
180 **Verhandlungsausschuß,** *m.*, negotiating committee
181 **Verhandlungsbericht,** *m.*, record/minutes of the case/of proceedings (*Protokoll[2])

182 **Verhandlungsfreiheit,** f., freedom to negotiate

183 **Verhandlungspartner,** m., (other) negotiating party

184 **Verhandlungsstaat,** m., negotiating state
(*See* VCLOT 2 *in Annex* 14.)

185 **Verhandlungsvollmacht,** f., power(s)/authority to negotiate/to conduct negotiations
(*Vollmacht)

186 **Verhandlungsweg** m., **auf dem/in dem,** by negotiation

187 **Die Abkommen werden im Verhandlungsweg ausgearbeitet** (CUN 43), The agreements shall be negotiated

188 **Verifikation,** f. (= Verifizierung, f.), verification

189 **Verifikationsabkommen,** n. (TNPNW), verification agreement

190 **verjährbar,** adj., subject to limitation/prescription

191 **Verjährbarkeit,** f., limitation, prescription

192 **verjähren,** to be/become void/barred by prescription/limitation, to lapse

193 **verjährt,** adj., lapsed, barred by limitation/prescription

194 **verjährter Anspruch,** lapsed right/entitlement/claim

195 **Verjährung,** f., limitation, prescription, lapse of time (EExt 10)
(*Erlöschen)

196 **Verjährungsfrist,** f., period of limitation/prescription

197 **Verkehr¹,** m., traffic, transport

198 **Verkehr²,** m., communication

199 **im Verkehr mit der Regierung** (VCDR 27), in communicating with the government

200 **Der Empfangsstaat gestattet und schützt den freien Verkehr der Mission** (VCDR 27), The receiving state shall permit and protect free communication on the part of the mission

201 **Verkehr³,** m., intercourse

202 **der gegenseitige Verkehr zwischen den Mitgliedern der Völkerrechtsgemeinschaft,** mutual intercourse between the members of the international community

203 **diplomatischer Verkehr,** diplomatic intercourse

204 **zwischenstaatlicher Verkehr,** international/intergovernmental intercourse, intercourse between states

205 **Verkehrsabkommen,** n., transport agreement

206 **Verkehrsausschuß,** m., transport committee

207 **Verkehrsfreiheit,** f. (VCDR 35), freedom of communication

208 **verklagbar,** adj., liable to process

209 **Diese Personen sind jederzeit verklagbar,** A charge may be brought against these persons at any time

210 **verklagen,** to bring an action/charge against, to take proceedings against

211 **verkünden,** to pronounce, to deliver (*e.g. a judgment*)
(*verlesen)

212 **Verkündung,** f., pronouncement

213 **verlängern,** to extend, to prolong, to renew

214 **Das Abkommen wird um jeweils 5 Jahre stillschweigend verlängert,** The Convention shall be tacitly extended for successive periods of 5 years
(*Geltungsdauer erneuern/verlängern)

215 **Verlängerung,** f., extension, prolongation, renewal

216 **die Verlängerung von Teil II des Abkommens** (EMA 31), the prolongation of Part II of the Agreement

217 **ausdrückliche Verlängerung,** explicit extension

218 **stillschweigende Verlängerung,** tacit/implied extension
(*verlängern)

219 **Verlängerungsprotokoll,** n., protocol of extension

220 **verleihen,** to grant

221 **Rechte/Staatsangehörigkeit (usw) verleihen,** to grant rights/nationality (etc.)

222 **Wirksamkeit/Wirkung verleihen,** to give effect

223 **den Empfehlungen des Ausschusses Wirksamkeit verleihen,** to give

effect to the recommendations of
the committee
224 **verlesen,** to read, to deliver
225 **(das Urteil) wird in öffentlicher Sit-**
zung verlesen (SICJ 58), (the judgment) shall be read in open court
226 **verletzen,** to violate, to infringe, to
injure
227 **verletzter Staat,** injured state, state
against whom the wrong/delin-
quency has been committed
228 **Verletzung,** *f.,* violation, infringement, breach, injury
229 **Verletzung einer Bestimmung,** violation of a provision
230 **Verletzung wesentlicher Form-**
vorschriften (ECSC 33), infringement of an essential procedural
requirement
231 **Verletzung der Verpflichtungen**
(EAEC 142), infringement of the
obligations
232 **Verletzung einer internationalen**
Verpflichtung (SICJ 36), breach of
an international obligation
233 **Verletzung des Völkerrechts,** violation of international law
234 **behauptete Verletzung,** alleged violation
(*Verantwortlichkeit)
235 **Verlust,** *m.,* loss
236 **Verlust eines Gebiets/der Staats-**
angehörigkeit, loss of (a) territory/
nationality
237 **Verlustgrund,** *m.,* reason for (the)
loss
(Verlust der *Staatsangehörigkeit)
238 **verlustig gehen/werden,** to lose,
to forfeit
239 **eines Rechtes verlustig gehen,** to forfeit a right
240 **. . . so kann eine solche Person der**
Rechte für verlustig erklärt werden
(GC IV 5), . . . such person shall be
regarded as having forfeited the
rights
241 **Vermächtnis,** *n.,* legacy
242 **Die Zentrale kann Zuwendungen**
und Vermächtnisse entgegennehmen
(ICPCP 11), The Centre may
receive gifts and legacies
243 **vermitteln,** to mediate

244 **vermittelnd,** *adj.,* mediatory
245 **vermittelnde Tätigkeit,** mediatory
function
246 **Vermittler,** *m.,* mediator
247 **ein Verzeichnis qualifizierter Juri-**
sten als Vermittler (VCLOT An), a
list of conciliators consisting of
qualified jurists
248 **Vermittlung,** *f.,* mediation
249 **durch Vermittlung des Generalse-**
kretärs der UN (ICCPR 4), through
the intermediary of the Secretary-
General of the UN
250 **Vermittlungsausschuß,** *m.,* mediation committee
251 **Vermittlungskommission,** *f.,*
mediation commission; joint conference (SICJ 12)
252 **Vermittlungsvorschlag,** *m.,*
mediatory proposal
253 **Vermögen,** *n.,* property
254 **Vermögen der Mission,** property of
the mission
255 **bewegliches Vermögen,** movable
property
256 **bewegliches Vermögen des Ver-**
storbenen (VCDR 39), movable
property of the deceased
257 **Der Rat kann bewegliches und**
unbewegliches Vermögen erwer-
ben und darüber verfügen, The
Council shall have the capacity to
acquire and dispose of movable
and immovable property
258 **unbewegliches Vermögen,** immovable property
259 **soweit es sich um unbewegliches**
Vermögen handelt (CCFTD 1), as
far as immovables are concerned
260 **privates, im Hoheitsgebiet des**
Empfangsstaates gelegenes unbe-
wegliches Vermögen (VCDR 34),
private immovable property situated in the territory of the receiving state
261 **Vermögen veräußern,** to dispose of
property
(*Rechtspersönlichkeit)
262 **Vermögensabgabe,** *f.,* property
tax/levy
263 **Vermögensgegenstand,** *m.,* property, item of property

264   im Inland erworbene Vermögens-
       gegenstände (VCDR 39), property
       acquired in the country
265   Vermögenswert, *m*., property,
       asset
266   die Vermögenswerte des Fonds
       (EPU), the assets of the fund
267   der Rat, seine Vermögenswerte und
       Guthaben (PrivExCE 3), the Coun-
       cil, its property and assets
268   rückerstattete   Vermögenswerte,
       restituted property
269   vermuten, to presume
270   Vermutung, *f*., presumption
271   gesetzliche Vermutung, legal pre-
       sumption, presumption of law
272   unwiderlegbare Vermutung, con-
       clusive/irrebuttable presumption
273   widerlegbare Vermutung, incon-
       clusive/rebuttable presumption
274   Vermutung entkräften/widerlegen,
       to rebut a presumption
275   vernehmen, to question, to examine,
       to hear the evidence of
276   Die Zeugen werden nacheinander
       und jeder für sich vernommen (HgI
       25), The witnesses are heard in suc-
       cession and separately
277   Vernehmung, *f*., examination, ques-
       tioning
278   Die Vernehmung der Zeugen erfolgt
       durch den Vorsitzenden (HgI 26),
       The examination of witnesses is
       conducted by the President
279   veröffentlichen, to publish (*treaty,
       etc.*), to disclose
       (*Abstimmungsergebnis)
280   Veröffentlichung, *f*., publication,
       disclosure
281   Veröffentlichungspflicht, *f*., duty
       to publish/disclose
282   die dem Sekretariat der UN über-
       tragene   Veröffentlichungspflicht,
       the duty to publish incumbent on
       the Secretariat of the UN
283   Verordnung, *f*., regulation
284   verpflichten, to obligate, to bind
285   die Artikel 11–13 können einen
       Staat nicht verpflichten, . . . (WEUS
       15), the provisions of Articles
       11–13 above shall not require any
       state . . .

286   dieser Artikel ist nicht so auszulegen,
       als verpflichte er einen Vertragsstaat
       . . ., no provision of this article shall
       be construed to require/as requiring
       any contracting state to . . .
287   sich verpflichten, to undertake, to
       pledge oneself
288   Die Vertragsparteien verpflichten
       sich, dem Rat Informationen
       zuzuleiten (CICES 5), The con-
       tracting parties undertake to
       furnish to the Council informa-
       tion
289   verpflichtet, *adj*., obliged, bound
290   die Staaten sind verpflichtet . . ., it
       is the duty of states to/it is incum-
       bent upon states to . . .
291   die Organisation ist verpflichtet . . .
       (PPELDO 25), the organization
       shall be required to . . .
292   Verpflichtung, *f*., obligation, duty,
       undertaking, commitment
293   Verpflichtungen, die auf Verträgen
       beruhen/sich aus Verträgen ergeben,
       obligations arising from treaties
294   Verpflichtungen aus dem Überein-
       kommen (ILOC 24.8), obligations
       arising out of the convention
295   in der Charta der UN enthaltene
       Verpflichtungen, obligations em-
       bodied in the Charter of the UN
296   Einhaltung/Erfüllung einer Ver-
       pflichtung, compliance with/observ-
       ance of an obligation
297   Nichteinhaltung/Nichterfüllung ei-
       ner Verpflichtung, failure to comply
       with/observe an obligation, non-ob-
       servance of/non-compliance with an
       obligation
298   Verletzung einer Verpflichtung,
       breach/violation of an obligation
299   die ihnen obliegenden Verpflich-
       tungen, the obligations incumbent
       upon them
300   vertragliche Verpflichtungen, con-
       tractual obligations
301   die für die Parteien verbindlichen
       vertraglichen   Verpflichtungen
       (ECPSD 26), the contractual
       obligations which are binding on
       the parties
302   völkerrechtliche   Verpflichtungen,

international obligations, the obligations at/under international law

303 **Verpflichtungen bestätigen,** to confirm obligations

304   **die Regierung bestätigt hiermit ihre Verpflichtung, . . .,** the government hereby confirms its obligation to . . .

305 **Verpflichtungen einhalten,** to comply with/to observe obligations

306 **von Verpflichtungen entbinden,** to release from obligations

307 **Verpflichtungen erfüllen,** to fulfil obligations

308 **Verpflichtungen genügen,** to comply with/to observe obligations

309   **die Staaten genügen der Verpflichtung dadurch, daß . . .,** states comply with the/their obligation by . . .

310 **Verpflichtungen nachkommen,** to fulfil/to carry out obligations

311 **Verpflichtungen übernehmen,** to assume/to accept obligations

312   **als heiligen Auftrag die Verpflichtung übernehmen . . .,** (CUN 73), to accept as a sacred trust the obligation . . .
(*abweichen, *hinfällig, *entbinden, *Treu und Glauben)

313 **Verrat,** *m.,* treason, act of treason

314 **Verrechnungswährung,** *f.,* currency of account

315 **versammeln,** to assemble

316 **Versammlung,** *f.,* assembly

317 **Generalversammlung,** General Assembly

318 **Vollversammlung,** Plenary Assembly

319 **beratende Versammlung,** consultative assembly

320 **Versammlungsfreiheit,** *f.,* freedom of assembly

321 **Versammlungs- und Vereinigungsfreiheit zu friedlichen Zwecken** (CERD/UDHR), freedom of peaceful assembly and association

322 **verschicken,** to transfer (*i.e. a population to another area*), to evacuate

323 **Unmittelbar nach Beendigung der Feindseligkeiten wird die so ver-**

schickte Bevölkerung in ihre Heimat zurückgeführt (GC IV 49), Persons thus evacuated shall be transferred back to their homes as soon as hostilities have ceased

324 **Verschickung,** *f.,* transfer, evacuation

325 **Verschickungen oder Räumungen,** transfers or evacuations

326   **Die Schutzmacht wird von Verschickungen und Räumungen verständigt, sobald sie stattgefunden haben** (GC IV 49), The protecting power shall be informed of any transfers and evacuations as soon as they have taken place

327 **verschleppen,** to deport

328 **Verschleppter,** *adj.n.,* deported person

329 **Verschleppung,** *f.,* deportation

330 **verschlüsseln,** to encode, to put in code, to encipher

331 **verschlüsselte Nachrichten,** messages in code or cipher (VCDR 40)

332 **Verschlüsselung,** *f.,* code, encoding

333 **Verschollener,** *adj.n.,* missing person

334   **die Todeserklärung von Verschollenen** (UNCDD), declaration of death of missing persons

335 **Verschollenheit** *f.* **von Personen** (UNCDD), disappearance of persons

336 **versehen mit,** to append (*signature*), to affix (*a seal*)

337 **verseuchen,** to pollute

338 **Verseuchung,** *f.,* pollution (*radioaktiv*)

339 **versklaven,** to enslave

340 **Versklavung,** *f.,* enslaving, enslavement

341   **die Versklavung einer Person** (SCS 6), the act of enslaving another person (*Sklaverei*)

342 **verstaatlichen,** to nationalize

343 **Verstaatlichung,** *f.,* nationalization

344 **verständigen,** to inform, to bring to the notice of

345   **sich verständigen,** to come to an understanding/agreement

346 **Verständigung**, *f.*, understanding, conciliation

347 **die vom Vermittler vorgeschlagenen Mittel der Verständigung** (HgI 5), the means of reconciliation proposed by the mediator

348 **Verstoß**, *m.*, infringement, violation, contravention

349 **Verstoß gegen,** infringement of

350 **Verstöße gegen die Vorschriften ahnden,** to punish infringements of the regulations (*Zuwiderhandlung)

351 **vertagen,** to adjourn, to postpone

352 **sich vertagen,** to adjourn (*beraten)

353 **Vertagung**, *f.*, adjournment, postponement

354 **Vertagungsantrag**, *m.*, motion for adjournment

355 **verteidigen,** to defend

356 **Verteidigung**, *f.*, defence

357 **die Stärke und Bewaffnung der Streitkräfte für die bodenständige Verteidigung** (WEU II 5), the strength and armaments of the inland defence forces

358 **Verteidigungsausschuß**, *m.*, defence committee

359 **Verteidigungsbeitrag**, *m.*, **deutscher** (CRFF), German Defence Contribution

360 **Verteidigungskrieg**, *m.*, defensive war

361 **Verteidigungspakt**, *m.*, defence treaty/pact (*see note to* *Vertrag *in* Annex* 1)

362 **zweiseitige Sicherheits- und Verteidigungspakte,** bilateral security and defence treaties

363 **Vertrag**, *m.*, treaty (*see Annexes* 1, 2, 3)

364 **Vertrag universalen/wirtschaftlichen (usw) Charakters,** treaty of a universal/economic (etc.) nature/character

365 **Vertrag zur Gründung des/der . . . ,** treaty establishing . . .

366 **Vertrag zugunsten Dritter,** treaty *pro tertio*, treaty in favour of a third party

367 **Vertrag zugunsten/zu Lasten von Drittstaaten** (VCLOT 35), treaty providing for rights/obligations for third states

368 **Abänderung eines Vertrags,** amendment of a treaty (*see note to* *Vertrag modifizieren)

369 **Ablehnung eines Vertrags,** repudiation of a treaty

370 **Änderung eines Vertrags,** amendment of a treaty

371 **Vorschläge zur Änderung eines mehrseitigen Vertrags mit Wirkung zwischen allen Vertragsparteien** (VCLOT 40), proposals to amend a multilateral treaty as between all the parties (*see note to* *Vertrag modifizieren)

372 **Anpassung eines Vertrags,** adjustment of/to a treaty

373 **Anwendung eines Vertrags,** application of a treaty

374 **Ausführung eines Vertrags,** execution of a treaty

375 **Auslegung eines Vertrags,** interpretation/construction of a treaty

376 **Austritt aus einem Vertrag,** withdrawal from a treaty

377 **Beendigung eines Vertrags,** termination of a treaty

378 **grundlegende Änderung der Umstände als Grund für die Beendigung eines Vertrags** (VCLOT 62), fundamental change of circumstances as a ground for terminating a treaty

379 **Beitritt zu einem Vertrag,** accession to a treaty

380 **Bindekraft eines Vertrags,** binding force of a treaty

381 **Bruch eines Vertrags,** breach/violation/rupture of a treaty

382 **Durchführung eines Vertrags,** execution of a treaty

383 **Einhaltung eines Vertrags,** observance of/compliance with a treaty

384 **Eintragung eines Vertrags,** registration of a treaty

385 **Erfüllung eines Vertrags,** fulfilment of a treaty

386 **Erlöschen eines Vertrags,** termination of a treaty

387 **Geltung eines Vertrags,** validity of a treaty

388   Geltungsbereich eines Vertrags, scope of a treaty (VCLOT), area of application of a treaty, territory to which the treaty applies

389   räumlicher Geltungsbereich eines Vertrags (VCLOT 29), territorial scope of a treaty

390   Gültigkeit eines Vertrags, validity of a treaty

391   Heiligkeit eines Vertrags, sanctity of a treaty

392   Kündigung eines Vertrags, denunciation of a treaty

393   Modifikation eines Vertrags, modification of a treaty (see note and example to *Vertrag modifizieren)

394   Nachprüfung eines Vertrags, review of a treaty

395   Nichtigkeit eines Vertrags, nullity of a treaty

396   Nichtrückwirkung eines Vertrags, non-retroactivity of a treaty

397   Öffnung eines Vertrags, opening of a treaty (for accession, etc.)

398   Paraphierung eines Vertrags, initialling of a treaty

399   Partner eines Vertrags, party to a treaty (see *Vertragspartei)

400   Ratifikation/Ratifizierung eines Vertrags, ratification of a treaty

401   Registrierung eines Vertrags, registration of a treaty

402   Rücktritt von einem Vertrag, withdrawal from a treaty

403   Sinn und Tragweite eines Vertrags, meaning/import and scope of a treaty

404   Suspendierung eines Vertrags, suspension of a treaty

405   Ungültigkeit eines Vertrags, invalidity of a treaty

406   Unterzeichnung eines Vertrags, signing/signature of a treaty

407   Urschrift eines Vertrags, original text of a treaty

408   Verletzung eines Vertrags, violation/breach of a treaty

409   Veröffentlichung eines Vertrags, publication of a treaty

410   Weitergeltung eines Vertrags, continuance in force of treaties

411   Wiederanwendung eines Vertrags, resumption of the operation of a treaty

412   Ziel und Zweck eines Vertrags, aim/object and purpose of a treaty (see also under *Vertrags- compounds)

413   allgemeiner Vertrag, general treaty (see note to *allgemein)

414   aufeinanderfolgende Verträge, successive treaties

415   die Anwendung aufeinanderfolgender Verträge über denselben Gegenstand (VCLOT 30), the application of successive treaties relating to the same subject matter

416   besonderer Vertrag, special treaty

417   bestehender Vertrag, existing treaty, treaty already in force

418   bilateraler Vertrag, bilateral treaty

419   früherer Vertrag, previous treaty

420   Der frühere Vertrag findet nur insoweit Anwendung, als er mit dem späteren Vertrag vereinbar ist (VCLOT 30), The earlier treaty applies only to the extent that its provisions are compatible with those of the later treaty

421   geschlossener Vertrag, (i) treaty not open for accession, closed treaty; (ii) concluded treaty

422   mehrseitiger Vertrag, multilateral treaty

423   multilateraler Vertrag, multilateral treaty

424   Einige multilaterale Verträge bezeichnen sich selbst als allgemein oder universal, Some multilateral treaties designate themselves as general or universal (see note to *allgemein)

425   nichtiger Vertrag, void treaty

426   Die Bestimmungen eines nichtigen Vertrags haben keine rechtliche Gültigkeit (VCLOT 69), The provisions of a void treaty have no legal force

427   normativer Vertrag, law-making treaty, normative treaty

428   normsetzender Vertrag, law-making treaty, normative treaty

429   offener Vertrag, treaty open for accession

430   **ratifikationsbedürftiger   Vertrag,**
       treaty requiring ratification
431   **rechtschöpfender Vertrag** (= recht-
       setzender   Vertrag),   law-making
       treaty
432   **regionaler Vertrag,** regional treaty
433   **späterer Vertrag,** subsequent treaty
       (früherer *Vertrag)
434   **unanwendbar gewordener Vertrag,**
       treaty that has become non-
       applicable
435   **ursprünglicher   Vertrag,**   original
       treaty
436   **zweiseitiger Vertrag,** bilateral treaty
437   **einen Vertrag abändern/ändern,** to
       amend a treaty (*see note to* *Vertrag
       modifizieren*)
438   **einen Vertrag auslegen,** to inter-
       pret/to construe a treaty
439   **einen Vertrag beenden,** to terminate
       a treaty
440   **einem Vertrag beitreten,** to accede
       to a treaty
441   **einen   Vertrag   durchführen,**   to
       execute a treaty
442   **einen Vertrag eingehen,** to enter into
       a treaty
443   **einen Vertrag einhalten,** to observe
       a treaty, to comply with a treaty, to
       respect a treaty, to observe/to com-
       ply with the provisions of a treaty
444   **einen Vertrag eintragen,** to register
       a treaty
445   **einen Vertrag erfüllen,** to fulfil (the
       provisions of) a treaty
446   **einen Vertrag erneuern,** to renew a
       treaty
447   **einen   Vertrag   stillschweigend/**
       ausdrücklich erneuern, to tacitly/
       expressly renew a treaty
448   **sich an einen Vertrag halten,** to
       observe/to comply with (the provi-
       sions of) a treaty
449   **sich über alle Verträge hinwegset-**
       zen, to set aside/to disregard all
       treaties
450   **einen Vertrag kündigen,** to de-
       nounce/to terminate a treaty
451   **einen Vertrag modifizieren,** to mod-
       ify a treaty (VCLOT *seems to make
       a distinction, not always found else-
       where, between* **modifizieren**/modify

by only SOME *of the parties, and*
ändern/amend *by* ALL *the parties.*
*See the following example, and that
given under* Änderung eines *Vertrags.)
452   **Zwei oder mehr Vertragsparteien**
       eines mehrseitigen Vertrags kön-
       nen eine Übereinkunft schließen,
       um den Vertrag ausschließlich im
       Verhältnis zueinander zu modi-
       fizieren (VCLOT 41), Two or
       more of the parties to a multi-
       lateral treaty may conclude an
       agreement to modify the treaty as
       between themselves alone
453   **einen Vertrag öffnen,** to open a
       treaty
454   **einen Vertrag zum/für den Beitritt**
       öffnen, to open a treaty for acces-
       sion
455   **Verträge in Übereinstimmung mit**
       dem Grundsatz der Universalität
       für den Beitritt aller Staaten öff-
       nen, to open treaties for the
       accession of all states in accor-
       dance with the principle of uni-
       versality
456   **einen Vertrag paraphieren,** to initial
       a treaty
457   **einen Vertrag ratifizieren,** to ratify a
       treaty
458   **einen Vertrag registrieren,** to regis-
       ter a treaty
459   **Alle Verträge und sonstigen inter-**
       nationalen Übereinkünfte, die ein
       Mitglied der UN schließt, werden
       so bald wie möglich beim Se-
       kretariat registriert und von ihm
       veröffentlicht (CUN 102), Every
       treaty and every international
       agreement entered into by any
       member of the UN shall as soon
       as possible be registered with the
       Secretariat and published by it
460   **einen Vertrag schließen,** to conclude
       a treaty (*see* *Rechtspersönlichkeit,
       *Widerspruch)
461   **einen Vertrag suspendieren,** to sus-
       pend a treaty
462   **einen Vertrag verlängern,** to ex-
       tend/to renew a treaty
463   **einen Vertrag veröffentlichen,** to

publish a treaty (*see* *Vertrag registrieren)

464   **einem Vertrag zuwiderhandeln,** to violate a treaty, to act in violation of a treaty

465   **vertraglich,** *adj.*, contractual, by treaty

466   **in vertraglicher Form,** in the form of a treaty

467   **vertragliche Regelung,** regulation by treaty, contractual regulation (*contrast with* *Vertragsregelung)

468   **vertragliche Verpflichtung,** contractual obligation (*see* *Freiheit entziehen)

469   **vertraglich eingeräumt/gewährt,** granted/accorded/conferred by treaty

470   **vertraglich vereinbart,** arranged/agreed by treaty

471   **Vertragsabänderung,** *f.*, amendment/modification of a treaty (*see note to* *Vertrag modifizieren)

472   **Vertragsablauf,** *m.*, expiration of a treaty

473   **Vertragsabschluß,** *m.*, conclusion of a treaty (*Vertragsschluß)

474   **Vertragsabschlußverfahren,** *n.*, procedure for concluding a treaty

475   **einphasiges Vertragsabschlußverfahren,** single-phase procedure for concluding a treaty

476   **mehrphasiges Vertragsabschlußverfahren,** multi-phase procedure for concluding a treaty (*see Annex 2*)

477   **Vertragsänderung,** *f.*, amendment/modification of a treaty (*see note to* *Vertrag modifizieren)

478   **Vertragsauslegung,** *f.*, interpretation/construction of a treaty

479   **Vertragsbestimmung,** *f.*, provision/term of a treaty

480   **Vertragsbezeichnung,** *f.*, title/designation of a treaty

481   **Vertragsbruch,** *m.*, violation/breach of a treaty, act in violation of/violating a treaty

482   **vertragsbrüchig,** *adj.*, in breach of/acting in breach of a treaty

483   **der vertragsbrüchig gewordene Teil,** the party acting in breach of the treaty

484   **Vertragsdauer,** *f.*, duration of a treaty

485   **Nach Ablauf dieser Zeit erneuert sich die Vertragsdauer auf ein Jahr,** At the end of this period the treaty shall be renewed for a further period of one year

486   **Vertragsentwurf,** *m.*, draft (of a) treaty

487   **Vertragserfüllung,** *f.*, fulfilment of a treaty

488   **Unmöglichkeit der Vertragserfüllung als Grund für die Beendigung des Vertrags** (VCLOT 61), impossibility of performing a treaty as a ground for terminating it

489   **Vertragsfähigkeit,** *f.*, capacity to enter into/to conclude a treaty/treaties

490   **Vertragsfähigkeit der Staaten: Jeder Staat besitzt die Fähigkeit, Verträge zu schließen** (VCLOT 6), Capacity of states to conclude treaties: Every state possesses capacity to conclude treaties

491   **Vertragsfreiheit,** *f.*, freedom to enter into/to conclude treaties/a treaty

492   **Vertragsgegenstand,** *m.*, subject matter of a treaty

493   **Vertragsinhalt,** *m.*, substance/provisions of a treaty

494   **Vertragsöffnung,** *f.*, opening of a treaty (*Vertrag öffnen)

495   **Vertragsparaphierung,** *f.*, initialling of a treaty

496   **Vertragspartei,** *f.* (= Vertragsteil, *m.*/Vertragspartner, *m.*), party to a treaty, contracting party

497   **(Übereinkünfte), denen auch andere Völkerrechtssubjekte als Vertragsparteien angehören** (VCLOT 3), (agreements) to which other subjects of international law are also parties

498   **Vertragsparteien dieses Vertrags,** parties to the present treaty

499   **Hohe Vertragsparteien,** High Contracting Parties

500 **ursprüngliche Vertragsparteien,** original (contracting) parties (ohne *Vorbehalt, *Verantwortlichkeit, *and* VCLOT 2 *in Annex* 14)
Vertragspartner, *m.* = *Vertragspartei, f.*

501 **Vertragspflicht,** *f.*, contractual obligation

502 **Vertragspraxis,** *f.*, practice as to treaties

503 **Vertragsrecht¹,** *n.*, contract law, law of contractual obligations

504 **Vertragsrecht²,** *n.*, treaty law, law of treaties, law relating to/governing treaties

505 **fortschreitende Entwicklung des Vertragsrechts** (VCLOT Pr), progressive development of the law of treaties

506 **Vertragsrecht³,** *n.*, law created by/arising under treaties

507 **Abänderung von Gewohnheitsrecht durch Vertragsrecht,** modification of custom/customary law by law created by treaties
(*For adjectival collocations, see under e.g.* *Recht *and* *Völkerrecht.*)

508 **Vertragsregelung,** *f.*, regulation (provided for) in a treaty (*contrast* *vertragliche Regelung)

509 **Vertragsregierung,** *f.*, contracting government

510 **Vertragsregistrierung,** *f.*, registration of a treaty
(* Vertrag registrieren)

511 **Vertragsrevision,** *f.*, revision of a treaty

512 **vertrag(s)schließend,** *adj.*, contracting

513 **vertragsschließende Partei,** contracting party
(*Vertragspartei)

514 **vertragsschließende Regierung** (= Vertragsregierung, *f.*), contracting government

515 **vertragsschließende Seite,** contracting party

516 **die Hohen Vertragsschließenden Teile** (WEU I), the High Contracting Parties

517 **Vertragsschluß,** *m.*, conclusion of a treaty

518 **die zum Vertragsschluß ermächtigten/berechtigten Organe,** the organs/agents authorized/empowered to conclude a treaty

519 **Vertragsschlußrecht,** *n.*, right to conclude a treaty

520 **Vertragsschuld,** *f.*, contract(ual) debt

521 **eingeforderte Vertragsschulden** (HgI 53), contract debts claimed

522 **die Eintreibung von Vertragsschulden, die Staaten gegenüber fremden Staatsangehörigen gemacht haben,** the recovery of contract debts which states have incurred towards foreign nationals

523 **Vertragssicherheit,** *f.*, contractual security, security created by contract

524 **Vertragssprache,** *f.*, language of a treaty

525 **Vertragsstaat,** *m.*, contracting state, state party to a treaty, state party (*In the pl., English usage varies between* states parties *and* states party *depending on whether* party *is considered to possess an adjectival function; this is shown clearly in the following examples; also SCS 3 under* wirksame *Maßnahmen.*)

526 **die Vertragsstaaten eines Kollektivvertrags/dieses Übereinkommens (usw),** the states party to a collective treaty/the present Convention (etc.)

527 **eine vom Generalsekretär am Sitz der UN anberaumte Sitzung der Vertragsstaaten** (CERD 8), a meeting of states parties convened by the Secretary-General at UN headquarters (*see* VCLOT 2 *in Annex* 14)
Vertragsteil, *m.* = *Vertragspartei, f.*

528 **Vertragstext,** *m.*, text of a treaty

529 **vorläufiger Vertragstext,** draft treaty, draft wording of a treaty

530 **den Vertragstext aushandeln,** to negotiate the text of a treaty

531 **Vertragstreue,** *f.*, compliance with/observance of a treaty

532 **Vertragsunterzeichnung,** *f.*, signing/signature of a treaty

533 **vertragsvereitelnd,** *adj.*, prejudicial to a treaty, calculated to prejudice/frustrate/thwart/impair a treaty/the terms/aims/provisions of a treaty
(*vereiteln)

534 **Vertragsverhandlung,** *f.*, negotiation of a treaty

535 **Vertragsverlängerung,** *f.*, extension/renewal of a treaty

536 **Vertragsverletzung,** *f.*, violation of a treaty, an act in violation of/violating a treaty, breach of a treaty

537 **Vertragsveröffentlichung,** *f.*, publication of a treaty
(*Vertrag registrieren)

538 **Vertragsverpflichtung,** *f.*, contractual obligation/commitment, obligation/commitment arising under (the terms of) a treaty

539 **Vertragswerk,** *n.*, instrument(s) constituting a treaty

540 **Vertragswirkung,** *f.*, effect of a treaty

541 **das Ende der Vertragswirkung,** termination of the effect of a treaty

542 **Vertragswortlaut,** *m.*, wording of the treaty (text)

543 **Vertragsziel,** *n.* (= Vertragszweck, *m.*), aim/purpose/object of the treaty

544 **Erreichung des Vertragsziels oder des Vertragszwecks** (VCLOT 60), accomplishment of the object or purpose of the treaty
(implizierte *Befugnisse)

545 **Vertragszuwiderhandlung,** *f.*, (act in) violation of a treaty

546 **vertreten¹,** to represent

547 **Ein Missionschef kann den Entsendestaat bei jeder internationalen Organisation vertreten** (VCDR 5), A head of mission may act as representative of the sending state to any international organization

548 **Der Gouverneursrat kann Personen bestimmen, die ihn gegenüber anderen Organisationen vertreten** (IAEA VI, I), The Board of Governors may appoint persons to represent it in its relations with other organizations

549 **durch Beobachter/Delegierte/Delegationen vertreten,** represented by observers/delegates/delegations

550 **vertreten²,** to substitute for, to replace (*see* *Vertreter²)

551 **Vertreter¹,** *m.*, representative, envoy

552 **Im Sinne der Artikel 9–12 bezieht sich der Ausdruck „Vertreter" auf alle Vertreter, stellvertretende Delegierte, Berater, technische Sachverständige und Delegationssekretäre** (PrivExCE 12), In Articles 9–12 above, the expression "representatives" shall be deemed to include all representatives, alternate representatives, advisers, technical experts and secretaries of delegations

553 **ad hoc Vertreter,** ad-hoc envoy/representative

554 **bevollmächtigter Vertreter,** accredited representative (ECER 9), (fully) authorized representative

555 **diplomatischer Vertreter,** diplomatic representative/envoy/agent (*see* *Diplomat)

556 **rangältester Vertreter,** highest ranking/senior representative/envoy

557 **ständiger Vertreter,** permanent representative/envoy

558 **stellvertretender Vertreter,** alternate representative, alternate, substitute
(*Delegierter)

559 **Vertreter²,** *m.*, alternate, substitute

560 **Kann ein Delegierter an einer Ratssitzung nicht teilnehmen, so kann er durch einen Vertreter ersetzt werden; dieser hat für die Dauer dieser Sitzung alle Befugnisse des Delegierten** (CICES 6), A delegate who is not present at a meeting of the Council may be replaced by a substitute who shall have all the powers of the delegate for that meeting
(*Stellvertreter)

561 **Vertretung¹,** *f.*, (diplomatic) mission, post

562 **diplomatische Vertretung,** diplomatic mission

563 **konsularische Vertretung,** consular post

564   **ständige Vertretung,** permanent mission

565   **Vertretungen austauschen,** to exchange missions

566   **Vertretung²,** *f.*, representation

567   **diplomatische Missionen als Vertretungen von Staaten** (VCDR Pr), diplomatic missions as representing states

568   **diplomatische/konsularische/ständige/ Vertretung,** diplomatic/consular/ permanent/ representation

569   **Vertretungsbefugnis,** *f.* (= Vertretungsmacht, *f.*), authority/power to represent/of representation

570   **Vertretungsrecht,** *n.*, right of representation, right to represent

571   **verurteilen,** to sentence

572   **Verurteilung,** *f.*, (passing of) sentence, sentencing

573   **Verurteilungen und Hinrichtungen ohne vorhergehendes Urteil eines ordentlich bestellten Gerichtes** (GC I 3), the passing of sentences and the carrying out of executions without previous judgment pronounced by a regularly constituted court

574   **Verurteilung zum Tode,** sentence of death

575   **alle Verurteilungen zum Tode** (GC IV 74), any judgment involving a sentence of death

576   **verwahren,** to act as depositary, to keep custody of

577   **Urkunden, Notifikationen und Mitteilungen entgegennehmen und verwahren** (VCLOT 77), to receive and keep custody of instruments, notifications and communications

578   **Verwahrer,** *m.* (= *Depositar, m.*), depositary

579   **Einzelne oder mehrere Staaten, eine internationale Organisation oder der leitende Verwaltungsbeamte einer internationalen Organisation können Verwahrer sein** (VCLOT 76), The depositary may be one or more states, an international organization or the chief administrative officer of the organization (*see* VCLOT 76–77 *in Annex* 15)

580   **Verwahrregierung,** *f.* (= ver-

wahrende Regierung), depositary government

581   **Diese werden hiermit zu Verwahrregierungen bestimmt** (MNTB), These are hereby designated the Depositary Governments

582   **Die Verwahrregierungen übermitteln den Regierungen der Unterzeichnerstaaten und beitretenden Staaten beglaubigte Abschriften,** Duly certified copies (of this treaty) shall be transmitted by the depositary Governments to the Governments of the signatory and acceding states

583   **Verwahrstaat,** *m.*, depositary state

584   **Verwahrstelle,** *f.*, depositary

585   **verwalten,** to administer

586   **verwaltend,** *adj.*, administering

587   **die verwaltende Behörde von Treuhandgebieten,** the administering authority of trust territories

588   **Verwaltung,** *f.*, administration

589   **Verwaltungsabkommen,** *n.*, administrative agreement

590   **Verwaltungsakt,** *m.*, administrative act/measure

591   **Verwaltungsangelegenheit,** *f.*, administrative matter/affair

592   **die laufenden Verwaltungsangelegenheiten der Mission** (VCDR 19), the current administrative affairs of the mission

593   **Verwaltungsausschuß,** *m.*, administrative committee

594   **Verwaltungsbeamter,** *adj.n.*, administrative official

595   **Höchster Verwaltungsbeamter der UN ist der Generalsekretär,** The chief administrative official of the UN is the Secretary-General

596   **Verwaltungsfunktion,** *f.*, administrative function

597   **Verwaltungsgebiet,** *n.*, administrative territory

598   **Verwaltungsgericht,** *n.*, administrative court/tribunal

599   **Verwaltungsgerichtsbarkeit,** *f.*, administrative jurisdiction

600   **Verwaltungsgrenze,** *f.*, administrative border/boundary

601   **Verwaltungshilfe** *f.*, **gegen**

seitige,mutual administrative assistance

602 **Verwaltungskonferenz,** *f.*,
administrative conference

603 **Verwaltungsmacht,** *f.*, administrative power/authority, administering
power/authority

604 **die UN, soweit sie Verwaltungsmacht eines Hoheitsgebiets sind**
(CFIMT XIII), the UN in cases
where they are the administering
authority for a territory

605 **Verwaltungsmaßnahme,** *f.*,
administrative measure/action

606 **Verwaltungsorgan,** *n.*, administrative organ/body

607 **Verwaltungspersonal,** *n.*,
administrative staff, clerical staff

608 **Verwaltungsrat,** *m.*, administrative
council

609 **Verwaltungsrecht,** *n.*, administrative law

610 **Verwaltungsstelle,** *f.*, administrative body/agency/authority

611 **diplomatische oder konsularische
Verwaltungsstellen** (ECSM 15),
administrative diplomatic and consular authorities

612 **zentrale Verwaltungsstelle,** central
administrative body/agency/author-
ity, administrative centre

613 **Verwaltungsübereinkommen,** *n.*,
administrative agreement (*see note
to* *Vertrag *in Annex* 1)

614 **Verwaltungsvereinbarung,** *f.*,
administrative agreement (*see note
to* *Vertrag *in Annex* 1)

615 **Verwaltungsvorschrift,** *f.*,
administrative regulation/provision
(* Rechtsvorschrift)

616 **verweigern,** to refuse, to deny, to
refuse to grant

617 **Verweigerung,** *f.*, refusal, denial

618 **Verweigerung der Anerkennung,**
refusal to grant recognition

619 **Verweigerung des Rechtsschutzes,**
denial of justice

620 **verweisen,** to remit, to refer

621 **eine Sache/einen Fall an ein anderes
Gericht verweisen,** to remit/to refer
a matter/a case to another court

622 **Verweisung,** *f.*, remittal, referring,

reference

623 **Verwendung,** *f.*, use, application

624 **bestimmungswidrige Verwendung**
(IAEA IX), unauthorized diversion

625 **verwirklichen,** to achieve, to
realize

626 **Verwirklichung,** *f.*, achievement,
realization

627 **die Verwirklichung von Rechten und
Grundsätzen** (ES 31), the effective
realization of rights and principles

628 **Verwundeter,** *adj.n.*, wounded
(person)

629 **Abtransport der Verwundeten** (GC
I), transport of the wounded

630 **Aufsuchung der Verwundeten** (GC
I), search for the wounded

631 **Behandlung der Verwundeten,**
treatment of the wounded

632 **die menschliche/unmenschliche
Behandlung der Verwundeten,**
(GC 1), the humane/inhumane
treatment of the wounded

633 **Bergung der Verwundeten,** removal
of the wounded

634 **die Bergung, der Austausch und
der Abtransport der auf dem
Schlachtfeld gebliebenen Verwundeten** (GC I 15), the removal,
exchange and transport of the
wounded left on the battlefield

635 **Evakuierung der Verwundeten,**
evacuation of the wounded

636 **die Evakuierung und der
Austausch von Verwundeten und
Kranken aus einer belagerten oder
eingeschlossenen Zone** (GC I 15),
the evacuation or exchange of
wounded and sick from a besieged
or encircled area

637 **Los der Verwundeten,** condition of
the wounded

638 **Verbesserung des Loses der Verwundeten** (GC I), amelioration of
the condition of the wounded
(*See full title of* GC I *in abbreviated
treaty title list*)

639 **Verzeichnis,** *n.*, list, schedule
(* Oberschiedsrichter)

640 **Verzicht,** *m.*, renunciation, waiver

641 **Der Verzicht muß stets ausdrücklich
erklärt werden** (VCDR 32/45), The

waiver must always be express/shall
in all cases be express

642 **Verzicht auf Bedingungen/Immuni-
tät,** waiver of conditions/immunity

643 **Verzicht auf Krieg,** renunciation of
war

644 **Veto,** *n.,* veto

645 **(ein) Veto (gegen . . .) einlegen,** to
veto . . .

646 **aufschiebendes Veto,** suspensive
veto

647 **Vetorecht,** *n.,* right of veto

648 **vielrassisch,** *adj.* (CERD 2), multiracial
(*Rassenintegrierung)

649 **Vielvölkerstaat,** *m.,* multinational
state
Vierer- = *Viermächte-

650 **Viermächteabkommen,** *n.,* four-
power/quadripartite agreement

651 **Viermächteausschuß,** *m.,* four-
power/quadripartite committee,
committee of four

652 **Gemeinsamer Viermächteausschuß**
(TORG), Joint Four-Power Commission

653 **Viermächteerklärung,** *f.,* four-
power/quadripartite declaration

654 **Viermächtegruppe,** *f.,* four-
power/quadripartite group

655 **Viermächtekontrolle,** *f.,* four-
power/quadripartite control

656 **Viermächteübereinkommen,** *n.,*
four-power/quadripartite agreement

657 **Viermächteverantwortlichkeit,**
f., four-power/quadripartite responsibility

658 **Viermächteverwaltung** *f.* **von
Berlin,** Four-Power Administra-
tion of Berlin
Vierparteien- = *Viermächte-

659 **Visitation,** *f.,* visitation, visit and
search

660 **Visitationsrecht,** *n.,* right of visit
and search
(*Durchsuchungsrecht)

661 **Vizekonsul,** *m.,* vice-consul

662 **Volk,** *n.,* people (*both in English and
German a term that defies satisfac-
tory definition. According to context
and/or emotive content may be better
translated by* nation, population,

inhabitants, *etc. See e.g. under*
*Staatsvolk.)

663 **wir die Völker der UN** (CUN Pr), we
the peoples of the UN

664 **die Nationen und Völker der Welt,**
the nations and peoples of the world

665 **das gute Einvernehmen unter den
Völkern der Welt,** good understanding between the peoples/nations of
the world

666 **friedliebende Völker,** peace-loving
peoples

667 **zivilisierte Völker,** civilized peoples
(*Freundschaft, *Rechtsgarantie)

668 **Völkerbund,** *m.,* League of Nations

669 **Völkerbundsrat,** *m.,* Council of the
League of Nations

670 **Völkerbundsversammlung,** *f.,*
Assembly of the League of Nations

671 **Völkerfamilie,** *f.,* family of nations

672 **Völkergemeinschaft,** *f.,* community of nations

673 **Völkergemeinschaftsgebiet,** *n.,*
international territory

674 **Völkergewohnheitsrecht,** *n.,*
international custom, customary
international law

675 **Völkergewohnheitsrecht besteht aus
denjenigen Verhaltensregeln, die
bisher von Völkerrechtssubjekten in
ihrem gegenseitigen Verkehr
beobachtet worden sind,** Customary
international law consists of those
rules of conduct that have been
observed by subjects of international law in intercourse with each
other

676 **Regeln/Sätze des Völkergewohnheitsrechts** (VCCR Pr), rules of customary international law

677 **wie jedes andere Völkergewohnheitsrecht . . .,** like any other rule/
right under customary international
law

678 **partikulares Völkergewohnheitsrecht,** particular customary international law

679 **regionales Völkergewohnheitsrecht,**
regional customary international law

680 **universales Völkergewohnheitsrecht,**
universal customary international
law

681 völkergewohnheitsrechtlich,
     adj., under customary international
     law, according to international cus-
     tom
682 **Verstoß gegen völkergewohnheits-
     rechtliche Regeln,** infringement/
     breach of the rules of international
     custom
683 **Völkerhöflichkeit,** *f.*, comity (of
     nations), *comitas gentium*
684 **Völkerkriegsrecht,** *n.*, interna-
     tional law of war
685 **Völkermoral,** *n.*, international mor-
     ality
686 **Völkermord,** *m.*, genocide
687 **Die folgenden Handlungen sind zu
     bestrafen: (a) Völkermord, (b) Ver-
     schwörung zur Begehung von Völker-
     mord, (c) unmittelbare und öffent-
     liche Anreizung zur Begehung von
     Völkermord, (d) Versuch, Völker-
     mord zu begehen, (e) Teilnahme am
     Völkermord (PCG 3),** The following
     acts shall be punishable: (a) Geno-
     cide, (b) Conspiracy to commit
     genocide, (c) Direct and public in-
     citement to commit genocide, (d)
     Attempt to commit genocide, (e)
     Complicity in genocide
     (*see* PCG 1–4 *in Annex* 11)
688 **Völkermordhandlung,** *f.*, act of
     genocide
689 **Völkerrecht,** *n.*, international law,
     law of nations
690 **das Völkerrecht als ein universales
     Recht,** international law as a univer-
     sal (system of) law
691 **nach Völkerrecht,** in accordance
     with/under/at international law
692 **Grundsätze des Völkerrechts,** prin-
     ciples of international law
693 **Kodifizierung des Völkerrechts,**
     codification of international law
694 **die fortschreitende Entwicklung
     des Völkerrechts sowie seine Kodi-
     fizierung begünstigen (CUN 13),**
     to encourage the progressive de-
     velopment of international law
     and its codification
695 **Normen des Völkerrechts,** rules of
     international law
696 **Normen des Völkerrechts, die**

     universal akzeptabel sind, rules of
     international law that are univer-
     sally acceptable/accepted
697 **Prinzipien des Völkerrechts,** princi-
     ples of international law
698 **Es ist unzulässig, sich auf eines
     oder einige Prinzipien des Völker-
     rechts zu berufen, um andere
     Prinzipien zu umgehen oder zu
     verletzen,** It is inadmissible to
     invoke one or several principles of
     international law in order to
     evade or to violate other princi-
     ples
699 **Quellen des Völkerrechts,** sources of
     international law (*see* *Rechts-
     quelle; *also* SICJ 38 *in Annex* 20. *For
     further nominal expressions see
     under the extensive list of* *Völker-
     rechts- *compounds.*)
700 **allgemeines Völkerrecht,** general
     international law
701 **Unter „allgemeines Völkerrecht"
     versteht man die Normen des Völ-
     kerrechts, die für die Mehrzahl
     der Staaten gelten,** "General
     international law" is understood
     as that body of rules which are
     considered valid by the majority
     of states
702 **Regeln des allgemeinen Völker-
     rechts (VCDR 41),** rules of gen-
     eral international law
703 **geschriebenes Völkerrecht,** written
     international law
704 **klassisches Völkerrecht,** classical
     international law
705 **kodifiziertes Völkerrecht,** codified
     international law
706 **öffentliches Völkerrecht,** public
     international law
707 **partikulares Völkerrecht,** particular
     international law
708 **Als „partikulares Völkerrecht"
     werden diejenigen Normen
     bezeichnet, die nur zwei oder
     wenige Staaten verpflichten,** "Par-
     ticular international law" is the
     term applied to such rules as obli-
     gate only 2 or a few states
709 **privates Völkerrecht,** private inter-
     national law, conflict of laws

710 **regionales Völkerrecht,** regional international law
711 **ungeschriebenes Völkerrecht,** unwritten international law
712 **universales Völkerrecht,** universal international law
713 **Es gibt völkerrechtliche Regeln, die für alle Staaten gelten, das sogenannte ,,universale Völkerrecht",** There are rules of international law that apply to all states: these one calls "universal international law"
714 **zwingendes Völkerrecht,** coercive international law, coercive rules of international law
715 **Völkerrechtler,** *m*., international jurisconsult, international jurist, expert/specialist in international law
716 **die Lehrmeinungen der fähigsten Völkerrechtler** (SICJ 38), the teachings of the most highly qualified publicists
717 **völkerrechtlich,** *adj*., of/under/at international law (*often best translated by simply* international, *as in many of the following expressions*)
718 **völkerrechtliche Beziehungen,** international relations
719 **völkerrechtliches Delikt,** international wrong/offence/delinquency/delict
720 **völkerrechtliche Dienstbarkeiten,** international servitudes
721 **völkerrechtliche Geltung,** validity under/at international law, international validity
722 **völkerrechtliches Gericht,** international court/tribunal
723 **völkerrechtliche Gerichtsbarkeit,** international jurisdiction
724 **völkerrechtliches Gewohnheitsrecht,** international custom, customary international law (*see* *Völkergewohnheitsrecht)
725 **völkerrechtlicher Grundsatz,** principle of international law
726 **völkerrechtliche Gültigkeit,** validity under/at international law, international validity
727 **völkerrechtliche Haftung,** international responsibility/liability

728 **völkerrechtliche Handlung,** international act
729 **völkerrechtliche Lehrmeinungen,** theories/doctrines of international law
730 **völkerrechtliche Nichtigkeit,** nullity under international law
731 **völkerrechtliche Normen,** rules/standards of international law, international rules/standards
732 **völkerrechtliche Person,** international person
733 **völkerrechtliche Persönlichkeit,** international personality
734 **völkerrechtliche Pflicht,** international duty/obligation
735 **völkerrechtliche Praxis,** international practice
736 **völkerrechtliche Rechte,** rights under international law
737 **die völkerrechtlichen Rechte und Pflichten eines Staates,** the rights and duties resting on/incumbent upon a state under international law
738 **völkerrechtliche Rechtsperson,** international legal person
739 **völkerrechtliche Rechtspersönlichkeit,** international legal personality, personality in international law
740 **völkerrechtliche Regel,** international rule, rule of international law
741 **völkerrechtlicher Schutz,** international protection, the protection offered by international law
742 **völkerrechtliche Staatenhaftung,** international responsibility of states, responsibility of states under international law
743 **völkerrechtliche Strafgerichtsbarkeit,** international criminal jurisdiction
744 **völkerrechtliches Strafrecht,** international criminal law
745 **völkerrechtliche Streitigkeit,** international dispute
746 **völkerrechtliche Übung,** international usage
747 **völkerrechtliches Unrecht,** international wrong/delinquency
748 **völkerrechtliche Verantwortlichkeit,** international responsibility

749 **völkerrechtliche Verbindlichkeit,** international obligation

750 **völkerrechtliches Verbrechen,** international crime/offence (*see note to* *Verbrechen)

751 **völkerrechtlicher Verkehr,** international intercourse, intercourse between states

752 **völkerrechtliche Verpflichtung,** international obligation, obligation arising under international law

753 **völkerrechtlicher Vertrag,** international treaty

754 **völkerrechtlich bedeutungslos/ belanglos,** of no significance under international law

755 **völkerrechtlich bindend,** binding under international law

756 **völkerrechtlich unzulässig,** inadmissible under international law

757 **völkerrechtlich verbindlich,** binding under international law

758 **völkerrechtlich zulässig,** admissible under international law
(*See also under* *international, *and* *Völker-* *and* *Völkerrechts-* *compounds.*)

759 **Völkerrechtsdelikt,** *n.*, international wrong

760 **Völkerrechtsdenken,** *n.*, school of (thought in) international law

761 **Völkerrechtsdoktrin,** *f.*, doctrine of international law

762 **völkerrechtsgemäß,** *adj.*, in accordance with/in conformity with international law (*völkerrechtskonform)

763 **Völkerrechtsgemeinschaft,** *f.*, international community, society/ community of states (* Völkerrechtssubjektivität)

764 **Völkerrechtsgrundsatz,** *m.*, principle of international law (Prinzipien des *Völkerrechts)

765 **Völkerrechtskommission,** *f.*, International Law Commission (ILC)

766 **völkerrechtskonform,** *adj.*, in accordance with/in conformity with international law

767 **Neue Völkerrechtsnormen sollen möglichst völkerrechtskonform sein,** New rules of international law should conform to existing international law as far as possible

768 **Verträge sind grundsätzlich völkerrechtskonform, d.h. sie müssen so weit wie möglich in Übereinstimmung mit der bisherigen Völkerrechtslage auszulegen sein,** One of the principles of treaties is that they are in accordance with international law, i.e. they must, wherever possible, be capable of an interpretation/ construction that is not at variance with the existing state of international law

769 **Völkerrechtskonzeption,** *f.*, concept of international law

770 **Völkerrechtskreis,** *m.*, school of (thought in) international law

771 **Die drei Völkerrechtskreise sind der anglo-amerikanische, der kontinental-europäische und der sowjetische,** The three schools of thought in international law are the Anglo-American school, the Continental school, and the Soviet school

772 **Völkerrechtslehre,** *f.*, theory of international law

773 **klassische Völkerrechtslehre,** classical theory of international law

774 **Völkerrechtsmißbrauch,** *m.*, abuse of international law

775 **Völkerrechtsnorm,** *f.*, rule of international law

776 **Völkerrechtsperson,** *f.*, international person, person in international law

777 **Völkerrechtspersönlichkeit,** *f.*, international legal personality, personality in international law (* Rechtspersönlichkeit, * Völkerrechtssubjektivität)

778 **Völkerrechtsprinzip,** *n.*, principle of international law (Prinzipien des *Völkerrechts)

779 **Völkerrechtsquelle,** *f.*, source of international law (* Rangunterschied; *see also* SICJ 38 *in Annex* 20)

780 **Völkerrechtsregel,** *f.*, rule of international law (* vorgehen[2])

781 **Völkerrechtssatz,** *m.,* rule of international law

782 **jeder anwendbare einschlägige Völkerrechtssatz (VCLOT 31),** any relevant rule of international law applicable

783 **Völkerrechtssitte,** *f.,* international custom

784 **Völkerrechtssubjekt,** *m.,* subject of international law
(*Träger)

785 **Völkerrechtssubjektivität,** *f.,* (possession of) international (legal) personality, status of/as a subject of international law

786 **Ein neues Mitglied der Völkerrechtsgemeinschaft muß handlungsfähig sein, während ein schon bestehender Staat seine Völkerrechtssubjektivität nicht durch eine vorübergehende Handlungsunfähigkeit (z.B. durch kriegerische Besetzung) verliert,** A new member of the international community/society of states must possess full capacity, whereas an existing state does not lose its international personality by virtue of a temporary incapacity (e.g. resulting from belligerent occupation)

787 **Völkerrechtstheorie,** *f.,* theory of international law

788 **Völkerrechtsverletzung,** *f.,* violation/breach of international law

789 **völkerrechtswidrig,** *adj.,* contrary to/in violation/breach of international law

790 **Völkerrechtswidrigkeit,** *f.,* violation/breach of international law, an act/conduct constituting a violation/breach of international law

791 **Völkerrechtswissenschaft,** *f.,* science of international law, academic study of international law

792 **Völkerrechtswissenschaftler,** *m.,* international jurisconsult, international jurist, expert/specialist in international law
(*Völkerrechtler)

793 **Völkersitte,** *f.,* international custom

794 **Völkerstrafgerichtsbarkeit,** *f.,* international criminal jurisdiction

795 **Völkerstrafrecht,** *n.,* international criminal law
(*Inpflichtnahme)

796 **Völkervertragsrecht,** *n.,* international law of treaties

797 **Volksaufgebot,** *n., levée en masse*

798 **Volkserhebung,** *f.,* popular rising

799 **Volksgruppe,** *f.* (CERD 1/7), ethnic/ethnical group
(ethnische *Gruppe)

800 **Volksstaat,** *m.,* republic

801 **Volkstum,** *n.,* ethnic origin (*see* CERD 1 *in Annex* 12)

802 **Volkszugehörigkeit,** *f.,* ethnic origin (CERD 4), nationality
(*Staatsangehörigkeit, *Staatszugehörigkeit)

803 **volljährig,** *adj.,* of (full) age, having attained (his) majority

804 **Volljähriger,** *adj.n.,* person of full age, person who has attained his majority

805 **Volljährigkeit,** *f.,* majority, age of majority, full age
(*Minderjährigkeit)

806 **Vollmacht,** *f.,* authority; (*frequently in pl.:* **Vollmachten** = full power(s), *pleins pouvoirs,* credentials)

807 **die Vollmacht, die erforderlich ist (WMO 23),** such authority as may be required

808 **Die Vollmachten der Delegierten werden zur Prüfung vorgelegt (ILO 2),** The credentials of delegates shall be subject to scrutiny

809 **Ausstellung der Vollmachten,** issue of full power(s)

810 **Austausch der Vollmachten,** exchange of full powers

811 **nach Austausch ihrer in guter und gehöriger Form befundenen Vollmachten,** having exchanged their full powers found (to be) in good and due form

812 **Hinterlegung der Vollmachten,** deposit of full powers

813 **Mitteilung der Vollmachten,** communication of full power(s)

814 **Prüfung der Vollmachten,** examination/scrutiny of full powers

815 **Vollmachten ausstellen,** to issue full power(s)

816   die vom Staatsoberhaupt auszu-
       stellenden Vollmachten, the full
       power(s) that must be issued by
       the head of state
817   Vollmachten   austauschen,   to
       exchange full powers
818   Vollmachten hinterlegen, to deposit
       full powers
819   Vollmachten vorlegen, to present
       full powers
820   Vollmachten vorweisen, to exhibit/to
       present full powers
       (See also VCLOT 2 in Annex 14.)
821   Vollmachtenprüfungsausschuß,
       m., credentials committee
822   Vollmachtenurkunde, f., creden-
       tials
823   Vollmitglied, n., full member
824   Vollsitzung, f. (= *Plenarsitzung,
       f.), plenary session/sitting, full ses-
       sion (see note to *Sitzung)
825   Der Gerichtshof tagt in Vollsit-
       zungen, The full court shall sit (SICJ
       25), The Court of Justice shall sit in
       plenary session (EEC 165)
826   vollstreckbar, adj., enforceable,
       capable of implementation
827   vorläufig vollstreckbar, provision-
       ally enforceable
828   Vollstreckbarkeit, f., enforceabil-
       ity
829   vollstrecken, to enforce, to execute,
       to implement
830   ein Urteil/eine Entscheidung voll-
       strecken, to execute/enforce an
       award/judgment/decision
831   Vollstreckung, f., enforcement,
       execution
832   Vollstreckung   eines   Urteils,
       enforcement/execution of an award/
       judgment
833   Vollstreckungsaufschub, m., stay
       of enforcement/execution
834   Vollstreckungsgewalt¹, f., execu-
       tive
835   Vollstreckungsgewalt², f., juris-
       diction
836   Vollstreckungsmaßnahme,   f.,
       enforcement measure/action
837   Der Küstenstaat darf Vollstrek-
       kungs- oder Sicherungsmaßnahmen
       gegen das Schiff ergreifen (GCTS

       20), The coastal state may levy ex-
       ecution against or arrest the ship
838   Gegen einen Diplomaten dürfen
       Vollstreckungsmaßnahmen nur un-
       ter der Voraussetzung getroffen wer-
       den, daß sie durchführbar sind
       (VCDR 31), No measures may be
       taken in respect of a diplomatic
       agent except provided that the mea-
       sures concerned can be taken
839   Vollstreckungsorgan, n., execu-
       tive organ/body
840   Vollversammlung, f., General
       Assembly
841   vollziehen, to execute
842   vollziehende Gewalt, executive,
       executive authority
843   Vollziehung, f., execution
844   Vollzug, m., execution
845   Vollzugsausschuß, m., executive
       committee
846   Vollzugsgewalt, f., executive,
       executive authority
847   Vollzugskommission, f., executive
       commission/committee
848   Vollzugs- und Verbindungskommis-
       sion, executive and liaison commit-
       tee
849   Vollzugsorgan, n., executive
       organ/body
850   Vorabentscheidung, f., prelimi-
       nary decision
851   im Wege der Vorabentscheidung
       entscheiden, to make a preliminary
       decision
852   Vorbehalt, m., reservation
853   ohne Vorbehalt, without reserva-
       tion
854   ohne Vorbehalt der Genehmi-
       gung/Ratifizierung (usw.), without
       reservation as to/in respect of
       approval/ratification (etc.)
855   sie können Vertragspartei werden:
       (a) indem sie es ohne Vorbehalt
       der Ratifizierung unterzeichnen;
       (b) indem sie es unter Vorbehalt
       der Ratifizierung unterzeichnen
       und danach ratifizieren (RMCE
       8), (who) may become parties to
       the Agreement either by: (a) sig-
       nature without reservation in
       respect of ratification; (b) signa-

ture with reservation in respect of ratification followed by ratification

856 **unter Vorbehalt,** subject to/with reservation

857 **die unter Vorbehalt beitretenden Mitglieder,** (new) members acceding subject to reservation

858 **unter Vorbehalt folgender Bestimmungen,** subject to the following provisions/terms

859 **von diesen Vorbehalten abhängig,** conditional on these reservations

860 **Annahme des Vorbehalts,** acceptance of the reservation (*see* *vorbehaltend*)

861 **Tragweite des Vorbehalts,** scope of the reservation

862 **Wirkung des Vorbehalts,** effect of the reservation

863 **die Wirkung des Vorbehalts erlischt am . . .,** such a reservation shall cease to have effect on . . .

864 **hinderlicher Vorbehalt,** inhibitive reservation

865 **Ein Vorbehalt gilt als hinderlich, wenn mindestens zwei Drittel der Vertragsstaaten Einspruch dagegen erheben** (CERD 20), A reservation shall be considered inhibitive if at least two thirds of the states parties to this Convention object to it

866 **unvereinbarer Vorbehalt,** reservation incompatible (with . . .)

867 **Mit dem Ziel und Zweck dieses Übereinkommens unvereinbare Vorbehalte sind nicht zulässig** (CERD 20), A reservation incompatible with the object and purpose of this Convention shall not be permitted

868 **unzulässiger Vorbehalt,** inadmissible reservation

869 **zulässiger Vorbehalt,** admissible/permissible reservation

870 **Vorbehalte zu diesem Abkommen sind nicht zulässig,** Reservations to this agreement shall not be permitted

871 **Vorbehalte anbringen / erheben / er-**

klären, to make/to formulate reservations

872 **Jeder Staat kann spätestens bei der Ratifizierung einen oder mehrere der in den Artikeln . . . vorgesehenen Vorbehalte erklären; andere Vorbehalte sind nicht zulässig** (CCFTD 18), Any state may, not later than the moment of its ratification, make one or more of the reservations mentioned in Articles . . .; no other reservation shall be permitted

873 **der den Vorbehalt anbringende Staat** (VCLOT 20), the reserving state

874 **Vorbehalte zulassen,** to admit/to permit of reservations

875 **Dieser Vertrag läßt Vorbehalte nicht zu,** The present treaty shall not admit/permit of reservations

876 **Vorbehalte zurücknehmen/zurückziehen,** to withdraw/to abandon reservations

(*See also* VCLOT 2 *in Annex* 14 *and* VCLOT 19/20 *in Annex* 21.)

877 **vorbehalten,** to reserve

878 **vorbehalten, sich,** to reserve (the right/the option)

879 **vorbehaltend,** *adj.*, making the reservation

880 **Die Annahme eines Vorbehalts durch einen einzigen Staat bewirkt, daß der vorbehaltende Staat gegenüber dem annehmenden Staat zum Vertragspartner wird,** The acceptance of a reservation by an individual state has the effect of the state making the reservation becoming a party to the treaty as against the state accepting the reservation

881 **vorbehaltlich,** *prep.* (+ *gen.*), subject to, pending, except as provided in

882 **vorbehaltlich der Bestimmungen der Artikel . . .,** subject to the provisions of Articles . . .

883 **vorbehaltlich der endgültigen Entscheidung** (SICJ 41), pending the final decision

884 **vorbehaltlich einer entsprechenden Verpflichtung** (SICJ 36), on condition of reciprocity

885 **Vorbehaltserklärung,** *f.*, reservation, statement/formulation of a
reservation
886 **vorbehaltslos,** *adj.*, without reserva-
tion(s)
887 **Vorbehaltsurteil,** *n.*, provisional/
reserved judgment/award
888 **Vorbereitungsausschuß,** *m.*, preparatory committee
889 **Vorbeugungsmaßnahme,** *f.*, preventive measure/action
890 **Vorbeugungs- oder Zwangsmaßnahmen ergreifen** (CUN 2), to take preventive or enforcement action
891 **Vorgängerstaat,** *m.*, predecessor
state
892 **vorgehen**[1], to proceed, to act
893 **vorgehen**[2], to have precedence over
894 **Die allgemeinen Regeln des Völkerrechts sind Bestandteil des Bundes-
rechts. Sie gehen den Gesetzen vor**
(GG 25), The general rules of international law shall be an integral part
of federal law. They shall take precedence over the laws
895 **der Grundsatz, daß die Spezialnorm
der allgemeinen Norm vorgehe,** the
principle that a special(ized) rule
shall have/take precedence over a
general rule
896 **Vorgehen,** *n.*, act, conduct, action
897 **in der Erkenntnis, daß zur
Beseitigung der bestehenden Hindernisse ein . . . Vorgehen erforderlich
ist,** recognizing that the removal of
existing obstacles calls for . . . action
898 **vorgelagert,** *adj.*, (situated) in front
of, off, adjacent to
899 **die der Küste vorgelagerten Inseln,**
the islands situated off-shore/lying
close to/off the coast
900 **Gewässer, die den in Anlage I
aufgeführten Küsten vorgelagert sind**
(FC 12), waters adjacent to the coasts
listed in Annex I
901 **vorgesehen,** *adj.*, provided for, set
out, set forth
902 **in den Artikeln . . . vorgesehene Be-
fugnisse/Maßnahmen (usw.),** au-
thority/action (etc.) provided for in
Articles . . .
903 **Vorkehren,** *n.* (= Vorkehrung, *f.*),

arrangement (*as a unilateral act*),
measure (*see note to* *Vertrag *in*
Annex 1)
904 **vorladen,** to summon
905 **Vorladung,** *f.*, summoning
906 **die Vorladung von Zeugen und
Sachverständigen** (FC An), the summoning and hearing of witnesses
and experts
(*Ladung)
907 **Vorlage,** *f.*, presentation, submission,
exhibition
908 **Der Gerichtshof kann von den
Bevollmächtigten die Vorlage aller
Urkunden verlangen** (SICJ 49), The
court may call upon the agents to
produce any document
909 **die Vorlage von Vollmachten,** presentation of full power(s)/credentials
910 **vorläufig,** *adj.*, provisional
911 **vorläufige Anwendung,** provisional
application
912 **vorlegen**[1], to submit, to refer (*e.g. a
dispute or a matter*)
913 **vorlegen**[2], to present, to exhibit
(*e.g. credentials*)
914 **Vorlegung**[1], *f.*, submission, referring,
referral
915 **Vorlegung**[2], *f.*, presentation, exhibition
(* Vorlage)
916 **Vormund,** *m.*, trustee, guardian
917 **als Vormund für Entmündigte handeln,** to act as trustee for persons
lacking/who have lost full capacity/
who are legally incapacitated
918 **Vormundschaft,** *f.*, trusteeship,
guardianship
919 **Vorrang**[1] *m.* **vor,** precedence/order
of precedence over (*e.g. of judges/
diplomats*)
920 **Dieser Antrag ist mit Vorrang zu
behandeln** (ECER 26), Any such
motion shall have priority
(*Anciennität)
921 **Vorrang**[2] *m.* **vor,** supremacy/prima-
cy over (*e.g. of international law
over state law*)
(*vorgehen[2])
922 **Vorrang-Klausel,** *f.*, precedence
clause
(* vorgehen[2])

923 Vorrecht, *n.* (*usu. in pl.*), privilege
924 **Vorrechte und Befreiungen,** privileges and immunities
925 **Die Vertreter im Ministerkomitee genießen während der Ausübung ihrer amtlichen Tätigkeit folgende Vorrechte und Befreiungen** (PrivExCE 9), Representatives at the Committee of Ministers shall, while exercising their functions, enjoy the following privileges and immunities
926 **Die Vorrechte und Befreiungen werden den Richtern nicht zu ihrem persönlichen Vorteil gewährt, sondern um die unabhängige Ausübung ihres Amtes zu gewährleisten,** Privileges and immunities are granted to judges not for the personal benefit of the individuals themselves but to ensure the independent performance of their duties
927 **jeder Mißbrauch der in diesem Protokoll vorgesehenen Vorrechte, Befreiungen und Erleichterungen** (PPELDO 22), any abuse of the privileges, immunities and facilities provided for in this protocol
928 **Vorrechte und Immunitäten,** privileges and immunities
929 **soweit der Empfangsstaat nicht zusätzliche Vorrechte und Immunitäten gewährt . . .** (VCDR 38), except insofar as additional privileges and immunities may be granted by the receiving state
930 **Ihre Vorrechte und Immunitäten bleiben bis zu ihrer Ausreise/Abreise,** Their privileges and immunities shall subsist until the time of their departure
931 **Vorrechte und Immunitätsrechte,** privileges and immunities (*See under* *Befreiung von, *Immunität von *for list of privileges.*)
932 **Vorsatz, *m.*,** intention, intent
933 **in dem Vorsatz . . .,** intending . . . (*in preamble*)
934 **mit Vorsatz,** wilfully, with (malicious) intent, deliberately

935 **eine mit Vorsatz begangene Handlung oder Unterlassung** (VCLD IV 2), an act or omission done with intent (*vorsätzlich)
936 **vorsätzlich , *adj.*,** wilful, intentional, deliberate, with (malicious) intent
937 **ein vorsätzlich begangenes Unrecht,** a wilfully committed wrong
938 **die vorsätzliche oder fahrlässige Unterbrechung eines unterseeischen Kabels** (GCHS 27), the breaking of a submarine cable done wilfully or through culpable negligence
939 **Vorschlag, *m.*,** proposal
940 **der Vorschlag wird für alle Vertragsregierungen am . . . wirksam,** the proposal shall become effective for all contracting parties on . . .
941 **auf Vorschlag der Kommission** (EEC 8), on a proposal from the Commission
942 **Annahme des Vorschlags,** acceptance/adoption of the proposal
943 **vorschlagen,** to propose, to make a proposal, to nominate
944 **von den Vertragsparteien vorgeschlagene Sachverständige** (ES 25), experts nominated by the contracting parties
945 **vorschreiben,** to prescribe, to require, to lay down
946 **Vorschrift, *f.*,** provision, regulation, rule
947 **Gesetze und Vorschriften,** laws and regulations, laws and other legal provisions
948 **allgemeine Vorschrift,** general regulation
949 **(inner)staatliche Vorschrift,** national/domestic/internal regulation
950 **allgemein übliche Vorschrift,** generally applicable rule
951 **universale Vorschrift,** universal regulation (*Rechtsvorschrift)
952 **Vorsichtsmaßnahme, *f.*,** precautionary measure
953 **Vorsitzender, *adj.n.*,** chairman (*Obmann)
954 **Vorspruch, *m.*,** preamble (*for samples see Annex* 4)

955 **Vorstand**, *m*., board, board of directors
956 **Der Ausschuß wählt seinen Vorstand für 2 Jahre** (CERD 10), The committee shall elect its officers for a term of two years
957 **vorstehend**, *adj*., preceding, foregoing
958 **der vorstehende Artikel/Absatz (usw.)**, the preceding/foregoing article/paragraph (etc.)
959 **Vorvereinbarung**, *f*., preliminary agreement (*see note to* *Vertrag *in* Annex* 1)
960 **Vorverfahren**, *n*., preliminary procedure, preliminaries
961 **Vorvertrag**, *m*., preliminary treaty (*see note to* *Vertrag *in* Annex* 1)
962 **Vorzugsbehandlung**, *f*., preferential treatment
963 **Vorzugsbehandlung eines Diplomaten bei der Gepäckkontrolle**, preferential treatment of a diplomatic agent in respect of the inspection of the/his luggage

W

1 **Waffen,** *f.pl.,* arms, weapons, armaments

2 **ABC-Waffen,** ABC weapons

3 **atomare Waffen,** atomic weapons

4 **biologische Waffen,** biological weapons

5 **chemische Waffen,** chemical weapons

6 **ferngelenkte Waffen,** guided missiles

7 **herkömmliche/konventionelle Waffen,** conventional weapons

8 **(thermo)nukleare Waffen,** (thermo)-nuclear weapons

9 **die Waffen (offen) führen,** to carry arms (openly)

10 **zu den Waffen greifen,** to take up arms

11   **aus eigenem Antrieb zu den Waffen greifen (GC I),** to spontaneously take up arms

12   **bevor sie zu den Waffen greifen** (HgI 2), before an appeal to arms

13 **die Waffen niederlegen/strecken,** to lay down arms

14 **die Waffen (offen) tragen,** to carry arms (openly)
(*see* NATA An *and* WEU III An *in Annex* 18)

15 **Waffenart,** *f.,* type of armaments

16 **Waffenbestände,** *m.pl.,* quantities/stocks of weapons/armaments

17 **Waffengebrauch,** *m.,* use of weapons/arms

18 **Waffengewalt,** *f.,* force, armed force, force of arms

19 **Waffenhandel,** *m.,* trade in arms, arms traffic

20   **allgemeine Überwachung des Waffen- und Munitionshandels,** general supervision of the trade in arms and ammunition

21 **Waffenruhe,** *f.,* suspension of hostilities

22 **Waffenstillstand,** *m.,* armistice, truce, cease-fire

23   **Verletzung der Bedingungen des Waffenstillstandes,** violation of the terms/conditions of the armistice

24 **Waffenstillstandsabkommen,** *n.,* armistice agreement (*see note to* *Vertrag *in Annex* 1)

25 **Waffenstillstandsangebot,** *n.,* armistice offer

26 **Waffenstillstandskommission,** *f.,* armistice commission

27 **Waffenstillstandsdelegation,** *f.,* armistice delegation

28 **Waffenstillstandsverhandlungen,** *f.pl.,* armistice negotiations

29 **Waffenstillstandsvertrag,** *m.,* armistice treaty (*see note to* *Vertrag *in Annex* 1)

30 **Wahl,** *f.,* election, ballot, vote

31   **alle Wahlen erfolgen in geheimer Abstimmung (ECER 38),** all elections shall be decided by secret ballot

32   **geheime Wahl,** secret ballot

33   **in geheimer Wahl aus einer Liste von Personen gewählt, die von . . . benannt worden sind (CERD 8),** elected by secret ballot from a list of persons nominated by . . .

34 **wählbar,** *adj.,* eligible (for election)

35   **Nur diese Personen sind wählbar,** Only these persons are eligible

36 **Wählbarkeit,** *f.,* eligibility (for election)

37 **Wahlkonsul,** *m.,* honorary consul/consular officer

38 **Wahlordnung,** *f.,* method/system of voting, voting regulations

39 **wahrnehmen,** to perform, to exercise, to fulfil, to discharge, to uphold

40   **die Hoheitsgebiete, deren internationale Beziehungen der Staat wahrnimmt (SF 91),** the territories for the international relations of which the state is responsible

41   **Aufgaben/Funktionen wahrnehmen,** to perform/discharge/exercise functions

42   **Interessen wahrnehmen,** to uphold/protect interests

43   **Rechte wahrnehmen,** to uphold/protect rights
(*Wahrnehmung)

44 **Wahrnehmung,** *f.*, performance, exercise, discharge, fulfilment
45   **Wahrnehmung von Aufgaben,** performance / discharge / exercise / fulfilment of duties/functions
46   **vom Empfangsstaat zur Wahrnehmung ihrer Aufgaben zugelassen** (VCCR 10), admitted to the exercise of their functions by the receiving state
47   **die wirksame Wahrnehmung ihrer Aufgaben gewährleisten** (VCDR Pr), to ensure the efficient performance of their functions
48   **der Mission jede Erleichterung zur Wahrnehmung ihrer Aufgaben gewähren** (VCDR 26), to accord full facilities for the performance of the functions of the mission
49   **Die Generalversammlung kann Nebenorgane einsetzen, soweit sie dies zur Wahrnehmung ihrer Aufgaben für erforderlich hält** (CUN 22), The General Assembly may establish such subsidiary organs as it deems necessary for the performance of its functions (* Erfüllung, *wahrnehmen)
50 **Wahrung,** *f.*, protection, preservation
51   **Wahrung der Rechte/Interessen,** protection / preservation / upholding of rights/interests
52 **Währung,** *f.*, currency
53   **Landeswährung,** local/national currency
54 **Währungsabkommen,** *n.*, monetary agreement
55 **Währungsausschuß,** *m.*, monetary committee
56 **Währungsgebiet,** *n.*, currency/monetary area
57   **Zahlungsverkehr in den Währungen und zwischen den Währungsgebieten der Vertragsparteien** (EMA 8), transactions in the currencies and between the monetary areas of the contracting parties
58 **Währungshoheit,** *f.*, monetary sovereignty
59 **Währungskonferenz,** *f.*, monetary conference

60 **Währungspolitik,** *f.*, monetary policy
61 **Währungsreform,** *f.*, currency reform
62 **Wahrzeichen,** *n.* (GC I), emblem
63   **Wahr- und Schutzzeichen** (GC I), emblem and distinctive sign
64 **Wanderarbeiter,** *m.* (ES), migrant worker
65 **Wanderung(sbewegung),** *f.*, migration
66   **Wanderungsbewegung zwecks Siedlung** (ILO), migration for settlement
67   **Wanderungsbewegung zur Erlangung von Beschäftigung** (ILO), migration for employment
68 **Wappen,** *n.*, emblem, coat of arms
69   **Der Entsendestaat ist berechtigt, seine Nationalflagge und sein Wappen zu benutzen** (VCCR 29), The sending state shall have the right to the use of its national flag and coat of arms
70 **Waren,** *f.pl.*, goods, products
71   **Austausch von Waren,** exchange of goods
72   **Bewertung der Waren,** valuation of goods (*see* * Zollwert)
73 **Warenbeschreibung,** *f.*, description of goods
74 **Warenverkehr,** *m.*, (visible) trade, trade in goods
75   **Liberalisierung des Warenverkehrs** (EMA Pr), liberalization of trade
76   **freier Warenverkehr** (EEC), freedom of movement for goods
77   **internationaler Warenverkehr auf der Straße** (ICC Pr), international transport of goods by road
78 **Wasser,** *n.*, water, waters
79   **das darüber befindliche Wasser** (GCF), the superjacent water/waters (* Gewässer, *Festlandsockel)
80 **Wasserfläche** *f.* **von Buchten** (GCTS), water area(s) of bays
81   **die größtmögliche Wasserfläche** (GCTS 7), the maximum area of water
82 **Wassergrenze,** *f.*, water frontier/boundary
83 **Wasserrecht** *n.*, **internatio-**

nales, law of international waters/rivers/waterways

84 **Wege, im/aufdem,** by, by means of
85 **im Wege des Boykotts** (ECSC 65), by boycott
86 **im Wege eines Schiedsverfahrens** (ECSC 65), by arbitration
87 **im Wege gütlicher Verhandlung** (EAEC 14), by friendly means
88 **im Wege unmittelbarer Verhandlungen zwischen ihnen,** by direct negotiation between them
89 **im Wege eines Vertrags,** by treaty, by way of (a) treaty
90 **auf diplomatischem Wege,** through diplomatic channels
91 **auf gütlichem Wege,** amicably
92 **Wegnahme,** *f.*, seizure, capture, expropriation
93 **gewaltsame Wegnahme** (IAEA IX), forcible seizure
94 **eine völkerrechtswidrige Wegnahme ausländischen Eigentums,** the seizure of foreign property/alien property in violation of international law (*Prisenrecht)
95 **Wegnahmerecht,** *n.*, right of seizure
96 **Wehrhoheit,** *f.*, military sovereignty
97 **Wehrmachtgefolge,** *n.*, army followers
98 **Wehrpflicht,** *f.*, military obligations, (duty to do/complete) national service
99 **die Wehrpflicht nur gegenüber einer der Vertragsparteien erfüllen** (CRMN 5), to fulfil military obligations in relation to one of the parties only (*i.e. in the case of dual/multiple nationality*)
100 **weigern,** to refuse, to refuse to grant
101 **Weigerung,** *f.*, refusal
102 **Weigerungsrecht,** *n.*, right to refuse/of refusal
103 **Weisung,** *f.*, instruction, directive
104 **Bei der Wahrnehmung ihrer Dienstobliegenheiten dürfen . . . (sie) . . . von keiner Stelle außerhalb der Organisation irgendwelche Weisungen erbitten oder entgegennehmen** (IAEA VII), In the performance of their duties . . . (they) . . . shall not seek or receive instructions from

any source external to the Agency

105 **Weisungsbefugnis,** *f.* (= Weisungsrecht, *n.*), authority/power to give directives/instructions
106 **Der Generaldirektor untersteht der Weisungsbefugnis und Kontrolle des Gouverneursrates** (IAEA VII), The Director-General shall be under the authority of and subject to the control of the Board of Governors

Weisungsrecht, *n.* = *Weisungsbefugnis, *f.*

107 **Weiteranwendung,** *f.*, continued application
108 **Weiteranwendung der übrigen Vertragsbestimmungen,** (VCLOT 44), continued performance of the remainder of the treaty
109 **der Gültigkeit des Vertrags, seinem Inkraftbleiben oder seiner Weiteranwendung stillschweigend zustimmen** (VCLOT 45), to acquiesce in the validity of the treaty or in its maintenance in force or in operation

Weitergabe, *f.* = *Weiterleitung, *f.*
weitergeben = *weiterleiten

110 **Weitergeltung,** *f.*, continuance in force
111 **weiterleiten** (= weitergeben), to transmit, to pass on (*e.g. documents*)
112 **Weiterleitung,** *f.* (= Weitergabe, *f.*), transmission
113 **an den Präsidenten zur Weiterleitung zu richten,** to be addressed to the President for transmission
114 **weiterliefern** (EExt), to re-extradite (*i.e. to a third state*)
115 **Weiterlieferung,** *f.* (EExt), re-extradition
116 **Weltabkommen,** *n.*, universal agreement/convention, world-wide agreement/convention
117 **Weltfrieden,** *m.*, universal peace, world peace, peace of the world, international peace
118 **Weltfrieden und Welteintracht,** universal peace and harmony
119 **der Weltfrieden und die internationale Sicherheit** (CUN 73), international peace and security
120 **die Herstellung und Wahrung des Weltfriedens** (CUN 26), the estab-

lishment and maintenance of international peace

121 **den Weltfrieden aufrechterhalten,** to maintain universal peace

122 **den Weltfrieden gefährden,** to endanger/jeopardize universal peace

123 **den Weltfrieden wahren (CUN 1),** to strengthen universal peace (*Frieden)

124 **Weltgemeinschaft,** *f.,* international/universal community, community of (all) states

125 **Welthandel,** *m.,* world trade, international trade, commerce of the world (CFIMT)

126 **die harmonische Entwicklung und Ausweitung des Welthandels (EFTA 2),** the harmonious development and expansion of world trade **Weltsicherheitsrat,** *m.* = *Sicherheitsrat, *m.*

127 **Wettbewerb,** *m.,* competition

128 **die Errichtung eines Systems, das den Wettbewerb innerhalb des Gemeinsamen Marktes vor Verfälschungen schützt (EEC 3),** the institution of a system ensuring that competition in the Common Market is not distorted

129 **redlicher Wettbewerb (EEC Pr),** fair competition

130 **Wettbewerbsbedingung,** *f.,* condition of competition

131 **Handel unter gerechten Wettbewerbsbedingungen (EFTA 2),** trade in conditions of fair competition

132 **wettbewerbsbeschränkend,** *adj.* (EFTA), restrictive, restrictive of competition

133 **wettbewerbsbeschränkende Praktiken,** restrictive practices

134 **Wettbewerbstarif,** *m.,* competitive tariff

135 **Wettrüsten,** *n.,* arms/armaments race

136 **Widerbeklagter,** *adj.n.,* defendant on a counterclaim

137 **Widerhandlung,** *f.,* contravention

138 **Widerklage,** *f.,* counterclaim, counter-action, cross-action, counter-suit

139 **Immunität von der Gerichtsbarkeit in** bezug auf eine Widerklage, die mit der Hauptklage in unmittelbarem Zusammenhang steht (VCDR 32), immunity from jurisdiction in respect of any counterclaim directly connected with the principal claim

140 **Erwiderung auf die Widerklage,** reply to the counterclaim

141 **Widerkläger,** *m.,* party/defendant bringing the counterclaim

142 **Widerruf,** *m.,* revocation, withdrawal

143 **Widerruf der Anerkennung,** withdrawal of recognition

144 **die Rechtswirkung des Widerrufs der Anerkennung entspricht der der ursprünglichen Nichtanerkennung,** the legal effect of the withdrawal of recognition is the same as that of non-recognition in the first place

145 **widerrufen,** to revoke, to withdraw

146 **Widerspruch,** *m.,* contradiction

147 **Staaten können Verträge schließen, die mit früheren Abkommen in Widerspruch stehen,** States may conclude treaties which are in contradiction to previous agreements

148 **soweit sie im Widerspruch zu diesem Abkommen stehen,** in so far as they are inconsistent with the present convention

149 **Widerstand,** *m.,* resistance

150 **bewaffneter Widerstand,** armed resistance

151 **Widerstandsbewegung,** *f.,* resistance movement

152 **Widerstandsgruppe,** *f.,* resistance group

153 **Widerstandskraft,** *f.,* power to resist

154 **gemeinsame Widerstandskraft gegen bewaffnete Angriffe (NAT 3),** collective capacity to resist armed attack

155 **wiederanwenden,** to reapply, to revive

156 **Wiederanwendung,** *f.,* revival, reapplication, renewed application/operation

157 **die Wiederanwendung eines Vertrags nach Friedensschluß,** the revival of a treaty after peace is concluded

158 **Wiederaufbauprogramm,** *n.,* recovery programme

159 **Wiederaufnahme**, *f.*, resumption (*e.g. of relations*), readmission (*e.g. to membership*), review (*e.g. of a case*) (*Revision)

160 **Wiederaufnahmeantrag**, *m.*, application for readmission/review

161 **Wiederaufnahmeverfahren**, *n.* (SICJ 61), proceedings in/for revision

162 **Wiederausfuhr**, *f.*, re-exportation

163 **wiederbenennen**, to renominate

164 **Wiederbenennung**, *f.*, renomination

165 **wiederbewaffnen**, to re-arm

166 **Wiederbewaffnung**, *f.*, re-armament

167 **Wiedereinbürgerung**, *f.*, recovery of nationality

168 **Wiedereingliederungsfonds**, *m.* (AACER), Resettlement Fund

169 **wiederernennen**, to reappoint

170 **Wiederernennung**, *f.*, reappointment

171 **Die Mitglieder des Schiedshofs werden für einen Zeitraum von 6 Jahren ernannt. Ihre Wiederernennung ist zulässig** (HgI 44), The members of the court are appointed for a term of 6 years. These appointments are renewable

172 **wiedereröffnen**, to re-open, to resume

173 **Wiedereröffnung**, *f.*, resumption, re-opening

174 **Wiedererwerb**, *m.*, recovery, re-acquisition

175 **wiedererwerben**, to recover, to re-acquire

176 **wiedergutmachen**, to compensate (for)

177 **Wiedergutmachung**, *f.*, compensation, reparation, restitution, indemnification

178 **unvollkommene Wiedergutmachung** (PHR 50), partial reparation

179 **Wiedergutmachungsausschuß**, *m.*, Reparation Commission

180 **Wiedergutmachungsleistung**, *f.*, (payment made as) compensation/reparation

181 **wiederinkraftsetzen**, to revive (in *Kraft setzen)

182 **Wiederkaperer**, *m.*, recaptor

183 **wiederkapern**, to recapture

184 **Wiederkaperung**, *f.*, recapture

185 **wiedervereinigen**, to re-unite

186 **Wiedervereinigung**, *f.*, re-unification

187 **wiedervorlegen**, to resubmit (*report, budget, etc.*)

188 **Wiedervorlegung**, *f.*, resubmission

189 **Wiederwahl**, *f.*, re-election

190 **Ihre Wiederwahl ist zulässig** (PHR 40), They may be re-elected

191 **wiederwählbar**, *adj.*, eligible for re-election, capable of re-election

192 **Die Mitglieder des IGHs sind wiederwählbar**, The members of the ICJ may be re-elected

193 **wiederwählen**, to re-elect

194 **Ausscheidende Mitglieder können nicht unmittelbar wiedergewählt werden** (CUN 23), A retiring member shall not be eligible for immediate re-election

195 **Wille**, *m.*, will, consent

196 **Nach der positivistischen Auffassung gründet sich das Völkerrecht ausschließlich auf den staatlichen Willen**, The positivist concept holds that international law is based exclusively on consent between states

197 **Wille des Volkes**, will of the people

198 **Der Wille des Volkes bildet die Grundlage für die Autorität der öffentlichen Gewalt** (UDHR 21), The will of the people shall be the basis of the authority of government

199 **fester Wille**, (firm) resolve

200 **in dem festen Willen** (= gewillt), determined (*in preamble*)

201 **in dem festen Willen, die Grundlagen für einen immer engeren Zusammenschluß der europäischen Völker zu schaffen** (SF 49), determined to establish the foundations of an ever closer union among the European peoples

202 **Willensübereinstimmung**, *f.*, agreement, consensus, mutual consent

203 **wirksam,** *adj.,* effective, operative, having efficacy

204 **wirksam werden,** to become effective/operative, to take effect

205 **Diese Erklärung wird mit dem Ablauf dieser Frist wirksam (ECSM 24),** Such notification shall take effect at the end of the period (*Inkrafttreten, in *Kraft treten)

206 **Wirksamkeit,** *f.,* effect, effectiveness, efficacy

207 **eine Organisation, die alle Garantien für Wirksamkeit bietet (GC I 10),** an organization which offers all guarantees of efficacy

208 **Wirksamkeit verleihen** (+ *dat.*), to give effect to

209 **außer Wirksamkeit setzen (CSMW 1),** to deprive of effect

210 **Wirkung,** *f.,* effect

211 **der Vertrag gilt mit Wirkung von dem Tag an dem . . .,** the treaty shall apply as from the date on which . . .

212 **die Absicht des Staates, der Unterzeichnung diese Wirkung beizulegen (VCLOT 12),** the intention of the state to give that effect to the signature

213 **bindende Wirkung,** binding effect

214 **Abgaben gleicher Wirkung,** charges with equivalent effect

215 **Wirkungsweise,** *f.,* operation (*Überprüfung)

216 **Wirtschaftsattaché,** *m.,* economic attaché

217 **Wirtschaftsausschuß,** *m.,* economic committee

218 **Wirtschafts- und Sozialausschuß (EEC, UN),** Economic and Social Committee

219 **Wirtschafts- und Finanzausschuß,** Economic and Financial Committee

220 **Wirtschaftsblockade,** *f.,* economic blockade

221 **Wirtschaftskommission,** *f.,* economic commission

222 **Wirtschaftskrieg,** *m.,* economic war(fare)

223 **Wirtschaftskriegführung,** *f.,* economic war(fare)

224 **Wirtschaftsrat,** *m.,* economic council

225 **Wirtschafts- und Sozialrat,** Economic and Social Council (UN)

226 **Wirtschaftssanktion,** *f.,* economic sanction

227 **Wirtschaftsverkehr,** *m.,* trade

228 **Wissenschaftsattaché,** *m.,* scientific attaché

229 **Wohl,** *n.,* welfare, well-being

·230 **das allgemeine Wohl,** common welfare, common well-being (*Wohlergehen)

231 **Wohlergehen,** *n.,* welfare, well-being

232 **Ziele des internationalen Friedens und des allgemeinen Wohlergehens der Menschheit (UNESCO),** objectives of international peace and of the common welfare of mankind

233 **wohnhaft,** *adj.,* resident

234 **dauernd/ständig wohnhaft,** permanently/normally resident

235 **im Empfangsstaat ständig wohnhafte Personen,** persons permanently resident in the receiving state

236 **Wohnland,** *n.* (TDRef), country of residence

237 **Wohnort,** *m.,* (permanent) (place of) residence

238 **Wohnort in dem Gebiet des Mitgliedstaats,** (permanent) residence in the territory of the member state

239 **Wohnsitz,** *m.,* place of (habitual) residence, place of domiciliation. (*Strictly speaking,* **Wohnsitz** *and* **Domizil** *are not equivalents of* domicile *in the sense of this term in English law, although many international texts will indicate such an equivalence.*)

240 **Personen, die ihren Wohnsitz in . . . haben,** persons normally/ordinarily resident in . . ., persons domiciliated in . . .

241 **Wortlaut,** *m.,* wording, text

242 **Geschehen in den Haag, am 5. Oktober 1961, in französischer und englischer Sprache, wobei im Falle von Abweichungen der französische Wortlaut maßgebend ist (CCFTD 20),** Done at The Hague, the 5th October 1961, in French and English, the French text prevailing in the case

of divergence between the two texts

243 **Wortlaut und Sinn des Vertrags,** letter and spirit of the treaty

244 **verbindlicher Wortlaut,** authentic text

245   **wobei jeder Wortlaut gleichermaßen verbindlich ist,** both texts being equally authentic

246 **in vollem Wortlaut,** *in extenso* (*beglaubigter Wortlaut, *maßgebender Wortlaut, *Übereinkunft)

247 **Wunsch,** *m.,* **in dem** (= von dem Wunsch geleitet/beseelt), desiring, desirous of, moved by the desire (*all in preamble*)

248 **Würde,** *f.,* dignity

249   **Würde der Mission,** dignity of the mission

250   **persönliche Würde,** personal dignity, dignity of the person

251 **Würdenträger,** *m.,* dignitary

Z

1 **Zahlungsabkommen,** *n.,* payments agreement (*see note to* *Vertrag *in Annex* 1)

2 **Zahlungsausgleich,** *m.,* settlement(s)

3 **multilaterales System des Zahlungsausgleiches** (EMA), multilateral system of settlements

4 **Zahlungsausgleichssystem,** *n.* (EMA), system of settlements

5 **Zahlungsbeschränkung,** *f.,* restriction on payments

6 **Zahlungsbeziehungen,** *f.pl.,* payments relations

7 **Zahlungssystem,** *n.,* payments system

8 **Zahlungsunion,** *f.,* payments union

9 **Zahlungsverkehr,** *m.,* payments, payments transaction(s)

10 **Zahlungsverkehrs-Ausschuß,** *m.* (EMA), Payments Committee

11 **Zedent,** *m.,* cedant (state) (*abtretender Staat)

12 **Zeitpunkt,** *m.* **(des Beitritts usw),** date (of accession, etc.)

13 **Zeitraum,** *m.,* term, period

14 **für einen Zeitraum von 2 Jahren gewählt,** elected for a term of 2 years

15 **nach einem angemessenen Zeitraum,** after a reasonable period of time (*Wiederernennung)

16 **Zensur,** *f.,* censorship

17 **. . . unterliegt nicht der Zensur, . . .** shall not be subject to censorship/no censorship shall be applied to . . . (amtlicher *Nachrichtenverkehr)

18 **Zentralausschuß,** *m.,* central committee

19 **Zentralkomitee,** *n.,* central committee

20 **Zentralkommission,** *f.,* central commission

21 **Zentralkommission für die Rheinschiffahrt** (SF 31), Central Commission for the Navigation of the Rhine

22 **Zentralstelle,** *f.,* central office

(ICCC), centre (WMO), central agency (*Stelle)

23 **zerklüftet,** *adj.,* indented

24 **Wenn eine Küste sehr zerklüftet ist, kann die Grundlinie aus geraden Linien bestehen, die zwischen geeigneten markanten Punkten gezogen werden,** In localities where the coast is deeply indented the base line can consist of straight lines drawn between appropriate prominent points (*Einschnitt)

25 **Zerklüftung,** *f.,* indentation (*Einschnitt)

26 **Zermürbungskrieg,** *m.,* war of attrition

27 **zerteilen,** to dismember, to partition

28 **Zerteilung,** *f.,* dismemberment, partition

29 **Zession,** *f.* (= *Abtretung, *f.*), cession

30 **Zessionar,** *m.,* cessionary state

31 **Zessionsvertrag,** *m.,* treaty of cession (*see note to* *Vertrag *in Annex* 1)

32 **Zeuge,** *m.,* witness

33 **Vernehmung von Zeugen,** hearing of witnesses

34 **eine Liste von Zeugen und Sachverständigen, deren Vernehmung sie wünscht** (HgI 19), a list of witnesses and experts whose evidence it wishes to be heard

35 **Vorladung von Zeugen,** summoning of witnesses

36 **als Zeuge aussagen,** to depose/give evidence as a witness

37 **Der Diplomat ist nicht verpflichtet, als Zeuge auszusagen** (VCDR 31), A diplomatic agent is not obliged to give evidence as a witness

38 **als Zeuge erscheinen,** to appear as witness

39 **einen Zeugen aufrufen,** to summon/to call a witness, to require (the

attendance of) a witness to testify/
give evidence

40 **einen Zeugen hören/vernehmen,** to
question/to interrogate a witness

41 **einen Zeugen vorladen,** to summon/
to call a witness, to require (the
attendance of), a witness to testify/
give evidence

42 **Zeugenaussage,** *f.*, evidence, tes-
timony, deposition

43 **Beweismittel und Zeugenaussagen**
(SICJ 52), proofs and evidence

44 **Zeugenpflicht,** *f.* (= Zeugnispflicht, *f.*), obligation to give evi-
dence/to appear as witness, liability
to give evidence
Zeugnispflicht, *f.* = *Zeugenpflicht, *f.*

45 **Ziel,** *n.*, objective, aim, purpose

46 **die Ziele und Grundsätze der UN,**
the purposes and principles of the
UN

47 **Ziel der Organisation ist es, . . .**
(IAEA II), the Agency shall seek to
. . .

48 **dem Geist und den Zielen der UN
zuwiderlaufen** (PCG Pr), to be contrary to the spirit and aims of the
UN

49 **sie werden sich von den Zielen und
Prinzipien leiten lassen, die in . . .
niedergelegt sind,** they shall be
guided by the aims and principles set
forth in . . .
(*Zielsetzung)

50 **Zielsetzung,** *f.*, aims, purposes,
objectives

51 **Zielsetzung: Die Assoziation hat zum
Ziele . . .** (EFTA 2), Objectives:
The objectives of the Association
shall be . . .

52 **Zirkularnote,** *f.*, circular note

53 **zivil,** *adj.*, civilian, civil

54 **zivile Dienstgruppen** (CRFF 45),
civilian service units

55 **zivile Kriegsopfer,** civilian war victims

56 **Zivilbevölkerung,** *f.*, civilian population, civilians

57 **Zivilgericht,** *n.*, civilian court, civil
court

58 **Zivilgerichtsbarkeit,** *f.*, civil

jurisdiction

59 **Zivilgerichtsbarkeit des Aufnahme-
staates** (NATOSF VIII), jurisdiction of the courts of the receiving
state

60 **Zivilinternierter,** *adj.n.*, civilian
internee (GC), interned civilian

61 **Zivilinternierung,** *f.*, civil internment

62 **Zivilkrankenhaus,** *n.*, civilian hospital

63 **Zivilluftfahrt,** *f.*, civil aviation

64 **Zivilluftfahrzeug,** *n.*, civil aircraft

65 **Zivilpersonal,** *n.*, civilian personnel

66 **Zivilperson,** *f.*, civilian

67 **verwundete oder kranke Zivilpersonen** (GC I), civilian wounded or sick

68 **Zivilprozeßrecht,** *n.* (= Zivilverfahrensrecht, *n.*), law relating
to/governing civil procedure

69 **Zivilrecht,** *n.*, civil law

70 **Zivilverfahren,** *n.*, civil procedure,
civil action

71 **im Falle eines von einem Dritten
angestrengten Zivilverfahrens**
(PPELDO 5), in respect of a civil
action by a third party
Zivilverfahrensrecht, *n.* =
*Zivilprozeßrecht, *n.*

72 **Zoll,** *m.*, customs, customs duty

73 **Abschaffung der Zölle und
mengenmäßigen Beschränkungen**
(EEC 3), elimination of customs
duties and of quantitative restrictions

74 **Zölle und sonstige Abgaben gleicher
Wirkung** (EFTA 3), customs duties
and other charges with equivalent
effect

75 **autonome Zölle,** autonomous duties
(*Abgabe[1])

76 **Zollabfertigung,** *f.*, customs clearance

77 **Zollabgabe,** *f.*, customs charge/duty

78 **Zollabkommen,** *n.*, customs agreement (*see note to* *Vertrag *in Annex
1)

79 **Zollbefreiung,** *f.*, exemption from
customs duties

80 **Zollbehandlung,** *f.*, tariff treatment

81 **Waren, welchen die Zollbehandlung
der Zone zusteht/gewährt wird**

(EFTA 3/4), goods which are eligible/shall be accepted as eligible for area tariff treatment

82 **Zollbereich,** *m.*, customs area
83 **Zollbuße,** *f.* (ICCA), customs penalty
84 **Zollerleichterungen,** *f.pl.*, customs facilities
85 die gleichen Zollerleichterungen hinsichtlich ihres persönlichen Gepäcks wie die Diplomaten (PPELDO 14), the same customs facilities as regards their personal luggage as are accorded to diplomatic agents
86 **Zollflughafen,** *m.* (CAC), customs airport
87 **Zollfreiflughafen,** *m.* (CAC), customs-free airport
88 **Zollfreiheit,** *f.*, duty-free treatment (GATT 28), freedom from customs duties
89 **Zollgebiet,** *n.* (CCC), customs territory
90 **Zollgesetz,** *n.*, customs law
91 **Zollhoheit,** *f.*, customs sovereignty
92 **Zollkontingent,** *m.*, tariff quota
93 **Zollkontingenten für welche die Zollsätze niedriger liegen oder gleich null sind** (GATT 25), tariff quotas at a reduced rate of duty or duty-free
94 **zollrechtlich,** *adj.*, (relating to) customs
95 **zollrechtliche Gesetze und Vorschriften,** customs laws and regulations
96 **zollrechtliche Überwachung eines Küstenstaates,** customs control/supervision exercised by a littoral state over entry (and exit) of goods
97 **Zollrückvergütung,** *f.* (EFTA), drawback
98 **Unter ,,Zollrückvergütung" ist jede Einrichtung für teilweise oder gänzliche Rückerstattung von Zöllen zu verstehen** (EFTA 7), "Drawback" means any arrangement for the refund, wholly or in part, of duties
99 **Zollsatz,** *m.*, rate of (customs) duty (*Zollkontingent)
100 **Zollschutz,** *m.* (GATT), tariff protection

101 **Zolltarif,** *m.*, customs tariff
102 **gemeinsamer Zolltarif,** common customs tariff
103 **Zolltarifrecht,** *n.* (GATT), tariff laws
104 **Zolltarifverhandlung,** *f.*, customs tariff negotiation
105 **Zolltechnik,** *f.*, customs technique (CCC Pr), customs procedures (CCC III), technical customs matters (CCC X)
106 **Zollüberwachung,** *f.*, customs supervision
107 **Zollunion,** *f.*, customs union
108 **Zollvereinbarung,** *f.*, customs agreement (*see note to* *Vertrag *in* Annex 1*)
109 **Zollverfahren,** *n.*, customs procedure
110 **Zollverschluß,** *m.*, customs seal
111 **Zollverwaltung,** *f.*, customs administration
112 **Zollvorschrift,** *f.*, customs regulation, law relating to customs (CAC 22)
113 **Zollwert,** *m.*, customs value, value for customs purposes
114 **Ausschuß für den Zollwert,** (Customs) Valuation Committee
115 **Ermittlung des Zollwerts,** valuation for customs purposes (GATT VII), determination of the value for customs purposes
116 **Zone,** *f.*, zone, belt, area
117 **Als ,,Zone" gelten alle Gebiete, auf die dieses Übereinkommen Anwendung findet** (EFTA 1), The Area of the Association shall be the territories to which this Convention applies
118 **Zonen, deren Betreten aus Gründen der nationalen Sicherheit verboten oder geregelt ist** (VCDR 26), zones entry into which is prohibited or regulated for reasons of national security
119 **innerhalb der Zone zwischen der 6. und der 12. Meile von der Basislinie des Küstenmeeres aus gemessen** (GCTS), within the belt between 6 and 12 miles measured from the baseline of the territorial sea

120 **angrenzende Zone,** contiguous zone
121 **atomwaffenfreie Zone,** zone free of atomic weapons
122 **belagerte Zone** (GC IV), besieged area
123 **eingeschlossene Zone** (GC I), encircled area
124 **entmilitarisierte Zone,** demilitarized zone
125 **neutrale Zone,** neutral zone
126 **neutralisierte Zone,** neutralized zone
127 **strategische Zone,** strategic area (CUN 82), strategic zone
128 **Zonenursprung,** *m.* (EFTA), Area origin
129 **Zufahrt,** *f.*, access, ingress
130 **die Zufahrt und Ausfahrt von dritten Staaten durch Blockade behindern,** to disturb the ingress and egress/access and departure of ships of third states by a blockade
131 **freie Zufahrt,** free access
132 **Zufahrtsrecht,** *n.*, right of access
133 **Zuflucht,** *f.*, asylum
134 **Zuflucht zu Maßnahmen nehmen** (IMF 1), to resort to measures
135 **Zufluchtsland,** *n.* (= Asylland, *n.*), country of asylum, country granting asylum
136 **Zufluchtsstaat,** *m.*, state of asylum, state granting asylum
137 **Zugang,** *m.*, access
138 **freier Zugang,** free access (*see* *Binnenstaat)
139 **gleicher Zugang,** equal access
140 **nach dem Grundsatz des gleichen Zugangs zu den Versorgungsquellen** (EAEC 52), on the principle of equal access to resources
141 **unbehinderter Zugang,** unimpeded access
142 **zugelassen,** *adj.*, admitted, permitted, registered
143 **alle zum Gerichtshof zugelassenen Staaten,** all states entitled to appear before the court
144 **zulassen,** to admit, to permit, to declare (as) admissible/permissible
145 **jemanden zur Wahrnehmung seiner Aufgaben zulassen** (VCCR 14), to admit someone to the exercise of his functions

146 **zulässig,** *adj.*, admissible, permitted
147 **nicht zulässig,** inadmissible, not permitted
148 **Zulässigkeit,** *f.*, admissibility, permissibility
149 **Zulassung,** *f.*, admission
150 **(vorläufige) Zulassung des Leiters einer konsularischen Vertretung** (VCCR 10/13), (provisional) admission of heads of consular posts
151 **Zulassung zu einem Gebiet,** admission to a territory
152 **Zulassungsantrag,** *m.* (= Aufnahmeantrag, *m.*), application for admission (*e.g. to an organization*)
153 **Zulassungsausschuß,** *m.*, committee on/for admission
154 **zurechnen,** to attribute
155 **das Tun oder Unterlassen einem Völkerrechtssubjekt zurechnen,** to attribute an act or omission to a subject of international law
156 **zurückführen,** to return, to send home, to repatriate (*verschicken)
157 **Zurückführung,** *f.*, repatriation, transfer (back)
158 **zurücknehmen,** to revoke, to withdraw
159 **Eine Notifikation kann jederzeit zurückgenommen werden, bevor sie wirksam wird** (VCLOT 68), A notification may be revoked at any time before it takes effect
160 **zurücktreten,** to withdraw
161 **von einem Vertrag zurücktreten,** to withdraw from a treaty
162 **Eine Vertragspartei kann von diesem Übereinkommen zurücktreten** (SF 115), Any party may denounce this Convention in so far as it is concerned
163 **Zusammenarbeit,** *f.*, cooperation
164 **jene Zusammenarbeit zu fördern, von der der Friede der Welt abhängt** (CAC Pr), to promote that cooperation on which the peace of the world depends
165 **die Mitgliedstaaten koordinieren in enger Zusammenarbeit . . .** (EEC 6), the member states shall, in close cooperation, coordinate . . .

166 friedliche Zusammenarbeit, peaceful cooperation
167 internationale Zusammenarbeit, international cooperation
168 internationale Zusammenarbeit auf den Gebieten der Wirtschaft, des Sozialwesens, der Kultur, der Erziehung und der Gesundheit (CUN 13), international cooperation in the economic, social, cultural, educational and health fields
169 zusammenkommen, to meet, to assemble
170 die nach Art. 18 zusammenkommenden Vertragsparteien, the contracting parties meeting in conformity with Art. 18
171 Zusammenschluß, m., union
172 durch diesen Zusammenschluß ihrer Wirtschaftskräfte (EEC Pr), by pooling their resources
173 die Grundlagen für einen immer engeren Zusammenschluß der europäischen Völker schaffen (EEC Pr), to lay the foundations of an ever closer union among the peoples of Europe
174 regionale Zusammenschlüsse (EAEC), regional unions
175 zusammensetzen, sich, to be composed (of)
176 Zusammensetzung, f., composition
177 die Zusammensetzung der Generalversammlung, the composition of the General Assembly
178 zusammentreten, to meet (*Tagung)
179 Zusatzabkommen, n., supplemental/supplementary agreement (see note to *Vertrag in Annex 1)
180 Zusatzartikel, m., supplementary/additional article
181 Zusatzklausel, f., rider
182 Zusatzprotokoll, n., supplementary protocol
183 Einzelheiten sind im Zusatzprotokoll geregelt, Details shall be regulated in the supplementary protocol
184 Zusatzvereinbarung, f., supplementary agreement
185 zuständig, adj., competent, authorized, having jurisdiction, responsible

186 als zuständig erachtet/angesehen, regarded as competent
187 zuständig für, competent for, having jurisdiction in respect of/over
188 zuständiges Gericht, competent court
189 das Gericht ist für . . . zuständig (CRPG An), the tribunal shall have jurisdiction over . . .
190 zuständige Stellen, competent authorities/organs
191 örtlich zuständig, competent ratione loci (UNCDD), having local jurisdiction/competence (*Zuständigkeit, zuständiges *Gericht, *Strafgericht)
192 Zuständigkeit, f., competence, jurisdiction, responsibility
193 Zuständigkeit des Gerichts/Gerichtshofs, competence/jurisdiction of the court/court of justice
194 Ergibt sich die Zuständigkeit der Gerichte von mehr als einer Vertragspartei, so sind zuständig . . ., . . . und . . . (VCLD XI), Where jurisdiction would lie with the courts of more than one contracting party, jurisdiction shall lie with . . ., . . . and . . .
195 Wird die Zuständigkeit des Gerichtshofs bestritten, so entscheidet dieser (SICJ 36), In the event of a dispute as to whether the court has jurisdiction, the matter shall be settled by the decision of the court
196 in/unter die Zuständigkeit des . . . fallen, to fall/to come within/to come under the jurisdiction/competence of . . .
197 Angelegenheiten, die in die Zuständigkeit dieser Organe fallen (IAEA III), matters within the competence of these organs
198 Teilung der Zuständigkeit (ECE VII), division of responsibility
199 Zuständigkeit zu einem Vertragsabschluß, power/authority to conclude a treaty
200 ausschließliche Zuständigkeit eines Staates, exclusive jurisdiction of a state

201   **Fragen, die nach Völkerrecht in die ausschließlich innerstaatliche Zuständigkeit fallen** (ECPSD 27), questions which by international law are solely within the domestic jurisdiction (of states)

202   **innere/innerstaatliche Zuständigkeit eines Staates,** domestic jurisdiction of a state

203   **Angelegenheiten, die wesentlich/im wesentlichen zur inneren Zuständigkeit eines Staates gehören,** matters (which are) essentially within the domestic jurisdiction of a state

204   **örtliche Zuständigkeit,** local jurisdiction

205   **die Zuständigkeit anerkennen,** to recognize the competence/jurisdiction (*Gerichtsbarkeit)

206   **Zuständigkeitsbereich,** *m.*, competence, (field of) jurisdiction

207   **ein Eingriff in den ausschließlichen Zuständigkeitsbereich eines Staates,** intervention in the exclusive jurisdiction of a state

208   **im Rahmen seines Zuständigkeitsbereiches** (ECE VII), within its scope

209   **alle Fragen, die in seinen fachlichen Zuständigkeitsbereich fallen** (ECE III), any questions which fall within its technical field of competence (*Gerichtsbarkeit)

210   **zustehen** (+ *dat.*), to enjoy, to be granted

211   **Einer Vertragspartei, die ihren Beitrag nicht geleistet hat, stehen keine Rechte aus diesem Übereinkommen zu** (CINES 14), A contracting party which has not paid its contribution shall not enjoy any rights under this Conventon

212   **zustellen,** to serve, to serve notice of (*e.g. award/judgment*)

213   **zustimmen,** to consent, to agree

214   **Zustimmung,** *f.*, consent, assent, agreement

215   **Die Zustimmung eines Staates, durch einen Vetrag gebunden zu sein, kann durch Unterzeichnung,** Austausch von Urkunden, die einen Vertrag bilden, Ratifikation, Annahme, Genehmigung oder Beitritt oder auf eine andere vereinbarte Art ausgedrückt werden (VCLOT 11), The consent of a state to be bound by a treaty may be expressed by signature, exchange of instruments constituting a treaty, ratification, acceptance, approval or accession, or by any other means if so agreed

216   **ausdrückliche oder stillschweigende Zustimmung,** express or implied consent

217   **freie Zustimmung,** free consent

218   **parlamentarische Zustimmung,** parliamentary approval, approval by parliament

219   **Zustimmungserklärung,** *f.*, notice of acceptance, notice/declaration of consent

220   **Zuwachs,** *m.*, accretion (*Anschwemmung *and note*)

221   **zuweisen,** to confer (on), to assign (to)

222   **zuwiderhandeln,** to violate, to act in violation of

223   **Zuwiderhandlung,** *f.*, offence, infringement, violation

224   **Zuwiderhandlungen gegen,** offences against

225   **Zuwiderhandlungen gegen die Bestimmungen des vorliegenden Abkommens** (GC I 49), acts contrary to the provisions of the present Convention

226   **die für jede Zuwiderhandlung verhängte Strafe,** the penalty imposed for each infringement/offence

227   **angebliche Zuwiderhandlung,** alleged offence

228   **strafbare Zuwiderhandlung,** punishable offence

229   **Verstöße gegen die Artikel III und IX stellen Zuwiderhandlungen dar, die nach dem Recht des Hoheitsgebietes strafbar sind** (PPSO An), Any contravention of articles III and IX shall be an offence punishable under the law of the relevant territory (strafbare *Handlung)

230 **zuwiderlaufen,** to be contrary to, to
     be against the spirit of
231 **Handlungen, die den Vertragsbe-**
     stimmungen zuwiderlaufen, acts
     which are contrary to/in opposition
     to the provisions of the treaty
232 **Zwang,** *m.,* compulsion, coercion,
     constraint
233 **körperlicher oder seelischer Zwang**
     (GC IV), physical or moral coercion
234 **Befreiung von jedem behördlichen**
     Zwang genießen (PPELDO 5), to be
     immune from any form of adminis-
     trative constraint
235 **Zwangsaktion,** *f.,* enforcement
     action/measure
     (*Zwangsmaßnahme)
236 **Zwangsarbeit,** *f.,* forced labour
237 **die Anwendung der Zwangsarbeit**
     oder der Arbeitspflicht (SC 5), the
     recourse to compulsory or forced
     labour
238 **Nur erwachsene, arbeitsfähige Per-**
     soen männlichen Geschlechts, die
     offenbar nicht unter 18 und nicht
     über 45 Jahre alt sind, dürfen zu
     Zwangs- oder Pflichtarbeit heran-
     gezogen werden (ILOC 29.11), Only
     adult able-bodied males who are of
     an apparent age of not less than 18
     and not more than 45 years may be
     called upon for forced or compul-
     sory labour
     (*Pflichtarbeit)
239 **Zwangsaufenthalt,** *m.,* entorced
     residence
240 **die Zuweisung eines Zwangsaufent-**
     halts (GC IV), the placing in
     assigned residence
241 **jemandem einen Zwangsaufenthalt**
     auferlegen, to impose assigned resi-
     dence on someone, to subject some-
     one to assigned residence
     Zwangsdurchführung, *f.* =
     *Zwangsvollstreckung, *f.*
242 **Zwangsgewalt,** *f.,* coercive power,
     jurisdiction
243 **Das Missionsgebäude unterliegt**
     nicht der Zwangsgewalt des Emp-
     fangsstaates, The premises of the
     mission are exempt from/are not
     subject to the jurisdiction of the
     receiving state
244 **Zwangsgewalt über ... ausü-**
     ben, to exercise jurisdiction
     over ...
245 **Zwangsmaßnahme,** *f.,* coercive
     measure, enforcement measure/ac-
     tion, measure to enforce
246 **ein Staat, gegen den die Organisa-**
     tion Vorbeugungs- oder Zwangs-
     maßnahmen ergreift (CUN 2), any
     state against which the UN is taking
     preventive or enforcement action
247 **gemeinsame internationale Zwangs-**
     maßnahmen (CUN 45), combined
     international enforcement action
248 **Zwangsmittel,** *n.,* coercive means,
     means of enforcement
249 **Zwangsrepressalie,** *f.,* forcible
     reprisal
250 **Zwangsverschickung,** *f.* (GC IV),
     forcible transfer
251 **Zwangsverwaltung,** *f.,* sequestra-
     tion
     (*Beschlagnahme)
252 **Zwangsvollstreckung,** *f.* (=
     Zwangsdurchführung, *f.*). enforce-
     ment, execution, coercive execution
253 **Zweck,** *m.,* purpose, aim
254 **Zweck des Vertrags,** aim of the
     treaty
255 **Zweck der Organisation ist es, ...**
     (WMO 2), the purposes of the
     organization shall be:
256 **zu friedlichen Zwecken,** for peaceful
     purposes
     (*Ziel)
257 **zweckdienlich,** *adj.,* relevant, per-
     tinent, expedient
258 **Den Zeugen und Sachverständigen**
     werden alle zweckdienlichen Fragen
     ... vorgelegt (SICJ 51), Any relev-
     ant questions are to be put to the
     witnesses and experts
259 **die Herstellung zweckdienlicher**
     Beziehungen zwischen der Organisa-
     tion und der UN (IAEA XVI), the
     establishment of an appropriate
     relationship between the Agency
     and the UN
260 **in dem ihr zweckdienlich er-**
     scheinenden Umfang (ICCC 14), so
     far as it considers expedient

261 **Zweifelsfall,** *m.*, case of doubt
262 **im Zweifelsfall,** where doubt exists, in case of doubt, in cases where doubt exists
263 **Zweikammersystem,** *n.*, bicameral system
264 **zweiseitig,** *adj.*, bilateral
265 **zwingen,** to coerce, to enforce
266 **zwingend,** *adj.*, mandatory, compulsory, compelling, coercive, imperative, cogent
267 **zwingendes Völkerrecht,** mandatory (etc.) international law, mandatory (etc.) rules of international law
268 **aus zwingenden Rechtsgründen,** for imperative/cogent legal reasons
269 **Zwischenabkommen,** *n.*, interim agreement
270 **Zwischenbericht,** *m.*, interim report
271 **zwischenstaatlich,** *adj.*, intergovernmental, international, interstate, between states
272 **zwischenstaatliche Beziehungen,** international relations, interstate relations, relations between states
273 **zwischenstaatliche Konferenz,** intergovernmental/international conference
274 **zwischenstaatliche Organisation,** intergovernmental/international organization
275 **zwischenstaatliche Streitfälle** (ICCC Prot), disputes between states
276 **Zwischenurteil,** *n.*, interim/interlocutory award/judgment
(*For examples and collocations see under* * Urteil.)

PART II: ANNEXES

LIST OF ANNEXES

Annex 1: Note on the use of the terms "Vertrag/Treaty"

1. In principle there is no distinction as between the various designations used for specific international instruments (i.e. **Vertrag, Pakt, Abkommen, Übereinkommen, Konvention, Übereinkunft, Vereinbarung, Protokoll,** etc.), as such instruments are all subject to the principle of "pacta sunt servanda — treaties shall be observed". On the whole, the designation chosen will depend on one or more of the following considerations:
   (a) the solemnity or political significance of the instrument: a highly significant political instrument is most likely to be designated **Vertrag,** e.g. **der Grundvertrag, der Vertrag zur Gründung der EWG;**
   (b) whether it is bilateral or multilateral;
   (c) whether it is an addition to or a clarification of an already existing instrument;
   (d) the subject matter: e.g. if dealing with predominantly technical or scientific matters, **Vertrag** or **Pakt** are not likely to be used.

2. There is, however, no entirely systematic way of translating these various designations. Normally it is fairly safe to use the equivalent pairs **Vertrag:** *treaty,* **Pakt:** *pact,* **Protokoll:** *protocol,* although variations occur (e.g. **Völkerbundpakt:** *Covenant of the League of Nations,* **Inkrafttreten dieses Vertrags:** *entry into force of this Convention* in CSMW 3.
   It must also be noted that the designation used in *official* versions — whether original or translated — may well be changed in *unofficial* references/publications, such as textbooks. The change from **Übereinkommen** to **Konvention,** for example, is particularly common, hence e.g. the frequent **Diplomatenkonvention** for **(Wiener) Übereinkommen über diplomatische Beziehungen.**

3. The major difficulty probably lies with the complex **Abkommen, Übereinkommen, Konvention, Vereinbarung** on the one hand, and *agreement, convention, arrangement* on the other. The following may serve as a general guide:
   (a) **Abkommen.** Previously used more or less indiscriminately for bilateral and multilateral instruments (hence = *agreement* or *convention*). Since 1956 (according to SF) to be used only for bilateral instruments. This results in such variations as **Internationales Weizenabkommen** (1953), but **Internationales Weizenübereinkommen** (1956); **Dreierabkommen/Dreierübereinkommen,** etc.
   (b) **Übereinkommen.** On the basis of the comments in 3(a), used for multilateral instruments, hence = *agreement* or *convention.*
   (c) **Konvention** = **Übereinkommen,** but it is more likely to be encountered in unofficial texts. Occasionally = *covenant.*
   Conversely:
   (d) *Agreement.* If bilateral normally = **Abkommen,** if multilateral normally = **Übereinkommen/ Konvention.**
   (e) *Convention.* Normally = **Übereinkommen/Konvention.** On the few occasions where a convention is bilateral, then = **Abkommen.**
   (f) *Arrangement.* If unilateral normally = **Vorkehrung,** if bilateral or multilateral normally = **Vereinbarung. Regelung** may be used for either.

4. There are, however, many variations from the above general guide. *Agreement* may have to be translated by **Vereinbarung** (less formal than **Abkommen**), as **Abmachung** (normally referring to the more abstract meaning of *consensus*) or as **Übereinkunft,** which, especially in the plural, may have the sense of *instrument(s).* (See some examples under both *Abmachung and *Übereinkunft.)
   If there are *special agreements* within an *agreement* the more normal **Sonderabkommen** may be replaced by **Sondervereinbarung.**
   (*See also under Article* 2.1(a) *of* VCLOT *in Annex* 14.)

5. In any case, the golden rule must be to find the word actually used in the title of any international instrument that already exists. For instruments still in gestation, provisional titles are likely to exist, even in languages which will not be used for authentic versions; these provisional titles should be obtained from the experts, and used unless there are strong reasons for not doing so.

Annex 2: Typical stages in the conclusion of a treaty

1. **Konferenz** — conference

   (a) **Teilnehmer** — participants
   Vertreter der Staaten — representatives of the states
   (Delegierte der Staaten) — (delegates of the states)

   Vertreter zwischenstaatlicher Organisationen — representatives of intergovernmental organizations

   Vertreter internationaler Organisationen — representatives of international organizations

   Beobachter — observers

   (b) **Vorlage der Vollmachten** — **presentation of full powers/credentials**
   Verhandlungsvollmachten — power(s) to negotiate the treaty
   Abschlußvollmachten — power(s) to conclude the treaty

   (c) **Verhandlungen** — **negotiations**

   (d) **Einigung über** — **agreement on**
   den vorläufigen Vertragstext — the provisional text of the treaty
   den endgültigen Vertragstext — the final text of the treaty

   (e) **Paraphierung** oder **Unterzeichnung** — **initialling** or **signature**

2. **Zustimmung des Parlaments** — **approval of parliament**

3. **Ratifizierung** — **ratification** (may or may not be the same as stage 2)

4. **Vorbehalte** — **reservations**

5. **Austausch/Hinterlegung der Ratifikationsurkunden** — **exchange/deposit of instruments of ratification**

6. **Registrierung/Veröffentlichung des Vertrags** — **registration/publication of the treaty**

7. **Inkrafttreten** — **entry into force** (may take place any time after item 3 above)

8. **Kündigung/Erlöschen** — **denunciation/termination**

Annex 3: Typical structure of a treaty

1. **Überschrift**   **heading** (title, normally with indication of subject matter)

2. **Präambel**   **preamble** (general statement of motives, aims and purpose of the treaty, reference to previous similar treaties, sometimes with list of signatory states/parties)

3. **Vertragstext**   **text of the treaty** (the detailed regulation of the subject matter)

The text will always be arranged under

    Artikel   **articles**
and may be further arranged in one or more of the following:

    Kapitel   **chapter**
    Teil   **part**
    Abschnitt   **section**
Each of the above 3 types of subdivision will normally be introduced by a concise heading indicating its content.

The last few articles will normally be called the
    Schlußbestimmungen   **final provisions**
which may regulate any or all of the following:

    Vertragsdauer   duration of the treaty
    Unterschrift   signature
    Paraphierung   initialling
    Kündigung   denunciation/termination
    Revision   revision
    Abänderung/Modifikation modification
    Ratifizierung   ratification
    Beitritt   accession
    Inkrafttreten   entry into force
    Vertragssprachen/maßgebende Texte languages of the treaty/authentic texts
    Ort/Datum des Vertragsabschlusses place/date of conclusion of the treaty

4. **Anhang/Anlage**   **annex/appendix** (may contain prescribed format of relevant forms/documents, reservations, further provisions, etc.)

5. **Schlußakte der Konferenz**   **final act of the conference** (e.g. full list of participating/represented states/organizations, committees, indication of future conference/related codification, etc.)

Annex 4: Samples of preambles

1. From ICCPR

Präambel	Preamble
DIE VERTRAGSSTAATEN DIESES PAKTES,	THE STATES PARTIES TO THE PRESENT COVENANT,
IN DER ERWÄGUNG, daß nach den in der Charta der Vereinten Nationen verkündeten Grundsätzen die Anerkennung der allen Mitgliedern der menschlichen Gesellschaft innewohnenden Würde und der Gleichheit und Unveräußerlichkeit ihrer Rechte die Grundlage von Freiheit, Gerechtigkeit und Frieden in der Welt bildet,	CONSIDERING that, in accordance with the principles proclaimed in the Charter of the United Nations, recognition of the inherent dignity and of the equal and inalienable rights of all members of the human family is the foundation of freedom, justice and peace in the world,
IN DER ERKENNTNIS, daß sich diese Rechte aus der dem Menschen innewohnenden Würde herleiten,	RECOGNIZING that these rights derive from the inherent dignity of the human person,
IN DER ERKENNTNIS, daß nach der Allgemeinen Erklärung der Menschenrechte das Ideal vom freien Menschen, der bürgerliche und politische Freiheit genießt und frei von Furcht und Not lebt, nur verwirklicht werden kann, wenn Verhältnisse geschaffen werden, in denen jeder seine bürgerlichen und politischen Rechte ebenso wie seine wirtschaftlichen, sozialen und kulturellen Rechte genießen kann,	RECOGNIZING that, in accordance with the Universal Declaration of Human Rights, the ideal of free human beings enjoying civil and political freedom and freedom from fear and want can only be achieved if conditions are created whereby everyone may enjoy his civil and political rights, as well as his economic, social and cultural rights,
IN DER ERWÄGUNG, daß die Charta der Vereinten Nationen die Staaten verpflichtet, die allgemeine und wirksame Achtung der Rechte und Freiheiten des Menschen zu fördern,	CONSIDERING the obligation of States under the Charter of the United Nations to promote universal respect for, and observance of, human rights and freedoms,
IM HINBLICK DARAUF, daß der einzelne gegenüber seinen Mitmenschen und der Gemeinschaft, der er angehört, Pflichten hat und gehalten ist, für die Förderung und Achtung der in diesem Pakt anerkannten Rechte einzutreten,	REALIZING that the individual, having duties to other individuals and to the community to which he belongs, is under a responsibility to strive for the promotion and observance of the rights recognized in the present Covenant,
VEREINBAREN folgende Artikel:	AGREE upon the following articles:

2. From CERD

INTERNATIONALES ÜBEREINKOMMEN ZUR BESEITIGUNG JEDER FORM VON RASSENDISKRIMINIERUNG	INTERNATIONAL CONVENTION ON THE ELIMINATION OF ALL FORMS OF RACIAL DISCRIMINATION
Die Vertragsstaaten dieses Übereinkommens—	The States Parties to this Convention—
eingedenk der Tatsache, daß die Charta der Vereinten Nationen auf dem Grundsatz der angeborenen Würde und Gleichheit aller Menschen beruht und daß alle Mitgliedstaaten gelobt haben, gemeinsam und einzeln mit der Organisation zusammenzuwirken, um eines der Ziele der	considering that the Charter of the United Nations is based on the principle of the dignity and equality inherent in all human beings, and that all Member States have pledged themselves to take joint and separate action, in cooperation with the Organization, for the achievement of one

249

Vereinten Nationen zu erreichen, das darin besteht, die allgemeine Achtung und Beachtung der Menschenrechte und Grundfreiheiten für alle ohne Unterschied der Rasse, des Geschlechts, der Sprache oder der Religion zu fördern und zu festigen;

eingedenk der in der Allgemeinen Erklärung der Menschenrechte enthaltenen feierlichen Feststellung, daß alle Menschen frei und an Würde und Rechten gleich geboren sind und daß jeder ohne irgendeinen Unterschied, insbesondere der Rasse, der Hautfarbe oder der nationalen Abstammung, Anspruch hat auf alle in der genannten Erklärung aufgeführten Rechte und Freiheiten;

in der Erwägung, daß alle Menschen vor dem Gesetz gleich sind und ein Recht auf gleichen Schutz des Gesetzes gegen jede Diskriminierung und jedes Aufreizen zur Diskriminierung haben;

in der Erwägung, daß die Vereinten Nationen den Kolonialismus und alle damit verbundenen Praktiken der Rassentrennung und der Diskriminierung verurteilt haben, gleichviel in welcher Form und wo sie vorkommen, und daß die Erklärung vom 14. Dezember 1960 [Entschließung 1514 (XV) der Generalversammlung] über die Gewährung der Unabhängigkeit an Kolonialgebiete und Kolonialvölker die Notwendigkeit einer raschen und bedingungslosen Beendigung derartiger Praktiken bejaht und feierlich verkündet hat;

eingedenk der Erklärung der Vereinten Nationen vom 20. November 1963 [Entschließung 1904 (XVIII) der Generalversammlung] über die Beseitigung jeder Form von Rassendiskriminierung — einer Erklärung, die feierlich bekräftigt, daß es notwendig ist, jede Form und jedes Anzeichen von Rassendiskriminierung überall in der Welt rasch zu beseitigen sowie Verständnis und Achtung zu wecken für die Würde der menschlichen Person;

in der Überzeugung, daß jede Lehre von einer auf Rassenunterschiede gegründeten Überlegenheit wissenschaftlich falsch, moralisch verwerflich sowie sozial ungerecht und gefährlich ist und daß eine Rassendiskriminierung, gleichviel ob in Theorie oder in Praxis, nirgends gerechtfertigt ist;

in erneuter Bekräftigung der Tatsache, daß eine Diskriminierung zwischen Menschen auf Grund ihrer Rasse, ihrer Hautfarbe oder ihres Volkstums freundschaftlichen und friedlichen Beziehungen zwischen den Völkern im Wege steht und daß sie geeignet ist, den Frieden und die Sicherheit unter den Völkern sowie das harmonische Zusammen-

of the purposes of the United Nations which is to promote and encourage universal respect for and observance of human rights and fundamental freedoms for all without distinction as to race, sex, language or religion,

considering that the Universal Declaration of Human Rights proclaims that all human beings are born free and equal in dignity and rights and freedoms set out therein, without distinction of any kind, in particular as to race, colour or national origin,

considering that all human beings are equal before the law and are entitled to equal protection of the law against any discrimination and against any incitement to discrimination,

considering that the United Nations has condemned colonialism and all practices of segregation and discrimination associated therewith, in whatever form and wherever they exist, and that the Declaration on the Granting of Independence to Colonial Countries and Peoples of 14 December 1960 [General Assembly Resolution 1514 (XV)] has affirmed and solemnly proclaimed the necessity of bringing them to a speedy and unconditional end,

considering that the United Nations Declaration on the Elimination of All Forms of Racial Discrimination of 20 November 1963 [General Assembly resolution 1904 (XVIII)] solemnly affirms the necessity of speedily eliminating racial discrimination throughout the world in all its forms and manifestations and of securing understanding of and respect for the dignity of the human person,

convinced that any doctrine of superiority based on racial differentiation is scientifically false, morally condemnable, socially unjust and dangerous, and that there is no justification for racial discrimination, in theory or in practice, anywhere,

reaffirming that discrimination between human beings on the grounds of race, colour or ethnic origin is an obstacle to friendly and peaceful relations among nations and is capable of disturbing peace and security among peoples and the harmony of persons living side by side even within one and the same State,

leben der Menschen sogar innerhalb eines Staates zu stören;

in der Überzeugung, daß das Bestehen von Rassenschranken mit den Idealen jeder menschlichen Gesellschaft unvereinbar ist;

beunruhigt durch die in einigen Gebieten der Welt immer noch bestehende Rassendiskriminierung und durch die auf rassische Überlegenheit oder auf Rassenhaß gegründete Apartheids-, Segregations- oder sonstige Rassentrennungspolitik einiger Regierungen;

entschlossen, alle erforderlichen Maßnahmen zur raschen Beseitigung aller Formen und Anzeichen von Rassendiskriminierung zu treffen sowie rassenkämpferische Doktrinen und Praktiken zu verhindern und zu bekämpfen, um das gegenseitige Verständnis zwischen den Rassen zu fördern und eine internationale Gemeinschaft zu schaffen, die frei ist von jeder Form der Rassentrennung und Rassendiskriminierung;

eingedenk des 1958 von der Internationalen Arbeitsorganisation angenommenen Übereinkommens über Diskriminierung in Beschäftigung und Beruf und des 1960 von der Organisation der Vereinten Nationen für Erziehung, Wissenschaft und Kultur angenommenen Übereinkommens gegen Diskriminierung im Unterrichtswesen;

in dem Wunsch, die in der Erklärung der Vereinten Nationen über die Beseitigung jeder Form von Rassendiskriminierung niedergelegten Grundsätze zu verwirklichen und die möglichst rasche Annahme praktischer Maßregeln in diesem Sinne sicherzustellen —

sind wie folgt übereingekommen:

convinced that the existence of racial barriers is repugnant to the ideals of any human society,

alarmed by manifestations of racial discrimination still in evidence in some areas of the world and by governmental policies based on racial superiority or hatred, such as policies of apartheid, segregation or separation,

resolved to adopt all necessary measures for speedily eliminating racial discrimination in all its forms and manifestations, and to prevent and combat racist doctrines and practices in order to promote understanding between races and to build an international community free from all forms of racial segregation and racial discrimination,

bearing in mind the Convention concerning Discrimination in respect of Employment and Occupation adopted by the International Labour Organization in 1958, and the Convention against Discrimination in Education adopted by the United Nations Educational, Scientific and Cultural Organization in 1960,

desiring to implement the principles embodied in the United Nations Declaration on the Elimination of All Forms of Racial Discrimination and to secure the earliest adoption of practical measures to that end,

have agreed as follows:

3. From VCLOT

WIENER ÜBEREINKOMMEN ÜBER DAS RECHT DER VERTRÄGE

Die Vertragsstaaten dieses Übereinkommens –

in Anbetracht der grundlegenden Rolle der Verträge in der Geschichte der internationalen Beziehungen;

in Erkenntnis der ständig wachsenden Bedeutung der Verträge als Quelle des Völkerrechts und als Mittel zur Entwicklung der friedlichen Zusammenarbeit zwischen den Völkern ungeachtet ihrer Verfassungs- und Gesellschaftssysteme;

im Hinblick darauf, daß die Grundsätze der freien Zustimmung und von Treu und Glauben sowie der Rechtsgrundsatz *pacta sunt servanda* allgemein anerkannt sind;

VIENNA CONVENTION ON THE LAW OF TREATIES

The States Parties to the present Convention,

Considering the fundamental role of treaties in the history of international relations,

Recognizing the ever-increasing importance of treaties as a source of international law and as a means of developing peaceful co-operation among nations, whatever their constitutional and social systems,

Noting that the principles of free consent and of good faith and the *pacta sunt servanda* rule are universally recognized,

252

in Bekräftigung des Grundsatzes, daß Streitigkeiten über Verträge wie andere internationale Streitigkeiten durch friedliche Mittel nach den Grundsätzen der Gerechtigkeit und des Völkerrechts beigelegt werden sollen;

eingedenk der Entschlossenheit der Völker der Vereinten Nationen, Bedingungen zu schaffen, unter denen Gerechtigkeit und die Achtung vor den Verpflichtungen aus Verträgen gewahrt werden können;

im Bewußtsein der in der Charta der Vereinten Nationen enthaltenen völkerrechtlichen Grundsätze, darunter der Grundsätze der Gleichberechtigung und Selbstbestimmung der Völker, der souveränen Gleichheit und Unabhängigkeit aller Staaten, der Nichteinmischung in die inneren Angelegenheiten der Staaten, des Verbots der Androhung oder Anwendung von Gewalt sowie der allgemeinen Achtung und Wahrung der Menschenrechte und Grundfreiheiten für alle;

überzeugt, daß die in diesem Übereinkommen verwirklichte Kodifizierung und fortschreitende Entwicklung des Vertragsrechts die in der Charta der Vereinten Nationen verkündeten Ziele fördern wird, nämlich die Wahrung des Weltfriedens und der internationalen Sicherheit, die Entwicklung freundschaftlicher Beziehungen und die Verwirklichung der Zusammenarbeit zwischen den Nationen;

in Bekräftigung des Grundsatzes, daß die Sätze des Völkergewohnheitsrechts weiterhin für Fragen gelten, die in diesem Übereinkommen nicht geregelt sind —

haben folgendes *vereinbart:*

Affirming that disputes concerning treaties, like other international disputes, should be settled by peaceful means and in conformity with the principles of justice and international law,

Recalling the determination of the peoples of the United Nations to establish conditions under which justice and respect for the obligations arising from treaties can be maintained,

Having in mind the principles of international law embodied in the Charter of the United Nations, such as the principles of the equal rights and self-determination of peoples, of the sovereign equality and independence of all States, of non-interference in the domestic affairs of States, of the prohibition of the threat or use of force and of universal respect for, and observance of, human rights and fundamental freedoms for all,

Believing that the codification and progressive development of the law of treaties achieved in the present Convention will promote the purposes of the United Nations set forth in the Charter, namely, the maintenance of international peace and security, the development of friendly relations and the achievement of co-operation among nations,

Affirming that the rules of customary international law will continue to govern questions not regulated by the provisions of the present Convention,

Have agreed as follows:

Annex 5: Samples of final provisions

1. From VCLOT

TEIL VIII

SCHLUSSBESTIMMUNGEN

ARTIKEL 81

Unterzeichnung

Dieses Übereinkommen liegt für alle Mitgliedstaaten der Vereinten Nationen, einer ihrer Sonderorganisationen oder der Internationalen Atomenergie-Organisation, fur Vertragsparteien des Statuts des Internationalen Gerichtshofs und für jeden anderen Staat, den die Generalversammlung der Vereinten Nationen einlädt, Ver-

PART VIII

FINAL PROVISIONS

ARTICLE 81

Signature

The present Convention shall be open for signature by all States Members of the United Nations or of any of the specialized agencies or of the International Atomic Energy Agency or parties to the Statute of the International Court of Justice, and by any other State invited by the General Assembly of the United Nations to become a

tragspartei des Übereinkommens zu werden, wie folgt zur Unterzeichnung auf: bis zum 30. November 1969 im Bundesministerium für Auswärtige Angelegenheiten der Republik Österreich und danach bis zum 30. April 1970 am Sitz der Vereinten Nationen in New York.

party to the Convention, as follows: until 30 November 1969, at the Federal Ministry for Foreign Affairs of the Republic of Austria, and subsequently, until 30 April 1970, at United Nations Headquarters, New York.

ARTIKEL 82

Ratifikation

Dieses Übereinkommen bedarf der Ratifikation. Die Ratifikationsurkunden werden beim Generalsekretär der Vereinten Nationen hinterlegt.

ARTICLE 82

Ratification

The present Convention is subject to ratification. The instruments of ratification shall be deposited with the Secretary-General of the United Nations.

ARTIKEL 83

Beitritt

Dieses Übereinkommen steht jedem Staat zum Beitritt offen, der einer der in Artikel 81 bezeichneten Kategorien angehört. Die Beitrittsurkunden werden beim Generalsekretär der Vereinten Nationen hinterlegt.

ARTICLE 83

Accession

The present Convention shall remain open for accession by any State belonging to any of the categories mentioned in article 81. The instruments of accession shall be deposited with the Secretary-General of the United Nations.

ARTIKEL 84

Inkrafttreten

1. Dieses Übereinkommen tritt am dreißigsten Tag nach Hinterlegung der fünfunddreißigsten Ratifikations- oder Beitrittsurkunde in Kraft.

2. Für jeden Staat, der nach Hinterlegung der fünfunddreißigsten Ratifikations- oder Beitrittsurkunde das Übereinkommen ratifiziert oder ihm beitritt, tritt es am dreißigsten Tag nach Hinterlegung seiner eigenen Ratifikations- oder Beitrittsurkunde in Kraft.

ARTICLE 84

Entry into force

1. The present Convention shall enter into force on the thirtieth day following the date of deposit of the thirty-fifth instrument of ratification or accession.

2. For each State ratifying or acceding to the Convention after the deposit of the thirty-fifth instrument of ratification or accession, the Convention shall enter into force on the thirtieth day after deposit by such State of its instrument of ratification or accession.

ARTIKEL 85

Authentische Texte

Die Urschrift dieses Übereinkommens, dessen chinesischer, englischer, französischer, russischer und spanischer Wortlaut gleichermaßen verbindlich ist, wird beim Generalsekretär der Vereinten Nationen hinterlegt.

ZU URKUND DESSEN haben die unterzeichneten, von ihren Regierungen hierzu gehörig befugten Bevollmächtigten dieses Übereinkommen unterschrieben.

ARTICLE 85

Authentic texts

The original of the present Convention, of which the Chinese, English, French, Russian and Spanish texts are equally authentic, shall be deposited with the Secretary-General of the United Nations.

IN WITNESS WHEREOF the undersigned Plenipotentiaries, being duly authorized thereto by their respective Governments, have signed the present Convention.

GESCHEHEN ZU WIEN am 23. Mai 1969.

DONE AT VIENNA, this twenty-third day of May, one thousand nine hundred and sixty-nine.

2. From CSE

ARTIKEL 16

(a) Dieses Übereinkommen bedarf der Ratifizierung; die Ratifikationsurkunden werden so bald wie möglich beim Generalsekretär des Ständigen Ausschusses des Brüsseler Vertrages hinterlegt.

(b) Dieses Übereinkommen tritt für die Unterzeichnerstaaten, die es ratifiziert haben, zwei Monate nach dem Tage der Hinterlegung der dritten Ratifikationsurkunde in Kraft. Für jeden anderen Unterzeichnerstaat tritt es mit dem ersten Tage des Monats in Kraft, der auf den Monat folgt, in dem seine Ratifikationsurkunde hinterlegt worden ist.

(c) Dieses Übereinkommen bleibt zeitlich unbegrenzt in Kraft vorbehaltlich des Rechtes einer jeden Vertragspartei, es durch schriftliche Erklärung gegenüber dem Generalsekretär zu kündigen; die Kündigung wird sechs Monate nach Eingang beim Generalsekretär wirksam.

(d) Der Generalsekretär unterrichtet die anderen Unterzeichner von der Hinterlegung jeder Ratifikationsurkunde und von jeder Kündigung.

Zu Urkund dessen haben die von ihren Regierungen hierzu gehörig befugten Unterzeichneten dieses Übereinkommen unterschrieben und mit ihren Siegeln versehen.

Geschehen zu Brüssel am 17. April 1950 in englischer und französischer Sprache, wobei jeder Wortlaut gleichermaßen verbindlich ist, in einer Urschrift, die im Archiv des Generalsekretariats der Ständigen Kommission des Brüsseler Vertrages hinterlegt wird; der Generalsekretär übermittelt jeder Unterzeichnerregierung eine beglaubigte Abschrift.

[Unterschriften]

ARTICLE 16

(a) The present Convention shall be ratified and the instruments of ratification shall be deposited as soon as possible with the Secretary-General of the Brussels Treaty Permanent Commission.

(b) It shall enter into force between those signatories which have ratified it two months after the day on which the third instrument of ratification shall have been deposited and shall enter into force for each of the other signatories on the first day of the month following that in which its instrument of ratification is deposited.

(c) The present Convention shall continue in force subject to the right of each Contracting Party to withdraw by giving notice to the Secretary-General which shall take effect six months after its receipt by him.

(d) The Secretary-General will inform the other signatories of the deposit of each instrument of ratification and of each notice of withdrawal.

In witness whereof the undersigned, duly authorized by their respective Governments, have signed the present Convention and have affixed thereto their seals.

Done at Brussels this 17th day of April, 1950, in English and French, both texts being equally authoritative, in a single copy which shall be deposited in the archives of the Secretariat-General of the Brussels Treaty Permanent Commission, and of which a certified copy shall be transmitted by the Secretary-General to each of the signatory Governments.

[Signatures]

Annex 6: Sample of exchange of notes

EXCHANGE OF NOTES BETWEEN THE GOVERNMENT OF THE UNITED KINGDOM OF GREAT BRITAIN AND NORTHERN IRELAND AND THE FEDERAL REPUBLIC OF GERMANY, BRINGING INTO FORCE THE AGREEMENT BETWEEN THE TWO GOVERNMENTS FOR THE EXTRADITION OF FUGITIVE CRIMINALS

No. 1
Her Majesty's Ambassador at Bonn to the German Minister for Foreign Affairs

1596   *British Embassy,*
Your Excellency,   *Bonn, July 16, 1960.*

Acting upon instructions from Her Majesty's Principal Secretary of State for Foreign Affairs, I have the honour to propose that the Agreement between the Government of the United Kingdom of Great Britain and Northern Ireland and the Government of the Federal Republic of Germany for the Extradition of Fugitive Criminals, signed at Bonn on the 23rd of February, 1960, should enter into force on the 1st of September, 1960.

If the foregoing proposal is acceptable to the Government of the Federal Republic of Germany, I have the honour to suggest that this Note together with Your Excellency's reply in that sense should constitute the Exchange of Notes provided for in Article VII of the said Agreement.

I have, &c.

CHRISTOPHER STEEL.

No. 2
The German State Secretary in the Ministry of Foreign Affairs to Her Majesty's Ambassador at Bonn

Herr Botschafter,   *Bonn, den 16. Juli 1960.*

ich beehre mich, den Empfang Ihrer Note Nr. 1596 vom 16. Juli 1960 zu bestätigen, mit welcher vorgeschlagen wird, daß die am 23. Februar 1960 in Bonn unterzeichnete Vereinbarung zwischen der Regierung der Bundesrepublik Deutschland und der Regierung des Vereinigten Königreichs Großbritannien und Nordirland über die Auslieferung flüchtiger Verbrecher am 1. September 1960 in Kraft tritt.

Ich beehre mich, Ihnen mitzuteilen, daß die Regierung der Bundesrepublik Deutschland mit diesem Vorschlag einverstanden ist und daß Ihre Note und diese Antwort den im Artikel VII der genannten Vereinbarung vorgesehenen Notenwechsel darstellen.

Genehmigen Sie, etc.,

A. H. van SCHERPENBERG.

[Translation of No. 2]

Mr. Ambassador,   *Bonn, July 16, 1960.*

I have the honour to acknowledge receipt of your Note No. 1596 of the 16th of July, 1960, in which you propose that the Agreement between the Government of the Federal Republic of Germany and the Government of the United Kingdom of Great Britain and Northern Ireland for the Extradition of Fugitive Criminals, signed at Bonn on the 23rd of February, 1960, shall enter into force on the 1st of September, 1960.

I have the honour to inform you that the Government of the Federal Republic of Germany is in agreement with this proposal, and also agree that your Note and the present reply shall be regarded as constituting the Exchange of Notes envisaged in Article VII of the said Agreement.

Please accept, etc.,

A. H. van SCHERPENBERG.

Annex 7: Sample immunities and exemptions

1. From VCDR

ARTIKEL 31

1. Der Diplomat genießt Immunität von der Strafgerichtsbarkeit des Empfangsstaats. Ferner steht ihm Immunität von dessen Zivil- und Verwaltungsgerichtsbarkeit zu; ausgenommen hiervon sind folgende Fälle:

(a) dingliche Klagen in bezug auf privates, im Hoheitsgebiet des Empfangsstaats gelegenes unbewegliches Vermögen, es sei denn, daß der Diplomat dieses im Auftrag des Entsendestaats für die Zwecke der Mission in Besitz hat;

(b) Klagen in Nachlaßsachen, in denen der Diplomat als Testamentsvollstrecker, Verwalter, Erbe oder Vermächtnisnehmer in privater Eigenschaft und nicht als Vertreter des Entsendestaats beteiligt ist;

(c) Klagen im Zusammenhang mit einem freien Beruf oder einer gewerblichen Tätigkeit, die der Diplomat im Empfangsstaat neben seiner amtlichen Tätigkeit ausübt.

2. Der Diplomat ist nicht verpflichtet, als Zeuge auszusagen.

3. Gegen einen Diplomaten dürfen Vollstreckungsmaßnahmen nur in den in Absatz 1 Buchstaben a, b und c vorgesehenen Fällen und nur unter der Voraussetzung getroffen werden, daß sie durchführbar sind, ohne die Unverletzlichkeit seiner Person oder seiner Wohnung zu beeinträchtigen.

4. Die Immunität des Diplomaten von der Gerichtsbarkeit des Empfangsstaats befreit ihn nicht von der Gerichtsbarkeit des Entsendestaats.

ARTIKEL 32

1. Auf die Immunität von der Gerichtsbarkeit, die einem Diplomaten oder nach Maßgabe des Artikels 37 einer anderen Person zusteht, kann der Entsendestaat verzichten.

2. Der Verzicht muß stets ausdrücklich erklärt werden.

3. Strengt ein Diplomat oder eine Person, die nach Maßgabe des Artikels 37 Immunität von der Gerichtsbarkeit genießt, ein Gerichtsverfahren

ARTICLE 31

1. A diplomatic agent shall enjoy immunity from the criminal jurisdiction of the receiving state. He shall also enjoy immunity from its civil and administrative jurisdiction, except in the case of:

(a) a real action relating to private immovable property situated in the territory of the receiving state, unless he holds it on behalf of the sending state for the purposes of the mission;

(b) an action relating to succession in which the diplomatic agent is involved as executor, administrator, heir or legatee as a private person and not on behalf of the sending state;

(c) an action relating to any professional or commercial activity exercised by the diplomatic agent in the receiving state outside his official functions.

2. A diplomatic agent is not obliged to give evidence as a witness.

3. No measures of execution may be taken in respect of a diplomatic agent except in the cases coming under sub-paragraphs (a), (b) and (c) of paragraph 1 of this article, and provided that the measures concerned can be taken without infringing the inviolability of his person or of his residence.

4. The immunity of a diplomatic agent from the jurisdiction of the receiving state does not exempt him from the jurisdiction of the sending state.

ARTICLE 32

1. The immunity from jurisdiction of diplomatic agents and of persons enjoying immunity under Article 37 may be waived by the sending state.

2. Waiver must always be express.

3. The initiation of proceedings by a diplomatic agent or by a person enjoying immunity from jurisdiction under Article 37 shall preclude him

an, so können sie sich in bezug auf eine Widerklage, die mit der Hauptklage in unmittelbarem Zusammenhang steht, nicht auf die Immunität von der Gerichtsbarkeit berufen.

4. Der Verzicht auf die Immunität von der Gerichtsbarkeit in einem Zivil- oder Verwaltungsgerichtsverfahren gilt nicht als Verzicht auf die Immunität von der Urteilsvollstreckung; hierfür ist ein besonderer Verzicht erforderlich.

from invoking immunity from jurisdiction in respect of any counterclaim directly connected with the principal claim.

4. Waiver of immunity from jurisdiction in respect of civil or administrative proceedings shall not be held to imply waiver of immunity in respect of the execution of the judgment, for which a separate waiver shall be necessary.

ARTIKEL 34

Der Diplomat ist von allen staatlichen, regionalen und kommunalen Personal- und Realsteuern oder -abgaben befreit; ausgenommen hiervon sind:

(a) die normalerweise im Preis von Waren oder Dienstleistungen enthaltenen indirekten Steuern;

(b) Steuern und sonstige Abgaben von privatem, im Hoheitsgebiet des Empfangsstaats gelegenem unbeweglichem Vermögen, es sei denn, daß der Diplomat es im Auftrag des Entsendestaats für die Zwecke der Mission im Besitz hat;

(c) Erbschaftssteuern, die der Empfangsstaat erhebt, jedoch vorbehaltlich des Artikels 39 Abs. 4;

(d) Steuern und sonstige Abgaben von privaten Einkünften, deren Quelle sich im Empfangsstaat befindet, sowie Vermögenssteuern von Kapitalanlagen in gewerblichen Unternehmen, die im Empfangsstaat gelegen sind;

(e) Steuern, Gebühren und sonstige Abgaben, die als Vergütung für bestimmte Dienstleistungen erhoben werden;

(f) Eintragungs-, Gerichts-, Beurkundungs-, Beglaubigungs-, Hypotheken- und Stempelgebühren in bezug auf unbewegliches Vermögen, jedoch vorbehaltlich des Artikels 23.

ARTICLE 34

A diplomatic agent shall be exempt from all dues and taxes, personal or real, national, regional or municipal, except:

(a) indirect taxes of a kind which are normally incorporated in the price of goods or services;

(b) dues and taxes on private immovable property situated in the territory of the receiving state, unless he holds it on behalf of the sending state for the purposes of the mission;

(c) estate, succession or inheritance duties levied by the receiving state, subject to the provisions of paragraph 4 of Article 39;

(d) dues and taxes on private income having its source in the receiving state and capital taxes on investments made in commercial undertakings in the receiving state;

(e) charges levied for specific services rendered;

(f) registration, court or record fees, mortgages dues and stamp duty, with respect to immovable property, subject to the provisions of Article 23.

2. From PPELDO

ARTIKEL 14

1. Die Vertreter der Mitgliedstaaten, die an den Tagungen des Rates und seiner nachgeordneten Stellen teilnehmen, genießen bei der Ausübung ihres Amtes sowie während der Reise zum

ARTICLE 14

1. Representatives of Member States attending meetings of the Council and of its subordinate bodies shall enjoy, while exercising their functions and in the course of their journeys to and from the

und vom Tagungsort folgende Vorrechte und Befreiungen:

(a) Immunität von Festnahme oder Haft sowie von der Beschlagnahme ihres persönlichen Gepäcks;

(b) Immunität von der Gerichtsbarkeit, auch nach Beendigung ihres Auftrags, bezüglich der von ihnen in Ausübung ihres Amtes vorgenommenen Handlungen einschließlich ihrer mündlichen und schriftlichen Äußerungen;

(c) Unverletzlichkeit aller ihrer amtlichen Schriftstücke und Urkunden;

(d) das Recht, Verschlüsselungen zu verwenden sowie Urkunden oder sonstige Schriftstücke durch Sonderkurier oder in versiegelten Behältern zu empfangen;

(e) Befreiung für sich und ihre Ehegatten von allen Einreisebeschränkungen und von der Meldepflicht für Ausländer;

(f) die gleichen Erleichterungen hinsichtlich der Währungs- und Devisenvorschriften wie die Vertreter ausländischer Regierungen mit vorübergehendem amtlichen Auftrag;

(g) die gleichen Zollerleichterungen hinsichtlich ihres persönlichen Gepäcks wie die Diplomaten.

2. Die Vorrechte und Befreiungen werden den Vertretern der Mitgliedstaaten nicht zu ihrem persönlichen Vorteil gewährt, sondern um ihre vollständige Unabhängigkeit bei der Ausübung ihres Amtes im Zusammenhang mit der Organisation zu gewährleisten.

place of meeting, the following privileges and immunities:

(a) immunity from arrest and detention, and from seizure of their personal luggage;

(b) immunity from jurisdiction, even after the termination of their mission, in respect of acts, including words spoken and written, done by them in the exercise of their functions;

(c) inviolability of all their official papers and documents;

(d) the right to use codes and to receive documents or correspondence by special courier or sealed bag;

(e) exemption for themselves and their spouses from all measures restricting entry and from aliens' registration formalities;

(f) the same facilities in the matter of currency and exchange control as are accorded to the representatives of foreign Governments on temporary official missions;

(g) the same customs facilities as regards their personal luggage as are accorded to diplomatic agents.

2. Privileges and immunities are accorded to representatives of Member States, not for their personal advantage, but in order to ensure complete independence in the exercise of their functions in connection with the Organization.

Annex 8: The staff of the mission

From VCDR

ARTIKEL 1

Im Sinne dieses Übereinkommens haben die nachstehenden Ausdrücke folgende Bedeutung:

(a) der Ausdruck „Missionschef" bezeichnet die Person, die vom Entsendestaat beauftragt ist, in dieser Eigenschaft tätig zu sein;

(b) der Ausdruck „Mitglieder der Mission" bezeichnet den Missionschef und die Mitglieder des Personals der Mission;

ARTICLE 1

For the purpose of the present Convention, the following expressions shall have the meanings hereunder assigned to them:

(a) the "head of the mission" is the person charged by the sending state with the duty of acting in that capacity;

(b) the "members of the mission" are the head of the mission and the members of the staff of the mission;

(c) der Ausdruck „Mitglieder des Personals der Mission" bezeichnet die Mitglieder des diplomatischen Personals, des Verwaltungs- und technischen Personals und des dienstlichen Hauspersonals der Mission;

(d) der Ausdruck „Mitglieder des diplomatischen Personals" bezeichnet die in diplomatischem Rang stehenden Mitglieder des Personals der Mission;

(e) der Ausdruck „Diplomat" bezeichnet den Missionschef und die Mitglieder des diplomatischen Personals der Mission;

(f) der Ausdruck „Mitglieder des Verwaltungs- und technischen Personals" bezeichnet die im Verwaltungs- und technischen Dienst der Mission beschäftigten Mitglieder ihres Personals;

(g) der Ausdruck „Mitglieder des dienstlichen Hauspersonals" bezeichnet die als Hausbedienstete bei der Mission beschäftigten Mitglieder ihres Personals;

(h) der Ausdruck „privater Hausangestellter" bezeichnet eine im häuslichen Dienst eines Mitglieds der Mission beschäftigte Person, die nicht Bediensteter des Entsendestaats ist;

(i) der Ausdruck „Räumlichkeiten der Mission" bezeichnet ungeachtet der Eigentumsverhältnisse die Gebäude oder Gebäudeteile und das dazugehörige Gelände, die für die Zwecke der Mission verwendet werden, einschließlich der Residenz des Missionschefs.

(c) the "members of the staff of the mission" are the members of the diplomatic staff, of the administrative and technical staff and of the service staff of the mission;

(d) the "members of the diplomatic staff" are the members of the staff of the mission having diplomatic rank;

(e) a "diplomatic agent" is the head of the mission or a member of the diplomatic staff of the mission;

(f) the "members of the administrative and technical staff" are the members of the staff of the mission employed in the administrative and technical service of the mission;

(g) the "members of the service staff" are the members of the staff of the mission in the domestic service of the mission;

(h) a "private servant" is a person who is in the domestic service of a member of the mission and who is not an employee of the sending state;

(i) the "premises of the mission" are the buildings or parts of buildings and the land ancillary thereto, irrespective of ownership, used for the purposes of the mission including the residence of the head of the mission.

Annex 9: Human rights

From CERD

ARTIKEL 5

Im Einklang mit den in Artikel 2 niedergelegten grundsätzlichen Verpflichtungen werden die Vertragsstaaten die Rassendiskriminierung in jeder Form verbieten und beseitigen und das Recht jedes einzelnen, ohne Unterschied der Rasse, der Hautfarbe, des nationalen Ursprungs oder des Volkstums, auf Gleichheit vor dem Gesetz gewährleisten; dies gilt insbesondere für folgende Rechte:

(a) das Recht auf Gleichbehandlung vor den Gerichten und allen sonstigen Organen der Rechtspflege,

ARTICLE 5

In compliance with the fundamental obligations laid down in article 2 of this Convention, States Parties undertake to prohibit and to eliminate racial discrimination in all its forms and to guarantee the right of everyone, without distinction as to race, colour, or national or ethnic origin, to equality before the law, notably in the enjoyment of the following rights:

(a) the right to equal treatment before the tribunals and all other organs administering justice;

(b) das Recht auf Sicherheit der Person und auf staatlichen Schutz gegen Gewalttätigkeit oder Körperverletzung, gleichviel ob sie von Staatsbediensteten oder von irgendeiner Person, Gruppe oder Einrichtung verübt werden,

(c) die politischen Rechte, insbesondere das aktive und passive Wahlrecht auf der Grundlage allgemeiner und gleicher Wahlen, das Recht auf Beteiligung an der Regierung und an der Führung der öffentlichen Angelegenheiten auf jeder Ebene sowie das Recht auf gleichberechtigten Zugang zum öffentlichen Dienst,

(d) sonstige Bürgerrechte, insbesondere
  (i) das Recht auf Bewegungsfreiheit und freie Wahl des Aufenthaltsortes innerhalb der Staatsgrenzen,
  (ii) das Recht, jedes Land einschließlich des eigenen zu verlassen und in das eigene Land zurückzukehren,
  (iii) das Recht auf die Staatsangehörigkeit,
  (iv) das Recht auf Ehe und auf freie Wahl des Ehegatten,
  (v) das Recht, allein oder in Verbindung mit anderen Vermögen als Eigentum zu besitzen,
  (vi) das Recht zu erben,
  (vii) das Recht auf Gedanken-, Gewissens- und Religionsfreiheit,
  (viii) das Recht auf Meinungsfreiheit und freie Meinungsäußerung,
  (ix) das Recht, sich friedlich zu versammeln und friedliche Vereinigungen zu bilden,

(e) wirtschaftliche, soziale und kulturelle Rechte, insbesondere
  (i) das Recht auf Arbeit, auf die freie Wahl des Arbeitsplatzes, auf gerechte und befriedigende Arbeitsbedingungen, auf Schutz gegen Arbeitslosigkeit, auf gleiches Entgelt für gleiche Arbeit, auf gerechte und befriedigende Entlohnung,
  (ii) das Recht, Gewerkschaften zu bilden und ihnen beizutreten,
  (iii) das Recht auf Wohnung,
  (iv) das Recht auf öffentliche Gesundheitsfürsorge, ärztliche Betreuung, soziale Sicherheit und soziale Dienstleistungen,
  (v) das Recht auf Erziehung und Ausbildung,
  (vi) das Recht auf eine gleichberechtigte Teilnahme an kulturellen Tätigkeiten,

(f) das Recht auf Zugang zu jedem Ort oder Dienst, der für die Benutzung durch die Öffentlichkeit vorgesehen ist, wie Ver-

(b) the right to security of person and protection by the State against violence or bodily harm, whether inflicted by governmental officials or by any individual, group or institution;

(c) political rights, in particular the rights to participate in elections—to vote and to stand for election—on the basis of universal and equal suffrage, to take part in the Government as well as in the conduct of public affairs at any level and to have equal access to public service;

(d) other civil rights, in particular:
  (i) the right to freedom of movement and residence within the border of the State;
  (ii) the right to leave any country, including one's own, and to return to one's country;
  (iii) the right to nationality;
  (iv) the right to marriage and choice of spouse;
  (v) the right to own property alone as well as in association with others;
  (vi) the right to inherit;
  (vii) the right to freedom of thought, conscience and religion;
  (viii) the right to freedom of opinion and expression;
  (ix) the right to freedom of peaceful assembly and association;

(e) economic, social and cultural rights, in particular:
  (i) the rights to work, to free choice of employment, to just and favourable conditions of work, to protection against unemployment, to equal pay for equal work, to just and favourable remuneration;
  (ii) the right to form and join trade unions;
  (iii) the right to housing;
  (iv) the right to public health, medical care, social security and social services;
  (v) the right to education and training;
  (vi) the right to equal participation in cultural activities;

(f) the right of access to any place or service intended for use by the general public, such as transport, hotels, restaurants, cafés,

kehrsmittel, Hotels, Gaststätten, Cafés,
Theater und Parks.

theatres and parks.

Annex 10: Extradition

From ExFC

ARTIKEL III

Artikel II des Vertrages von 1872 wird durch nachstehenden Artikel ersetzt:
,,Auslieferung wird gegenseitig für die folgenden Straftaten gewährt, wenn sie nach den Gesetzen des ersuchenden und ersuchten Gebietes auslieferungsfähig sind:

1. Mord und andere zum Tode eines Menschen führende verbrecherische Handlungen, einschließlich Versuch, Verabredung und Verbindung zur Tat;
2. vorsätzliche Tötung geringerer Schwere und grob fahrlässige Tötung;
3. Abtreibung mittels Drogen oder Werkzeugen, einschließlich vollendetem Versuch;
4. vorsätzliche Körperverletzung;

5. Doppelehe;
6. Vornahme unzüchtiger Handlungen unter Androhung oder Anwendung von Gewalt;
7. Beischlaf mit einem Mädchen unter 16 Jahren, einschließlich Versuch;

8. Erzwingung oder Erschleichung des außerehelichen Beischlafs;
9. Kuppelei;
10. Freiheitsberaubung;
11. Entführung;
12. Kindesraub, Kindesaussetzung und rechtswidrige Vorenthaltung eines Kindes;
13. Einbruchsdiebstahl, Diebstahl, Unterschlagung und Veruntreuung;
14. Raub;
15. Erpressung;

16. Hehlerei;

17. Betrug und Untreue;

18. Urkundenfälschung;

ARTICLE III

For Article II of the Treaty of 1872 the following Article shall be substituted:
"Extradition shall be reciprocally granted for the following crimes, provided that the crime charged constitutes an extradition crime according to the laws of the territory from which and to which extradition is desired:

1. Murder or attempt or conspiracy to murder.

2. Manslaughter.

3. Administering drugs or using instruments with intent to procure the miscarriage of women.
4. Maliciously wounding or inflicting grievous bodily harm, or assault occasioning actual bodily harm.
5. Bigamy.
6. Indecent assault.

7. Unlawful sexual intercourse, or any attempt to have unlawful sexual intercourse, with a girl under sixteen years of age.
8. Rape.

9. Procuration.
10. Kidnapping or false imprisonment.
11. Abduction.
12. Stealing, abandoning, exposing or unlawfully detaining a child.
13. Burglary, housebreaking, larceny or embezzlement.
14. Robbery with violence.
15. Threats, by letter or otherwise, with intent to extort money or other things of value.
16. Receiving any money, valuable security or other property, knowing the same to have been stolen or unlawfully obtained.
17. Fraud by a bailee, banker, agent, factor or trustee, or by a director, member or public officer of any company; fraudulent conversion; or obtaining money, valuable security or goods by false pretences.
18. Forgery, or uttering what is forged.

19. (a) Falschmünzerei, Münzverfälschung und Inverkehrbringen falschen Geldes;

(b) die vorsätzliche und rechtswidrige Herstellung sowie der vorsätzliche und rechtswidrige Besitz von Instrumenten, die für Falschmünzerei geeignet oder bestimmt sind;

(c) der Versuch, eines der unter (a) oder (b) aufgeführten Verbrechen zu begehen;

20. Meineid und Anstiftung zum Meineid;
21. Sachbeschädigung;
22. vorsätzliche Brandstiftung;
23. vorsätzliche Gefährdung von Personen im Eisenbahnverkehr;

24. Konkursstraftaten;
25. Straftaten im Zusammenhang mit dem Handel mit Betäubungsmitteln, einschließlich Versuch;
26. Piraterie sowie andere Straftaten, die auf hoher See gegen Personen oder Sachen begangen werden;
27. Sklavenhandel.

Auslieferung wird auch für die Teilnahme an einer der oben erwähnten Straftaten gewährt, wenn die Teilnahme nach den Gesetzen des ersuchenden und des ersuchten Gebietes strafbar ist.

Die Auslieferung kann abgelehnt werden, wenn der Verfolgte wegen der Straftat, die dem Ersuchen um Auslieferung zugrunde liegt, nach dem Recht der ersuchenden Partei der Todesstrafe unterliegt, während das Recht der ersuchten Partei für einen solchen Fall die Todesstrafe nicht vorsieht."

19. (a) Counterfeiting or altering money, or bringing into circulation counterfeited or altered money.

(b) Knowingly and without lawful authority making or having in possession any instrument for the counterfeiting of money.

(c) Attempts to commit any crime mentioned in (a) or (b) above.

20. Perjury or subornation of perjury.
21. Malicious damage to property.
22. Arson.
23. Any malicious act done with intent to endanger the safety of any persons travelling or being upon a railway.
24. Crimes against bankruptcy law.
25. Crimes or attempted crimes in connection with the traffic in dangerous drugs.
26. Piracy and other crimes committed on the high seas against persons or things.
27. Dealing in slaves.

Extradition is also to be granted for participation in any of the aforesaid crimes, provided that the participation is punishable by the laws of the territory from which and to which extradition is desired.

Extradition may be refused if under the law of the requesting Party the person sought is liable to the death penalty for the crime on which the request for his extradition is based but the law of the requested Party does not provide for the death penalty in a similar case."

Annex 11: Genocide

From PCG

ARTIKEL II

In dieser Konvention bedeutet Völkermord eine der folgenden Handlungen, die in der Absicht begangen wird, eine nationale, ethnische, rassische oder religiöse Gruppe als solche ganz oder teilweise zu zerstören:

(a) Tötung von Mitgliedern der Gruppe;

(b) Verursachung von schwerem körperlichem oder seelischem Schaden an Mitgliedern der Gruppe;

ARTICLE II

In the present Convention, genocide means any of the following acts committed with intent to destroy, in whole or in part, a national, ethnical, racial or religious group, as such:

(a) Killing members of the group;

(b) Causing serious bodily or mental harm to members of the group;

(c) vorsätzliche Auferlegung von Lebensbedingungen für die Gruppe, die geeignet
sind, ihre körperliche Zerstörung ganz oder
teilweise herbeizuführen;

(d) Verhängung von Maßnahmen, die auf die
Geburtenverhinderung innerhalb der
Gruppe gerichtet sind;

(e) gewaltsame Überführung von Kindern der
Gruppe in eine andere Gruppe.

(c) Deliberately inflicting on the group conditions of life calculated to bring about its
physical destruction in whole or in part;

(d) Imposing measures intended to prevent
births within the group;

(e) Forcibly transferring children of the group
to another group.

ARTIKEL III

Die folgenden Handlungen sind zu bestrafen:

(a) Völkermord,

(b) Verschwörung zur Begehung von Völkermord,

(c) unmittelbare und öffentliche Anreizung zur
Begehung von Völkermord,

(d) Versuch, Völkermord zu begehen,

(e) Teilnahme am Völkermord.

ARTICLE III

The following acts shall be punishable:

(a) Genocide;

(b) Conspiracy to commit genocide;

(c) Direct and public incitement to commit
genocide;

(d) Attempt to commit genocide;

(e) Complicity in genocide.

ARTIKEL IV

Personen, die Völkermord oder eine der sonstigen in Artikel III aufgeführten Handlungen
begehen, sind zu bestrafen, gleichviel ob sie regierende Personen, öffentliche Beamte oder private Einzelpersonen sind.

ARTICLE IV

Persons committing genocide or any of the
other acts enumerated in article III shall be
punished, whether they are constitutionally responsible rulers, public officials or private individuals.

Annex 12: Racial discrimination

From CERD

ARTIKEL 1

In diesem Übereinkommen bezeichnet der Ausdruck „Rassendiskriminierung" jede auf der
Rasse, der Hautfarbe, der Abstammung, dem
nationalen Ursprung oder dem Volkstum beruhende Unterscheidung, Ausschließung, Beschränkung oder Bevorzugung, die zum Ziel oder
zur Folge hat, daß dadurch ein gleichberechtigtes
Anerkennen, Genießen oder Ausüben von Men-
schenrechten und Grundfreiheiten im politischen,
wirtschaftlichen, sozialen, kulturellen oder jedem
sonstigen Bereich des öffentlichen Lebens
vereitelt oder beeinträchtigt wird.

ARTICLE 1

In this Convention, the term "racial discrimination" shall mean any distinction, restriction or
preference based on race, colour, descent or
national or ethnic origin which has the purpose or
effect of nullifying or impairing the recognition,
enjoyment or exercise, on an equal footing, of
human rights and fundamental freedoms in the
political, economic, social, cultural or any other
field of public life.

Annex 13: Prisoners of war

From GC III

ARTIKEL 12

Die Kriegsgefangenen unterstehen der Gewalt der feindlichen Macht, nicht jedoch der Gewalt der Personen oder Truppenteile, die sie gefangen haben. Der Gewahrsamsstaat ist, unabhängig von etwa bestehenden persönlichen Verantwortlichkeiten, für die Behandlung der Kriegsgefangenen verantwortlich.

ARTICLE 12

Prisoners of war are in the hands of the enemy power, but not of the individuals or military units who have captured them. Irrespective of the individual responsibilities that may exist, the detaining power is responsible for the treatment given them.

ARTIKEL 13

Jeder Kriegsgefangene ist auf Befragen nur verpflichtet, seinen Namen, seinen Vornamen, seinen Dienstgrad, sein Geburtsdatum und seine Matrikelnummer zu nennen, oder wenn diese fehlt, eine andere gleichwertige Angabe zu machen.

ARTICLE 13

Every prisoner of war, when questioned on the subject, is bound to give only his surname, first names and rank, date of birth, and army, regimental, personal or serial number, or failing this, equivalent information.

ARTIKEL 17

Die Kriegsgefangenen müssen jederzeit mit Menschlichkeit behandelt werden. Jede rechtswidrige Handlung oder Unterlassung seitens des Gewahrsamsstaates, die den Tod oder eine schwere Gefährdung der Gesundheit eines in seinen Händen befindlichen Kriegsgefangenen zur Folge hat, ist untersagt und gilt als schwere Verletzung des vorliegenden Abkommens. Insbesondere dürfen an den Kriegsgefangenen keine Verstümmelungen oder medizinischen oder wissenschaftlichen Versuche irgendwelcher Art vorgenommen werden, die nicht durch die ärztliche Behandlung des betreffenden Kriegsgefangenen gerechtfertigt sind und nicht in seinem Interesse liegen.

Die Kriegsgefangenen werden ferner jederzeit geschützt, insbesondere auch vor Gewalttätigkeit oder Einschüchterung, Beleidigungen und öffentlicher Neugier.

ARTICLE 17

Prisoners of war must at all times be humanely treated. Any unlawful act or omission by the detaining power causing death or seriously endangering the health of a prisoner of war in its custody is prohibited, and will be regarded as a serious breach of the present Convention. In particular, no prisoner of war may be subjected to physical mutilation or to medical or scientific experiments of any kind which are not justified by the medical, dental or hospital treatment of the prisoner concerned and carried out in his interest.

Likewise, prisoners of war must at all times be protected, particularly against acts of violence or intimidation and against insults and public curiosity.

Annex 14: Definitions of some terms in treaties

From VCLOT

ARTIKEL 2

Begriffsbestimmungen

1. Im Sinne dieses Übereinkommens:

(a) bedeutet „Vertrag" eine in Schriftform

ARTICLE 2

Use of terms

1. For the purposes of the present Convention:

(a) "treaty" means an international agreement

geschlossene und vom Völkerrecht bestimmte internationale Übereinkunft zwischen Staaten, gleichviel ob sie in einer oder in mehreren zusammengehörigen Urkunden enthalten ist und welche besondere Bezeichnung sie hat;

(b) bedeutet „Ratifikation", „Annahme", „Genehmigung" und „Beitritt" jeweils die so bezeichnete völkerrechtliche Handlung, durch die ein Staat im internationalen Bereich seine Zustimmung bekundet, durch einen Vertrag gebunden zu sein;

(c) bedeutet „Vollmacht" eine vom zuständigen Organ eines Staates errichtete Urkunde, durch die einzelne oder mehrere Personen benannt werden, um in Vertretung des Staates den Text eines Vertrags auszuhandeln oder als authentisch festzulegen, die Zustimmung des Staates auszudrücken, durch einen Vertrag gebunden zu sein, oder sonstige Handlungen in bezug auf einen Vertrag vorzunehmen;

(d) bedeutet „Vorbehalt" eine wie auch immer formulierte oder bezeichnete, von einem Staat bei der Unterzeichnung, Ratifikation, Annahme oder Genehmigung eines Vertrags oder bei dem Beitritt zu einem Vertrag abgegebene einseitige Erklärung, durch die der Staat bezweckt, die Rechtswirkung einzelner Vertragsbestimmungen in der Anwendung auf diesen Staat auszuschließen oder zu ändern;

(e) bedeutet „Verhandlungsstaat" einen Staat, der am Abfassen und Annehmen des Vertragstextes teilgenommen hat;

(f) bedeutet „Vertragsstaat" einen Staat, der zugestimmt hat, durch den Vertrag gebunden zu sein, gleichviel ob der Vertrag in Kraft getreten ist oder nicht;

(g) bedeutet „Vertragspartei" einen Staat, der zugestimmt hat, durch den Vertrag gebunden zu sein, und für den der Vertrag in Kraft ist;

(h) bedeutet „Drittstaat" einen Staat, der nicht Vertragspartei ist;

(i) bedeutet „internationale Organisation" eine zwischenstaatliche Organisation.

2. Die Bestimmungen des Absatzes 1 über die in diesem Übereinkommen verwendeten Begriffe beeinträchtigen weder die Verwendung dieser Begriffe noch die Bedeutung, die ihnen im innerstaatlichen Recht gegebenenfalls zukommt.

concluded between States in written form and governed by international law, whether embodied in a single instrument or in two or more related instruments and whatever its particular designation;

(b) "ratification", "acceptance", "approval" and "accession" mean in each case the international act so named whereby a State establishes on the international plane its consent to be bound by a treaty;

(c) "full powers" means a document emanating from the competent authority of a State designating a person or persons to represent the State for negotiating, adopting or authenticating the text of a treaty, for expressing the consent of the State to be bound by a treaty, or for accomplishing any other act with respect to a treaty;

(d) "reservation" means a unilateral statement, however phrased or named, made by a State, when signing, ratifying, accepting, approving or acceding to a treaty, whereby it purports to exclude or to modify the legal effect of certain provisions of the treaty in their application to that State;

(e) "negotiating State" means a State which took part in the drawing up and adoption of the text of the treaty;

(f) "contracting State" means a State which has consented to be bound by the treaty, whether or not the treaty has entered into force;

(g) "party" means a State which has consented to be bound by the treaty and for which the treaty is in force;

(h) "third State" means a State not a party to the treaty;

(i) "international organization" means an intergovernmental organization.

2. The provisions of paragraph 1 regarding the use of terms in the present Convention are without prejudice to the use of those terms or to the meanings which may be given to them in the internal law of any State.

Annex 15: Function of depositaries

From VCLOT

| TEIL VII | PART VII |

VERWAHRER, NOTIFIKATIONEN, BERICHTIGUNGEN UND REGISTRIERUNG

DEPOSITARIES, NOTIFICATIONS, CORRECTIONS AND REGISTRATION

ARTIKEL 76

Verwahrer von Verträgen

1. Der Verwahrer eines Vertrags kann von den Verhandlungsstaaten im Vertrag selbst oder in sonstiger Weise bestimmt werden. Einzelne oder mehrere Staaten, eine internationale Organisation oder der leitende Verwaltungsbeamte einer internationalen Organisation können Verwahrer sein.

2. Die Aufgaben des Verwahrers haben internationalen Charakter; der Verwahrer ist verpflichtet, diese Aufgaben unparteiisch wahrzunehmen. Insbesondere wird diese Verpflichtung nicht davon berührt, daß ein Vertrag zwischen einzelnen Vertragsparteien nicht in Kraft getreten ist oder daß zwischen einem Staat und einem Verwahrer über die Erfüllung von dessen Aufgaben Meinungsverschiedenheiten aufgetreten sind.

ARTICLE 76

Depositaries of treaties

1. The designation of the depositary of a treaty may be made by the negotiating States, either in the treaty itself or in some other manner. The depositary may be one or more States, an international organization or the chief administrative officer of the organization.

2. The functions of the depositary of a treaty are international in character and the depositary is under an obligation to act impartially in their performance. In particular, the fact that a treaty has not entered into force between certain of the parties or that a difference has appeared between a State and a depositary with regard to the performance of the latter's functions shall not affect that obligation.

ARTIKEL 77

Aufgaben des Verwahrers

1. Sofern der Vertrag nichts anderes vorsieht oder die Vertragsstaaten nichts anderes vereinbaren, hat ein Verwahrer insbesondere folgende Aufgaben:

(a) die Urschrift des Vertrags und der dem Verwahrer übergebenen Vollmachten zu verwahren;

(b) beglaubigte Abschriften der Urschrift sowie weitere Texte des Vertrags in den nach dem Vertrag erforderlichen zusätzlichen Sprachen zu erstellen und sie den Vertragsparteien und den Staaten zu übermitteln, die berechtigt sind, Vertragsparteien zu werden;

(c) Unterzeichnungen des Vertrags entgegenzunehmen sowie alle sich auf den Vertrag beziehenden Urkunden, Notifikationen und Mitteilungen entgegenzunehmen und zu verwahren;

ARTICLE 77

Functions of depositaries

1. The functions of a depositary, unless otherwise provided in the treaty or agreed by the contracting States, comprise in particular:

(a) keeping custody of the original text of the treaty and of any full powers delivered to the depositary;

(b) preparing certified copies of the original text and preparing any further text of the treaty in such additional languages as may be required by the treaty and transmitting them to the parties and to the States entitled to become parties to the treaty;

(c) receiving any signatures to the treaty and receiving and keeping custody of any instruments, notifications and communications relating to it;

(d) zu prüfen, ob die Unterzeichnung und jede sich auf den Vertrag beziehende Urkunde, Notifikation oder Mitteilung in guter und gehöriger Form sind, und, falls erforderlich, den betreffenden Staat darauf aufmerksam zu machen;

(e) die Vertragsparteien sowie die Staaten, die berechtigt sind, Vertragsparteien zu werden, von Handlungen, Notifikationen und Mitteilungen zu unterrichten, die sich auf den Vertrag beziehen;

(f) die Staaten, die berechtigt sind, Vertragsparteien zu werden, von dem Zeitpunkt zu unterrichten, zu dem die für das Inkrafttreten des Vertrags erforderliche Anzahl von Unterzeichnungen oder von Ratifikations-, Annahme-, Genehmigungs- oder Beitrittsurkunden vorliegt oder hinterlegt wurde;

(g) den Vertrag beim Sekretariat der Vereinten Nationen registrieren zu lassen;

(h) die in anderen Bestimmungen dieses Übereinkommens bezeichneten Aufgaben zu erfüllen.

2. Treten zwischen einem Staat und dem Verwahrer über die Erfüllung von dessen Aufgaben Meinungsverschiedenheiten auf, so macht dieser die Unterzeichnerstaaten und die Vertragsstaaten oder, wenn angebracht, das zuständige Organ der internationalen Organisation darauf aufmerksam.

(d) examining whether the signature or any instrument, notification or communication relating to the treaty is in due and proper form and, if need be, bringing the matter to the attention of the State in question;

(e) informing the parties and the States entitled to become parties to the treaty of acts, notifications and communications relating to the treaty;

(f) informing the States entitled to become parties to the treaty when the number of signatures or of instruments of ratification, acceptance, approval or accession required for the entry into force of the treaty has been received or deposited;

(g) registering the treaty with the Secretariat of the United Nations;

(h) performing the functions specified in other provisions of the present Convention.

2. In the event of any difference appearing between a State and the depositary as to the performance of the latter's functions, the depositary shall bring the question to the attention of the signatory States and the contracting States or, where appropriate, of the competent organ of the international organization concerned.

Annex 16: Amendment and modification of treaties

From VCLOT

ÄNDERUNG UND MODIFIKATION VON VERTRÄGEN

ARTIKEL 39

Allgemeine Regel über die Änderung von Verträgen

Ein Vertrag kann durch Übereinkunft zwischen den Vertragsparteien geändert werden. Teil II findet auf eine solche Übereinkunft insoweit Anwendung, als der Vertrag nichts anderes vorsieht.

AMENDMENT AND MODIFICATION OF TREATIES

ARTICLE 39

General rule regarding the amendment of treaties

A treaty may be amended by agreement between the parties. The rules laid down in Part II apply to such an agreement except in so far as the treaty may otherwise provide.

ARTIKEL 40

Änderung mehrseitiger Verträge

1. Sofern der Vertrag nichts anderes vorsieht, richtet sich die Änderung mehrseitiger Verträge nach den folgenden Absätzen.

2. Vorschläge zur Änderung eines mehrseitigen Vertrags mit Wirkung zwischen allen Vertragsparteien sind allen Vertragsstaaten zu notifizieren; jeder von ihnen ist berechtigt,

(a) an dem Beschluß über das auf einen solchen Vorschlag hin zu Veranlassende teilzunehmen;

(b) am Aushandeln und am Abschluß einer Übereinkunft zur Änderung des Vertrags teilzunehmen.

3. Jeder Staat, der berechtigt ist, Vertragspartei des Vertrags zu werden, ist auch berechtigt, Vertragspartei des geänderten Vertrags zu werden.

4. Die Änderungsübereinkunft bindet keinen Staat, der schon Vertragspartei des Vertrags ist, jedoch nicht Vertragspartei der Änderungsübereinkunft wird; auf einen solchen Staat findet Artikel 30 Absatz 4 Buchstabe (b) Anwendung.

5. Ein Staat, der nach Inkrafttreten der Änderungsübereinkunft Vertragspartei des Vertrags wird, gilt, sofern er nicht eine abweichende Absicht äußert,

(a) als Vertragspartei des geänderten Vertrags und

(b) als Vertragspartei des nicht geänderten Vertrags im Verhältnis zu einer Vertragspartei, die durch die Änderungsübereinkunft nicht gebunden ist.

ARTIKEL 41

Übereinkünfte zur Modifikation mehrseitiger Verträge zwischen einzelnen Vertragsparteien

1. Zwei oder mehr Vertragsparteien eines mehrseitigen Vertrags können eine Übereinkunft schließen, um den Vertrag ausschließlich im Verhältnis zueinander zu modifizieren,

(a) wenn die Möglichkeit einer solchen Modifikation in dem Vertrag vorgesehen ist oder

(b) wenn die betreffende Modifikation durch den Vertrag nicht verboten ist und
   (i) die anderen Vertragsparteien in dem

ARTICLE 40

Amendment of multilateral treaties

1. Unless the treaty otherwise provides, the amendment of multilateral treaties shall be governed by the following paragraphs.

2. Any proposal to amend a multilateral treaty as between all the parties must be notified to all the contracting States, each one of which shall have the right to take part in:

(a) the decision as to the action to be taken in regard to such proposal:

(b) the negotiation and conclusion of any agreement for the amendment of the treaty.

3. Every State entitled to become a party to the treaty shall also be entitled to become a party to the treaty as amended.

4. The amending agreement does not bind any State already a party to the treaty which does not become a party to the amending agreement; article 30, paragraph 4 (b), applies in relation to such State.

5. Any State which becomes a party to the treaty after the entry into force of the amending agreement shall, failing an expression of a different intention by that State:

(a) be considered as a party to the treaty as amended; and

(b) be considered as a party to the unamended treaty in relation to any party to the treaty not bound by the amending agreement.

ARTICLE 41

Agreements to modify multilateral treaties between certain of the parties only

1. Two or more of the parties to a multilateral treaty may conclude an agreement to modify the treaty as between themselves alone if:

(a) the possibility of such a modification is provided for by the treaty; or

(b) the modification in question is not prohibited by the treaty and:
   (i) does not affect the enjoyment by the

Genuß ihrer Rechte auf Grund des Vertrags oder in der Erfüllung ihrer Pflichten nicht beeinträchtigt und

(ii) sich nicht auf eine Bestimmung bezieht, von der abzuweichen mit der vollen Verwirklichung von Ziel und Zweck des gesamten Vertrags unvereinbar ist.

2. Sofern der Vertrag in einem Fall des Absatzes 1 Buchstabe (a) nichts anderes vorsieht, haben die betreffenden Vertragsparteien den anderen Vertragsparteien ihre Absicht, eine Übereinkunft zu schließen, sowie die darin vorgesehene Modifikation zu notifizieren.

other parties of their rights under the treaty or the performance of their obligations;

(ii) does not relate to a provision, derogation from which is incompatible with the effective execution of the object and purpose of the treaty as a whole.

2. Unless in a case falling under paragraph 1 (a) the treaty otherwise provides, the parties in question shall notify the other parties of their intention to conclude the agreement and of the modification to the treaty for which it provides.

Annex 17: Recourse to arbitral bodies

From CSE

ARTIKEL 15

(a) Etwa erforderliche Maßnahmen zur Anwendung dieses Übereinkommens sind durch Vereinbarungen zwischen den zuständigen Behörden der Vertragsparteien zu treffen.

(b) Streitigkeiten zwischen zwei oder mehreren Vertragsparteien über die Auslegung oder Anwendung dieses Übereinkommens werden durch unmittelbare Verhandlungen beigelegt.

(c) Kann eine Streitigkeit nicht innerhalb von drei Monaten, vom Beginn der Verhandlungen an gerechnet, beigelegt werden, so ist sie einer Schiedsstelle, deren Zusammensetzung und Verfahren durch Vereinbarung zwischen den Vertragsparteien festgelegt werden, zur Schlichtung vorzulegen.

(d) Die Schiedsstelle entscheidet nach den Grundsätzen und im Geiste dieses Übereinkommens; ihre Entscheidung ist endgültig und bindend.

ARTICLE 15

(a) Arrangements for the application of the present Convention will, if required, be made between the competent authorities of the Contracting Parties.

(b) Any disagreement between two or more of the Contracting Parties arising out of the interpretation or application of the present Convention shall be resolved by direct negotiation.

(c) If any such disagreement cannot be resolved by such negotiation within a period of three months from the commencement of the negotiation, the disagreement shall be submitted to arbitration by an arbitral body whose composition and procedure shall be determined by agreement between the Contracting Parties.

(d) The decision of the arbitral body shall be given in accordance with the fundamental principles and spirit of the present Convention and shall be accepted as final and binding.

Annex 18: Atomic, biological and chemical weapons

1. From NATA Annex

Par. 11

BEGRIFFSBESTIMMUNGEN

Par. 11d:

,,(d) Der Ausdruck ,,Atomwaffe" bedeutet jede Vorrichtung, welche — mit Ausnahme ihres

Section 11

DEFINITIONS

Section 11d:

"(d) The term "atomic weapon" means any device utilizing atomic energy exclusive of the

Beförderungs- oder Antriebsmittels (falls dieses Mittel ein abtrennbarer und teilbarer Bestandteil der Vorrichtung ist) — Atomenergie verwertet, und deren hauptsächlicher Zweck darin besteht, als Waffe, Waffenprototyp oder Waffenerprobungsvorrichtung verwendet oder dazu entwickelt zu werden."

means for transporting or propelling the device (where such means is a separable and divisible part of the device), the principal purpose of which is for use as, or for development of, a weapon, a weapon prototype, or a weapon test device."

2. From WEU III Annex II

I. Atomwaffen

(a) Als Atomwaffe gilt jede Waffe, die Kernbrennstoff oder radioaktive Isotope enthält oder eigens dazu bestimmt ist, solche aufzunehmen oder zu verwenden und welche — durch Explosion oder andere unkontrollierte Kernumwandlung des Kernbrennstoffes oder durch Radioaktivität des Kernbrennstoffes oder der radioaktiven Isotope — Massenzerstörungen, Massenschäden oder Massenvergiftungen hervorrufen kann.

(b) Als Atomwaffe gilt ferner jeder Teil, jede Vorrichtung, jede Baugruppe oder Substanz, welche eigens für eine unter (a) aufgeführte Waffe bestimmt oder für sie wesentlich ist.

(c) Als Kernbrennstoff gemäß der vorangehenden Definition gilt Plutonium, Uran 233, Uran 235 (einschließlich Uran 235, welches in Uran enthalten ist, das mit mehr als 2,1 Gewichtsprozent Uran 235 angereichert wurde) sowie jede andere Substanz, welche geeignet ist, beträchtliche Mengen Atomenergie durch Kernspaltung oder -vereinigung oder eine andere Kernreaktion der Substanz freizumachen. Die vorstehenden Substanzen werden als Kernbrennstoff angesehen, einerlei in welchem chemischen oder physikalischen Zustand sie sich befinden.

I. Atomic Weapons

(a) An atomic weapon is defined as any weapon which contains, or is designed to contain or utilize, nuclear fuel or radioactive isotopes and which, by explosion or other uncontrolled nuclear transformation of the nuclear fuel, or by radioactivity of the nuclear fuel or radioactive isotopes, is capable of mass destruction, mass injury or mass poisoning.

(b) Furthermore, any part, device, assembly or material especially designed for, or primarily useful in, any weapon as set forth under paragraph (a) shall be deemed to be an atomic weapon.

(c) Nuclear fuel as used in the preceding definition includes Plutonium, Uranium 233, Uranium 235 (including Uranium 235 contained in Uranium enriched to over 2.1 per cent by weight of Uranium 235) and any other material capable of releasing substantial quantities of atomic energy through nuclear fission or fusion or other nuclear reaction of the material. The foregoing materials shall be considered to be nuclear fuel regardless of the chemical or physical form in which they exist.

II. Chemische Waffen

(a) Als chemische Waffe gelten alle Einrichtungen oder Geräte, die eigens dazu bestimmt sind, die erstickenden, toxischen, reizerregenden, lähmenden, wachstumsregelnden, die Schmierwirkung zerstörenden und katalytischen Eigenschaften irgendeiner chemischen Substanz für militärische Zwecke auszunutzen.

(b) Vorbehaltlich der unter (c) getroffenen Regelung sind chemische Substanzen, die derartige Eigenschaften besitzen, und für die Ver-

II. Chemical Weapons

(a) A chemical weapon is defined as any equipment or apparatus expressly designed to use, for military purposes, the asphyxiating, toxic, irritant, paralysant, growth-regulating, anti-lubricating or catalysing properties of any chemical substance.

(b) Subject to the provisions of paragraph (c), chemical substances, having such properties and capable of being used in the equipment or

wendung in Einrichtungen und Geräten gemäß (a) in Frage kommen, in dieser Definition einbegriffen.

(c) Von dieser Definition gelten als ausgenommen die unter (a) und (b) genannten Geräte und die Mengen von chemischen Substanzen, die nicht über den zivilen Friedensbedarf hinausgehen.

apparatus referred to in paragraph (a), shall be deemed to be included in this definition.

(c) Such apparatus and such quantities of the chemical substances as are referred to in paragraphs (a) and (b) which do not exceed peaceful civilian requirements shall be deemed to be excluded from this definition.

III. Biologische Waffen

(a) Als biologische Waffen gelten alle Einrichtungen oder Geräte, die eigens dazu bestimmt sind, schädliche Insekten oder andere lebende oder tote Organismen oder deren toxische Produkte für militärische Zwecke zu verwenden.

(b) Vorbehaltlich der unter (c) getroffenen Regelung sind in dieser Definition Insekten, Organismen und ihre toxischen Produkte eingeschlossen, soweit sie nach Art und Menge für die Verwendung in den unter (a) genannten Einrichtungen oder Geräten in Frage kommen.

(c) Von dieser Definition gelten als ausgenommen die unter (a) und (b) aufgeführten Einrichtungen und Geräte sowie die Mengen von Insekten, Organismen und ihren toxischen Produkten, die über den zivilen Friedensbedarf nicht hinausgehen.

III. Biological Weapons

(a) A biological weapon is defined as any equipment or apparatus expressly designed to use, for military purposes, harmful insects or other living or dead organisms, or their toxic products.

(b) Subject to the provisions of paragraph (c), insects, organisms and their toxic products of such nature and in such amounts as to make them capable of being used in the equipment or apparatus referred to in (a) shall be deemed to be included in this definition.

(c) Such equipment or apparatus and such quantities of the insects, organisms and their toxic products as are referred to in paragraphs (a) and (b) which do not exceed peaceful civilian requirements shall be deemed to be excluded from the definition of biological weapons.

Annex 19: International Court of Justice

1. From SICJ

Artikel 1

Der durch die Charta der UN als Hauptrechtsprechungsorgan der UN eingesetzte Internationale Gerichtshof wird nach Maßgabe dieses Statuts errichtet und nimmt seine Aufgaben nach Maßgabe seiner Bestimmungen wahr.

Article 1

The International Court of Justice established by the Charter of the United Nations as the principal judicial organ of the United Nations shall be constituted and shall function in accordance with the provisions of the present Statute.

Artikel 2

Der Gerichtshof besteht aus unabhängigen Richtern, die ohne Rücksicht auf ihre Staatsangehörigkeit unter Personen von hohem sittlichen Ansehen ausgewählt werden, welche die in ihrem Staat für die höchsten richterlichen Ämter erforderlichen Voraussetzungen erfüllen oder Völkerrechtsgelehrte von anerkanntem Ruf sind.

Article 2

The Court shall be composed of a body of independent judges, elected regardless of their nationality from among persons of high moral character, who possess the qualifications required in their respective countries for appointment to the highest judicial offices, or are jurisconsults of recognized competence in international law.

ARTIKEL 3

1. Der Gerichtshof besteht aus 15 Mitgliedern, von denen nicht mehr als eines Angehöriger desselben Staates sein darf.

2. Wer im Hinblick auf die Mitgliedschaft beim Gerichtshof als Angehöriger mehr als eines Staates angesehen werden kann, gilt als Angehöriger des Staates, in dem er gewöhnlich seine bürgerlichen und politischen Rechte ausübt.

ARTICLE 3

1. The Court shall consist of 15 members, no two of whom may be nationals of the same state.

2. A person who for the purposes of membership in the Court could be regarded as a national of more than one state shall be deemed to be a national of the one in which he ordinarily exercises civil and political rights.

2. From CUN

KAPITEL XIV

Der Internationale Gerichtshof

ARTIKEL 92

Der Internationale Gerichtshof ist das Hauptrechtsprechungsorgan der Vereinten Nationen. Er nimmt seine Aufgaben nach Maßgabe des beigefügten Statuts wahr, das auf dem Statut des Ständigen Internationalen Gerichtshofs beruht und Bestandteil dieser Charta ist.

CHAPTER XIV

The International Court of Justice

ARTICLE 92

The International Court of Justice shall be the principal judicial organ of the United Nations. It shall function in accordance with the annexed Statute, which is based upon the Statute of the Permanent Court of International Justice and forms an integral part of the present Charter.

ARTIKEL 93

1. Alle Mitglieder der Vereinten Nationen sind ohne weiteres Vertragsparteien der Satzung des Internationalen Gerichtshofs.

2. Ein Staat, der nicht Mitglied der Vereinten Nationen ist, kann zu Bedingungen, welche die Generalversammlung jeweils auf Empfehlung des Sicherheitsrats festsetzt, Vertragspartei des Statuts des Internationalen Gerichtshofs werden.

ARTICLE 93

1. All Members of the United Nations are ipso facto parties to the Statute of the International Court of Justice.

2. A state which is not a Member of the United Nations may become a party to the Statute of the International Court of Justice on conditions to be determined in each case by the General Assembly upon the recommendation of the Security Council.

ARTIKEL 94

1. Jedes Mitglied der Vereinten Nationen verpflichtet sich, bei jeder Streitigkeit, in der es Partei ist, die Entscheidung des Internationalen Gerichtshofs zu befolgen.

ARTICLE 94

1. Each Member of the United Nations undertakes to comply with the decision of the International Court of Justice in any case to which it is a party.

Annex 20: Sources of international law

From SICJ

ARTIKEL 38

1. Der Gerichtshof, dessen Aufgabe es ist, die ihm unterbreiteten Streitigkeiten nach dem Völkerrecht zu entscheiden, wendet an

ARTICLE 38

1. The Court, whose function it is to decide in accordance with international law such disputes as are submitted to it, shall apply:

(a) internationale Übereinkünfte allgemeiner oder besonderer Natur, in denen von den streitenden Staaten ausdrücklich anerkannte Regeln festgelegt sind;

(b) das internationale Gewohnheitsrecht als Ausdruck einer allgemeinen, als Recht anerkannten Übung;

(c) die von den Kulturvölkern anerkannten allgemeinen Rechtsgrundsätze;

(d) vorbehaltlich des Artikels 59 richterliche Entscheidungen und die Lehrmeinung der fähigsten Völkerrechtler der verschiedenen Nationen als Hilfsmittel zur Feststellung von Rechtsnormen.

2. Diese Bestimmung läßt die Befugnis des Gerichtshofs unberührt, mit Zustimmung der Parteien *ex aequo et bono* zu entscheiden.

(a) international conventions, whether general or particular, establishing rules expressly recognized by the contesting states;

(b) international custom, as evidence of a general practice accepted as law;

(c) the general principles of law recognized by civilized nations;

(d) subject to the provisions of Article 59, judicial decisions and the teachings of the most highly qualified publicists of the various nations, as subsidiary means for the determination of rules of law.

2. This provision shall not prejudice the power of the Court to decide a case *ex aequo et bono,* if the parties agree thereto.

Annex 21: Reservations

From VCLOT

Abschnitt 2: Vorbehalte

ARTIKEL 19

Anbringen von Vorbehalten

Ein Staat kann bei der Unterzeichnung, Ratifikation, Annahme oder Genehmigung eines Vertrags oder beim Beitritt einen Vorbehalt anbringen, sofern nicht

(a) der Vertrag den Vorbehalt verbietet;

(b) der Vertrag vorsieht, daß nur bestimmte Vorbehalte gemacht werden dürfen, zu denen der betreffende Vorbehalt nicht gehört, oder

(c) in den unter Buchstabe (a) oder (b) nicht bezeichneten Fällen der Vorbehalt mit Ziel und Zweck des Vertrags unvereinbar ist.

ARTIKEL 20

Annahme von Vorbehalten und Einsprüche gegen Vorbehalte

1. Ein durch einen Vertrag ausdrücklich zugelassener Vorbehalt bedarf der nachträglichen Annahme durch die anderen Vertragsstaaten nur, wenn der Vertrag dies vorsieht.

2. Geht aus der begrenzten Zahl der Verhandlungsstaaten sowie aus Ziel und Zweck eines Vertrags hervor, daß die Anwendung des Ver-

Section 2. Reservations

ARTICLE 19

Formulation of reservations

A State may, when signing, ratifying, accepting, approving or acceding to a treaty, formulate a reservation unless:

(a) the reservation is prohibited by the treaty;

(b) the treaty provides that only specified reservations, which do not include the reservation in question, may be made; or

(c) in cases not falling under sub-paragraphs (a) and (b), the reservation is incompatible with the object and purpose of the treaty.

ARTICLE 20

Acceptance of and objection to reservations

1. A reservation expressly authorized by a treaty does not require any subsequent acceptance by the other contracting States unless the treaty so provides.

2. When it appears from the limited number of the negotiating States and the object and purpose of a treaty that the application of the treaty in its

trags in seiner Gesamtheit zwischen allen Vertragsparteien eine wesentliche Voraussetzung für die Zustimmung jeder Vertragspartei ist, durch den Vertrag gebunden zu sein, so bedarf ein Vorbehalt der Annahme durch alle Vertragsparteien.

3. Bildet ein Vertrag die Gründungsurkunde einer internationalen Organisation und sieht er nichts anderes vor, so bedarf ein Vorbehalt der Annahme durch das zuständige Organ der Organisation.

4. In den nicht in den Absätzen 1 bis 3 bezeichneten Fällen und sofern der Vertrag nichts anderes vorsieht,

(a) macht die Annahme eines Vorbehalts durch einen anderen Vertragsstaat den den Vorbehalt anbringenden Staat zur Vertragspartei im Verhältnis zu jenem anderen Staat, sofern der Vertrag für diese Staaten in Kraft getreten ist oder sobald er für sie in Kraft tritt;

(b) schließt der Einspruch eines anderen Vertragsstaats gegen einen Vorbehalt das Inkrafttreten des Vertrags zwischen dem den Einspruch erhebenden und dem den Vorbehalt anbringenden Staat nicht aus, sofern nicht der den Einspruch erhebende Staat seine gegenteilige Absicht eindeutig zum Ausdruck bringt;

(c) wird eine Handlung, mit der die Zustimmung eines Staates, durch den Vertrag gebunden zu sein, ausgedrückt wird und die einen Vorbehalt in sich schließt, wirksam, sobald mindestens ein anderer Vertragsstaat den Vorbehalt angenommen hat.

5. Im Sinne der Absätze 2 und 4 und sofern der Vertrag nichts anderes vorsieht, gilt ein Vorbehalt als von einem Staat angenommen, wenn dieser bis zum Ablauf von zwölf Monaten, nachdem ihm der Vorbehalt notifiziert worden ist, oder bis zu dem Zeitpunkt, wenn dies der spätere ist, in dem er seine Zustimmung ausgedrückt hat, durch den Vertrag gebunden zu sein, keinen Einspruch gegen den Vorbehalt erhebt.

entirety between all the parties is an essential condition of the consent of each one to be bound by the treaty, a reservation requires acceptance by all the parties.

3. When a treaty is a constituent instrument of an international organization and unless it otherwise provides, a reservation requires the acceptance of the competent organ of that organization.

4. In cases not falling under the preceding paragraphs and unless the treaty otherwise provides:

(a) acceptance by another contracting State of a reservation constitutes the reserving State a party to the treaty in relation to that other State if or when the treaty is in force for those States;

(b) an objection by another contracting State to a reservation does not preclude the entry into force of the treaty as between the objecting and reserving States unless a contrary intention is definitely expressed by the objecting State;

(c) an act expressing a State's consent to be bound by the treaty and containing a reservation is effective as soon as at least one other contracting State has accepted the reservation.

5. For the purposes of paragraphs 2 and 4 and unless the treaty otherwise provides, a reservation is considered to have been accepted by a State if it shall have raised no objection to the reservation by the end of a period of twelve months after it was notified of the reservation or by the date on which it expressed its consent to be bound by the treaty, whichever is later.

PART III

ENGLISH REGISTER

The Register contains all the English words and phrases included in Parts I and II of the Glossary, and lists the precise reference(s) to where they can be found there. The arrangement of entries in the Register is based on the same criteria as those used in Part I (see p. v of the Introduction). The only departure from strict alphabetical order is to permit plural entries to immediately follow singular entries (e.g. *acts* entries follow *act* entries and precede *action* entries).

There are three categories of references in the Register:

1. to major headwords in Part I—these references are given in bold type;
2. to sub-entries, derived phrases or examples in Part I—these are given in normal type;
3. to the Annexes in Part II, also given in normal type.

The references in categories 1 and 2 consist of a *letter plus number* corresponding to the running numbers of entries in Part I (e.g. V372 = *to be found under* 372 *in letter* V). The references in category 3 consist of AN *plus number* (e.g. AN4 = *to be found in Annex* 4).

In the case of multiple references the three categories are each arranged in alphabetical and numerical order, and are separated where appropriate by a semi-colon (e.g. B10, S303, T12; AN3, AN12 or **B19, F24;** B22, D18, F26). The three categories are not intended, however, to imply in all cases a hierarchy of usefulness: the user will appreciate that because of the pattern of entries in Part I, the sub-entries and examples are often more significant than the major headwords themselves (e.g. *Meer, Recht,* etc., function as no more than convenient common language headings under which are listed the various technical phrases). The references printed in bold may consequently not always be the most important.

In Part I many of the noun sub-entries are in the plural form. Hence, although many plural forms have been eliminated from the Register in the interest of simplicity, the user should check whether the collocation or phrase required is listed as a plural form. As explained above, such plural entries are situated for convenience immediately after the singular entries, regardless of whether this disrupts strict alphabetical order.

a posteriori   **N50**
abide by (to)   **E72**
abolish (to)   K321
abrogate (to)   **A639**
absence of, in the   **E421;** E422
abstain from (to)   **E240**
abstention   **S682**
abuse   **M256, U38**
abuse. in   **M259**
abuse of law, in   R357
abuse (to)   **M258, U37**
abusive   **M259**
accede, invite to (to)   B235
accede, subject to reservation (to)   B226
accede to (to)   **B222;** B223, B224, B225
accede to, right to   T81
accede, willing to   **B242**
acceding   **B183, B227**
acceding, subsequently   B184, B229
accept (to)   **A446, A666, E239**
acceptable   **G179**
acceptable, not   **U108;** G180, G181
acceptance   **A437, A657, E238;** A438; AN14
acceptance clause   **A444**
acceptance, condition of   **A664**
acceptance, deferred   A441
acceptance, formal   A439
acceptance, instrument of   **A445**
acceptance, notice of   **Z219**
acceptance, notification of   **A442;** A443
acceptance, subsequent   A441; AN21
access   **D216, Z129, Z137**
access, equal   Z139, Z140
access, free   Z131, Z138
access, right of   **Z132**
access, unimpeded   Z141
accession   **B230, T76;** AN5, AN14
accession, applying for   **B242**
accession, be open for (to)   B233, B234; AN5
accession by acceptance   T83
accession by approval   T83
accession by ratification   T83
accession by signature   T83
accession clause   **B239**
accession, clause of   **B239**
accession, condition of   **B236**
accession, declaration of   **B237**
accession, effect (to)   B231
accession, instrument of   **B237, B241;** B231,
  B238; AN5
accession, right of   **B240**
accession to a treaty   T80
accommodation   **R85**
accord   **E89**
accord (to)   **G362**
accordance   **E89**
accordance with, in   **G164;** E90, M37, M38
accordance with the annexed statute, in   G166

accordance with the charter, in   G165
accorded by treaty   V469
account   **A80, R95, R97;** R98
account, annual   **J3, J5**
account, audited annual   J6
account, currency of   **V314**
account, not taken into   **U91**
account, period of   **A81, R112**
account, unit of   **R101;** R102, R103
accounting   **A80**
accredit (to)   **A194, B136**
accreditation   **B144**
accredited   **B138**
accredited, longest   **D68**
accredited to the head of state   A195, B140
accrediting   **A196**
accretion   **A475, Z220**
accusation   **B398**
accuse of (to)   **B396**
achieve (to)   **V625**
achieve, failure to   N145
achievement   **V626**
acquiesce (to)   **W109**
acquire (to)   **E477**
acquired   **E485**
acquisition   **E476, E482**
acquisition *in rem*   D95
acquisition of real rights   D95
acquisition, reason for   **E481**
acquisition, territorial   **G38;** E483, T100
act   **A197, A203, H63, T23, T186, V896**
act, administrative   **V590**
act against the state   H65
act, aggressive   **A405, A407**
act, belligerent   H76
act, charged with   L42
act, commit (to)   H94
act, conclusive   H75, K192
act, confirmation of   H99
act, constituent   **G547**
act, constitutional   **V113**
act, criminal   **D31, S719**
act, discriminatory   D167
act, fail to perform (to)   H97
act, final   **S200;** AN3
act, general   **G188**
act harmful to the enemy   H66
act, hostile   **A405, A407;** H74
act implying intent   K192
act in an official capacity   H68, H70
act in the law   R314
act, international   H93, V728
act, judicial   H78
act, legal   **R314, R329**
act, malicious   **AN10**
act, non-war aggressive   A406
act, notification of   M332
act of a state, sovereign   **S609**

act of aggression **A405, A407**
act of hostility H74
Act, official **A245, A260;** A261, H70
act, omit to perform an (to) H97
act or omission T187, U188
act, penal **S719**
act, perform (to) **H94, H98**
act performed as part of their duties H70
act performed in a private capacity H77
act performed outside their duties H67
act performed without authorization H99
act, person committing the **T28**
act, private H77
act, punishable **S719;** H69; AN11
act, refrain from (to) **H95, H96**
act, retaliatory **V154**
act, sovereign **H237, H250;** H235
act, tortious **D31**
act, unilateral **A200, H73**
act, unlawful H91
act with legal effect H64
act without legal effect H64
act, wrongful H91
acts at international law R316
acts contrary to the provisions Z225
acts, foreign A199
acts, legislative G341
acts, non-sovereign N151
acts prejudicial to peace A201
acts, unfriendly A202
act (to) **H30, V892**
act illegally (to) R449
action **A197, H32, H63, K61, M48, T23, V896**
action, administrative **V605**
action, adoption of A198
action against, bring (to) **V210**
action agreed upon by the parties E187
action, alternative M58
action, base on (to) K74
action, bring (to) **K81;** K70, K73, S75
action brought, prior to R333
action brought, subsequent to R332
action, by means of **K88**
action, by means of legislative **G349;** G340
action, capable of **H100**
action, cause of **K80**
action, civil **Z70;** Z71
action, collective **K120, K126**
action, commencement of **K79**
action, common H34
action, concerted E190
action, directly concerned in K64
action, disciplinary **D179**
action, file (to) K71
action, grounds for **K80**
action, hostile **A398, A405, A407, F71**
action *in rem* D96
action, incapable of **H108**

action, individual **E201**
action, initiate (to) K70, K73
action, initiation of **K79**
action, institute (to) K70, K73
action, joint H34
action, judicial **G272;** R389
action, legislative G348, M62
action, liberty of E294, H105, H106
action, lodge (to) K71
action, pass (to) K75
action, policing **P116**
action, preventive **P129, V889;** V890
action, preventive and enforcement P130
action, prompt and effective H33, M73
action, protective military M222
action, real D96, K65, K66, L103; AN7
action, refer (to) K75
action relating to AN7
action relating to succession K62, N30
action, start (to) K73
action, statement of **K78**
action, submit (to) K71
action, taking of A198
action with respect to breach of the peace M51
action, withdrawal of **K86**
action, written **K78**
actions, admissible K67
actions, inadmissible K67
actions prejudicial to peace A201
actions, set of M52
active **T32**
activity **T35**
activity, engage in (to) T54
activities **G286, G308**
activities, annual report of T36
activities, assumption of T38
activities, commence (to) T52
activities, conduct (to) H31
activities, continuation of T43
activities, description of **T62**
activities, exercise of T40
activities, field of **T61**
activities, humanitarian T47
activities, scope of **T61**
activities, suspension of T42
activities, termination of T41
adhere to (to) **B222, E72**
adhere to, promise to (to) **E75**
adherence **B230**
adherence, instrument evidencing B232
adhering **B227;** B185
adhesion **B230**
adjacent **A395**
adjacent to **V898**
adjacent to (to be) **A393, G484**
adjoin (to) **A393, G484**
adjoining **A395**
adjourn (to) **V351;** V352

adjournment   V353
adjournment, motion for   V354
adjudication   A174; A175
adjudications, arbitral   R391
adjustment   A455, B297, O78
adjustment, pacific   F301
adjustment, peaceful   B298
adjustments to the treaties   A456
administer (to)   V585
administering   V586
administration   V588
administration, occupying   B355
administrative power   V603
admissibility   Z148
admissible   Z146
admissible, declare as (to)   Z144
admission   A657, Z149
admission, application for   A660, A662, Z152
admission as a member   A658
admission, committee on   Z153
admission, condition of   A664
admission, party applying for   A661
admission, state applying for   A661
admission to membership   A658
admit (to)   A666, Z144
admitted   Z142
adopt (to)   A176, A446, U30
adoption   A177, A437, E55, U27; T149
adoption of a common policy   E57
adoption, specific   A178
adoption theory   A179
adoption, unrestricted   U28
advise (to)   K38, K40
adviser   R61; R62
advisory   B268, G577, G580
advocate   B510
aequitas   B595
affair   A372
affairs, conduct of   G297; G298
affairs, domestic   A377
affairs, execution of   G297
affairs, external   A376
affairs, foreign   A376
affairs, internal   A377
affairs, intervention in   A378
affect (to)   B333, B335
affect, adversely (to)   B49
affect, not to   U94, U98
affirm (to)   B245
affirmation   B247
affirming   B248; AN4
affix (to)   V336
afford (to)   E105
aforesaid   G177
age, full   V805
age, of full   M365
age of majority   M366
age, person of full   V804

agency   A237, D88, E122, O83, O90, S641; O92
agency, ad-hoc   S642
agency, administrative   V610
agency, central   Z22
agency, central administrative   V612
agency, competent   D91
agency, executive   E500
agency, governmental   R497; S646
agency, impartial   S647
agency, intergovernmental   E124
agency, military   M214
agency, non-governmental   S645
agency of necessity   G299
agency, regional   E123, R505
agency, special   S424, S427
agency, specialized   S428; F7, O91
agency, subordinate   S643
agenda   T5
agenda, approve (to)   T10
agenda, approved   T8
agenda committee   T14
agenda, draft   T15
agenda, draw up (to)   T11
agenda, exhaust (to)   T12
agenda, final   T8
agenda, fix (to)   T11
agenda, item on   T16
agenda, overload (to)   T13
agenda, place items on (to)   T6
agenda, point on   T16
agenda, provisional   T9
agenda, withdraw items from (to)   T7
agent   A180, B509, P190; B510
agent, civilian   M228
agent, diplomatic   D97; D98, D121 (*see also
     under* diplomatic agent)
agent, enemy   F51
agent, military   M228
agent, special   A181
aggression   A183, A398, A405, A407
aggression, acts of   F255
aggression, armed   A402, A403, M210
aggression, military   M210
aggression, policy of   A410
aggression, suppress acts of (to)   A408
aggression, unprovoked   A404
aggression, war of   A409
aggressive act   A405
aggressive war   A409
aggressor   A184, A390
aggressor, determination of   A391, B475
aggressor state   A392; A389
agree (to)   A74, E83, U1, U10, V51, Z213; U2
agree as follows (to)   V52
agree upon (to)   V51
agreed   V56
agreed by treaty   V470
agreed, it has been   E178

agreed, it is   E177
agreed, unless otherwise   A77, A302, G112
agreed upon   **V56**
agreement   **A59, A75, A108, E85, E176, E191, U3, U7, U11, V60, W202, Z214; AN1**
agreement, administrative   **V589, V613, V614**
agreement, agricultural   **L40**
agreement, amending · **A296; AN16**
agreement between the parties   E193
agreement, bilateral   V68
agreement, bring parties to (to)   V158
agreement, by   **E185, E189, G585;** E183
agreement, by unanimous   B373
agreement, collective   **G275**
agreement, come to (to)   **A74, E83, U1;** V345
agreement, commercial   **H35**
agreement, common   E181
agreement, constitute (to)   V61
agreement, cultural   **K463**
agreement, declaration of   **E184**
agreement, draft   **V70;** V71
agreement, extension of   A697
agreement, failure to observe   N136
agreement for   A60
agreement, in common   E179
agreement, in the spirit of   G134
agreement in writing   V67
agreement, intergovernmental **R491;** A67
agreement, interim   **Z269**
agreement, international   A62, A66; AN14
agreement, memorandum of   **V60**
agreement, monetary   **W54**
agreement, mutual   E181
agreement, naval   **F139**
agreement, non-observance of   N136
agreement of a cultural nature   A61
agreement of a technical nature   A61
agreement of association   **A576**
agreement on A60
agreement, oral   V65
agreement, partial   **T74**
agreement, preliminary   **V959**
agreement, principal   **H125**
agreement, quadripartite   **V650, V656**
agreement, reach (to)   **A74, U1;** E86
agreement, regional   **R508;** A64
agreement, secret   **G123**
agreement, special   **S165, S417, S433;** S166, S434; AN1
agreement, supplemental   **Z179**
agreement, supplementary   **E362, Z179, Z184**
agreement, three-power   **D197, D201**
agreement to the contrary   G113
agreement to the contrary, in absence of   V54
agreement, tripartite   **D197, D201**
agreement, universal   **W116;** A65
agreement with, in   U12
agreement, world-wide   **W116**

agreements entered into   U13
agreements, general or particular   A63
agreements, local   U9
agrément   **A185;** E429
agrément, grant (to)   A189
agrément, granted (to be)   A186, A188
agrément, issue (to)   A189
agrément, receive (to)   A186, A188
agrément, refuse to grant (to)   A190
agrément, withdraw (to)   A187
agriculture   **L39;** M92
aid   **B186**
aid, government   B187
aid, legal   **R336**
aid station   **R574**
aide-mémoire   **A193**
aim   **Z45, Z50, Z253**
aim, primary   **H132**
aim, principal   **H132**
air attaché   **L146**
air corridor   **L127**
air domain   **L122**
air forces   **L136**
air, freedom of   **L121;** L133
air incident   **L147**
air regulations   **L145**
air, rules of   **L143**
air supremacy   **L123**
air traffic   **L140**
air transport   **L140**
air transport agreement   **L141, L144**
air transport committee   **L142**
air transport convention   **L144**
air warfare   **L128**
air warfare, law of   **L129**
aircraft   **L119**
aircraft, civil   **Z64**
aircraft, military   **M201**
aircraft, national   L120
airspace   **L122, L130**
airspace above   L132
airspace over territorial sea   L131
airspace, prohibited   **L135**
airspace, sovereignty over   **L124;** L125
airspace, superincumbent   L132
airworthiness   **L137**
airworthiness, certificate of   L138
alien (*adj.*)   **A740**
alien (*noun*)   **A733, F244, S594;** F245
alien, enemy   A734, F52
alien, undesirable   U109
aliens, duty of to register   **A735**
aliens, international laws relating to   F243
aliens, law governing   **F241**
aliens, law relating to   **A736, F241**
aliens' registration   **A737**
aliens, registration of   **A737**
aliens, status of   **A739**

all states clause   **A206**
alleged   **A362, B173**
allegiance, duty of   **T162, T163;** T164
allegiance, oath of   **T161**
alliance   **B677**
alliance, agreement of   **B678**
alliance, defensive   **D10**
alliance, treaty of   **B678, B681**
alliances, policy of   **B680**
alteration   A283
alternate (*adj.*)   **S653**
alternate (*noun*)   **S654, V559;** S655, V558
alternative   **A298**
ambassador   **B646;** M290
ambassador, roving   **S422**
ambassadors, conference of   **B647**
amend (to)   **A1, A278;** A289
amend, proposal to   AN16
amended   **A45**
amending   **A279**
amending protocol   **A295**
amendment   **A3, A282**
amendment, acceptance of   A286
amendment by agreement   A4
amendment, consider (to)   B267
amendment, draft   **A293**
amendment, instrument of   **A5**
amendment, proposal for   **A297;** A287, A288
amendment, propose (to)   A291, A292
amendment, proposed   **A6, A297**
amendment, protocol of   **A295**
amendment to the annex   A290
amiables compositeurs   B598
amicable   **G585**
amicably   W91
amnesty   **A215**
amnesty clause   **A216**
amnesty, general   **G189**
analogy, by   **S368**
anchorage   **R457;** R458
angary   **A360**
angary, right of   **A361**
annex   **A416, A430;** A418; AN3
annex, amendment to   B267
annex (to)   **A448, B180, E172**
annexation   **A449, A450, A472, E173**
annexation by armed force   E175
annexation, declaration of   **A452**
annexation of the occupied territory   E174
annexation, prohibition of   **A454**
annexation, right of   **A453**
annexation, territorial   **G37**
annexed   **B202**
annexed hereto   B137, U8
annul (to)   N153, R631
annulment   **N158, N159, R632**
Anschluss   **A472**
anxious   **B485;** B254

anxious to achieve   B488
apartheid, policies of   S303
apostolic   **P5**
apostolic delegate   D17
appeal   **B325, B402, R358, R369;** R364, R365
appeal at law   **R358**
appeal, court of   **B328**
appeal, file (to)   B326, R362
appeal, ground of   **B329**
appeal, lodge (to)   B326, R362, R363
appeal, notice of   **B331**
appeal, party lodging the   **B404**
appeal, period allowed for   **R368**
appeal, reasons for   **B329**
appeal, right of   R366
appeal, subject to (to be)   R367
appeal, susceptible of (to be)   R367
appeal, tribunal of   **B328**
appeal, without   **U86;** A356, R359
appeal (to)   R362
appeal against (to)   **A357**
appealable   **A355**
appealed against   **B327**
appealing   **B404**
appease (to)   **B409**
appeasement   **B410**
appeasement, policy of   **B411**
appel   S142
appellant   **B330, B404**
append (to)   **B180, V336**
appended   **B202**
appendix   **A416, A430;** A417; AN3
applicability   **A525, G148, G562**
applicable   **A521, G561;** A550
applicable (to be)   **A549**
applicable, become (to)   A522
applicable, cease to be (to)   A552
applicable to the case   A523
applicant   **A517**
application   **A508, A531, G148, I83, V623**
application, area of   **G154**
application, continued   **W107**
application, disagreement arising out of   AN17
application, ensure (to)   A553
application, extend (to)   A546, A556
application, extension of   A538, A539
application, field of   **A557**
application, full   A541, A542
application, improper   M260
application, postpone (to)   A545
application, provisional   A543
application, renewed   **W156**
application, scope of   **A557;** A558
application, suspend (to)   A547, A555
application, terminate (to)   A544
application, termination of   A537
application, territorial   **G154;** A561, G157
application, wide scope of   A559

application, written **K87;** S762
apply (to)   **A527, A549, G135;** W211
apply, cease to (to)   **A845;** A552, G563
apply for (to)   **B16**
apply in whole or in part (to)   A528, A551
apply *mutatis mutandis* (to)   G139
apply provisionally (to)   A529
apply restrictively (to)   E133
apply to (to)   **E447;** A526
applying   A515
appoint (to)   **A504, B258, B428, B443, E152, E426**
appointed   E424
appointed, duly   E425
appointment   A505, B259, B429, B445, E154, E428
appointment, certificate of   **A507, B446, E435**
appointment, letter of   **A507, B446, E434, E435**
appointment, make (to)   **E431**
appointment, power of   **E159, E433**
appointment, regularity of   E430
apportion (to)   **U68**
appropriate   G56
approval   B603, G183; AN14
approval *a posteriori*   N52
approval as provided for in constitution   G185
approval by parliament   Z218
approval certificate   **G187**
approval clause   **G186**
approval in accordance with constitution   G185
approval, instrument of   **B605, G187;** H214
approval of parliament   AN2
approval, parliamentary   E81, Z218
approve (to)   **B369, B593, G182**
approximate (to)   **A385**
approximation   A386
approximation of municipal laws   A387
approximation of national laws   R418
approximation of provisions   R439
arbiter   S121
arbiter, duties of   **S124**
arbiter, office of   **S124**
arbiters, list of   **S127, S128**
arbiters, panel of   **S116, S127, S128**
arbitrable   B189, S101
arbitral   S99, S125
arbitral award,   **S131;** S132
arbitral award, enforcement of   S134
arbitral award, final   S141
arbitral award, foreign   S134
arbitral award, recognition of   S133, S134
arbitral award, request for   S135
arbitral award, setting aside of   S136
arbitral award, subject matter of   S137
arbitral award, validity of   S138
arbitral body   **S154;** S155; AN17
arbitral body, permanent   S132
arbitral procedure   **S159, S168**

arbitral process, by   S169
arbitral tribunal   **S93, S112**
arbitral tribunal, award of   **S131**
arbitral tribunal, by   **S99**
arbitral tribunal, chairman of   O33
arbitral tribunal, member of   **S107**
arbitral tribunal, mixed   S98
arbitral tribunal, rules of   **S108**
arbitration   S103, S109, S129, S159, S168; B201
arbitration agreement   **S87, S88, S157, S165;** S158
arbitration, appeal to court of   S97
arbitration arrangement   **S88**
arbitration board   **S154**
arbitration board, appoint (to)   S156
arbitration body   **S154**
arbitration, by   **S99, S125;** W86
arbitration, by means of   S169
arbitration, by recourse to   S169
arbitration clause   **S114;** S115
arbitration, commercial   **H53**
arbitration, commission of   **S117**
arbitration, committee of   **S90**
arbitration compromise   **S120, S164**
arbitration, compulsory   **S104**
arbitration, conditions of   S89
arbitration, court of   **S93, S105, S112**
arbitration, member of court of   **S107**
arbitration, mixed court of   S98
arbitration, party requesting   S161
Arbitration, Permanent Court of   S106, S635
arbitration, private   S162
arbitration, recourse to court of   S97
arbitration, request for   S135
arbitration, right to resort to   S92
arbitration, right to submit to   **S91**
arbitration, rules of court of   **S108**
arbitration, seek recourse to (to)   S130
arbitration, settlement by   S100
arbitration, subject of   G101
arbitration, subject of G101
arbitration, submit to (to)   S163; AN17
arbitration, system of   **S111**
arbitrator   S121
arbitrator, chief   **O6;** O8
arbitrator, duties of   **S124**
arbitrator, office of   **S124**
arbitrator, presiding   **O31;** O7
arbitrator, sole   **E207;** O7
arbitrators   S116
arbitrators, list of   **S127, S128**
arbitrators, panel of   **S127, S128**
archive   A571
area   Z116
area, besieged   Z122
area, currency   **W56**
area, encircled   Z123

area, monetary **W56**; W57
area origin **Z128**
area, prohibited **S469**
area, restricted **S469**
area, strategic Z127
areas, metropolitan M380
areas, non-metropolitan M379
argument **R281**
argument, conclusion of **S201**; S202
argument, final **S201**
argument, point of **R281**
arguments by both parties **K268**
arguments, oral development of R282
arise (to) **E332**
arise from (to) **E471, H182**
arm (to) **B512**
armament **B517, R650**
armaments **W1**
Armaments, Agency for Control of R657
armaments committee **R653**
armaments, control of **R656**
armaments, limitation of **R654, R655**
armaments not to be manufactured R659
armaments production **R658**
armaments race **R660, W135**
armaments, reduction of **T75**
armaments, regulation of R651
armaments, stocks of **W16**
armaments to be controlled R652
armaments, type of **W15**
armed **B513, G399, M209**
armies in the field H148
arming **B517**
armistice **W22**
armistice agreement **W24**
armistice commission **W26**
armistice delegation **W27**
armistice negotiations **W28**
armistice offer **W25**
armistice treaty **W29**
armistice, violation of terms of W23
arms **R650, W1**
arms, before an appeal to W12
arms, carry openly (to) W9, W14
arms embargo E217
arms, lay down (to) W13
arms limitation **R654, R655**
arms race **R660, W135**
arms, take up (to) W10
arms, take up spontaneously (to) W11
arms, trade in **W19**; W20
arms traffic **W19**
arms, use of **W17**
army **H147**
army followers **H149, W97**
army number **M83**
arrange (to) **V51**
arranged by treaty V470

arrangement **A75, M352, V60, V157, V903; AN1**
arrangement, bilateral V69
arrangement, budgetary **B668**
arrangement, consultative **K246**
arrangement, extension of A697
arrangement, proceedings leading to **V162**
arrangement, special **S431, S433**
arrangements, voisinage **N4, V66**
arrangements made by the General Assembly **A76**
arrest **F85**
arrest, lawful F86
arrest, provisional **A791**
arrest (to) **A412**
arrival **E112**
arrive (to) **E114**
article **A573, G106**
article, additional **Z180**
article, final **S203**
article, supplementary **Z180**
articles for use of the mission G107
articles imported free of duty G108
assemble (to) **V315, Z169**
assembly **V316**
assembly, annual **J12**
assembly, consultative V319
assembly, freedom of **V320**
assembly, freedom of peaceful V321
assembly, general **G200, H129**
assembly, main **H129**
assent **E191, Z214**
assert (to) G144
asserting **G146**
assertion **G146**
assessor **B206**; B207
asset **V265**; V267
assets of the fund V266
assign to (to) **Z221**
assistance **B186, B208**
assistance, legal **R336**; R337
assistance, mutual B209
assistance, mutual administrative **V601**
assistance to vessels in distress **H184**
assistance, treaty of **B212**
associate (to) **A579**
association **A574, A580, G322, V12, V75**
association agreement **A576**
association, council of **A577**
association, freedom of **V76**
association, multilateral A575
Association, Regional **R509**
association, right of **V77**
association treaty **A578**
associations, guaranteeing H20
assume (to) **A518, F90**
assumption **A519**
asylum **A582, Z133**

asylum, afford (to)   A584
asylum, apply for (to)   A583
asylum, country granting   **Z135**
asylum, country of   **Z135**
asylum, diplomatic   D122
asylum, grant (to)   A584
asylum, request (to)   A583
asylum, right of   **A585**
asylum, state granting   **Z136**
asylum, state of   **Z136**
atomic arms race   **A594**
atomic energy   **A586**
atomic energy, peaceful use of   A587
atomic energy, practical application of   A588
atomic information   **A590**
atomic information, dissemination of   A591
atomic information, safeguarding of   A591
atomic war   **A592**
atomic warfare   **A493**
attach (to)   **P95**
attaché, commercial   **H37**
attaché, cultural   **K464**
attaché, economic   **W216**
attaché, military   **M197**
attaché, naval   **M27**
attaché, scientific   **W228**
attachment   P96
attack   A398
attack, armed   A402, A403, G400, M210
attack, imminent threat of   A399
attack, in the event of   A399
attack, military   M210
attack on the person   A400
attack, unprovoked   A404
attack (to)   **A388**
attain, failure to   **N144**
attend (to)   **B243**
attest (to)   **B136**
attestation   B144
attested   B138
attribute (to)   **Z154; Z155**
attrition, war of   **Z26**
audience   A595
audience, farewell   **A91**
audience, grant (to)   A598
audience, private   A596
audience, public   A596
audience, request (to)   A597, A599
auditing   R109
auditing committee   **R108**
auditor   R107
auditors, committee of   **R108**
authentic   A896, M44
authentic, equally   A897, V16; AN5
authenticate (to)   **B136;** A900
authenticated   B138
authenticated, hereby   B137
authentication   B144

authoritative   M44
authority   A258, B98, B175, B554, D88, E394, E419, G371, H229, K156, M10, R494, S641, V806
authority, administering   **V603;** V587, V604
authority, administrative   **V603, V610**
authority, central administrative   V612
authority, competent   B179, D91, S650, S651; AN14
authority derives from B101
authority, executive   **V846;** G382, V842
authority, exercise (to)   G383
authority, full   M11
authority, issuing   B177
authority, judicial   **G256;** G379
authority, law-making   **R298**
authority, legislative   **G345, G346;** G374
authority, military   **M199**
authority, occupational   **B344**
authority of supervision   **K273**
authority, official   B176
authority, power to delegate   **K159**
authority, public   B178
authority, responsible   B179
authority, supervisory   **K273**
authority, supreme   G375, G378, R495
authority to conclude   **A97**
authority to legislate   **G345, G346**
authority under the present charter   B99
authorities, judicial   **J17;** G231
authorities, judicial and administrative   G257
authorities, occupation   B342
authorities, occupying   B342
authorization   B294, B511, B554, E394, E419, G183, L71, L74
authorization, prior or subsequent   G184
authorization, special   **S421**
authorization to conclude   **A97**
authorize (to)   **B97, B289, B553, E415, G182, L73**
authorized   B120, B290, B504, E416, K155, Z185
authorized, duly   B122, B505
authorized thereto   B123
authorized to conclude a treaty   B292, E418
authorized to negotiate a treaty   B293
authorized to represent   E417
authorized to that effect   B123
auto-limitation   S312
auto-limitation, doctrine of   **S313**
autonomous   A901, S309, S326
autonomy   A902, S311, S319, S327
auxiliaries, naval   **K448**
aviation, civilian   **Z63**
award   R404, S470, U325, U360
award, annul (to)   S147
award, arbitral   **S131; S132**
award, assert (to)   S150

blockade, raise (to)   B630
blockade, right of   **B638**
blockade, rule of effectiveness of a   B629
blockade, run a (to)   B632
blockade runner   **B636**
blockade, state of   **B641**
blockade, violate a (to)   B632
blockades, law governing   **B639**
blockade (to)   B635
board   **A237, R56, S641, V955**
board, advisory   **B280**
board, disciplinary   **D180**
board, executive   **E497, E501**
Board, Managing   **D162**
board of control   **K271, K283**
board of directors   **V955**
Board of Governors   **G468**
Board of Governors, outgoing   A145
Board of Management   **D162**
board, supervisory   **K271, K283**
body   **K297, O83, S641**
body, ad hoc   O85
body, administrative   **V606, V610**
body, advisory   **K247;** K298, O86
body, arbitral   AN17
body, auxiliary   **H195**
body, central administrative   V612
body, consultative   **K247**
body, corporate   **K297**
body corporate   K302
body, deliberative   K298
body, executing   E498
body, executive   **E500, V839, V849**
body, governing   O87
body, impartial   S648
body, legislative   K299
body, national   K301
body, permanent   O89
body, public   K302
body, subordinate   O88
body, subsidiary   **H195;** H196, H197, S644
body, supervisory   U55
bombardment, naval   S292
bona fide   **G584;** G432, G433
bond   **B617, B687**
booty   **B497, K394**
border   **G475**
border, adjustment of   **G474, G491**
border, administrative   **V600**
border dispute   **G493**
border, drawing of   **G485, G500**
border, national   **L20**
border, natural and artificial   N78
border, rectification of   **G474**
border, regulation of   **G491**
border treaty   **G499**
border (to)   **G484**
bound   **A424, G53, G117, V289;** G54

bound by a treaty   AN14
boundary   **G475**
boundary, administrative   **V600**
boundary line   **G489**
boundary river   **G486**
boundary, territorial   **H253**
boundaries, delimit (to)   **A51**
boundaries, draw up (to)   **A51**
boycott, by   W85
breach   **B654, V228**
break off (to)   **A11, U158**
breaking off   **A12, U159**
bring before (to)   **B60;** B62
budget   **B666, H139**
budget, administrative   B667
budget, annual   **J8, J9**
budget, draft   **H143, H145**
budget estimate   **H145**
budget, extraordinary   H140
budget, ordinary   H141
budget, proposed   **H143, H146**
budget, supplementary   **N53**
budgetary   **B668**
buffer state   **P202**
burden   **L41**
bureau   **A237, B682, B689, P127**
business   **G286**
business, despatch of   **G289**
business, official   **A256;** A257

cabotage   **K1, K530**
cabotage privileges   **K2**
call (to)   **A270, E25**
call upon (to)   **B60;** B61, V908
called   **A271**
camera, in   O47
camera, session in   **G127**
cancel (to)   N153, R631
cancellation   **R632**
candidacy, condition of   **A664**
candidate   **B242, K14**
candidate, stand as (to)   **K15**
capability to appear as party   **P18**
capable, legally   **G290, G293**
capable of action   **H100**
capable of only limited action   H102
capacity   **E5, T35**
capacity, act in this (to)   T33
capacity, acting in a sovereign   H236
capacity, acts in a private   I45
capacity, advisory   **E10, T46**
capacity as an expert   **E8, E11**
capacity, civil   R305
capacity, consultative   **E12**
capacity, deprivation of   **E259**
capacity, deprive of (to)   **E257**
capacity, enjoying   **H100**

capacity, full **G294**
capacity, full civil   R306, R383
capacity, in an advisory   A621
capacity, in an official   **A238**
capacity, lacking   **H108**
capacity, lacking full   **G314; G291**
capacity, legal   **G294, R300;** R301, R302,
R303, R382, R408, R411
capacity, limitation of   G295
capacity, limitation on   H107
capacity, limited   H106
capacity, mediatory   T51
capacity of a legal person   R304
capacity, of limited   H102
capacity, official   E9
capacity, party lacking   **H109**
capacity, party possessing   **H103**
capacity, person enjoying   **H103**
capacity, person lacking   **E258, H109**
capacity, person possessing   **H103**
capacity, personal   E13
capacity, possessing full   **G290**
capacity, possessing legal   **R299**
capacity, possessing limited   G292
capacity to act   H101, R301
capacity to act, lacking   **H108**
capacity to act, party lacking   **H109**
capacity to act, party possessing   **H103**
capacity to act, person lacking   **H109**
capacity to conclude a treaty   V490
capacity to contract   R381
capacity to resort to arbitration   **S91**
capitulate (to)   **K35**
capitulation   **K32**
capitulation, treaty of   **K34**
capitulation, unconditional   B40, K33
captivity   **G76**
captivity, conditions of   **G77**
captor   **K23**
captor state   **N89**
capture   **G73, W92**
capture card   **G78**
capture (to)   **G74**
careless   **F18**
carelessness, recurrent   F20
cargo   **F176, L7**
cargo, dangerous   L10
cargo declaration   **F177**
cargo, prohibited   L10
cargo, put down (to)   L8
cargo, warehousing of   L9
cargo ship   **F178**
cargo, take on (to)   L8
cargo, warehousing of   L9
carnet de passage en douane   **G490**
carry (to)   **B369**
carry out (to)   **A712**
cartel, international   I148

case   **A379, F24, R399, S12**
case, adjudication of   A382
case before the court   A421
case, bring before the court (to)   A422
case, conduct of   L95, V86
case, criminal   **S718**
case, deal with (to)   B63
case, judges appointed for specific   S14
case law   **F28**
case of doubt   **Z261**
case, pending   A420
case, primary   **H123**
case, primary matter of   **H123**
case, refer to another court (to)   V621
case, remit to another court (to)   V621
case, settle (to)   S15
case, submission of   **K79**
cases and counter-cases   S225
cases, categories of   A381
cases, decided   **R388**
cases, leading   L93
cases referred to the court   A380
case-book   **F29**
casus belli   **K402**
casus foederis   **B679**
catch   **F35**
category   **G552, K36**
category and class   K95
cease (to)   **A111, E153**
cease-fire   **W22**
cedant (*adj.*)   **A142**
cedant (*noun*)   **Z11**
cede (to)   **A139**
ceding   **A142**
cemetery, military   **M202**
censorship   **Z16**
censorship, apply (to)   N44
censorship, subject to   Z17
censure, adopt a motion of (to)   M295
censure, introduce a motion of (to)   M296
censure, motion of   **M294, T1**
censure, table a motion of (to)   M296
centre   **Z22**
centre, administrative   V612
ceremonial   **P185**
ceremony   **P182**
certification   **B144**
certified   **B138**
certified, duly   A244, B139
certified, officially   A244
certify (to)   **B136**
cessation   **A112, E155, E411**
cession   **A146, Z29**
cession, treaty of   **A147, Z31**
cessionary   **Z30**
chairman   **O31, V953; O32**
chairman, elect (to)   M299
challenge (to)   **A357**

chamber **K3**
chamber, decision of K5
chamber, form (to) **K6**
chamber, judgment given by K4
Chancellor K18
chapel, right of **K20**
chaplain **F80, S274;** S275
chaplains attached to armed forces F81
chaplains of the armed forces **S275**
chapter **K29;** K31; AN3
chapters, set out in (to) K30
character **C1**
character, coercive C5
character, cultural C7
character, general C2
character, hostile F55
character, non-binding **U256**
character, non-compulsory **U256**
character, non-obligatory **U256**
character, non-war C8
character, recommendatory **E228;** C3
character, technical C7
character, universal C4
characteristic **M191**
charge **A24, B398, L41, O9**
charge against, bring (to) **V210**
charge, countervailing **A728**
charge, criminal B399
charge, file (to) B399
charge, official **A254**
charges, fiscal F125
charges, internal A31
charges, levy (to) A39
charges, national A34
charges of equivalent effect A25
charges, reimburse (to) A41
charges, related A30
charges, remit (to) A40
charge (to) **B20, B60, B493**
charge with (to) **B396**
chargé d'affaires **G309;** M290
chargé d'affaires *ad interim* G310, G311, G313
chargé d'affaires *en pied* G312
chargé d'affaires *en titre* G312
charged **B21;** B22
charged with a penal offence B397
charged with execution of duties B494
chart, maritime **S269**
charts, officially recognized S270
charter **C9, S61**
charter, amendment of **S63**
charter, in accordance with **S64;** G165
charter, review of R577
check **N32**
check (to) **N31**
Chief Judge, pertaining to **H122**
cipher **C16**
cipher, messages in V331

ciphering section **C15**
ciphering service **C15**
citizen **A367, S540, S588**
citizenship **S591;** S592
citizenship, deprivation of **A693**
citizenship, deprive of (to) **A692**
citizenship papers **E35, N74**
civic **S589**
civil **S589, Z53**
civil law **Z69**
civil procedure, law governing **Z68**
civilian (*adj.*) **Z53**
civilian (*noun*) **Z66**
civilian, interned **Z60**
civilians **Z56**
civilization **K461**
civilization common to all K462
claim **A491, A508, I68**
claim, bring (to) **K81**
claim, commencement of **K79**
claim, extinction of A495
claim, governmental **R492**
claim, grounds for **K80**
claim, initiation of **K79**
claim, lapse of A495
claim, lapsed V194
claim, legal **R277**
claim, principal **H118;** W139
claim, statement of **K61, K78, K87**
claim, submitting the **A515**
claim, territorial **G33;** T99
claim, withdrawal of **K86**
claims against A493
claims arising out of the war A492
claims, disposal of A494
claims, lodge (to) A498, A502
claims, make (to) A498
claims, opposing A496
claims, present (to) A502
claims, reconcile opposing (to) A497
claim (to) A500, G144
claim, entitled to **A503**
claimant **A517**
claimant, state which is the A516
claiming **I68**
clarification **A645, K91**
clarify (to) **A644, K90**
class **K93, R9, R28;** K94, R10
class, distinction of **R34**
classification **K96**
classification, international K97
classification of patents, system of K99
classification, system of K98
clause **K100**
clause, arbitral **S114;** S158
clause, blocking **S467**
clause, final **S205, S209**
clause, general **G191**

clause, most-favoured-nation **M146**
clause, optional **F22**
clause, *rebus sic stantibus* K101
clause, restrictive **S467**; S468
clause, secret **G125**
clear (to) **A20**
clearance **A21**
clearance of cargo and passengers A22
clearing **A727**
clemency, act of **G466**
closed **G318**
coast **K523**; K524
coast, curvature of K526
coast, general direction of K525
coat of arms **W68**; W69
cobelligerency **K393**
cobelligerent **M328**
code **C16, S206, V332**
code clerk **C14**
code, criminal **S715**
code, messages in V331
code, penal **S715**
code, put into (to) **V330**
codes, right to use **C17**
codification **K103, K113**; V694
codification conference **K105**
codification treaty **K106**
codified **K108**; K109
codified in a treaty K111
codify (to) **K107**
coerce (to) **Z265**
coercion **Z232**
coercion, physical or moral Z233
coercive **Z245, Z266**
coexistence **K114**
coexistence, peaceful F306, K115
cogent **Z266**
cogent legal reasons Z268
coimperial **K116**
coimperial form of government K117
coimperium **K118**; K168
collect (to) **E170**
collection **E171**
collective **K119**
colonialism **K137**
colonialist **K138**
colours, national **L17, N61**
combat **K7**
combat zone **K13**
combat, hors de K8, K9
combatant **K141**
combatant, illegal K142
combatant, legal K143
comitas gentium **V683**
comity of nations **V683**
command, military M211
commerce **H28, H57**
commerce, freedom of **H42**

commerce of the world **W125**
commission **B130, B431, E434, K147**; B432, B433
commission, advisory **B285**; K148
commission, arbitral **S117**; S118
commission, central Z20
commission, consultative **B285**
commission, economic **W221**
commission, examining **P201**
commission, executive **V847**
commission, functional **F3**
commission, interim **I124**
commission, member of **K152**
commission, mixed advisory K149
Commission on Narcotic Drugs **S791**
commission, permanent K150
commission, place of **B135**
commission, preparatory K151
commission, special **S425**
commission, specialized **F3**
commission, technical **F3**
commission, time and place of B131
commissioner **K146, K152**; M298
commissioner-general **G192**
commit (to) **B124**
commit, conspiracy to B133
commit, incitement to B132
commitment **B614, V292**
commitment arising under a treaty **V538**
commitment, contractual **V538**
committee **A823, K144**
committee, ad-hoc A825
committee, administrative **V593**
committee, advisory **B281**; A826
committee, advisory and technical K145
committee, appropriate A836
committee, arbitral **S90**
committee, auxiliary **H185**
committee, budgetary **H142**
committee, central **Z18, Z19**
committee, competent A836
committee, consultative **B281**; A826
committee, coordinating **K296**
committee, directing **D159**
committee, disciplinary **D176**
committee, drafting **R455**
committee, economic **W217**
Committee, Economic and Financial W219
Committee, Economic and Social W218
committee, entitled to sit on T79
committee, executive **E497, V845, V847**; A830
committee, executive and liaison V848
committee, general **P127**
Committee, Governmental Social **R496**
committee, intergovernmental A824, A837
committee, interim **I123**
committee, intersessional A831
committee, joint A828

committee, legal affairs **R280**
committee, main **H115**
committee, management A830
committee, managing A830
committee, manpower **A566**
committee, military **M198**
committee, ministerial **M250**
committee, mixed A829
committee, monetary **W55**
committee, negotiating **V180**
committee of control **K272**
committee of four **V651**
committee of ministers **M250, M251**
committee of three **D198**
committee of ways and means H142
committee, organizing **O119**
committee, permanent A834
committee, planning **P108**
committee, preparatory **V888**
committee, procedural **V107**
committee, programme **P166**
committee, quadripartite **V651**
committee, regional **R509;** A833, R507
committee, restricted A827
committee, select A827
committee, senior **O1**
committee, special **S419**
committee, specialized **F1**
committee, standing A834
committee, steering **D159;** D160
committee, subordinate A832
committee, subsidiary **N87**
committee, supervisory **K272, U54**
committee, technical **F1;** A835
committee, three-power **D198**
committee, tripartite **D198**
committing **B130**
common **G169**
communicate (to) **M329, U25;** M331
communication **M330, U26, V198**
communication, free N41, V200
communication, freedom of **V207**
communication, means of **N36**
communication, official A242
communication, oral M368
communications **N35, N38, N40, N42**
communications ban **N37**
communications blackout **N37**
communications, official N39, N43, N44
communiqué **K153**
communiqué, joint K154
community **G171**
community, international **V763, W124**
community of all states **W124**
community of free nations G172
community of states **V763;** G173, V786
community, universal **W124**
company **G322**

compatibility with **V55**
compatible with **V50**
compelling **Z266**
compensate (to) **E265**
compensate for (to) **W176**
compensation **A727, E266, S69, S77, W177**
compensation, application for **E270**
compensation, beneficiary of **S78**
compensation, claim (to) S70
compensation, claim for **E270, S74**
compensation, claim to **E269**
compensation for occupational accidents E267
compensation for victims of persecution E268
compensation, obligation to pay **S79**
compensation, pay (to) S73
compensation, payment made as **W180**
compensation, payment made in **S77**
compensation, receive (to) S71
compensation, recover (to) S72
compensation, right of **S75**
compensation, right to **E269, S74**
compensation, rights of S76
compensation, without **E271**
competence **K156, Z192, Z206**
competence, agreements establishing the B157
competence, come under (to) Z196
competence, division of **K161;** K162
competence, domestic K158
competence, fall within (to) Z196
competence, having local Z191
competence, international K157
competence, lack of **U282**
competence, lacking **U281**
competence, legislative **G346**
competence, matters within Z197
competence, national K158
competence, not possessing **U281**
competence, power to delegate **K159**
competence, recognize (to) Z205
competence, state K158
competence, technical field of Z209
competence theory **K160**
competence to legislate **G346**
competence to make decisions **B384**
competent **K155, Z185**
competent for Z187
competent, not **U281**
competent *ratione loci* Z191
competent, regarded as Z186
competent to make decisions B379
competition **W127**
competition, condition of **W130**
competition, distorted W128
competition, fair W129, W131
competition, restrictive of W132
complainant **K84**
complainant's case, statement of V101
complaint **B400, K61**

complaint, answer to the   **K77**
complaint, bring (to)   **K81**
complaint, by means of   **K88**
complaint, directly concerned in   K64
complaint, file (to)   K72
complaint, grounds for   **K80**
complaint, individual   **I71**
complaint, meet (to)   K68, K69
complaint, party entering the   **B403**
complaint, refer (to)   K76
complaint, right to enter   B401
complaint, right to lay   B401
complaint, withdrawal of   **K86**
complaint, written   **K78, K87**
complement   **E360**
complement (to)   **E359**
complementary   **E361**
compliance with   **E74**
comply with (to)   **E72, E353, N27**
comply with, failure to   **N130, N134; N135**
comply with, promise to   **E75**
composed of (to be)   **Z175**
composition   **V157, Z176**
composition proceedings   **V162**
compromis   **K163, S165**
compromise   **K163, S120, S164**
compromise, arbitral   **S164**
compromise peace   **K165**
compromise, readiness to reach   **K164**
compromise solution   **K166**
compulsion   **Z232**
compulsory   **O28, V14, Z266**
concern (to)   **B333**
concerned   **B490, B495**
concert (to)   **A114**
concession   **K289**
concession contract   **K290**
concession treaty   **K290**
conciliation   **V157, V346; S110, V164**
conciliation commission   **V160**
conciliation commission, special   V161
conciliation committee   **V159**
conciliation procedure, adopt (to)   V163
conciliation, procedure of   **V162**
conciliator, appoint (to)   B444
conciliators, list of   V247
conclude (to)   **A92, S198**
concluded   **A50, G319**
conclusion   **A94**
conclusions   **B284**
conclusive   **K190**
concordat   **K193**
condition   **A648, B33, L115**
condition of, on the   V884
condition, on the   B35
condition, subject to the   A649, B35, M42, M43
conditions, accept (to)   B37
conditions, impose (to)   B38

conditions, living   **L51**
conditions of, under   M37
conditions of employment   **B360**
conditions, under   M39
conditions, uniform   B36
conditions, upon   M40
conditions, waiver of   B34
conditions, working   **B360; B361**
conditions of life   L52
condominium   **K167; K168**
conduct   **L94, V896**
confederation   **D2, S515; S516**
confer on (to)   **U44, Z221**
conference   **K169; K170, K171**
conference, adjourn (to)   K175
conference, administrative   **V602**
conference, annual   **J10**
conference badge   **T88**
conference card   **T89**
conference, convene (to)   K174
conference, convoke (to)   K174
conference for revision   **R586**
conference, general   **G193; K173**
conference, intergovernmental   Z273
conference, joint   **V251**
conference, maritime   **S290**
conference members   **K177**
conference, monetary   **W59**
conference on K172
conference on maritime shipping   **S290**
conference, participants at   **K177**
conference, postpone (to)   K175
conferred   **U46**
conferred by treaty   V469
confirm (to)   **B437**
confirmation   **B438**
confirming their intentions   B439
confiscate (to)   **E235, K178**
confiscating   E236
confiscation   **E211, E237, K179**
conflict   **A701, K132, K180**
conflict, armed   A702, A703, K184, N104
conflict, belligerent   A703
conflict, military   A704, K184
conflict, non-belligerent   A705
conflict, non-war   A705, K182, N168
conflict not of international character   K181
conflict of laws, rules governing   **K135**
conflict of non-war character   K182
conflict, party to   **K189; K183, M13**
conflict, powers in   K183
conflict, rule of   **K133; K134**
conformity with, in   U12, U13
congress badge   **T88**
congress card   **L72, T89**
connection   **V25**
connection, qualifying   B618
conscience, public   O39

contingent **K264**
contingents, national air-force K265
continuity **K266**
contraband **B2, K254, S213**
contraband, absolute B4, K255, K257
contraband cargo **B6**
contraband, conditional K256
contraband, destination of B3
contraband goods **B2, S213**
contraband, law of **B7**
contraband, relative B5
contract debt **V520**
contract debts, recovery of V522
contract debts claimed V521
contract law **V503**
contracting **V512**
contractual **V465**
contradiction **E108, W146**
contradiction to agreements, in W147
contrary, to the **A281, A298, G109;** B462,
  B463
contrary A281, A298, **G109;** B468, B471
contrary to (be) **Z230;** Z48
contravention **V348, W137;** Z229
contribution **B213, B220;** B214
contribution, annual **J4**
contributions, committee on **B218**
contributions due B216, B217
contributions, scale of **B219**
contributions, unpaid B216, B217
contributions, voluntary B215
control **K275**
control action **K279**
control, board of **K283**
Control Council Law **K280**
control document **K274**
control, international I151
control, measure of **K279**
control, quadripartite **V655**
control, right of **K281;** K282
control (to) **K278**
convene (to) **A270, E25**
convened **A271**
convening **E27**
convention **K284, U3; AN1** (*see also under*
  treaty)
convention, aerial navigation **L118**
convention, application of the present A535
convention, aviation **L118**
convention, bound to apply B317
convention, conclude (to) U6
convention, conclusion of **K286**
convention, consular **K232**
convention, cultural **K463**
convention, denounce (to) K491, Z162
convention, denunciation of K498
convention, draft **K287**
convention, duration of the present G159

convention, expiry of B56
convention, fishing **F116**
convention, intergovernmental **R498**
convention, invoke (to) B316
convention of inquiry **U215**
convention on K285
convention revising this convention U5
convention, scope of G156
convention, territorial extension of G155
convention, text of **K288**
convention, universal **W116**
convention, world-wide **W116**
conviction **U58**
conviction, in the U59
convinced U59
convocation **E27**
convocation, letter of **E28**
convoke (to) **E25**
cooperation **Z163**
cooperation, in close Z165
cooperation, international Z167, Z168
cooperation, peaceful Z166
co-opt (to) **K292**
co-option **K293**
coordinate (to) **K294**
coordination **K295**
coordination committee **K296**
copy **A14, A99, A706**
copy, certified **A15, A100, B141**
copy, duly certified A101
copy, in a single **A707, U307, U308; AN5**
copyright **U283**
copyright, acquisition of U285
copyright, enjoyment of U284
copyright proprietor U286
copyright, protection of U287
corps **K303**
corps, consular K305
corps, diplomatic K304
corps, volunteer **F237**
correct **O65, O80, O82**
correction **B312**
correction in the text B313
correspondence **B652, B653, K306, S229, S231**
correspondence, by S220
correspondence, by direct S230
correspondence, official A243, K307
correspondence, receive by courier (to) S228
correspondent S34
co-signatory **M343**
co-signatory government **M344**
co-signatory state **M345**
costs, divide (to) U69
council **R56**
council, administrative **V608**
council, advisory **B204, K248**
council, bureau of R57
council, composition of R58

council, consultative **K248**
council, economic **W224**
Council, Economic and Social W225
council, executive **E501**
council, interim **I125**
council, ministerial **M251**
council of ministers **M251, M253**
council, parliamentary R59
council, permanent R60
council, scientific advisory B205
council, standing R60
Council vote A119
counsel **B210, R290, R294;** B211, B510
counsel, assisted by R295
counsel, domestic R292
counsel, engage (to) R291
counsel, free legal R293
counsel, legal **R290**
counsellor **B648**
counter-action **W138**
counter-arguments, by means of **K268**
counter-case **G85**
counterclaim **W138;** W139
counterclaim, defendant bringing **W141**
counterclaim, defendant on **W136**
counterclaim, party bringing **W141**
counterclaim, reply to W140
counterfeiting **F30**
counterfeiting of money AN10
counter-memorial **G84**
counter-memorials **K77**
counter-reprisal **G82**
counter-reprisal, resort to (to) G83
counter-suit **W138**
country **L15**
country, home **H157, H160, H175**
country, native **H160, H164**
country, neighbouring **N1**
country, non-aligned L16
country of domicile **H160**
country of origin **H164, H175;** H165
country, own **H160;** H161
country, signatory U235
courier **K509**
courier ad hoc K512
courier, consular K511
courier, diplomatic K510
courier, receive papers by (to) K513
course, in due **F158**
court **E319, G152, I102**
court, administrative **V598**
court, before the **A419**
court, civil **Z57**
court, civilian **Z57**
court, competence of G269
court, competent G226, G227, G228
court, constitute the (to) G265
court, constitutional **V115**

court costs **G270**
court costs, bear a share of (to) G271
court, criminal **S705**
court, entitled to appear before Z143
court, expenses of **G270**
court, full T4
court, impartial G224
court, independent and impartial G225
court, international G221, V722
court, international military M206
court, law of the G227
court martial **M203, M205**
court, member of G218, G266, M300
court, military **M203, M205**
court, national G220
court of appeal **B328**
Court of International Justice, Permanent
  (PCIJ) G263
court of justice **G259**
Court of Justice, International (ICJ) G261;
  AN19
Court of Justice of the EC G260
court, official language of **G273**
court, order of the **B371**
court, penal **S705**
court, permanent G223
court, power of B100
court, premises of G219
court, regularly constituted G222, V573
court, rules of G304
court, under control of L96
covenant **K284, S61;** AN1
credentials **B145, V806, V822;** AN2
credentials, alterations in B146
credentials committee **V821**
credentials, deliver (to) B149
credentials, hand over (to) B149
credentials, order of presentation of B148
credentials, present (to) B149
credentials, presentation of B147
credentials, subject to scrutiny (to be) V808
credentials, true copy of B150
creditor **G435**
creditor state **G436**
crew **B339, S187**
crew, civil members of B349
crew document **B343**
crew list **B346**
crew, member of **B348**
Crew's Effects Declaration E383
crime **V41**
crime against humanity V43
crime against peace V42
crime, country in which committed B134
crime, international V750
criminal **S717**
criminal law **S715**
cripple **B358;** B359

criteria established by the council   M192
criteria, fundamental technical   M193
criterion   M191
cross (to)   U37
cross-action   W138
crossing, illegal   U38
cruelty, acts of   G470
culpable   S232
cultural   K466
cultural activities   K468
cultural agreement   K463
cultural attaché   K464
cultural expert   K485
cultural experts, committee of   K486
cultural heritage   K467
cultural property   K469; K470
Cultural Property, Commissioner-General
   for   K480
cultural property, depositary of   K484
cultural property, immovable   K478
cultural property, immunity of   K483
Cultural Property, International Register
   for   K472
cultural property, movable   K473, K474
cultural property, national   K476
cultural property, refuge for   B299
cultural property, registration of   K479
cultural property, repatriation of   K482
cultural property, restoration of   K481
cultural property under special
   protection   K471
cultural value, object of   K469
cultural value, objects of European   K475
culture   K461
curiosity, public   N94
currency   W52
currency, local   L23; W53
currency, national   L23; W53
custody   G366, O9; O10
custody, entrust to third state (to)   M280
custody, keep (to)   V577; AN15
custody of original text   AN15
custody, take into (to)   G367
custom   G49, G415, G418, S370
custom, by   G416
custom, codified international   K112
custom, international   V674, V783, V793;
   G422, G423, G427, I143, V724
customary   G416, G428
customary international law   G422, G427
customary law   G418
customary law, of   G428
customary law, rules of   G429
customs   Z72
customs administration   Z111
customs agreement   Z78, Z108
customs airport   Z86
customs area   Z82

customs charge   Z77
customs clearance   Z76
customs, constitutional   V128
customs control   Z96
customs duty   E40, Z72, Z77; E41
customs duty, rate of   Z99
cutoms duties, elimination of   Z73
customs duties, exemption from   Z79
customs duties, freedom from   Z88
customs facilities   Z84; Z85; AN7
customs law   Z90
customs, law relating to   Z112
customs laws and regulations   Z95
customs matters, technical   Z105
customs office, inland   I91
customs office en route   D246
customs office of departure   A724
customs penalty   Z83
customs procedure   Z109
customs procedures   Z105
customs purposes, valuation for   Z115
customs purposes, value for   Z113
customs regulation   Z112
customs, relating to   Z94
customs seal   Z110
customs sovereignty   Z91
customs supervision   Z106; Z96
customs tariff   Z101
customs tariff, common   Z102
customs tariff, establishment of   E56
customs tariff negotiation   Z104
customs technique   Z105
customs territory   Z89
customs union   Z107
customs valuation committee   Z114
customs value   Z113
customs-free airport   Z87

damage   S68, S80
damage, nuclear   N287
damage suffered   G206
damage (to)   S67
Danube Commission   D188
date   Z12
date, effective   I89
dates fixed   A273
dates prescribed   A273
dead   G66
dead, collect the (to)   G69
dead, despoil the (to)   G68
dead, find the (to)   G69
dead, found   G67
dead, list of the   G65
deal with (to)   B63, B64
dean   D11, D193
dean, duties of   D194
debate   A849

debate in plenary session **P111**
debellatio **D7**
debt, contractual **V520**
debtor state **S238**
decartellization **D12**
deceit **T67**
deception **T67**
decide (to) **A815, B369, E272, E321**
decide by unanimous vote (to) **B370**
decide *ex aequo et bono* (to) E274; AN20
decided **E324**
decided by a majority of members E284
decided, finally E289
decided, unless otherwise E276
decipher (to) **D8, E326**
deciphering **D9, E327**
decision **A854, B371, B388, E277; B389**
decision, abide by (to) E309, E310, E311
decision at first instance E292
decision, binding E302
decision binding on all member states E303
decision by competent judicial authority E283
decision, carry out (to) B376
decision, comply with (to) E309, E310
decision, consider (to) B275
decision, contrary E275
decision creating legal precedent **G542**
decision, deliver (to) E312
decision establishing a principle of law **G542**
decision *ex aequo et bono* **B599**
decision, execute (to) B376
decision, final **E229;** E288, E297, E299
decision, final judicial E301
decision, free E293
decision, give (to) E305
decision, give effect to (to) B378
decision, grounds of **E317**
decision, grounds on which based **E317**
decision, hand down (to) E308
decision, implementation of D229
decision in effect E299
decision in force E299
decision, in the annex to B372
decision, judicial **B371;** E295, E300
decision, make (to) B377
decision making **B388**
decision of the last instance E298
decision, power of **E316, E318**
decision, preliminary **V850;** V851
decision, pronounce (to) E305, E308, E312
decision, pronouncement of E286
decision, provisional E304
decision, pursuant to E283
decision, reach (to) **E272;** E308
decision, refer for (to) E315
decision, render (to) E305, E306
decision, reserve (to) E313
decision, submit for (to) E315

decision, take (to) B377
decision, unanimous B373, E287
decision with final effect E288, E296, E299
decisions **B388, R388**
decisions, arbitral R391
decisions by international courts E278
decisions by organs of organizations E279
decisions delivered by the ICJ R392
decisions, in reaching its E281
decisions in the form of directives E280
decisions in the form of judgments E280
decisions of international courts E278
decisions of the General Assembly B375
decisive **M44**
declaration **D13, E380**
declaration, agreed E391
declaration, conflicting E385
declaration, contrary G110
declaration, deposit (to) E393
declaration, general E384
declaration, joint E387, E391
declaration, make (to) E392
declaration of death **T130;** T131
Declaration of Health, Maritime **S267**
declaration, original E390
declaration, quadripartite **V653**
declaration, subsequent E388, E389
declaration, three-power **D199**
declaration to the contrary E385, E386
declaration, tripartite **D199**
declaration, universal E384
declaratory **D14**
declare (to) **E378**
declare solemnly (to) E379
decode (to) **D8, E326**
decoding **D9, E327**
decolonization **E247**
decolonize (to) **E246**
decretion **A102**
deduce (to) **A71**
deed **T23**
deed, criminal **S719**
deed, penal **S719**
deem (to) **F90**
deemed (to be) **G135**
defaulting **S65;** S66, S236
defence **V356**
defence committee **V358**
Defence Contribution, German **V359**
defence forces, inland V357
defence, inland B644
defence, internal B644
defence, national **L22**
defence pact **V361**
defence treaty **V361**
defence treaty, bilateral V362
defend (to) **V355**
defendant **A371, B244**

defendant's answer **K77; V101**
defendant's rejoinder **D210**
deferred **N50**
deficit, accounting **R99**
deficit, cumulative accounting R100
definition **B153**
definitions and general provisions B154
definitive **E230**
delegate **B23, D16, D24, T87, U178**
delegate, alternate D28
delegate, apostolic D17
delegate, designate as (to) **B453**
delegate, permanent D27
delegate, principal **H117**
delegate, send as (to) **A78**
delegate, substitute D28
delegate's card **T89**
delegates, represented by D25, D26
delegates, voting S686
delegate (to) **A78, B20, D23, U44**
delegated **B21, U46**
delegation **A79, D18, D29, U49**
delegation, act of **D29**
delegation, commercial **H40**
delegation, head of **C13, D20, D21; C11, D19**
delegation theory **D22**
deleted **G353**
deliberate (to) **B265**
deliberate (*adj.*) **V936**
deliberately V934
deliberation **B273**
deliberation, power of **B282**
deliberations, participate in (to) B279
deliberations, present at (to be) B278
deliberations, secret B276, B277, G121
deliberative **B268**
delict **D31**
delict, international V719
delicto, in flagrante T24
delimit (to) **A51**
delimitation **G485, G500**
delimitation, line of **G489**
delimitation, territorial T98
delimiting **A52**
delinquency **U143**
delinquency, international V719, V747
delinquent **S234**
deliver (to) **A853, V211, V224**
delivery **U17**
demand (to) **E170**
demarcation **A52, D33**
demarcation line **D34**
demarcation, principles of geographic A54
demilitarization **E254**
demilitarize (to) **E253**
demobilization **D36, E256**
demobilize (to) **D35, E255**
denaturalized **A725**

deneutralization **E261**
deneutralize (to) **E260**
denial **V617**
denial of justice V619
denounce (to) **K488; K489, N153, Z162**
denouncing K490
denunciation **K492; G163, K493, K494, K495, K498; AN2**
denunciation clause **K505**
denunciation, except in the event of K499
denunciation, instrument of **K501, K508**
denunciation, not subject to **U133; U134**
denunciation, notice of **K500, K507**
denunciation, right of **K506; R644**
denunciation, subject to **K487**
deny (to) **V616**
depart from (to) **A148**
departure **A82, A800; A160**
departure, final A83, A801
dependence **A56**
dependent **A55, N183**
deport (to) **D43, V327**
deportation **D42, V329**
deported person **V328**
deposit **D41, H216, H218, L14**
deposit, mineral **L14**
deposit of instruments H217
deposit (to) **D40, H213; H214; AN15**
depositary **D44, H220, V578, V584; D45, D46, V579; AN15**
depositary, act as (to) **V576**
depositary, duties of **D47**
depositary, functions of **D47; AN15**
depositary government **D49, V580; V581, V582**
depositary state **D50, H219, V583; M327**
depositing, act of **H218**
deposition **D41, Z42**
depositor **H215**
deprivation of effect A842
deprive (to) **A817**
deputy **S653, S654**
deratting certificate **E262**
dereliction **D51**
derive from (to) **B332**
derogate from (to) **A148**
derogating **A153**
derogating from A149
derogation **A151, A157, D52; A159**
derogation from A150
derogation, in **A153; A155**
derogation, incompatible AN16
derogation, right of A158
desertion **F10**
designate (to) **B452**
desire, moved by **W247**
desiring **W247**
desirous of **W247**

despoil (to) **A798**
despoliation **A799**
destination **B473**
destination, customs office of **B480**
destination, hostile **F46;** F53
destination, non-quota countries of Q21
destination, port of **B479**
destination, territory of **B476**
destination, territory of final B477
destination, territory of intended B478
destructive **A137**
details, giving **A359**
details, together with **A359**
detain (to) **G70**
detaining **G368**
détente **E331**
detention **G71, G73, G76, G366**
detention, place of **G72, G369**
determination **B474, E322**
determined **E324, G413, W200;** W201
determining **M44**
detrimental to (to be) **G59**
deviance **A157**
deviate from (to) **A148**
deviating **A153**
deviation **A151;** A159
deviation from A152
devoid of content **H209**
devolve on (to) **O17;** O19
differ from (to) **A148**
differences, regardless of U200
dignitary **W251**
dignity **W248**
dignity, personal W250
diplomacy **D115**
diplomacy, ad-hoc D116
diplomacy, by D158
diplomacy by conference K176
diplomacy, direct D117
diplomacy, permanent D119
diplomacy, secret **G124;** D118
diplomat **D97**
diplomatic **D120**
diplomatic agent **A745, D97;** D121; AN7, AN8
diplomatic agent, appointment of D104
diplomatic agent, arrival of D103
diplomatic agent, departure of D99
diplomatic agent, dismissal of E251
diplomatic agent, final departure of D100
diplomatic agent, household of D105, D106
diplomatic agent, immunities of D101, D107; AN7
diplomatic agent, official residence of D102
diplomatic agent, person of D108, D109
diplomatic agent, privileges of D110
diplomatic agents, convention on **D113**
diplomatic agents, law relating to **D112**
diplomatic asylum D122

diplomatic bag, D124, D144
diplomatic bag, deliver (to) K515
diplomatic bag, detain (to) K516
diplomatic bag, take possession of (to) K517
diplomatic channel D157
diplomatic channels, through the D158
diplomatic corps D143
diplomatic custom D139
diplomatic documents D151
diplomatic envoy **A745;** D153
diplomatic immunities D142
diplomatic intercourse D152
diplomatic list D145
diplomatic mission D155
diplomatic note D146
diplomatic passport **D111**
diplomatic post D155
diplomatic privileges D149, D156
diplomatic privileges, law governing **D112**
diplomatic rank D150
diplomatic relations D125
diplomatic relations, break off (to) D134, G284
diplomatic relations, breaking off of D126
diplomatic relations, convention on **D113**
diplomatic relations, desire to establish D129
diplomatic relations, establish (to) D135
diplomatic relations, establishment of D127
diplomatic relations, initiate (to) D135
diplomatic relations, maintenance of D128
diplomatic relations, re-establish (to) D138
diplomatic relations, re-establishment of D132
diplomatic relations, resume (to) D138
diplomatic relations, resumption of D132
diplomatic relations, sever (to) D134
diplomatic relations, severance of A13, D126
diplomatic relations, suspend (to) D137
diplomatic relations, suspension of D131
diplomatic relations, willingness to establish D129
diplomatic representation D155
diplomatic representative **A745;** D153
diplomatic rights, law governing **D112**
diplomatic service D141
diplomatic staff D147
diplomatic staff, member of D148; AN8
diplomatic visa **D114**
direct **U136**
direction **V145**
directive **R603, V145, W103**
directives, authority to give **W105**
directives of the General Assembly R604
Director, Regional **R510**
Directors, Conference of **D161**
director-general **G190**
disadvantage, of **N48**
disagreement, resolve (to) AN17
disappear (to) **U173**

disappearance U169
disarm (to) A84, E335
disarmament A85, E336
disarmament agreement A87
disarmament conference A88
disarmament control A89
disarmament convention A87
disarmament, general and complete A86
disarmament negotiations A90
disarmament, partial T75
discharge D228, E250, E356, W44
discharge (to) D227, E249, E353, N27, W39
disciplinary D178
disclose (to) V279
disclose, duty to V281
disclosure V280
discriminate (to) D163
discrimination D168; D165
discrimination, act of D167, H71
discrimination, act of racial H72
discrimination, eliminate racial (to) R41
discrimination, incite racial (to) R42
discrimination, incitement to racial R40
discrimination, justify racial (to) R43
discrimination on grounds of D170
discrimination on grounds of nationality S548
discrimination, prohibit racial (to) R44
discrimination, racial R39; AN4, AN9,
  AN12
discriminatory D164
discriminatory treatment D171
discuss (to) B265
discussion A849, B273
discussion, adjournment of A851
discussion among governments A852
discussion, basis of D174; D175
discussion, question under A850
disembarkation A812
disembarkation card A814
disembarkation, port of A813
dismember (to) Z27
dismemberment Z28
dismiss (to) E249
dismissal E250
dismissal, not subject to U85
dismissal, powers of E252
disposal V148
disposal, final V149
disposition V148
disposition, testamentary V150
disputant S781
dispute A701, M141, S731, S744, S750, S761;
  M144
dispute, amicable settlement of E398
dispute, arbitral settlement of S741
dispute, at S759, S784
dispute between states S529; S747, S749
dispute, engaged in (to be) S742

dispute, in S759, S784
dispute, in the event of M142
dispute, international S747, S749, V745
dispute, involved in S732
dispute, judicial settlement of S740
dispute, legal R414
dispute, legitimate interest in S765
dispute, local S748
dispute, pacific settlement of E399
dispute, party to S755, S780
dispute, peaceful settlement of E399
dispute, powers strangers to S733
dispute, regulate (to) S736, S738
dispute, resolve (to) S737
dispute, resolve by peaceful means (to) S751
dispute, settle (to) S736, S738
dispute, settlement by arbitration S741
dispute, settlement of S739, S743
dispute, subject matter of S735
dispute, subject of S752; G103, S166
dispute, submit to arbitration (to) S763
dispute, submit to ICJ (to) S762
dispute, summary account of S753
dispute, territorial T107
dispute, under S759, S784
disputes arising out of contracts P163
dispute (to) A357, S742
disputed S759, S784
dissenting A153
dissenting opinions A154
dissolution A655
dissolve (to) A654
distinction U195, U198
distinction, without U196, U197, U199
distinguish (to) U194
district, consular A250
disturb (to) B335
disturbance, civil L19
divergence W242
diversion, unauthorized V624
division, racial R52
doctrine L80, L83
doctrine, current L82
doctrine, eclectic E213
doctrine, legal R355
doctrine, ruling L81
document D183, S221, S226, U290
document, constituent G549
document of identity I4
document of identity, official I5
document, produce (to) V908
document, validity of A883
documents, administrative U293
documents, authoritative U297
documents, basic U298
documents constituting a treaty U291
documents, diplomatic D151
documents, exchange of A860

entitle (to) **B289**
entitled **B290**
entitled (to be) R152
entitled to, legally R278
entitled to (to be) A480
entitlement **B294**
entitlement, create (to) B159
entitlement, lapsed V194
entitlement to, claim (to) A500
entity, non-state N187
entity, state-like S514
entrance point O54
entrusted to U45
entry **E112**
entry, measures restricting AN7
entry, regulations on **E116**
enumerate (to) **A613**
enumerated **A633**
environment, contamination of R5
envoy **G278, V551;** G279, M290
envoy, ad-hoc **S420, S422;** V553
envoy, diplomatic D153, V555
Envoy Extraordinary G280
envoy, highest ranking V556
envoy, permanent V557
envoy, senior V556
envoy, special **S420, S422**
equal **G456**
equal force, having G457
equal rights **G441**
equal rights and duties G450
equal rights and self-determination G442
equal rights, enjoying **G440**
equal rights of men and women G443
equal rights, on the basis of **G440**
equal value, of **G456**
equality **G441, G445, G454, G458**
equality before the law G446
equality, in full G444
equality of states G447, G455
equality, principle of **G452**
equality, sovereign G448, G449, G450, G451
equality, vote resulting in S679
equally authentic **G456**
equally authentic character **G458**
equipment, military **K423**
equitable **B592;** B596
equitably **B594**
equitably, decide (to) B597
equity **B595, B602**
equity, concept of **B600**
equity, principles of **B602**
equivalent **G456**
establish (to) **A665, B536, E46, E117, E438;**
  B530
establishment **A656, E55, E119, E439, N206**
establishment, articles intended for E120, U42
establishment, articles of **U41**

establishment, freedom of **N207**
establishment, goods of **U41**
establishment, right of **N208**
establishment, treaty of **N209**
estate **E343, N29**
estate duty **E344;** AN7
etatism **E490**
ethnic **E491;** AN12
ethnical **E491;** AN11
etiquette **E493, P182**
evacuate (to) **R82, V322;** V323
evacuation **R90, V324;** V325, V326
evidence **A804, B523, B545, B546, Z42**
evidence, admissibility of B526
evidence, admissible B528
evidence, admit (to) B531
evidence, closing of B535
evidence, conclusive B527
evidence, consideration of **B552**
evidence, furnish (to) B529
evidence, furnishing of **B539**
evidence, give (to) **A805**
evidence, give as a witness (to) A806
evidence, give as an expert (to) A806
evidence, giving of **B539**
evidence, having the force of **B541**
evidence, hear (to) **V275**
evidence, hearing of **B533, B538**
evidence, obligation to give **Z44**
evidence, oral B548
evidence, presentation of **B532, B537, B539**
evidence, presumptive B524
evidence, procure on the spot (to) B534
evidence, proofs and Z43
evidence, provide (to) B529
evidence, relevance of B525
evidence, relevancy of B525
evidence, rule of **B551**
evidence, state (to) B549
evidence, submit (to) B550
evidence, taking of **B533, B538**
evidence, tender (to) B550
evidence, written B548
ex aequo et bono **B597**
ex officio A236, K309
exact (to) **E170**
exacting **E171**
examination **P198, U211, V277**
examine (to) **K278, P194, U210, V275**
exceed (to) **U37**
except that M42
excessive G52
exchange **A859**
exchange, free A861
exchange (to) **A862;** A863
exclave **E512**
exclude (to) **A817**
exclusion **A818**

execute (to) A712, D227, D263, V829, V841
executing A715
execution D228, D264, E494, V831, V843, V844, Z252
execution, capable of D261
execution, coercive Z252
execution, effective AN16
execution, impossibility of U107, U277
execution, incapable of U276
execution, levy (to) V837
execution measure E496
execution, measure of E496
execution, measures ensuring S350
execution, not capable of D262
execution, stay of V833
executive (adj.) A715, G296
executive (noun) E499, V834, V846; V842
exempt (to) B68
exempt from (to) I25
exemption B70, S250; AN7
exemption, accord (to) B92
exemption from B75
exemption from aliens' registration B78
exemption from arrest and prosecution S252
exemption from customs duties and inspection B89
exemption from detention and prosecution B86
exemption from dues and taxes B76
exemption from immigration restrictions B80
exemption from judicial process B82, B83
exemption from legal process B83, B84, B85
exemption from personal arrest or detention B81
exemption from personal services and contributions B87
exemption from prosecution B82
exemption from residence permit B77
exemption from social security B88
exemption from taxation B79
exemption, grant (to) B92
exemption in respect of B74
exemption, waive (to) B90, B93
exequatur E503
exequatur, grant (to) E506
exequatur, granted (to be) E505
exequatur, issue (to) E506
exequatur, pending delivery of E470
exequatur, receive (to) E505
exequatur, refuse to grant (to) E507
exequatur, withdraw (to) E509
exercise A878, G146, W44
exercise, effective A881
exercise, impartial A221
exercise, incompatible with A223
exercise, independent A221
exercise (to) A873, W39
exhaust (to) E442

exhaustion E444
exhibit (to) V913
exhibition V907, V915
exile E510
exile, government in E511
existing B440
existing or hereafter arising V23
exit A800
exit visa A802, A803
expedient Z257; Z260
expedition, punitive S704
expel (to) A817, A887; A888
expert E513, G576, S29
expert, chief O3
expert committee S23
expert opinion G572, S25, S28
expert opinion, give (to) G573
expert's report S26
experts, ad-hoc working group of S36
experts, best qualified technical S33
experts, committee of S23; S24
experts, corresponding S34
experts, group of S27
experts, highly qualified technical S33
experts, list of S37
experts of acknowledged impartiality S30
experts of high moral standing S30
experts of highest integrity S35
experts of recognized competence S35
experts on missions for the organization S31, S32
experts, panel of S37
expiration A68, E411
expiration, reasons for E414
expire (to) A70, E408
expiry A68, B55
explicit A698
exploit (to) A689
exploitation A690
exploitation of natural resources A691
exploration A677, E352
explore (to) A676, E351
explosions, nuclear test N288
export duty A718
export licence A710
export prohibition A717
export restriction A708
export restriction, quantitative A709
export, restriction on A708
export (to) A711
exportation, restriction on A708
exporting A713
exporting member state A714
express A698
express or implied A699
expropriate (to) E235
expropriation E237, W92
expulsion A818, A892

expulsion, collective   **K121**
expulsion of a member   A819
expulsion of aliens, collective   K122
expulsion order   **A894**
expulsion order, issue (to)   A895
expulsion procedure   **A893**
extant   B440
extend (to)   **A694, E474, V213**
extend tacitly (to)   V214
extend to (to)   **E447**
extension   A696, E451, E475, V215
extension, explicit   V217
extension, implied   V218
extension of extinction period   **S76**
extension, protocol of   **V219**
extension, tacit   V218
exterritorial   E514
exterritoriality   E515
extinct, become (to)   **E408;** R194
extinction   E411, U169
extinction, period of   E412
extinction, reason for   **E414**
extinguished (to be)   **U173**
extraditable   A788
extraditable offences   A790
extradite (to)   **A767, U24**
extradite, failure to   **N127**
extradite, obligation to   **A794**
extradition   A770; AN10
extradition action   **A793**
extradition agreement   **A784**
extradition, allow (to)   A781, A782
extradition, convention on   **A792**
extradition crime   A789; AN10
extradition, give reasons for (to)   A779
extradition, grant (to)   A780
extradition, make a request for (to)   A787
extradition, mutual   A774
extradition of fugitive criminals   A771
extradition of nationals   A776, A783
extradition of the person claimed   A772
extradition, offence for which requested   A786
extradition, offences for which allowed   A773
extradition, offences for which excluded   A773
extradition, purpose of   **A796;** A797
extradition, refuse (to)   A775, A776, A777
extradition, request (to) A778
extradition, request for   **A785**
extradition treaty   **A795**
extra-judicial   A838
extraordinary   A844

facilitate (to)   **E401, F167**
facilitate, in order to   E406
facilitation   E403
facilitation, measure of   **E407**

facility   E403
facilities, nuclear   N283
facilities, peaceful nuclear   N284
fact   T63; T64
fact, question of   B305, S734
fact, relevant questions of   T31
facts   S18, T29
facts, ascertaining of   **T66**
facts, brief statement of   S20
facts, clarification of   S22
facts, elicit (to)   U212
facts, elucidate (to)   T30
facts, elucidation of   S22
facts found   T65
facts of the case   **T26**
facts on which based   S19
facts, statement of   T27
facts, summary of   S21
fail (to)   **U181**
failing   E421
failing such procedure   E423
failure to act   **N149, U151, U185, U187;** U152
failure to attain   **N144**
failure to fulfil   **N140**
fair   A383, B592
fairly   B594
fairness, concept of   **B600**
faith   G430
faith, in bad   G431
faith, in good   **G584;** A759, G432, G433
faith whereof, in   **U288**
fallen   G66
family law   **F31**
family rights   **F32**
family, the human   G324
fate   L115
fault, at   **S65, S234**
Federal   B676
Federal Law Gazette   **B672**
federation   B670, D2, V12
federation, member of   **B674**
federation, national   **D2**
fee   G51
fee, official   **A254**
fiction   F88; F89
fiction, legal   **F88**
fiction, maintain (to)   **F90;** F91
field   B296, G5
final   E230
final and binding   AN17
financial year   **H144**
findings, embodying its   B305
fire, suspension of   **F87**
fiscal   F124
fish   F92
fish, stock of   **F94**
fish (to)   **F96**
fish habitually (to)   F97, F98

forcible reprisal   **Z249**
foregoing   V957
foreign   **A740**
forfeit (to)   **V238**
form   **F169**
form, in due   **G129**
form, good and due   F170
form, in due   **G129**
form, in due and proper   AN15
form, in written   **S219**
form, proper   **F171;** F170
form, written   **S217**
formal   **F171, F172**
formality   **F173**
formalities, facilitation of   E404
formally accepted   A440
formation, instrument of   **G549**
forum   **F174**
forum for discussion   F175
forum, state of the   **G274**
foundation   **G510**
founded in fact and law   B158
Four-Power Administration of Berlin   **V658**
four-power agreement   **V650, V656**
four-power committee   **V651**
four-power control   **V655**
four-power declaration   **V653**
four-power group   **V654**
four-power responsibility   **V657**
fraud   **T67;** T68; AN10
fraud, obtain by (to)   U356
free   **F181**
free and equal in rights   F183
free articles   **F197;** F193
free choice of employment   F185
free exchange of ideas   F184
free flow of ideas   F188
free goods   **F197;** F193
free movement   **F238**
free movement of workers   F186
free port   **F198**
free practice of religion   F191
free state   **F232**
free to (to be)   **F233**
free trade area   F199
freedom   **F200**
freedom, assure (to)   F228
freedom, deprive of (to)   F225
freedom, ensure (to)   F227, F228
freedom, exercise (to)   F224
freedom, foundation of   F201
freedom from arbitrary arrest   F219
freedom from slavery and servitude   F216
freedom, fundamental   AN12
freedom, grant (to)   F227
freedom, individual   F222
freedom of association   **K102;** F217
freedom of belief   **G434**

freedom of coalition   **K102**
freedom of commerce and industry   H43
freedom of commerce and navigation   H44
freedom of communications   F218
freedom of conscience   **G414**
freedom of expression   F189, F213
freedom of fishing   F207
freedom of movement   **B521, F238**
freedom of movement and travel   B522
freedom of movement for capital   F190, F240
freedom of movement for goods   F240
freedom of movement for persons   F190, F240
freedom of movement for services   F190
freedom of movement for workers   F239
freedom of navigation   F214
freedom of opinion   **M140;** F208, F212
freedom of passage through the air   F187
freedom of religion   **R532**
freedom of speech   **R456;** F220
freedom of speech, complete   F221
freedom of the air   F210
freedom of the high seas   F209, F211
freedom of the open sea   F209, F211
freedom of thought   **G55, M140;** F208, F212
freedom of transit   F205
freedom of worship   F191
freedom, secure (to)   F228
freedom to correspond   F215
freedom to fly in   **F152**
freedom to fly over   **F152**
freedom to fly through   **F152**
freedom to hold opinions   F212
freedom to receive information   F206
freedom, withdraw (to)   F225
freedoms, fundamental   **G508;** M162
freight   **F176**
friendly means, by   W87
friendship   F246
friendship, agreement of   **F248**
friendship, create and preserve (to)   F247
friendship, treaty of   **F249**
frontier   **G475**
frontier, adjustment of   **G474**
frontier, cross (to)   G476
frontier, crossing of   **G495**
frontier crossing point   **G494**
frontier dispute   **G493**
frontier, drawing of   **G500**
frontier line   **G489**
frontier, national   **L20, S606**
frontier, natural and artificial   N78
frontier, rectification of   **G474**
frontier river   **G486**
frontier traffic   **G497**
frontier treaty   **G499**
frontier violation   **G498**
frontier worker   **G471, G487;** G472, G488
frontier worker's card   **G473**

frontier zone **G501;** G502
frontiers in lakes G477
frustrate (to) **V78**
fuels, irradiated K46
fuels, irradiated nuclear K47
fulfil (to) **E72, E353, N27, W39**
fulfil, failure to **N140**
fulfil in good faith (to) E354
fulfil, promise to **E75**
fulfilment E356, W44
fulfilment of **E74**
full age **V805**
full member **V823**
full powers **U179, V806; AN2, AN14**
full powers, communication of V813
full powers, deposit (to) V818
full powers, deposit of V812
full powers, examination of V814
full powers, exchange (to) V817
full powers, exchange of V810
full powers, exhibit (to) V820
full powers, having communicated M333
full powers, issue (to) V815, V816
full powers, issue of V809
full powers, present (to) V819, V820
full powers, scrutiny of V814
function A614, F319, T35
function, administrative **V596**
function, advisory A620, G578, G581, G582,
    G583, T46
function, consultative A620
function, mediatory T51
function, official **A265;** A622, T44
functions, admitted to exercise of W46
functions, area of **A631**
functions assigned to them F321
functions, assumption of **D70**
functions, authorized U47
functions, continuation of T43
functions, continue to discharge (to) T57
functions, delegate (to) A628
functions, delegation of A618
functions, description of **T62**
functions, discharge (to) A625, F324
functions, entrust (to) A628
functions, exceed (to) A626
functions, exercise (to) A624, A630, F323,
    F325, T53
functions, exercise impartially (to) U139
functions, exercise of A619, F320, O25, T40
functions, fulfil (to) A625, F324
functions, fulfilment of A616
functions, humanitarian A623
functions, in virtue of K309
functions, limits of A617
functions, on the termination of their D56
functions, perform (to) A624, A630, F323,
    F325

functions, performance of A615, A619, A880,
    F320
functions, range of **A631**
functions, scope of **A631, T61**
functions, suspend (to) T56
functions, take up (to) A247, T52
functions, taking up of **A246**
functions, terminate (to) T55
functions, termination of B57, T41, T45
fund F166
fund, special **S423**
funds M337
further (to) **F167**

general A207
General Assembly **G200, V840**
General Assembly, composition of Z177
general secretary **G197**
generally recognized A208
Geneva Cross **G202**
genocide G203, V686; V687; AN11
genocide, act of **V688**
genocide, attempt to commit V687
genocide, complicity in V687; AN11
genocide, conspiracy to commit V687; AN11
genocide, incitement to commit V687
geographical R83
good G567
good faith, in T160
good offices D58, D61
good offices, lend (to) D62, D63
good offices committee D60
good offices of impartial bodies D59
good-neighbourliness N6
good-neighbourly G586
goods W70
goods, contraband **B2**
goods, description of **W73**
goods, enemy F58
goods, exchange of W71
goods, freedom of movement for W76
goods, international transport of W77
goods, trade in **W74**
goods, valuation of W72
govern (to) **R473, R485**
governing body **D159**
government R486, S600
government affected R487
government agency **R497; S646**
government, authority of W198
government concerned R487
government, contracting **V509;** R490
government, *de facto* R488
government, *de jure* R488
government, defaulting S236
government delegate **R493, R499**
government, depositary **D49**

government, legitimate R489
government, non-contracting **N202**
government, non-participating **N194**
government, non-signatory **N197**
government representative **R499**
government, signatory **U230, U232**
government, signatory and acceding U233
government signatory hereto U234, U237
government, sovereign .S603, S604, S625
grade A135
grant E107, E469
grant (to) **B553, E105, E468, G362, V220**
grant, refuse to (to) **V616, W100**
granted (to be) **E79, Z210**
granted by treaty V469
granting E107, E469
Graves Registration Service **G469**
ground for appeal **B329**
ground for terminating V488
ground forces **L32**
grounds G504
grounds of, on G507
group G552
group, ad-hoc **G554**
group, ethnic **V799; G555**
group, ethnical **V799; G556; AN11**
group, national G556, G557
group of three **D200**
group, planning **P109**
group, quadripartite **V654**
group, racial **R45; G556, G558**
group, racial or ethnical **R46**
group, religious G556, G559
group, special working **S418**
group, specialized **F2**
group, technical **F2**
group, three-power **D200**
group, tripartite **D200**
group, working **A564**
groups, rights of minority **G560**
guarantee B687
guarantee, collective **K124**
guarantee, judicial **R308; R309**
guarantee, legal **R308**
guarantee (to) **B684, G364**
guarantor B683
guarantor, act as (to) **B684**
guarantor, stand as (to) **B684**
guardian V916
guardianship V918
guidance R603
guide line **R603**
guided by (to be) Z49
guilty S234
guilty of a wrong S237
guilty of an act S237
gunshot range **K16**

hand down (to) **F25**
hand over (to) **U34**
handing over **U17, U35**
harbour H2
harbour works **H7**
harbour works, permanent H8
harmonization A117, H114
harmonize (to) **A114, H113**
harmony, universal W118
hatred, racial **R47**
head C10
head of post **L90**
head of post, acting L91
head of post, admission as L92
head (to) **L89**
heading AN3
headquarters, UN S377
hear (to) **A426, V169**
hearing A427, S387, V176; V177
hearing in court V179
hearing of witnesses A428
hearings V176
hegemony H151
hereinafter F160; N46
hereinafter called F161
heritage E342
high commissioner **H226**
high commissioner, office of **H227**
High Contracting Party P17, S305, T73, V6, V499
high seas **H260; M100, S260**
high seas, freedom of **M110**
high seas open to all nations S262
high treason **H228, L21**
historic H222
holy H152
Holy See H154
home country **H160**
home of each judge **H162**
home state **H164**
honour E2
honour, acts injurious to E3
hospital L45
hospital, civilian **Z62**
hospital locality **S53**
hospital nurse **H188**
hospital orderly **H188**
hospital ship **L46; L49**
hospital ship, military L47, L48
hospital train **L50**
hospital zone **S56**
hostage G131
hostages, execution of **G132**
hostages, shooting of **G132**
hostile A137, F50, N120
hostile destination F53
hostile relations F54
hostile to security A138

immunity, jurisdictional   B323
immunity, personal   **P75**; I38, I39
immunity, procedure to obtain   U271
immunity, relative   I40
immunity, right of   **I59**
immunity, secure (to)   I56
immunity, waive (to)   B90, B91, B93, I47, I48, I49, I57
immunity, waiver of   **I61**; I31, I32, I33, I34; AN7
immunity with regard to   I13, I17
immunity, withdrawal of   U272
immunities and facilities   B71
immunities and privileges   B72, B73
impair (to)   **B49, B335, V78**; B338
impairment   **B51**
impartial   **U137**; U138
impartiality   **N178, U140**
impartiality, with complete   U142
impartially   U141
imperative   **Z266**
imperative legal reasons   Z268
implement (to)   **D227, E353, V829**
implementation   **D228, E356**
implementation, capable of   **D225, V826**
implementation, impossibility of   **U107**
implements of war   **K423**
implied   **I66, K190, S667**
imply (to)   **I65**
import   **E38**
import authorization   **E44, E48**
import duty   **E59**
import formalities   **E47**
import licence   **E44, E48, E51**
import prohibition   **E58**
import quota   **E49, E53**
import restriction   **E54**
import restrictions, quantitative   E43
imports, restrictions on   **E42**
import (to)   **E45**
importance   **B24**
importation   **E38**
importation, country of   **E50**
importation, monopoly of   **E52**
importation papers, temporary   E39
importation, quantitative restrictions on   E43
importation, restrictions on   **E42**
impose on (to)   **A607**
imposed   **A610**
imposing   **A612**
imposition   **A612**; I98
impossible to execute   **U106**
imprison (to)   **G70**
imprisonment   **G71**
imprisonment, place of   **G72**
improper   **M259**
in extenso   W246
in rem   **D94**

inadmissibility   **U280**
inadmissible   **U279**; Z147
inalienability   **U74**
inalienable   **U72, U252**
inaugurate (to)   **E46**
incapable of action   **H108**
incapacitated   **G314, G315**
incapacity   **G316**
incapacity, legal   **G316**
incapacity, temporary   V786
incapacity to act   **H110**
incapacity to conduct legal business   **G316**
incident, aerial   **L147**
incident, nuclear   N285, N286
incite (to)   **A673**
incitement   **A674**
income   **E100**
incompatibility   **U260**; U261
incompatible   **U257**; V867
incompatible with   AN21
incompatible with object of the treaty   U259
incompetence   **U282**
inconsistency   **U260**
inconsistent   **U257**
inconsistent with   W148
inconsistent with purposes of the UN   U258
incontestability   **U87**
incontestable   **U86**
incorporate (to)   **I78**; I79
incorporation   **I75, I80**; I76
incorporation, automatic   I81
incorporation theory   **I77**
incumbent (*adj.*)   **A610, O21**; U48
incumbent on (to be)   **O17**; O18
incumbent upon   V299
incumbent upon states   V290
incumbent (*noun*)   **T134**
incumbent of international rights   T136
incumbent of rights and duties   T135
indemnification   **W177**
indentation   **E29, E129, Z25**
indentation not regarded as a bay   E130
indented   **Z23**; E30
independence   **S311, U79**
independence, attain (to)   U80
independence, declaration of   **U81**
independence, gain (to)   U80
independence, treaty of   **U84**
independence, unilateral declaration of   U82
independence, war of   **U83**
independent   **S309, U75**
indispensable   **U72**; U73
individual   **E204**; P50, P51
individual, rights of   **I73**
individuals, group of   **P80**
individuals, private   E205
infancy   **M245**
infant (*adj.*)   **M243**

infant (*noun*)   **M244**
infer (to)   **A71**
inflict on (to)   **A607**
inflicting   **A612**
influence, sphere of   **M12**
inform (to)   **B255, M329, V344**; K38, K40
information   **N35**
information agency   **I74**
information centre   **I74**
informed of (to be)   K41
informing   **B256**
infringe (to)   **B49, U50, V226**
infringement   **V228, V348, Z223**
infringement, alleged   A363, B174
infringement, penalty imposed for   Z226
infringements, punish (to)   V350
ingress   Z129
inhabitants   **V662**
inhabitants, native   B499
inherent   **U252**
inheritance   **E343**
inheritance duty   **E344**
inhibitive   **H208**
initial (to)   **P6**
initialling   **P7**; P8; AN2
injunction   **V145**
injunction, interim   V147
injure (to)   **S67, V226**
injury   **S68, S80, V228**
injustice   **U114**
inland waterway   **B624**
innocent   **U150**
inoperative   **U115, U278**
inquire into (to)   **U210**
inquiry   **A645, U211**; A646
inquiry, commission of   **U218**
inquiry, committee of   **U216**
inquiry, conduct (to)   **U210**; U214
inquiry convention   **U215**
inquiry, means of   **A647**
inquiry procedure   **U219**
inquiry, procedure for committees of   **U217**
inquiry, procedure of   **U219**
insert (to)   **A667**
insertion   **A659**
inspect (to)   **K278**
inspection   **K275**
inspection, aerial   **L126, L139**
inspection of personal baggage   K276
inspections, conduct of   D233
installation   **A432, E119**
installation, coastal   **K527**
installation, first   E121
installation, fixed coastal   K528
installation state   **A433**
instance   **I102**
instance, first   I103
instance, higher   I104

instance, lower   I105
institute (to)   **E117**
institution   **E122, I106, T137**
institution, bilateral   I108
institution, intergovernmental   I112
institution, international   I109
institution, multilateral   I110
institution, regional   I111
institution, responsible   T138
institutions of the association   I107
instruction   **W103**
instructions, authority to give   **W105**
instructions, power to give   **W105**
instructions, seek or receive (to)   **W104**
instrument   **E380, U290**
instrument, agreement in a single   U292
instrument, constituent   **G549**; AN21
instrument, in a single   AN14
instrument in writing   K497
instruments, agreement in two or more related   U292; AN14
instruments, basic   U298
instruments, exchange of   A860
instruments, in two or more related   AN14
instruments, texts of   U8
insurgent   **I113**
integration, racial   **R48**
integrity   **I114**
integrity, territorial   G14, I115, I116, S596, T108
intending   **G413**; A104, V933
intent   **A103, V932**
intent, act done with   V935
intent, declaration of   **A107**
intent, with malicious   **V936**; V934
intention,   **A103, V932**
intention, affirm (to)   B246
intention, affirming their   B249
intention, contrary   A106; AN21
intention, expression of   AN16
intentional   **V936**
intercourse   **V201**
intercourse between states   V204, V751
intercourse, diplomatic   D152, V203
intercourse, intergovernmental   V204
intercourse, international   V204, V751
intercourse, mutual   V202
intercourse, neighbourly   N5
interdependence   **A57**
interdiction   **V32**
interest   **I117**
interest, in the common   G176
interest, injured   I122
interest, injury to private   P156
interest, legitimate   I120, S765
interest, parties having the same   **S756**
interest, private   **P155**
interest, public   I121

interests of the community of states   I118
interests, preservation of   W51
interests, protect (to)   W42
interests, protection of   I119, W51
interests, uphold (to)   W42
interests, upholding of   W51
interfere (to)   **E94, I199**
interference   **E96**
intergovernmental   **Z271**
interim   **E163**
interim agreement   **Z269**
interim injunction   E165
interim measures   E164
interim provision   **U19**
interlocutory judgment   **Z276**
intermediary   **M341;** V249
intermediary, act as (to)   M342
intern (to)   **I186**
internal   **B643, I92**
international   **I126, V717, Z271**
international act   AN14
international administrative law   I177
international airport   I134
international authority   I129
international canal   I147
international cartel   I148
international character   I132
international character, exclusively   I133
international civil aviation   I180
international community   **W124**
international conference   I149
international conflict   I150
international cooperation   I181
international court   I139
international court of justice   I141
international criminal jurisdiction   I168
international criminal law   I169, V744
international custom   **V674;** I143; AN20
international custom, according to   **V681**
international custom, breach of rules of   V682
international dispute   I170
international friction   I164
international functions   I138
international inland waterway regulations   I131
international internal waters   I130
international jurisdiction   I140
international law   **V689;** I162
international law, abuse of   **V774**
international law, academic study of   **V791**
international law, admissible under   V758
international law, binding under   V755, V757
international law, breach of   **V790**
international law, classical   V704
international law, classical theory of   V773
international law, codification of   V693
international law, codified   V705
international law, coercive   V714
international law, coercive rules of   V714

International Law Commission   **V765**
international law, concept of   **V769**
international law, contrary to   **V789**
international law, customary   **V674;** V675
international law, doctrine of   **V761;** V729
international law, enforceability of   E487
international law, general   V700, V701
international law, governed by   AN14
international law, in accordance with   **V762, V766;** V691, V768; AN20
international law, in breach of   **V789**
international law, in conformity with   **V762, V766**
international law, in violation of   **V789**
international law, inadmissible under   V756
international law, mandatory   Z267
international law, of no significance under   V754
international law of the sea   **S298**
international law of treaties   **V796**
international law of war   **V684**
international law, particular   V707, V708
international law, particular customary   V678
international law, possibility of enforcing   E487
international law, primacy of   P140
international law, principle of   **V764, V778**
international law, principles of   V692, V697, V698
international law, private   P161, V709
international law, progressive development of   V694
international law, public   V706
international law, regional   V710
international law, regional customary   V679
international law, rule of   **V775, V780, V781;** V695, V696, V731, V740
international law, rules of customary   V677
international law, rules of general   V702
international law, school of   **V760, V770**
international law, school of thought in   V771
international law, science of   **V791**
international law, source of   **V779;** R395, V699; AN20
international law, specialist in   **V715**
international law, standards of   V731
international law, subject of   **V784**
international law, theory of   **V772, V787;** V729
international law, under   **V717;** V691
international law, universal   V712, V713
international law, universal customary   V680
international law, unwritten   V711
international law, validity under   V721, V726
international law, violation of   **V788, V790;** V233
international law, written   V703
international morality   **V685**
international obligations   I175
international officer   I128

international official I128
international order of states I167
international peace I137, W119
international person V776; I156
international personality I158
international practice I159, I174
international protection I165
international régime I163
international regulations I178
international river I135, I172
international rivers, law of I136
international sanitary regulations I142
international security I166
international staff I157
international station I127
international treaty law I176
international trusteeship system I173
international waterways I179
internationalization I184
internationalization of rivers I185
internationalize (to) I182
internationalized I183
internee I188
internee, civilian Z60
Internee Committee I187
internee, military M207
internee, transfer of I189
internment I190
internment camp I192; I193
internment card I191
internment, civilian Z61
internment, military M208
internment, place of I194
internuncio I195; M290
interpret (to) A746, I198; A749
interpretation A750, I196; A752
interpretation, authentic A753
interpretation, disagreement arising out of
 AN17
interpretation, extensive A756
interpretation, legal R279
interpretation, means of A760
interpretation, principle of A758
interpretation, protocol of A763
interpretation, provisions relating to A757
interpretation, restrictive A754, A755
interpretation, rule of A764; A766
interpretation, rules governing the A765
interpretation, supplementary means of A761,
 A762
interpretation, supreme principle of A759
interstate Z271
intervene (to) E69, E94, E135, I199
intervene, duty not to E99, I208
intervene in domestic affairs (to) E95
intervene, intention to I204
intervene, right to I207
intervention E70, E71, E96, E136, I200

intervention, act of I205
intervention action I206
intervention, armed E97, G402, M220
intervention by using armed force G402
intervention, collective K125
intervention, inadmissible E98
intervention measure I206
intervention, military E97, M220
intervention, non-justifiable U114
intervention, prohibition against E99
intervention, prohibition of I208
intervention, right of I207
interventionism I201
interventionist I202
interventionist action I203
interventionist measures I203
intimidate (to) E137
intimidation E138
intimidation, measure of M55
introduce (to) E46
introduction E55
invade (to) E36
invalid U115
invalidate (to) U116
invalidity U119
invest in (to) U44
invested U46
investigation, impartial and conscientious
 P199, T30
inviolability U263, U265; AN7
inviolability, infringe (to) U267
inviolability of frontiers U268
inviolability of papers and documents U270
inviolability of the person U266
inviolability, personal U273
inviolable U262, U264
invite (to) E91
invite to accede (to) E92
invite to participate (to) E92
invocation B322
invoke (to) B314; G144, U117
invoking B322
invoking, by B324
irrevocability U74
irrevocable U72
island I99; I100
islands, chain of I101
islands, fringe of I101
islands situated offshore V899
issue A857, E469
issue, at S759, S784
issue between the parties S746
issue, country of A858
issue, points at S785
issue, relevant to the B305
issue (to) A855, E468
issuing A857
item S12

jurisdiction over, exercise (to)   Z244
jurisdiction over, have (to)   Z189
jurisdiction over, having   Z187
jurisdiction, personal   **P74; S602**
jurisdiction, persons subject to   H181
jurisdiction, recognize (to)   G251, G252,
   Z205
jurisdiction, recognize as compulsory (to)
   G253, G254, G255
jurisdiction, regular   G246
jurisdiction, solely within   Z201
jurisdiction, territorial   T102
jurisdiction, territories placed under   G237
jurisdiction to legislate   **G345**
jurisdiction, voluntary   G241
jurisprudence   **R310**
jurisprudence, history of   **R318**
jurist   **R311**
jurist, international   **V715, V792**
juristic   **J16**
jus cogens   R145
jus in bello   **K441**
jus sanguinis   **A110**
jus soli   **T112**
just   **A383, B592**
justice   **G212**
justice, administration of   **R384**; R385
justice and peace in the world   F201
justice, court of   **G259**
justice, denial of   **J20, R423**; V619
justice, fundamental principles of   G213
justice, impede the course of (to)   G214
justice, obstruction of   R386
justice, proper administration of   R387
justiciable   **J19**
justification   **B160**
justify (to)   **B155**
justly   **B594**

killing   **T132**
killing with malice aforethought   T133

labour, compulsory   **P103;** Z237, Z238
labour detachment   **A565**
labour, forced   **Z236;** P104, Z237, Z238
labour laws   **A567**
labour, protection of   **A568**
labour unit   **A565**
lacking   **E421**
laissez-passer   **A882**
land area   **L24;** H242, L25
land boundary   **L26**
land domain   **L24**
land forces   **L32**
land frontier   **L26**
land, no-man's   **N218**

land power   **L31**
land territory   **L24;** H247, K533
land warfare   **L27, L29**
land warfare, law of   **L30**
land warfare, laws and customs of   L28
land, freedom to   **L36**
land, right to   **L37**
landing   **L33**
landing forces   **L38**
landing, freedom of   **L36**
landing, liberty of   **L36**
landing, right of   **L37**
language, official   **A264**
language, working   **A569; A570**
lapse   **E411, U169**
lapse of time   **V195**
lapse, reasons for   **E414**
lapse (to)   **E408, U173, V192**
lapsed   **V193**
law   **G325, R113**
law, abuse of   **R356**
law, applicable   R117
law applicable   R118
law applied by the court   R366
law arising under treaties   **V506**
law, attitude to   **R279**
law, by   R115
law, by operation of   K312, R115, R436
law, civil   **Z69;** R123
law, codified   R130
law, commercial   H52
law, comparative   **R419;** R144
law, compatible with   **G351**
law, consistent with   **G351, R273**
law, constitutional   **S616, V123**
law, contrary to   **R448**
law, course of   **R444**
law created by treaties   **V506**
law, criminal   **S715**
law, customary   **G418;** K109
law, dispositive   R124, R133
law district   **R351**
law, domestic   G343, R126, R127
law, enacted   **G325**
law, existing   R122
law, existing customary   G420
law, foreign   R121
law, general   R116
law, general customary   G419
law, general principles of   R320
law, generally recognized principles of
   R321
law governing aerial warfare   **L129**
law governing airspace   **L134**
law governing aliens   **F241**
law governing land warfare   **L30**
law, history of   **R318**
law, humanitarian   **H262**

legal assistance **R336**
legal capacity **R300**; R301, R302, R303, R382, R408, R411
legal capacity, possessing R299
legal claim **R277**
legal consultancy T48
legal counsel **R290**
legal counsel, free R293
legal dictum **R400**
legal dispute **R414**
legal doctrine **R355**
legal effect, having **R450**
legal efficacy **R345**
legal force **R345**
legal force, having **R348**
legal guarantee **R308**
legal interpretation **R279**
legal matter **R307**
legal measures R325
legal opinion, advisory **R326**
legal order **R374**
legal person **R378**
legal personality **R380**; R381
legal position **R352, R406**
legal presumption V271
legal principle **R319, R400**
legal proceedings, institute (to) R446
legal process, after due V92
legal process, by R445
legal protection **R401**
legal provision **R425**
legal question **R307**
legal reasons, cogent Z268
legal recourse **R453**
legal relationship **R296, R420**; R421
legal remedy **R283, R444**
legal remedy, local R286
legal remedies, exhaustion of local R288
legal right **R277**
legal scholar **R311**
legal status **R352, R406**; R274, R407, R412
legal status, possessing R299
legal successor **R371**
legal system **R374, R417**
legal theory **R355**
legal transaction **R314**
legal validity **R324**
legal view **R279**
legality **L65, R276**
legality, principle of **L66**
legalization **L60, L64**; U301
legalization, consular L62
legalization, diplomatic L61
legalize (to) **L63**
legate **L67**
legate, apostolic L68
legation **G281, L69**; G282
legation, duty to establish **G283**

legation, duty to maintain G284
legislate, power to G339
legislating, act of **G338**
legislation **G338, R425**; M62, R427, R428
legislation, by means of **G349**; G340
legislation, deprivation of effect of A842, R441
legislation, domestic G342
legislation, enact (to) G337
legislation, in accordance with R434
legislation, municipal G342
legislation, national G342
legislation, process of adopting **G338**
legislation, process of making **G338**
legislation, repeal of R440
legislation, subject to R429
legislative **G333, G336**
legislature K300
legitimacy **L76, R276**
legitimacy, constitutional L78
legitimacy, principle of **L79**
legitimate (to) **L73**
legitimate **L70, R275**
legitimation **L74**
legitimation card **L72, T89**
legitimist **L75**
letter **B659**
letters, exchange of **B653**
letters of credence **B145**
letters of marque and reprisal **K21**
letters of recall **A10**
letters of request **R338**
letters rogatory **R338**; E460, H80, R339
letters rogatory, execute (to) R341
letters rogatory, execution of R340
lettres de créance **B145**
lettres de récréance **L99, R531**
levée en masse **L100, V797**
level **A135**
level, regional R503, R504
levies **U66**
levies, assessment of U67
levy (to) **E370, U68**
liability **H21, S233, V5, V8, V22**; H12, H18
liability, absolute H19
liability, absolve of (to) V6
liability, assume (to) V24
liability, contract (to) V24
liability, contractual H26
liability for, bear (to) **V3**
liability, international H27, V727
liability, limit (to) H23
liability, limitation of H24
liability of the state H25
liability under international law H27
liable **H11, H15, S232, V4**; H17
liable for (to be) **H15, V3**
liable, hold (to) **H15**; H13, H23
liable, jointly and severally H12

liable to (to be)   **U189;** U190
liable to process   **V208**
liaison   **V25**
liaison committee   **V28**
liaison group   **V29**
liaison office   **V30**
liaison office, ILO   V31
liberalization, list of   **L101**
liberate (to)   **B67**
liberation   **B69**
liberation army   **B94**
liberation front   **B95**
liberation, war of   **B96**
liberty   **F200**
liberty, at (to be)   **F233;** F234
liberty, deprive of (to)   **F225, F226**
liberty, exercise (to)   F224
liberty, individual   **F222, F223**
liberty, withdraw (to)   F225
licit   **R275**
life at sea   **M156**
life at sea, saving   M157
life, deprivation of   **T132**
limit   **A52, E134, G482**
limit, territorial   **H253;** H254
limits permitted by international law   G483
limit (to)   **B390, E131**
limitation   **B391, V191, V195**
limitation, barred by   **V193**
limitation, become void by (to)   **V192**
limitation due to race   B393
limitation, period of   **V196**
limitation, subject to   **V190**
line   **L105**
line, low-tide   **N215**
line, low-water   **N215;** N216
line, median   **M338;** L107, M339, M340
link   **B617, V25**
link, genuine   **B618, V26**
liquidate (to)   **A654, L110**
liquidation   **A655, L108**
liquidation of the fund   L109
list   **L111, V639**
list, general   **G276**
list (to)   **A358, A613**
listed   **A364, A633**
litigant   **S780**
litigation, value in   **S782;** S783
local   **O120**
locality in which situated   S378
locality, inspection of   **A683, A686**
locality, visit of   **A686**
localities, visit (to)   A684, A685
located, country in which   S379
location   **D84, S374**
location of the secretariat   S376
lodging   **A42**
lose (to)   **V238**

loss   **V235**
loss, reason for   **V237**
lot   **L113**
lot, drawing   L114
low-tide   **T181**
low-water line   M340

maintain (to)   **A668, E365**
maintenance   **A670, E366**
majority   **M123, V805**
majority, absolute   M124, M125
majority, age of   **M246, V805**
majority, approved by   B46
majority decision   **M130**
majority, having obtained   **V803**
majority, person who has attained   **V804**
majority, qualified   M127
majority, relative   M128
majority report   **M129**
majority, simple   M126
majority vote   **S680**
majority vote, decide by (to)   S681
malice aforethought, with   T133
malicious   **V936;** AN10
management   **L94**
mandate   **M16, M22, M25;** H242
mandate, duration of   M18
mandate system   **M24**
mandate, territories under   M26
mandate territory   **M21**
mandatory   **Z266**
maritime   **M30** (*see also* **See-** *compounds under* S265–S297)
mass destruction   **M32;** AN18
mass destruction, weapons of   **M33**
mass forcible transfer   **M35**
mass transfer   **M34**
master   **K26, S189;** S190
master's certificate   **K28**
material   **S688**
material, military   K424
materials, fissionable   S689, S690
matter   **A372, F179, S12**
matter, adjust (to)   S16
matter, administrative   **V591;** V592
matter, amicable settlement of   A373
matter, criminal   **S718**
matter, deal with (to)   B63, B64, S13
matter in dispute   **S750**
matter, legal   **R307**
matter, let drop (to)   **B190**
matter, procedural   **V108**
matter, refer to another court (to)   V621
matter, settle (to)   S15
matters within the provisions of   A374
matters within the purposes of   A375
meaning   **B26, S365;** B27

meaning and scope   S366
meaning, determine (to)   B28
means   M335, M337
means, appropriate   M336
means, by pacific   F292; F304
means, by peaceful   F292
means, coercive   Z248
means of, by   W84
means of enforcement   Z248
means, pacific   F299
means, subsidiary   H192; AN20
means, supplementary   H192; H194
measure   H32, M36, M48, V903
measure, administrative   V590, V605
measure, coercive   Z245
measure, collective   K126; K127
measure decided upon   M50
measure, disciplinary   D179
measure ensuring   M49
measure, individual   E203
measure intended to prevent   M53
measure, interim   U20; M70
measure, judicial   G272
measure, legislative   G347; M62, M63, R442
measure of brutality   M228
measure of execution   E496
measure of preparation for war   M351
measure of protection, military   M222
measure, precautionary   V952
measure, preventive   P129, V889; M68
measure providing   M49
measure, punitive   S710
measure, retaliatory   V155
measure to enforce   M57
measure to ensure   M49
measure to facilitate   M56
measure to overcome   M54
measure to provide   M49
measure to remove   M54
measure, transitional   U20
measures, abstain from (to)   M81
measures, adopt (to)   M75, M77, M80
measures, alternative   M58
measures, appropriate   M61
measures appropriate for   G58
measures, by legislative   R442
measures calculated to   G58
measures, carry out (to)   M74
measures, cease (to)   M76
measures, discriminatory   M59
measures, domestic   M64
measures, effective   M71, M72
measures, execute (to)   M74
measures, forbid (to)   M82
measures, immediate and effective   M67
measures in dispute   A534
measures, initiate (to)   M75
measures, introduce (to)   M75

measures, military   M65
measures, proscribe (to)   M82
measures, provisional   M69, M70
measures, refrain from (to)   M81
measures, resort to (to)   M77, M78, M79
measures, restrictive   M60
measures, standstill   S666
measures, suitable   M61
measures, take (to)   M80
measures, temporary   M70
measures, urgent military   M66
mediate (to)   V243
mediation   V248
mediation commission   V251
mediation committee   V250
mediatization   M85; M87
mediatization of the individual   M86
mediator   V246
mediatory   V244
mediatory proposal   V252
medical   S44
medical aircraft   S50
medical duties   S45
medical equipment   S51
medical establishment   S48
medical establishment, fixed   S49
medical material   S51
medical personnel   S54
medical service   S41
medical service, regular   S43
medical transport   S55
medical unit   S46
medical unit, mobile   S42, S47
meet (to)   T2, Z169, Z178
meeting   S387, T17
meeting, extraordinary   T19
meeting, ministerial   M255
meeting, ordinary   T20
meeting, secret   G127
meetings held in public   S397
meetings, publicity of   S389
member   M297
member, associated   M307
member, cease to be (to)   A810
member country   M324
member, expulsion of   A819
member, federal   B674
member, founding   G548; M315
member, full   V823; M313
member government   M325
member, initial   G548; M315
member, non-permanent   M311, M312
member, ordinary   M313
member, original   G548; M315
member, outgoing   M309
member, permanent   M314
member, regular   M313
member, retiring   A808, M309, M310

member, special **S426**
member state **G459, M326**
member state, original U317
member, withdrawing M309
members mentioned by name A366
members specified by name A366
membership **M316**
membership, admission to A658
membership, application for **A660, A662;**
M321
membership, applying for **B242**
membership, associate M308
membership, benefits arising from M319
membership, condition of **A664**
membership, expiration of M322
membership, expiry of M322
membership open to governments M317
membership, original U316
membership, recommend and approve for
(to) M320
membership, request for M321
membership, rights arising from M319
membership, state applying for **A661**
membership, termination of M322
membership, universality of M323
memorandum **M150**
merchant ship **H54**
merchant vessel **H54**
merchantman **H54**
method **M335, M352, M357, V80**
method of selecting V85
methods, appropriate M353
metropolitan territory **H158, M374**
migration **W65**
migration for employment W67
migration for settlement W66
military **B513, M209**
military operations, close of E158
Military Security Board M224
Military Staff Committee **G198;** G199
militia **M229**
mindful E65
Minister Resident **M254**
minor (*adj.*) **M243**
minor (*noun*) **M244;** G291
minority **M230, M245**
minority, age of **M245;** M246
minority, alien M232
minority, ethnic M231
minority, foreign M232
minority group **M230**
minority group, member of **M241**
minority groups, law governing **M237**
minority groups, protection of **M239**
minority groups, rights of **M238**
minority, linguistic M236
minority, national M233
minority, racial M234

minority, religious M235
minority report **M242**
minority rights **M238**
minority treaty **M240**
minutes **N212, P177**
minutes, agreed N214
minutes, correct (to) P180
minutes, draw up (to) P178, P181
minutes, joint N213
minutes of the case **V181**
minutes, rectify (to) P180
missiles, guided W6
missing person **V333;** V334
mission **A678, B645, G281, M261, V561**
mission, administrative staff of M276
mission, archives of M264
mission, carry out (to) A682
mission, commercial **H47**
mission, communication on the part of M281
mission, dignity of W249
mission, diplomatic **V561;** M283, V562
mission, diplomatic staff of M274; AN8
mission, duty to establish **G283**
mission, duty to maintain **G283**
mission, exceed (to) A627
mission, execute (to) A682
mission, head of **M289;** G311, K94, M266,
M290, R22; AN8
mission, inviolability of U269
mission, member of **M292;** M263, M265,
M266, M268, M269; AN8
mission, member of staff of M271, M272,
M273; AN8
mission, military M225
mission, offices forming part of M262
mission, peace of the F257
mission, permanent V564
mission, permanent diplomatic M284
mission, premises of **M291;** M277, M278,
M279, M280, R87; AN8
mission, property of M282
mission, recall (to) M287
mission, recall permanently (to) M288
mission, recall temporarily (to) M288
mission, residence of head of M278
mission, sacred A681, M285
mission, security of G365
mission, service staff of M275
mission, staff of **M293;** M270; AN8
mission, termination of A680
missions, exchange (of) V565
missions, humanitarian T47
missions, temporary official A679
misuse **M256;** U39
misuse (to) **M258**
mobilization **M348, M349;** M351
mobilization, general **G196;** M350
mobilize (to) **M347**

modification   A3, A282, M354; A161, M355
modification, draft   **A293**
modification, instrument of   **A5**
modification, proposed   **A6**
modified   A45
modify (to)   **A1, A278, M356**
modifying   A279
monetary   W54
monism   M359
monist (*adj.*)   **M361**
monist (*noun*)   **M360**
monitor (to)   **K278**
monitoring   K275
monopoly of a commercial character   H49
monopolies, state   S534
monument, centre containing   **D37**
morality   M362, S371
morality, international   **V685;** I153, S373
morality, law relating to   **S372**
morality, public   O44
morality, requirements of   O70
morals   S371
moratoria   S665
mother country   **M374**
mother country, separation from   M375
motion   A508
motion, file (to)   A513
motion, filing the   **A515**
motion for   A512
motion of no confidence   **M294**
motion, procedural   **V106**
motion, submit (to)   A513
mouth   O52
movable   B518
movables   M346
movement, free   R526
multilateral   M132, M363
multilaterality   M364
multiracial   V648
municipal   I92
munition   M369
munitions and implements of war   M370
munitions, trade in   M371
murder   T132
mutatis mutandis   **S368**
mutineer   M195
mutiny   M194
mutiny (to)   **M196**
mutual   G86

name of, in the   **N54, N56**
nascent   S599
nation   V662
nations and peoples of the world   **V664**
nations, community of   **S517, V672**
nations, family of   **V671**

nations of the world, understanding between   V665
national (*adj.*)   **I92, S532**
national service, duty to complete   **W98**
national (*noun*)   **A367, S540, S588, S626;** S627
national, enemy   F66
national of full age   S544
national, undesirable   S545, S546, U110
national who is a minor   S544
nationals, local   S543
nationals of a member state   A368
nationals of Contracting Parties   S542
nationals of other states   A370
nationals of the sending state   A369
nationals, UN   S541
nationality   N63, S547, S591, S628, V802; N64, S592, S629, S630
nationality, acquire (to)   S577, S578
nationality, acquisition by adoption   S553
nationality, acquisition by birth   S558
nationality, acquisition by legitimation   S560
nationality, acquisition by marriage   S555, S559
nationality, acquisition by naturalization   S556
nationality, acquisition by previous nationality   S554
nationality, acquisition by service of the state   S557
nationality, acquisition of   **S585;** S552
nationality decrees   **S584**
nationality, deprivation of   **A693**
nationality, deprive of (to)   **A692;** S571, S576
nationality, deprived of   **A725**
nationality, dual   **D192;** S569
nationality, enemy   F61
nationality, former   S551
nationality, give up (to)   S572, S573
nationality, grant (to)   S580
nationality, grant of   N65
nationality, lose (to)   S581
nationality, loss by acquisition of foreign nationality   S565
nationality, loss by denaturalization   S562
nationality, loss by marriage to foreign national   S563
nationality, loss by recovery of nationality   S568
nationality, loss by renunciation   S567
nationality, loss by service of foreign state   S564
nationality, loss by territorial changes   S566
nationality, loss of   **S586;** S561
nationality, multiple   **M133;** M134, S570
nationality, opt for (to)   S579
nationality, person with multiple   **M135**
nationality, possess (to)   S575
nationality, recover (to)   S583
nationality, recovery of   **W167**
nationality, renounce (to)   S582

nationality, retain (to)   S574
nationality, retention of   S551
nationality, without distinction as to   S549
nationalization   **V343**
nationalize (to)   **V342**
NATO Annual Review   **N67**
NATO Commands   **N68**
NATO Military Authorities   **N71**
NATO Military Committee   **N69**
NATO Military Staffs   **N70**
natural   **N76**
naturalization   **E32, N73**
naturalization, certificate of   **E35, N74**
naturalization, collective   **K123**
naturalization, entitled to (to be)   **E34**
naturalization, entitlement to   **E33**
naturalization, letters of   **E35, N74**
naturalize (to)   **E31, N72**
nature   **C1**
nature, binding   **V18**
nature, recommendatory   **C3**
nature, universal   **U130**
nature, unlawful   **I9**
navicert   **N85**
navicert system   **N86**
navigable   **S184**
navigation   **S177**
navigation agreement   **S180**
navigation, freedom of   **S182; F214**
navigation, interfere unjustifiably with (to)
   S179
navigation, maritime   **S289**
navigation treaty   **S183**
Navy List   **R29**
necessary   **E347**
necessity   **B47, E349, N279**
necessity, imperative military   **N281**
necessity, military   **K440; M216**
necessity, urgent military   **M217**
negligence   **F19**
negligence, through culpable   **V938**
negligent   **F18, S232**
negotiate (to)   **A730, V168**
negotiate, authority to   **V185**
negotiate, freedom to   **V182**
negotiate, power to   **V185**
negotiating   **A732**
negotiating party   **V183**
negotiating state   **V184**
negotiation   **A732, V170**
negotiation, by   **V186**
negotiation, by direct   **W88**
negotiation, direct   **AN17**
negotiation, resolve by (to)   **V171**
negotiation, settle by (to)   **V171**
negotiation, settled by   **M144**
negotiations, adjournment of   **V175**
negotiations, authority to conduct   **V185**

negotiations, breaking off of   V172
negotiations, commencement of   V173
negotiations, conduct of   V174
negotiations, power to conduct   **V185**
negotiations pursuant to   A638
negotiations, start of   V173
neighbourly   **N2**
neutral   **N95**
neutralism   **N100**
neutralist (*adj.*)   **N102**
neutralist (*noun*)   **N101**
neutrality   **N103; N104**
neutrality, absolute   N107
neutrality, armed   N108
neutrality, benevolent   N113
neutrality, breach of   **N114, N118**
neutrality, declaration of   **N115**
neutrality, in violation of   **N120**
neutrality, law governing   **N117**
neutrality, permanent   N109, N111
neutrality, perpetual   N109, N111
neutrality, right of   **N116**
neutrality, state of   N105, N106
neutrality, status of   N105
neutrality, treaty of   **N119**
neutrality, unconditional   N112
neutrality, violation of   **N118**
neutrality, voluntary   N110
neutralization   **N99**
neutralize (to)   **N97**
neutralized   **N98**
news ban   **N37**
nominate (to)   **E426, N58, V943**
nominated   **E424**
nomination   **E428, N219**
nomination, make (to)   **E431**
nomination, power of   **E433**
nomination, regularity of   **E430**
nominations committee   **E432, N220**
non grata   **N221**
non grata, declare (to)   N222, N223
non-aggression   **N124, N125**
non-aggression, pact of   **N126**
non-aggression, treaty of   **N126**
non-applicable   **U115**
non-attainment   **N144**
non-autonomous   **N128, N183**
non-belligerence   **N171**
non-belligerency   **N171**
non-belligerent   **N166, N170**
non-binding   **U255**
non-citizen   **S594**
non-combatant   **N162, N165**
non-compliance   **N130, N134**
non-compulsory   **U255**
non-contractual   **N201**
non-criminal   **N191**
non-discrimination   **N131**

non-discrimination clause   **N133**
non-discriminatory   D172
non-discriminatory basis   **N132**
non-discriminatory trade policies   D173
non-extradition   N127
non-fulfilment   N140
non-government delegate   **N179**
non-governmental   N185
non-intervention   N138, N160
non-intervention, duty of   **N139**
non-judicial   N180
non-justiciable   N161
non-justifiable   U112
non-mandatory   U255
non-member   N172
non-member government   **N173**
non-member state   **N174**; N175
non-national   S594; A370
non-neutral   N176
non-neutrality   N177
non-nuclear-weapon power   **N163**
non-nuclear-weapon state   **N164**
non-obligatory   U255
non-observance   N129, N130, N134
non-participant   N193
non-participating   N194
non-participation   N192
non-permanent   N189
non-prejudicial to peace   **N146**
non-proliferation   N199
non-proliferation treaty   **N200, N292**
non-quota   Q21
non-recognition   W144
non-resident   A733
non-retroactive   N181
non-retroactivity   N182
non-self-governing   N128
non-signatory   N196
non-sovereign   N150
non-state   N185
non-submission   N123
non-validity   N147
non-war   N166
norm   N224
norm, non-validity of   **N148**
norm, validity of   N148
normalization   N244
normalize (to)   **N242**
normative   N248, N249, N251
not contestable   A356
notarial acts   U299
notary, act as (to)   B117
note   A435, N254
note, circular   **Z52**
note, collective   **K128**
note, diplomatic   D146, N255
note, identical   N256
note in reply   A520; V61

note verbale   **V11**
notes   E395
notes, exchange of   **N257, N258**; N259; AN6
notes, exchange of diplomatic   N260
notes, interpretative   **E395**; A436
note (to)   K41
notice   B256, F310; K503, K504
notice, bring to (to)   **V344**
notice, due   B257
notice of, give (to)   **B255**; B257, K40
notice, period of   **K502**
notification   M330, N261, N269; N262, N270, N271
notification, instrument of   **N264**
notification, official   A242
notification, oral   M368
notification, prior   N267
notification, receipt of   M334, N263
notification received   E67
notification, revoke (to)   Z159
notifications, revocation of   R637
notify (to)   **B255, M329, N265**; N266
notify by instrument in writing (to)   K497
notifying   N262
notifying party   **N268**
notifying state   **N268**
noting   A274, A384
notwithstanding   U99; A155, U101
notwithstanding the provisions   A156
nuclear   N282
nuclear energy   **K48**
nuclear energy, peaceful development of   K50
nuclear energy, peaceful use of   K49
nuclear explosive device   **K55**
nuclear explosives   **K56**
nuclear fuel   **K45**; AN18
nuclear fuel, factory using   K43
nuclear installation   **K42**; K43
nuclear installation, operator of   K44
nuclear material   **K53**; K43
nuclear material, special   K54
nuclear research   **K51**
nuclear research, joint   K52
nuclear weapon state   **K59**
nuclear weapon test   **K60**
nuclear weapon test explosions   K58
nuclear weapons   **K57**
nuclear weapons, proliferation of   V47
nuclear weapons, test explosions of   K58
null   N289
null and void   **H209, R630**; N154
nullify (to)   N153
nullity   N155
nullity, appeal based on   **N157**
nullity, declaration of   **N158**
nullity, judgment of   **N159**
nullity under international law   V730
nunciature   N290

offence in connection with taxes **A44**
offence, intentional H90
offence, international V719, V750
offence, minor **U51**
offence, party committing the **T28**
offence, penal B397, H79
offence, penalty imposed for Z226
offence, petty **U51**
offence, political H89
offence, punishable H79, Z228, Z229
offence, security H84
offences against Z224
offences, concurrence of H81
offences, statement of B131
offender T28
office A217, A237, B682, B691
office, assume (to) A226, A227
office, assumption of **A246, D70;** A218, T38
office, before taking T39
office, by virtue of K309
office, central **Z22**
office, continuation in A224
office, continue in (to) A235
office, continue to exercise (to) A230
office, dismissal from **A253**
office, dismissed from (to be) A232, E245
office, duration of term of M19
office, entering into **A246**
office, entry into **D70**
office, exercise (to) A228
office, exercise conscientiously (to) A229
office, exercise impartially (to) A229
office, expiration of term of M20
office, hold (to) A230, A231
office, local seniority of A277
office, occupy (to) A233
office, on assuming A249
office, on leaving A268
office, permanent **B692**
office, prior to assuming T39
office, prior to assumption of A219
office, relieved of (to be) E245
office, remain in (to) A230
office, removal from **A253**
office, removed from (to be) A232
office, seniority of **A275;** A276
office, take up (to) A226
office, taking up of **A246**
office, term of **A252, A262, A267, M16;** A263, A269, M18
offices, good D58
officer B15, B29
officer, career consular **B318**
officer of an organization **A266**
officers B689; V956
officers, international B32
officers of the organization B31
official (*adj.*) **A238, D79**

official (*noun*) **B15**
official, administrative **V594**
official, chief administrative **V595**
official of an organization **A266**
officials, category of G553
omission N149, U151, U185, U187; H92
omit (to) **U181**
omitted G353
open (*adj.*) **U89;** S396
open (to be) **A651**
open cities U275
open court, in S398
open for (to be) O36
open for accession **A652;** AN5
open for signature **A653;** AN5
open to challenge **A355**
open (to) **A650, O51**
opened (to be) **A651**
opened for signature U245
opening O53
operation A531, W215
operation, bring into (to) G150
operation, come into (to) **R451**
operation, extension of A540
operation, in **G140**
operation, military **K11;** K12
operation of, by **K308;** R436
operation, period of **G158**
operation, put into (to) G144
operation, renew the period of (to) G162
operation, renewed **W156**
operation, suspend (to) A846
operation, suspension of E157
operations G286, G308, T58; G287, T59, T60
operations, international G288
operative G561, W203
operative, become (to) W204
operative in law **R450**
opinion, A476, M136; S652
opinion, advisory **B163, G572, R326;** R327
opinion, chief expert's **O2**
opinion, counsel's **R326**
opinion, deliver an advisory (to) G575
opinion, difference of **M141**
opinion, dissenting M137
opinion, expert **B163**
opinion, give (to) **B162**
opinion, give an advisory (to) G573, G574, R328
opinion, separate M138
opinion, unanimous A477, A478
opposing G115
opposite G109, G115
opposition S142
opposition to, in Z231
opt for (to) **O61**
option O62
option clause **O63**

option, right of **O64**
optional **F21**
oral **M367**
order **O66, V145**
order, constitutional **V121; O74**
order, good **O66**
order, international O75, O76
order, maintenance of O67
order, maintenance of public O71
order of things, peaceful F301
order, public O69, O70
order, statutory **R422**
orders for conduct of the case V146
orderly **K336**
orderly, armed K337
ordre public O69, O73
organ **E122, O83, S641**
organ, administrative **V606**
organ, advisory **B286, K247**
organ, auxiliary **H195**
organ, consultative **B286, K247**
organ, executing A716
organ, executive **V839, V849;** A716
organ of state **S615;** S535
organ, principal **H119**
organ, principal judicial **H121;** AN19
organ, special **S427**
organ, subordinate N26
organ, subsidiary **H195, N88;** W49
organ, supervisory **U55**
organism **L56**
organisms, sedentary L57
organization **O90, V12**
organization, accede to (to) O117
organization, accession to O113, T80
organization, admission to O109, O115
organization, admit to (to) O118
organization, affiliated O95
organization, apply for admission to (to) O110
organization, central **D1, D2**
organization, expulsion from O111
organization, governmental O94, O103, S536
organization, humanitarian **H198;** O98
organization, impartial O106
organization, industrial **B320;** B321
organization, intergovernmental O108
organization, international O99
organization, join (to) O117
organization, member of M303
organization, membership of O114
organization, multiracial R49
organization, national **D1**
organization, non-governmental N188
organization, non-governmental international O101
organization, non-official international O100
organization, official O94
organization, overhead **D1**

organization, professional **B320**
organization, public international O102
organization, regional R506, R507
organization, semi-official O97
organization, specialized intergovernmental S429
organization, supranational O104, O105
organization, suprastate O105
organization, technical **F6;** F5, O96
organization, withdraw from (to) O116
organization, withdrawal from O112
organizations, workers' and employers' O93
organize, right to **V77**
origin **U310**
origin, area of **U320**
origin, certificate of **U323**
origin, country of **U321**
origin, ethnic **V801, V802;** U311; AN12
origin, national **U312**
origin, rules of **U322**
origin, territory of **U320**
original (*adj.*) **U313**
original (*noun*) **U304, U324**
otherwise agreed A302
otherwise established A299
outlaw (to) **A166**
outlawry **A173**
outvote (to) **U43**
overdue **F26**
overrule (to) **U43**
overstep (to) **U37**

pacific **F292, N166, P32**
pacific blockade F294
pacific settlement F293
pacifism **P33**
pacifist (*adj.*) **P35**
pacifist (*noun*) **P34**
pact **P3;** AN1
pact, military M226
pains **B253**
panel **L111**
paper **A882, S221, S226**
papers, discharged A885
papers, present one's (to) A890
papers, receive by courier (to) S228
papers, show one's (to) A890
papers, undischarged A885
pardon **B152, G462**
pardon, grant (to) **B151**
pardon, petition for **G463**
pardon, petition for (to) G465
pardon, prerogative of **G467**
pardon, reject petition for (to) G464
pardon, right of **G467**
pardon, submit petition for (to) G465
pardon (to) **B151**

parentage **F33**
parentage, registration of F34
parity **P9**
parity clause **P10**
part **T69; T71; AN3**
part, in **T95**
part, in whole or in T96
part, integral **B434**
partial agreement **T74**
participant **T87; AN2**
participate in (to) **B243**
participate, right to **T86;** T81
participating country **T90**
participating government **T91**
participating state **T92**
participation **T76**
participation by acceptance T83
participation by approval T83
participation by ratification T83
participation by signature T83
participation by virtue of T82
participation, clause regulating **T85**
participation, exclude from (to) **S468**
participation in a treaty T80
participation in an organization T80
participation on basis of equal rights T84
participation, right of **T86**
participation subject to reservations T78
participation without a vote T77
particular **P19**
partisan **P24**
partisan movement **P25**
partisan warfare **P26**
partition **Z28**
partition (to) **Z27**
partnership **G322**
party **M297, P11, S304, T72; AN14**
party, ability to appear as **P18**
party, acquiring **G39**
party acquiring territory **G39**
party, adverse **G80**
party against whom complaint is entered **B405**
party appealed against **B327**
party appealing **B330, B404**
party before the court **G267, G268**
party bringing the action P14
party, cease to be (to) **A810**
party concerned **B492;** B491
party, contracting **V496;** P16
party, defaulting P15
party, defendant P13
party, defending **A371**
party, denouncing **K490**
party, extinction of U171
party filing the motion **A517**
Party, High Contracting P17, S307, T73, V6
  V499
party in the same interest S757

party, injured **G285;** G207
party lacking full capacity **G315**
party legally capable **G293**
party, negotiating **V183**
party, neutral **N96**
party, opposing **G80;** G116
party, opposite **G80**
party opting for **O60**
party, original contracting **V500**
party possessing full capacity **G293**
party, protesting **P173**
party, ratifying **R78**
party, recognizing **A311**
party seeking recourse **A462**
party, signatory **U231**
party, state entitled to become **AN16**
party submitting the protest **P173**
party submitting the request **A517**
party, the other **G80;** G81
party, third **D205**
party to a legal transaction P12
party, working **A564**
pass **P27**
pass, official **D85**
pass, allow to (to) **D251**
pass on (to) **W111**
pass through (to) **D214**
passage **D216, D247, D254**
passage, allow (to) **D251**
passage, allow free (to) D249, D252
passage, ensure free (to) D250
passage, free D218, D248
passage, innocent D219, D220, D221, D222
passage, liberty of **F152**
passage, permit free (to) D252
passage, rights of **D255**
passage, unhindered D218
passenger **F14**
passenger document **F16**
passenger list **F17**
passengers, embarking and disembarking F15
passport holder **P28**
passport, Nansen **N60**
patent **P29**
patent application **P30**
patents, classification of **P31**
payment **L87**
payment, claim for **L88**
payment due F27
payment, entitlement to **L88**
payments **Z9**
payments agreement **Z1**
Payments Committee **Z10**
payments policy, non-discriminatory D173
payments relations **Z6**
payments, restriction on **Z5**
payments system **Z7**
payments transactions **Z9**

payments union **Z8**
peace **F250**
peace and security **F262**
peace, armed F259
peace based upon justice F258
peace, breach of **F274;** F254, F255
peace, conclude (to) F267
peace, conclusion of **F281**
peace conference **F278**
peace, consolidate (to) F265
peace, consolidation of F256
peace, desire for **F288**
peace, disruptive of **F283**
peace, efforts to achieve **F270**
peace, endanger (to) F266
peace, endanger universal (to) W122
peace, endangering **F277**
peace, enduring F260
peace, establishment of international W120
peace, in the maintenance of **F275**
peace, in time of F290
peace, international **W117;** F261
peace, jeopardize universal (to) W122
peace, lasting F260
peace, likely to endanger **F277**
peace, maintain (to) F263, F264
peace, maintain universal (to) W121
peace, maintaining **F275**
peace, maintenance of F251, F252, F262
peace, maintenance of international W120
peace negotiations **F284**
peace observation commission **F272**
peace observer **F271**
peace observer commission **F272**
peace of the mission F257
peace of the world **W117;** Z164
peace offensive **F279**
peace, prejudicial to **F283**
peace, restore (to) F268
peace settlement **F280**
peace, state of **F291**
peace, strengthen universal (to) W123
peace, strengthening of F256
peace, threat to **F269;** F253, F255, F266
peace treaty **F285**
peace treaty, by **F286**
peace, universal **W117;** W118
peace, will for **F288**
peaceful **F292**
peace-loving **F308**
peacetime **F289**
peacetime, in F290
penal **S717**
penal code **S715**
penal court **S705**
penalize (to) **B481**
penalty **S694;** Z226
penalty, collective **K129**

pendency **A423, R331, S758**
pending **A419, R330;** V881
pending the final decision V883
penetrate (to) **D211**
penetration **D212**
penetration, peaceful D213
people **V662**
people, will of W198
peoples, civilized V667
peoples, ever closer union among W201
peoples of the UN, we the V663
peoples, peace-loving V666
perform (to) **A712, A873, E72, E353, W39**
perform, promise to E75
performance **A878, D228, E356, W44**
performance, continued W108
performance, efficient W47
performance, facilities for W48
performance of E74
performance, supervening impossibility of
    E358
performing **A715**
period **D3, F310, Z13**
period, accounting **A81**
period, aforesaid F313
period, after a reasonable Z15
period, current F314
period, expiry of F312
period, financial **R112**
period, interim **U22**
period, transitional **U22;** U23
permanent **S631**
permissibility **Z148**
permissible, declare as (to) **Z144**
permission **B554, E394, G183**
permit **B554, E394, P27**
permit (to) **B553, G182, Z144**
permitted **U89, Z142, Z146**
perpetrate (to) **B124**
perpetration **B130**
persecute (to) **V134;** V135
persecution **V138**
persecution, national V139
persecution, political V139
persecution, racial **R53;** V139
person **P36**
person against whom complaint is entered
    B405
person appealed against **B327**
person appealing **B330, B404**
person, artificial legal P48
person, attack on P38
person before the law **R378;** R379
person, convicted R366
person, dead **G66**
person, denaturalized **A725**
person deprived of nationality **A725**
person, dignity of W250

person, enemy F62
person entitled to restitution P57
person, extradited **A726**
person, fallen **G66**
person, human P39, P54
person, immunity of the I38
person in international law **V776;** P61
person, incapacitated **G315**
person, individual protected E206
person, injured **B357, G285**
person, international P47, P61, V732
person, international legal **V738**
person, inviolability of P40, U267
person, juridical P48
person killed in action **G66**
person killed on active duty **G66**
person lacking full capacity **G315;** G291, V917
person, legal P48, P49
person, missing P60
person, natural P49, P56
person, naturalized **E63**
person, neutral **N96**
person of dual nationality **D191**
person or entity P49
person, persecuted P59
person possessing full capacity **G293**
person, protected P44, P45, P46
person, repatriated P58
person, respect for P37
person sustaining damage **G285**
person, wounded **V628**
persons, disappearance of **V335**
persons, freedom of movement for P83
persons, law relating to **P81**
persons, movement of **P82**
persona non grata **P62;** P63
personality P85
personality in international law **V777;** V739
personality in law **R380**
personality, international P86, P88, V733, V786
personality, international legal **V777, V785;** V739
personality, judicial P87
personality, juridical **R380;** P52, P53, P87, R409
personality, legal **R380;** P87, R381
personnel, civilian **Z65**
personnel office **P71**
persuaded U59
pertaining S6
pertinent S6, Z257
petition A508, B325, B402, G354, P89, S221; G355
petition, accept (to) G358, G359, P91
petition, admissible G357
petition, examine (to) G359
petition filed pursuant to S222

petition, inadmissible G356, G361
petition, reject (to) G360, G361
petition, right of **P92;** P93
petition (to) B326
petitions, register of **P94**
petitions submitted to the tribunal A511
petitioner G209, P90
pillage B288
pillage (to) **B287**
piracy P106, S280; AN10
piracy, acts of S283
piracy, suppress (to) S281
pirate P105, S279
pirate aircraft **S284**
pirate ship **S285**
place S380
place under (to) **U208**
plaint K61
plaintiff (*adj.*) **K82**
plaintiff government K83
plaintiff party **K84;** P14
plaintiff state **K84**
plaintiff (*noun*) **K84**
plaintiff, appear as (to) K85
plant A432
plea E109, P107, R281
plea, admit (to) E111
plea, declare admissible (to) E111
plea, raise (to) E110
pleadings P107
pleadings, written **S221**
plebiscite P110
pledge oneself (to) **V287**
pleins pouvoirs **U179, V806**
plenary debate **P111**
plenary session **P112**
plenary session, constitute (to) P115
plenipotentiary B507
plenipotentiaries, appointed as their B508
plenipotentiaries, conference of **B506**
plenipotentiaries, undersigned U168, U204; AN5
plenum P112, P114
plunder B288
plunder (to) **A798, B287**
plundering A799
police action **P116**
policy, aggressive A411
policy, commercial **H50;** H51
policy committee **G541**
policy, monetary **W60**
policy, public O69, O72
policies, general R605
pollute (to) **V337**
pollution V338
population B498, S624, V662
population, civilian **Z56**
population, exchange of **B502**

population, indigenous   B499
population, local   B500
population, national   **S624**
population, native   B499
population, permanent   B501, S625
port   **H2**; H3
port administration   **H10**
port health authorities   **H9**
port of arrival   **E93**
port of call   H6
port of discharge   **E248**
port of disembarkation   **A813**
port of embarkation   **E127**
port of registry   **H159, R511**
port, peace of   **R649**; H5
port time   H4
portion   **T69**
position   S652
position, legal   **R352**
positivism   **P117**
positivist (*adj.*)   **P119**
positivist (*noun*)   **P118**
possess (to)   **B424**
possession   **B423, B425**
possession, overseas   B427
post   **V561**
post, diplomatic   D155
postpone (to)   **V351**
postponement   **V353**
pouch   **K514**
pourvoi en cassation   **N157**; S142
power   **B98, E419, G371, K156, M1, M12**
power, administering   **V603**
power, administrative   **V603**
power, allied   M2
power, associated   M3
power, belligerent   M8
power, capturing   M6
power, coercive   **Z242**
power, colonial   **K139**
power concerned   M4
power, constituent   G380
power, constitutional   G381
power, detaining   **G368, G370**
power, disciplinary   **D177**
power emanates from the people   G372
power, enemy   M5
power, exclusive   B108
power, executive   **E499**; G382
power, exercise (to)   G383
power, hostile   M5
power, law-making   **R298**; B102
power, legislative   **G345**; G374
power, mandatory   **M23**
power, maritime   **S276**
power, naval   **S276**
power, neutral   M9
power, normative   K317

power, occupant   **B417, O55**
power, occupational   **B344**
power, occupying   **B347, B417, O55**
power of supervision   **K273**
power, opposing   M7
power politics   **M15**
power, protecting   **S254**; S255
power, protectory   **P168**
power, seizure of   **M14**
power, special   **S421**; B109
power, supervisory   **K273**
power to conclude   **A97**
power to legislate   **G345**; B102
power, victorious   **S362**
powers, abuse of   U39
powers, abused   B118
powers accorded   B111
powers agreed on by treaty   B119
powers and duties   O26
powers as agreed by treaty   B119
powers conferred   B111
powers conferred by treaty   B112, B119
powers, curtailed   B113
powers, delegation of   B104, B105, D30
powers, exercise impartially (to)   U139
powers, exercise of   B103
powers, full   **B511, U179, V806**; AN2
powers granted   B111
powers, implied   B114, B115
powers, limited   B113
powers listed   B106
powers, misuse of   U39
powers notary   B116
powers, reduced   B113
powers, restricted   B113
powers, separation of   **G398**
powers set forth   B107
powers, special   **S435**
powers, specific   B110
powers specified   B107
powers, transfer of   B105
practice   **P125, P131, U61**; U62
practice accepted as law   G423
practice as between states   **S528**
practice, current   P133
practice, diplomatic   P132
practice, international   I174, P134, V735
practice, prevailing   P133
practice, without prejudice to   U64
practices, discriminatory   P126
practices, recommended   R606
practices, restrictive   W133
practices, standard   **M372**
preamble   **P121, V954**; AN3, AN4
precedence   **R21, R30**; R18, R23
precedence and etiquette   R31
precedence, ceremonial   P186, R33
precedence clause   **V922**

precedence, order of   **R21, R30, V919**
precedence over   **V919**
precedence over, have (to)   **V893;** V895
precedence, take (to)   R22, V894
precedent   **P135, P136**
precedent, creating   **G542, G546**
preceding   **V957**
predecessor in title   **R424**
predecessor state   **V891**
preferential   **V962**
prejudice   **B51**
prejudice to, without   **U99;** A558, B52, B336,
   I49, P123, U94; AN14
prejudice (to)   **B49, B335, G59, P122;** B50,
   B337, F316, G60
prejudicial   **A137, N48**
prejudicial to a treaty   **V533**
prejudicial to security   A138
preliminaries   **V960**
preliminary procedure   **V960**
premises   **R85**
premises, acquisition of   R89
premises, buildings and   R86
prescribe (to)   **V945**
prescribed, as   **O65, O80;** M37
prescription   **V191, V195**
prescription, acquisitive   **E446**
prescription, barred by   **V193**
prescription, become void by (to)   **V192**
prescription, period of   **V196;** E412
prescription, subject to   **V190**
present (to)   **U34, V913**
present   **A562, B440**
present and voting   A563, S686
present at (to be)   **B243**
presentation   **U35, V907, V915**
presentation of credentials, order of   U36
preservation   **E366, W50**
preservation, measure of   **E368**
preserve (to)   **E365**
press attaché   **P137**
press, freedom of   **P138**
presume (to)   **V269**
presumption   **V270**
presumption, conclusive   V272
presumption, inconclusive   V273
presumption, irrebuttable   V272
presumption, legal   V271
presumption of law   V271
presumption, rebut (to)   V274
presumption, rebuttable   V273
prevail (to)   M47, W242
preventive   **P128**
previous   **B625, F315**
primacy   **P139**
primacy over   **V921**
principle   **G518, P141**
principle, acts inconsistent with   G520

principle, acts not compatible with   G521
principle, declaration of   **G543**
principle, fundamental   **G516**
principle, legal   **R319**
principle, matter of   **G544**
principle, most-favoured-nation   **M147**
principle of continuity of states   G530
principle of effectiveness   G522, G540
principle of effectivity   G522
principle of equal rights   G526, G527
principle of equal treatment   G525
principle of equality at law   G528
principle of equality of states   G537
principle of freedom of the seas   G533
principle of independence of all states
   G529
principle of justice   G524
principle of legality   G531, G536
principle of legitimacy   G532
principle of non-intervention   G534
principle of proportionality   G535, G538
principle of reciprocity   G523
principle of self-determination   G527
principle of sovereign equality   G529
principle of the rule of law   G539
principle, question of   **G544;** G545
principles and arrangements   U4
principles and spirit of the convention   G519
principles, equitable   B597
principles, evade (to)   V698
principles, humane penological   S728
principles, invoke (to)   V698
principles of law, derived from   K109
principles of the UN   H31
principles, violate (to)   V698
prior   **F315**
priority, have (to)   V920
prisoner of war   **K410;** AN13
Prisoner of War, Capture Card for   **K422**
prisoner of war, humane treatment of   K413
prisoner of war, internment of   K417
prisoner of war, labour camp for   K414
prisoner of war, medical needs of   K412
prisoner of war, repatriation of   K415
prisoner of war, spiritual needs of   K412
prisoner of war, transfer of   K418
prisoner of war camp   **K407**
Prisoner of War Mail   **K408, K409**
prisoner, take (to)   **G74**
Prisoners of War, Central Agency   K420
Prisoners of War, Central Information
   Agency   K419
private law   **P159**
private law, relating to   P162
privateer   **F196, K25**
privateering   **K22**
privilege   **P164, V923;** B73
privileges, abuse of   M257, V927

privileges and immunities   P165, R303, V924, V928; AN7
privileges, diplomatic   D149
privileges, enjoy (to)   V925
privileges, exercise (to)   A876
privileges, grant (to)   V926
privileges, grant additional (to)   V929
prize   P142
prize award   **P151**
prize court   **P144**
prize court, international   I160, P145, P147
prize court, national   P146
prize crew   **P148**
prize judgment   **P151**
prize law   **P149, S264**
prize, seized in   P143
problem   F179
procedural motion   **V106**
procedure   M352, M357, V80
procedure, advisory   **G579**
procedure, arbitral   **S109**
procedure, civil   **Z70**
procedure, code of criminal   **S713**
procedure, constitutional   V104, V119, V129, V132
procedure, current   V89
procedure, determine its own (to)   V81
procedure, emergency   **D203**
procedure, established   V88, V89
procedure, expedited   **D203**
procedure, general rules of   G305
procedure, multilateral   V93
procedure, observe rules of (to)   G306
procedure, peaceful and orderly   F303
procedure, preliminary   **V960**
procedure, question of   **V108**
procedure, rules of   **G300;** G301, G302
procedure, standard   **M372, M373**
procedure, summary   **S214;** V87, V103
procedures, customary constitutional   V128
proceed (to)   **V892**
proceeding   K61
proceedings   P189, V80, V176
proceedings against, take (to)   **V210**
proceedings by default   **A162**
proceedings by way of appeal   **R369**
proceedings by way of remedy   **R369**
proceedings, commencement of   R335
proceedings, criminal   **S720, S722;** V102
proceedings for revision   **R587**
proceedings, initiate (to)   **K81**
proceedings, initiate criminal (to)   S725
proceedings, institute legal (to)   P192, R446
proceedings, institution of   R334
proceedings, judicial   V90
proceedings, legal   V90
proceedings, main   **H128**
proceedings, minutes of   **V181**

proceedings, non-criminal   V96
proceedings, obligation to take   S723
proceedings of the General Assembly   V84
proceedings, oral   V94, V95
proceedings, party to   **P191**
proceedings, public   V97
proceedings, regular   V98
proceedings, written   V99, V101
process   V80
process, constitutional   V105, V124, V129
process, judicial   V90
process, legal   V90
process, peaceful and orderly   F303
process (to)   **A20**
processing   A21
processing of passengers   A23
procès-verbal   **P177**
procès-verbal, draw up (to)   P179
proclaiming   B251
proclaiming as their principal aim   B252
proclamation   B250
produce, marine   **M108, M117;** M91
products   W70
products, marine   **M108, M117;** M91, M92
programme, supplementary   **E363**
prohibit (to)   **V13**
prohibited   V38
prohibited (to be)   V37
prohibition   V32
prohibition, order (to)   V36
prohibitions and restrictions   V35
proliferate (to)   **V45**
proliferation   V46
prolong (to)   **V213**
prolongation   V215; V216
promote (to)   **F167**
pronounce (to)   **A853, F25, V211**
pronounced (to be)   **E364**
pronouncement   V212
pronouncement, judicial   **R602**
pronuncio   P167
proof   B523, B545, B546
proof, apportion the burden of (to)   B544
proof, apportion the onus of (to)   B544
proof, burden of   **B542**
proof, conclusive   B527
proof, having the force of   **B541**
proof, impose the burden of (to)   B543
proof, impose the onus of (to)   B543
proof, onus of   **B542**
proof, state (to)   B549
proof, submit (to)   B550
proof, tender (to)   B550
proper   A383, G129
property   E15, G568, S8, V253, V263, V265
property, acquire (to)   E21
property and assets   E16
property, claimed   S11

property, confiscate (to)   E20, E22
property, cultural   G570 (*see under* cultural
 property)
property, dispose of (to)   V261
property, enemy   F79; E18, F56, F70
property, immovable   I11, L102; E19, G571,
 S9, S10, V258
property, inalienable   U254
property, item of   V263
property levy   V262
property, movable   M346; E17, G569, S9, S10,
 V255, V256, V257
property, personal   M346
property, private   P152
property, private enemy   F63, P153, P154
property, private immovable   V260
property, public enemy   F67
property, real   I11
property, restituted   V268
property right   E24
property, seize (to)   E20
property, sequestrate (to)   E23
property tax   V262
proportionality   V166
proportionality, principle of   V167
proportionate   Q17
proposal   V939
proposal, acceptance of   V942
proposal, adoption of   V942
proposal, make (to)   V943
proposal, on a   V941
proposal to amend   A297
propose (to)   V943
proscribed   V38
proscription   V32
prosecute (to)   V137
prosecution   S722, V141; V142
prosecution, temporary protection from   S724
protect (to)   G364
protected   G320
Protected Person, Central Information
 Agency   P46
protection   O9, S243, W50; H242
protection against abuses   S248
protection at law   R401
protection by the law   R401
protection, diplomatic   S249
protection, international   V741
protection of citizens abroad   S245
protection of civilian population   S246
protection of honour   S244
protection of interests   S255
protection of nationals abroad   S245
protection offered by international law   V741
protector   P168
protectorate   P169
protectorate, treaty of   P170
protest   P171

protest, lodging of   A43
protest note   P174
protest, submission of   A43
protest, submit (to)   P172
protocol   P175, P182; AN1
protocol, amending   A295; P176
protocol, chief of   P187
protocol, final   S210
protocol, optional   F23
protocol, secret   G126
protocol, special   S430
protocol, supplementary   Z182; Z183
prove (to)   B536; B530
provide (to)   B450
provide for (to)   G362; AN16
provide otherwise (to)   AN16
provided for   V901
provided that   M42
provision   B454, M36, V946
provision, accepted   B464
provision, administrative   V615
provision, alternative   B462, B463
provision, contradictory   B468
provision, contrary   B468, B471
provision contrary to national law   B472
provision, final   S205; AN3, AN5
provision, general   B461
provision, interim   U19
provision, legal   R425; R426
provision listed above   B470
provision, necessary   B466
provision, penal   S693
provision, preceding   B470
provision, restrictive   B465
provision set forth above   B470
provision set out   A365
provision, special   S431; S434
provision, statutory   G332; R426
provision to the contrary   B462, B463, B471
provision, transitional   U19
provision, violation of   V229
provisions, adoption of   B455
provisions, application of   B456
provisions, carrying out of   B458
provisions, compliance with   B458
provisions, constitutional   V126
provisions, discharge of   B458
provisions, execution of   B457
provisions, failure to discharge   B459
provisions, failure to fulfil   B459
provisions, fulfilment of   B458
provisions, give effect to (to)   A554
provisions, harmonization of   R443
provisions, implementation of   B457
provisions, in accordance with   G167
provisions in force   K326
provisions, infringement of   B460
provisions laid down by law   R439

provisions laid down by legislation   R443
provisions, miscellaneous   B469
provisions, non-compliance with   B459
provisions of law, by adopting   R442
provisions, offence against   B460
provisions, performance of   B457
provisions referred to   A365
provisions, subject to the following   V858
provisional   P188, V910
proviso   A648, M36
pseudo-official   O49
public (adj.)   O37
public (noun)   O46
publication   V280
publicists, most highly qualified   V716
publish (to)   V279
publish, duty to   V281; V282
punish (to)   A191, B481
punishable   S691
punishment   A192, B483, S694, S726
punishment, collective   K129
punishment, degrading   S699
punishment, disciplinary   D181
punishment, enforcement of   S726
punishment, execution of   S726
punishment, inhuman   S700
punitive   S710
purpose   Z45; Z253
purpose, primary   H133
purpose, principal   H133
purposes   Z50
purposes, commercial   H62
purposes, for peaceful   Z256
purposes of the UN   H31, Z46
pursuance of, in   G164
pursuant to   A637, G164; G506, M37
pursue (to)   N12, V136
pursuing   N13
pursuit   N8, V140
pursuit, hot   N8; N9, N10
pursuit, in   N13

quadripartite   V650
qualification   Q1
qualification, criterion of   Q2
quantitative   M151
quarantinable   Q6
quarantinable animal products   Q8
quarantinable diseases   Q7
quarantinable plant products   Q8
quarantine   Q3
quarantine certificate   Q9
quarantine law   Q4
quarantine measure   Q5
quarantine measure, agricultural   P97
quarantine measures, public health   M158
quarantine purposes   Q11; Q12

quarantine regulation   Q10
question   F179
question, budgetary   B669
question, legal   R307
questions in dispute   S760
questions, relevant   Z258
question (to)   V275
questioning   V277
quorum   B384, Q15; B381, B385, G265, Q16
quorum (to be)   B379
quorum, constitute (to)   B379; B382, B386
quorum, existence of   B384
quota   K262, Q18
quota, basic   A719
quota basis, on a   Q17
quotas, enlargement of   K263
quotas, exceeding the   Q19
quota-free   Q20

race   R36
race, doctrine of equality of   R38
race, doctrine of inequality of   R38
racial   R54
racial discrimination   R39; AN4, AN9, AN12
racist activity   R50
radio contact   F326
radio reconnaissance   F318
radioactive   R1
radioactive contamination   R6, R7
radioactive débris   R3
radioactive products   R2
radioactive substances   R4, R5
radioactive waste   R2
range of cannon, rule of   K17
rank   R9, R28
rank, alteration of   R20
rank, change of   R20
rank, comparable   R12, R16, R17
rank, diplomatic   D150, R14, R15
rank, distinction of   R34
rank, equal   G454
rank, having highest   R19
rank, of comparable   R25
rank, of equal   G453, R25
rank, of highest   R27
rank, priority of   R18
rank after (to)   R24
ranking, highest   R19, R27
ranking, senior   R19, R27
rapporteur   R309
rapporteur-général   H116
ratification   R63, R79; AN2, AN5, AN14
ratification clause   R70
ratification, declaration of   R69
ratification, deposit of instruments of   R73; AN2

ratification, exchange of instruments of   R72; AN2

ratification, formal   R66

ratification, imperfect   R81

ratification, incomplete   R81

ratification, instrument of   **R69, R71;** H214, R80; AN5

ratification, registration of   R65

ratification, require (to)   B45

ratification, requiring   **R68**

ratification, reservation in respect of   **R74**

ratification, subject to   B45, R64, R80; AN5

ratification, subsequent   R67

ratify (to)   **R75**

ratify subsequently (to)   F163, R76

ratione materiae   **P41**

ratione personae   **P41**

re-acquire (to)   **W175**

re-acquisition   **W174**

read (to)   **V224**

readmission   **W159**

readmission, application for   **W160**

real   **D94**

realization   E376, V626

realize (to)   **V625**

reapplication   **W156**

reapply (to)   **W155**

reappoint (to)   **W169**

reappointment   **W170**

re-arm (to)   **W165**

re-armament   **W166**

reason   B160, G504

reasons   **B160**

reasons, cogent legal   Z268

reasons for appeal   **B329**

reasons for the award   B161

reasons for the judgment   B161

reasons, give (to)   **B155**

reasons on which based   G505

reasons on which judgment is based   B161

reasons, state (to)   B156

reasonable   A383, B592

reasonably   **B594**

rebel   A675

recall   A9

recall, letters of   **A10**

recall (to)   **A7**

recall permanently (to)   A8

recall temporarily (to)   A8

recalling   E64, H221; AN4

recaptor   **W182**

recapture   **W184**

recapture (to)   **W183**

receipt   E60, E82

receipt, thirty days after   E61

receive (to)   **E79, E218**

received   **E66**

received (to be)   **E68**

reciprocal   **G86**

reciprocity   **G89**

reciprocity clause   **G95**

reciprocity, declaration of   **G94**

reciprocity, on condition of   G92

reciprocity, on the basis of   G90

reciprocity, subject to   G93

reciprocity, treaty of   **G96**

reckless   **F18**

recognition   A313, E376

recognition, accord (to)   A343

recognition, act of   **A347**

recognition at international law   A339

recognition, collective   A334

recognition, constitutive doctrine of   A325, A350

recognition, constitutive effect of   A319

recognition, constitutive theory of   A325

recognition *de facto*   A316

recognition *de jure*   A317

recognition, declaration of   **A351**

recognition, declaratory doctrine of   A324, A349

recognition, declaratory theory of   A324

recognition, declare (to)   A343

recognition, doctrine of   **A348;** A323

recognition, earlier   A333

recognition, effect of   A318

recognition, evidentiary doctrine of   A349

recognition, evidentiary theory of   A324

recognition, express   A330

recognition, formal   A332

recognition, general   A329

recognition, grant (to)   A343

recognition, implicit   A331, A336

recognition, implied   A331, A336, K191

recognition, imply (to)   A337

recognition, instrument of   **A353**

recognition, international   A339

recognition, legal effect of   A321

recognition, levels of   A136

recognition of a state   A314

recognition, original   A338

recognition, practice as to   **A352**

recognition, practice of   **A352**

recognition, premature   A341, A342

recognition, prior   A333

recognition, refusal of   A326

recognition, refusal to grant   A326

recognition, refuse (to)   A344

recognition, refuse to grant (to)   A344

recognition, retroactive effect of   A320

recognition, subsequent   A335

recognition, theory of   A323

recognition, treaty of   **A354**

recognition under international law   A340

recognition, withdraw (to)   **A16;** A345, A346

regulation, general   G305, V948
regulation, interim   **U21**
regulation, internal   V949
regulation made by the General Assembly
   R477
regulation, national   V949
regulation, pacific   F302
regulation, present   B442
regulation provided for in a treaty   **V508**
regulation, special   **S431**
regulation, statutory   **R422**
regulation, subsequent   B442
regulation, technical   **F9**
regulation, transitional   **U21**
regulation, universal   V951
regulations   **G300**; G303
rejoinder   **D210**; V101
relation   **B557**
relation, legal   **R296**; R297
relations between states   B559, B585
relations, bilateral   B565, B584
relations, break off (to)   B586
relations, breaking off of   B560
relations, consolidation of   B563
relations, consular   B578
relations, cultural   B579
relations, diplomatic   B566, D125 (*see also*
   under **diplomatic** relations)
relations, economic   B582
relations, enter into with (to)   B589
relations, establish (to)   B587
relations, establishment of   B561
relations, financial   B568
relations, goodneighbourly   B575
relations, hostile   B567, F54
relations, international   B576, B577, B581,
   B585, V718
relations, interstate   B585
relations, maintain (to)   B588, B590
relations, maintenance of   B562
relations, multilateral   B580
relations, mutual   B572
relations, neighbourly   N3
relations, normalization of   B564, N246
relations, pacific   B569
relations, peaceful   B569
relations, peaceful and harmonious   B570
relations, reciprocal   B572
relations, rupture of pacific   B571
relations, scientific   B583
relations, sever (to)   B586
relations, severance of   B560
relations with other organizations   B558
relationship, appropriate   Z259
relationship, legal   **R420**; R421
release   **F231**
release (to)   **F229**
release from (to)   **B67, E233**

release on parole or promise (to)   F230
relevance   **E372**
relevant   **S6, Z257**; S7
relief   **H205**
relief agency   **H206**
relief, collective   **S39**
relief consignment   **H204**
relief consignment, collective   **S38**
relief consignment, individual   **E202**
relief organization   **H198**
relief parcel   **H199**
relief shipment   **H204**
relief shipment, collective   **S38**
relief shipment, individual   **E202**
relief society   **H186**
relief supplies   **H190**
relief supplies, medical   H191
relieve of (to)   **E233, E244**
remark, final   **S211**
remedy   **R358, R369**
remedy, judicial   R403
remedy, legal   **R283**
remedies, application of   R284
remedies, domestic   R285, R360, R370, S13
remedies, effective   R289
remedies, exhaust local (to)   R447
remedies, exhaustion of local   R288
remedies in law   **R444**
remedies, internal   R285, R360
remedies, local   R286, R287, R360, R361
remedies, national   R285, R360
remit (to)   **V620**
remittal   **V622**
removal   **A112**
removal, not subject to   **U85**
remove (to)   **A111**
renew (to)   **E436, V213**
renew tacitly (to)   G163
renewal   **E437, V215**
renominate (to)   **W163**
renomination   **W164**
renunciation   **V640**
renunciation of war   V643
re-open (to)   **W172**
re-opening   **W173**
reparation   **E266, R535, W177**
reparation, claim for   **R536**
Reparation Commission   **W179**
reparation, make (to)   **E265**
reparation, partial   W178
reparation, payment made as   **W180**
reparation purposes   **R537**
reparation, right to   **R536**
repatriate (to)   **H168, H170, H173, R539, R626,**
   R638, Z156
repatriation   **H169, H171, H174, R540, R627,**
   R639, Z157; R629
repatriation certificate   **H172**

reservation in respect of   V854
reservation in respect of approval   V854
reservation in respect of ratification   V854, V855
reservation, inadmissible   V868
reservation incompatible with   V866
reservation, inhibitive   V864, V865
reservation, make (to)   V871, V872
reservation, making the   **V879**
reservation, objection to   AN21
reservation, permissible   V869
reservation, permit of (to)   V874, V875
reservation, scope of   V861
reservation, state making the   V880
reservation, statement of   **V885**
reservation, subject to   V856
reservation, with   V855, V856
reservation, without   **V886;** V853, V855
reservations, abandon (to)   V876
reservations, conditional on   V859
reservations, withdraw (to)   V876
reserve (to)   **V877, V878**
reserving state   V873
reservoir   **L14**
Resettlement Fund   **W168**
residence, assigned   Z240, Z241
residence, country of   **A604, W236**
residence, enforced   **Z239**
residence, official   **D93**
residence, permanent   W238
residence, place of   **W237, W239**
residence, privilege of   **A606**
residence, state of   **A605**
residence, take up (to)   **N204;** N205
resident (*adj.*)   **A470, W233**
resident, normally   W234, W240
resident, ordinarily   W240
resident, permanently   A471, W234, W235
resist, capacity to   W154
resist, power to   **W153**
resistance   **W149**
resistance, armed   W150
resistance group   **W152**
resistance movement   **W151**
resolution   **B371, E322, R557**
resolution concerning the protocol   E323
resolution, draft   **R558**
resolve, firm   W199
resolve (to)   **E321, L116, R473**
resolve by direct negotiation (to)   AN17
resolved   **E324, G413**
resort   **A463, I68**
resort to regional agencies   A467
resort to (to)   **A459;** A461, Z134
resources   **B642, H201, M337, R520, S82;** H202
resources, by pooling   Z172
resources, conservation of   S83
resources, conservation of living   S85

resources, conservation of natural   H203
resources, exploitation of natural   N84
resources, living   R521, S84
resources, living marine   M119
resources, marine   **M118;** M94
resources, natural   **B642, N83;** R522, S86
resources of the high seas   S85
respect   **A167**
respect for   **E74**
respect for territorial integrity   A171
respect for the dignity of a state   A168
respect for the honour of a state   A168
respect for the principle of   A169
respect of, in   **H211**
respect, universal   A172, A210
respect (to)   **A163, R559;** E73
respondent   **B327**
respondent in appeal proceedings   **B406**
responsibility   **H21, V5, V8, Z192**
responsibility, contractual   H26
responsibility, disciplinary   V7
responsibility, division of   Z198
responsibility for, accept (to)   **H15**
responsibility for, bear (to)   **V3**
responsibility, international   H27, V727, V748
responsibility, lack of   **U282**
responsibility, lacking   **U281**
responsibility, limitation of   H24
responsibility, not possessing   **U281**
responsibility of states, international   V742
responsibility, penal   V7
responsibility, primary   **H126;** H127
responsibility, quadripartite   **V657**
responsibility, termination of   H22
responsible   **H11, V4, Z185**
responsible for (to be)   **H15, V3**
responsible, hold (to)   H13, H14, V9
responsible, not   **U281**
restitute (to)   **R561, R615**
restituted, property to be   R562
restitutee   **R619**
restitution   **R563, R616, W177**
restitution action   **R572**
restitution, action for   **R572, R623**
Restitution Agency   **R618**
Restitution Appeals, Court of   **R620**
restitution, application for   **R568**
restitution claim   **R617;** R567
restitution, claim for   **R566, R568**
Restitution Court   **R621**
Restitution Court, Supreme   R622
restitution, entitled to   **R569;** R570
restitution, external   R564
restitution in kind   **N75**
restitution law   **R625**
restitution legislation   **R625**
restitution, person entitled to   **R571, R619**
restitution request   **R568**

restitution, right of   **R566, R617**
restitution, right to   **R624**
restrict (to)   **B390, E131**
restricted   B394
restriction   **B391, E134**
restriction, progressive abolition of   B392
restriction, quantitative   B395
restrictions, elimination of quantitative   Z73
restrictive   **E132, H208;** W132
resubmission   **W188**
resubmit (to)   **W187**
resume (to)   **W172**
resumption   **W159, W173**
retaliate against (to)   **V152**
retaliation   **V153**
retaliatory act   **V154**
retire (to)   **A141, A807**
retiring   **A144**
retiring member   A808
retorsion   **R573**
retroaction   **R648**
retroactive   **R646**
retroactivity   K318
retrograde   **R630**
retrogressive   **R630**
retrospective   **R646**
return   **R627**
return (to)   **R626, Z156**
re-unification   **W186**
re-unite (to)   **W185**
revenue   **E100**
revenue duty   **F126;** F127
revenue, loss of   **E101;** E102
review   **N32, P198, R576, U32, W159**
review, application for   **W160**
review commission   **P201**
review, comprehensive   U33
review group   **P200**
review, open to   N33
review, subject to   N34
review (to)   **N31, U31;** R575
revise (to)   **A1, A278, N31, N91, R575**
revise in whole or in part (to)   A2
revised   **A45**
revising   **A279**
revision   **A3, A282, N32, N92, R576**
revision, acceptance of   A286
revision, application for   **R583**
revision clause   **R585**
revision conference   **R586**
revision, draft   **A293**
revision, instrument of   **A5**
revision, make application for (to)   R584
revision, make request for (to)   R581, R584
revision procedure   **R587**
revision, proceedings for   **W161**
revision, proposed   **A6**
revision, request (to)   R582

revision, request for   **R583**
revival   **W156**
revive (to)   **W155, W181**
revocation   **R636, W142**
revoke (to)   **W145, Z158;** R631
revoking   **R632**
reword (to)   **N91**
reworded   **N93**
rewording   **N92**
rider   **Z181**
right   **A479, B294, R146**
right, basic   **G517**
right, by virtue of   K311
right, exclusive   R177
right, extinction of   U172
right, forfeit (to)   R207, V240
right, fundamental   **G517**
right, hold (to)   R204
right, holder of   **R342**
right, inalienable   **N79;** R191
right, inherent   **N79;** R178, R185
right, legal   **R277**
right, natural   **N79**
right of   A480, R209
right of a hearing by a tribunal   A487
right of accession   **B240**
right of adequate standard of living   R214
right of angary   **A361**
right of annexation   **A453**
right of appeal   **B407;** R267, R366
right of asylum   **A585**
right of benefits   A485
right of, claim (to)   A500
right of collective bargaining   R242
right of complaint   **B407;** R267
right of control   **K281**
right of derogation   A158
right of economic protection   R215
right of education   R222
right of effective protection of the law   A490
right of equal pay for equal work   R238
right of equal protection of the law   A484
right of equal rights   R237
right of equal treatment   R236
right of equality   R237
right of establishment   R246
right of fair and impartial trial   R247
right of fair remuneration   R234
right of fair trial   R235
right of favourable conditions of work   R212
right of favourable remuneration   R213
right of free access   R228
right of free choice of profession   R224
right of free decision   R225
right of freedom of association   R230
right of freedom of decision   R225
right of freedom of expression   R226
right of freedom of movement   R231

right of freedom of residence   R227
right of hot pursuit   R245
right of immunity   I59
right of independence   R261
right of just conditions of work   R212
right of just remuneration   R213
right of legal protection   R215
right of liberty   R229
right of limitation of working hours   A482
right of nationality   A489, R258
right of objection   E150
right of ownership   E24
right of pardon   G467
right of peaceful assembly and association
   R262
right of peaceful enjoyment of possessions
   R210
right of periodic holidays with pay   A486
right of petition   B407, P92
right of property   R220
right of protection against unemployment
   R249
right of protection and assistance   R250
right of recognition as a person before the
   law   A481
right of requisition   B366
right of respect for dignity of the person
   R211
right of rest and leisure   A483
right of safe working conditions   R254
right of sanctuary   A585
right of search and seizure   D270
right of security   R255
right of security of the person   R248, R256
right of self-defence   R252, R253
right of self-defence, collective   R241
right of self-defence, individual   R241
right of self-determination   R251
right of self-help   R252
right of settlement   R246
right of social and medical assistance   R232
right of social protection   R215
right of social security   R257
right of special protection   R217, R218
right of stoppage   A414
right of supervision   K281
right of the protection of the law   A488
right of visit and search   D269
right of withdrawal   A870
right, possessor of   R342
right, reserve (to)   R208
right to   A480, R209 (see also under right of)
right to accede   B240
right to bargain collectively   R242
right to choose one's residence   R271
right to complain   R267
right to engage in gainful occupation   R216
right to fish   F99, F117; F100

right to form and join professional associations
   R266
right to form and join trade unions   R266
right to form associations   R272
right to found a family   R239, R269
right to marry   R219, R268
right to own property   E24; R221
right to petition for pardon   R270
right to stop   A414
right to stop and search   A414; A415
right to use the flag   R223
right to wage war   R243
rights, abolition of   R161
rights, accord (to)   R202
rights, acquired   R180
rights and benefits   R158, R159, R160
rights and duties   R154
rights and duties, imposition of   I98
rights and privileges   R159
rights arise from   R195
rights arising from   R149
rights arising hereafter   R153
rights arising under   R151
rights, assignment of   R163
rights, civil   B686; R179; AN9
rights, civil law   R179
rights, claim (to)   R200, R203
rights, cultural   R184; AN9
rights, delegate (to)   R201
rights, delegation of   R166
rights, deprivation of   E264
rights, deprive of (to)   E263
rights, destruction of   R162
rights, economic   R192; AN9
rights, enjoyment of   R170
rights, equal   G441; R182
rights, equal and inalienable   AN4
rights, equality of   G441
rights, equivalent   R182
rights, exercise (to)   R196, R203
rights, exercise of   R165
rights, existing   R153
rights, extinction of   R169, R175
rights, forgo (to)   R197
rights, grant (to)   A608
rights, human   M159; AN9
rights, impose (to)   R155
rights, in asserting their   G147
rights in civil law   R179
rights, individual   I73; R148
rights, invoke (to)   R200, R203
rights lapse   R193
rights, lapse of   R169, R175, U172
rights, lapsed   V194
rights, maintenance of   R172
rights, nature and extent of   R157
rights, observance of   R164
rights of individuals   R148

rights of passage   **D255**
rights, person deprived of   **E258**
rights, person lacking full   **E258**
rights, political   M173, R187; AN9
rights, possess (to)   R204
rights, preservation of   R176, W51
rights, protect (to)   W43
rights, protected   R181
rights, protection of   R171, R172
rights, put into effect (to)   R203
rights, real   D95
rights, respect for   R164
rights resulting from   R150
rights, retain (to)   R198, R199
rights, securing of   R172
rights, social   M174, R189
rights, sovereign   **H229, H255**; H256, R188, S439
rights, subrogation of   R173
rights, suspension of   R167, R168
rights, territorial   R190
rights, transfer (to)   R205
rights, transfer of   R173, R174
rights under international law   V736, V737
rights, uphold (to)   W43
rights, upholding of   R176, W51
rights, violate (to)   R147
rights, withdrawal of   R167
rightful   R275
riot, civil   **L19**
rising, popular   **V798**
river   **F153**
river, international   F154
river, internationalized   F155
river, navigable   F156
rivers, law of international   **W83**
roadstead   R457; R458
roadsteads, demarcate (to)   R459
roll call   A123
rule   **H176, N224, R460, R476, V946**
rule, adhere to (to)   R470
rule, adherence to   R462
rule, apply as a (to)   I76
rule, basic   **G515**
rule, breach of   R463, R465
rule, break (to)   R471
rule codified in a treaty   K111
rule, cogent   N238
rule, constitutional   **V131**; V130
rule, contractual   N236
rule created by treaty   N236
rule, customary   **G417**; N233
rule, enforce (to)   G151
rule, establish (to)   N241
rule established by custom   N234
rule, foreign   H178, N232
rule, future   B442
rule, general   N229

rule, generally applicable   V950
rule, infringe (to)   R472
rule, infringement of   R465
rule, interim   **U21**
rule, international   N235, N240, R469, V731, V740
rule, lay down (to)   R484
rule, mandatory   N238
rule, non-self-executing   N184
rule, observance of   R462
rule, observe (to)   R470
rule of international law   N237
rule of municipal law   N225
rule of procedure   **G300, V111**
rule, peremptory   N238, N239
rule, present   B442
rule prohibiting   **V39**
rule, recognized   N230
rule relating to war(fare)   **K456**
rule, restrictive   R466, R467
rule, self-executing   A524, R468
rule, subsequent   B442
rule, transitional   **U21**
rule, violate (to)   R472
rule, violation of   R465
rules applicable to all ships   R461
rules, binding nature of   N228, V20
rules, body of   R464
rules in force, governed by   R431
rules of law, determination of   R373; AN20
rules of the court   **V109**
rules, sum of   N227, R464
rules, total body of   N227
rules with regard to   R484
rupture   B654

sabotage   **S1**
sabotage, act of   **S2**
sabotage, serious acts of   S3
sabotage (to)   **S5**
saboteur   **S4**
sacred   **H152**
safe conduct pass   **P27**
safeguard   **S340, S351, S353**
safeguard, measure of   **S353**
safeguard (to)   **G364**
safeguarding   **S351**
safeguards agreement   **S352**
safeguards system   **S354**
safety at sea   S332
safety locality   **S342**
safety, maritime   S332
safety measure   **S340**
safety standard   **S341**
safety, standard of   **S341**
safety zone   **S347**; S348
said   **G177**

settlement, peaceful B198, E399, R482
settlement, special S431
settlement, suitable terms of R481
settlements, multilateral system of Z3
settlements, system of Z4
sever (to) A11
severance A12
shelf S413
shelf, area of S414
shelf, continental F83, K260, K261, S413; A53, F84
ship S170
ship, arrest of on high seas S263
ship, enemy F64
ship, government S617; S618, S619
ship, pursued S176
ship, pursuing N14
ship, registered S175
ship, registration of R515
ship, registry of R515
ship, safety of S194; S195
ship, sea-going S288
ship, state S617
ship's document S188
ship's papers S192
ships, access and departure of Z130
ships engaged in fishing S171
ships engaged in international voyages S173
ships engaged in whaling S171
ships, ingress and egress of Z130
ships, naval K448
ships, non-registered S175
ships of war K449
ships, operation of S172
shipping S177
shipping agreement S180
shipping engaged in international trade I146, S178
shipping, maritime S289
shipping services S181
shipping treaty S183
shipwrecked members of armed forces S186
show of hands H111
show of hands, vote by (to) H112
si omnes clause A205, S369
sign (to) U201, U228
sign, invitation to U244
signal, auditory S81
signal to stop, visual or auditory S356
signal, visual S355
signatory (adj.) U236
signatory state S364
signatory (noun) S363, U230
signature U202, U241; AN2, AN5
signature ad referendum U249
signature, append (to) U203, U204
signature, at the time of U247
signature, deferred U248

signature, instrument of U251
signature, one month from date of U243
signature, opened for U245
signature, protocol of U250
signature, subsequent U248
signature with reservation U246
signature without reservation U246
significance B24
signing U241
single chamber E87
sit (to) T2; G217
sitting S387
sitting, last S388
sitting, plenary V824
situated B65
situated off V898
situation L11, S18
situation, in consideration of L13
situation of fact L12
slave S403
slave taking refuge S404
slave trade S405; S410
slave trade, prevent and suppress (to) S407
slave trade, repression of S406
slaves, dealing in AN10
slavery S408; S409, S410
slavery, held in S410
slavery, similar to S411; S412
social charter S456
social fund S457
social security fund S458
social security institution S458
social security scheme S459
social security system S459
society G322, G323
society, aid H186
society, multiracial M131
society of states V763
society, relief H186
Society, Voluntary Aid H187
solemn F42
solemnly declare (to) F43
solemnly undertake (to) F44
solidarity S415, V48; V49
solidarity of mankind S416
solution L117
solution, ex aequo et bono B601
solve (to) L116
source Q13
source material A720, A722
source, secondary H200
source, subsidiary H200
source, supplementary H200
sources, hierarchy of R35
sources, order of precedence of R13, R32
sources, ranking of R13
sovereign (adj.) H234, S436

state, extinction of   S477
state, federal   **B675;** S490
state, foreign   S481, S491
state, free   **F232**
state frontier   **S606**
state having no sea-coast   B622
state, head of   **S614**
state, home   **H157, H164**
state, host   **E220;** E219
state, hostile   **F78;** F65
state, independent   S507, S509
state, injured   S493, V227
state jurisdiction   **S600**
state, land-locked   **B621**
state liability   H25
state, littoral   **A457, K538**
state, maritime   **K538;** S496
state member   **T94**
state, mother   **A213**
state, multinational   **V649;** S498
state, nascent   S599
state, national   **N66**
state, native   **H164**
state, negotiating   AN14
state, neighbouring   N7
state, neutral   H107, S501
state, neutralized   S502
state, new   S499, S500
state, newly emerged   S499
state, non-coastal   **B621**
state, non-contracting   **N203**
state, non-participating   **N195**
state, non-signatory   **N198**
state, non-unitary   **N137;** E78
state, occupant   **B417;** B416
state, occupied   S505
state, occupying   **B417;** B416, S504
state of origin   **H164**
state organ   **S615**
state organs   S535
state, parent   **A213;** A214
state party   **V525;** V526, V527; AN4
state party to a treaty   **V525**
state, peace-loving   S492
state, peripheral   **R8**
state practice   **S528**
state, previous   B627
state, protected   S484
state, puppet   **M29**
state, pursuing   N15
state, ratifying   **R78**
state, receiving   **A663, E220;** E219
state, recipient   **E220;** E219
state, recognition of   S473
state, recognized   S479
state, requested   S488
state, requesting   S487
state requesting admission   S483

state requesting membership   S483
state, reserving   V873
state responsibility   **S520;** H25
state, riparian   **U65**
state security   **S621**
state security, act endangering   S622
state security, breach of   S622
state seeking recourse   **A462**
state, semi-sovereign   S494
state, sending   **E329**
state, signatory   **U230, U235**
state, sovereign   S508
state sovereignty   **S607;** S446
state succession   **S526**
state, successor   **E480, S527**
state system   **S530**
state, territories of   S608
state territory   **S595**
state territory, acquisition of   S597
state territory, loss of   S597
state, third   **D205, D206;** S485; AN14
state, treaty-breaking   S510
state, tutelary   **A213**
state, unitary   **E77**
state within a federation   **G459**
states, community of   **S517, V763;** G173, S518
states, composite   **S531**
states, contesting   S732
states, continuity of   S475
states, equality of   **G455, S519;** G447
states, legitimacy of   L77
states, responsibility of   **S520**
states, society of   **V763**
states, sovereignty of   S446
states, succession of   **S476, S526**
states, union of   **S531**
state (to)   **E378**
statehood   **S538**
stateless   **S523**
stateless person   **S524**
statelessness   **S525**
state-like   **S513**
statement   **A804, D38;** S652
statement, make (to)   **A805**
statement, unilateral   AN14
statement, written   **D38**
status   **C1, R9, R28, S636, S640**
status, enemy   F68
status, equal   **G454**
status, hostile   F55
status, international   **S638**
status, legal   **R352;** R274, R407, R412
status, of equal   **G453**
status of forces agreement   **T184**
status, possessing legal   **R299**
statute   **G325, S61, S639**
statute, amendment of   **S63**
statute, general review of   R580

statute, in accordance with   S64; G166
statute of the ICJ, party to   M305
statutory   G350
steering committee   L97
steering group   L98
stem from (to)   B332
step   M48
stop (to)   A412
stop and search, right to   A415
stop and search (to)   A412
stoppage   A413
stoppage, right of   A414
stopping and anchoring   D217
straits   M101
straits agreement   M105
straits closed to warships   M102
straits, control of   M106; M104
straits used for international navigation   M103
stretcher bearer, auxiliary   H189
strike, right to   S730
study group   S787
sub-commission   U180; H197
sub-committee   U154; U155
sub-division   U175
sub-division, political   U176
sub-group   U177
subject (adj.) to   U99, V881; U100, V856, V857
subject to (to be)   U189, U207
subject to state's jurisdiction   U227
subject (noun)   S788
subject capable of transactions   S790
subject matter   G97
subject matter of a punishable act   G100
subject of a treaty   G104
subject of arbitral proceedings   G101
subject of arbitration   G101
subject of international law   S789
subject of judicial proceedings   G99
subject of the dispute   G103
subject with legal capacity   S790
subject to (to)   U208, U220
subjected   U226
subjugated   U226
subjugation   U223
subjugation by armed force   U225
subjugation to foreign jurisdiction   U224
submission   A42, U223, V907, V914
submission of a protest   A43
submit (to)   U160, V912
submit, failure to   N123
submit to (to)   U221, U222
subordinate   N24, U174
sub-paragraph   B659, U153; B660
subsequent   N19, N50, S461
subsequently   F158, F162
subsidiary   N24
substance of a punishable act   G100
substantiate (to)   B536; B530

substitute   E441, S653, S654, V559; V558, V560
substitute, method of appointing   S657
substitute for (to)   V550
succeed to (to)   N18
succeeding   N19
succession   E343, N16
succession duty   E344
succession of states   N17
succession, partial   T93
successor in title   N22, R371
successor organization   N21
successor state   N23, S792
sue (to)   K81; K70, K85
suit   K61; V142
suit, commencement of   K79
suitable   G56
summary record   K521
summon (to)   L1, V904
summoned before the commission   L2
summoned, duly   L4
summoning   L3, V905
summoning of witnesses and experts   V906
summons   L3
summons, renewed   L5
summons, verbal   L6
superiority, racial   R37
superjacent   B66
supersede (to)   A72
supervise (to)   B17, U52
supervision   B18, K275, U53; B19
supervision and inspection, rights of   K277
supervision, international   I151
supervision, right of   K281
supervisory committee   U54
supplement   E360
supplement (to)   E359
supplementary   E361
supplementary agreement   Z179
supply contractors   H150
suppress (to)   U156, U162
suppression   U157, U165
suppression of illicit traffic   U166
supranational   U29
supremacy   H229, P139, V921
surety   B683
surety, stand as (to)   B684
suretyship   B687
surplus, accounting   R110
surplus, cumulative accounting   R111
surrender   A770, U17
surrender, postponed or conditional   U18
surrender, unconditional   B40
surrender (to)   A767, U24
suspend (to)   A639, A817, A845, E153, S793,
   U158; K321
suspended   A636
suspension   A642, A818, A839, A847, E155,
   S794, U159

transit route, misuse of   T156
transit state   **D240, D260**
transit, state of   **D240, D260**
transit traffic   **D242, T154**
transit, traffic in   **D234, D241, D242**
transit, unhindered   D218, D236
transit visa   **D259**
transitional provision   **U19**
transmission   **U26, W112;** W113
transmit (to)   **U25, W111**
transport   **V197**
transport agreement   **V205**
transport committee   **V206**
transport, inland   **B623**
travel and transport, maritime   P84
travel document   **R529**
traverse   **E108**
treason   **L21, V313**
treason, act of   **V313**
treasures, national   K477
treatment   **B164**
treatment, cruel   B168
treatment, customs   B172
treatment, degrading   B166
treatment, discriminating   B165
treatment, discriminatory   B165, D171
treatment, equal   **G437;** G438, R385
treatment, equal social and medical   G439
treatment, equality of   **G437**
treatment, fiscal   B170
treatment, humane   B169
treatment, humiliating   B167
treatment, inhuman   B171
treatment, most-favoured-nation   **M145**
treatment, preferential   **V962;** V963
treatment, reciprocal   G91
treatment, tax   B170
treaty   **S623, V363;** AN1, AN14
treaty, accede to (to)   V440
treaty, accession to   V379
treaty, act in violation of (to)   V464
treaty, act violating   **V536, V545**
treaty, acting in breach of   **V482**
treaty, adjustment of   V372
treaty, aim of   **V543;** V412
treaty already in force   V417
treaty, amend (to)   V437; AN16
treaty, amend by agreement (to)   AN16
treaty, amendment of   **V471, V477;** V368, V370; AN16
treaty, application of   V373
treaty, area of application of   V388
treaty, authentic text of   A899
treaty, authorized to conclude   **V518**
Treaty, Basic   **G551**
treaty between states   **S623**
treaty, bilateral   V418, V436
treaty, binding force of   V380

treaty, breach of   **V481, V536;** V381, V408
treaty, by   **V465;** W89
treaty, by way of   W89
treaty, capacity to conclude   **V489;** V490
treaty, collective   **K131**
treaty, commercial   **H59**
treaty, compliance with   **V531;** V383
treaty, comply with (to)   V443, V448
treaty, concessionary   K291
treaty, conclude (to)   V460
treaty, concluded   V421
treaty, conclusion of   **V473, V517;** AN2
treaty constituting   **G550**
treaty, construction of   **V478;** V375
treaty, construe (to)   V438
treaty, continuance in force of   V410
treaty, denounce (to)   V450
treaty, denunciation of   V392
treaty, depositary of   AN15
treaty, designation of   **V480**
treaty, disregard (to)   V449
treaty, draft   V529
treaty, draft of   **V486**
treaty, draft wording of   V529
treaty, duration of   **V484**
treaty, earlier   V420
treaty, effect of   **V540**
treaty, enter into (to)   V442
treaty establishing   **G550;** V365
treaty, execute (to)   V441
treaty, execution of   D230, V374, V382
treaty, existing   V417
treaty, expiration of   **V472**
treaty, extend (to)   V462
treaty, extension of   **V535**
treaty, failure to fulfil   N136
treaty, failure to observe   N136
treaty, freedom to conclude   **V491**
treaty, freedom to enter into   **V491**
treaty, fulfil (to)   V445
treaty, fulfilment of   **V487;** V385
treaty, general   **G201;** V413
treaty, impossibility of performing   V488
treaty in favour of third party   V366
treaty in force   G141, G142
treaty, in the form of   V466
treaty, individual   **E200**
treaty, initial (to)   V456
treaty, initialling of   **V495;** V398
treaty, instrument constituting   **V539**
treaty, international   **S623;** V753
treaty, interpret (to)   H105, V438
treaty, interpretation of   **V478;** V375
treaty, invalidity of   V405
treaty, invoke (to)   B316
treaty, language of   **V524**
treaty law   **V504**
treaty, law created by   V507

valid at law **R322**
valid in law **R322**
validate (to)   G144
validity   **G148, G562, G566**; R325
validity, acquiesce in (to)   W109
validity at law   **R324**
validity expires   G563
validity, extend the period of (to)   G162
validity in international law   G153
validity in law   **R324**
validity in municipal law   G152
validity, international   V721, V726
validity, legal   **R324**
validity, period of   **G158, G566**
validity, prejudice (to)   G564
validity, renew the period of (to)   G162
validity terminates   G563
value for customs purposes   **Z113**
variance   **A157**
variance, at (to be)   **A148**
variance, states at   S732
vassal state   **V1**
vassalage   **U193, V2**
verbal note   **V11**
verdict   **U360**
verification   **V188**
verification agreement   **V189**
version   **F40**
vessel   **S170**
vessel, enemy   F64
vessel, foreign   A742
vessel, government   S620
vessel, sea-going   **S288**
vessel, surface   **U57**
veto   **V644**
veto, right of   **V647**
veto, suspensive   V646
veto (to)   V645
vice-consul   **V661**; K229
view, in   **A274, A384**
view, legal   **R279**
views, exchange of   **M139**
violate (to)   **U50, V226, Z222**
violation   **B654, V228, V348, Z223**
violation, alleged   A363, B174, V234
violation, in   **M259**
violation of, act in (to)   **Z222**
violence   **G403**
violence, act of   **G403**
violence, unlawful   G396
virtue of, by   **A637, K308**; U48
visa   **S357**
visa, collective   **S40**
visa, obligation to obtain   **S358**
visa, permanent   **D6**
visas, abolition of   S359
visit and search   **D267, V659**
visit and search, belligerent right of   D271

visit and search, right of   **D269, V660**
visit (to)   **D266**
visitation   **V659**
void   **H209, N152**
void, declare (to)   N153
voisinage   **N2**
vote   **A118, A130, S672, W30**
vote, affirmative   **J13**
vote by correspondence   A125
vote, by unanimous   B373
vote, cast (to)   **A115**; S673
vote cast "against"   **N90**
vote cast "for"   **J13**
vote, casting   A816
vote, deciding   S677
vote, give the deciding (to)   **A815**
vote in writing   A125
vote, negative   **N90**
vote, open   A124
vote, put questions to the (to)   A120
vote, secret   A121
vote, unanimous   **E161**
votes cast by delegates   S674
votes, equal division of   **S676**
votes, equality of   **S676**; S677
votes, majority of   **S680**
votes, number of   **S683**
votes, total number of   **G277**
vote (to)   **A115**; A128, S673
vote, entitled to   **S670**
vote individually (to)   A116
vote, right to   **S685**
voting   **A118, S668**
voting, abstain from (to)   A126, A127, E243, S675
voting by call   A123
voting, method of   **W38**
voting power   **S685**
voting power, suspension of   S687
voting power, total   S684
voting procedure   **A132**; A133
voting regulation   **A134, W38**
voting, result of   **A130**
voting right   **S685**
voting rule   **A134**
voting, system of   **W38**
voyage, continuous   R524, R527
voyage, doctrine of continuous   R525, R528

waive (to)   **A639**
waiver   **A642, V640**; AN7
waiver, express   V641
waiver of conditions   V642
waiver of immunity   V642
war   **K340**
war, act of   **K429**
war, aggressive   **A409**

waters, historic   G407
waters, internal   **B619, E4;** G408, G409, K533
waters, land-locked   G410
waters, law of international   **W83**
waters, superjacent   **G405, G406, W79**
waters, territorial   **H252, T109;** H242, L25, T103
waterway, inland   **B624**
waterways, law of international   **W83**
weapons   **W1**
weapons, ABC   W2
weapons, atomic   W3; AN18
weapons, biological   W4; AN18
weapons, chemical   W5; AN18
weapons, conventional   W7
weapons, nuclear   W8
weapons, stocks of   **W16**
weapons, thermonuclear   W8
weapons, use of   **W17**
welfare   **W229, W231**
welfare, common   **G175;** W230
welfare of mankind   W232
well-being   **W229, W231**
well-being, common   **G175;** W230
whereas   **A274, A384, E473**
wilful   **V936**
wilfully   **V934**
wilfully committed   V937
will   **W195**
will and testament, last   V150
will, common   **G174**
will of the people   **W197**
wind up (to)   **A654**
winding up   **A655**
wireless communication   **F326**
withdraw (to)   **A141, A807, A864, E209, E340, W145, Z158, Z160;** A809
withdrawal   **A811, A865, E210, E341, R636, R640, W142**
withdrawal from a treaty   A867
withdrawal from an organization   A866
withdrawal, notice in writing of   **A872, R645**
withdrawal, notice of   **A868, A872, R642;** AN5
withdrawal, notification of   **A869**
withdrawal, right of   **A870, R643;** R644
withdrawal, written notice of   **A872**
withdrawing   **A144**
witness   **Z32**
witness, appear as (to)   Z38
witness, call (to)   Z39, Z41
witness, give evidence as (to)   Z36
witness, interrogate (to)   Z40
witness, obligation to appear as   **Z44**
witness, question (to)   Z40
witness, require to give evidence (to)   Z39
witness, require to testify (to)   Z39
witness, summon (to)   Z39, Z41
witness, summoning of   Z35
witness whereof, in   **U288;** U289; AN5

witnesses and experts   Z34
witnesses, examination of   **B533, B538;** V278
witnesses, hear (to)   V276
witnesses, hearing of   **B533, B538;** A428, Z33
witnesses, put questions to (to)   Z258
word (to)   **F39**
wording   **F40, T115, W241**
wording, authentic   M46
wording, revised   F41
worker, migrant   **W64**
world peace   **W117**
world trade   **W125**
world trade, harmonious development of   W126
world trade, harmonious expansion of   W126
world-wide   **W116**
wounded   **V628**
wounded, condition of   V637, V638
wounded, evacuation of   V635, V636
wounded, exchange of   V634
wounded, humane treatment of   V632
wounded, inhumane treatment of   V632
wounded, removal of   V633
wounded, search for   V630
wounded, transport of   V629
wounded, treatment of   V631
writ   **K61**
writing, in   **S219;** S218, S220
writing, not in   **M367**
written   S219
wrong   **D31, U143**
wrong, cessation of   U144
wrong, commit (to)   U147
wrong, international   **V759;** V719, V747
wrong, redress for   R633
wrong, retaliation against   U145, U146
wrongful   **U148**

year, current financial   R105
year, financial   **R104**
year, preceding financial   R106
yearbook   **J1**
yearbook, statistical   J2

zone   **Z116**
zone, contiguous   **A473, K259;** A474, Z120
zone, demilitarized   Z124
zone free of atomic weapons   Z121
zone, neutral   Z125
zone, neutralized   Z126
zone of military operations   **K10**
zone, prohibited   **S469, V40**
zone, restricted   **S469**
zone, strategic   Z127
zone, three-mile   **D202**
zones entry into which prohibited   Z118